INFORMATION PROCESSING
SYSTEMS FOR MANAGEMENT

The Irwin Series in
Information and Decision Sciences

Consulting Editors

ROBERT B. FETTER   CLAUDE MCMILLAN
Yale University   *University of Colorado*

INFORMATION PROCESSING SYSTEMS FOR MANAGEMENT

Donna Hussain

K. M. Hussain

New Mexico State University

1981

Richard D. Irwin, Inc.
Homewood, Illinois 60430

ISBN 0–256–02482–0
Library of Congress Catalog Card No. 80–82451

Printed in the United States of America

3 4 5 6 7 8 9 0 K 8 7 6 5 4 3 2

PREFACE

Few businesses have been left untouched by the computer revolution. The computer is being increasingly used for operations, control, and planning as well as to improve office efficiency. Managers today need to know how computers work and how they can be applied to a firm's operations.

The purpose of this book is to provide managers and students of management with a basic understanding of processing systems. Though the text includes a brief overview of hardware, software, peripherals, and communications, the primary focus is on the development and administration of information systems and on computer applications. Omitted is an explanation of the internal workings of a computer, flowcharting, how to program, and the history of computers that are topics presented in introductory computer science texts.

Use of this textbook does not require a course prerequisite. The book is a stand-alone text, written for the upper division undergraduate or the masters student. An instructor's manual has been prepared to accompany the text. Included in the manual are more than 1,000 multiple-choice questions for reviews or exams, plus supplementary diagrams, photos, and summary lists in the form of transparency masters which can be used in the classroom.

The authors wish to thank colleagues and reviewers who read the manuscript and provided helpful comments and corrections. We are particularly indebted to Marvin Rothstein, Leslie Spencer, Deane Carter, and Steve Hallam, for their constructive criticisms. A special word of gratitude must also be given to our secretaries, Elida Lechuga and Betty Stacey.

Donna Hussain
K. M. Hussain

CONTENTS

Data and data elements: *Data elements by function. Data elements by source.*
Selecting data elements for collection. Data element dictionary: *Descriptors of
a DED.* Organization of data: *Logical organization. Physical representation of
input.* Common data base.

Data collection. Codes: *Types of codes. Selection of coding structure. Principles
of code design. Problems.* Validation: *Validity checks.*

Directories: *Information repository for users. Information repository for software.*
Adding descriptors to the DED. Organization of a DED/DD system. Data base
administrator (DBA). Resources for data administration.

Overview of DBMS. Operations of a DBMS. Architecture. Features and functions
of DBMS. Data base administrator. Retrieval: *Types of queries. Query languages.
Classes of users.* Costs and benefits of a DBMS. Implementation: *When to implement. Preparing for implementation.* Growth of DBMS.

The development process: *Feasibility study (Activity 15–20). Overall systems planning (Activity 20–30). Specifying the systems requirements (Activity 30–40). Design (Activity 40–50) and implementation (Activity 50–60) of the system.
Organizational adjustments (Activity 30–60). Testing the solution (Activity 60–
70). Conversion (Activity 70–80). Project management (Activity 30–80). Operation
(Activity 80–90) and evaluation (Activity 80–100). Recycling.* Role of managers.

Phase one: Organizing for a feasibility study. Phase two: Search for solutions.
Phase three: Feasibility analysis. *Economic feasibility. Financial feasibility. Organizational feasibility. Technological feasibility. Other feasibility considerations. Feasibility decision.* Phase four: Choice of a solution: *Selecting project personnel.*
Duration of a feasibility study.

Data collection: *The traditional approach. The innovative approach. The hybrid approach.* Tools and techniques of data collection: *Literature search. Interviews. Meetings. Study organization plan (SOP). Accurately defined system (ADS). Other instruments of data collection.* Documentation. Identifying users' objectives, policies, and constraints: *Stating objectives, policies, and constraints.* Performance specifications. Approval procedures. Project management: *Selection of project management technique.*

Design management (300–390, Figure 13.1). Operational and hardware specifications (300–310–390). Model selection and development (300–330–390). Documentation standards (300–340). Testing specifications (300–350). Organizational specifications (300–355). Programming specifications (300–360). Quality and control specifications (300–370). Input and output specifications (300–375–380–382–390): *Output (300–375). Input (375–380). Files (380–390). Forms (380–382). Procedures (382–390).* Formal design techniques. Revise project schedule (390–395). Management approval (395–400).

Implementation: *Programming activities. Hardware selection and installation. File preparation. Organizational considerations.* Testing the solution: *Levels of testing. Testing responsibility.* Conversion. Evaluating the systems development process.

Operations. Evaluation of operations. Evaluation of applications: *Efficiency. Effectiveness.* Maintenance and redevelopment: *System modification.* Maintenance and redevelopment management.

Protection of data. Countermeasures to threats: *Access control. Auditing.* How much control and security? Control points: *Control of procedure and code manuals (Circle 1, Figure 16.2). Form control (Circle 2). Data collection (Circle 3). Data preparation (Circle 4). Operations (Circle 5). Data files (Circle 6). Programming controls (Circles 7,8). Processing (Circle 9). Output (Circle 10). Teleprocessing (Circle 11).* Control responsibility of management.

Location of EDP. EDP relationship with user departments. EDP departmental organization. Nature of human resistance. Overcoming resistance. Human factors.

tion of CAD hardware. CAD software. Applications of CAD. Cost of CAD. Future of CAD. Predictions for future use of computers in manufacturing.

Electronic mail: *Use of electronic mail. Scenario of future use of electronic mail. Advantages and disadvantages of electronic mail. Future of electronic mail.* Teleconferencing. War room (multimedia center). Electronic fund transfer: *EFT uses. Resistance to EFT. Pros and cons of EFT.* Word processing (WP): *Nature of word processing. When word processing? Computer resource requirements of word processing. Future of word processing.*

Office tasks. Electronic office components: *Software. Processing, storage, and retrieval. Copying and distribution components.* A day of work in an electronic office. Case study results. Implementation considerations. Future of the electronic office.

Computers for hobbyists. The home computer: *Uses of stand-alone home computers.* Home computers connected to other computers: *Extension of EFT. Home shopping. Electronic home offices.* Home computers connected to data base services: *Sample data base services of the future.* Equipment considerations: *Telephone. TV. Cable TV.*

PART ONE

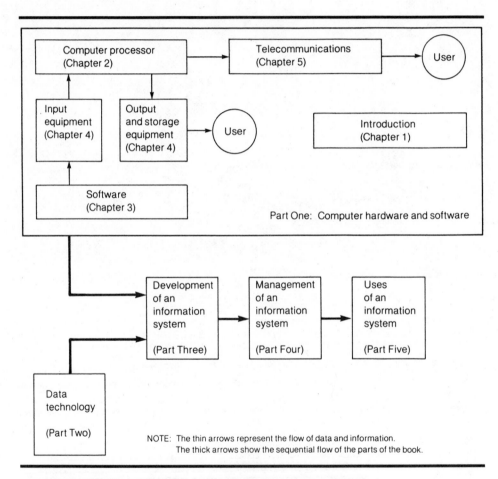

Computer processor
(Chapter 2)

Telecommunications
(Chapter 5)

User

Input
equipment
(Chapter 4)

Output
and storage
equipment
(Chapter 4)

User

Introduction
(Chapter 1)

Software
(Chapter 3)

Part One: Computer hardware and software

Development
of an
information
system

(Part Three)

Management
of an
information
system

(Part Four)

Uses
of an
information
system

(Part Five)

Data
technology

(Part Two)

NOTE: The thin arrows represent the flow of data and information.
The thick arrows show the sequential flow of the parts of the book.

COMPUTER HARDWARE
AND SOFTWARE

Computer technology required for a computerized information system is the subject of Part One. The relationship of the chapters of this part is shown in the diagram.

Central to all computer technology is the computer itself. Students of management for whom this text is written need general knowledge about computers, not technical details of how computers are constructed and operate. They are like car owners who can be good drivers without understanding the design and mechanics of internal combustion engines. Chapter 1 discusses the impact of information technology on business. In Chapter 2, the main components of a computer and component capabilities in general terms are described. The chapter also tells what computer equipment can and cannot do.

Given input, computer programs are needed to instruct the computer in processing so that desired results are achieved. These programs, called software, are the subject of Chapter 3. Again, technical details are omitted. Instead, the chapter presents an overview of types of programs used in processing. Also given is an introductory classification of languages that are used to write programs. Languages used most frequently in business processing are identified, and their capabilities and limitations briefly discussed.

Chapter 4 discusses input and output equipment and how output is stored for later use. Once programs process data, the output generated must be transmitted to a manager or user. The destination for the output is sometimes remote from the place of processing. Equipment and a set of procedures for efficient, effective, and secure transmission of output are required. Chapter 5, on telecommunications, deals with this subject.

1

INFORMATION FOR BUSINESS MANAGEMENT

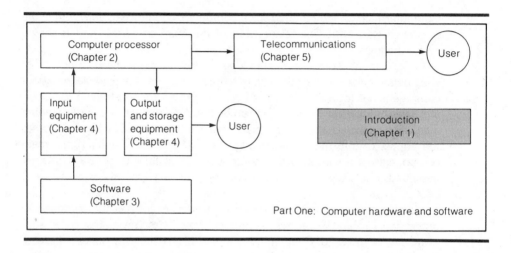

Ages, such as the stone, bronze, medieval, and industrial ages, have been used to describe the passage of human history. The dramatic development of computers in recent years has led to the birth of a new age, the age of information. In this chapter the technology of information as it relates to business management is examined.

GROWTH OF INFORMATION TECHNOLOGY

Businesspeople first felt the impetus of the age of information in the 1950s when electronic computers reached the market. The first computer, the ENIAC, made calculations in milliseconds, matching in one day 300 days of manual computation. By the 1970s, computer speeds reached nanoseconds (billionths of a second). Business applications such as those listed in Figure 1.1 are now solved in only a fraction of a second. No longer must businesses be run by hunch and intuition. Information on which to base decisions can now be processed by computer at incredible speeds.

Everyone recognizes that technological advances in transportation in the last century have reshaped the American life-style. We are no longer limited to walking, but travel by jet, an increase in speed by a factor of 100, from 4 mph to roughly 400 mph. The speed of processing information by computer, however, has increased by a factor of one million. Accessibility of information will ultimately transform society as profoundly as did the invention of the jet or the internal combustion engine.

Speed is not the only aspect of computer development to make prodigious improvement in recent years. Computers are getting smaller. Even purse and pocket models can now be purchased. Other characteristics such as system reliability, programmer productivity, and cost performance ratios have also made phenomenal advances, as shown in Table 1.1 and Figure 1.2. In spite of inflation, the price of information is dropping steadily. In 1950 the first computer cost $5 million. Today there are over a million computers, many models costing less than $100. Although information can be processed at reduced cost, total expenditures for data processing are on the rise (see Table 1.2) due to increased demand for information, rising salaries of EDP personnel, and the expense of sophisticated software. This is a good indication of how the business community values information as a resource.

5

FIGURE 1.1
The computer performs its functions at incredible speeds

In the computer, the basic operations can be done within the order of a

NANOSECOND

One thousandth of a millionth of a second.

Within the half second it takes this spilled coffee to reach the floor, a fairly large computer could —

$\left(\begin{smallmatrix}\text{given the information}\\\text{in magnetic form}\end{smallmatrix}\right)$

Debit 2000 checks to 300 different bank accounts,

and *examine the electro- cardiograms of 100 patients and alert a physician to possible trouble,*

and *score 150,000 answers on 3000 examinations and evaluate the effectiveness of the questions,*

and *figure the payroll for a company with a thousand employees.*

and a few other chores.

Courtesy International Business Machines Corporation

Many improvements in computers can be traced to the development of integrated circuitry and the use of small chips made of silicon, an element second to oxygen in abundance, on which circuitry is crammed. Modern technology also enables us to send data by satellite at 1200 million bits per second compared with an average of 1 bit per second on a telephone line. Data storage devices are needed when transmitting such large amounts of data,

TABLE 1.1
Comparison of selected characteristics normalized over time (1955 base year)

	1955*	1965	1975	(estimated) 1985
Number of computers	1	22.5	225	1,100
Performance/Cost	1	100	10,000	1,000,000
Programmer productivity	1	2.0	2.7	3.6
System reliability	1	5	24	120

* Values for 1955 are normalized at 1. Figures for subsequent years are relative, not absolute.

Source: T. A. Dolotta et al., *Data Processing in 1980–1985: A Study of Potential Limitations to Progress* (New York: Wiley-Interscience, 1976), pp. 173, 175.

FIGURE 1.2
Projected computer performance

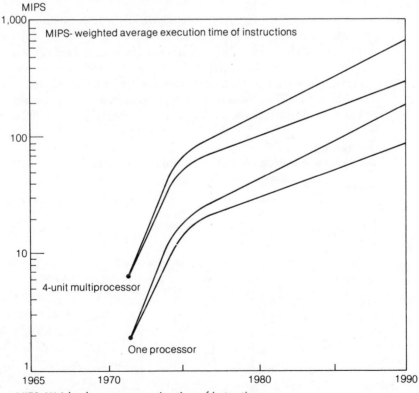

MIPS: Weighted average execution time of instructions.

Source: Adapted from Rein Turn, *Computers in the 1980s* (New York: Columbia University Press, 1974), p. 91.

TABLE 1.2
Expenditures for data processing in the United States (in billion dollars)

Year	Total data processing industry	All research and development
1970	21	41
1975	41	51
(estimated)		
1980	82	63
(estimated)		
1985	164	79

Source: T. A. Dolotta et al., *Data Processing in 1980–1985: A Study of Potential Limitations to Progress* (New York: Wiley-Interscience, 1976), pp. 173, 176.

but again, costs are dropping per unit stored and the devices themselves are becoming smaller and more compact (see Figure 1.3). Today data bases of over a trillion bits of stored data (one million million bits) are not uncommon.

Of course, computers have limitations. They lack human skills such as intuitive reasoning, associative recall, creativity, recognition of all patterns in written and spoken words, hearing, smelling, feeling, and tasting. Also, computers require human intervention. Without direction they cannot operate. Through research, however, some of these limitations may be eliminated in the near future. For example, prototype models are being developed which follow voiced instructions, and have some "intelligent" capabilities.

FIGURE 1.3
Space for one million characters of storage over time

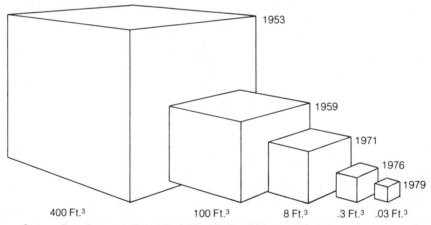

400 Ft.³   100 Ft.³   8 Ft.³   .3 Ft.³   .03 Ft.³

Source: *Data Processor,* (Special edition, March 1979), pp. 7–8.

PREDICTIONS FOR THE FUTURE

The potential of computers is vast. Future computers may think and teach themselves to do new tasks, like HAL, a computer in the film, *2001: A Space Odyssey.* Factories may be automated to operate on the basis of programmed decisions produced in automated offices, as predicted by the Nobel prizewinner Herbert Simon. Shopping may be done on home screens instead of at shopping centers. Advertising and news may be produced on computer terminals rather than on the printed page. Society may become cashless and checkless, with funds transferred electronically. The convergence of the computing and telecommunications industries may result in computers being as common and necessary for businesses as telephones are today. Constraints on these developments are more organizational, political, and regulatory than technological or economic, making it difficult to forecast when such projections will become reality.

It is harder to predict future misuse of computer technology. Will computers attempt to take control as did the computer in *2001,* or team up with foreign computers to take over the world as in the film *Colossus, the Forbin Project?* Will computers become monsters as in Michael Crichton's *The Terminal Man* and Ira Lewis's *This Perfect Day?* Will computers and large data banks monitor people's lives as perceived by Orwell in *1984* or direct a spy network as in Len Deighton's *Billion-Dollar Brain?* Will the ultimate robot prove ultimately uncontrollable as in John Barth's *Giles, Goat Boy?* Or become a lover as in Karl Bruchner's *The Hour of the Robots?* Will Karl Capek's play, *R.U.R.,* which depicts a dehumanized computerized version of man as a technological slave become reality? Will man no longer be dominant in society but become a markedly inferior species as in Olaf Johannesson's *Tales of the Big Computer?* Is it possible that fiction will become fact? No one can answer these questions with certainty, but knowledge of computer technology and information systems should help readers evaluate the likelihood of such imaginary scenarios becoming reality.

Since it generally takes a 5- to 20-year gestation period from invention to commercial application of new computer technology, professionals studying past trends and current research and development can make generalizations about the performance of computer systems to be marketed in this century with some measure of certainty. It is predicted that:

1. Computers will be more convenient for access, more compact, and more compatible with computer-related equipment manufactured by a wide range of vendors.
2. Computers will be simpler to use. For example, they will be conversational in mode, carrying on dialogues with users to help determine their needs, making it easy for nontechnical personnel to communicate with the computer system. Voice recognition equipment, optical character recognition equipment, and the development of computer microfilm

technology will help make the use of computers faster and cheaper as well.

3. Languages and the control of data bases will evolve, helping human-machine interface.

4. Copiers will have their own memory and intelligence, and will be integrated into computer systems for both on-site and remote-site processing.

5. Computer processing and copier technology will converge with teleprocessing, to make instant correspondence and transfer of information between offices economically possible even when long distances separate them.

6. Interorganizational communications will be electronic, bypassing the post offices in many cases.

7. Teleconferences will be held by management at all levels, decreasing the time and cost of business traveling.

8. Transmission of data will be done by satellites. For on-land transmission, glass optic fibers will be used that are 1/200th inch in diameter, having a capacity a billion times that of scarce copper wire used in today's telephone cable.

9. Robots will increasingly displace manufacturing personnel, and computers will be used in the areas of numerical control, process control, and computer-aided design, thereby increasing both efficiency and productivity.

10. Computers designed for special purposes will be compact, reliable, and cheap enough to be part of many household and industrial products.

To take full advantage of these trends, knowledge of computer technology and computerized information systems is essential for managers of the future. Providing this background is the purpose of this text.

IMPACT OF INFORMATION TECHNOLOGY ON BUSINESS

Formerly the two principal economic resources of business were capital and labor. A third primary resource has now been added: information. Access to information enables management to answer questions and solve problems and, in so doing, achieve corporate goals. Without information, decisions are intuitive and expedient, but not necessarily economically rational. The information provided by computer systems not only makes decision making more effective than in the past, but enables businesses to realize objectives never before possible. For example, a mail order company with the objective of good customer relations was never able to satisfy this aim when using manual inventory control, for customers were frequently inconvenienced by out-of-stock notices. When a computer system was installed to monitor warehouse contents and reorder items when a predetermined stock level was reached, the new system resulted in prompt fulfillment of orders and satisfied customers.

But information system technology places a burden on managers. They must understand what information systems can do, and participate in the development of systems for their own special needs. This involves the ability to define problems, objectives, and constraints specifically, in operational terms. Otherwise the manager will become a victim as in W. W. Jacob's story, "The Monkey's Paw," in which the owner of a monkey's paw was awarded three wishes. The first wish for $200 was granted, but it was recompense for the life of his son who was mangled while operating a machine. The second wish, for the son's return, was granted in the form of a mutilated ghost knocking at the door. The man's third wish, for the disappearance of this ghost, left him bereaved yet no richer than at the start of the story.

Managers, like the owner of the monkey's paw, must learn how to frame their wishes. An information system produces what is asked, but this may not be what the manager really wants, nor information that could have, or should have, been produced. In order to exploit information technology, knowledge about computers and their capabilities is required. New skills and new patterns of decision making must be learned. A different cadre of business managers is now in demand.

ROLE OF MANAGEMENT IN DEVELOPING INFORMATION SYSTEMS

What information is needed, why, for whom, and when are specifications on which the design of an information system is based. Determining these specifications is the responsibility of management, though analysts and consultants may assist in this determination. Implementation of the system is more technical, a responsibility of computer personnel, though liaison with management is necessary when making organizational changes required for the new system. Implementation transforms design specifications into the desired finished product: the new information system.

A distinction between user (management) and developer (systems analyst) is often made when discussing the development of information systems, but it is the authors' position that both groups are developers. They must cooperate, understand each other's capabilities and limitations, and support one another throughout the development process. Development is a highly interactive process. But as Schoderbek states, "Too often in the past top management has relinquished its responsibility by allowing the EDP [*electronic data processing*] group to determine its own objectives, set up its own standards, and measure its own performance. This is management by default."[1]

A lack of interest on the part of management can lead to serious undesirable consequences. According to Ackoff, "Managers who are not willing to invest some of their time in this [*development*] process are not likely to use a

---

[1] P. P. Schoderbek, ed., *Management Systems* (New York: John Wiley & Sons, Inc., 1967), p. 291.

management control system well, and their system in turn, is likely to abuse them."[2]

To effectively discharge their role in the development of information systems, managers should understand basic analytic tools, they should have fundamental knowledge of information systems and data organization, and should comprehend the process of developing an information system. This book discusses all of these topics.

OUTLINE OF BOOK

The text is divided into five parts. Part One presents computer technology needed for a computerized information system. The discussion of the basic components of computers and computer-related equipment is in general non-technical terms. The section on computer hardware in this part includes a look at input, output, and storage equipment, and the use of telecommunications for transferring data and information. Computer software, programs to instruct the computer on the processing of data, is also introduced.

Though much of the information in Chapters 1–4 can be found in introductory textbooks, the emphasis in this book is on recent developments. For example, Chapter 2 includes a discussion on microelectronics; Chapter 3, dialogue and interactive languages; and Chapter 4, scanners, COM (computer output on microfilm), voice recognition, and terminals with intelligent, graphic, and interactive capabilities.

Data, another component of an information system, is defined and the related technology discussed in Part Two. Since the cost per bit of random access storage of data has dropped steadily since 1970 with every indication that this trend will continue, businesses today are collecting increasingly large amounts of data. To use data effectively requires a basic knowledge of data organization, storage, and retrieval techniques, all described in this part of the text.

The development of an information system is the subject of Part Three. No two information systems are alike because every organization has unique output needs, but common to all systems are procedures for determining the needs of the information system and specific steps for designing and implementing the system, testing it, and converting the old to the new. The activities in each of these stages are presented.

The management of an information system is also important if the system is to be effective and economically efficient. Part Four discusses how to operate, maintain, evaluate, control, and organize an information system.

Information systems in businesses have many applications. These are discussed in Part Five. Sample functional applications are presented, integrating the principles and concepts described in the first four parts of this text. Also

---

[2] R. L. Ackoff, "Management Misinformation Systems," *Management Science,* Application (Series B), vol. 14, no. 4 (December 1967), p. 136.

introduced are the use of computers for planning and control by top and middle management, numerical control, robots, process control, computer-aided design, electronic fund transfer, electronic mail, teleconferencing, and word processing.

The last two chapters look to the future, describing how the electronic office and personal computers will function when business applications are expanded. Though predictions about technology often prove near-sighted, particularly in a fast-paced field such as computer science, the authors do attempt to alert readers about some of the social and economic implications of tomorrow's computerized society.

A more detailed outline of the contents of this book can be obtained by reading in a series the part introductions which describe chapter contents within each part, or reading the summaries that appear at the end of each chapter.

A list of key terms and concepts introduced in the text and a set of discussion questions are at the end of each chapter, followed by a selected annotated bibliography for further study. Some chapters have a set of exercises as well.

A contextual definition of terms and concepts presented in the book is found in the Appendix, "Glossary in Prose."

DISCUSSION QUESTIONS

1. Why should business students study computer processing and computerized information systems?
2. Need a businessperson know about a computer? What understanding of a computer and a computer system is necessary? Why?
3. Is the need for information systems for business increasing or decreasing? What is the future trend? How does it depend on the nature, size, and complexity of the business?
4. What is the difference between mechanization, automation, and computerization?
5. Give examples of users of computerized information in business and industry.
6. Give several possible examples of businesses without computerized information systems failing.
7. What are the major trends in computers and computing in terms of speed, reliability, cost-effectiveness, and size? Are these trends expected to continue? If so, for how long and to what extent?
8. Distinguish between user and developer.
9. State briefly your view of the limitations of computers and your agreement or disagreement with the many fictional views described in this chapter.
10. Would you agree that persons who like computers tend to be technologists, scientists, and mathematicians, and those who dislike computers, humanists?
11. Our current dependence on computers is dangerous. Do you agree with this statement? Why?
12. Give examples of misuse of information technology.

13. What is the role of a manager in the development and maintenance of an information system?

14. What capabilities must a manager have in order to effectively participate in the development of an information system?

15. What are some of the potential capabilities of information technology?

EXERCISE

1. Read the article by Harold J. Leavitt and Thomas L. Whistler, "Management in the 1980s," *Harvard Business Review,* vol. 36, no. 6 (November–December 1958), and a follow-up by J. G. Hunt and P. F. Newell, "Management in the 1980s Revisited," *Personnel Journal,* vol. 16, no. 1 (January 1971). Both these articles are printed in Gordon B. Davis and Gordon C. Everest, *Readings in Management Information Systems* (New York: McGraw-Hill Book Co., 1976), pp. 266–84.

Identify the predictions made on information technology and the effect advances in technology will have on management, business organization structure, and management information systems. Have predictions mentioned in these articles already become a reality? Are the authors' assumptions wrong? Do you anticipate that the predictions will become true in the 1980s? Why is it difficult and dangerous to predict advances in computer technology and the implications of such advances?

SELECTED ANNOTATED BIBLIOGRAPHY

Baer, Robert M. *The Digital Villain.* Reading Mass.: Addison-Wesley Publishing Co., Inc., 1972.

The subtitle of this book is: *Notes on the Numerology, Parapsychology, and Metaphysics of the Computer.* Despite the foreboding subtitle, this is a delightful book on computers in fiction. It cites extensively from many books, films, and plays where a computer is usually the villain. It also discusses the social implications in the event that fiction becomes reality.

Dolotta, T. A., et al. *Data Processing in 1980–1985: A Study of Potential Limitations to Progress.* New York: John Wiley & Sons, Inc., 1976. 191 pp.

There are seven authors of this book, all from industry, including representatives of the computer industry. They focus on the main stream of large, general-purpose business-oriented data processing systems and predict changing demands on both the data processing industry and on management. The appendix has a set of tables that include predictions on expenditures and personnel required for 1980–85.

Futurist, vol. 12, no. 5 (October 1978).

This issue has three articles on the future as it will be affected by computing technology—"Checkless/Cashless Society? Don't Bank on It!" "Electronic Meetings: Utopian Dreams and Complex Realities," and "Videoconferencing via Satellite: Opening Government to the People." The first two articles are rather critical about computing euphoria. The topics are relevant to everyone in business.

Information Systems in the 1980s. Boston: Arthur D. Little, Inc., 1978.

The chapter "The Corporate Computer in the 1980s" by Frederick G. Withington is a fairly nontechnical discussion of the very technical subject of computer technology. The author is an authority on the subject and has predicted computer technology before with good success.

This reference is difficult to find but worth the extra effort. The booklet also has three other articles which forecast development regarding distributed systems, the office of the future, and systems planning in the 1980s. All are worth reading.

Martin, James. *The Wired Society.* Englewood Cliffs, N.J.: Prentice-Hall, Inc., 1978. 300 pp.

This is an excellent book written without technical jargon on the future of information technology, especially with regard to telecommunications. It makes predictions for the next two decades and discusses the social and economic implications of information technology. The author paints scenarios of a 3½-day workweek with education, shopping, and work done at a computer terminal at home; of EFT (electronic fund transfer) almost eliminating the need for cash and checks; of wrist transmitters and common satellite transmission; and of 6 billion people on the planet bombarded with video media bringing news, advertising, shopping, polling, and other daily activities within the reach of a home computer terminal.

Simon, H. A. "What Computers Mean for Man and Society." *Science,* vol. 195, no. 4283 (March 18, 1977), pp. 1186–91.

The author looks into the present and the future of computers and their impact on society, especially in relation to control and privacy, the nature of work, and shifts in the structure of business employment. The author, a Nobel prizewinner in economics, has been a keen commentator on decision making and artificial intelligence, and the relationship between the two.

Turn, Rein. *Computers in the 1980s.* New York: Columbia University Press, 1977. 257 pp.

This book is a set of predictions by a senior analyst at RAND corporation. The author looks at developments in CPU hardware, peripherals, communication systems, and computer systems until 1990 and tells the reader how to revise these predictions as certain developments occur. The forecast assumes no super-technological breakthrough.

In Part Four of the book the author discusses specific innovations which include modularity of systems and networks, software transferability, greater failure-tolerant systems, and increased viability of human-machine interface.

2

THE COMPUTER PROCESSOR

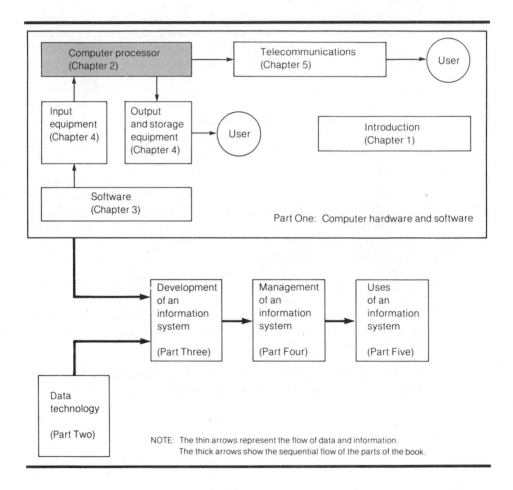

An information system is an organized set of components designed to produce intelligence required for decision making. In a business context, the information is for management. The system itself has four main components: input, output, computer programs, and the processor. The relationship between these parts is shown in Figure 2.1. The subject of this chapter is the processor. The

FIGURE 2.1
Main components of an information system

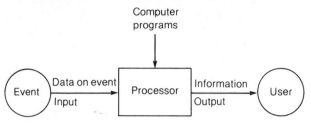

other components and the design of the system will be discussed in chapters that follow.

JUSTIFICATION FOR COMPUTER PROCESSORS

Following a transaction, data on the event must be handled according to predetermined procedures and decision rules to generate desired information. This can be done by hand, called **manual processing,** but when computations are complex and large in volume, such processing can be slow, monotonous, inaccurate, and costly. Machine processing is then recommended, often called simply **data processing.**

Data processing was first used by Herman Hollerith in 1896 to speed up processing of 1890 census data. The machine processing was done with greater accuracy and in one third the time that previous manual census processing had required.

Hollerith developed a card on which data could be represented by holes, a card known as the **Hollerith card** which has since been produced in such massive quantities by IBM that it is more commonly called the **IBM card.** When data processing was in its infancy these cards often contained data for one record, such as all sales data for one transaction, so that processing cards became known as **unit record processing.** The machines used were electrical and performed primarily accounting operations, which explains why they were called **electrical accounting machines** or **EAM** equipment. As the amount of data to be processed increased, this equipment proved slow and expensive to use. It was replaced by the electronic computer for **electronic data processing,** known as **EDP.**

Although both EAM and EDP require the initial investment of costly equipment, large volume data processing reaches a **break-even point** where use of the equipment is economically justified. Savings in processing occur for added volume beyond this point. Figure 2.2 illustrates this concept. In this figure variable costs are shown by the slope of the total cost lines. It will be noted that the slope of *AB* for manual processing is steeper than *CD,* the slope of machine processing. (*CD* includes EAM and other office machines such as bookkeeping equipment.) That means that the variable

FIGURE 2.2
Break-even points for machine and computer processing

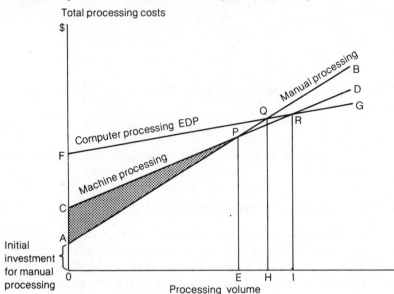

cost per unit processed is higher in manual processing, though the fixed cost *OA* (desk, pencil, paper) is lower. The break-even point *P,* representing volume processing *OE,* is the point beyond which machine processing is warranted. For less volume, manual processing remains more economical, the shaded area showing the savings that would accrue if manual instead of machine processing were used.

The slope of computer processing is even flatter, though initial costs are higher. The break-even point compared to manual processing *(AB)* is *Q,* for volume *OH.* A much higher volume of data processing *(OI)* is needed when compared to machine processing *(CD)* before EDP becomes economically justified.

This figure is merely a model. In an actual case, the starting point on the *X* axis would depend on the equipment used, and the slope of manual processing would depend on the wage scale. But the general concept that this figure illustrates would still apply. As the volume of data processing increases, the switchover from manual to machine to computer processing becomes economically justified. For large volume processing, beyond *OI* in Figure 2.2, computer processing is the cheapest way to generate information.

THE DIGITAL COMPUTER

Computers may be classified in terms of the type of data processed. When data is discrete, a **digital computer** is used. When data is processed continuously, such as monitoring temperature, pressure, and flow of liquids in manufacturing, an **analog computer** is used. A **hybrid computer** handles both discrete and continuous data. Since businesses usually deal with discrete digital data, digital computers are most commonly used for management decision making.

The main components of a digital computer system are shown in Figure 2.3. The **central processor (CPU)** in this system has three parts: the **arithmetic and logic unit,** the **memory and storage unit,** and the **control unit.**

Input data is stored in the memory until it is ready to be processed. Also stored are instructions concerning computations to be performed—calculations such as addition and multiplication which are carried out by the arithmetic unit, which also does logical operations such as comparisons. The control unit coordinates the sequence of instructions and flow of data between units.

Intermediate calculations and other information related to the transformation of input are also stored. If the volume of data to be stored is too large for the **internal memory** or **main memory,** it can be stored in **external memory** or **secondary storage** on devices such as magnetic tapes or disks. Some manufacturers have developed **virtual memory,** which enables secondary storage to be treated as an extension of the internal memory, thereby effectively expanding internal storage capacity.

Digital computers have changed greatly since the UNIVAC computer be-

FIGURE 2.3
The organization of a digital computer system

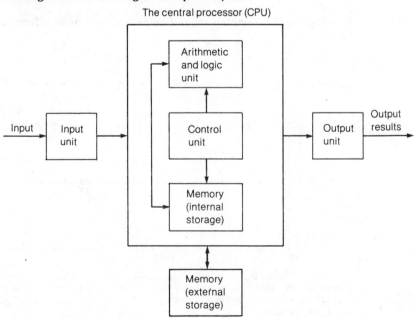

came commercially available in 1951. The changes came in large jumps of performance, referred to as **generations** of computers, instead of slowly and gradually as might be expected. In the first generation, **vacuum tubes** were used; in the second, **transistors;** in the third, **integrated circuits.** A further comparison of these three generations is found in Table 2.1.

TABLE 2.1
Comparison of three generations of computers

Major characteristics	First generation	Second generation	Third generation
Electronic circuitry	Vacuum tubes	Transistors	Integrated circuits
Size	Room size	Closet size	Desk-top to chip
Speed	1 microsecond	100 nanoseconds	5 nanoseconds
Reliability (relative) . . .	1	1,000 times	100,000 times
Software	Machine language User-written	Symbolic language Canned programs	Higher level languages Query and interactive languages
Operating mode	Batch	Online Real time Time sharing	Distributed processing Microprocessing Microcomputers Minicomputers

FIGURE 2.4
Development of components and computer systems as a function of time

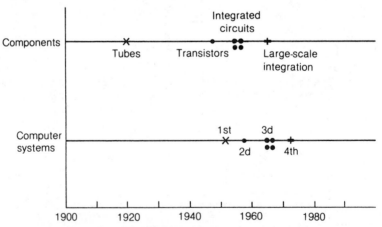

Source: Adapted by permission of the publisher, from John T. Soma, *The Computer Industry: An Economic-Legal Analysis of its Technology* (Lexington, Mass.: Lexington Books, D. C. Heath and Company, 1976), p. 10. Copyright 1976 D. C. Heath and Company.

Some authors identify a fourth generation, **large-scale integration.** A time scale showing when these generations were developed appears in Figure 2.4.

CPU ADVANCES

All digital data can be represented by unique arrangements of the digits 0 and 1. These **binary digits,** called **bits,** can be represented by two states (on and off in a switch, different states of electrons in a vacuum tube, or by high and low voltage in a transistor). The answers to true-false statements, for example, can be coded in binary digits; that is, off = false, on = true. The British mathematician Boole designed algebra (Boolean algebra) using the true-false concept for a logical analysis that is electronically represented in gates. A **gate** controls the flow of information by providing an output signal only when the input signals are in prescribed states. Combinations of gates enable computations such as addition, subtraction, multiplication, division, and comparisons. It is the production method of these gates that changed with the generations of digital computers. The first vacuum tube gates proved unreliable. These gates were replaced by the transistor which proved 1,000 times more reliable. Transistors were in time replaced by integrated circuits that proved 100 times more reliable still. Thus the progression to integrated circuits from the vacuum tube represented an improvement of reliability by a factor of 100,000.

While reliability was advancing, costs were decreasing. The vacuum tube gate cost about $10. Only one cent was required for an integrated circuit gate in the late 70s.

Other characteristics of digital computers have been affected by technological developments as well. The early vacuum tubes were large, consumed much electrical power, and generated considerable heat. Air conditioning and frequent maintenance were required. Transistors are smaller, cheaper, generate less heat, and consume less power. Integrated circuits made quantum jumps in all these areas, but especially in size. The technology that made this possible was **microelectronics,** a photolithography process for fabricating millions of elements of circuitry onto thin wafers of silicon. The wafers are divided into individual **dice** or **chips,** each of which forms at least one complete electronic circuit which is photographically etched. Integrated circuitry contains many interconnections that previously had to be joined manually; thus there is a saving in labor and materials and less chance of human error causing malfunction. Integrated circuits consume little power and their small size means short distances of circuitry must be traveled, resulting in increased speeds of processing.

Chip technology is also used in **memory units.** A three-quarter-inch diameter wafer can hold over 100 square silicon chips, each able to store 64,000 bits of information. The cost in 1979 was less than $\frac{1}{10}^5$ cent per bit compared to $\frac{1}{10}$ cent per bit in magnetic tape storage used in the first generation of computers, making storage costs 10,000 times cheaper.

MODES OF PROCESSING

Batch processing

In the first generation of digital computers **batch processing** was used. This technique is still employed though faster processing methods have been developed. Many persons use batch processing when paying bills. They do not write checks immediately upon receipt of bills, but collect them, waiting until the monthly paycheck arrives, at which time all bills are paid at once. Writing checks in a batch saves time since checkbook, pen, stamps, and envelopes must be located and put back only once a month instead of numerous times. In computer batch processing, either the computer operator or the system itself collects jobs in batches, resulting in a significant reduction in overhead costs since repetitive handling of each job is eliminated. Batch processing of data reduces processing costs, though a processing delay of hours or days may result.

Delay in batch processing is compounded when the source of data is remote from the computer. The use of **telecommunication lines** (the telephone, for example) to transfer data to the CPU reduces this delay. Special control programs for receiving, checking, scheduling, and observing priorities for data processing services are added to the system when such **remote processing** is employed. Businesses that have multiple sources of data generation use remote processing for input **(remote job entry).**

Equipment not directly connected to a computer is called **offline. Online** means users have direct connection to the computer system. Online systems gained prominence in second generation computers. Their capability gave users at terminals direct access to the computer for both input and output. But since telecommunications proved much slower than the computing capabilities, a system was developed for sharing a computer between many users at many terminals, a system called **time sharing.**

Time sharing

Fair-use rules had to be developed with time-sharing systems. First-come, first-served had the disadvantage that users with small jobs had to wait until users with long jobs were serviced. A **round-robin service** was initiated in which all users were given a small slice of computing time in turn. Since second generation computers which first used round-robin service had microsecond (millionths of a second) processing speeds, most users got fast service and had the illusion of owning the computer. Time sharing has proved particularly valuable to small businesses unable to afford computers and software equipment of their own, and many firms that formerly used batch processing switched to time sharing for convenience and faster processing, even though the cost of information processed by this mode was higher. Time sharing is still widely used, although problems with data security and priority processing can arise. A summary of the advantages and disadvantages of time sharing appears in Table 2.2.

Time sharing does not always provide immediate access to computing power which some businesses require. For example, banks may want quick access at all times to the status of a customer's current balance. For instantaneous processing and continuous updating of the data base, **real-time systems** were developed in the second generation of computers.

TABLE 2.2
Time sharing

Characteristics
   Central computer accessible to multiple users for input and output.
   Telephonic connections between computer and user at remote sites.

Advantages
   Enables small user to have access to a large computer system, sharing overhead
      costs with other users.
   Reduces overhead cost even for large user.
   Provides access to data bases and generalized applications programs.
   Faster response than batch.
   Enables interactive and conversational use of computer.
   No geographic restriction except for cost of transmission.
   Convenience of use.

Disadvantages
   When system is down, all users sharing the system are affected.
   Higher cost than batch processing.
   Loss of security. Data is subject to violation either due to accident or design.
   Response time can drop with increase in number of users, especially those with
      large scientific problems to process.
   Possible loss of priority when large competitive demands are placed on system.

Real time

Real-time systems process both input and output data continuously and simultaneously. They are used to monitor data and to detect undesirable deviations from predetermined standards and then provide feedback information for control. For example, the computer may process continuous data on an industrial process and issue instructions for controlling that process, such as monitoring pressure and shutting off valves when pressure gets too high. Though real-time processing is instantaneous, the speed of output will depend on need, taking only a fraction of a second in some cases or minutes in others, depending on the time required to make the necessary correction or the urgency of information processed. Such a system must be online; hence it is called an **online real-time** system or **OLRT.**

Distributed processing

Distributed data processing, the relocation and distribution of computing capability from a central location to remote sites such as branch offices, warehouses, and plants, is one of the results of the development of third generation computers. Giving local levels more autonomy through distributed processing results in decentralization, changing the organizational structure of firms and their patterns of decision making. The impact of such processing on management will be discussed in Part Four at length.

Two technological developments have made distributed data processing feasible: **teleprocessing** (see Chapter 5) and **microelectronics,** including microprocessors, microcomputers, and minicomputers. Microelectronics, in drastically reducing computing cost, have made one-site data processing practical. The nature and implications of microelectronics is the subject of the remaining parts of this chapter.

MICROELECTRONICS

Microelectronics became possible as a result of advances made in solid-state physics and integrated circuitry. In the early stages of microelectronics, the concentration of circuit components that were integrated was small, called **small-scale integration (SSI).** Conventional transistor circuitry as found in radios was used. This circuitry consumed much electric current and developed heat which limited the number of transistors that could be put on one chip. These problems were overcome by **metal oxide semiconductor (MOS) technology** which enabled greater concentration of circuitry per chip, or **large-scale integration (LSI).** A comparison of LSI and SSI appears in Table 2.3.

In 1964, Gordon E. Moore, then working for Fairchild, noted that the

TABLE 2.3
Summary of SSI and LSI

Characteristic	Small-scale integrated circuits	Large-scale integrated circuits
Components per circuit	1–32	1,000–262,000
Size of computer	Desk or desk-top size	Typewriter size to chip size
Speed of computer	100 nanoseconds	5 nanoseconds
Main memory	Magnetic core	LSI circuits
Mode of processing	Time sharing Online real time	Distributed processing Microprocessors Microcomputers Minicomputers

number of components per circuit had a linear relationship over time. He correctly predicted that circuit complexity would double each year. The graph in Figure 2.5 shows the transition that has been made from small through medium to large-scale integration. Technology still hasn't reached the limits imposed by the laws of physics. Further miniaturization is still possible.

FIGURE 2.5
Components per circuit over time

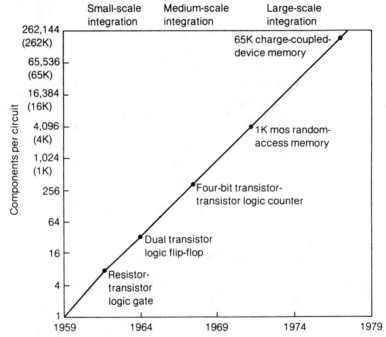

Note: The number of components per circuit in the most advanced integrated circuits has doubled every year since 1959, when the planar transistor was developed.
Source: Robert N. Noyce, "Microelectronics," *Scientific American,* vol. 237, no. 3 (September 1977), p. 67.

Other dramatic differences between SSI and LSI are the relative cost per gate (see Figure 2.6) and the relative rate of failure per gate (see Figure 2.7). In both figures SSI and LSI are superimposed over the curves for vacuum tubes and transistors. Some authors consider LSI such a great advance that they advocate it represents a fourth generation of computers.

Microprocessors

LSI technology means that an entire CPU can now be placed on a single chip. **Microprocessors,** designed to perform specific functions in products

FIGURE 2.6
Relative costs per gate over time

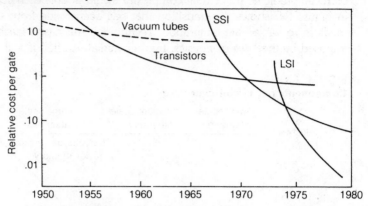

Source: John S. Mayo, "The Role of Microelectronics in Communication,"
Scientific American, vol. 237, no. 3 (September 1977), p. 208.

FIGURE 2.7
Relative failure rate of gate over time

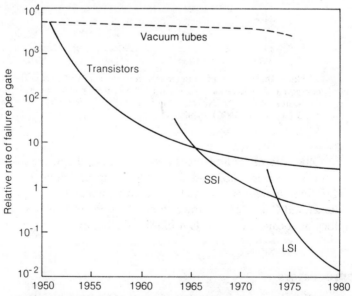

Source: John S. Mayo, "The Role of Microelectronics in Communication,"
Scientific American, vol. 237, no. 3 (September 1977), p. 208.

and to make needed adjustments necessary for changed conditions, utilize this miniaturization. Through **sensors,** a microprocessor can collect input on performance, evaluate it against preset standards, and through an actuator make control adjustments. For example, in cars, a microprocessor can optimize consumption of fuel by sensing the air environment (temperature, velocity, density) and adjusting the mixture of air and fuel accordingly. A user may also change the microprocessor's **microcode** (program) from one control application to another.

TABLE 2.4
Uses of microprocessors

Industrial products	*Consumer products*
Aircraft subsystems	Automobile subsystems
Blood analyzers	Blenders
Cash registers	Burglar alarms
Communication devices	Calculators
Copying machines	Cameras
Dictating machines	Clocks
Gasoline pumps	Clothes dryers
Lab equipment control	Dishwashers
Machine control	Electric slicing knives
Measuring instruments	Fire alarms
Medical diagnostics	Food blenders
Pacemakers	Hair dryers
Robots	Heating systems
Scales	Microwave ovens
Scanners	Monitoring of home utilities
Taxi meters	Fuel/heat/water/light
Telephone switching	Ovens
Testing instruments	Pinball machines
Toasters	Radios
Traffic lights	Refrigerators
TV camera	Slow cookers
Vending machines	Stereo systems
etc.	Telephones
	Television sets
	Washing machines
	Watches
	etc.

Table 2.4 is a list of products where microprocessors are commonly used. Many of these need more than one micro. Uses of microprocessors in an airplane are shown in Figure 2.8. Table 2.5 summarizes current and potential use of microprocessors in automobiles. A study by Arthur D. Little predicts that by 1987 the microprocessor industry will have 400 million chip-based consumers, with an annual market of $40 billion in 1978 dollars.[1]

---

[1] A single copy of the results of this $2 million study costs $35,000. A report of this study appears in *Economist,* vol. 270, no. 7073 (March 24–30, 1979), p. 49.

FIGURE 2.8
Use of microprocessors in aircraft

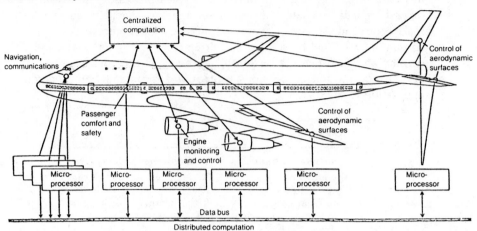

Modern jet aircraft depend on a variety of sophisticated systems for navigation, communication, passenger comfort and safety, engine control, and the control of aerodynamic surfaces. At present the sensors that monitor these various systems transmit their data to a central computer, which generates the control signals needed to keep the systems working properly. The miles of cables required for such centralized systems have become a significant fraction of the total cost of modern aircraft. In principle, various systems of aircraft could be controlled locally by microprocessors with a great saving in cable costs, increased reliability, increased computing power, and lower maintenance costs. Such distributed computing networks are under active examination for a wide variety of similar applications.

Source: Hoo-Min D. Toong, "Microprocessors," *Scientific American,* vol. 237, no. 3 (September 1977), p. 160.

TABLE 2.5
Uses of microprocessors in an automobile

Accessory control	Exhaust gas control
Air conditioning control	Locking doors
Belt buckling control	Maintenance analysis
Braking control	Skid control
Collision avoidance system	Speed control
Comfort control	Steering control
Control of subsystems such as level of fuel,	Theft deterrent control
driver's seat, and mirror adjustments	Trip information (distance to
Emission control	destination, driving range, etc.)
Engine control	Vehicle diagnosis
Air-fuel mixture	Vehicle performance analysis
Ignition timing	

Microcomputers

When microprocessors are given additional memory and input/output capabilities they are called **microcomputers.** A microcomputer can also be constructed on a chip or chips and may be much smaller than a fingertip,

**FIGURE 2.9
A microcomputer on a chip placed against
a fingertip**

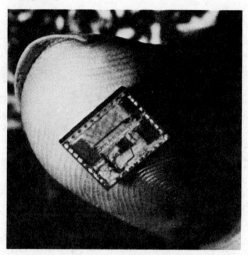

Courtesy Intel Corporation

as illustrated in Figure 2.9. One of these chips can be a microprocessor, an enlarged photograph of which appears in Figure 2.10 with its main functional components identified. A functional representation of this microprocessor within a microcomputer, shown in Figure 2.11, corresponds with the basic components of a computer illustrated in Figure 2.3.

Minicomputers

Unlike a microcomputer designed for a specific application, a **mini-computer** is a general-purpose computer. The term ***mini*** originally meant smaller in memory capacity, lower in cost, slower in speed, and smaller in size than other computers on the market. When microprocessors were developed, they were much smaller than minis, but the term mini continued to apply to small general-purpose computers. Taking advantage of diminished costs of components, minis have continued to add to their computing capacity without proportionately raising in cost, so that today minis are comparable to what were former medium-scale computers, blurring the lines of division between the two. Some authors consider the term minicomputer an anachronism[2] and argue that larger computers and minis will soon merge into one.[3]

---

[2] Myles E. Walsh, "Where Have All the Minis Gone? *Infosystems,* vol. 25, no. 7 (July 1978), pp. 62–73.

[3] Frederick W. Miller, "The Impending Merger of Minis and Main Frames," *Infosystems,* vol. 25, no. 4 (April 1978), pp. 45–46.

FIGURE 2.10
Components of the Intel 8086 microprocessor

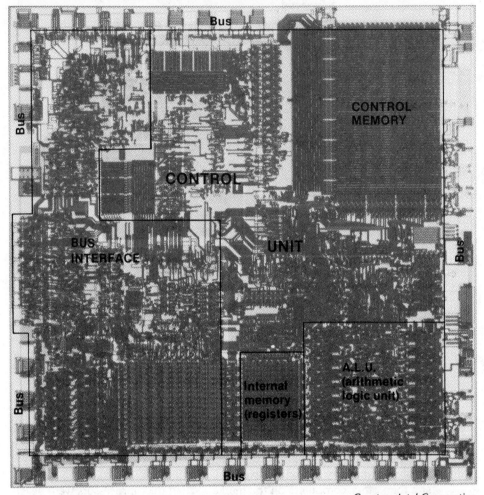

Courtesy Intel Corporation

Even in size minis are no longer physically small. The PDP-11 is six feet high and occupies 14 by 18 inches of floor space. This does not include a printer but does include storage devices like the **magnetic cassette** and the **floppy disk.** (The nonrigid floppy is preferable to former disks which required large disk drive units and had to be extremely level for operation.)

Minis are still limited in computing capacity for they continue to have lower processing speeds, a relatively small memory, few peripheral units for input-output (I/O) and less software support than medium- or large-scale computers. The low speed is the result of an architectural characteristic: small

word size where a word is a unit of storage. This small width of word reduces the number of instructions that can be fetched from memory at one time. The word size varies between 8 and 18 bits. If a mini has 16 bits per word, and floating point calculations (with decimal numbers) are being computed, this requires 64 bits; that is, four fetches from memory, instead of one fetch with a 64-bit machine, resulting in low speed of processing.

The CPU and memory of minicomputers can be built from microprocessors and chips. Different **configurations** can be constructed for varying applications as shown in Figure 2.12. As prices for microprocessors drop, it may become possible to have hundreds or even thousands of processors working in parallel on a common problem. This would increase machine intelligence (artificial intelligence), conceivably bringing it near to human intelligence.

FIGURE 2.11
Basic components of a microcomputer

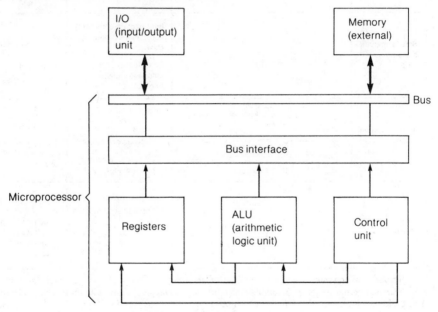

Because of the adaptability and flexibility of minicomputer configurations, over a third of the production is bought by companies called **original equipment manufacturers (OEMs)** who resell the minis with their own software as a **package** for applications in accounting, sales, control of manufacture, and other specialized business functions. Such packages enable small businesses with low budgets and nontechnical personnel to purchase and use a computer.

The characteristics, advantages, and limitations of minicomputers are summarized in Table 2.6. Both minis and micros are least effective when applica-

FIGURE 2.12
Configurations of micro and mini hardware

Micro hardware hierarchy		Capabilities	Typical uses and users
Level	Representation		
Chips		Custom design of a hardware system for particular need	Hardware designers
Modules		Small development system for learning microprocessor characteristics Small-user programs (under 1 K)	Beginning users of microprocessors Elementary prototyping User evaluation of microprocessor
Small computer system (SCS)	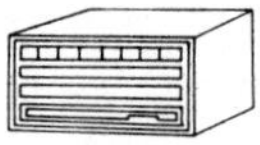	Intermediate-complexity applications programs (1-10 K) Some higher-level language capability (e.g. BASIC)	Personal computer Hobbyist
Full development system (FDS)	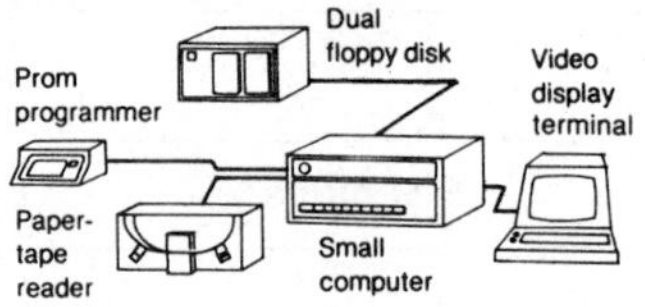 Prom programmer / Dual floppy disk / Video display terminal / Paper-tape reader / Small computer	Full software development Hardware debugging Higher-level language programming	Software-applications programming Debugging of hardware target system
Multiprocessor system	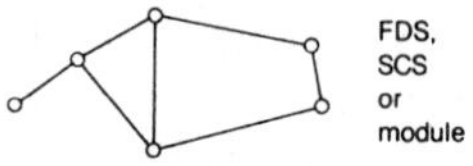 FDS, SCS or module	Distributed computing Tightly coupled parallel processing	Process automation Coordination and control on a distributed and local basis

Microprocessor systems can be arranged in an ascending hierarchy of hardware and software in which smaller components are assembled into successively larger systems with more powerful capabilities. The building blocks are the families of chips designed for various functions. To solve an application problem, for example the control system of an airplane, designers usually assemble modules or small computer systems and provide them with a suitable program for the task. Chips and modules have become so cheap (less than $30 for a microprocessor and less than $300 for a single-board module) that a major cost in engineering an application is the cost of developing the software to create the final program for the "target" system. Improvements in semiconductor technology are steadily making it possible for systems at each level to include more of capabilities once assigned to level above.

Source: Adapted from Hoo-Min D. Toong, "Microprocessors," *Scientific American,* vol. 237, no. 3 (September 1977), pp. 154–55.

TABLE 2.6
Characteristics, advantages and limitations of a minicomputer

Characteristics
16-bit word
4–28000 word storage
Low cost (10–25000 $)
Integrated circuit technology used for both
CPU and memory

Advantages
Ease of use
Low cost
Flexibility through external programs
Adaptability to different configurations

Limitations*
Cannot perform complex programs
Slow speeds of computing due to small word size
Less software support
Many manufacturers are new to the field
Has limited peripherals

* Many of these limitations are being overcome in newer models.

FIGURE 2.13
Price-performance ratios for micros, minis, and large-scale computers

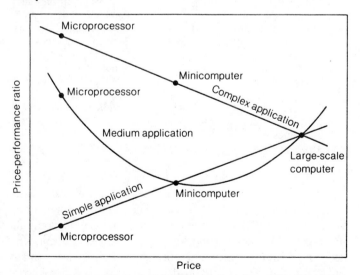

Source: Reprinted by permission from A. L. Scherr, "Distributed Data Processing," *IBM System Journal,* vol. 17, no. 4 (1978), p. 330. © 1978 by International Business Machines Corporation.

tions are complex, as shown in Figure 2.13. For simple problems, the price performance ratio of microprocessor is least (best). As complexity increases, minicomputers become cost-effective until a point is reached where only large-scale computers are economically justified. The curves in Figure 2.13 indicate that there are areas where micros, minis, and large computers have a respective comparative advantage.

Uses of minicomputers are listed in Table 2.7. It is predicted that by 1986 applications will increase 100 times, and the price per mini will drop to less than $100. This will be primarily due to better exploitation and integration of LSI, greater demand for distributive processing, and pressure on manufacturers and software houses for better price performance ratios.

TABLE 2.7
Uses of a minicomputer

Current	Future
Bank terminals	Badge and credit-card checking
Blood analyzer	Bartenders
CAI (computer-assisted instruction)	Elevator control
Cash register	Gas pump control
Communication	Medical diagnosis
Storing and forwarding	Online calculations in hotel
messages	Hotel bill
Monitoring telephone lines	Restaurant
Education	Tip
Input validation on terminals	Passenger movement control
Instrumentation	Physician control of
Mixers (e.g., paint and	information on patients
other substances)	Plant schedule control
Numerical control	Process control
Personal computer	Security and access control
Printing	Shopping scales
Editing	Simulation
Typesetting	Stock and commodity applications
Page layout	Typewriters
Process control	Vending machines
Stand-alone computer for small	
businesses	
Text editing	

The sale of desk-top minicomputers to businesspersons and homeowners as **personal computers** is a potentially explosive market for minis. Software is being developed for entertainment (games) and computing applications such as checkbook balancing, keeping a calendar of events, calculating income taxes, monitoring investments, updating address lists, and typing letters. A California Supreme Court justice has even used a minicomputer to index data from a trial. Neither cost nor hardware technology limit the widespread use of minis at present. It is rather a reluctance to learn how to use computers and a lack of understanding of their capabilities that is slowing sales. When these problems are overcome, there will be a revolution in the way we live, work, and do business.

COMPUTER HARDWARE IN THE FUTURE

The 1980s will see greater use of micros and minis in different combinations and networks. In addition, there will be still more powerful computers. One development that shows great promise for the future is the **Josephson computer** being developed by IBM, named after the Englishman who theorized that electrical flow becomes faster at low temperatures because of lack of resistance. The Josephson computer will operate at −269°, its circuits, referred to a cryogenic devices, sitting in liquid helium at 4°C. On/off switching will be at 7 billionths of a second, enabling 70 million instructions per second (70 mips). This computer is roughly 14 times faster than the most powerful IBM computer of the 1970s. The basic components, the Josephson junctions, are very fragile, however, and had a high rejection rate in early production. This production problem has now been overcome. The Josephson computer only awaits engineering to fit into a three-pound package, a package projected for the mid-1980s.

Another development, also at IBM, is the introduction of a totally new family of circuits called **current injection logic** which utilize a thousand times less energy than transistor circuits and operate at about 13 picoseconds,[4] twice or thrice as fast as Josephson circuits. Another promising line of research is being conducted at the Herrit-Watt University in Edinburgh on electronic **lasers** to make an optical switch turn on and off at a trillionth of a second. Such speed, combined with the Josephson computer, makes computers with 250 mips a distinct possibility in the 1990s.

A **distributed array processor,** using thousands of microprocessors in parallel, is also under development. This processor, however, has limited speed, for it depends on conventional integrated circuits. Another major problem is that it requires considerable power. A 250 mips computer with conventional architecture would consume around 20,000 watts and would melt as soon as it was turned on. Circuitry problems may be resolved by VLSI (very large-scale integration) and VHSIC (very high-speed integrated circuits). Chips are projected that are one hundredth the width of human hair, containing lines half a micron in size. A single chip could contain entire systems for a radar network, a library, or factory. We may someday have an information-system-on-a-chip, or an office-on-a-chip.

Research isn't simply limited to arrays of microprocessors. Approaches such as pipelines or multiprocessors are also being studied. With so many

---

[4] As an analogy, a picosecond is to a second what a second is to 31,710 years. In contrast, a nanosecond is to a second what a second is to 30 years.

lines of research, the technologies that will actually produce the supercomputers of the future are hard to predict.

It should be recognized, however, that what is technically feasible may not be implemented in the near future. Chips, for example, were in short supply in 1980, with shortages predicted for the following five years, one reason being that the semiconductor industry was not earning enough profit to finance its own phenomenal growth, while decline in profits had scared away venture capital. Furthermore, investment costs have become so high that few new firms can afford to enter the market. A basic chip-making facility built for $2 million in the 1960s cost at least $50 million in 1980. Many firms which manufactured chips in-house in the past, now buy chips on the open market due to production problems at their own facilities, adding to chip demand.[5]

Even with an abundant supply of chips, time is required to design new products based on chips, time is needed to develop secondary technologies to take advantage of the raw intelligence of microelectronics, and time is essential to gain the confidence of consumers in intelligent products. The 80s will see an increase in the use of microchips, but the increase may not constitute a microelectronic revolution as was once predicted.

SUMMARY AND CONCLUSIONS

This chapter has discussed the evolution of computers. Minicomputers have more computing capacity than the first electronic computer, ENIAC; are 20 times faster; have a larger memory; are thousands of times more reliable; consume the power of a light bulb rather than that of a locomotive; and occupy 1/30,000 the volume. They also cost less than 1/10,000 as much.[6] (See Figure 2.14 for a comparison of components per chip and cost per component.) Minicomputers can be purchased by mail order or at local hobby stores. The trend is continuing toward further miniaturization, faster speeds, greater reliability, and lower costs. Past improvements were due to technological changes in the basic components of the CPU, which evolved from the vacuum tube to transistors, and from SSI to LSI and chip technology. Technological advances have resulted in increased concentration of circuitry (gate density) by a factor of 100, or two magnitudes (10^2). Another two orders of magnitude are predicted for the 1980s. Yet another order of magnitude is necessary to approach the gate density of the human brain.

Micros and minis are being incorporated in home products making them "smart." That is, they are able to evaluate the environment and the desires of the user and activate correcting adjustments where necessary. In the future,

---

[5] "All That Is Electronic Does Not Glitter," *The Economist,* vol. 274, no. 7122 (March 1–7, 1980), pp. 53–54.

[6] Robert N. Noyce, "Microelectronics," *Scientific American,* vol. 237, no. 3 (September 1977), p. 65.

FIGURE 2.14
Trends in microelectronics

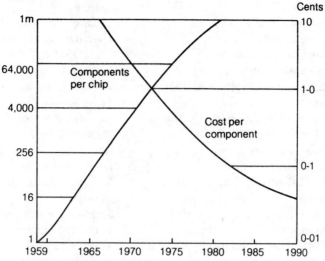

Source: "Survey on Microelectronics," *Economist,* vol. 274, no. 7122 (March 1–7, 1980), p. 3.

they will commonly appear in clocks, thermostats, light switches, radios, toasters, vacuum cleaners, and so forth. Micros and minis will also appear in industrial products, in the factory, and in communications. These applications will be discussed at greater length in Part Five.

Micros, minis, and **maxis** (large) computers can only do what they are programmed to do. Their intelligence is based on the instructions that tell the CPU how to process data. This subject, **programming,** is examined in Chapter 3.

KEY WORDS

Analog computer	Dice
Arithmetic and logic unit	Digital computer
Batch processing	Distributed array processor
Binary digits	Distributed data processing
Bits	Electrical accounting machines
Break-even point	(EAM)
Central processor (CPU)	Electronic data processing (EDP)
Chip	External memory
Configurations	External storage
Control unit	Floppy disk (floppy)
Current injection logic	Gate
Data processing	Generations

Hollerith card
Hybrid computer
IBM card
Integrated circuits
Internal memory
Internal storage
Josephson computer
Large-scale integration (LSI)
Lasers
Machine intelligence (artificial intelligence)
Main memory
Magnetic cassette
Manual processing
Maxis
Memory and storage unit
Memory units
Metal oxide semiconductor (MOS) technology
Microcode
Microcomputers
Microelectronics
Microprocessors
Mini
Minicomputer

Modes of processing
Offline
Online
Online real time (OLRT)
Original equipment manufacturer (OEM)
Package
Personal computers
Programming
Real-time systems
Remote job entry
Remote processing
Round-robin service
Secondary storage
Sensors
Small-scale integration (SSI)
Telecommunication lines
Teleprocessing
Time sharing
Transistors
Unit record processing
Vacuum tubes
Virtual memory
Word

DISCUSSION QUESTIONS

1. What are the economic considerations and conditions that can justify the use of computers?
2. Distinguish between manual, machine, and computer processing in terms of:
   a. Equipment used.
   b. Economic justification.
3. Distinguish between batch, time-sharing, interactive, online, and online-real-time processing. Give an example of each mode of processing in business.
4. List the main advantages of computer processing over:
   a. Manual processing.
   b. Machine processing.
5. Are computers capable of making logical choices? Explain.
6. What is the effect of an increase in:
   a. Volume of processing.
   b. Fixed cost.
   c. Variable cost.
   on the break-even point between computer processing and other means of processing?
7. Give three examples from business and industry for each of the following modes of processing:

      a. Batch.
      b. Online.
      c. Online real time.
      d. Time sharing.
      e. Offline.

8. Distinguish between:
      a. Business and scientific computer.
      b. Analogue and digital computer.
      c. Discrete and continuous computations.
      d. General-purpose and special-purpose computer.
      e. Small and large computer.
      f. Microcomputer and microprocessor.
      g. Microcomputer and minicomputer.

9. What is meant by the microelectronic revolution? Has this revolution affected you? How? Will it affect businesses? How?

10. What unique hardware features are required for a system operating in an OLRT environment rather than a batch environment?

11. What is meant by computer generations? How have computer generations affected the user in business?

EXERCISE

1. In the table below check the appropriate column for the best mode of processing for each application listed.

	Mode of processing			
Application	Batch	Time sharing	Online	OLRT
Airline reservations				
Hotel nationwide reservations				
An auto dealer				
Accounting				
Contract calculations				
with buyer				
Instructor keeping grades				
University keeping grades				
University admissions				
University registration				
University computing for class				
University alumni records				
Retailer point-of-sales				
credit checking				
Bank account status				
monthly ledger				
Wholesale inventory				
For perishables				
For nonperishables				
and stable demand				
Large data base computing				
and computing for sale				

SELECTED ANNOTATED BIBLIOGRAPHY

On modes of processing

Awad, Elias M. *Introduction to Computers in Business.* Englewood Cliffs, N.J.: Prentice-Hall, Inc., 1977. Chaps. 4 and 6.

Chapter 4 is a discussion of the general and specific purposes of analog, digital, and hybrid computers. Also discussed are minis, micros, and computers of different sizes from portable to large-scale computers.

House, William C., ed. *Data Base Management.* New York: Petrocelli Books, 1974. Part V, pp. 330–97.

Included are five chapters on processing methods: batch, remote access, dedicated, time sharing, and real time. An excellent coverage of the subject.

Mader, Chris, and Hagin, Robert. *Information Systems: Technology, Economics and Applications.* Chicago, Ill.: Science Research Associates, Inc., 1974. Pp. 291–309.

This text has an excellent chapter (13) on time sharing and interactive computing. The emphasis is on the economics and applications to business.

Sackman, Harold. *Mass Information Utilities and Social Excellence.* Princeton, N.J.: Auerbach Publishers, 1971. 254 pp.

The author has had many years of experience working with time sharing, especially at Rand, using large systems for defense. He discusses the implications of mass time sharing on home managers, businesspersons, and society. He subscribes to the philosophy that every individual possesses the right of free access to knowledge and that "information power ultimately resides in the public." Sackman also discusses the issue of individual and collective human intelligence being affected by computers.

On microelectronics

Firebaugh, Morris, et al. "A Feast of Microcomputers." *Personal Computing,* vol. 2, no. 11 (November 1978), pp. 60–81.

This article reviews the use of microcomputers for education, home, and business. It discusses 15 computers in terms of their hardware, software, prices, and capabilities. The systems are each evaluated and rated. This article will, of course, soon be outdated, but such articles appear periodically in many journals such as *Datamation* and *Personal Computing.*

Roland, John. "The Microelectronic Revolution." *The Futurist,* vol. 13, no. 2 (April 1979), pp. 81–90.

A futurist view and a very optimistic one. Roland discusses the applications of microcomputers in business and everyday life, applications in which security and privacy of information are protected. A provocative look at micros and their effect on society.

Scientific American. *Microelectronics.* San Francisco: W. H. Freeman and Co., 1977. 145 pp.

This softcover book is a reprint of the September 1977 special issue of *Scientific American* on microelectronics. It has 11 articles written on the entire range of microelectronics, including the technical aspects of circuitry and production. But throughout, the text is successfully addressed to the layman in nontechnical language. There are numerous stand-alone diagrams, including many that are multicolor, contributing to an easier understanding of the material.

The subjects covered include the concepts and manufacturing of microelectronic circuits and chips, both CPU and storage chips, personal computers, and the application of computers to instrumentation, process control, communication, and data processing. In most cases, the state of the art is reviewed and future trends identified. A superb and understandable discussion of a very technical subject.

3

SOFTWARE

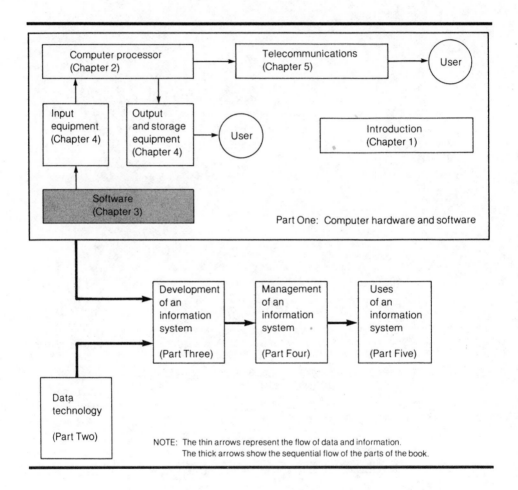

Computer hardware is circuitry and metal. What gives life to a computer, the ability to perform calculations and process information, are **programs.** Programs are sets of instructions and decision rules for processing. Unlike **hardware** that is physical, hard, and something that can be touched, programs represent decision logic, the intellectual process for solving problems. Being the antithesis of hardware, programs are called **software.**

In this chapter two principal categories of software will be discussed: **operating systems** and **application programs.** Some authors list a third classification, **data base management systems (DBMS)** since these programs are needed to administer large data bases. Because of the importance of DBMS to business, an entire chapter, Chapter 9, will be devoted to this subject.

Every computer has an operating system unique to that model that is often provided by the manufacturer. Programs for operation usually concern only data processing personnel, not users. However, since their functions should be understood by managers, an overview of operating systems is included in this chapter. Applications programs consist of detailed instructions for processing and generating information, serving as the interface between user and hardware. All programs are written in **programming languages,** many of which are technical. Though the actual instructions are written either by EDP personnel, analysts, or programmers working for the users, the objective of each program and the logic used are decisions that should be made by management. Only by understanding the capabilities of different programming languages and their comparative advantages can managers participate wisely in program preparation. A section in this chapter compares and evaluates the main languages for business processing to give future business managers this needed background.

As the price of computer terminals continues to drop, a new class of software is emerging which enables users to directly converse and interact with computers, using English-like languages. Because of the ease in using these new languages, they offer great promise. This chapter concludes with sections on **terminal interactive languages** and natural language research.

DATA PROCESSING

A computer does computations by using arithmetic **operators** (add, subtract, multiply, etc.). But what operators should be used, which data must be processed, and the sequence of operations to be performed must all be specified by programs. The composition of data and how it is processed are factors that determine how programs will be written and what programming languages are most appropriate. But in order to explain this further, the structure of data first needs to be discussed.

STRUCTURE OF DATA

The most elemental data used by management is numeric (0–9), alphabetic (A–Z), or special symbols (i.e., /, $, %, and including the operators +, −, ÷, ×). Variables that users need to record, such as name, date, price, and so forth are called **data elements,** the values of which are expressed by a combination of **characters.** For example, alphabetic characters are used to represent the data element "name," and a combination of numeric characters and alpha characters would represent the data element "invoice number" (e.g., AC325).

Related data elements constitute a **record.** An accounts payable record might consist of a vendor's name, identification number, and amount of sale. All accounts payable records for all vendors would constitute a **file,** an accounts payable file. Businesses generally have many functional files, including a payroll file, a production file, an asset file, and so forth.

A function that includes transactions, events like goods delivered or received, or accounts paid or received, has a **transaction file** in which transactional data of a temporary nature is recorded. Permanent data on the function is kept on a **master file,** which is periodically updated from the transaction file, the latter being destroyed or kept as backup once updating takes place. The updated master is used in processing.

Updating requires processing of two files, transferring relevant information from the transaction file to the master. If data on both files were at random, merging the two would be a complex task. As an analogy, imagine placing one thousand letters, each addressed to a specific customer, in preaddressed envelopes which are in no special order. The task would be simplified by sorting and stacking both letters and envelopes in alphabetical order by last name of customer, then matching and merging the two piles while stuffing the envelopes. In batch processing, records on both the transaction and master file must be **sorted** before data on the two files can be merged. In real-time processing, where transactions are entered at random (as they occur) on the transaction file, only the master must be sorted. Sorting of computer data is seldom done by name because names are long and not unique. Instead, a unique identification, known as a **key data element,** must appear in both files.

Table 3.1 shows data in a master file before and after sorting by identification number. This sorting is not done manually but done by computer program. Data on the transaction file is also sorted by vendor number. The applications program then instructs the computer to deduct the amounts paid listed on the transaction file from the corresponding record of amount due on the master file.

The master file when updated is then ready for additional processing. In Table 3.1, processing concluded with a printout made of the updated master resorted alphabetically. Other processing might be performing computations with master file figures such as calculating totals, balances, or averages. The

TABLE 3.1
Updating a master file

Unsorted records on master file

3000510	Hall, A. E.	$120.20
3285000	Adams, J. M.	210.00
2003250	Jackson, K. M.	150.00

(Each record has ID number of vendor, name of vendor, and amount payable, in that order.)

Master file
(Sorted by vendor number in ascending sequence)

2003250	Jackson, K. M.	$150.00
3000510	Hall, A. E.	120.00
3285000	Adams, J. M.	210.00

Transactional file
(Sorted by vendor number listing amounts paid)

2003250	$100.00
3285000	110.00

Master file after updating

2003250	Jackson, K. M.	$ 50.00
3000510	Hall, A. E.	120.00
3285000	Adams, J. M.	100.00

Updated master file resorted into alphabetic sequence (output)

Adams, J. M.	3285000	$100.00
Hall, A. E.	3000510	120.00
Jackson, K. M.	2003250	50.00

results might then be **classified** into categories, **summarized** and **reported** for use by different levels of management. All of these operations, summarized in Figure 3.1, are common business applications done by computer according to programmed instructions. These instructions are written in a form a computer can understand, called a **programming language.** How these languages work will now be explained.

PROGRAMMING

Signals (off and on of electric current, or two levels of voltage in a transistor) are used in computers to represent the **binary digits** 0 and 1. These digits are the only digits used in the binary number base; therefore all numbers commonly used in the base ten number system rewritten in binary configurations will be recognized by the computer's circuits in the CPU (for example, $1001 = 9$, $10011001 = 153$).

Machine language, the most elemental programming language, was the first programming language developed. Instructions in machine language are a series of base ten numbers which are converted internally by the computer

FIGURE 3.1
Basic business operations by the CPU

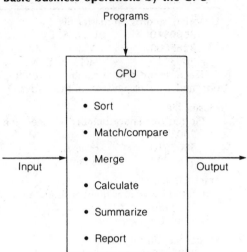

into binary digits recognized by the CPU. Figure 3.2 shows a machine language instruction for an early computer, the IBM 1620. The instruction has three parts. The first two digits represent the operation code (add, subtract, move data, etc.). In this example, code 21 represents add. The data will, therefore, be channeled through circuitry that will perform addition (other circuitry exists for other arithmetic operations). The second and third parts are **operands,** where data is stored, called a **storage location** or **address.** In this case the data in storage location 14000 is 120; the data in storage location 12002 is 30. The machine instruction 211400012002 means: find data stored in operand 1, add it to data stored in operand 2, and then store the result in operand 1. That is, take the data 120 (which in this case is regular weekly pay in dollars), add it to data 30 (overtime pay), and store the result 150 in location 14000.

Writing programs in **machine language** has many drawbacks.

1. It is necessary to keep track of storage locations and their contents, for contents keep changing, as in the example above. Location 14000 switched from regular daily pay to total weekly pay.
2. It is necessary to remember operation codes.
3. There are many instructions to write, one for each machine command.
4. The language is **machine dependent.** Each CPU has a unique circuitry design so that the form and structure of instructions used may vary from one manufacturer to another, and possibly from one model to another as well. A machine language program is written for a specific computer, sometimes even for a specific model. It is usually not **portable** from one computer to another.

To overcome some of these problems the first **assembly language** was developed in the 1950s. An instruction in this language, also for the IBM 1620, with the same meaning as the previous example, 211400012002, is: A RGP OTP. Here the numeric operation code 21 is replaced by the alphabetic code A, and the addresses have been replaced by variable names RGP (regular pay) and OTP (overtime pay). The computer has an internal program, called an **assembler,** to convert alphabetic letters (and symbols) into binary digits. The assembler also converts storage location names when new variables are stored there: RGP becoming TP (total pay). In other words, the assembler

FIGURE 3.2
An example of machine language instruction

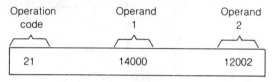

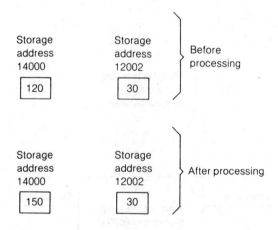

converts the assembly language program, the **source program,** into its machine language equivalent, the **object program.** This process is shown in Figure 3.3

Assembly programs are less difficult to write than programs in machine language, for the need to remember storage locations and contents is eliminated. Also, alphabetic operation codes are easier to remember than numeric codes, especially when the abbreviations are meaningful. But criticisms 3 and 4 remain: a large number of instructions still must be written and the language is nonportable.

As a result, **high level programming languages** have been developed,

FIGURE 3.3
Assembly language translation process

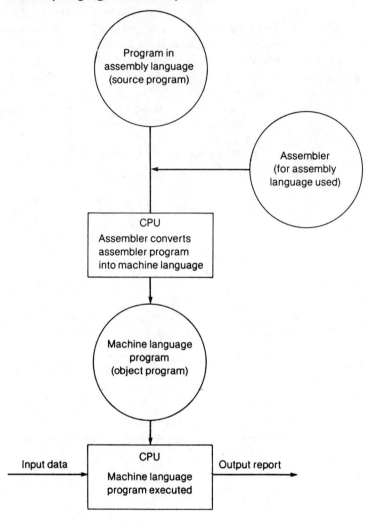

languages closer to English. Instructions in COBOL, a language commonly used for business applications, look like this:

ADD REGULAR-PAY, OVERTIME-PAY GIVING TOTAL-PAY
or   PAY = REGPAY + OVTPAY
or   PAY = RGP + OTP

As with assembly languages, a translation of these instructions is done internally before the program is executed. But for high level languages, the translation is done by a **compiler,** not an assembler. This translation process is shown in Figure 3.4.

FIGURE 3.4
Language translation by compiler

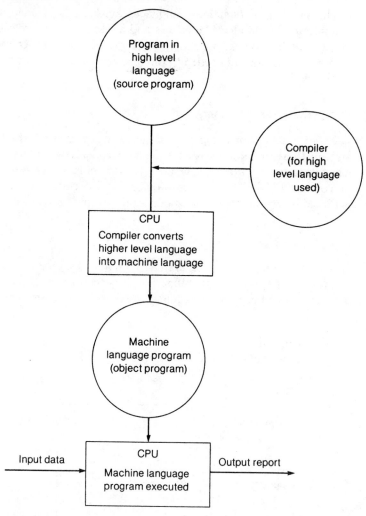

High level languages overcome all of the drawbacks of machine languages. The computer keeps track of storage locations and contents. Operation codes are familiar symbols. A major gain over machine or assembly languages is that few instructions are necessary. In 1957 when FORTRAN was developed, a set of 47 FORTRAN instructions equaled approximately 1000 machine language commands.[1] Furthermore, high level languages are portable, provided the other computer has an appropriate compiler. In addition, because instructions resemble English, high level languages are easier to learn, quicker

---

[1] Richard A. McLaughlin, "The IBM 704: 36 Bit Floating-Point Money Maker," *Datamation*®, vol. 21, no. 8 (August 1975), p. 45.

and less tedious to write and modify, and easier to check for errors. In addition, many such languages are self-documenting.

The number of high level languages available is steadily increasing. A classification of high level languages and a discussion of a selected few commonly used in business processing will appear later in this chapter. But first, other types of software needed to run a computer and an information system will be discussed.

CLASSIFICATION OF SOFTWARE

There are two main types of software: **operating systems software** and **applications software.** The latter generally is custom-made for a particular problem or environment, whereas the former is concerned with the operation of the CPU and its peripheral equipment. The classification of all software is shown in Figure 3.5. These subdivisions are discussed next.

Operating systems software

The operating system for a small computer may consist of only a few control and processing programs. For large computer systems, however, a complex set of programs is required to coordinate, control, and allocate the

FIGURE 3.5
Types of software

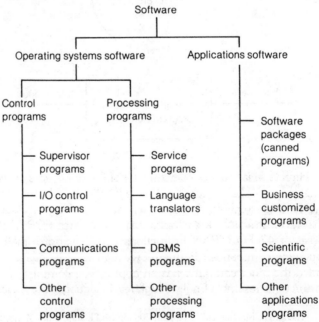

systems resources. These programs are provided by the vendor of the CPU and are especially necessary for systems that handle large volumes of interrelated data and for systems using communications networks, real-time, time-sharing, or distributed processing. The objectives of operating software are to maximize efficiency of operations, minimize human intervention, and facilitate the task of the programmer in accessing data and/or peripheral equipment. To achieve these objectives, two main sets of programs exist: **control programs** and **processing programs.**

CONTROL PROGRAMS

The **supervisor,** also called the **executive, monitor,** or **controller,** is the most important control program of a computer system. It coordinates all the hardware of the computer system and handles job scheduling, queuing, and storage allocation. It also keeps logs and does job accounting for each job processed. Finally, the supervisor communicates with the human operator through the console regarding the status of computer system operations.

I/O control programs are a collection of subroutines for the input of data and output of information dealing with the actual physical location and format of data and its logical organization into data elements, records, and files. These programs handle input/output scheduling, error corrections, and various functions necessary to create and maintain files. For business applications, I/O control programs may constitute between 30–45 percent of all programmed instructions.

Communications programs perform message switching and remote inquiry. Other control subroutines exist for specialized functions. But, in essence, control programs manage data (input, output, storage, and retrieval), execute processing programs, and govern job preparation and scheduling.

Some manufacturers offer control program facilities. For example, IBM's Systems Management Facilities (SMF) provides the base for user written control programs for monitoring jobs and utilization of equipment. SMF also collects the necessary data for user specified analytical reports for accounting and costing purposes.

PROCESSING PROGRAMS

Service programs are a subclassification of processing software, performing calculations and other repetitive routines such as sorting and merging needed so frequently in business applications. Other service programs include automatic program testing and debugging software. Many service programs are unique to a machine, manufacturer, or environment so they will not be specifically mentioned due to the lack of generality in their use.

Assemblers, compilers, and **interpreters** (translation programs to convert applications program languages into machine language) are also classified as processing programs.

Another set of processing programs, the **data base management system (DBMS),** is used to administer large data bases. In addition, there are **housekeeping** or **utility programs.** These consist of programs needed for standard and frequent operations such as listing data in storage, called **dumping,** or converting data from one storage medium to another.

Applications software

SOFTWARE PACKAGES

Many firms have similar information requirements. Programs using common decision rules to perform statistical computations, sorting, merging, and standard applications such as payroll and inventory control, can serve many organizations. Businesses needing such programs can save development costs and time by purchasing predeveloped **software packages** with self-supporting documentation for their needs. These programs may require modification, but generally they are ready for immediate use, a convenience that parallels that of canned food. Hence the term **canned programs** is used. The advantages and limitations of canned programs as well as criteria for their evaluation are shown in Table 3.2.

Software packages are available for **scientific** and **business programs,** and also for DBMS. Many computer vendors provide such packages free

TABLE 3.2
Software packages

Advantages
Time is saved by the organization (compared to tailor-made system).
Time and worry over debugging reduced.
Cheaper because the development cost is distributed over many users.
Systems analysts, a scarce resource, are freed for other tasks.
Necessary modification requires less commitment of resources than initial development.

Disadvantages or limitations
Programs for complex applications are often too generalized to be useful. When specific, they may need extensive modification to fit local needs.
Programs may require unavailable hardware.
Resistance to canned programs is common. Users prefer programs developed for their own special needs.
Purchase hampers the development of in-house program design and implementation capability.

Criteria for evaluating package
Quality and completeness of documentation.
Ease of installation.
Ease of use.
Vendor technical support.
Throughput.
Efficiency.
Amount of training required.

as a service to their customers. Other packages can be leased or purchased from **software houses,** companies that develop software.

BUSINESS PROGRAMS

Although software packages exist for many general applications, programs must be customized for specialized or unusual applications. Businesses may

FIGURE 3.6
The tower of Babel of programming languages

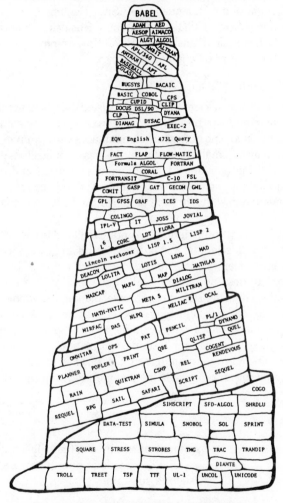

And the Lord said, . . . let us go down, and there confound
their language, that they may not understand
one another's speech (Genesis, 11:6-7)

Source: Adapted from Jean E. Sammet, *Programming Languages: History and Fundamentals* (Englewood Cliffs, N.J.: Prentice-Hall, Inc., © 1969, front cover. Reprinted by permission.

have unique requirements for even common programs such as sales reporting or payroll, in which case in-house programs must be written for these needs.

A large number of languages exist for business operation applications. In 1969 Jean Sammet characterized the overabundance of such languages as a Tower of Babel (see Figure 3.6). But her implicit warning has been ignored. In recent years languages have proliferated, adding to the confusion of users and dividing the ranks of professionals. Even languages for special applications such as artificial intelligence, query, and text processing have multiplied. Among the leading languages for business problems are APL (A Programming Language), BASIC (Beginner's All-purpose Symbolic Instruction Code), COBOL (Common Business Oriented Language), FORTRAN (Formula Translation), PL/1 (Programming Language 1), and RPG (Report Program Generator).

SCIENTIFIC PROGRAMS

In the past a clear distinction existed between applications software for scientific problems and for business problems. In the natural sciences, complex formulas involving numerous computations are common, but input and output are relatively small. In contrast, business applications in the past generally required the handling of large volumes of input and output but the actual computations were relatively simple and repetitive. As a result, computer hardware and software were designed for either scientific or business applications.

This distinction is fading. Computers like the IBM 360 are now designed to meet both scientific and business needs and programming languages available today claim capability over the entire range of problems.[2] Furthermore, many business applications, as in the area of planning and control, have scientific characteristics. For example, planning is often computation-intensive, involving statistics and regressive equations as found in scientific programming, though still a large volume of input and output must be processed as in other business applications. Calculating the optimal mix of production levels (linear programming) is another business problem involving complicated scientific formulas.[3] Equations like the following must be solved:

$$a_{i1} x_1 + \cdots + a_{ij} x_j + \cdots + a_{in} x_n \leq b_i$$

where:

a_{ij} = amount of resource i (first subscript)
required to produce one unit of product j
(second subscript)

---

[2] Traditionally, 25 percent of applications (or 90° of a pie) were scientific applications and 75 percent (270°) were business oriented. When IBM manufactured a computer that served all 100 percent of users' needs (or 360° of the pie), the computer was called the IBM 360.

[3] For a survey of programs used for scientific problems, see H. R. Schucany et al., "A Survey of Statistical Packages," *Computing Surveys*, vol. 4, no. 2 (June 1972), pp. 65–79.

$$x_j = \text{level of product } j$$
$$b_i = \text{available resource } i$$
$$n = \text{total number of products}$$

LANGUAGES USED IN BUSINESS

Today many business problems involve hundreds of equations for tens of products resulting in complex matrix calculations. These applications use a scientific-type language such as FORTRAN. APT and ADAPT are other languages used for business applications with a scientific orientation such as numerical control (automated production).

Business problems that involve probabilities (such as the probability of customer arrival and of customer sale, etc.) that cannot be solved by models like linear programming or regression equations must be **simulated.** That is, the problems must be repeatedly solved for different values of variables to answer the question, "What if this variable changes x percent?" Though **simulation programs** can be written in FORTRAN, specialized programming languages have been developed that facilitate repeated calculations for "What if?" type questions. The most common of such simulations languages in the United States are GPSS and SIMSCRIPT.

The features of FORTRAN IV, GPSS, and SIMSCRIPT are listed in Table 3.3 and the performance of each when used to solve a queuing and an inventory problem are compared. SIMULA, a mathematically powerful simulation language with similar capabilities, does not appear in the table though this language is used extensively in Europe, since the SIMULA compiler is not readily available in the United States.

Some languages have modified versions such as FORTRAN IV, for example, or COBOL '74. The chart in Table 3.4 is an evaluation by Edwards and Broadwell of the six languages most commonly used in business. Comparative programming costs are shown in Figure 3.7. Note that the initial fixed cost for program development is low for APL, BASIC, and FORTRAN, and high for PL/1, RPG, and COBOL. For a small number of runs (up to point *A*) APL is cheapest, BASIC is most economical from point *A* to *B,* and thereafter COBOL is least costly in spite of its high development cost.

Both APL and BASIC have an advantage not listed in Table 3.5 or shown in Figure 3.7. They are **interactive languages.** The problem is stated, a specific key on the terminal is pressed, and the answer is computed. There is no need to specify the format of input or output as required when using the other four languages. APL is also very powerful mathematically. For example, one command will produce a set of random numbers or compute statistics. But additional mathematical characters have been added to the language to generate this computing power, the use of which often makes business programmers uneasy. Many prefer BASIC, a simpler language to learn, available on many minis, but understandably less powerful.

Though FORTRAN does not solve many business problems efficiently

TABLE 3.3
Comparison of simulation languages used for business

General characteristics	FORTRAN IV	GPSS	SIMSCRIPT 2.5
Availability	Available on almost all computers	On IBM Equipment only (provided by vendor)	Available from CAI Company (consulting company)
Compiler internal storage requirement	Relatively small	Medium	Relatively large
Easy to learn	Very easy	Easy	Difficult
Readability of program	Medium	Easy	Medium
Self-documenting	No	No	A little
Run time characteristics	*FORTRAN IV*	*GPSS*	*SIMSCRIPT 2.5*
Queuing problem			
Time to learn (hours)	10	6	15
Time to write (hours)	8	4	12
Time to validate (hours)	8	12	15
Execution time (seconds)	1.64	1.53	2.21
Number of instructions	148	22	85
Max core used (kilobyte)	128	128	288
Large capacity storage (kilobyte per hour)	0.05	0.34	0.92
Inventory problem			
Time to learn (hours)	12	8	17
Time to write (hours)	10	5	15
Time to validate (hours)	8	10	12
Execution time (seconds)	3.92	2.44	3.19
Number of instructions	167	15	142
Max core used (kilobyte)	128	128	288
Large capacity storage (kilobyte per hour)	0.12	0.51	0.97

Source: Y. S. Fang, "Comparison of Simulation Languages" (1979), unpublished paper.

TABLE 3.4
Language comparison

Characteristics	APL	BASIC	COBOL 1974	FORTRAN IV	PL/1	RPG II
Number of instructions	6	10	62	12	21	27
Number of characters	150	250	1550	300	525	675
Entry time	1.2	2	12.4	2.4	4.2	4.6
Compile time (minutes)	0.066	0.024	0.03	0.012	0.033	1.5
Time to validate (seconds)	0.024	0.0144	0.123	0.0144	0.124	1.5
Time to write (days)	0.5	0.9	5.6	1.1	1.9	2.4
Self-documentation	No	No	Yes	No	Yes	No
Easy language rule	Moderate	Difficult	Easy	Moderate	Easy	Easy
Easily readable	No	Moderate	Yes	Moderate	Moderate	No
Widely available	Moderate	Moderate	Yes	Yes	Moderate	Moderate
Machine independent	Moderate	Moderate	Yes	Yes	Moderate	Yes

Source: Adapted from Perry Edwards and Bruce Broadwell, *Data Processing: Computers in Action* (Belmont, Calif.: Wadsworth Publishing Co., Inc., 1979), pp. 284–85. © 1979 by Wadsworth, Inc. Used by permission of the publisher.

FIGURE 3.7
Cost of programming selected languages

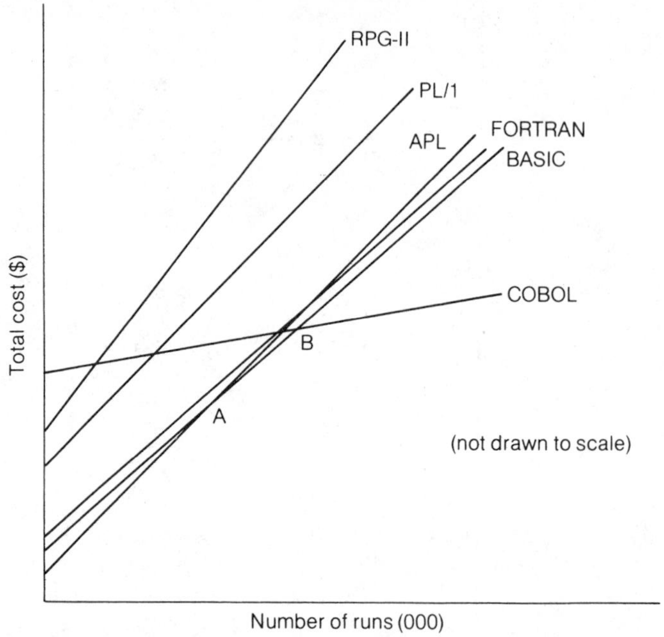

Source: Perry Edwards and Bruce Broadwell, *Data Processing* (Belmont, Calif.: Wadsworth Publishing Co., Inc., 1979), p. 287. © 1979 by Wadsworth, Inc. Reprinted by permission of the publisher.

and is too mathematical for many business programmers, it is still commonly used for both operations and planning in business. One reason is that the language is taught at most universities, providing a large cadre of FORTRAN programmers. Also, the FORTRAN compiler is widely available.

Both COBOL and RPG are more business-oriented than FORTRAN. Of the two, COBOL has better computational capability. It also includes special features like the SORT verb (which enables sorting of data), and its design permits it to handle and manipulate large input and output files. When the Department of Defense required COBOL for all their computers, computer manufacturers started supplying COBOL compilers. By the 1970s, COBOL had become the most widely used business language.

IBM attempted to develop a programming *lingua franca* with PL/1. This language has business as well as scientific capabilities and is also a very high level language. Among the special features included is text processing. PL/1 has not become a universal language as was once predicted, however, in part because its features have made it so complex. Meanwhile, as hardware has evolved and the costs of terminals have dropped, interactive languages have gained in appeal. Also the emergence of DBMS has made it possible to access large data bases with much of the data manipulation and processing handled by the system. Language needs have consequently changed. Many businesses need terminal interactive languages that permit nontechnical personnel to query the system from a terminal for information needed in decision making. This chapter will conclude with a discussion of such interactive languages.

TERMINAL INTERACTIVE LANGUAGES

The growing use of terminals for data entry by clerks and information retrieval by management has led to the development of **terminal interactive languages.** These languages have a special capability: computer-directed or computer-prompted queries assist in data collection and retrieval. The questioning which appears on the terminal may be menu selection, fill in the blanks, or parametric requests.

Question and answer techniques

MENU SELECTION

In menu selection the user is offered a list of choices. For example, three reports, each numbered, will be briefly described. The user merely types 2 if the second report is the one desired. The advantage of this method of retrieval is that no knowledge of the system or data base is required. The disadvantage is slowness, for all of the choices must be explained.

FILL IN THE BLANKS

A checklist of questions with blanks to be completed prods the user into supplying all of the necessary input in this method of data collection. Intelligent terminals or real-time terminals may have the added capability of validating the data as soon as it enters the system. For example, the system may be programmed to provide the exact format of input to reduce possible errors. A nine-digit number required as input might be requested by a set of nine boxes, making any omission obvious.

This technique requires some training or knowledge to operate the system (e.g., ten digits might be required for a social security number, the last being a check digit). Careful programming, however, can train the user online by providing explanations or rephrasing questions when users make entry errors or need assistance.

PARAMETRIC REQUESTS

This technique is a form of dialogue between user and machine. The values of specific parameters are entered, the computer responds, new parameters are added, another response given, and so forth until the transaction is completed. For example, a salesperson wanting to know the availability of a given product might provide the product number and quantity desired as input. The system would answer yes or no. If available, the system might also list price in its response. The order might then be confirmed by the clerk and the client's name and address provided. Much of this exchange is in code, following a specified format and sequence. The user of this parametric technique must therefore be well trained.

Query languages

The questioning in the above-mentioned techniques must be in an English-like language in order for persons with little programming knowledge to enter and retrieve data. Examples of **query languages** that have been developed include ADAM (A Data Management System), MODEL 24, and SYSTEM 2000, all of which feature quick retrieval; COLINGO (Compile On Line and Go), which can be easily programmed online; FLORAL and QUERY BY EXAMPLE, two calculus-based languages; CUPID, FLORAL LP, and SQUARE which use two-dimensional notation; DSL/ALPHA that enables operations to be expressed in a relational data base; IQF (Interactive Query Facility language); and QUEL and SEQUEL II, which are key-word-based languages. Table 3.5 demonstrates how a statement in English is translated into a sample few of these languages.

A study comparing the effectiveness of SEQUEL and SQUARE, two IBM

TABLE 3.5
Examples of query languages

---

a. English:
Find employees working for Smith who make under $20,000.

b. SEQUEL: SELECT NAME
FROM PERSONNEL
WHERE MANAGER = 'SMITH'
AND SALARY <20000

c. SQUARE: EMP ('SMITH',<'20000')
NAME MANAGER,SALARY

d. QUERY BY EXAMPLE:

PERSONNEL	NAME	MANAGER	SALARY
	P*	Smith	<20000

e. IQF: (1) FROM PERSONNEL FILE
(2) FOR SMITH MANAGER
(3) AND FOR SALARY <20000
(4) LIST NAME

* P stands for print, identifying desired output.

languages listed in the table, found that the error rate for nonprogrammers using SEQUEL, a key-word language, was 51 percent whereas the rate for SQUARE, which features an explicit composition operator, was only 34 percent. Programmers got about two thirds of their queries correct in either language. With both user groups, 50 percent of the errors were judged clerical rather than conceptual. Each language required ten hours to learn.[4]

QUERY BY EXAMPLE, evaluated by Thomas and Gould, showed a query accuracy rate of 67 percent.[5] Less than two hours were required to learn this language. The effectiveness of IQF, studied by Gould and Ascher, showed an overall accuracy by nonprogrammers of 34 percent and an error rate of 28 percent.[6]

It is often assumed that, ideally, computers should be programmed in natural languages. This is possible at the present time, though processing is very costly and computer time is inefficiently used. This postulate has been refuted by Small and Weldon who studied English versus SEQUEL, concluding:

> The common assumption that ordinary, everyday English is the ideal way to communicate with computers is not supported by the present results. Subjects were not reliably more accurate using English than using SEQUEL. They were reliably faster using SEQUEL, suggesting that the structured language is easier to use.[7]

Schneidermann, not satisfied with Small and Weldon's experimental design, questioned this finding.[8] He objected to the fact that subjects were required to use tables, feeling this constrained them in formulating questions to resolve problems. Schneidermann experimented on his own, asking subjects to choose a department where they would like to be transferred, based on departmental information acquired by query from a data base, such as employees' names, salaries, managers, job descriptions, age of personnel, and years of employment. Fourteen percent of the queries were invalid using SEQUEL, 55 percent invalid using English. Imaginative questions, ones that had no answers in the data base, were asked in English, such as, "How often are raises awarded?" "What is the personality of managers?"

The above studies indicate that a formal query language helps structure user requests. English may be too flexible, inappropriate for queries. Or per-

---

[4] P. Reisner, R. Royce, and D. Chamberlin, "Human Factors Evaluation of Two Data Base Query Languages: SQUARE and SEQUEL," *IBM Technical Report* (RJ 1478, 1974).

[5] J. Thomas and J. Gould, "A Psychological Study of Query-by-Example," *AFIPS National Computer Conference Proceedings* (Montvale, N.J.: AFIPS Press, 1975), pp. 439–45.

[6] J. Gould and R. Ascher, "Use of an IQF-like Query Language by Non-Programmers," *IBM Research Report* (RC 5279, 1975).

[7] D. W. Small and L. J. Weldon, "The Efficiency of Retrieving Information from Computers Using Natural and Structured Query Languages," Rep. SAI-78-655-WA. (Arlington, Va.: Science Applications, 1977).

[8] Ben Schneidermann, "Improving the Human Factors Aspect of Database Interactions," *ACM Transactions on Database Systems,* vol. 3, no. 4 (December 1978), pp. 433–37.

haps a natural language is not a natural query language, as Montgomery suggests.[9] Certainly factors such as the quantitative background of users and their abilities (right-brain visual intuitive thinking versus left-brain verbal deductive thinking) affect individual success with formal query languages. The function for which the language is used (for example, production and inventory control) also plays a role. The ideal may prove to be formal languages as an alternative to, not as a substitute for, natural language programming.

NATURAL LANGUAGE RESEARCH

At the present time much language research is being conducted. In 1977, 52 separate projects on artificial intelligence were cataloged.[10] Natural languages have an obvious advantage: no training in programming language structure is required, though users must still understand the function of a computer and be able to formulate, organize, and analyze problems. Research is also being conducted in this latter area. It is hoped techniques will be developed to help users identify needs and formulate problems so that computers can be of assistance.

For example, there are several prototype languages under development that engage the user in a dialogue, trying to determine what information is needed through questions and answers. The assumption here is that the user either doesn't know or can't express needs in terms the computer understands. A sample output of one such language, RENDEZVOUS, appears in Table 3.6. Note that the menu technique is used in this example. The computer's method of restating and clarifying the user's request is called a **clarification response.** The program also utilizes a **stroking dialogue,** congratulating or sympathizing with the user (in this sample, "Good!"), a technique found in diagnostic and psychiatric discourse.[11]

Another dialogue technique, not included in Table 3.6, is the **contributive response,** where entirely new information is introduced by the computer such as, "These parts are also supplied by the foreign firm ABC."

Using a mix of the above techniques, the user is guided in framing a request for information while being reminded of the range of options available. In the case of RENDEZVOUS, the main objective of the program is to understand the user's requirements and to match this need for information with what the system and its data base can provide.

IBM, the developer of RENDEZVOUS, also uses dialogue in a system

[9] C. A. Montgomery, "Is Natural Language an Unnatural Query Language?" *Proceedings National ACM Conference* (New York: Association of Computing Machinery, 1972), p. 1075.

[10] Association of Computing Machinery, Special Interest Group on Artificial Intelligence, 1977.

[11] For an early and classical example, see the work by Joe Weizenbaum and his ELIZA program. J. Weizenbaum, "ELIZA—A Computer Program for the Study of Natural Language Communication between Man and Machine," *Communications of the ACM,* vol. 9, no. 1 (January 1966), pp. 36–45.

TABLE 3.6
Sample query dialogue with RENDEZVOUS

SYSTEM: Please proceed.

USER: Give me a list of the part numbers, quantities, and suppliers of Houston parts.

SYSTEM: You are requesting (among other things) a listing of quantities of parts. Do you want:
          1. Quantities on hand
          2. Quantities on order
          3. Quantities shipped?

USER: I want quantities on order.

SYSTEM: Fine! Now, with regard to "Houston Parts," do you mean:
          1. Parts supplied by Houston suppliers
          2. Parts supplied to Houston projects
          3. Parts associated with Houston in some other way?

USER: I mean Item 2.

(NOTE: Nothing prevents the user from responding in a manner which is incomprehensible to the system—for example, "le deuxieme"—but if he does, the system tightens up the dialogue by: "Please reply by means of one of the numerals 1 or 2 or 3." How response 3 would be treated is discussed later.)

SYSTEM: Good! I need one more piece of information. In the listing of part numbers, quantity on order, and suppliers, how do you want suppliers to be identified:
          1. By number
          2. By name
          3. Some other way?

USER: By name and by city.

SYSTEM: O.K. This is what I understand your query to be: "Find all combinations of part number, quantity on order, supplier name, and supplier city such that the supplier supplied the part to a project located in Houston." Is this what you intended?

(We now follow two possibilities. Case 1: the user is satisfied.)

USER: Yes.

SYSTEM: Do you want the listing to be ordered in any special way?

USER: Yes, by part number and then by supplier number.

This ends the dialogue in Case 1. The system now proceeds to interpret the relational calculus formula for the user's query—a formula that it has been synthesizing in its store, partly from the original statement by the user, and partly from the succeeding dialogue.

(Case 2: the user is not satisfied.)

USER: I have changed my mind.

(NOTE: The system does not understand this idiom, but is fully aware of its inability to understand, so it tightens up the dialogue as follows.)

TABLE 3.6 *(continued)*

SYSTEM:　Please select item 1 or 2 below:
　　　　　　1.　The re-statement is satisfactory.
　　　　　　2.　The re-statement is *not* satisfactory.

USER:　　　2.

SYSTEM:　If your intent can be expressed by making minor changes in my restatement, please type it in with your changes incorporated. If you change is major, you may re-state your query in your own terms.

This is where we leave the dialogue in Case 2.

> Source: E. F. Codd, "Seven Steps to RENDEZVOUS with the Casual User," in J. W. Klimbe and K. L. Koffeman, *Data Base Management* (Amsterdam: North-Holland Publishing Co., 1974), pp. 181–82.

to customize applications for accounting. An example of such a dialogue is shown in Table 3.7. Yet another example is NPGS work done at Yale University, a sample output of which appears in Table 3.8. Here a problem on queuing is expressed in English and the equivalent simulation language in GPSS is automatically generated. This shows how powerful specialized languages like GPSS in simulation can be used by a manager without programming knowledge of that language, though in this case some understanding of queuing was obviously required.

The results of the above research projects, and of other similar projects, such as LSNLIS, NPL, RAIN, REL, REQUEST, as well as SHRDL, are impressive and promising. However, it must be recognized that these programs apply only to a very limited set of problems. The language used is a restricted subset of English with a very narrow vocabulary and conceptual range. Natural language dialogue with computer recognition of the full range of grammatical subtleties and syntactic diversities of English is still under research. What is needed is a computer that can converse with a user on any subject, interpret requests for information meaningfully, and one that can learn from the dialogue how the user makes decisions (frame of reference, style of management, even idiosyncracies) so that the data supplied is appropriate.

There is a danger, however, that natural language communication will give users the illusion that the computer fully understands their problems, and that solutions proposed are indisputably correct. Further research is necessary not only in language development but in techniques for evaluating solutions and testing for correctness.

FUTURE OF SOFTWARE

In 1970, in an out-of-court settlement, IBM agreed to price and sell hardware and software separately. This decision enabled small innovative software houses to enter into competition with computer giants and, as a result, a

TABLE 3.7
Hypothetical customizing dialogue (IBM)

IN ORDER FOR ME TO CREATE A BILLING PROGRAM FOR YOU I WILL NEED TO GET CERTAIN INFORMATION FROM YOU ABOUT WHAT YOU WANT. FEEL FREE TO ASK QUESTIONS AS WE GO ALONG.

WOULD YOU LIKE YOUR SYSTEM TO BE TRANSACTION ORIENTED OR BATCH ORIENTED?

what is a transaction oriented system?

IN A TRANSACTION ORIENTED SYSTEM AN INVOICE IS PRODUCED IMMEDIATELY WHEN AN ORDER ARRIVES.

i want invoices to be produced just once a day at 5 p.m.

DO YOU WANT A SEPARATE INVOICE FOR EACH ORDER OR DO YOU WANT THE ORDERS GROUPED BY CUSTOMER?

separate invoices.

ARE THE CUSTOMER'S NAME AND ADDRESS FURNISHED ON EACH ORDER OR MUST THEY BE LOOKED UP IN THE CUSTOMER MASTER FILE?

looked up; is it possible to specify a different address on an order?

NO, NOT IF THEY ARE TO BE LOOKED UP IN THE CUSTOMER MASTER FILE.

how would i handle an order from a new customer?

BY "NEW CUSTOMER" DO YOU MEAN ONE WHO IS NOT IN THE MASTER FILE?

yes.

YOU WOULD HAVE TO MAKE AN ENTRY FOR HIM IN THE CUSTOMER MASTER FILE BEFORE THE ORDER IS PROCESSED.

okay.

DOES THE SAME TAX RATE APPLY TO ALL CUSTOMERS?

yes, 5%.

TO SUMMARIZE YOUR REQUIREMENTS:
   INVOICES ARE TO BE PRODUCED IN A BATCH AT 5 PM EACH DAY.
   A SEPARATE INVOICE WILL BE PRODUCED FOR EACH ORDER.
   THE CUSTOMER'S NAME AND ADDRESS WILL BE LOOKED UP IN THE
      CUSTOMER MASTER FILE.
   A TAX RATE OF 5% APPLIES TO ALL CUSTOMERS.

DO YOU HAVE ANY FURTHER QUESTIONS?

what does an invoice look like?

(SYSTEM PRINTS A SAMPLE INVOICE)

how is extended price calculated?

THE EXTENDED PRICE FOR AN ITEM IS CALCULATED BY MULTIPLYING THE UNIT PRICE BY THE QUANTITY.

that's all.

TABLE 3.8
Problem statement in NPGS

1. when a vehicle arrives at a station, it leaves there immediately if the length of the line at a pump in the station is not less than 2.
2. 75 percent of the vehicles are cars and a fourth are trucks.
3. there is just 1 pump.
4. a simulation run time of 8 hours is desired.
5. ask questions for further info.
6. HOW OFTEN DO THE VEHICLES ARRIVE AT THE STATION?
7. the arrivals of vehicles are normally distributed with a mean of 8 minutes.
8. WHAT IS THE STANDARD DEVIATION OF THE NORMAL DISTRIBUTION?
9. 1 minute.
10. OTHERWISE, WHAT DO THE VEHICLES DO?
11. what?
12. AFTER ARRIVING AT THE STATION, IF THE LENGTH OF THE LINE AT THE PUMP IN THE STATION IS NOT LESS THAN 2, THE VEHICLE WILL LEAVE THE STATION. OTHERWISE, WHAT DO THE VEHICLES DO?
13. they are serviced.
14. WHERE ARE THE VEHICLES SERVICED?
15. at the pump.
16. HOW LONG ARE THE VEHICLES SERVICED AT THE PUMP IN THE STATION?
17. vehicle service times are exponential.
18. THE TIME FOR THE VEHICLES TO BE SERVICED AT THE PUMP IN THE STATION IS EXPONENTIALLY DISTRIBUTED. WHAT IS THE MEAN OF THE EXPONENTIAL DISTRIBUTION?
19. 5 minutes for cars and 9 minutes for trucks.
20. AFTER BEING SERVICED AT THE PUMP IN THE STATION, WHAT DO THE VEHICLES DO?
21. leave the station.
22. WHAT IS THE BASIC TIME UNIT TO BE USED IN THE MODEL?
23. 30 seconds.
24. THE PROBLEM STATEMENT IS COMPLETE.
25. how often does a vehicle arrive at the station?
26. THE TIME BETWEEN ARRIVALS OF THE VEHICLES AT THE STATION IS NORMALLY DISTRIBUTED, WITH A MEAN OF 8 MINUTES AND A STANDARD DEVIATION OF 1 MINUTE.
27. the standard deviation of the time between arrivals should be 2 minutes.
28. are vehicles serviced at the pump?
29. YES, THE VEHICLES ARE SERVICED AT THE PUMP IN THE STATION.
30. state the complete problem in english.
31. THE VEHICLES ARRIVE AT THE STATION. THE TIME BETWEEN ARRIVALS OF THE VEHICLES AT THE STATION IS NORMALLY DISTRIBUTED, WITH A MEAN OF 8 MINUTES AND A STANDARD DEVIATION OF 2 MINUTES. 75 PERCENT OF THE VEHICLES ARE CARS, AND THE REST ARE TRUCKS. AFTER ARRIVING AT THE STATION,

TABLE 3.8 *(continued)*

IF THE LENGTH OF THE LINE AT THE PUMP IN THE STATION IS LESS THAN 2, THE VEHICLE WILL BE SERVICED AT THE PUMP IN THE STATION. OTHERWISE, THE VEHICLE WILL LEAVE THE STATION. THE TIME FOR THE VEHICLES TO BE SERVICED AT THE PUMP IN THE STATION IS EXPONENTIALLY DISTRIBUTED, WITH A MEAN OF 5 MINUTES FOR THE CARS, AND 9 MINUTES FOR THE TRUCKS. AFTER BEING SERVICED AT THE PUMP IN THE STATION, THE VEHI- CLES LEAVE THE STATION.

THE SIMULATION IS TO BE RUN FOR 8 HOURS, USING A BASIC TIME UNIT OF 30 SECONDS.

Source: G. E. Heidorn, "Automatic Programming through Natural Language Dialogue: A Survey," *IBM Journal of Research and Development,* vol. 20, no. 4 (July 1976), p. 303. Copyright 1976 by International Business Machines Corporation; reprinted with permission.

large number of applications programs with a variety of capabilities and options appeared on the market. In the 1980s, applications software will become even more "friendly," that is, designed for users with little knowledge of computer systems, the former cryptic terminal responses replaced by conversational exchanges, and the coding and command structure simplified. A greater use of parameters will let users state a need with the computer itself translating this need into computer language and guiding the user toward a programmed solution.

As software becomes increasingly sophisticated, a larger percentage of the total system cost will be software costs, up from 10 percent to 40–50 percent for minis, approaching 90 percent (up from 50%) for large systems. More special-purpose packages and small systems with improved reliability will appear in the 80s, many packages being sold off-the-shelf. The user will also benefit from greater discipline in design and improved techniques in programming, such as structured programming.

In addition, there may be a noticeable shift in the comparative popularity of programming languages in the 1980s. PASCAL, competing with BASIC for minis, is gaining converts for all types and sizes of computers. This language, named after a French mathematician, was first developed by Niklaus Wirth in the 1960s. It retains the block structure of ALGOL but gave up ALGOL's cumbersome grammar and syntax for free form coding, elegance, and simplicity. It is a powerful and easy language to use, falling somewhere between FORTRAN and COBOL.

Another reason for PASCAL's importance is that it serves as a base for other languages. One example is ADA, a language named after Ada Augusta, the Countess of Lovelace, the world's first programmer. ADA, developed and implemented by the U.S. Department of Defense, is designed for numerical applications, systems programming, embedded programs, and real-time applications. A computer using this language based on Steelman specifications[12] is scheduled for 1980. Many forecast ADA to be the language of the future. This is largely due to the fact that the Department of Defense is a major user of computers. In the 1970s, over $3 billion a year was spent by the department on software, and every indicator points to greater allocations in the future. ADA, however, is not as appropriate as COBOL for business processing and lacks COBOL's elegant data structures. COBOL has survived competition in the past, and may well remain the favorite language of the business community in the future. As expressed by one business programmer:

> BASIC is easy,
> PL/1 is powerful,
> FORTRAN is fast,
> but COBOL's the one.

SUMMARY

Business data processing includes sorting, merging, calculating, summarizing, and reporting. To perform such processing, software is needed: applications software which specifies decision rules and sequencing necessary for processing; operating software necessary for translating applications programs into machine language, and software for operating computer hardware. Figure 3.8 shows the hierarchy of communications with computers from the movement of electrons to query languages.

FIGURE 3.8
Hierarchy of communication with computers

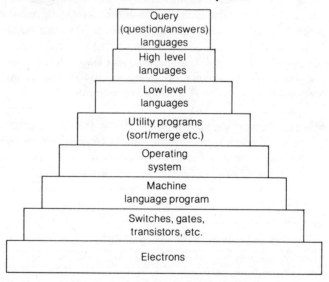

---

[12] Steelman is the name of one of its set of requirements. The earlier versions were called Strawman, Woodenman, and Ironman. Other versions are Sandman and Pebbleman.

Implementing programs requires programming languages. The most efficient to run in terms of computer time is machine language but this language is complex and difficult to learn. Languages closer to natural languages take more computer running time but are easier to learn and faster to write. Because skilled programmers are an expensive, scarce resource while computer time is becoming cheaper, a distinct shift is being made from machine efficiency, favoring inefficient but high level languages. Even operating systems are no longer written in machine language. Users have always preferred high level languages for business applications programs, the higher the better, though language ranking within the high level category is subjective, depending on one's need and background. The languages discussed in this chapter are arranged according to the authors' view of their levels in Figure 3.9.

FIGURE 3.9
High and low level language spectrum

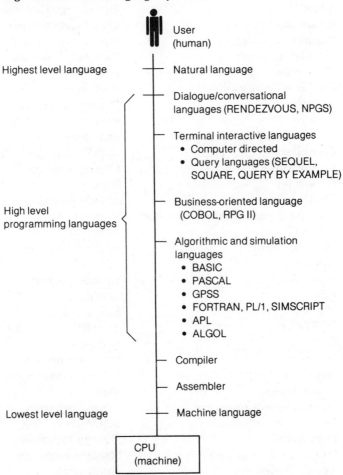

Software that will enable a manager to enter input and generate output from a terminal in a conversational mode and in a language close to English is the trend of the future. Businesspeople want simple, versatile programs that are reliable, readable, verifiable, and maintainable. Research in this direction is very active and promising.

KEY WORDS

ADA
Address
APL
Application programs
Applications software
Assembler
Assembly language
BASIC
Binary digits
Business programs
Canned programs
Characters
Clarification response
Classify
COBOL
Communications programs
Compiler
Contributive response
Controller
Control programs
Data base management systems
  (DBMS)
Data elements
Dumping
Executive
File
Fill in the blanks
FORTRAN
GPSS
Hardware
High level programming
  languages
Housekeeping programs
Interactive languages
Interpreter
I/O control programs
Key data element

Machine dependent
Machine language
Master file
Menu selection
Monitor
Object program
Operand
Operating system software
Operating systems
Operators
Parametric requests
PL/1
Portable
Processing programs
Programming languages
Programs
QUERY BY EXAMPLE
Query languages
Record
RENDEZVOUS
Report
RPG
Scientific programs
SEQUEL
Service programs
SIMSCRIPT
Simulated
Simulation program
Software
Software houses
Software packages
Sort
Source program
SQUARE
Storage location
Stroking dialogue
Summarize

Supervisor
Terminal interactive languages
Transaction file

Updating
Utility programs

DISCUSSION QUESTIONS

1. Describe *(a)* in narrative and *(b)* by flowchart, the basic steps in processing data for a particular application such as payroll or accounts receivable.

2. What is an operating system? Why is it sometimes called the "underwear" system to the hardware and software system?

3. What is the difference between a natural language, such as English, and a formal programming language? Under what circumstances would it be desirable for programming languages to approach natural languages?

4. Name two compiler languages used in business. How are they different? When would each be used?

5. Which programming languages are most suitable for business applications? Give examples.

6. What factors must be considered when selecting a programming language for a given specific business problem?

7. Which programming language would you recommend for an application that is primarily:
   a. Computational (using a mathematical model).
   b. A problem in simulation.
   c. A problem in retrieval.
   d. Rearranging data.
   e. Generation of a report.
   f. A combination of *(d)* and *(e)* with some computations?

8. What is a utility program? Are such programs useful in business processing? Give three examples. Where would you obtain a utility program?

9. What is a software package? Give three examples. How are packages used and where can one obtain them?

10. Would software packages be more appropriate for small rather than large businesses? Why? What are the limitations of such software packages? What are some advantages?

11. Why is COBOL a common programming language used in business? Will it be superseded by ADA?

12. Can a computer language resemble natural language? Should it?

13. What are the limitations of all translator languages, including compilers?

14. What are the advantages and disadvantages of a machine language? When are machine languages used for business applications?

15. What knowledge of programming is essential for a middle or top business manager? If a language must be learned, what language would you recommend for each level of management?

16. What is an interactive programming language and interactive processing? How is interactive processing different from batch processing?

17. Distinguish between:
    a. Source and object program.
    b. Low and high level languages.
    c. Applications and systems programs.
    d. Systems and utility programs.
    e. Interactive and intelligent terminals.
    f. Minicomputer and large size computer.
18. What are the major categories of software?
19. What are the functions of an operating system?
20. Does every computer application require a computer program? Explain.
21. What are interactive and conversational computing? Are online, real time, and/ or time sharing necessary for interactive or conversational computing?
22. Distinguish between a transaction and master file. Give examples from files for a marketing department, accounting office, and university.
23. Comment on this statement: Computers are neutral and unbiased. They only do what they are instructed to do. Who then is responsible for a computer error?
24. Comment on this statement: Computers and information are amoral.
25. How does sorting, merging, and updating vary in complexity between batch and online–real-time systems? What additional resources are required for the additional complexity?

EXERCISE

1. An interactive system involves a set of activities that must be performed in a specific sequence. Rearrange the steps below to meet the sequence requirements:
    a. User types in a reply (to the question).
    b. User thinks about the questions for a while.
    c. Computer asks a question.
    d. Computer asks another question.
    e. The above steps are repeated.
    f. Computer does some processing.

SELECTED ANNOTATED BIBLIOGRAPHY

Edwards, Perry, and Broadwell, Bruce. *Data Processing.* Belmont, Calif.: Wadsworth Publishing Co., Inc., 1979, pp. 173–292.

This is a module on programming languages including a sample business-type problem solved in BASIC, FORTRAN IV, COBOL 1974, RPG II, PL/1, and APL and an evaluation of these languages. Well written with enough detail to appreciate the special characteristics of each language.

Heidorn, G. E. "Automatic Programming through Natural Language Dialogue: A Survey." *IBM Journal of Research and Development,* vol. 20, no. 4 (July 1976), pp. 302–13.

An excellent survey of the use of natural languages for programming. Applications for queuing, accounting, and customized business are discussed. Numerous examples of output are displayed. The article also includes a discussion of research issues.

O'Brien, James A. *Computers in Business Management, An Introduction.* Homewood, Ill.: Richard D. Irwin, Inc., 1979, pp. 150–74.
An excellent treatment of software. Nothing on languages but a survey of all programs needed to run a computer system.

Pratt, Terrence W. *Programming Languages: Design and Implementation.* Englewood Cliffs, N.J.: Prentice-Hall, Inc., 1975, 530 p.
This is a text for computer science courses on programming languages. However, it is neither technical nor mathematical. It describes seven languages (FORTRAN, ALGOL 60, COBOL, PL/1, LISP 1.5, SNOBOL 4, and APL) and evaluates them in terms of structure, simplicity, clarity and unity of language concept, ease of extension, external support, and efficiency.

Sammet, Jean E. "The Use of English as a Programming Language." *Communications of the ACM,* vol. 9, no. 3 (March 1966), pp. 228–30.
This 1966 article has a high ratio of still pertinent and provocative problems raised per page.

Schneidermann, B. "Improving the Human Factors Aspect of Database Interactions." *ACM Transactions on Database Systems,* vol. 3, no. 4 (December 1978), pp. 417–39.
This is a survey of query languages. It classifies interaction modes, types of users, query features, and methods of retrieval. Field studies in evaluating the effectiveness of the natural and query languages are discussed. Also a good list of 52 references is included.

Wegner, Peter. "Programming Languages—the First 25 Years." *IEEE Transactions on Computers,* vol. C–25, no. 12 (December 1976), pp. 1207–25.
The author discusses 30 milestones in the history of programming. Thirteen milestones concern development. Evaluated are assemblers, FORTRAN, ALGOL 60, COBOL 61, ALGOL 68, SIMULA 67, and LISP. Ten milestones are programming concepts and theories, and the remaining seven concern software engineering technology. The article is descriptive with the technical portion separated so it can be easily skipped. The author captures the sense of excitement and the enormous variety of activity that was characteristic of the first 25 years of programming.

4

INPUT, OUTPUT, AND STORAGE EQUIPMENT

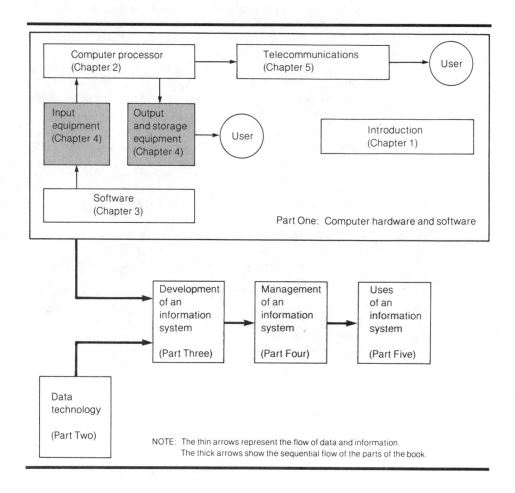

Computer processor (Chapter 2)

Telecommunications (Chapter 5)

User

Input equipment (Chapter 4)

Output and storage equipment (Chapter 4)

User

Introduction (Chapter 1)

Software (Chapter 3)

Part One: Computer hardware and software

Development of an information system (Part Three)

Management of an information system (Part Four)

Uses of an information system (Part Five)

Data technology (Part Two)

NOTE: The thin arrows represent the flow of data and information. The thick arrows show the sequential flow of the parts of the book.

All computers need **peripheral devices** to support the CPU. This includes equipment for input, output, and storage (the topic of this chapter) and communication equipment (the subject of Chapter 5). It is important that students of business understand the capabilities and limitations of peripherals since they constitute the major share of hardware costs, sometimes as much as

90 percent. Formerly these devices were technical, the jurisdiction of data processing personnel. But the trend is toward less expensive, easier to operate machines. Managers today help select peripherals and supervise their use. Of these peripherals, input equipment is the most troublesome from management's point of view since input is human-intensive, prone to error. Users, not skilled EDP operators, prepare input and operate input equipment, often at remote sites where technical assistance is unavailable. Minimizing errors and seeing that the equipment is used efficiently is management's responsibility.

The effectiveness of storage devices also depends on input equipment, for most output placed in storage becomes input at a later point in time.

Furthermore, input equipment is the greatest bottleneck in computing operations. CPU speed is measured in nanoseconds, input speed in seconds. **Input bound** systems result when data waiting to be processed by high speed computers backlogs due to the slowness of input equipment. Correcting this situation through purchase of new devices or revised approaches to input preparation is also a problem for management.

Before examining input, output, and storage devices in detail, the relationship between these peripherals, as depicted in Figure 4.1, should be explained. An example may prove helpful. A transaction file (**cards, tape,** or **disk**) is input; an updated master (also cards, tape, or disk) is output. This master will be stored until it serves as input for subsequent updating and processing. For example, the updated master of the day's transactions would serve as input for the next day's processing. Thus, the master has two states: **intermediate output** and input. Output, such as a journal listing, might

FIGURE 4.1
Input, output, and storage

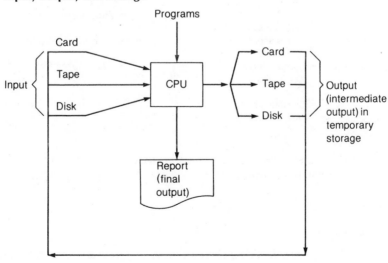

also be in a **terminal** (final) state, a finished product that would not be stored.

This chapter examines the characteristics and uses of input, output, and storage devices, including specialized and advanced equipment since such machines will reduce, possibly eliminate, the problem of I/O bound systems in the future.

INPUT CONVERSION

Input is generated by humans who collect data to be processed by the computer. Coding this data onto a machine-readable medium such as cards, disk, or tape is done by **conversion equipment.** Then the data is read by input equipment before being processed by the CPU. Figure 4.2 shows

FIGURE 4.2
Input conversion to machine-readable form

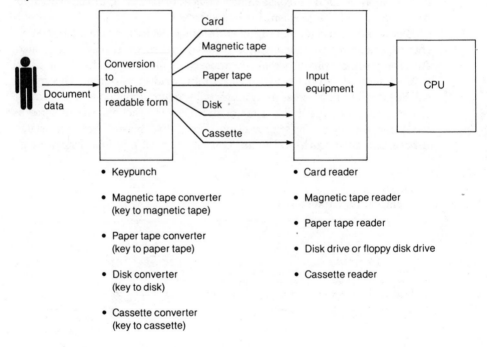

this process. Input devices may be **offline,** not directly connected to the computer, or **online,** in which case the interface would be part of the computer itself.

Input devices

Cards are still widely used for input. Figure 4.3 shows some of the conversion equipment needed before cards can be machine-read. Note that some-

FIGURE 4.3
Equipment to convert data to cards as machine-readable input

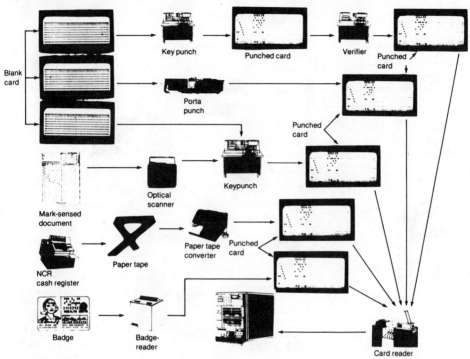

times two machines are required; that is, an **optical scanner** and a **keypunch** when cards are produced from a mark-sensed document.

Noncard input to a computerized system is illustrated in Figure 4.4. The top path, in which a document is encoded on **magnetic tape,** is an example of offline input. But this same document read directly into a scanner is converted online (bottom path) since the scanner transmits directly to the CPU. The **badge reader,** used in production plants or **terminals,** such as a **CRT** (cathode ray tube terminal), are other online input devices.

The characteristics of offline input are summarized in Table 4.1. Online input is reducing in price, becoming increasingly competitive with labor-intensive offline equipment. Also online conversion eliminates human error that occurs offline. A discussion follows of terminal and recognition devices, two online devices.

Terminals

Terminals connected to the computer CPU can be used exclusively for input or for both input and output. Figure 4.5 shows the variety of terminals available. An **intelligent terminal** is one that is programmable. It might incorporate a minicomputer capable of performing computing tasks independ-

FIGURE 4.4
Noncard input to a computerized information system

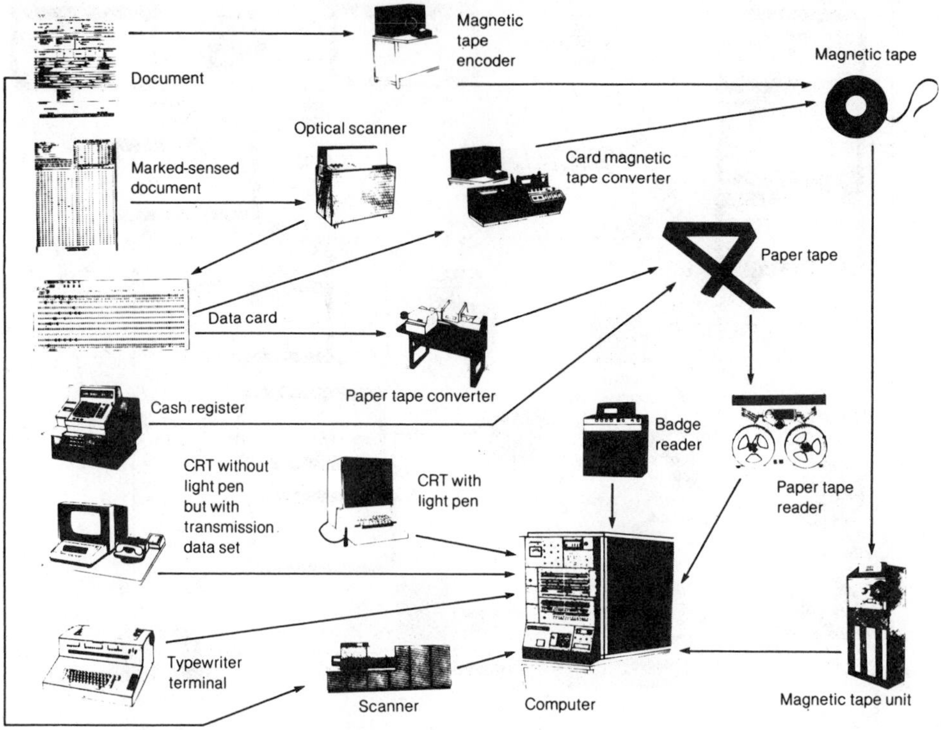

ent of the central CPU, such as editing and validating data at the point of entry, a feature that helps reduce operator errors. Such intelligent terminals are useful in banking, reservations at hotels, car rentals, insurance, and accounting applications where data entry volume is large. A **dumb terminal** lacks such computing capabilities but can still be used to enter data and programs, and solve problems online where processing is done by the central computer.

Teletype terminals (a typewriter terminal) can have both input and output capabilities. They may be used for entering data by keying the input or using push buttons for calling upon programs from the central computer facility to solve problems, and even for typing new programs into the system. Slowness is the major problem with this device. Input is limited by the operator's typing ability, and output by teletype speed.

A **cathode ray tube (CRT)** displays input or output on a screen resembling that of a TV. Information may appear character by character, or page by page. In either case, each character can be **addressed** (accessed) for making changes. The screen is a grid with characters at intersections of two coordinates. An operator can move a **cursor,** a symbol such as a dash, to locations on this grid by pressing a specific key. Wherever the cursor is sta-

TABLE 4.1
Characteristics of offline input devices

Equipment	Media	Primary functions	Typical I/O speed range*	Typical storage capacity	Major advantages and/or disadvantages
Card reader/punch	Punched card	Input and output 150–2,700 cpm	Input: 150–2,700 cpm Output: 80–650 cpm	80 or 96 characters per card	Low cost, but slow-speed and bulky media
Paper tape reader/punch	Paper tape	Input/output	Input: 50–2,000 cps	10 characters per inch	Simple and inexpensive, but fragile and bulky
Magnetic ink character recognition (MICR)	MICR paper documents	Direct input of MICR documents	700–3,200 cps 180–3000 dpm	—	Fast, high reliability reading, but documents must be preprinted, and the character set is not alphabetic
Optical character recognition reader (OCR)	Paper documents	Direct input from OCR typed documents	100–3,600 cps 180–1,800 dpm	—	Direct input from paper documents, but limitations on input format
Mark-sense scanner	Mark-sense documents	Input	1,000–2,500 mark positions per hour	One mark-sense sheet	Faster and more reliable than cards, but more expensive and limited to reading "marks"

* Cps = characters per second; bps = bytes per second; cpm = characters per minute; dpm = documents per minute.

Source: Adapted from James A. O'Brien, *Computers in Business Management* (Homewood, Ill.: Richard D. Irwin, 1975), pp. 85–86. © 1975 by Richard D. Irwin, Inc.

FIGURE 4.5
Classification of terminals

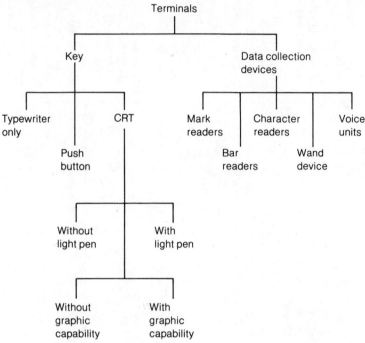

tioned, a character may be entered, filling the space or replacing an existing character. This process is slow, however. Furthermore, the page image will fade unless it is **refreshed** (continually redisplayed), a process that requires extra hardware capability, increasing the price of the CRT unit. There is the additional cost of an add-on printer if a hardcopy is desired. All the applications of a typewriter terminal can be done on a CRT but the latter is faster and quieter, and eliminates reams of paper. Ordering merchandise, recording inventory states, and accounting are examples of business applications for which the CRT is particularly well suited.

Some CRTs also have **graphic capabilities.** Lines and curves can be drawn on the tube so that vectors rather than characters are displayed. These are generated by a computer program which locates points on the screen matrix and joins them in the desired pattern.

There are many types of graphic CRT devices. In 1979 there were 72 models sold by 22 vendors. They differed in cost and sophistication, some having more control over image manipulation than others. Users could also select from a potpourri of special features including: a **joystick,** a control level for moving the cursor; a **data tablet** that digitizes the coordinates of points of a hand-drawn sketch; **blinking characters** (for emphasis), brightness, and color choice; **zooming** and **scaling** (enlargement and reduction); **character reversal** (black character on white background becoming white on black); **scroll display** (the lines move upward, disappearing from the top of the screen with new lines continuously added to the bottom); **protected formats** (prevention of inadvertent alteration or erasure); partial screen transmission; control over image placement on screen; and the ability to underline or overstrike a character. Other features available include communication capabilities; access to programming languages and editing; choice of storage devices; printing facilities; and automatic answering where residing programs enable responses to messages without human intervention.

The use of graphic CRTs for production design is an application that has been used extensively in the automotive and electronics industries. Visual display is also appropriate for computer-assisted instruction, drafting and mapping, chart preparation (for example, flowcharts, organization charts, or planning and scheduling charts such as Gantt, PERT, or CPM), blueprints, and layouts.

The slow and cumbersome cursor can be replaced by a **light pen** which resembles a pencil attached by cable to the CRT. The light pen, hand-held for operation, has a photo-sensitive element hardly larger than a pinhead at one end which creates electric impulses that are recognized by the CRT when the screen is touched. The CRT can be programmed so that this tool can draw on the screen or indicate a choice from a menu presented on the screen. For example, in a query dialogue, the question,

How do you want suppliers identified?
1. By number
2. By name
3. Some other way

might be answered by touching the light pen on 2 if name identification is desired. In other systems the cursor might have to be brought into position for keying 2.

The light pen is deceptive in cost. The pen itself is not expensive, but the software that must accompany it is.

Data scanning terminals

Some terminals scan documents such as inventory tags, plastic credit cards, or badges, converting the data on these into machine-readable form and storing the information for later processing. The data—unique marks or special **fonts**—need to be preprinted on the object to be scanned. Such online input terminals eliminate the labor and error of operator data conversion, and reduce the time required for data entry. However, documents in poor condition (smudges, creases, tears, or dirt) can be misread.

The **optical scanning** industry is highly competitive. In 1979, 81 products by 32 manufacturers were commercially available. Scanning terminals read three classifications of data: **marks, bars,** and **characters.** The advantages and disadvantages of equipment to scan these media are summarized in Table 4.2.

TABLE 4.2
Comparison of scanning terminals

	Mark-sense reader	*Bar code reader*	*Character reader*
Media	Marks on cards or documents	Bars on document or product	Characters on document
Speed/sec	500–4,000 mark positions	Application of UPC reader limited by clerk speed	110–2400 characters
Readable by human	Yes	Not easily	Yes
Accuracy	Depends on care in marking	Very high	High
Information density	Low (binary)	Medium (digital)	High (character)
Complexity of equipment	Simple	Simple	Complex-specialized
Cost	Low	Low	High
Problems	Marks are specialized	Bars must be preprinted	Format size is restricted
Advantages	Less danger of being misread Easy to complete Straightforward Errors known can be corrected easily	Easily and quickly read	Direct way to process printed documents like insurance premiums and turn-around documents Reduces stacks of paper
Disadvantages	Special documents required Sometimes requires special markers/pencils Unsuitable for extensive alphabetic data Assumption of careful entering not valid Inappropriate for volatile data	Bars must be preprinted Requires standardization in production of bar-coded products	Special input preparation equipment required Handprinting not foolproof to read Requires >10,000/day for use justification Problems of standardization

TABLE 4.2 *(continued)*

	Mark-sense reader	*Bar code reader*	*Character reader*

Applications	Market research
	Testing
	  (multiple-choice
	  exam grading)
	Inventory
	Meter reading
	  for billing and
	  accounting
	Time sheets
	Order forms
		Supermarket
		  checkout (UPC)
		Credit card checking
		Badge reading for
		  factory floor or
		  library use
		Tag reading for
		  point-of-sale use
		  in retail stores
			Office work
			Turn-around
			  documents
			Stock/shares
			Payroll data
			Mail sorting

One scanning device is a portable **wand,** resembling a plastic pistol connected by cable to the data collection terminal. The wand captures data through a sensor at its tip when waved past a bar tag or other encoded data (the universal product code, for example). In the NCR model an audible beep registers that the data has been read. In the Singer machine a key lights up. Such systems are used extensively in retail stores. At the time this text was written Montgomery Ward had approximately 16,000 wands in use in over 500 stores.

Voice recognition

Another pattern recognition device used for input is **voice recognition equipment.** These devices are conceptually similar to optical scanners in that patterns are traced and represented by a set of numbers (0 and 1 bits). However, converting speech, an airborne signal, into digital data is a far more complex process than reading marks or bars, for voice patterns include variables in sound, pitch, tone, and loudness. Voice data, once digitized, is then compared to a voice profile stored in the memory of the computer.

A major problem in voice recognition is that pronunciation varies from individual to individual, and a person's mood, circumstance, or health can also affect speech characteristics. Furthermore, telephone lines distort voice signals, as do factors such as humidity. An exact match of voice patterns is, therefore, almost an impossibility.

One method of overcoming some of the above problems is to store **voice profiles** of individual users. In a get-acquainted session the computer flashes on a screen vocabulary words which the user repeatedly vocalizes. The voice profile stored in the computer is, therefore, the user's own. Another approach is to store a set of standard voices for a limited vocabulary, a vocabulary chosen according to client's use of voice recognition equipment. Such an approach would permit travelers to request timetable or gate number information at railway stations or airports, for example.

At present, voice recognition is effective only for limited applications. Each word pronounced by a client must be surrounded by an overlay of silence extending $\frac{1}{10}$ to $\frac{1}{4}$ second. A string of words in a sentence or words spoken quickly require a storage capacity and processing time far too expensive for practical use. In the future, however, advances in technology of voice reproduction and reduction in memory costs will undoubtedly make voice recognition units even for large vocabularies cost-effective.

Voice recognition devices are currently in use in factories where the hands of an employee are busy so that data entry by typewriter or optical scanner would break hand motion, reducing throughput. The worker voices input through a headset, continuing prescribed hand tasks. Mail sorting in post offices and in large firms (such as Monsanto, a Missouri chemical company which processes 25,000 pieces of mail per day) is another practical application.

Voice recognition can also be used for identification purposes in restricted areas of factories, or as security in banking or cash dispensing. These latter examples, however, are better served by pattern recognition of signatures, fingerprints, and hand forms. These, surprisingly, are more unique than voice patterns, and vary less over time. Prototypes of such recognition devices have already been developed.[1] The steady drop in the price of minicomputers required for processing pattern recognition will ensure the manufacture and use of such devices in the future.

STORAGE DEVICES

Characteristics of the main storage devices on the market today are summarized in Table 4.3. The **cassette** and **floppy disk** are products of recent technology. Both are compact, cheap, and very simple to operate, though of the two, the floppy disk (or **diskette**) is more useful because it allows random access. The floppy comes in different sizes (5 to 8 inches in diameter) with single or double side, and has a capacity of up to 5 million bytes. This capacity can be increased by adding more floppy disk drives. The floppy represents a definite advance over storage devices of the 1960s which were bulky, had limited capacity, and required extremely level disk drives during processing. Today's floppy rotates freely within its jacket and can be handled, even transported in a notebook or attaché case without being damaged. It is readily replacing cards, cartridges, and even cassettes for cheap medium-size storage, complementing new storage technology of bubble memory, charged coupled devices (CCD), and random access memory (RAM) using metal-oxide-semiconductor technology (MOS) which provides fast access to large memories. A detailed discussion of the technology of such large memo-

---

[1] For an excellent discussion of this subject see D. J. Sykes, "Positive Personal Identification," *Datamation®*, vol. 24, no. 11 (November 1978), pp. 179–80, 183–84, and 186.

TABLE 4.3
Characteristics of external storage equipment

Equipment	Media	Primary functions	Typical I/O speed range	Typical storage capacity	Major advantages and/or disadvantages
Magnetic tape drive	Magnetic tape	Secondary storage (sequential access) and input/output	15,000–340,000 bps (bytes per second)	Up to 160 million characters per tape reel	Inexpensive with a fast transfer rate, but only sequential access
Magnetic tape cassette	Magnetic tape cassette	Secondary storage and input/output	3,000–5,000 cps (characters per second)	1–2 million characters/unit	Small, inexpensive, and convenient, but only sequential access
Magnetic strip storage unit	Magnetic strip cartridge	Mass secondary storage	Data transfer: 25,000–55,000 cps Access time: up to several seconds	Up to 500 billion bytes per unit	Relatively inexpensive, large capacity, but slow access time
Magnetic disk drive	Magnetic disk	Secondary storage (direct access) and input/output	Data transfer: 100,000–1,000,000 bps Access time: 20–200 ms (ms = microseconds)	Up to 100 million characters per disk pack	Large capacity, fast direct access storage device (DASD), but expensive
Floppy disk drive	Magnetic diskette	Input/output and secondary storage	10,000 cps	250,000 to 1,500,000 characters/disk	Small, inexpensive, and convenient, but slower and smaller capacity than other DASDs
Magnetic drum unit	Magnetic drum	Secondary storage and input/output	Data transfer: 230,000–1,500,000 bps Access time: 10–100 ms	Up to 200 million characters	Fast access time and large capacity, but expensive

Source: James A. O'Brien, *Computers in Business Management* (Homewood, Ill.: Richard D. Irwin, 1975), p. 85. © 1975 Richard D. Irwin, Inc.

ries is beyond the scope of this book.[2] But a brief look at bubble memory will give the reader some insight into recent developments in this area.

Bubble memories store information on a thin film of garnet in areas where the magnetic polarity can be reversed, a reversal that represents the binary states 0 and 1. These areas, when seen under a microscope, appear as bubbles, for which the memory is named. The great advantage of this device is that stored data is unaffected by a power failure. The memory can come on a chip with one million bits storage capacity. An increase in this density by a factor of four is projected for the mid-80s. At present, bubble memory costs less than CCDs and RAMs with MOS technology, and the fact that its price is expected to tumble greatly in the next few years means that bubble devices will commonly be used for large memories in the mid-80s. Technological advances are harder to predict for CCDs and RAMs. At present the former is 100 times faster than bubble memory; RAMs with MOS technology is 10,000 faster. But cost is a factor limiting their use.

OUTPUT PERIPHERALS

Figure 4.6 illustrates common **output devices** and media. The characteristics of major output equipment are summarized in Table 4.4.

Note that terminals and CRTs discussed earlier in this chapter as input devices serve for output as well. A printer is an example of equipment used solely for output. The disadvantage of computer printout is that it can be so voluminous that information which a manager needs is not always readily accessible. To overcome this problem, a terminal to **page** or **scroll** the output on a CRT screen can be used.

Computer output on microfilm

Output representing historical data needed for infrequent processing (for example, violation records of a police department, invoice files, student records at a university) or output that must be preserved as stipulated by law (for example, utility company records) can be produced on **microfilm** or **microfiche** called **COM (computer output on microfilm).** Figure 4.7 shows how this output is prepared, stored, and retrieved. The advantages and limitations of COM are summarized in Table 4.5. At the present time, COM is cost-effective only when output volume is large and the frequency of retrieval small.

Voice output

An output device that will become more common in the 1980s is **voice output.** This equipment reverses the process of voice recognition discussed

[2] For a good discussion, see Raymond P. Cupace, "Memories," *Electronics,* vol. 57, no. 22 (October 26, 1978), pp. 126–32.

FIGURE 4.6
Output devices and media

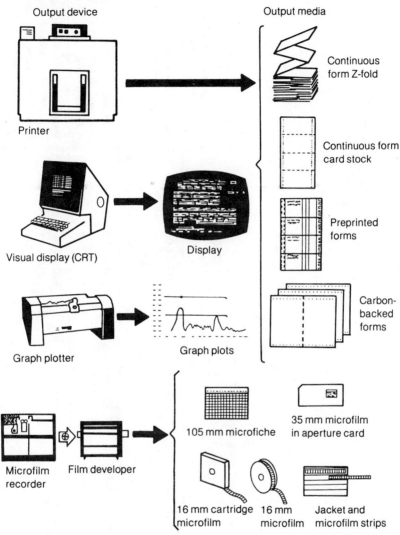

earlier. Digitized data of the human voice for a given vocabulary is stored in the computer memory. To verbalize a message, a microprocessor selects the desired words, strings them together, draws the digitized data for these words from the memory, and converts the data to an analog signal through filters and amplifiers. The advent of microprocessors and reduced costs for large memory capacity have resulted in recent improvement in speech synthesis. No longer is the output monotone as depicted in movies such as *Star Wars*. Computers can speak with variable pitch and loudness. They can phrase

TABLE 4.4
Characteristics of major output equipment

Equipment	Media	Primary functions	I/O Speed range	Major advantages and/or disadvantages
Line printer	Paper (hard copy)	Printed output of paper reports and documents	200–11,000 lpm (lines per minute) 10–400 cps (characters per second)	Fast and low-cost hard copy, but inconvenient and bulky
CRT terminal	"Soft" display	Keyboard input and output	250–50,000 cps output	Convenient and inexpensive, but limited display capacity and no hard copy
Plotter	Paper	Output	Resolution of up to 200 points per inch of output	Important when graphic output is needed; expensive, especially the table model that can plot back and forth
Computer output, on microfilm, (COM)	Microfilm spool/ strips/cartridge Microfiche Aperture card	Output that has archival significance	1,000–30,000 lpm	See Table 4.5

FIGURE 4.7
COM—computer output on microfilm

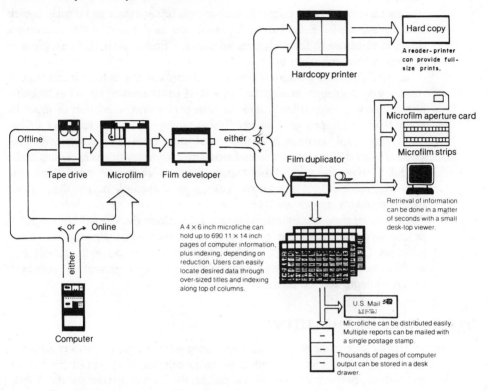

TABLE 4.5
Advantages and limitations of COM

Advantages
> Reduces printed paper volume dramatically (space occupied by film cassette or microfiche is 1 percent and 0.05 percent, respectively, of the paper equivalent) and hence is cheaper to store (cost of facility, insurance, security, and so forth) and mail.

> Fast in preparation—over 1 million frames per month in one shift.

> Faster (and much cheaper) to retrieve than a paper document (⅛ the time).

> More reliable; less down time than printer.

Disadvantages
> Requires special equipment to read and to print hard copy. Strange media, uncomfortable, causing eyestrain for some readers.

> Updating is expensive and time-consuming. Not appropriate for operational data.

> User cannot mark pages or make notes on microfilm or fiche.

> Poor file integrity (continuity) with microfiche. If one COM is removed and misplaced, its loss is difficult to detect. (Not so with microfilm.)

> High capital investment needed.

> Can raise organizational questions. In which department will the COM be located?

sentences with appropriate pauses and even reproduce regional and local accents.

One can expect voice output to increasingly replace dials and display boards in factories, airplanes, and even the family car as the cost of this equipment drops in response to technological advances. ("Fasten your seat belt, please," instead of that annoying buzz.)

Voice output has numerous educational applications as well. It can supplement visual display in **computer-assisted instruction,** or aid in teaching and translating foreign languages. In data processing, validation of input by audio feedback improves efficiency. Errors often pass undetected when operators check input documents against input entry on a CRT screen with eyes shifting from document to screen. Errors are caught more easily during audio validation when the eyes of the operator focus solely on the input document. However, voice output raises noise levels, a good example of how the solution to one problem creates another.

Eventually speech synthesis and voice recognition devices will be integrated in one piece of equipment, permitting verbal computer responses to voiced inquiries. One major benefit will be extended service to clients outside 8–5 working hours, for automated responses to phoned questions at any hour of day or night will be possible.

PERIPHERALS OF THE FUTURE

The development of faster and less labor-intensive peripherals is essential, otherwise bottlenecks in creation of data, storage, and output production will restrict the performance of the powerful CPUs projected for the 1980s. To speed input, data will be increasingly collected by scanners and optical readers, eliminating the current step of keying data which is not only time-consuming but subject to human error. Present identification systems are also inadequate for transactions such as fund transfers. Recognition of fingerprints, hand forms, signatures, and voice prints will replace the plastic identification card used today. Though such devices are technologically feasible at the present time, their cost is too high for common business use. For example, in 1980 signature analysis equipment was approximately $1,000; biometrics (analyzing the shape of the hand) $3,000; voice analysis $5,000; and fingerprint analysis $9,000. Based strictly on cost, signature analysis seems most promising, but voice recognition equipment has other business applications as well. Data entry, for example. As a result, voice recognition equipment will be increasingly common in the 80s.

The technology of sensors for input has not kept pace with CPU technology, in part because the market of suppliers is fragmented, but also because of the difficulty of finding venture capital for manufacturing such equipment. Besides, once data is recognized by sensors, there still remains the problem of interpreting and using this information.

CRTs, the mainstay of the terminal market in the 70s for both input and output, may well be displaced in the 80s because of user dissatisfaction with their flicker which causes eyestrain after one or two hours of work. The electronic beam scanning across the screen fades and needs to be refreshed: hence, the flicker. The CRT has also been opposed by unions for alleged dangerous X-ray emissions. The **plasma display** may be the CRT replacement. This device is essentially a grid of conductors between glass plates surrounded by neon gas. When a point on the screen is part of a desired image, the conductors intersecting at that point are energized making the gas there glow brightly and steadily. At present, plasma displays are more expensive than their CRT counterpart, but as demand increases in the 80s, the price should drop. A major disadvantage of plasma displays is that they lack the color and graphic capabilities of the CRT. Color graphics, especially interactive color graphics, have many applications for management at the control and planning level, providing information in a manner that is easily absorbed and understood especially when the terminal has adaptive keys for routines (of computations and figures), and a variety of character sets (special symbols, foreign alphabets, and so forth).

In the 1980s, present storage technology will be implemented. Lower storage costs for greater storage capacity can be expected, including archival mass storage systems that can store up to 470 billion characters (equivalent to 27 million pages of a typical newspaper). Lasers may also be used to record information for storage. However, the lasers burn the medium, which cannot then be reused, a major disadvantage.

Stored data has little value unless it can be efficiently retrieved. This requires an effective word-matching algorithm and software to implement the algorithm. SDC, a California company, is presently developing a records manager which matches key words in a query (concerning a letter or a memo) with words in the files and allows not only for a change in order of words but also for misspelling. The records manager has its own display and printer. Though it has a storage capacity of 75,000 full pages, holding information equivalent to information stored in 60 file cabinets, it is smaller in size than a single small file cabinet. When debugged and commercially available at cost-effective prices, it will have a great impact on the office of the future.

Another important change in peripherals of the future will be in the terminal market. The dollar value of terminals will increase an estimated 50 percent in the decade ending in 1988 while the expected number of terminals will double due to falling terminal prices. Furthermore, the mix of terminals will change. Dumb terminals and point-of-sale **(POS)** terminals have peaked in their demand and will be replaced by intelligent and specialty terminals, custom-built for applications such as brokerage terminals, industrial badge readers, hand-held portable terminals, and voice units, albeit those with limited functional vocabulary.

SUMMARY AND CONCLUSIONS

All computers require equipment for input and output. In cases where processing is spread over time, information needs to be stored. Equipment of input, output, and storage varies in structure and performance depending on the media of data handled. Figure 4.8 summarizes both available media and peripherals.

Some peripherals are both expensive and technical, acquired and maintained by EDP personnel though shared by all users in an organization. These include printers, plotters, large storage devices, and input conversion equipment. Other equipment, such as optical character readers and COM devices, though technical, may be under the user's jurisdiction. User responsibility is generally for media and equipment that is compact, easy to operate, and

FIGURE 4.8
Summary of input, output, and storage media and peripherals

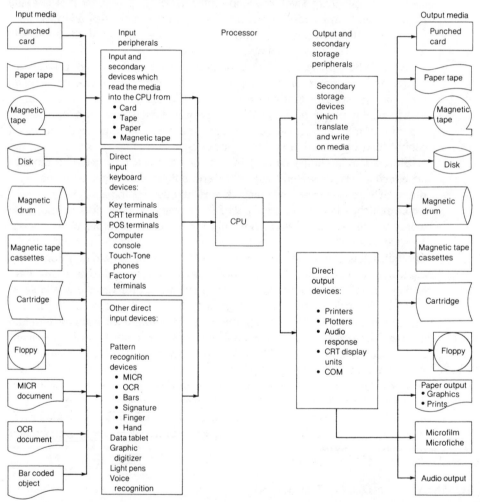

inexpensive—equipment that can be employed in conjunction with minis and micros in a distributive processing environment such as point-of-sale terminals (POS), data entry terminals, floppy diskettes and diskette drives, and scanners.

In discussing peripherals, no attempt has been made to identify actual equipment models, manufacturers, or prices because the industry is extremely volatile, with new competitors and equipment continually entering the market. Technological advances mean that performance is improving while prices are dropping, even with current inflation. When peripherals are needed, a cost-benefit study should be made of available equipment to determine which models are cost-effective in view of an individual firm's requirements.

KEY WORDS

Address	Light pen
Badge reader	Magnetic drum
Bars	Magnetic ink character
Blinking characters	recognition device (MICR)
Bubble memory	Magnetic tape
Cards	Marks
Card reader	Mark-sense scanner
Cassette	Microfiche
Cathode ray tube (CRT)	Microfilm
Character reversal	Offline
Characters	Online
COM (computer output on	Optical character recognition
microfilm)	(OCR) reader
Computer-assisted instruction	Optical scanner
Conversion equipment	Output devices
Cursor	Paging
Data scanning terminals	Peripheral devices
Data tablet	Plasma display
Disk	Point-of-sale terminal (POS)
Diskette	Printer
Dumb terminal	Protected formats
Floppy disk	Refresh
Font	Scaling
Graphic capability	Scroll display
Graph plotter	Terminal output
Input bound	Voice output
Intelligent terminal	Voice profile
Intermediate output	Voice recognition equipment
Joystick	Wand
Keypunch	Zooming

DISCUSSION QUESTIONS

1. What is the difference between online and offline devices? Give three examples of each. What circumstances favor each?
2. What peripherals have you personally used? Was your use multipurpose or for input, storage, or output?
3. Compare OCR with MICR. Cite examples in business where each has a comparative advantage.
4. Compare printers, CRTs, and COMs as computer output devices. Cite business examples where each has the comparative advantage. Explain.
5. Compare typewriter terminals and CRTs as I/O devices. Under what conditions would one be more desirable than the other?
6. When would voice input and voice output be appropriate? Why is voice recognition equipment limited in use at the present time?
7. How are checks processed in a modern bank using computers? What special equipment and input characteristics are required?
8. What is a light pen? Why is it not universally used?
9. Distinguish between:
   a. Remote and console terminals.
   b. Inquiry and response terminals.
   c. Badge and audio terminals.
   d. Visual and voice terminals.
   e. Tape and disk storage.
10. What peripherals would you use for an OLRT system in a large firm with a diversified set of sources for raw materials, many products, and a variety of production processes?
11. Are peripherals essential to the operation of a computer? Do they contribute to the performance of a computer? What is the proportion of peripheral cost to the total cost of hardware?
12. What is currently the main constraint to computer performance, CPU or peripherals? Cite examples.
13. What developments in the peripheral industry are expected in the next few years? What is the main obstacle to peripheral technological advance?
14. What are the factors that influence the selection of peripheral equipment?
15. How would selection of peripherals differ for OL and OLRT systems?

EXERCISE

1. Visit a computer room. Draw a block diagram of the hardware located in the computer room. Identify and label each hardware in terms of devices for input, output, storage, processing, or multipurpose use.

SELECTED ANNOTATED BIBLIOGRAPHY

Axner, David H., and Regan, Fonnie, H. "Alphanumeric Display Terminal Survey." *Datamation®*, vol. 24, no. 6 (June 1978), pp. 183–219.

170 products from 76 vendors are evaluated in this article in terms of model highlights, display features, communication facilities, keyboard, and peripheral pricing.

This survey will undoubtedly be outdated by the time this review is read. That is the nature of the computer industry, particularly with regard to peripherals. The purpose of this citation is to draw attention to surveys and evaluation articles that appear periodically in the literature, such as *Datamation®*, *Mini-Micro Systems, Infosystems, Datapro,* and *Data World.*

Datapro Research Corporation. *Datapro '70.*

This is a looseleaf reference service in three volumes on computer equipment, software, media, and supplies. New products are described and evaluated. For peripherals, see Volume 3. In addition to product briefs, there is a periodic update section called "All about __ ." Some of the topics covered are display terminals, printers, disk drives, disk packs, data entry devices, key entry and data collection equipment, COM, optical readers, and plotters. In each case, the state of the art is reviewed, the advantages and limitations discussed, vendors' names and addresses listed, and most important of all, models on the market are evaluated in detail.

Datapro is a consumer's guide written in nontechnical language. In a competitive and innovative industry, this is a valuable reference for anyone planning to acquire computer equipment. *Data World* is a similar reference service.

Steifel, M. "Floppy Disk System." *Mini-Micro Systems,* vol. 11, no. 10 (November 1978), pp. 37–51.

This is an editorial feature that examines with text and charts the companies and products that shape the industry.

Webster, Edward. "Figuring the Economics of the New Page Printers." *Datamation®*, vol. 24, no. 5 (May 1978), pp. 171–77.

A look at the benefits and cost of any peripheral is important. One does not have to be an economist to follow the analysis of this article. The evaluation procedure for printers used by Webster could be adapted to all equipment acquisition.

5

TELEPROCESSING

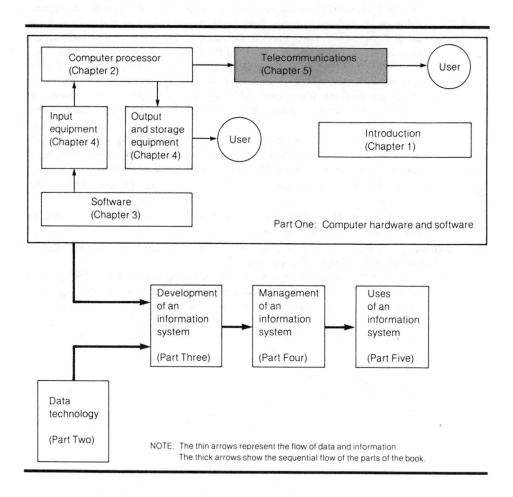

NOTE: The thin arrows represent the flow of data and information.
The thick arrows show the sequential flow of the parts of the book.

Though processing by computers is measured in nanoseconds, the user does not get the full benefit of this speed because of the time lapse in moving input data to the computer and output to the user. Cards and paper printouts create delays due simply to their bulk. Even if this problem is overcome by the use of more compact tape, disk, and cassette, the transfer of information is still time-consuming when dispersed locations such as sales offices, branch offices, warehouses, and plants of a business use a centralized computer.

Teleprocessing to instantly record input and output is one method of speeding operations. This involves the transfer of data and information between computers and remote points by telephone, satellite, or other communication channels. The term *teleprocessing,* first used by IBM, is often used as a synonym for telecommunications, data communication, or information communication. The term is also used to include communication of data and its related processing. Businesses that want instant information on inventory levels, production status, or bank balances find teleprocessing invaluable. So do airlines, hotels, and car rentals that require immediate reservation confirmations.

This chapter will consider data transmission channels, computer equipment configurations, procedures, and security of teleprocessing systems.

DATA TRANSMISSION

Data transmission is the transfer of data to and from the computer through telecommunication channels. The movement may be a few feet within a single office building or thousands of miles. Transmission methods can be characterized by three main variables: **types of channels, speed of transmission,** and **mode of transmission.**

Types of channels

A communication line or **channel** can be simplex, half duplex or full duplex. These channels are compared in Figure 5.1. The **simplex** enables communication of information in only one direction, from source to computer or from computer to user. No interchange is possible. There is no indication of readiness to accept transmission nor any acknowledgment of transmission received. A **half-duplex** system allows sequential transmission of data in both directions but this involves a delay when the direction is reversed. The ability to transmit simultaneously in both directions requires a **duplex** or **full duplex** system. Though more costly, this system decreases processing time because it enables output to be displayed on a terminal while input is still being sent.

Speed of transmission

Transmission of data is measured in **baud.** (Baud is both a singular and plural word, named after the inventor.) In most communication lines, a baud is one bit per second. The capacity of the channel is a data rate called **bandwidths** or **bands.** This gives a measure of the amount of data which can be transmitted in a unit of time. Table 5.1 compares different bands of transmission with their respective speeds and uses. Combining speeds, bandwidths,

FIGURE 5.1
Types of channels in telecommunications

Type	Transmission direction	Graphic representation	Example
Simplex	One direction only	 A ⟶ B	• Radio • Television
Half-duplex	One direction only at any one time. Can be in both directions in sequence	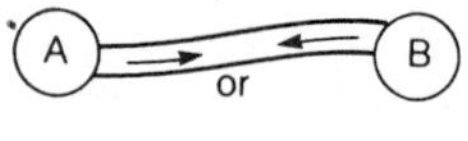 A ⟶ ⟵ B or	• Walkie-talkie • Intercom
Duplex or Full duplex	In both directions simultaneously	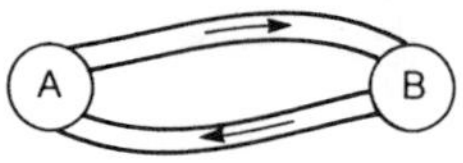 A ⟶ ⟵ B	• Picture-telephone • Dedicated separate transmission lines (such as a presidential "hot-line")

and types of channels, one has a spectrum of capabilities, the cheapest and most limited being a simplex telegraphic grade channel, the most versatile and expensive being a full duplex broadband system.

TABLE 5.1
Types of transmission of data

Channel bandwidth	Speed	Use
Telegraph grade	75 b/s (bits per second)	Printer and keyboard devices
Subvoice grade	45–180 b/s	Teleprinter, also used for telephone
Voice grade	600–4800 b/s	Communication (telephone)
Broadband	Usually 4800–9600 b/s, may go as high as 500,000 b/s	Computer-computer communications

Modes of communication services

Different modes of communication services are summarized in Table 5.2. Carriers in the United States are licensed by the Federal Communications Commission (FCC), which regulates public transmission by wire, radio, satel-

TABLE 5.2
The services offered by principal carriers in telecommunications

Name of service	Characteristics of service	Carrier
DATAPHONE	Uses telephone lines.	Bell System
WATS (Wide-Area Telephone Service)	Uses telephone lines but restricted to geographic area. Has fixed charges. Can be used with DATAPHONE.	Bell System
TWX (Teletypewriter Exchange Service)	Each subscriber has individual line with TWX number. Charges are based on length of call, time used, and established minimums. Used for low-speed business machines.	Bell System and other telephone companies.
TELEX	Similar to TWX except for limit on digits (7) that can be dialed. Has no minimum charge.	Western Union
ACS (Advanced Communication System)	Able to switch computer data between terminals at different speeds and formats.	AT&T (parent company of Bell)
SBS (Satellite Business System)	Intra-company communication for large businesses via satellite.	IBM, Aetna Life, and Communications Satellite Corp.
XTEN System	Envisages microwave and satellite transmission to rooftop antennas of subscribers in over 200 cities.	Xerox Corp. (filed for license in 1978)
VIEWDATA	Offers information services through the television.	Agency of British Government

lite, telephone, television, telegraph, facsimile (documents), and telephoto.[1] There are over 2,000 telecommunication carriers in the United States, the largest being AT&T for telephone, and Western Union for wire and microwave radio communications. In addition, there are specialized **common carriers,** such as MCI and Datron, that provide point-to-point or switched services in heavy traffic areas. These services send data over public lines passing through exchanges and switching facilities, so the term **switched line** is used. In contrast, there are private or **leased lines** which have full access to the line. Some companies with private lines connecting branches and plants refer to these lines as **tie lines.**

Some telecommunication services split data into **batches** or **packets,** transmitting over routes that are less busy during slack periods, and using routes that take advantage of the difference in time between east and west coast. The data is then reassembled at the receiving end. This concept is illustrated in Figure 5.2. Here a company wishes to transmit data between points 1 and 2. Instead of having its own communications system, the company pays for the services of a carrier that has the packet switching capability added to its transmission line. A carrier of this type is called a **value-added carrier.** The carrier can select one of many routes on its packet-switched

FIGURE 5.2
Packet switching

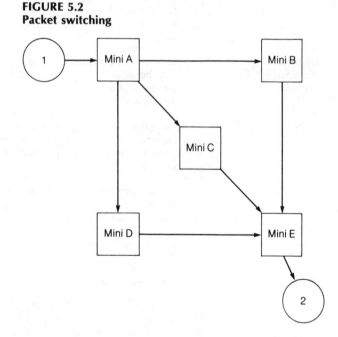

[1] For an excellent discussion of public carriers both in the United States and abroad, see R. J. Halsey et al. "Public Networks: Their Evolution, Interfaces and Status," *IBM Systems Journal,* vol. 18, no. 2 (1979), pp. 223–43.

network, such as ABE, ACE, or ADE. The packets transmitted could all follow the same route but alternate with other customer packets in transmission, or the packets could follow different routes according to line availability. The combination of routing and interspersing of packets is **transparent** to the user since the user does not necessarily know how it is done. This routing and sequencing of packets adds security for it makes it difficult to intercept an entire **message,** since it is split in parts.

The FCC, concerned with competitiveness in telecommunications, regulates the carriers and services offered. One of its far-reaching decisions was to allow a consortium, including IBM, to initiate a system for transmission of data between large organizations via satellite, a system in competition with AT&T. Another set of rulings will be made on a Xerox system which provides high speed communications to small businesses, offices, and large companies, integrating telecommunications with office copy machines. Competition between AT&T, IBM, and Xerox will benefit the consumer by providing a greater variety of services at competitive prices. This will lead to the electronic office, the merging of office equipment technology and computers with data communications. Adequate technology and corporate resources are available. Progress in this direction will in part depend on the consistency and liberalness of FCC policy.

EQUIPMENT AT THE USER'S END

A user needs a **terminal,** a **multiplexer** or **concentrator,** and a **modem** when transmitting and receiving data to and from a computer over a communication line.

Terminals

The types of terminal equipment used for sending and receiving data are summarized in Table 5.3. Some of these are only input equipment (Touch-Tone, voice, and badge reader), some are only output equipment (printer, COM, and audio response), while others have both input and output capabilities (keyboard and CRT terminals).

Special software is often needed for adding processing capabilities to the terminal and for polling the terminals. **Polling** is a set of rules by which each terminal is queried to determine whether or not it is ready for use.

Multiplexers

One problem with terminals is that their maximum speed of transmission is much less than that of a telecommunication line. To improve efficiency, a **multiplexer** is used to combine multiple lines from terminals of slow transmission speeds with one fast broadbeam transmission line. The multi-

TABLE 5.3
Terminals and other devices used for sending and receiving data

Device	Feature and capability of device
Terminal keyboard	Typewriter terminal.
Intelligent	Verifies data and enables correction prior to transmission. Could be a minicomputer with peripheral devices such as tape or disk.
Nonintelligent	Simple input and output device.
Video display unit	Has a video tube like a TV. Can have alphanumeric or graphic capability. Can also have a hard copy unit for printing.
Touch-Tone phone	Used for numeric data transmission by persons such as sales representatives.
Voice input	Acoustic features of person speaking can be checked for bona fide user. Expensive and relatively modern. Useful where identification of input source is essential.
Input reader	Card or tape readers.
Badge reader	Reads specially coded badges such as identification cards carried by factory workers.
Printer	Only for output.
COM	Computer output on microfiche or microfilm.
Audio response	Audio output only.

plexer functions at the terminal end in both receiving and transmitting data. This is illustrated in Figure 5.3.

Concentrator

A multiplexer assumes that all terminals need equal priority of access and have equal density of use. When some terminals operate less frequently than others, resulting in under-utilization of transmission lines, slow terminal lines are concentrated into a few faster channels for transmission. This is done by a device called a **concentrator.**

A concentrator serving many terminals will poll each terminal. If one is ready to transmit or needs to receive data, it is then engaged. A user may also initiate a request for service. If all channels are engaged, the user will get a busy signal and must wait in turn. Terminals share a channel, unlike multiplexing where each terminal has its own channel.

The number of channels and terminals per concentrator depends on the frequency of terminal use, the average time spent per usage, the cost of

FIGURE 5.3
Multiplexer

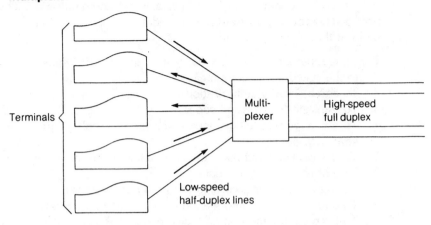

equipment, and cost of waiting by a user. A manager can specify limits to waiting time and maximum queue length and then use a queuing model to determine the optimal number of channels and terminals.

Unlike a multiplexer, the concentrator performs intelligent functions such as routing messages and checking for codes and errors. Some of these functions are performed by minicomputers which also control part of the communications network.

Modem

Data from a terminal or a computer is in **digital signals,** while the transmission is in **analog signals** (except for recent transmission modes such as satellites). A digital-analog converter, called a **modulator,** is used for sending data and an analog-digital converter, called a **demodulator,** is used for receipt of data. The modulator/demodulator is a **modem,** also commonly known as a **data set.** An illustration of the digital and analog signals and the conversions by a modem is shown in Figure 5.4.

FIGURE 5.4
Digital and analog signals

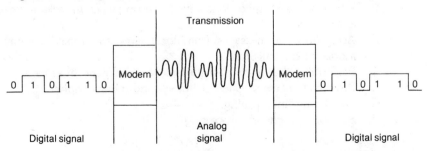

EQUIPMENT AT COMPUTER END

Though a modem is not used in satellite telecommunication, all systems need **interface equipment** between data transmission and the CPU to perform the following functions:

1. To compensate for the relatively slow speed of transmission compared to the speed of the computer.
2. To check security authorization.
3. To translate transmission codes.
4. To exchange recognition signals with the terminal, referred to as **handshaking.**
5. To detect errors and take corrective action where necessary.
6. To edit and pre-process data.
7. To route messages according to priority of messages.
8. To buffer and store information before routing, if necessary.
9. To keep communication and teleprocessing statistics.

Front-end processor

The interface can be performed by most general-purpose computers equipped for remote communications. But as the number of terminals serviced and the volume of data processed increases, the channels become clogged, the **buffer** (a storage device) swamped with messages for the CPU. Consequently, the efficiency and effectiveness of the computing system drops below acceptable levels. To alleviate the problem, teleprocessing functions are transferred from the CPU to special processing equipment called a **front-end processor** which can be programmed to relieve the CPU or host computer of teleprocessing responsibilities. The front-end programmable processor is cheaper and more easily maintained, programmed, and modified than the host computer because of its more limited and specialized functions and because of its detachment from the CPU.

Figure 5.5 shows a front-end processor having many ports or connection points for transmission lines and showing many terminal devices. But this is only one configuration. Many designs, with varying capabilities, are possible. Some of these capabilities are:

1. Message switching between terminals.
2. Performance of stand-alone data processing when the teleprocessing load is low or absent.
3. Acceptance of messages from local lines and mixed communication modes of transmission.
4. Performing the function of multiplexers and concentrators.
5. Providing access to external storage and other peripherals.
6. Facilitating time sharing.
7. Supporting network processing.

FIGURE 5.5
One configuration of a front-end processor

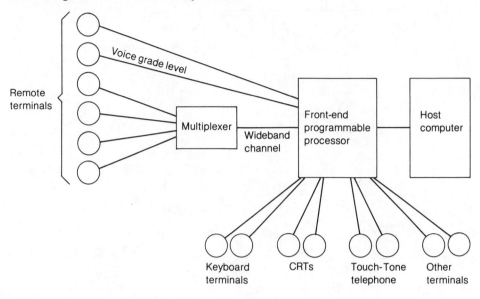

NETWORK PROCESSING

Computers can stand alone, but with increasing demands, and demands from physically dispersed locations, computers belonging to the same organization often need to share and exchange information. This requires that the computers be interconnected. Examples of possible configurations are shown in Figure 5.6. One is the **star network** which enables centralized control and sharing of resources, but the network is vulnerable because breakdown of the central computer will affect the entire system. To provide backup, the network may include more than one computer connected in a **ring.** If a computer breaks down, it can then be supported by a connected computer. But if the computers on both sides and/or the transmission lines fail, the network will no longer be effective. To reduce the effect of breakdown an **interconnected system** is needed. Added interconnections increase the cost of equipment and transmission lines, but backup is provided. As minicomputers become cheaper and more powerful, they will be used increasingly as interconnected computers in the network and as front-end processors.

The actual network configuration selected by management will depend on the reliability and promptness of responses required from the system. For example, a reservation system will have a greater need for fast response time than will a warehouse of durable goods. The cost of a network (including the possibility of a standby additional system) must be weighed against the benefits. In one sense, the selection is determined by the function performed by the teleprocessing system.

FIGURE 5.6
Computer network configurations

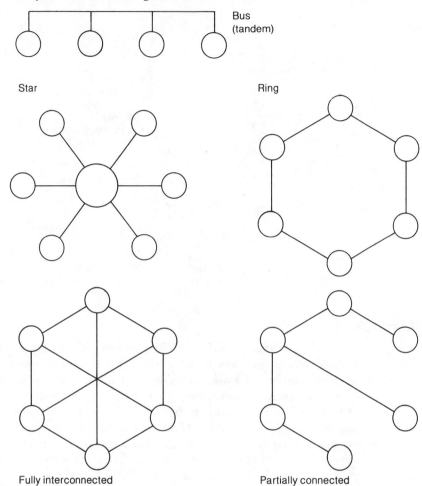

FUNCTIONS PERFORMED BY A TELEPROCESSING SYSTEM

There are three main functions performed by a teleprocessing system: **data entry, inquiry and transaction processing,** and processing from a remote point **(remote job entry).**

Data entry

Using telecommunications to enter data in a computer directly from a terminal avoids the need of recording data on a form, punching cards, and transporting input to the computer. It saves time and also reduces errors by the elimination of one step in the data recording process.

Examples of terminals used for data entry would be badge readers in an assembly plant, sensors in a factory to measure variables that must be controlled, and keyboard or Touch-Tone terminals for recording sales in a department store. These terminals are used as input devices to collect data for immediate use in an OLRT (online real-time) system or for later processing by a batch system.

Inquiry and transaction processing

In this application a terminal is used to make a query such as: Are ten items of product X in the warehouse? If not, how many are available? When can the complete order be filled? Can two reservations be confirmed on Flight TWA311 on January 6? What is the bank balance of account 7614? When a decision is made based on the computer response, the transaction is processed using the data base and a set of programs, and the dialogue ends. Then the initiator of the inquiry is informed that the transaction has been completed.

In this application, the terminal is used as an input-output device. Typewriter terminals are sufficient for short cryptic or coded messages. A CRT terminal is appropriate for longer output.

Remote job entry (RJE)

In **RJE,** a user enters data on a terminal and expects a solution from the computer. The program is sometimes provided on the terminal or called from external memory, but no updating of a data base is necessary as with a warehouse or reservation application. RJE might be used by an engineer solving a problem on a terminal in an office, for example, when the computer itself is located elsewhere. The terminal could be keyboard, CRT, or a graphics terminal.

Other functions

The above three modes of teleprocessing are not mutually exclusive. Many businesses, especially those with dispersed plants, warehouses, and sales offices, use all of them.

The actual functions performed and the equipment used will vary between industries and even within an industry, and will depend not only on size or complexity of the business but on management and its use of equipment. For example, within a plant there might be use of a computer as a calculator for RJE, but the terminals could be keyboard terminals or CRTs with "bells and whistles," such as light pens, attached printer, COM devices, or even color graphics. In some cases, these terminals might be replaced by minicomputers.

Once the devices have been selected, there are still many choices to be made, such as: Should a half-duplex line with a public carrier or a full-duplex leased private line be used? Would the ACS system by AT&T serve, or would the satellite transmission by IBM's SBS be preferable? Are individual terminal channels with a multiplexer needed, or should channels be shared? These choices must be made uniquely for each business, depending on the frequency and density of transmission, the need for security and access to a private line, and finally, the offerings of services and cost by the different public carriers.

SECURITY

Security is providing controlled access in order to maintain the confidentiality of data. Intrusion may take place at the terminal when transmission is initiated or during transmission.

One method to ensure security at the terminal end is the use of a predetermined signal of recognition called a **handshake.** The computer must recognize the signal before transmission of data can take place. Conventions and procedures for user identification and dialogue termination are also used. These are often specified by manufacturers of equipment, particularly producers of multiplexers and concentrators. Codes, conventions, procedures, and rules of handshaking are referred to as **protocol.**[2]

The violation of security during transmission occurs when a line is intercepted and eavesdropping takes place. To prevent interception, the message is sent in predetermined codes. **Encoding** or **encrypting** (a word from the Greek root *crypt:* to hide) can be done in one of two ways: **transposition** or **substitution.** In transposition, characters are exchanged by a set of rules. For example, the third and fourth characters might be switched so that 5289 becomes 5298. In substitution, characters are replaced. The number 1 may become a 3, so that 514 reads 534. Or the substitution may be more complex. A specified number might be added to a digit, for example, a 2 added to the third digit, making 514 read 516. Decrypting restores the data to its original value. This process is illustrated in Figure 5.7.

The **key** used in Figure 5.7 for coding the message is derived from a **key base** (base of data). It could be a random number key, or a key based on a formula or algorithm. The key base and the algorithm must be kept a secret, accessible only to bona fide users. As in all codes, the key must be difficult to break. Frequent changing of the key adds to the security of data.

The U.S. government is as concerned as business is regarding security of telecommunications. The 1974 Privacy Act entrusted the National Bureau of Standards with the security of federal data and produced a **data encryption standard (DES)** which has been accepted by most manufacturers of

---

[2] For more details, see P. E. Green, "An Introduction to Network Architectures and Protocols," *IBM Systems Journal,* vol. 18, no. 2 (1979), pp. 202–22.

FIGURE 5.7
Encrypting and decrypting of data in teleprocessing

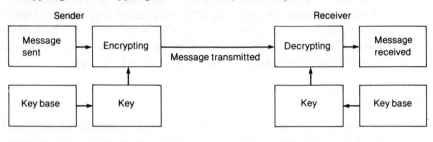

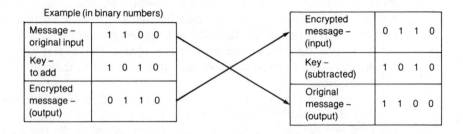

teleprocessing equipment. The DES incorporates transposition and substitution repeatedly in each encryption.

In addition to DES, some computer manufacturers have developed their own encryption products

> . . . IBM encryption products feed back part of the immediately proceeding, already transformed message and combine it with the plain text about to enter, and their sum is enciphered under control of the key. . . . Such is the security offered by that arrangement that its project work factor is considerable: the time needed to decipher the message encrypted by it would engage the most powerful of all present computers for many years, in which time the value of the information would have long faded and the key many times changed.[3]

This quote is based on the capabilities of computers in the 1970s. In future years decrypting may be faster, taking only weeks, possibly merely days or hours. When billions of dollars are at stake, as in the electronic transfer of funds, the ingenuity of intruders and the resources allocated to theft will increase.

In 1978, telecommunications security was broken by a computer consultant to a bank, enabling him to transfer the bank's money to a Swiss account for the purchase of Russian diamonds. The FBI which broke the case will

---

[3] L. Sandek, "Privacy, Security and Ciphers," *Data Processor,* vol. 21, no. 1 (January 1978), p. 5.

not state whether the bank was using DES or encrypting equipment. But certainly there is evidence that present-day security is not foolproof in spite of our knowledge of protocol, DES, and encrypting devices. This case was unusual in that it had a happy ending, at least for the bank. When the diamonds were resold, the bank's profit was many times the potential rate of return had the funds been legally invested in a savings account.

ERRORS

In teleprocessing, errors may be the result of **noise,** the addition of unintended signals caused by switching equipment of the transmission carrier, or noise caused by natural events such as a surge impulse due to lightning. **Fading,** the reduction of signals due to weak transmission, may also cause mistakes. Both noise and fading occur frequently on public telephone and telegraph lines. **Leased dedicated lines** are less prone to noise and fading but the cost of transmission on these lines is greater. In deciding which lines to use, management must compare this additional cost to the cost of losses in transmission.

One method of facilitating error detection is the odd (even) **parity check.** A bit of data is added to each set of bits representing a character so that the total number of 1 bits is odd (even). Upon receipt of the transmission, the bits are added and compared to the parity rule. When an error is detected, a signal is sent for retransmission of the data.

Checking for the use of a prescribed pattern of ones and zeros to represent characters is another method of tracing errors. Automatic checking of prescribed patterns of bits in a code makes this a self-checking code. This raises costs, however, since additional check bits must be transmitted and processed.

Fortunately, improved technology such as large- and small-scale integrated circuitry (LSI and SSI) is reducing the error rate in communication lines and improving reliability.

FUTURE OF TELECOMMUNICATIONS

The 1980s will be a period of great activity in satellite telecommunications,[4] a period both of challenges to the FCC and of court battles regarding integration of computers with satellites. Once regulations are clarified, competition between corporate giants (IBM, Xerox, AT&T), and other firms (for example, General Telephone and Electronic Corporation, and Continental Telephone Corporation) should spur the development of numerous equipment configurations for satellite teleprocessing. One such configuration, shown in Figure 5.8, has two earth stations both at the sending and receiving end. Whatever the configuration, satellites will transmit data, voice, video, and facsimile at

---

[4] For an excellent discussion, see Wade White and Morris Holmes, "The Future of Commercial Satellite Telecommunications," *Datamation®*, vol. 24, no. 7 (July 1978), pp. 94–102.

FIGURE 5.8
One configuration of a satellite communication

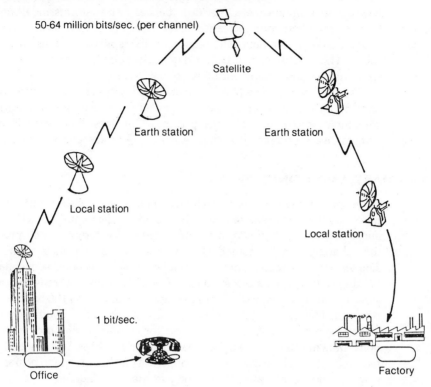

50-64 million bits/sec. (per channel)

Satellite

Earth station   Earth station

Local station

Local station

1 bit/sec.

Office   Factory

a rate of 60–1200 million bits/second. The constraint in speed is the earth relay from satellite station to user. Telephones, for example, can only transmit 1 bit/sec. Here, the high technology of optical fibers, replacing conventional copper wire, is very promising. Optical fiber can transmit pulses of information in the form of laser-emitted light waves. The light waves are detected and decoded at the receiver end by photo diodes, technology produced by the semiconductor industry. The transmitting media in between is glass fiber that is thinner than human hair, stronger than steel, and 80 times lighter than an equivalent copper conductor. Its capacity is one billion times the capacity of copper telephone wire in bits/second. But replacing existing telephone lines with glass fibers would be very expensive. Martin estimates the cost as equivalent to the entire U.S. moon program (allowing for inflation).[5] And, of course, firms with vested interests in existing equipment will resist changes in equipment standards.

---

[5] James Martin, *Wired Society* (Englewood Cliffs, N.J.: Prentice-Hall, Inc., 1978), pp. 166–67.

Optical fibers are already implemented in pilot projects in Atlanta and Chicago. In addition to the advantages of the fibers already mentioned, they have proven immune to electrical disturbances such as storms and disturbances from surrounding communication links. They are amenable to transmission of digital computer data and require fewer repeater stations than copper cables. The security is also tighter (light waves are hard to decode and light wave interception equipment does not yet exist).

Once the costs of glass fibers drop and line losses are reduced, it is conceivable that fiber optic cables may even prove more economical than satellite communications over high-density routes. Satellites, however, will retain a comparative economic advantage over long distances and rough terrain.

SUMMARY AND CONCLUSIONS

Teleprocessing is the use of telecommunication lines for transferring computer data between remote points. It is used for data entry as well as inquiry and transaction processing. It is also essential for remote batch processing, time sharing, and distributed data processing. The channels used may be simplex (one direction only), half-duplex (both directions sequentially), or full duplex (both directions simultaneously). The speed of transmission, measured in baud (bits/second), determines use. Seventy-five to 150 baud are appropriate for teleprinters, 600–4800 are voice grades, and broadbands with an average speed of 4500–9600 are used for computer-computer communications. Data may be sent by public, leased, or private lines. Value-added carriers have packet switching capabilities that permit batches of data to be transmitted over a choice of routes for reassembly at the receiving end.

Transmission can be by telephone lines, sea cables, radio, or satellite. These are shown in Figure 5.9, along with different input-output equipment options available. Devices and procedures required specifically for telecommunications are summarized in Table 5.4.

A major cost of teleprocessing is the equipment needed by user and computer which must be added to the communication channel. A variety of terminals for transmitting data are available. Some are input equipment only (card and tape readers, badge readers, Touch-Tone telephones); some are exclusively for output (printers, card punch, COM, audio response units); and some (keyboard terminals and CRTs) are used as both input and output devices. A multiplexer or concentrator is required so that a fast wideband channel may be used, and a modem is needed to convert signals (digital-analog-digital). A front-end processor that can be programmed (possibly a minicomputer) is also used to interface the transmission signal with the computer.

Teleprocessing costs include costs of transmission, security measures, protocols, error detection, special software, job control procedures, and backup. These expenses must be weighed against savings made by the elimination of the physical movement of data and savings as a result of sharing processing

FIGURE 5.9
Different transmission modes with different input and output devices

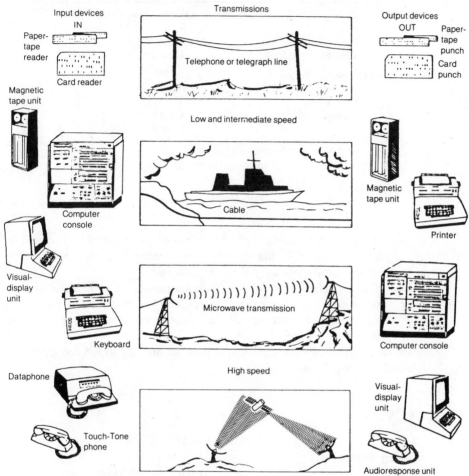

Source: Andrew Vazsonyi, *Introduction to Data Processing,* 3d ed. (Homewood, Ill.: Richard D. Irwin, 1980), p. 223. © 1980 by Richard D. Irwin, Inc.

facilities, computer programs, and data bases. In deciding whether or not to invest in teleprocessing, a business must consider the volume, density, direction, and distribution of its messages. It must also analyze the urgency of transmission and receipt of data. Available equipment must be examined, and choices made regarding the degree of security needed and acceptable error rates.

In the future, telemail, teleconferences, telediagnostics, invisible money, teleshopping, telenews, and telelectures served by satellite transmission and

TABLE 5.4
Devices and procedures needed for telecommunications

Interfacing	*Distribution of information*
Modems	Front-end processors
Terminal interfaces	Concentrators
Equipment interfaces	Line Controllers
Bandwidth sharing	Protocols
Concentrators	*Network control*
Multiplexers	Testing
Software multiplexing—polling	Diagnostics
Switching	Error detection
Store-and-forward switches	
Message	
Packet	
Circuit or line switches	

telepocket radios are possible applications. Since telecommunication channels are regulated by the FCC, the direction and development of teleprocessing in business will be largely shaped by this agency.[6]

The effect of teleprocessing on organizations will be considered in Part Four, with present and future business applications examined in Part Five. But before investigating the use of information, this text will explain what data is, how it is identified, collected, validated, organized, and managed (Part Two); and how data information systems are developed and operated (Parts Three and Four).

KEY WORDS

ACS	**DATAPHONE**
Analog signal	**Data set**
Band	**Data transmission**
Bandwidth	**Demodulator**
Batch	**Digital signal**
Baud	**Duplex**
Buffer	**Encoding**
Channel	**Encryption**
Common carrier	**Fading**
Communication modes	**Front-end processor**
Concentrator	**Full duplex**
Data encryption standard (DES	**Half-duplex**
Data entry	**Handshaking**

---

[6] For a discussion on the future of teleprocessing, see W. D. Frazer, "Potential Technological Implications for Computers and Telecommunications in the 1980s," *IBM Systems Journal,* vol. 18, no. 2 (1979), pp. 333–47.

Inquiry and transaction processing
Intelligent terminal
Interconnected system
Interface equipment
Key base
Leased dedicated line
Message
Modem
Mode of transmission
Modulator
Multiplexer
Network processing
Noise
Packets
Parity check
Polling
Processing modes
Protocol
Remote job entry (RJE)

Ring network
SBS
Security
Simplex
Speed of transmission
Star network
Substitution
Switched line
Teleprocessing
TELEX
Terminal
Tie line
Transposition
TWX
Types of channels
Value-added carrier
VIEWDATA
WATS
XTEN

DISCUSSION QUESTIONS

1. What is the difference between telecommunications, teleprocessing, and tele-transmission?
2. Why are telecommunications important to computer processing?
3. What functions do the following perform: modem, multiplexer, concentrator, front-end processor?
4. Contrast:
    a. Half-duplex and full duplex.
    b. Modulation and demodulation.
    c. Multiplexer and concentrator.
    d. Transmission and communications.
    e. Analog and digital signals.
    f. Encryption and decryption.
5. What are the advantages and disadvantages of a satellite system? Can the disadvantages be overcome with time and technological advances?
6. Discuss the factors which a firm must consider in choosing what type of telecommunication system to use.
7. What are the main components of a telecommunication system? Draw a diagram showing these components and their interrelationships.
8. What are the functions performed by a front-end processor? Under what circumstances is a front-end processor necessary or desirable? Give examples.
9. What are the different types of terminals used in teleprocessing? Why would you recommend each type? What other equipment could be used instead of a terminal?

10. Discuss a teleprocessing network. What functions does it perform? How is it controlled? What happens if there is a breakdown in one of the paths?

11. What is an intelligent terminal? Why and when would it be used?

12. Identify and compare at least three network designs in terms of cost, reliability, ease of implementation, and special equipment required. Give business or industrial examples where each type of network might be used.

13. What are the organizational and managerial considerations of a telecommunications network?

14. What types of networks are most common in business? Give examples of their use.

15. What network would you recommend for each of the following applications. (The number of computers in each network is in parenthesis.)
    a. Hotel reservation network (4).
    b. Airline reservation network (24).
    c. Warehouse network (3).
    d. Production plants (5).
    e. Insurance company (3).
    f. University (10).

16. What are current trends in telecommunications?

17. What are the obstacles in exploiting existing telecommunication technology? Why the delay?

18. Teleprocessing is one of the most important growth sectors of the computer industry. Do you agree or disagree with this statement? Explain.

19. Why are there more legal and regulatory problems with telecommunication systems than with on-site processing? What are the problems?

20. What elements in a telecommunication system are not found in a batch system?

SELECTED ANNOTATED BIBLIOGRAPHY

FitzGerald, Jerry, and Eason, Tom S. *Fundamentals of Data Communications.* New York: John Wiley & Sons, Inc., 1978.
An excellent text, covering communication concepts, hardware, software, and errors, as well as networks and common carriers.

IBM Systems Journal, vol. 18, no. 2 (1979), pp. 186–350.
This is a special issue on telecommunications, including IBM's own use of telecommunications, one of the most advanced telecommunications systems in existence, with 8200 devices, applications, and its communication architecture, the SNA. Also discussed are emerging international telecommunications standards and three excellent nontechnical articles by Halsey et al. on public networks, their evolution, interfaces, and status; an article by Frazer on the future of telecommunications; and a tutorial on network architecture and protocols by Greer.

Kimbleton, Stephen R., and Schneider, Michael G. "Computer Communication Networks: Approaches, Objectives and Performance Considerations." *Computing Surveys,* vol. 7, no. 3 (September 1975), pp. 129–73.
This comprehensive survey is addressed to the nonspecialist. It describes network functional components and their interaction. It advances the hypothesis that the

packet-switched networks provide the most appropriate technology for supporting multimodel traffic between hosts. The functional components of the packet switch are examined. The paper concludes with a description of three networking examples and identification of areas for future research. The article has a detailed bibliography of 191 references.

Martin, James.   *Telecommunications and the Computer.* 2d ed. Englewood Cliffs, N.J.: Prentice-Hall, Inc., 1976.
This book has detailed sections on transmission, switching, and imperfections. The latter includes noise and distortion, line failures, delays, and data errors. The book is very readable, well organized, and generously illustrated with photos and colored diagrams.

————. *Future Developments in Telecommunications,* 2d ed. Englewood Cliffs, N.J.: Prentice-Hall, Inc., 1977.
This is the fourth book written by the author on teleprocessing. It discusses the use of teleprocessing, its synthesis and technology. Like other Martin books, this one is very well organized and illustrated.

————. *Wired Society,* Englewood Cliffs, N.J.: Prentice-Hall, Inc., 1978, 300 p.
An excellent nontechnical discussion of telecommunications technology, including its social implications for future society.

Mayo, John S.   "The Role of Microelectronics in Communication." *Scientific American,* vol. 237, no. 3 (September 1977), pp. 192–208.
A well-illustrated nontechnical discussion of a technical subject. This issue is a special one on microelectronics as it relates to computing. It is also available in a separately bound volume as a *Scientific American Book.* Highly recommended as a tutorial for a layman on microelectronics, microprocessors, and microcomputers.

Ross, Ronald G.   *An Assessment of Current Data Base Trends.* Wellesley, Mass.: Q.E.D. Information Sciences, 1977, 96 p.
This monograph has interesting chapters on DBMSs for remote computing and minicomputers. It also has numerous product briefs, including Honeywell's 1-D-S/II; UNIVAC's DMS1100 and DMS/90; Cullinane Corporation's IDMS, Digital's DBMS–10; and CDC's DMS–170.

Sandek, Lawrence.   "Privacy, Security and Ciphers." *Data Processor,* vol. 21, no. 1 (January 1978), pp. 1–6.
This article traces the history of ciphers and cryptography and discusses cryptographic products. The equipment described is IBM equipment, but this bias is to be expected from an IBM journal.

Sanders, Ray W.   "Comparing Network Technology." *Datamation*®, vol. 24, no. 7 (July 1978), pp. 88–93.
This article discusses digital switching and includes a detailed survey of ten years of packet switching.

White, Wade, and Holmes, Morris.   "The Future of Commercial Satellite Telecommunication." *Datamation,*® vol. 24, no. 7 (July 1978), pp. 94–102.
An excellent, well-illustrated article on a little-documented subject. Has details on one system: TDMA (Time-Division Multiple Access).

PART TWO

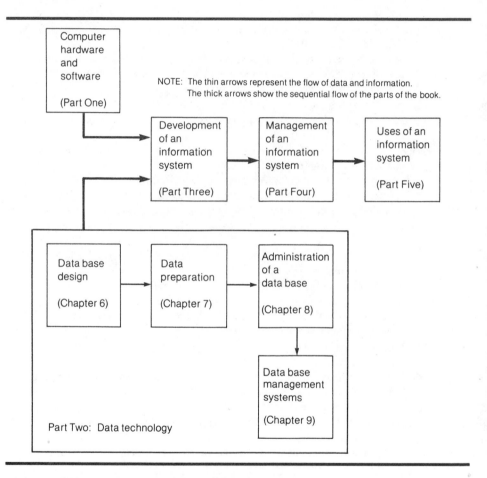

Computer
hardware
and
software

(Part One)

NOTE: The thin arrows represent the flow of data and information.
The thick arrows show the sequential flow of the parts of the book.

Development
of an
information
system

(Part Three)

Management
of an
information
system

(Part Four)

Uses of an
information
system

(Part Five)

Data base
design

(Chapter 6)

Data
preparation

(Chapter 7)

Administration
of a
data base

(Chapter 8)

Data base
management
systems

(Chapter 9)

Part Two: Data technology

DATA TECHNOLOGY

Technology relating to data, how data is created, organized, prepared, stored, accessed, maintained, and controlled is the subject of Part Two. Such technology is becoming increasingly important to business, for the reduced cost of hardware for data storage means that firms can afford large data bases comprising billions of characters of data. These data bases are the foundation on which management information systems are built. Though many of the activities related to data bases are technical and the responsibility of EDP personnel, managers must be involved in these activities to ensure that data needed for decision making is included in the base, and to ensure quality, security, and easy retrieval of needed data. The background knowledge provided in the chapters in Part Two is a prerequisite to understanding how management information systems are developed and maintained, the subjects of Parts Three and Four.

The chapter layout for Part Two is shown in diagram form. The design and content of data bases is the subject of Chapter 6. Chapter 7 examines three aspects of data preparation: data collection, coding, and validation. Data directories and the organization of a DED/DD system for implementing the data base are discussed in Chapter 8. The role of a data base administrator and the resources needed for data management are also reviewed. Program sets for automating many of the responsibilities of a data base administration are called data base management systems (DBMS). Chapter 9 introduces DBMS to the reader.

6

DESIGN OF A DATA BASE

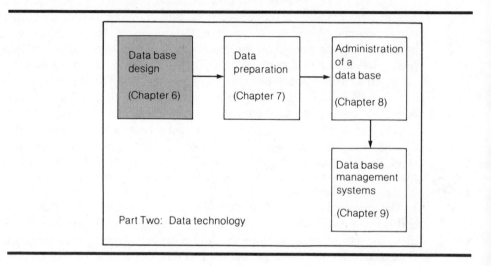

Part Two: Data technology

The data for a computerized information system must be in a machine-readable form and according to prescribed conventions. Such data is called a **data base.** A **common data base** consists of data shared by organizational units within a business, a sharing that is of great value when different units need to correlate data for effective decision making.

Managers should be involved in both creation and maintenance of a data base, since the information obtained from the base is for their use. Furthermore, the quality of information derived is very directly related to the quality of the data base itself. There is a cliché in data processing, GIGO: garbage in, garbage out. Therefore, the design of the base for a management information system should not be left to computer technicians either by delegation or default, for technicians lack the expertise, judgment, viewpoint, and motivation of managers, the ultimate users of the system. Managers themselves should be active in the design. But this requires that the manager understand how data bases work. Providing such an understanding is the objective of this chapter of the text.

This chapter opens with a definition of data and then outlines the types of data elements commonly collected by business and industry. How to determine the exact data elements an information system requires is then explained. To avoid misinterpretation of data elements, data element dictionaries must be prepared. The design and content of such dictionaries are therefore described. Finally, the difference between logical and physical organization of data within a data base is clarified, and the comparative advantages of cards, tape, and disks for input are reviewed.

DATA AND DATA ELEMENTS

Data is a fact or an observation. The data 3528 is abstract, meaningless unless it can be related or associated with a specific entity. It might be an invoice number, an account number, a machine part number, or the number might represent an employee, Mr. Jones. Data on other attributes about Mr. Jones might also be gathered, such as age, marital status, or address. An attribute for which data is collected is called a **data element.** Thus, the sex of employee Jones is a data element, the value of that data element being MALE, or the data element is a code representation meaning male—

such as 2. Name of the employee is also a data element. In this case the value is JONES. If an employee works seven hours, the data 7 is the value of the data element "hours worked." If the seven hours of work and the male employee Jones were related, they would form a logical grouping of data elements yielding the information, Jones is a male employee who has worked seven hours. If these data elements were associated with other data elements, such as academic record and date appointed, more information could be produced, creating a **logical record** of employee Jones.

There are many kinds of data elements. A summary list appears in Table 6.1. The list identifies data elements by function and source, and shows the person primarily responsible for their determination. Each data element in this table is explained below.

TABLE 6.1
Classification of data elements

Data elements by function	Person with prime responsibility
Transaction Reference	} Manager
Planning Linking Control Security	} Manager and analyst
Identification Checking Other data elements	} Analyst
Data element by source	

Raw data
  Observation
  Fact
  Assignment
Derived
Estimated
  Hunch
  Guesswork
  Statistical techniques
	} Manager

Data elements by function

TRANSACTIONAL DATA ELEMENTS

Most data elements in a common data base are created by transaction. For example, hiring an employee is a transaction which generates a whole series of values for data elements such as name, address, sex, and previous employment. When work hours are recorded, or salary checks issued, additional **transactional data** is created. Purchase of raw materials, or the sale of a product, would create values for still other transactional data elements.

REFERENCE DATA ELEMENTS

Sometimes data elements are needed for purposes of reference. Consider a transaction regarding the purchase of supplies. When the supplies are received, the vendor is paid an agreed amount and the transaction is recorded in the financial file. But occasionally the transaction must be traced and the invoice checked. To do this, the data system must include some means of reference to the invoice, such as the invoice number. This means of reference is a data element.

Other examples of **reference data elements** include purchase order numbers, personnel employment form sequential numbers, and transaction numbers.

DATA ELEMENTS FOR PLANNING

If variable and fixed cost coefficients are used to predict costs in the planning process, these are **planning data elements.** Other examples of planning data elements are future production coefficients or projected estimates of variables such as future sales. These data elements can be derived from historical data, may be based on the planner's value judgment, or may be normative and reflect what is wanted or hoped.

LINKING DATA ELEMENTS

Linking data elements are unique identifiers to permit integration of files. For example, a payment recorded in a receipts file can be deducted by computer from the balance owed by that same customer in the accounts receivable file when a link, such as the customer's account number, is used in both files. Linking data elements will be discussed in greater detail in this chapter.

CONTROL-RELATED DATA ELEMENTS

A number of variables in production are regulated by upper and lower control limits, predetermined maximum and minimum allowable values. When a variable exceeds or even approaches these limits, management is informed. These limits constitute values for **control-related data elements.** Other control limits or values are set in budgeting, advertising, sales, and quotas. Violation of these limits is defined as an **exception,** and an **exception report** is generated. The exception is then traced and resolved.

SECURITY-RELATED DATA ELEMENTS

To prevent unauthorized access to data, users often need to be assigned codes. One code may be used to identify a user's access to a certain file and another may specify what the user can do with the file (read, modify, delete, and so forth). These codes are values of special data elements related to the **security** of the system.

IDENTIFICATION DATA ELEMENTS

Transactional data needs to be **identified** as to where and when the transaction occurred and where the data is stored. For example, payroll needs to be identified by week, month, or year; sales by month or even day. Another type of identification could be that of data from different divisions, or even committees, in an organization.

CHECKING DATA ELEMENTS

Many transactions need to be checked for completeness and accuracy. This is sometimes done by matching a total that is provided as data with a total generated by the computer for the same set (or batch) of transactions. For example, a cashier may make transactions on a cash register and send these to be processed by computer along with a total generated by the cash register. The computer adds each transaction in the set and compares the total with that of the cash register. If it is the same, further processing takes place. If not, the inconsistency is identified, to be later traced and resolved. In this case, the total is the value of a **checking data element.** A checking data element does not appear in the output for the user but is nonetheless necessary.

Sometimes entries of numbers which are long or crucial for other computations need to be checked. The accuracy of social security numbers or employee numbers is a good example of such a problem. These numbers, used when making salary payments to employees, must be recorded accurately as input. To prevent input errors, a specific additional character or **check digit** is calculated by a special formula and is attached to each employee number. This check digit is recalculated by the computer each time the number is encountered in processing and compared with the original check digit added to the identification number. Any discrepancy is noted as an error in the input and processing is terminated until the error is corrected. In order for the check digit to be used by more than one user, the formula for generation needs to be defined and accepted by all users.

OTHER DATA ELEMENTS

There are other specialized data elements related to processing which are primarily of interest to EDP personnel. These will be mentioned briefly in a section on descriptors which follows later in the chapter.

Data elements by source

RAW DATA

Earlier, data was defined as an observation or a fact, that is, JONES being a value for the data element "name of employee." Sometimes coded values are assigned to data, such as codes to denote the professional classification of an employee or the department where the employee works. Both facts and **assigned data** are **primitive data,** data not derived from other data elements nor the result of processing. Primitive data is also called **raw data.**

DERIVED DATA ELEMENTS

Derived data is determined by manipulation or processing of data elements. For example, the data element "average number of hours worked per week per employee" is calculated by dividing the data element "total number of hours worked" by the data element "number of employees."

Another example would be values for the data element "age of employee." The value of this data could be derived from the employee's date of birth and the current date. This is sometimes called a **virtual data element.**

Though the actual computation is done by computer program, management is responsible for specifying derivation rules. In the above examples, the rules are obvious, but in many instances alternative ways of deriving data exist. For example, firms differ in procedures for calculating markups and discounts. When derived data is included in the data base, the formula or algorithm used must be defined and documented.

ESTIMATED DATA ELEMENT

Estimated data elements are neither primitive nor derived. The future cost of production, for example, cannot be observed, nor is it a fact. This data element must be calculated by a formula such as:

$$Y = bX$$

where $Y =$ future cost of production
$X =$ units of production
$b =$ future cost coefficient (variable cost per unit produced).

The coefficient b is the relationship between Y and X (Y/X) and must be estimated by statistical techniques based on historical data of Y and X, by hunch, or by the manager's perception of the relationship of Y and X. This data element b is an estimated data element. When multiplied by X, the answer is the estimated data element "future cost of production."

In this discussion of data elements, the original definition of data has been extended. Data can now be defined as raw data (an observation, fact, or assignment), derived data, or estimated data.

SELECTING DATA ELEMENTS FOR COLLECTION

The identification of specific data elements needed in an information system is deduced by studying the informational needs of management and output. For example, if a personnel report is expected to list the number of female professional employees with masters' degrees as output, the input for such a report must include data on the academic qualifications and sex of each employee. Similarly, if a report on accounts receivable is to show the distribution of aging of accounts (that is, the distribution of the time the accounts are outstanding), the input for the report must include the invoice dates so that aging can be calculated. If a report were to compare dollar value of sales for each sales representative with quotas, then both sales and quotas would have to be entered as input.

In a data base, data elements will often be used for generating more than one report. (A single report may be generated from one file. More often a report is generated from more than one file and a file contains data elements for many different reports.) Data elements needed for new reports may already exist in the common data base. To identify these existing data elements, an **input/output table (I/O table)** can be used, a technique developed by the economist W. Leontief. An example of an I/O table is shown in Table 6.2. The table has a horizontal axis listing output reports and files. The vertical axis lists data elements necessary for these reports. When new reports are added to the system, new columns are added to the table. Data elements already existing in the system required for these reports are checked off. These can be shared, resulting in economies in storage and processing. If the new report requires data never before collected, a new row to the I/O table may be necessary. Sometimes, however, needed data can be derived from existing data in the system. For example, if the company represented in Table 6.2 were to require the age of each employee for a new report, this information could be calculated from the date of birth already in the data base. However, if this new report were to be generated by a new file, File 3, this file would have to be linked to File 1 in order to derive age. That is, a common data element would have to appear in both files so that the computer could access information in the two files when processing. Derived data elements are not listed in an I/O table since they do not require the collection of additional data.

Other data elements excluded from an I/O table include the report heading names or column headings that appear on output. Also excluded are data

TABLE 6.2
Partial I/O table

Files / Data elements	File 1		File 2
	Report 1	Report 2	Report 3
1. Employee ID (identification no.)	x	x	x
2. Name	x	x	
3. Address	x	x	
4. Date of birth	x	x	
5. Sex		x	
6. Academic qualifications			x
7. Field of specialization			x
8. Years of experience			x
9. Year of first employment		x	

FIGURE 6.1
Analysis of information needs

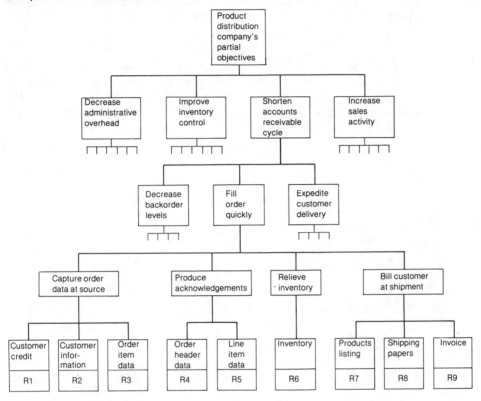

elements written into the applications programs such as norms for checking value weights and control-related data. Page numbers and subtotals of totals (derived data) would also be created by programs. In addition, the computer generates data such as time and date which appear on printouts at the time of processing. None of these data elements are included in an I/O table. Though the I/O table does not name all the data elements in the system, every data element that is listed in the table must exist in the data base.

To identify elements needed in a company's data base, corporate goals and the informational needs of management at all levels will have to be studied to arrive at the reports a computerized information system should produce. Thereafter an I/O table can be used to identify which data elements must be added to the data base.

An illustration of this process is shown in Figure 6.1. Here the information needs of a product distribution company are analyzed.[1] A chart has been

---

[1] For details see Thomas R. Finneran and J. Shirley Henry, "Structured Analysis for Data Base Design," *Datamation*®, vol. 23, no. 11 (November 1977), pp. 99–113.

prepared listing company goals; decreased administrative overhead, improved inventory control, shortened accounts receivable cycle, and increased sales activity. For simplicity's sake only one of the goals is subdivided in Figure 6.1, that of shortening the cycle of accounts receivable, and only one of these subgoals, filling orders quickly, is further traced to the report level. From the reports identified in the chart, an I/O table, Table 6.3, has been prepared. This I/O table would be merged to an I/O table previously compiled for data elements in the firm's data base (if one exits). By studying the table, analysts can learn which data elements need collection for the new reports and which already exist in the data base.

TABLE 6.3
I/O table for a distribution company

Data elements \ Reports	R1	R2	R3	R4	R5	R6	R7	R8	R9
Each customer record									
ID	x	x	x	x				x	x
Name	x			x				x	x
Credit rating	x								
Credit unit	x								
Sold-to address		x		x				x	x
Ship-to address		x		x				x	x
Shipping instructions		x		x				x	x
Product number		x		x				x	x
Sales tax rate		x		x					x
Territory code		x							
Each item record									
ID			x		x	x	x	x	x
Description			x		x	x	x	x	x
Order quantity			x		x	x	x	x	x
Price/unit			x		x				x
Ship from warehouse			x						
Warehouse location						x	x		
Discount					x				
Each shipment record									
ID							x	x	x
Ship date							x		
Bill location							x		
Ship warehouse location							x		
Ship quantity								x	x
Weight								x	
Freight class								x	
Net amount									x
Sales tax									x

Data elements for future requirements should also be included in a data base. Adding data elements after a common data base has been organized can be a costly and disruptive process, analogous to adding plumbing and electrical connections to a house after the walls have been painted. So data elements for future use should be incorporated in the base when the system is designed. However, predicting such elements is a far more difficult task than studying an I/O chart and deducing what data elements need collection for current reports. It is management's responsibility to make such predictions, to chart the company's future. Data element needs must be anticipated for the estimated life of the information system.

Managers and analysts designing the data base must be cognizant that future changes in management may occur or that shifts in the style of current decision makers may take place. The data base must be flexible in content and format to allow for such changes. For example, today's manager may want an analysis of sales in dollars per sales representative. In the future, the same manager or a later replacement may demand dollar sales per product. Such shifts in need for information must be possible within the framework of the data base.

DATA ELEMENT DICTIONARY

Data for operations, control, and planning may be shared by several levels of management (Figure 6.2), or sharing may occur along organizational lines (Figure 6.3). In both cases the use of the data varies from level to level.

For example, the value of the data element "dollar sales" by sales representative Smith is used at the control level to determine the performance of Smith, and over a period of time this data may determine whether a bonus is given or Smith is released. Smith's data reclassified in terms of products sold, com-

FIGURE 6.2
Flow of data between levels of management

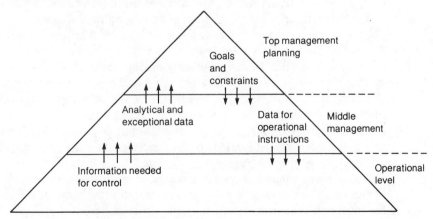

FIGURE 6.3
Flow of data along organizational lines

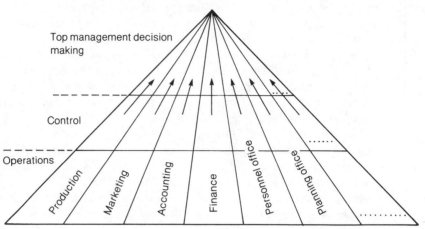

bined with sales data from the other sales representatives, is used at the planning level for future sales projections. The data could also be used to generate derived data such as average sales by sales representatives per month per product—data used in control and planning. This sales data may also be used at the regional, national, or international headquarters of the company. Thus, the value of Smith's dollar sales is data that is used at all levels of decision making. However, this shared use of data is possible only if all users interpret the data elements in the same manner, agreeing on data element definitions.

The need for common definitions arises whenever people wish to communicate with each other and have a large or complex vocabulary. Dictionaries are a reference for word definitions in natural languages, such as English and French. Data elements are also defined in dictionaries so that all data users know their exact meaning. A **data element dictionary (DED)** has to be designed for every information system using data elements.

Most spoken languages have words with more than one meaning and words that are synonyms. In designing a DED one must try to avoid such linguistic ambiguities. But since users generally prefer to retain their natural language words as names of data elements, and agreement on the meaning of technical terms is lacking in the field of data processing, data elements must be defined with enough detail in the DED so that no misinterpretation is possible. For example, a data element cannot be called "date," for there are many types of dates used to generate reports: date of birth, date of sale, date of employment, etc.

Sometimes a single data element may have several commonly used names. For example, the purchasing department may use the term "item" for what the inventory department calls a "part." In such cases of multiple names, the dictionary must provide cross-references, referring users to the exact name of the data element used by the information system.

A sample page from a DED is shown in Figure 6.4. A DED is simply a collection of pages of such data element definitions. But unlike single-volume French or English dictionaries, data element dictionaries are often in many volumes corresponding to functions such as personnel or production, and each level of decision making in an organization will have a dictionary set that differs in content from sets at other levels, for only data elements needed

FIGURE 6.4
Sample page of a DED

ABC COMPANY
DATA ELEMENT DICTIONARY

Name of Data Element	Marital status				
Variable Name	MARISTATUS				
Definition	Indicates whether or not a person is legally and currently married				
Classification & Coding	1. Unmarried 2. Married 3. Other				
Uses	For calculation of tax, deductions, and personnel profile				
Derivation Rules (if any)	Source is Personnel Form 201A to be completed by person concerned.				
Units (if any)	None				
Format	Numeric		Justification	N.A.	
Width of Field	One digit				
Validity Rules	Required [X] Definite Error	Range 1-3	Content	Other	
	Optional [ ] Possible Error				
PERSON PROCESSING FORM	Diana Sandalian				
Date Issued	02/10/81				
Status	Already implemented				
Comments	The "other category" is expected to be less than 5%. If more, or another category is needed such as divorced, further coding subclassification is advisable.				

for decision making at that level will be included. The set of functional DEDs needed at the division level will therefore differ in content from the DEDs required by the corporation headquarters, though there will be many data elements common to both sets. Definitions, however, must be consistent at all levels in all the functional DEDs. This consistency gives data **upward compatibility** and lets data collected at the operational level of the organization be uniformly interpreted when used at higher levels of the organization.

Small systems may use preprinted-form DED pages, filling in the blanks by typing in information on each data element. In larger systems the DED will be in machine-readable form, stored in the computer, and accessed by programs for screen display, or printout pages (corresponding to the sample). Computer programs can also use the information in the DED to generate reports and tables for analysis when the DED is in machine-readable form.

Descriptors of a DED

Data elements are described in a DED by characteristics and attributes called **descriptors.** Not all DEDs use the same descriptors and the order and design of a DED page may vary. Every information system has unique requirements and limitations. The DEDs are prepared with these specialized needs in mind. Constraints of space, the relative importance of descriptors, and logical groupings of descriptors (that is, technical descriptors) will also influence DED design.

The main descriptors of interest to managers are: name, definition, derivation algorithm, units, format, width of field, validity rules, version of issuance, identification, and status. These will be discussed in detail below.

NAME

The **name** of a data element must be unique, unambiguous, and easy to use and remember. Names must also be logical and meaningful terms.

Long names chosen to eliminate ambiguities may prove too cumbersome for convenience and efficiency in processing. As the name length increases, more storage and processing time is required. Therefore, long data element names are often abbreviated. An abbreviation will also fit easily on a printed computer report when space is limited. If abbreviations are used, they must be defined in the DED.[2]

DEFINITION

The **definition** explains the meaning of the data element. Examples of a practical application of the element may be included in the definition for

---

[2] For standard abbreviations of states and names of countries, see ANSI (American National Standards Institute) publications. ANSI is the source of most computer-related standards in the United States, including standards on codes, magnetic disks, magnetic tapes, data communication, and computer programming. For details, write: ANSI Inc., 1430 Broadway, New York, N.Y. 10018.

added clarity. Other data elements with similar or contrary meanings may be mentioned and the root of the term explained.

The origin of the data element should also be included in the definition. If a data element is raw data, the division originating the raw data should be mentioned. This will help users assess possible bias. If the data element is estimated, the manner of estimation is relevant.

The data element should be defined at the lowest level of aggregation in case this detail is needed at some future date. For example, sales information collected at the county level can be aggregated for state, regional, or national sales statistics. But if sales data is initially collected only at the state level, the data cannot provide management with information on county sales. When deciding what level of aggregation should be collected, one must weigh possible benefits from lower levels of aggregation against the cost of including possible nonessential data elements in the DED and the added cost of processing these data elements.

DERIVATION RULE

If data is derived, the **derivation rule** must be specified. In calculating ratios and coefficients, for example, the numerators and denominators in equations must be defined in unambiguous terms. This not only eliminates confusion and misunderstandings, but is essential for the programmer who will have to write the program instructions to derive the data.

In deriving data values it is also necessary to specify the level of accuracy required. For example, should a percentage value be calculated at one, two, or three decimal places? How should values be rounded to the first significant digit? Rounding is especially important when calculating financial values, for the rounding rule can make a significant dollar difference when values are repeatedly used in other calculations.

Problems of derivation also occur with alphabetic data. For example, in using the data element "name of employee," many computer programs limit the surname to ten characters even though many names are longer. How should a business abbreviate an 11-character name like Thorneberry? Let the employee choose an abbreviation or develop guidelines applicable to all names? What abbreviation guidelines should be selected? Initials? Truncations? The abbreviation rules used for data element values must be explicitly defined.

UNITS

The **units** of measure for the data element must be specified. For example, the data element "weight" with a value of ten needs a unit descriptor. Is it ten pounds or grams? The data element "length" must have a descriptor specifying FPS or metric units. Sometimes the units are included in the name of data element, such as "dollar sales." If not, a separate unit descriptor is needed.

FORMAT

The **format** of how the data elements are stated is also a descriptor to be included in the DED. This need arises in group data elements. A **group data element** is a composite data element of several individual data elements. For example, the data element "date of birth" (120565) is a composite of the data elements month, day, and year. The usual format is:

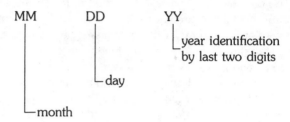

If this format, MMDDYY, is the desired format, it should be so stated. Otherwise a possible misunderstanding might arise. DDMMYY is the format used in England; other European countries use YYMMDD.

The format of a name is also important. A DED that defines an employee's name as a combination of surname, first name, and middle initial does not have an adequate definition since the format must convey the order of the name components as well as the separators between the component parts. Blanks used as separators can be confusing because they sometimes occur within a surname, as in Mac Donald or Van der Kamp. The format for additions to the surname such as Jr. or Sr. must also be expressed. Should shortened names (Liz for Elizabeth) or nicknames be allowed? This is not hairsplitting. A detailed specification is necessary. Names will not match in computer processing if the same format is not used consistently; that is, the same order of components, the same separators, and the exact same spelling.

Another formatting problem that must be clarified in the DED is the placement of data in a field wider than the data itself. Should the data start from the left or the right of the field? In the case of alphabetic data, it is customary to start from the left, called **left justified.** This facilitates reading a list of alphabetic data and is needed when sorting alphabetic data by computer. In contrast, numeric data starts from the right, called **right justified,** so as to avoid interpreting blank spaces in the field as zeros. For example, 345 appearing in a five character field that is left justified could be read by the computer as 34500. Left or right justification of the values of each data element must be stated.

WIDTH OF FIELD

The DED definition should also specify the **width of field** for each data element. Most width determinations are technical, made by analysts. Adding a check digit to a social security number is the type of technical decision an analyst would make. But many widths must be determined by management.

Determining potential maximum values for the data elements, for example. How many characters should be allowed for the data element "dollar value of sales per customer?" An amount of 2000 dollars would require a four-character field width. If the amount increased to 10000 dollars or more, the allowed field would be inadequate. On some computer printouts, the value of 12003 dollars would appear as 2003 if the field specification were four characters, ignoring the most significant digit. It is the manager's responsibility to predict maximum values so an adequate width of field will be allowed.

VALIDITY RULES

Many data elements have values that need to be checked for validity. These data elements should be identified and the **validity check rules** should be stated in the DED. The analyst can specify many of these rules. For example, a name field may not have numeric characters but may contain symbols such as hyphens, whereas the data element "weight" must have a numeric value. Some check rules, however, should be determined by managers instead of analysts. These include checks as to probable ranges of data element values. For example, a firm's check rule for age of employee could identify values under 15 and over 75 as definite errors and ages between 15–18 and 70–75 as possible errors. A manager can best state such ranges and can best identify which data elements need to be checked for allowable ranges. Managers also know what data is essential and cannot be missing from the input data.

IDENTIFICATION

Each data element is assigned a coded label to enable a unique and fast **identification.** A blocked decimal code structure has been successfully used for this purpose. An example of such a label is:

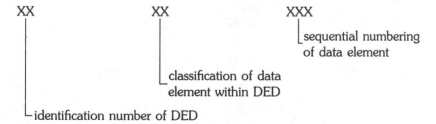

The first character or two characters identifies in which dictionary within the set of DEDs the data element appears. The next subfield identifies how the data element is classified within the DED. For example, one subclassification in the payroll file might be the rate; rate of pay, the tax deduction rate, the medical service deduction rate, and so forth. The third subfield can be a sequential identification of the data element itself. An example of this coding structure is shown in Table 6.4. In this chart the data element "health deduction

TABLE 6.4
Example of coding for data element identification

DED identification	Classification of data elements	Sequencing of data elements
03 Staff	01 Name	01 Surname
	•	02 First name
	•	03 Middle name
	•	04 Jr. and Sr. identification
	06 Payroll Rates	01 Rate of pay
		02 Health deduction rate
		03 Tax deduction rate

rate" (02) is classified under payroll rates (06) located in the staff DED (03). Its code identification number is 03.06.02.

The main purpose of subfields is to facilitate reference, processing, and analysis. For example, in searching for payroll rates in the staff file one need only search the codes 03.06 without being concerned with the remaining subfield codes.

In order to find a specific data element definition in a DED without knowing its identification code, an alphabetical index by data element name can be used. This index is generated by computer program once the DED sets are completed.

TABLE 6.5
Selected list of descriptors of interest to analysts and programmers

User relationship
Creation/specification responsibility
Transaction relationship
Program names
Synonym
Codes
Mode
Security code
Billing code
Access limitation
Logical/physical relationship
Medium of storage

STATUS

The **status** of data elements must also appear in the DED. A data element may be operational or under consideration for adoption. If the latter, it should be stated whether the data element has been approved but not yet implemented, or merely proposed. Some data elements have the status "superseded" but are still recorded for reference purposes.

OTHER DESCRIPTORS

The descriptors mentioned above are basic descriptors. But the list is by no means complete. Some additional descriptors of interest to the analyst and programmer are listed in Table. 6.5. A manager may not use these technical descriptors but they appear in the DED since the dictionary is designed for all users of the information system.

ORGANIZATION OF DATA

Once data is identified and defined in DEDs, it must be organized so that later processing and retrieval will be fast and efficient. There are two types of organization: logical and physical.

Logical organization is the grouping of data elements according to the user's view of data interrelationships for purposes of input and output. For example, the grouping of all data elements relating to payroll. This logical organization, the order in which data is collected and reported, may appear as input on cards. The cards in this case are physical representations of a logical set of data. Logical organization is a major concern of management, determining the facility with which data elements serve the informational needs of the user.

Physical organization, on the other hand, concerns technical personnel: programmers and data specialists. It is the physical storage on the data base's storage media of data elements in the data base. Since technicians, not management, are responsible for planning the storage location of every bit of data and for providing access to that data for retrieval and processing, only a brief discussion of the physical organization of data on data storage devices will be included in this chapter.

Logical organization

There are many steps to the logical organization of data. First, data elements required to produce a specified output must be determined. Then a **record** is formed by joining the related data elements with one another. An employee record would consist of related data elements such as name of employee, address, date of birth, department, and salary code. An invoice record might include customer identification, customer address, item(s) bought, purchase date(s), and price(s). All related records are then grouped into **file.** An employee personnel file, for example, would be a collection of all employee records. A business may have an advertising file, a payroll file, a marketing file, a production file, and so forth. These data files when integrated or linked to share data form a **common data base.**

A graphic representation of data organization from data element to the data base is shown in Figure 6.5. Theoretically, there is no limit to the number of data elements in a record, the number of records in a file, or files in a data base. In practice, however, the values of *k, m,* and *n* in Figure 6.5 are constrained by factors such as storage space on a tape or disk. Efficiency poses additional restraints. A file used primarily for accounts payable is more efficient when limited to data elements relevant to that application. Interdepartmental rivalry in many businesses also tends to limit file size. A unit which has created a file for a specific purpose may resist the enlargement of that

FIGURE 6.5
Data organization from data element to data base

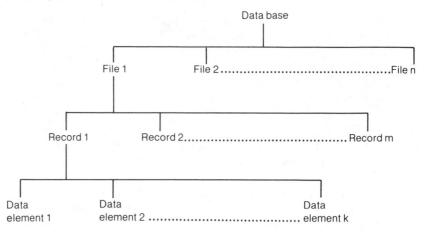

file by other departments, fearing that the expansion will result in loss of control over that file.

A common data base consists of **linked files.** Table 6.6 helps illustrate the concept of linkage. Key data elements in each file are in bold print, for these data elements appear in two or more files. They enable the computer to integrate information in disparate files. For example, the data element "item number" appears in the inventory and order files. Given an item number, a computer program can locate the invoice number and order the quantity from the Order Line Item File and can also list the item description as well as price and discount rate, information stored in the Inventory File. The use of a common data element in two or more files is therefore the link which permits file integration.

Figure 6.6 is another schema showing linkage. It also identifies the key data elements which integrate the files in Table 6.6. Note that there is no direct linkage between the Inventory and Customer Files, whereas the Order Line Item File is directly linked with two other files.

Data elements organized into records, files, and data base constitute levels of data, part of the **hierarchy of data.**

The hierarchy of data can be further disaggregated into a set of characters. The characters may be alphabetic (a–z), numeric (0–9), a combination of letters and numbers as commonly seen on license plates, called alphanumeric or alphameric, or special character symbols such as / * - , ' % #. Since a

TABLE 6.6
Data elements in each record in each file

Customer file Data elements for each customer	*Invoice header file* Data elements for each invoice
ID (customer) Name Address Credit rating Credit limit Territory code Sales tax code	**ID (customer)** **Invoice no.** Ship-to address Shipping instructions Purchase order number **Warehouse code**

Order line item file Data elements for each item	*Inventory file* Data elements for each item
Invoice no. **Item number** Order quantity	**Warehouse code** **Item number** Item description Item price Discount rate

computer cannot store characters per se, a still lower level of data organization is required. A character is represented by a set of **bytes,** each byte consisting of **bits,** generally eight bits to a byte. In most machines, bytes are aggregated further into **words** for efficient access on storage devices. The hierarchy of data is shown in Figure 6.7.

A bit (binary digit) can be recognized by the computer. The conversion of a character to a bit is done by input equipment so a manager is seldom concerned with data organization below the character level. The input which is collected and arranged in logical order by the manager, and the output which crosses the manager's desk, will be in characters, not bits or bytes.

FIGURE 6.6
Linking of files

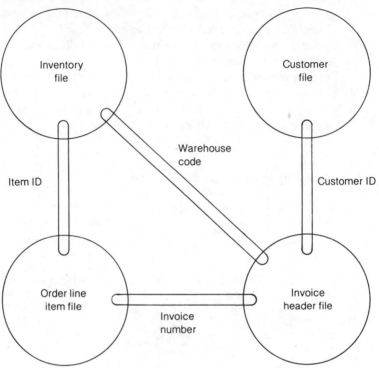

Physical representation of input

Some logical records are long, requiring many physical units of data, units such as cards. These units are called **physical records.** Physical records are grouped into **physical files** just as logical records are grouped into logical files.

To clarify the relationship between logical and physical files, imagine that a student taking Mktg. 310, Acctg. 329, and CS 330 keeps notes for these classes in separate notebooks. Mktg. 310 in one notebook would constitute one logical file in one physical file (one to one relationship). If the student kept notes for all three courses in a single notebook, the person would have three logical files in one physical file, a many-to-one relationship. If a second notebook were purchased when the first filled, the student would have three logical records in two physical records, a many-to-many relationship. In the latter case, the student would have to look through both notebooks when reviewing for an exam in marketing to find course material. The search would take less time if the notebook pages had been numbered and a list kept of page numbers containing marketing notes. For computerized data, the com-

FIGURE 6.7
Hierarchy of data for logical records and physical records on storage files

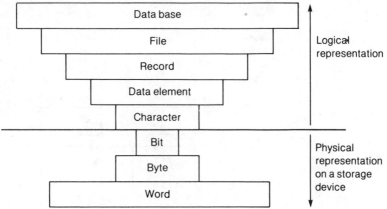

puter needs a similar aid to locate data belonging to a logical file on one or more physical files. Data is located by an **address** which "points" to the data's location on the physical file, thereby maintaining the continuity of the logical file just as the student notation of page numbers indicates directions to all marketing notes in different notebooks.

The space allocated a data element on a physical record is called a **field.** The group data element "date of birth" with the value 010375 has a field of six digits consisting of three **subfields** (day, month, and year); each subfield composed of two digits. Figure 6.8 illustrates the relationship between a data element field and subfields.

In much of data processing, physical records are **cards** and the physical space is measured in **columns** per card. In planning, the physical number of columns, called **width of field,** and the allocation (spacing or relationship) of the assigned columns are specified on a **data layout sheet.** Field width must be planned with care. An unnecessarily wide field will result in a waste of computer storage space and processing time. An insufficient width of field will necessitate restructuring the data base before data can be processed. For example, if only four columns are allocated to number of employees and the firm subsequently grows over ten thousand, data on the cards will have to be shifted to allow an additional column for the information. Then all the computer programs which use the data elements involved will have to be modified, for processing cannot take place unless the applications programs know the correct location of data on each physical record.

The card layout form in Figure 6.9 shows how the personnel file of John Doe, a logical record, is assigned space on a physical record. Each row represents a computer card. In this case, Doe's personnel file requires two cards, that is, two physical records for one logical record.

FIGURE 6.8
Field and subfields for data element "date of birth"

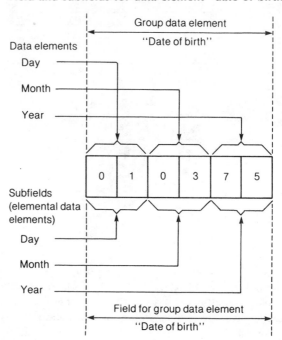

The use of cards becomes cumbersome when a logical record requires many physical records (ten cards per record are not uncommon); when a large number of logical records need processing (payroll for a firm of 120,000 employees, for example); and when processing is frequent (once a week or even once a month). In such cases, logical records on **tape** are preferable.

Figure 6.10 shows the transference to tape of a logical record stored on cards. Note that the employee number appears only once on tapes, whereas it must be restated on each card of the logical record. The data ID, identifying sequencing of cards, is also eliminated because its purpose is to identify related cards of each logical record. Instead a **header label** is used at the beginning of each tape to identify the logical records on the tape. The logical records themselves are separated by an **inter record gap (IRG)** which identifies the end of one logical record and signals the start of another. In planning the location of data on tape, a data layout is used to identify each data element and its sequencing. Data is located in processing by searching the entire tape.

The use of magnetic tape is appropriate for **sequential processing** when all logical records in a logical file need processing; for example, the reconciliation of bank accounts or payroll processing. But tape is inappropriate for handling individual logical records. An analogy can be made to taped music. For listening to a series of songs, tapes are excellent. But tapes do

FIGURE 6.9
Card form layout

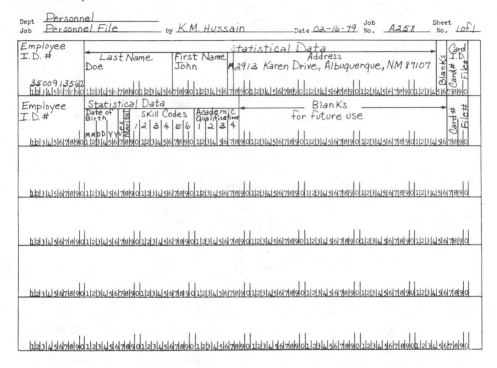

FIGURE 6.10
Illustration of the transformation of two physical cards for one employee record into one logical tape record

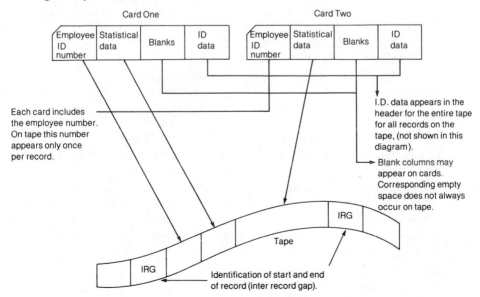

FIGURE 6.11
A logical record stored on
random storage disk

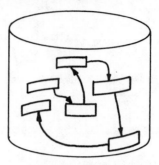

Data elements belonging to
one logical record are shown on
a disk system. Data elements are
stored where space is available
and the next data element in the
chain is identified by its address
(referred to as a **pointer** and indicated in Figure 6.11 as an arrow).

not let the listener hear a single song over and over, nor can the song order
be changed. When data of a single logical record is frequently needed then
a computer **disk** (a **random storage device**) is used instead of tape.

A representation of a logical record on magnetic disk is shown in Figure
6.11. The data is stored on tracks on the disk wherever there is space, so
the logical record may appear in several discontinuous parts. The order for
storing the logical record is not prescribed. Space availability and the time
of data collection will determine the location of the data on the disk. However,
the entire logical record can be retrieved, for each segment ends with a pointer
indicating the address where the data is continued on the disk.

Random processing or **direct access** is essential when data must
be retrieved quickly. However, this shortened response time costs more. Sequential processing is the most time-consuming but costs least. In between
are other forms of data processing which vary in response time and cost
performance.

Figure 6.12 shows the relationship of time and cost for three types of
processing. Economical batch processing with magnetic tape can be used
when response time is not critical. As response time is reduced and random processing is used, the cost increases rapidly. Eventually, batch
processing with an indexed sequential file becomes less expensive (where
data is stored sequentially on a disk, but indexed with the indexes being
accessed randomly) since it allows skipping over inactive portions of the
file and thus reduces input/output time.

FIGURE 6.12
Cost as a function of response time and mode of processing

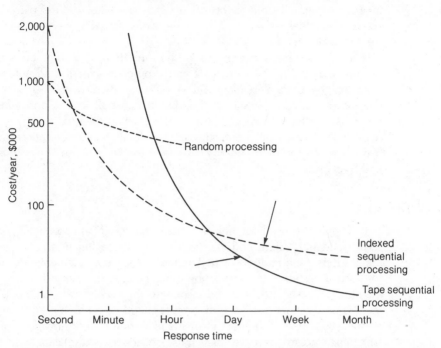

Source: Adapted from J. Emery, "Cost/Benefit Analysis of Information Systems," in J. Daniel Couger and Robert W. Knapp, *Systems Analysis Techniques* (New York: John Wiley & Sons, Inc., 1974), p. 415.

COMMON DATA BASE

Stored data when integrated makes up a **data base**. A **common data base** is merely a data base that has pooled data integrated for common use as a shared resource. A business may have one or more common data bases but need not place all its data in a common pool. Excluded may be specialized data, data used by only one group or department.

Determining what data to include in a common data base is often an arduous process. Users do not always agree on what is and what should be common data. They fear that security and privacy of data is endangered in a common pool. Managers who have built up an empire of data resist losing control over that data. They may not want others to know such data exists or share in its use. There may be genuine problems in reaching agreement on data element definitions and difficulties in coordinating the timing of data creation. Standardization means each user may have to change practices in collecting and handling data.

In deciding what constitutes a common data base, all potential users of that base should participate. When consensus is not possible, conflicts must be resolved or arbitrated by management at a higher level. Unfortunately, interorganizational politics too often determine what data is placed in the common data base when, instead, the decisions should be based on technological and economic factors.

Though user resistance may slow the formation of a common data base, its evolution should be systematic and progressive, for the advantages of a common pool of data are many. Data required by many users need be collected only once. A single operation will update data for all users. Consistent procedures are established for gathering and recording data for a common pool, making the data itself more reliable. And finally, communication improves because a common terminology defined in the DED is used by both analysts and managers.

SUMMARY

Data may be used for transactions, reference, planning, linking, control, security, identification, and checking. All of these functions have business applications. One method of determining which data elements are required for each application is to trace the input needed for every data element in the output. To see if the data base contains the needed data, an input/output table is used where each output is represented by a column and every data element by a row. If the data elements identified do not already exist in the I/O table and in the base, they must be added to the data base for the new application. Other data elements needed for processing, such as those required for linking, identification of data, security, and control, are determined by analysts.

Data elements must be defined in a DED, a data element dictionary. The descriptors for each data element will vary, but typically they include: label of identification, name of data element as it appears to the user and as it appears in the computer program, description, derivation rule, units of measure, format, width of field, and rules for validation.

Once the data elements for an application are identified, they must be conceptually organized into a logical entity. Related data elements constitute a record, related records constitute a file, and related files are a data base. The data is then collected. If the data is collected on cards, each card is a physical representation of one or more parts of the logical record. A set of cards can represent a set of records in a file. In cases of large amounts of data, the file can be on tape, which is appropriate for sequential processing, or on a disk, which is best for random processing. Whatever the form of storage, files must be linked by a common data element if they are to be related and the data shared. This common sharing of data reduces redundancy, storage space, processing time, data preparation, time and effort, and improves security and standardization. This sharing of a common data base also enables the data of different divisions to be correlated for preparation of computerized reports. But it does cause organization problems because users do not always want to pool data and are often unwilling to submit to the standardization and discipline required for such sharing.

KEY WORDS

Address	Identification label
Assigned data	Input/output table (I/O table)
Bit	Inter record gap (IRG)
Byte	Left (right) justification
Cards	Linked files
Characters	Linking data elements
Check digit	Logical organization
Checking data element	Logical record
Columns	Name
Common data base	Physical file
Control-related data elements	Physical organization
Data	Physical record
Data base	Planning data elements
Data element	Pointer
Data element dictionary (DED)	Primitive data
Data layout sheet	Random processing
Definition	Random storage device
Derivation rule	Raw data
Derived data	Record
Descriptor	Reference data elements
Direct access	Security-related data elements
Disk	Sequential processing
Estimated data elements	Status
Exception	Subfield
Exception report	Tape
Field	Transactional data
File	Unit
Format	Upward compatibility
Group data element	Validity check rules
Header label	Virtual data element
Hierarchy of data	Width of field
Identification data elements	Word

DISCUSSION QUESTIONS

1. Distinguish between data and information.
2. Classify types of data and give two examples of each.
3. Describe the hierarchy of a data base.
4. What is the difference between a data base and a common data base?

5. Conflicts arise when establishing common data bases. What are they? How can they be reduced or eliminated?

6. What are the benefits of a common data base?

7. What is the difference between the physical and logical structure of data? Is this relationship interchangeable (that is, physical to logical and logical to physical)?

8. What is meant by the phrase "bit and byte level" of a computer? What is a manager's relationship to this level?

9. Why is numeric data preferable to alphabetic? Why are numeric identifications preferable to names of individuals?

10. Why is a social security number a useful identification in computerized processing? What are the limitations of social security numbers?

11. The social security number is used as a personal identifier mainly for economic reasons. Do you agree with this statement?

12. The social security number has been printed on T-shirts to suggest depersonalization of the human being. Is that a justifiable image? Who is to blame for such an image? How can it be corrected?

13. Distinguish between:
    a. Alphabetic and alphameric field.
    b. Fixed and variable length of data field.
    c. Physical and logical files.
    d. Raw and derived data.
    e. Size and format of data.
    f. Identification and reference data elements.
    g. Direct and random access.
    h. Bit and byte.
    i. Header and IRG.
    j. Data element and data field.
    k. Left and right justification.

14. Compare planning data with data for control and operations in terms of:
    a. Reliability.
    b. Source.
    c. Contribution to decision making.

15. Is data privacy a right? How can privacy be protected? How can this protection be enforced?

16. Compare random processing with sequential processing. Give examples from business for each approach.

17. What is a subfield? Give an example other than dates where subfields occur? Why are subfields needed?

18. What are the special factors to be considered in designing a common data base (features not needed in a local data base)?

19. What are fixed and variable costs in designing a file? Why should the cost of maintaining the file be evaluated carefully? How do maintenance costs depend on the content of file? Give examples. How can maintenance costs be reduced?

20. How are decision rules used for determining what data elements to include and what to exclude in a data file?

EXERCISES

1. Design cards for a personnel file for the following data elements:
    Name
    Home address
    Date of birth (correct to the day)
    Sex
    Marital status
    University major
    Fixed montly salary
    Commission rate
    Assume two cards per person.

2. What type of processing would you recommend for the above file? Random, sequential or index sequential? Why? Explain.

3. If the personnel file above were used by managers to print lists of sales by each salesperson (with additional sales information provided), would you use random or sequential processing? Explain. What additional data is needed?

4. Trace one character used in a personnel data base (specify one if you do not have access to a personnel data base) through all the levels of hierarchy. Draw a diagram showing your hierarchy of data.

5. Check the most appropriate storage device and processing mode for the applications listed below.

Application	Storage media		Mode of processing	
	Tape	Disk	Random	Sequential
Airline reservations				
Hotel nationwide reservations				
An auto dealer Accounting				
Contract calculations with buyer				
Instructor keeping grades				
University keeping grades				
University admissions				
University registration				
University computing for class				
University alumni				
Retailer point of sales credit checking				
Bank account status monthly ledger				
Wholesaler inventory Perishables				

	Storage media		Mode of processing	
Application	Tape	Disk	Random	Sequential
Nonperishables and staple demand				
Large data base and computing for sale				

6. In the table below, check the data elements that should be included in a bank deposit file, production inventory file, and accounts payable file.

Data element	Bank deposit file	Production inventory file	Accounts payable file
Name of part			
Name of depositor			
Account number			
Address of vendor			
Address of deposit			
Part description			
Name of vendor			
Discount code			
Unit price			
Amount deposited			
Vendor account number			
Quantity ordered			
Quantity of goods			
Amount withdrawn ($)			
Safety check			
Price			
Invoice number			
Current stock on hand			
Balance ($)			
Invoice date			
Quantity sold			

SELECTED ANNOTATED BIBLIOGRAPHY

Bassler, Richard A. and Logan, Jimmie J., eds. *The Technology of Data Base Management Systems.* Arlington, Va.: College Readings, Inc., 1973.

This book of readings has many short, well-written articles on data bases. Especially recommended are sections on data base creation (pp. 37–38), need (pp. 39–40), file structuring (pp. 72–82), and maintenance (p. 103).

Canning, Richard G. "The Cautious Path to a Data Base." *EDP Analyzer,* vol. 11, no. 6 (June 1973), pp. 1–12.

This issue discusses data base problems. The advice offered is: develop long-range plans; have a series of short projects; have compatibility, maintainability, and convertability; get in-depth user involvement; and obtain management involvement where it counts.

House, William C., ed. *Interactive Decision-Oriented Data Base Systems.* New York: Mason/Charter, 1977, 470 p.

This book has many contributions on the general subject of data bases, including concepts and design.

Lyon, John K. *An Introduction to Data Base Design.* New York: John Wiley & Sons, Inc., 1971, 81 p.

This is an old book yet it does cover well the basic concepts of physical and logical organization of a data base. It also has five examples of data base design in business: banking; order entry sales and inventory; cost accounting; manufacturing; and report dissemination.

Walsh, Myles E. "Update on Data Dictionaries." *Journal of Systems Development,* vol. 29, no. 8 (August 1978), pp. 28–39.

The author discusses recent dictionaries on the market as to their facilities and capabilities, including those relating to security of data.

7

DATA PREPARATION: COLLECTION, CODING, AND VALIDATION

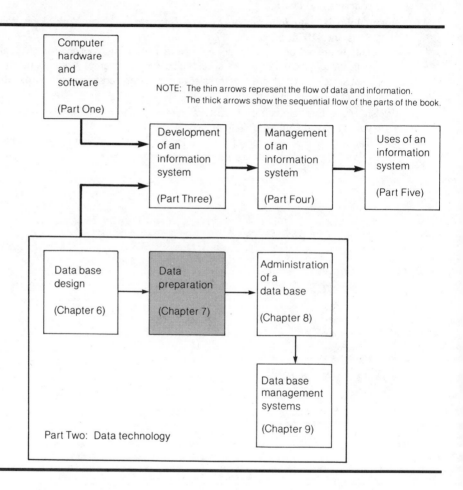

Once the data is designed, the data itself must be collected, coded, converted into machine-readable form, and validated before it can be used. These procedures, shown diagramatically in Figure 7.1, are called **data preparation**. Quality output of a management information system depends on quality input. It is up to management to provide guidelines for data preparation to ensure

FIGURE 7.1
Overview of data preparation

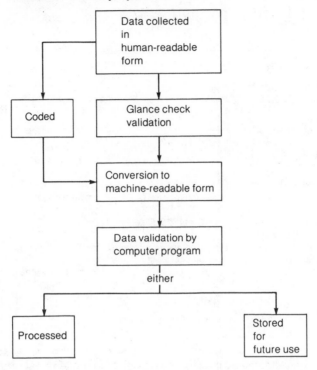

that data is complete, and coded for maximum processing efficiency and validity. Managers who participate in the development of information systems and utilize the reports generated need the knowledge of this aspect of data technology. Three aspects of data preparation, collection, coding, and validation, are dealt with in this chapter.

DATA COLLECTION

There are many methods of collecting data for a data base. These methods, shown in Figure 7.2, are classified into two general categories, **online** and **offline collection.** The characteristics and major advantages and disadvantages of input devices in this figure were described in Chapter 4. Identification of the person entering input data is particularly important for online systems when banking or POS terminal fund transfers are involved. Card identification is not foolproof, because stolen cards can be used to breach the system's security. More unique identification, such as pattern recognition equipment, is required, but such devices are expensive and not totally reliable at the present time.

FIGURE 7.2
Data collection

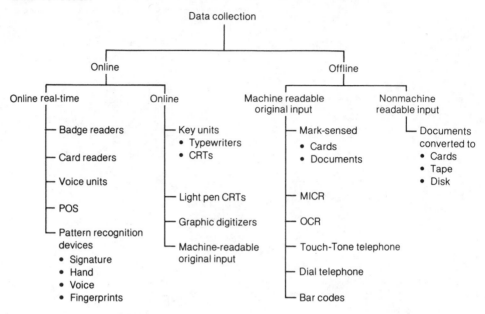

Original input in machine-readable form collected by online equipment can be validated by intelligence capability in the terminal or it can be validated for accuracy by programs at time of entering the data base. This is also the case with offline data in machine-readable form. Surprisingly, most data collected for a data base is still derived from documents. This data must be converted into machine-readable form such as cards, disks, or tape before being entered into the data base. The equipment required for this conversion was discussed in Chapter 4.

All data, whether collected on forms or directly by equipment, must have a prescribed format. Procedures and rules governing input are documented in an input manual. This manual is prepared after the output of an information system is decided and after the system's specifications have been determined. This text will present a detailed discussion of data collection in Chapter 12 of Part Three, which describes the cycle of development of an information system.

CODES

Codes are used for many purposes. During the Revolutionary War, two lanterns were hung in North Church in Boston to warn that British troops were arriving by sea. A more elaborate set of symbols is the Morse Code used for transmitting messages over wire or by flashing lights at sea. A kick under a bridge table can be a coded signal. A more subtle player was once expelled from a tournament for using finger signals, conveying high points by the way the cards were held.

Codes are also used in information systems. In this context, a code is a system of symbols for identifying attributes of data elements, simplifying natural language identification.[1] That is, a character or set of characters replace the natural language value of the data element. A firm might number its divisions, for example, and then substitute the number code for the division name in personnel records. This type of code aids systems analysis and design when established top-down through the corporation, with codes standardized in all divisions and subsystems.

Codes can also abbreviate natural language messages. The information, "Elida Glass, a female employee, born in December 1947, is working in the Welding Department of the Production Division" can be shortened by coding. Miss Glass can be identified by her social security number (585281928), her sex coded as 2, her birth month identified by number (12 for December), the year of birth coded by the last two digits (47), the Division of Production coded as 14, and the Department of Welding as 09. The coded record would be as follows:

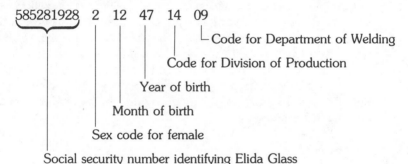

This coded form requires only 18 data columns (the input omits spacing) instead of the 118 columns of the English statement.

The use of a code also saves time when recording the data in machine-readable form such as keypunching, and when transmission of data is necessary. But the main use of codes is to facilitate classification of data and to speed processing. If codes are used to categorize data regarding product composition, for example, information on all wood products can be quickly retrieved by use of the wood code. Search and computing time for noncoded data is substantially more time-consuming. Though the time saved must be weighed against the time spent preparing codes and using them, the net savings in processing alone is often sufficient to economically justify coding.

---

[1] For another approach, see G. W. Patterson, "What Is a Code?" *Communications of the ACM,* vol. 3, no. 5 (May 1960), p. 315. Patterson states: "The most fundamental idea concerning a code is that of the existence of two languages, the source language (historically a natural language such as English) and the code language (usually made up of special signals created for the purpose at hand). . . . The code, properly speaking, is the system of rules that enables messages in the source language to be encoded into the code language."

Another advantage of a code is that it provides unique or near-unique identification. Much noncoded information is subject to semantic vagueness. It is possible for two employees to have the same name, and even the same middle initial. When duplication must be eliminated, a code such as an employee number or social security number would make each employee's record distinct. (Uniqueness of identification is not necessarily provided by a social security number, however, for some individuals have been issued two social security numbers by the government.)

Coding sometimes appears as output. This occurs when large amounts of data must be compressed onto one page. Generally, however, coded data is decoded by computer program for output reports. The computer simply scans a table to determine the meaning of each code in the output and prints the decoded information, a procedure called **table lookup.** The program will also determine format of the decoded information, providing spacing and the addition of symbols, such as dollar signs, to make the output readable.

It should be mentioned that the terms *code* and *coder* have more than one meaning in the computing field. In this chapter, the conversion of data from natural languages to code characters according to a set of rules is called **coding** or **encoding.** The person performing this operation is a **coder.** The special form used for this purpose is called a **coding sheet.**

In programming, another set of definitions is used. An abbreviated programming instruction is also called a code, and a programmer writing such an instruction will use coding sheets and be called a coder. Programmers, however, have a wider responsibility than coders as first defined. They design programs and specify program logic by preparing flowcharts, in addition to coding instructions.

Types of codes

ALPHABETIC AND NUMERIC CODES

The binary system used by computers to represent numerical concepts is one type of code. The number 9 coded as 1001 in binary appears a longer representation than the noncoded 9, but in fact speeds processing.

A **mnemonic symbol** is a code chosen to aid memory. M for male is an example of an alphabetic mnemonic symbol; 1 for single and 2 for married are numeric mnemonic codes. **Alphabetic codes** are often preferred by coders because their meaning seems so obvious, but in fact they are often misinterpreted when they appear as output. An M might mean married or manager to a user. Even MA, a two-letter code, would be ambiguous in this case.

Arbitrary **numeric codes** might instead be assigned. Though such a code is not easy to remember, processing is twice as fast for numeric codes when using data processing equipment that assigns two holes per character for letters on a punch card, and only one hole per numeric character. A common coding technique combines the advantage of mnemonic clues with numeric uniqueness and code speed, giving data elements **alphameric** (or **al-**

phanumeric) coded values. The product code CRB162 for a crib and a customized license plate, such as HAL62, are examples. Some commercial banks identify customer accounts by the first five characters of the surname followed by first and middle initials and a two digit number. The account of Arthur James Carswell might therefore be coded as CARSWAJ63.

Yet even alphanumeric codes can be misinterpreted unless designed with care. A firm which coded the Henry Building as H, and the O'Hare Building as OH printed the following room assignment for an important conference: 23OH. Some participants went to 23 O'Hare, the rest to 230 Henry. Caution must also prevail when using alphabetic characters so that undesirable permutations are not formed. Inept coding of the Sam Oliver Building (by using its first letters as a code) could cause a flood of complaints.

SEQUENTIAL CODES

Numbering accounts **sequentially** is a conceptually simple code. A unique identification is provided and the number shows the relative age of accounts, but that is all. No classification information is provided. Another weakness of numbering is apparent when employee numbers are assigned sequentially from an alphabetic personnel list. The names of new employees cannot be added to the alphabetic list without renumbering unless, when the sequential code was designed, numbers were skipped to allow for later insertions.

BLOCK CODES

The use of **block codes** is a more effective technique, permitting subclassification of data elements. The mail zip code is a good example. The first number identifies geographic area, the next two permit sorting within that area, and the final two digits identify the local post office from which a letter is to be delivered.

Blocks with assigned subfields for each subclassification of a data element are called **group classification codes.** Each subfield is coded independently. Numbers can therefore be repeated in one or more subclassifications, their position in the block determining code meaning. By adding subfields, more and more information can be conveyed. The number 93015181 might represent a straight-back wooden chair with side arms and green leather upholstery if the code were a composite of the following code groups:

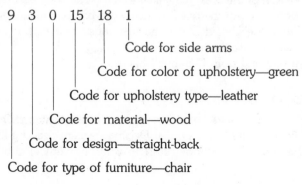

The size for each subclassification should be designed to allow for the addition of other codes at a later date. For example, if the furniture manufacturer expanded operations, producing 14 types of furniture, a block size with only one digit for type of furniture would not be wide enough.

Subclassifications facilitate processing for purposes of statistical analysis and other computations, but a blocked code often results in a long code. When the range of choices to be coded is small, a serial set of codes may expedite processing.

Another problem with group classification is that each subfield has to be wide enough to accommodate the maximum code value. If that maximum seldom occurs, the space is underutilized, making both storage and processing of the data element more expensive than necessary. To overcome this problem, some subclassifications are designed to have variable width, while keeping within the total width constraint of the code. For example, publishers use ISBN (International Standard Book Number) throughout the world. A sample book in this code is 0-256-01834-0.

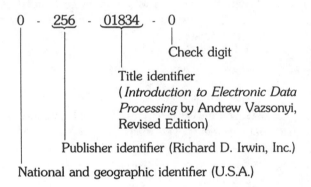

Only a few countries have a single digit for national identifier. Those chosen for the single digit are countries with many publishers and hundreds of titles printed per year, such as the United States and Britain. Countries with a smaller publishing industry are given wider identification blocks (Spain, 84; Indonesia, 929) and narrower publisher and title subfields. Certain numbers in the first block are codes which identify field widths. But in all cases the total width of the code remains the same. The code ensures that book orders will be filled with the titles, authors, and editions requested.

Within the United States the first code is deleted. American wholesalers and retailers use the truncated code, calling it SBN (Standard Book Number) when ordering from U.S. publishers.

DECIMAL CODES

Decimal codes are also used for subclassifications. One example of this coding structure is the Dewey Decimal System used by libraries. According to this system, a textbook on EDP would be numbered 651.84.

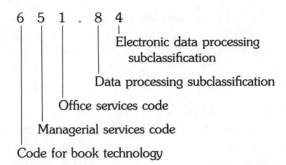

6 5 1 . 8 4

Electronic data processing
subclassification

Data processing subclassification

Office services code

Managerial services code

Code for book technology

The primary advantage of decimal codes is their expandability.

MAGNETIC INK CHARACTER CODE

This code was developed for a specific application: banking. A code written in **magnetic ink characters** is preprinted at the bottom of checks. In processing, the dollar amount of the written check is keyed manually on an **encoder** (similar to keypunch) which converts this figure into magnetic ink characters which are placed in the lower right-hand corner of the check, as in Figure 7.3. The check then passes through a **magnetic ink character recognition (MICR) reader** which validates the characters for completeness and readability. Invalid checks such as those that are torn or smudged are sorted into a pocket for later manual processing. The rest are sorted by

FIGURE 7.3
Sample of MIC (magnetic ink characters)

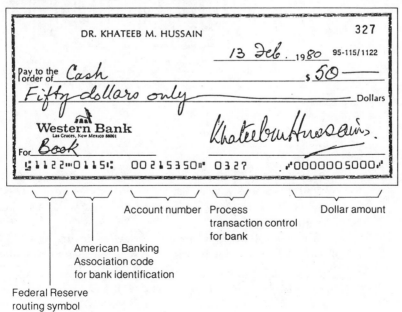

the MICR equipment according to block codes in the preprinted characters for routing, bank identification, account number, and process control, with the characters sending sorting signals to the MICR equipment as they pass the read-head. The data is then transferred to a storage device, such as a disk, which is later used for processing the bank's daily transactions.

UNIVERSAL PRODUCT CODE (UPC)

The **universal product code** is also a specialized code, in this case developed for retailing. This code, read by a scanner, is most commonly found on products in grocery stores. The manufacturers ID and the product or part ID, both numeric codes, are represented in each UPC symbol by a combination of black and white bars (the white being spacing). The width of these bars is significant, for each number is uniquely identified by bar

FIGURE 7.4
Universal product code

A UPC contains a number system character, ten data characters, and a check character. In addition, guard bars appear on each side and separate the two halves of the code.

width and color. The correspondence between each of the ten numeric digits and their bar codes is shown in Figure 7.4.

Once the scanner reads the code, identifying manufacturer and product, the computer searches a price list stored in its memory to determine price of the item. The directness of this operation reduces the speed of checkout by an estimated 30 percent.[2]

The bar code of the UPC may be extended to the U.S. Postal Service for all letter mail that can be machine processed. It is estimated that this

---

[2] *Computer World,* vol. 9, no. 8 (February 19, 1975), p. 1.

will reduce the error rate of misdirected mail from 2.2 percent to less than 1 percent and will speed processing at reduced cost.[3]

MISCELLANEOUS CODES

The coding systems described above can be combined into a variety of permutations. The code CARSWAJ63 mentioned earlier is a combination of name and sequential codes. Sequence codes can also be added to block and decimal codes.

Sometimes codes have embedded information. The personal ID code in Sweden includes year of birth. Some product codes include prices. The first four digits in product 35402620 might be the suggested sales price ($35.40), the last four the wholesale price ($26.20). This innocent-looking code can be used to calculate markup.

Color codes are also common. One prestigious university is now sending letters of acceptance on paper with a pink border and rejection letters bordered in black after a computer center mixup of address tapes which caused accepted students to receive rejection letters and vice versa. The color codes now alert computer operators, mail personnel, and the control clerk as to the nature of the letter so that extra care in computer processing will take place.

Selection of coding structure

The coding structure used for a data element must be chosen with great care. It affects error rates in coding, readability, and processing, as well as the morale of coders. The hardware and software components of an information system may also have to be modified. Van Court Hare states:

> The selection of a particular code that will be used, even though unique, offers a classic example of economic trade-offs. On the one hand, some capacity or investment in facilities is required to transmit, process, and manipulate codes. On the other hand the capacity required in each of these phases of processing is affected by the choice of code format. In general, the shorter the code, the smaller the cost of transmission storage, data entry, sorting and human handling. The longer code, however, requires less translation and "look-up" capacity and processing and often provides greater versatility in data extraction, statistical analysis, and category combination.[4]

Decisions on coding structures and data element subclassifications should not be delegated to analysts. Management should participate in the design of coding schemes and in code implementation.

---

[3] James Rawlings Sydnor, "Bar Coded Unique ZIP Codes Solve Postal Problems," *Journal of Systems Management,* vol. 29, no. 7 (July 1978), p. 18.

[4] Van Court Hare, Jr., *Systems Analysis: A Diagnostic Approach* (New York: Harcourt Brace Jovanovich, Inc., 1967), pp. 494–95.

Principles of code design

Once a code structure has been selected, codes must be assigned within the structure. The following are principles of code design.

1. Codes should be logical and meaningful whenever possible. Arbitrary alphabetic codes that have no relation to names, such as a rug coded CN, can be confusing to coders and result in inaccuracies. Numerical codes should also make sense. 1 for married and 2 for single should be reversed, for example.

2. Codes should be neutral, evoking no emotional response on the part of coders or users. Women's groups have objected to the use of 1 for male and 2 for female in sex coding. Many coders dismiss the number 13 as a coding option.

3. Codes should identify the lowest level of measurement or aggregation that will be needed during the lifetime of the coding structure.

4. Long codes should include a self-checking feature to ensure that codes are correctly transcribed and converted into machine-readable form. (An explanation of check digits appears later in this chapter.)

5. The code design should allow for expansion of data attributes. Lack of planning for such needs may require reprogramming and restructuring of data files to incorporate changes at a later date. The U.S. Postal Service wants to add four digits to the zip code to help identify postal routes and sets of postal boxes. A small Connecticut business has calculated that it would need to change 85 computer programs, expand 40 disk files, reprint 6 input documents, and recompile 81 control procedures for a 9-digit zip code. The nationwide cost of this code expansion would be high, not to mention the confusion and disruption that such a change would entail.

6. Codes should incorporate supplemental information embedded in the code wherever possible. For example, a personnel number that includes year of employment in two digits added to sequential numbering is a code that identifies employee records uniquely while providing useful information for statistical reports.

7. An "other" category that can be subclassified at a future date should be provided, since it is not always possible to anticipate all attributes of a data element that need coding.

8. Hyphens, decimals, or spaces should be added to long codes to help users remember them. The grouping of digits in social security numbers assists memorization, for example.

9. A standard coding system should be adopted, and codes defined for each data element that is coded in the DED. This will ensure that data elements within a firm's data base are uniformly coded. Imagine the confusion that would arise if a warehouse assigned color codes to products that differed from the color codes used by salespersons.

Problems

A major disadvantage of coding is that errors are frequently made converting data to code, errors which are not always easily detected. Computer programs can be written to check data entry against a list of accepted codes so that nonexistent characters will be spotted, but a legitimate code used incorrectly will pass undetected.

The credibility of data is often directly related to the origin of coding. Coding at the data source may lead to inadvertent errors due to a misunderstanding of the coding structure or carelessness in applying valid and relevant codes. Trained coders, selected and supervised with care and motivated as to the importance of their job, make fewer errors. Their work can be checked by sending a copy of the coded record to the division that collected the data, but this approach depends on the cooperation of individuals at the data source. What if the data were unfavorable to that division? Would motivation to make corrections exist? A statistical sample of a coder's work should therefore be regularly checked. If the coder's error rate exceeds previously set standards, that person should be fired or relocated. An information system with incorrect data as a result of incorrect coding has little value.

VALIDATION

Data (either coded or uncoded) ready for input should first be **glance-checked.** Once converted into machine language, content and meaning can be further validated by computer program. In computer science literature, validation is often called editing, but these two terms should not be interchanged. **Editing,** strictly defined, is correcting syntax such as adding hyphens, dollar signs, or commas to make output readable or eliminating zeros as in the number 0032, changes that can be made by programs during processing. **Validation,** however, concerns checking compliance of data with preset standards and verification of data correctness.

This validation may be of input, checking data on forms or CRT screens at the time of data collection. For example, an incorrect entry on an employment application might be caught by a clerk, and called to the applicant's attention for revision. Data converted into machine language can further be validated by computer program. If errors are detected, data must recycle back to the error source, as shown in Figure 7.5.

Invalid data may be the result of:

1. Incorrect or outdated source documentation (form or manual).
2. Entry error by data collector.
3. Misinterpretation of documentation on input preparation.
4. Coding errors.
5. Operator errors in data conversion (the largest single cause of input error).
6. Errors in data transmission and data handling (for example, lost data or incorrect sequencing).

FIGURE 7.5
Data validation

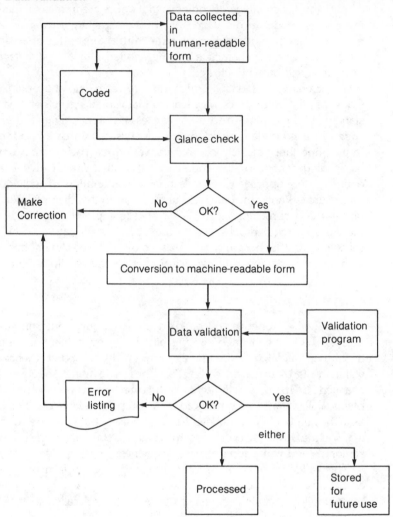

Validity checks

Data should be checked for completeness, format, range, reasonableness, consistency, sequence, and transaction count. The self-checking code should also be validated. It should be emphasized that decision rules for all validity tests need to be stated with care. Errors in data should not pass undetected nor should correct data be identified as invalid. The perspective of managers is needed in deciding which data elements require validation, and what validation rules should be applied.

COMPLETENESS

Data should be **complete.** When data has a prescribed length, such as nine digits for a social security number, all characters should be expressed. Completeness checks are necessary only when missing data will affect results. The computer could not process an order with a truncated product number or one with quantity blank, but the order could probably be filled if the client's middle initial were absent or a digit omitted from the client's phone number.

FORMAT

Character configuration can be specified in validation programs, and the data checked against these predetermined rules. For example, a validation program can be written to identify as an error an alphabetic character in a dollar data field, or numeric data in names. The check can divide the **format** into subfields. An address may be assigned numeric fields for house number and zip code, but alphabetic blocks for street and city.

RANGE

A check rule may state that data entry is limited to predetermined values, or a **range of values.** If M and F are used as sex codes, only these two characters would be valid in the sex code field. Any other letter or number would be listed as an error. Similarly, a range of values could be specified. If a firm's minimum wage/hour rate were $4 and the maximum $9, the computer could be programmed to identify as invalid data with values under or over these amounts, errors called **definite** or **fatal errors.** The computer might also be programmed to identify **possible** or **suspected errors,** data near the limits of acceptable values. For example, if few employees earned over $8, a listing of employees in the $8–9 range could be provided for recheck. The validation rule would be as follows:

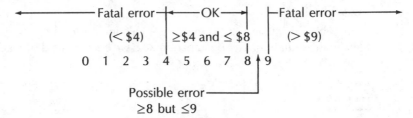

Fatal errors identified by the validation program would have to be traced and corrected. The data would then be reprocessed. An overriding code would permit processing of suspected data that proved valid.

REASONABLENESS

In any given situation a number of checks for **reasonableness** could be postulated. Date of employment cannot predate a worker's birth, the total of accounts receivable cannot be negative, a probationary student cannot graduate with honors, and so forth. The cost of processing such checks must be weighed against losses (monetary and credibility), should errors pass undetected. Such judgments require management's expertise.

CONSISTENCY

Data values can be checked by verifying them from more than one source. This may mean collecting the same raw data from two or more principals, or generating the values of a data element from input to be matched with the keyed value for that same data element. The latter method is used to check totals, for example. If the information on Table 7.1 were keypunched, a computer validity program could add $53.20, $32.80, and $39.90 in Batch I and match the total with the batch total $125.90 entered as input. Or each invoice total could be calculated by computer (price times quantity) and the product compared to the figure listed in the value column. Any discrepancy would be identified on an error listing. Most frequently, invalid data is a mistake in keying the input.

A **hash total** entered as input is also a useful check for **consistency.** All the data in one transaction is totaled even though the units are not the same. The computer then totals the "hash" independently, (320 + 16 + 3.20 + 53.20 in the first transaction in Figure 7.1) and compares the total with the keyed hash total. Since many transactions involve 80 to 100 characters, the hash total is an important validity check.

Duplicate processing is another method of checking for consistency. A firm which needed to determine a coefficient to two decimal places from complex calculations for the allocation of over $4 million used both COBOL and FORTRAN to make the calculations. Because of the large amount of money involved, it was helpful to compare calculations made by the two compilers which differed in rounding and truncation rules.

SEQUENCE

In Table 7.1 invoice 322 is missing. A validity test for **sequencing** would identify this situation. The document may have been mislaid or lost, in which

TABLE 7.1
Transaction data

	Invoice number	Quantity (units)	Price $	Value $	Batch total	Hash total
Batch 1	320	16	3.20	53.20		392.40
	321	8	4.10	32.80		365.90
	323	21	1.90	39.90	125.90	511.70
Batch 2	224	25	4.00	100.00		363.00
	325	31	4.20	130.20		490.40
	326	9	5.80	52.20		393.00
	327	5	6.10	30.50	312.90	681.60
				438.80	438.80	

case corrective action, such as recollection of the data, would take place. But often an explanation, such as a cancelled order, will be traced. In processing payrolls, logs are kept of checks damaged, destroyed by the printer, or checks left blank—a record that is searched when a sequence validity test flags an error.

TRANSACTION COUNT

When a given number of transactions are to be processed, this total is entered as input. The transactions are again counted during processing. An invalid state will be identified if the totals do not match. This will alert operators to a lost document, or records stuck to one another, or possibly even multiple processing of the same transaction.

SELF-CHECKING CODES

A code is sometimes used to check for transposition of data or data entry errors, situations that often occur in data elements consisting of a long string of digits. This code, called a **check digit,** is calculated by a prescribed set of rules based on the value of the digits in the number and their locational relationships. The code is then added to the data element number and recalculated every time that data element is processed. If the recalculated value does not coincide with the original check digit, an error is identified.

Modulus 10 is one technique for calculating a check digit. In this technique, the position of digits in a number are significant. Digits in odd positions (such as first, third, fifth, and so forth) are added for a subtotal. Digits in even positions are multiplied by 2 and the products added together for a second subtotal. The subtotals are then added and divided by ten. The remainder is the check digit.

For the number 142796538 the check digit according to these rules is 5. The new number, 1427965385 is determined as follows:

The number will be aligned in two rows, digits in odd positions separated from digits in even positions. The calculations are then performed:

					Multiplied by 2	Subtotal of digits in row
1	2	9	5	8	No	25
	4	7	6	3	Yes	40
					Total	65

Remainder when total is divided by 10 = 5
Check digit = 5
New number 1427965385

To test the working of the check digit, study the following example in which the value of one digit is changed.

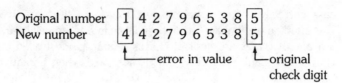

Original number   1 4 2 7 9 6 5 3 8 5
New number   4 4 2 7 9 6 5 3 8 5
                  ↑——error in value   ↑—original
                                       check digit

Calculation:

					Multiplied by 2	Subtotal of digits in row
4	2	9	5	8	No	28
4	7	6	3		Yes	40
					Total	68

Remainder after dividing total by 10 = 8
New check digit = 8
Original check digit = 5

New check digit does not equal original check digit. Therefore, an error exists. In the following example, two adjacent digits are transposed.

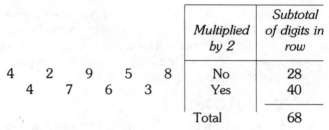

Original number   1 4 2 7 9 6 5 3 8 5
New number   (4 1) 2 7 9 6 5 3 8 5 ←—check digit
                  ↑—error from single transposition

Calculation:

					Multiplied by 2	Subtotal of digits in row
4	2	9	5	8	No	28
1	7	6	3		Yes	34
					Total	62

New check digit = 2
Original check digit = 5

New check digit does not equal original check digit. Therefore, an error exists. The problem with **Modulus 10** is that double transposition can take place without affecting the check digit (that is, 5431 transposed as 3154). **Modulus 11,** another method of calculating a check digit, overcomes this problem. In Modulus 11, digits in the value of the data element are assigned weights such as numbers in an ascending or descending scale. Each digit is then multiplied by its corresponding weighted value, and the products are totaled. The number that must be added to this total to make it divisible by 11 is the check digit. All types of transposition (double, triple, and so forth) and data entry errors are caught by this technique. This system has been adopted by the publishing industry for the ISBN check digit code. As an example, the check digit for the book ISBN 0–256–01834 is calculated as 0, the new number becoming 0–256–01834–0.

ISBN number	0	2	5	6	0	1	8	3	4
ISBN weights	10	9	8	7	6	5	4	3	2
Weighted values		0	18	40	42	0	5	32	9	8

(ISBN number multiplied by ISBN weight)

Weighted total: $0 + 18 + 40 + 42 + 0 + 5 + 32 + 9 + 8 = 154$
Number required to make total divisible by 11 = 0
Check digit = 0

If the check digit is calculated as 10, an X is used since only one character is assigned to the check digit. ISBN 0–256–02121–X for the revised edition of James A. O'Brien's text *Computers in Business Management: An Introduction* fits this pattern.

The use of a check digit does create problems. It adds to the length of numbers and increases data preparation effort, the time required for processing, and storage space requirements. The longer number is also harder to remember. But when reliability is important and the number is repeatedly used in processing, detection of errors may be worth the inconvenience and cost. Self-checking codes are commonly the last digit in identification numbers for employees, vendors, customers, accounts, and parts. Their use will identify posting of transactions to wrong accounts.

SUMMARY

Three aspects of data preparation have been discussed in this chapter: data collection, coding, and validation.

Coding is a brief unique representation of data used to facilitate classification, speed processing, and reduce costs in data preparation and storage. Each application requires codes tailored to the environment. That is why management should participate in code design. Technicians may have coding skill but lack perspective regarding the goals and operational limitations of the firm, factors that should be considered when designing coding for input and retrieval.

Computer validation of data takes place after it is coded in machine language. The rules of validation should be specified with care by management. Underspecification may lead to undetected errors, causing the system to produce unreliable information. Overspecification adds unnecessarily to processing costs. Validation tests include checks for completeness, format, range, reasonableness, consistency, sequence, and transaction count, and recalculation of check digits. Some errors will still escape detection—such as mistakes of data entry that fall within allowable ranges. But validation tests will improve the quality of information by reducing, even eliminating, obvious errors in input and output.

KEY WORDS

Alphabetic codes
Alphameric (alphanumeric) code
Block code
Check digit
Coder
Coding
Coding sheet
Completeness
Consistency
Data collection
Data preparation
Decimal code
Definite error
Duplicate processing
Editing
Encoder
Encoding
Fatal error
Format
Glance check
Group classification code

Hash total
Magnetic ink character code
Magnetic ink character
   recognition (MICR) reader
Mnemonic symbol
Modulus 10
Modulus 11
Numeric codes
Offline collection
Online collection
Possible error
Range of values
Reasonableness
Self-checking code
Sequential code
Suspected error
Table lookup
Transaction count
Universal product code (UPC)
Validation

DISCUSSION QUESTIONS

1. What are the principles of code design?
2. What are the disadvantages of using codes?
3. What approach to data collection would you advise for each of the following situations? Identify both input media and input equipment.
   a. Bank.
   b. Warehouse.
   c. Production plant.
   d. Sales office.
   e. Accounts payable.
4. What is the UPC? What are its advantages and disadvantages? Why is it not used universally in retail stores?
5. What are some of the applications of a bar code in industries other than the retail industry?

6. Identify situations in business and industry where optical scanning can be used effectively.

7. What is the need and significance of editing or validation? At what point in processing must they be performed? What additional resources are necessary?

8. Can the following errors be caught by validation? In each case state the validation rule.
   a. $93A2.4.
   b. DR. HUSS3IN.
   c. $3 2.64.
   d. WAGE $1686 per hour.
   e. Account number incorrect.
   f. Age incorrect by one year.
   g. Age incorrect by 100 years.

9. Within a firm, coding methods should be standardized or else there will be confusion and inefficiency. Comment. How can coding methods be standardized?

10. Describe how data is converted into machine-readable form. Why is this conversion important? How can data from a meter be converted into machine-readable form?

11. What are the rationale for coding data? What costs are involved?

12. What national attempt has been made at standardized codes? Why? What are the main obstacles to standardization?

13. Distinguish between:
    a. Data code and program code.
    b. Block code and group code.
    c. Code and coder.
    d. Decimal code and classification code.
    e. Alphabetic and numeric code.
    f. Alphameric and alphanumeric code.

14. When should a file be verified? Must all the contents be verified in each verification run?

15. What is the difference between verification of new data for content errors and editing for format errors? How is each done? Must each be done?

16. When is a check digit useful? Why? Give examples.

17. Why are codes used in information systems?

18. Explain six validation rules for data.

19. What are common causes for invalid data?

EXERCISES

1. Design codes for the data elements in Exercise 1, Chapter 6. Use alpha characters only for the month subfield code, use a block code to identify university, college (e.g., Business Ad), department (e.g., Economics), and major (e.g., Micro Economics).

2. Find the ISBN number for this text. Decode it. The identifier for the country of publication is the first digit, the publisher identifier the next three digits. All Irwin books should have these same digits. The title identifier is the next five

digits. Compare this ISBN number with other business books published by Irwin. What digits are the same?

3. The last digit of the ISBN is a check digit. Figure out the algorithm used for your book. Try the algorithm on another Irwin book. Does it work?

4. Calculate the check digit for the number 362815 using Mod 11 with 1, 2, 3, 4, 5, and 6 as weights. What is the new number with the check digit?

5. Compare the UPC code on a can of Campbell's cream of chicken soup with the code from some other product by Campbell. What parts of the codes are identical? Why? Which parts differ? Why?

SELECTED ANNOTATED BIBLIOGRAPHY

Anderson, Lauek, et al. "Self-Checking Digit Concepts." *Journal of Systems Development,* vol. 25, no. 9 (September 1974), pp. 36–42.
A very detailed description and comparison of seven check digit formulas, including Mod 11.

Clifton, H. D. *Business Data Systems.* Englewood Cliffs, N.J.: Prentice-Hall, Inc., 1978, pp. 229–35.
A good systematic discussion of coding classification and design.

Daniels, Alan, and Yeates, Donald. *Systems Analysis.* Palo Alto, Calif.: Science Research Associates, 1971, pp. 62–71.
An excellent discussion on functions of codes and design considerations. Sequence codes, group classification codes, block codes, significant digit codes, the Dewey Decimal Code, and nine types of check digit codes are reviewed.

Kohn, B. *Secret Codes and Ciphers.* Englewood Cliffs, N.J.: Prentice-Hall, Inc., 1968, 63 pages.
This is a small book with a large print, many diagrams, and amusing illustrations—a delight.

Savir, D., and Laurer, G. L. "The Characteristics and Decodability of the Universal Product Code." *IBM System Journal,* vol. 14, no. 1 (1975), pp. 16–34.
An excellent discussion on the development of the UPC, including characteristics, errors, and decoding. The decoding presentation is mathematical, but that part can be skipped and still much gained by the general reader.

Way, Peter. *Codes and Ciphers.* London: Aldus Books Limited, 1977, 144 p.
A nontechnical book with many illustrations with an interesting description of how codes have been used (successfully and unsuccessfully) during wars and in espionage.

8

ADMINISTRATION OF A DATA BASE

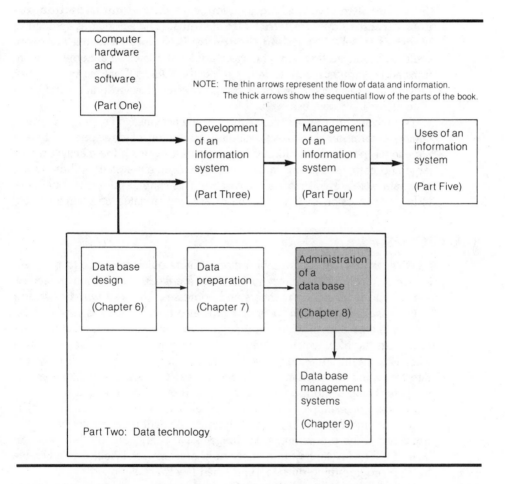

NOTE: The thin arrows represent the flow of data and information.
The thick arrows show the sequential flow of the parts of the book.

As data grows in volume within a business, a system is required to keep track of and manage all the data elements in the common data base. The data base itself can be utilized efficiently and effectively only when procedures for its control and use are well designed.

Knowledge of this aspect of data technology is needed when developing and implementing information systems. For example, a manager may wish to know which reports would be affected if values for a specific data element were no longer collected. A listing of who accesses data, and why, might prove useful. The ability to identify units creating data, or programs and files using particular data elements might also be required. This information can be generated by a set of programs which draws on all knowledge about the elements stored in the data element dictionaries of the firm and available in the data base. The tables or lists generated make up a **directory.**

Because of the close relationship between dictionaries and data directories, the two are often developed together, forming a **data element dictionary/ data directory system (DED/DD system).** (The acronym is sometimes shortened to **DD/D** for **data dictionary/directory.**) But the dictionary could be produced first and a directory added at a later date. Some software firms and computer manufacturers put together DED/DD systems which they provide to customers. Many businesses, however, develop unique DED/DD systems for their own use.

Technicians are responsible for most of the activities in creating and maintaining a common data base, including generation of directories, although a manager, personally, or through a committee, oversees these activities. For large and complex systems, a data base management system and the hiring of a data base administrator are advisable. This chapter presents a brief nontechnical discussion of how data bases are implemented and administered.

DIRECTORIES

Directories are lists or tables that facilitate quick reference to pertinent information. Consider a directory we utilize every day—a telephone directory. We refer to it for phone numbers and addresses. The **key word** or **index** in this case is family name. Data systems also have directories. These index data elements and provide information such as where data elements are located in the files, which programs and transactions use the elements, and who uses the information derived from the data elements. In data system directories, the key word indexed is either the data element name, or a **label,** the latter being a short, unique, and easy-to-process identifier substituted for the name. For example, FICA (for Federal Insurance Contributions Act) is a label commonly used in place of the data element name of *social security tax.* Since some programming languages have restrictions on the choice of label (FORTRAN limits the number of characters per label), it is advisable to keep programming rules in mind when labels are designed.

Because dictionaries and directories both provide organizational information about data elements, the two are closely related. In some cases, directories also define data elements, so they perform the function of dictionaries. The distinction between directories and dictionaries has been further clouded by many data processing practitioners who define **fixed data elements** (such as sex) in dictionaries, and **variable data elements** (such as marital status) in directories. However, not all data elements can be easily categorized in this manner. Some data elements are fixed over a period of time and then change, such as a name which changes upon marriage. Data element definitions may also change when managers change. There simply is no universally accepted distinction between dictionaries and directories in the data processing profession. By referring to dictionaries and directories jointly, as a DED/DD system, the need for making a hard and fast distinction between the two is avoided.

DED/DD systems have two primary functions: they serve as a repository of information for data processing personnel and users, and as an information source for applications and systems programs. Just how they facilitate and control the use of the data base is described below.

Information repository for users

INDEXES

One important function of a DED/DD system is that it documents information related to processing. This documentation also serves as a set of standards governing the creation and use of the data.

Accessing this information may prove laborious in large systems. An **index** can facilitate access, particularly when searching for data elements with compound or long names when one has forgotten the exact title or spelling of the element. In such cases a **KWIC (Key Word In Context)** or **KWOC (Key Word Out of Context)** index is helpful. The former is more commonly used because it identifies in alphabetic sequence every data element word without changing the order of words. Table 8.1 shows excerpts from a sample KWIC that would help a user trace the data element "employee job startdate." Note that in the alphabetic sequence this data element is listed three times: under E for employee, J for job, and S for startdate. The data element could therefore be traced if only one of the three words in its name were recalled.

This multiple indexing technique has other business applications as well. It may be employed in indexing a user's manual, a procedures manual, or even a chart of accounts.

Since some data element names are ambiguous or have names chosen for convenience rather than relevance, a descriptor called a **designator** is often added to the definition of a data element and is used for indexing that element. This descriptor is a set of **key words** reflecting the content and meaning of the data element. A convention is generally followed for ordering words in the designator name: the most general key word appears first, the most specific last. Thus, if the words "shortened name of employee" were chosen for the designator, the convention would require that this be written as "name employee shortened" since "name" is the most general key word and "shortened" the most specific. "Of" would be eliminated entirely.

Some key words occur frequently. These are designated **classwords** and

TABLE 8.1
KWIC extracts

	Data element number
EMPLOYEE-HISTORY-DATA	1.1.10
EMPLOYEE-JOB-STARTDATE	1.3.18
EMPLOYEE-JOB-STATUS	1.3.19
EMPLOYEE-JOB-TITLE	1.3.20
EMPLOYEE-NAME	1.2.02
EMPLOYEE-NUMBER	1.2.03
PAST-EMPLOYEE-NUMBER	1.2.13
•	
•	
•	
•	
•	
INVOICE-CREDIT	3.2.02
INVOICE-DATE	3.2.04
INVOICE-NUMBER	3.2.04
JOB-NUMBER	1.3.02
EMPLOYEE-JOB-STARTDATE	1.3.18
EMPLOYEE-JOB-STATUS	1.3.19
EMPLOYEE-JOB-TITLE	1.3.30
JOB-WAGE-RATE	1.3.24
•	
•	
•	
•	
•	
•	
SCHEDULED-COMPLETION-DATE	4.1.02
SCHEDULED-DUE-DATE	4.1.03
SCHEDULED-STARTDATE	4.1.04
SCHEDULED-WORKDATE	4.1.05
EMPLOYEE-JOB-STARTDATE	1.3.18
SUBASSEMBLY-COMPONENTS	5.2.03
SUBASSEMBLY-PART-LOCATION	5.2.05

should be used wherever applicable. This helps reduce synonyms. Examples of classwords are amount, salesperson, and part number.

Using designators and using key words in data element names and designators results in the grouping of similar data elements in indexes. Such groupings greatly facilitate the identification of duplications, synonyms, and inconsistencies in a DED. A manager administering a data base may be alerted to the need for modification or even reconstruction of the firm's DED by analyzing directory indexes.

TABLE TO IDENTIFY USERS OF DATA ELEMENTS

A DED/DD system can generate a directory to represent the relationship of each data element with user. Data elements form one axis, and user (current or potential) the other. The latter may represent organizational units, reports, models, or individuals. A matrix of this type (see Table 8.2) can help streamline the data base by identifying data elements which should be dropped (data elements collected but not used) and can help assess the relative importance of data elements in the system, an assessment of value to management for control, since heavily used data elements will require more careful monitoring than those used infrequently. For example, since PIN is a data element used by all organizational units in Table 8.2, the need for validation procedures of PIN input might be deduced from this matrix.

TABLE 8.2
Matrix to identify users of data elements

Users / Data elements	Organizational unit (departments coded)				
	1	2	3	• • •	• • •
PIN of employee (personal ID number)	x	x	x		
Name	x		x		
Address	x		x		
Sex	x		x		
Marital status	x		x		

MATRIX TO IDENTIFY DATA CREATORS

DED/DD systems may also generate a directory to identify organizational units that create and/or maintain each data element. This matrix tells management which units are responsible for correct, complete collection of data on time. When superimposed on the matrix showing organizational users, managers can identify data elements that are both created and used by a single organizational unit (see Table 8.3). The quality of data in such cases is generally high, for the creator as a later user has a vested interest in accuracy and completeness. Units that serve merely as collectors of data for others are less motivated and may become lax in the quality of data generated. The matrix is therefore a useful tool in data base administration for it helps monitor quality by pointing to potential weaknesses in data collection.

TRANSACTION MATRIX

It is sometimes desirable to identify the data elements used by each transaction. In the matrix, transactions can be either formal input documents and

TABLE 8.3
Matrix to identify creators and users of data elements

Data elements	Users — Organization unit (departments coded)				
	1	2	3	•••	•••
PIN of employee (personal ID number)	x	x	x		
Name	x		⊗		
Address	x		⊗		
Sex	x		⊗		
Marital status	x		⊗		
Educational highest degree		⊗			
Experience code		⊗			
Years of experience		⊗			
Language code	x				
State of birth	x				
Year of birth	x				
Medical benefit		⊗	⊗		
Deduction codes		⊗	⊗		
Tax code		⊗	⊗		
Wage rate		⊗	⊗		

Key: x = creator
      ○ = user

printed forms, or output forms. This matrix is generated to determine which transactions would be affected if a data element were redefined or deleted. Such information is useful in form and document control.

Information repository for software

ACCESS DIRECTORY

In processing, the computer sometimes uses tables generated by the DED/DD system. For example, the computer may check the level of security code needed for access to specific data elements or files before processing a user's job—information that is stored in a directory. In addition, the table referenced might specify the type of access permitted, that is, read or write. In a terminal environment, the data elements accessible by each terminal might also be listed, as well as the time of day when access is permitted. Special user access limitations and user account numbers for purposes of billing might also be drawn from the directory in processing. Computers programmed to refuse access to those not authorized generally log all requests to use the system, a log that will help alert managers to attempted security violations of the system.

Programs may be written for printing directory information stored in computer memory. For example, a manager or auditor may wish a printout of information in the security/access directory used by the computer in processing. The exact format of the printout would depend on the programmed instructions, for the information could be printed in a variety of sorting orders. A sample access directory is shown in Table 8.4.

TABLE 8.4
Access directory

User identification: 076–835–5623
Access limitation: 13 hours (of CPU time for current fiscal year)
Account No.: AS5842

Data elements	Type of access	Security level	Terminal number	Time lock
Customer No.	Read	10	04	08.00–17.00
Invoice No.	Read	10	04	08.00–17.00
Cash receipt	Read/Write	12	06	08.00–12.00

PROCESSING INFORMATION

The form of a data element, such as its mode of data representation, format, and compaction (if it is compacted), is information needed in processing. Though this is usually specified by programs, it may prove more economical to have this information in a directory that is machine-readable. In such cases, every time that data elements in the common data base are used, information necessary for processing is referenced from the DED/DD system.

A somewhat similar situation may arise in validating input data values for data elements entered into the system by several terminals. Instead of independent validity programs testing the input values, the validation rules can be stored in the DED/DD system and referenced by a DED/DD-driven validator. If the data does not pass the validation tests, diagnostics of error are sent to the originator of the data. Valid data is added to the data base and subsequently used in processing applications programs. This process is shown in Figure 8.1

LOCATIONAL INFORMATION

Once data is validated, it is stored on a storage device and the location is recorded. A stored set of data constitutes a **physical record.** When the data is a set of logically related values, it constitutes a **logical record.** Physical records therefore become repositories of stored logical records. When access to a logical record is needed, its physical location must be known. This information can be provided by a directory. DED/DD systems with locational information enable programmers to merely name logical records or data elements needed in processing without having to specify location. **Data**

FIGURE 8.1
DED/DD-driven centralized validator for input data to data base

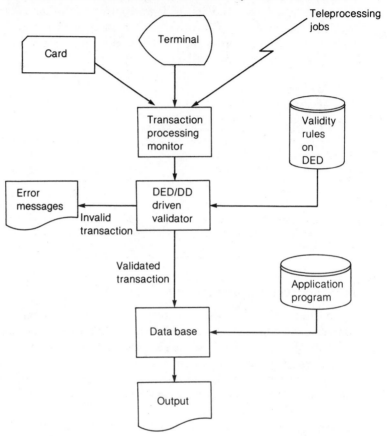

mapping, illustrated in Figure 8.2, referenced from a directory is particularly useful in a multistorage device system.

GENERATION OF TEST DATA

The rules for data validation discussed earlier include information on character composition and the permissible range of data values. This information, plus information on format available in the data dictionary, enables DED/DD systems to generate sample data needed to test computer programs before live data is collected. Even after live data is available, DED/DD generation of sample data is useful for maintenance programs which can then be tested without disturbing the live data stream.

The sample test data should be statistically designed (for example, a stratified random sample). It should include boundary conditions and exceptional values, information which is available in the DED/DD system.

FIGURE 8.2
Physical and logical mapping of data

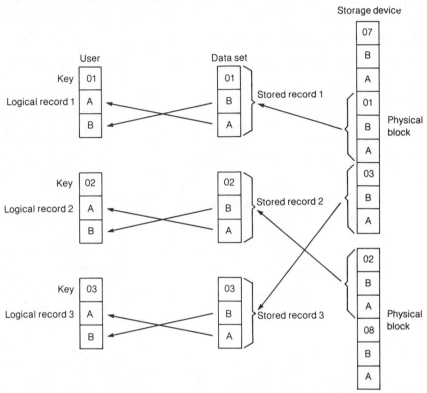

Source: Reprinted by permission from *Introduction to Data Management.* Student Text No. SC20–8096–0, p. 37. @ 1980 International Business Machines Corporation.

CODE FILE

Definitions of data elements can be extended to include subclassifications. A DED/DD system can then generate a **code file** from these definitions, listing names and codes of all subclassifications, a file to be referenced whenever the data element name or code is unknown.

Some argue that a code file should contain only large sets of frequently used codes, such as a chart of accounts of a diversified firm. Short, frequently used codes, such as a sex code, should be excluded (may be defined externally or in programs used). Others favor inclusion of all codes in a code file to facilitate data definition control, believing that this control justifies the higher cost required for equipment and processing.

Code files have many side benefits. The computer can generate updated code listings for users from the file. The file serves as an authority on codes and helps managers identify duplications of codes which need purging. Users must first check whether existing codes are applicable to their needs before adding new codes to the system.

ADDING DESCRIPTORS TO THE DED

Only a few of the many directories and indexes that can be produced by a DED/DD system have been mentioned. The information itself is generated by computer programs. In most cases this requires a trivial effort.[1] But there is an important cost component: the addition of descriptors to the DED to define terms and relationships needed in the reference tables. Examples of such descriptors include designator, synonym, user, data creator, codes for subclassification, mode (bit string, character string, packed decimal, and so

TABLE 8.5
Common descriptors used in DED/DD systems

Name (for ease in identifying and remembering)	Last date changed
	Designator
Definition	Synonym
Derivation algorithm (including accuracy level)	User relationship
	Creation/specification responsibility
Units (where relevant, e.g., dollars, meters)	Transaction relationship
Format	Potential use relationship
Justification	Codes
Width of field	Mode
Validity rules	Security code
Identification	Billing code
Version of issuance	Access limitation
Date of issuance	Logical/physical relationship
Status (effective, proposed or approved)	Medium of storage

forth), logical/physical relationship, and medium of storage.[2] One large firm studied listed 250 descriptors required for its use of COBOL, assembler source programs, Job Control Language, and operating system and software packages. This firm, however, is an exceptional case, requiring far more descriptors than usual.[3] Commonly used descriptors for DED/DD systems are listed in Table 8.5.

---

[1] The effort of writing a program that will generate a directory is not trivial in itself, but such programs can be purchased, or they are provided by vendors of computer equipment. Their use requires a trivial effort.

[2] For another list and one that is very formally described, see P. J. Plourd, "Elements of Data Dictionary Systems Design," *Proceedings of the 1973 CAUSE National Meeting* (Boulder, Colo., 1973), pp. 707–12.

[3] Richard G. Canning, "The Data Base Administrator's Function," *EDP Analyzer,* vol. 10, no. 11 (November 1972), p. 4.

ORGANIZATION OF A DED/DD SYSTEM

A DED/DD system requires considerable organization and control. In many firms a DED/DD committee is responsible for the content of the system and decides what equipment and software are required for developing and maintaining the system, what qualifications are desirable for personnel using equipment and software, and what procedures and mechanisms are needed for control, and so forth.

Control procedures are diagrammed in Figure 8.3. Although the ultimate authority to authorize change to the data base may rest with a DED/DD committee, as shown in this figure, in reality change commonly involves a sequence of approval steps in which users, programmers, analysts, and data processing management play a role. The exact personnel involved will depend on the organization's procedures in the past, the system's complexity, and personalities. For example, when a report is requested by management for which a new program is written, the programmer may find that data elements not in the data base are needed. This need may be brought to the attention of a data processing manager who will then request approval of the DED/DD committee for the additions. Some firms may skip this intermediate step, however, authorizing the programmers to approach the committee directly.

Not shown in Figure 8.3 is the duty of the committee to periodically review the existing DED for redundancies and duplications, and the important committee role in recognizing the need for revision of the DED due to changes in organizational needs, structure, and personnel.

In controlling the content of the DED/DD system, the committee also has the responsibility of resolving the differences which arise between organizational units. This duty can best be performed when the committee is a consortium of users with high level management positions so that the committee has the operational power and respectability to enforce decisions made— that is, power to overrule unilateral actions by users, to adjudicate conflicts, and to overcome resistance.

The committee must also state policy and provide guidelines for creating, maintaining, and monitoring the DED/DD system. Since implementation is often complex and technical, the committee may delegate this responsibility, retaining merely a supervisory role. The delegated responsibility goes to a **data base administrator** (sometimes called a **data manager** or **data controller**), a new position in many organizational structures.

The bottom half of Figure 8.3 shows validation programs (discussed in Chapter 7) to control data input, and directories to keep track of data elements in the system.

DATA BASE ADMINISTRATOR (DBA)

As mentioned above, a data base administrator is often delegated authority to coordinate, monitor, and control the data base and accompanying software,

FIGURE 8.3
Mechanism for controlling the DED/DD

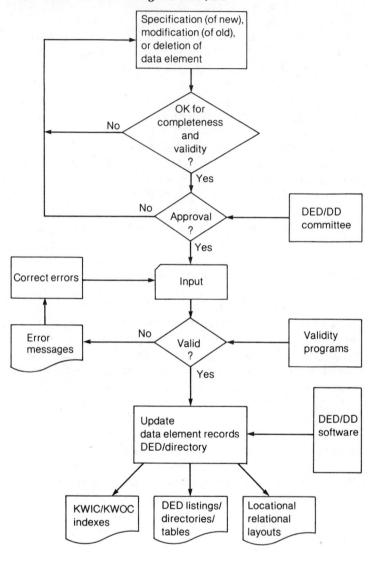

and responsibility for administering the total DED/DD system. Table 8.6 summarizes the data base administrator's duties. Data maintenance, the up-keep of active data, the storage of historical data, and the purging of useless data are primary tasks. Authorized changes to the data base must be made to dictionaries and directories under the data base administrator's supervision. Such changes may require moving data from one storage medium to another, a move which entails careful logging and tagging if data is to be quickly

TABLE 8.6
Functions of a data base administrator

Data base design	Retrieval
Content	Search strategies
Creation	Statistics
Reconciling differences	Access
Dictionary/Directory	Frequency of processing
Create	Space use
Maintain	User utilization
Data compression	Response time
Data classification/coding	Design operational
Data integrity	procedures
Backup	Access to data base
Restart/recovery	Access for testing
	Interfaces
Data base operation	Testing system
DED custodian/authority	
Maintain	*Monitoring*
Add	Quality of data
Purge	validity
Data base maintenance	Performance
Integrity	Efficiency
Detect losses	Cost
Repair losses	Use/utilization
Recovery	Security/privacy
Access for testing	Audit
Dumping	Compliance
Software for DED/DD	Standards
Utility programs	Procedures
Tables/indexes, etc., for	
end user	*Other functions*
Storage	Liaison/communications with:
Physical record structure	End users
Logical-physical mapping	Analysts/programmers
Physical storage device	Training on data base
assignments	Consultant on file design
Security/access	Design operational
Assign passwords	procedures
Assign lock/key	Access to data base
Modifying passwords/keys	Access for testing
Logging	Interfaces
Cryptography	
Modification	

and effectively accessed. Maintenance also includes checking for continuity and completeness of data. Continuity is especially important for planning data with longitudinal integration (integration over time). The modification of historical files is required when definitions of data elements and classifications change. Continuity is threatened by breakdowns in processing, particularly those of online systems where loss of data may result. Procedures for backup, recovery, and restart for all possible types of breakdowns, including natural disasters, must be planned.

A DBA is also responsible for the quality (accurateness and reliability) of the data base. **Logging** and **auditing** procedures should be established, and performance (access, utilization, cost, and response-time performance) monitored. Screening procedures to identify authorized users at minimal cost and inconvenience should be devised to protect the data from misuse. Security of access can be achieved through passwords or passkeys, and directories listing data to be accessed, the time of permissible access, and place.

Both legislative and executive powers are needed by data base administrators. They must not only make rules regarding data base content, access, security, recovery, logging, dumping, and auditing, they must also be able to enforce these rules for all users at all levels of the organizational hierarchy. This authority must extend even over data processing management and vice presidents, for individuals in these positions have been known to break the system for personal financial gain, as shown in a study by the Stanford Research Institute (see Table 8.7). A supervisor or committee should oversee the data administrator, safeguarding against abuse of such authority.

Governing a data base requires many talents. A DBA must be a " . . .

TABLE 8.7
Distribution of embezzlers by position

Position	Number of embezzlers*
Operations vice president, manager, clerk	32
Loan officer, manager	29
Teller	22
President	14
Cashier	8
Director, stockholder, officer	5
Vice president, EDP	4
EDP clerk	3
Bookkeeper	3
Trust officer	3
Programmer	3
Computer operator	3
Systems analyst	2
Chief teller	1
Auditor	1
Vice president	1
Proof department supervisor	1

* Includes 17 cases of collusion.
Source: Donn B. Parker, *Crime by Computer* (New York: Charles Scribner's Sons, 1976), p. 52. Copyright © 1976 by Donn B. Parker. Reprinted by permission of the publisher.

technician, politician, [*and*] consultant . . . who speaks with equal fluency the languages of both computers and human beings."[4] But since it is difficult to find all of these qualities in one person, data base administrators in large organizations generally select a balanced staff of assistants including data specialists with expertise in public relations and liaison work, and personnel qualified as trainers/educators.

Since data base administrators and staff are usually classified as data processing technical personnel, some organizational theorists recommend that they report to a data processing manager. Others argue that the data base administrator should report to a user committee. This gives users the feeling of being "custodians" of the data base.

RESOURCES FOR DATA ADMINISTRATION

Special equipment, such as cryptographic equipment, and special software are used to administer a data base. The terminal in the data base administrator's office may be the only terminal with authority to make changes to the DED/DD system, for example. In security-sensitive systems, the data base administrator's terminal may list all changes to the system that need to be monitored. Some systems will alert the DBA when a user tries many access codes from the same terminal in a short period of time for this may indicate an attempt to break a code. A timely response by the administrator may prevent breach of the system's security.

Software is also needed to generate reports related to use, operation, and monitoring of the data base. A list of reports and programs which support a DED/DD system appears in Table 8.8.

SUMMARY AND CONCLUSIONS

Data directories are extensions to the DED, providing reference information regarding data relationships of data elements defined in the DED. Data element relationships are of interest and importance in the maintenance of data, in designing data collection, and in reports. Each relationship can be expressed in tabular form like an input/output table, with the data element on the X axis, and the Y axis representing whatever organization, transaction, file, or program needs to be defined in terms of data elements. DED/DD software enables generation of printed lists and tables in response to simple commands.

Most comprehensive DED/DD systems contain information about and maintain relationships between entities in the following categories:

Applications program	Physical data base
Data base schema	Report
Data base subschema	Source document

---

[4] C. M. Travers, "Data Base Administrator—the Emerging Position," *Proceedings of the College and University Machine Records Conference* (1973), p. 8.

Data item   Transaction
Data field   User
Data file

   Centralizing all information on data elements in a DED/DD system improves efficiency in monitoring and control of data. All information regarding security and validity of data can be readily accessed, information that is needed by a data base administrator given responsibility for integrity, reliability, and operations of the data base.

TABLE 8.8
**Reports and programs to support the DED/
DD system**

Listings of DED
KWIC/KWOC indexes
Listings of directories
Testing data generator
Data division generator
JCL generator
Implementing hardware and software changes
Data validator
Access controller
Data definition controller
Data structure converter
Data storage assigner
Statistical reports on utilization
Comparison routine
Utility routines
   Logging
   Editing
   Dumping
   Garbage collector

   DED/DD systems can be used by businesses with data bases at any level of sophistication. The most basic use would be a DED as a repository of definitions of data elements. Directories and DED/DD software could be added for more developed bases. Large and complex data systems require a data base management system, the subject of the next chapter.

KEY WORDS

Access directory   Data base administrator
Classword   Data controller
Code file   Data dictionary/directory (DD/D)

Data element dictionary/ data directory system (DED/ DD)	Key word
	Key word in context (KWIC)
	Key word out of context (KWOC)
Data maintenance	Label
Data mapping	Logging
Descriptor	Logical record
Designator	Matrix
Directory	Physical record
Fixed data elements	Transaction matrix
Index	Variable data elements

DISCUSSION QUESTIONS

1. What are problems of security and privacy in a data base system for business firms?

2. What power accrues to the person responsible for the common data base? How can this power be misused? Can misuse be avoided? How?

3. What is the difference between a DED and a DD system?

4. What software is required (if any) to operate the DED, DD, or DED/DD system? Should such software be developed internally in each firm or be purchased from a vendor or software house?

5. List characteristics that are common in software for a:
   a. DED.
   b. DD.
   c. DED/DD system.
   What factors should be considered in selecting such software?

6. What special resources are required by a data base administrator?

7. List users of a:
   a. DED.
   b. DD.
   c. DED/DD.
   Give examples of use of each of these systems.

8. List tables in a data directory that are useful to:
   a. A user-manager.
   b. A programmer.
   c. Programs.
   d. A DBA.

9. How can access to a common data base be controlled? Discuss problems of access control.

10. To whom should the DBA report? Explain your answer.

11. A DBA needs staff assistance to manage a large and complex common data base. If only three staff members were assigned to a DBA, what assignments would you recommend each be given?

EXERCISE

1. Prepare a sheet for a DED for the data element "date of birth." Include in your descriptors the validity rules for each of the subfields for the data element "date of birth." If you feel you do not have sufficient information to do this exercise, then make a reasonable assumption, state it, and justify your assumption. How can this information in the DED be used by a data directory?

SELECTED ANNOTATED BIBLIOGRAPHY

Canning, Richard G.   "The Data Dictionary/Directory Function." *EDP Analyzer,* vol. 12, no. 11 (1974), pp. 1–12.
This article is a very good review of the basic components of a DED/DD system. It discusses examples of DED/DD implementation.

Lyon, John K.   *The Data Base Administrator.* New York: John Wiley & Sons, Inc., 1976, 170 p.
The author discusses the responsibilities of a data base administrator and tools used on the job. This book is written by a practicing computer scientist at Honeywell who has written extensively on the subject of data bases.

Uhrowczki, P. P.   "Data Dictionary/Directories." *IBM Systems Journal,* vol. 12, no. 4 (1973), pp. 332–50.
One of the earliest and still authoritative articles on the subject. It has a good discussion and diagrams on physical organization, logical organization, and reports generated by DED/DD systems. A good appendix on definitions of data base terms is included.

Walsh, Miles E.   "Update on Data Dictionaries," *Journal of Systems Management,* vol. 20, no. 8 (August 1978), pp. 28–39.
This article discusses the concept, implementation and use of data dictionaries and DED/DD systems. It has many samples of dictionary reports.

9

DATA BASE MANAGEMENT SYSTEMS

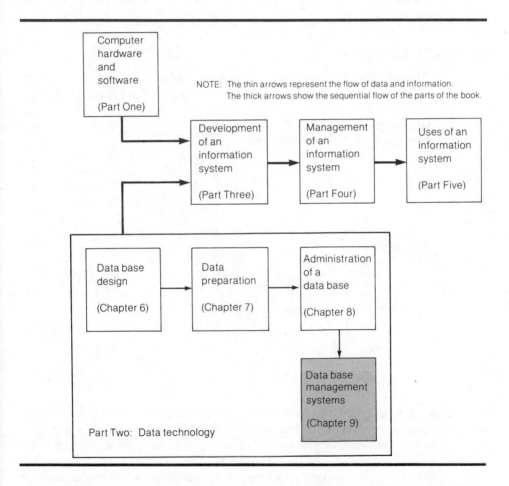

Computer
hardware
and
software

(Part One)

NOTE: The thin arrows represent the flow of data and information.
The thick arrows show the sequential flow of the parts of the book.

Development
of an
information
system

(Part Three)

Management
of an
information
system

(Part Four)

Uses of an
information
system

(Part Five)

Data base
design

(Chapter 6)

Data
preparation

(Chapter 7)

Administration
of a
data base

(Chapter 8)

Data base
management
systems

(Chapter 9)

Part Two: Data technology

Management of large data bases servicing a large number of users is an exceedingly complex task. Fast retrieval by programs using different languages is often needed. Remote access adds to problems of privacy and security of data. Users' programs must be protected, should the data base grow and need restructuring. In order to modify a large data base, the logical and physical organization of data must be known. Software to perform these functions is called a **data base management system (DBMS).**

In this chapter, the evolution of DBMS will be traced. The structure, features, and operation of such systems will be discussed, and both resources and problems of implementation will be examined. The chapter is an extension of Chapter 8, for a DBMS is essentially a way of facilitating the control and access of the data base. The subject matter is somewhat technical, but managers should be knowledgeable about this aspect of data technology to participate effectively in both development and implementation of information systems.

OVERVIEW OF DBMS

The very first computer-based information systems were simple applications using programs with their own sets of data as depicted in Figure 9.1 Though

FIGURE 9.1
Early configuration of data by many users

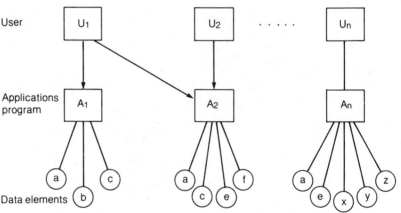

User 1 might have had need of information generated by both application programs A_1 and A_2, the data required by the programs was not integrated. Likewise, applications programs A_1 and A_2, both used some common data elements without any integration. Data elements such as *a* and *c* had to be collected, verified, and stored for more than one program, a wasteful duplication of effort.

The inefficiency of independent processing runs was replaced by integrated applications when common data bases were established. This required the corollary development of input/output routines and basic operating systems to manage the data base and to facilitate data access. The schema in Figure 9.2 shows this revised organization. Users no longer had exclusive control

FIGURE 9.2
Common data base and many users

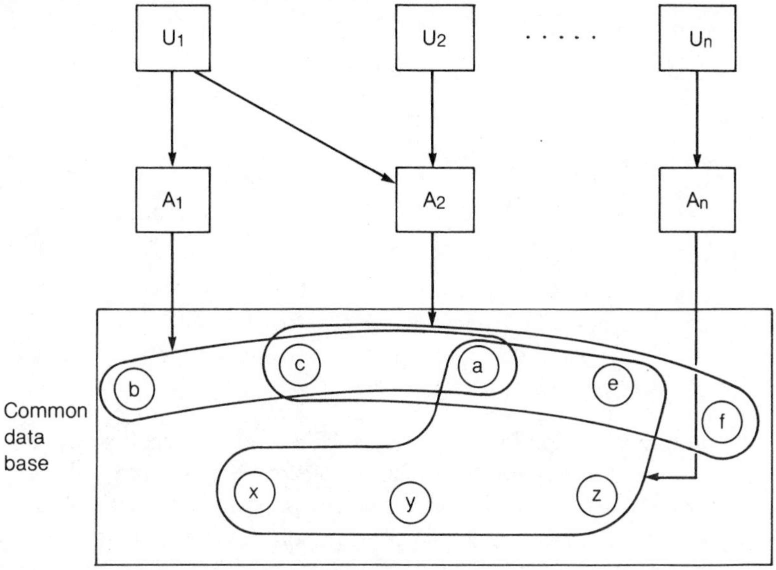

Note: Users and programs are able to access the data elements they need from the common data base.

of data, but integration meant additional systems using the data were feasible that were previously not available.

With the growth of common data bases and an increase in users, operating systems proved inadequate. Software to provide greater integration of data, complex file structures, and online access was in demand. Additional facilities for data base reorganization, data privacy, breakdown recovery, and independence of applications programs were needed. Supplementary software was developed to fulfill these needs, software called a data base management system (DBMS). The relationship of a DBMS to the data base, operating system, and user is shown in Figure 9.3.

Access to large and complex data bases is facilitated in DBMS by a **data manager.** The manager is not a person as the word suggests, but software which describes the logical and physical organization of the data base and enables manipulation of the base by programmers. This software, an interface between the data base and high level languages such as FORTRAN, COBOL, or PL/1 employed by users, comprises a **data description language (DDL)** and a **data manipulation language (DML).** The word "language" in DDL and DML is confusing, for DDL and DML are interface software, not names of programming languages such as FORTRAN. The relationship of DDL and DML to the data base and user is shown in Figure 9.4.

What the figure attempts to show diagramatically is that users may write

FIGURE 9.3
DBMS as an interface

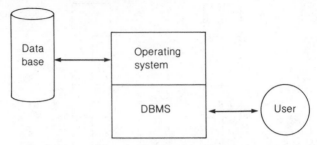

Source: Adapted from R. Clay Sprowls, *Management Data Bases*
(New York: John Wiley & Sons, Inc., 1978), pp. 71–72.

programs in high level languages, DDL and DML converts these instructions
into information that the operating system requires, while the data base manager guides the operating system in retrieving the needed data by keeping
track of the logical and physical organization of all data in the base. (Other
features and functions of a DBMS are described later in this chapter.)

DDL and DML can be embedded as a **guest** in high level languages,
called **host languages.** In this case, the user program would be a mixture
of both the host language and statements of DDL and DML. Some independent languages incorporate DDL and DML capabilities. These are called **self-
contained languages** (GIS, MARK IV, TDMS, and UL1 are examples).
Both host and self-contained languages are used in the batch mode. For
terminal use where rapid answers to questions are needed, a query language
is used which communicates through a teleprocessing monitor attached to
the DBMS.

To date, no standard implementation design for a DBMS has been accepted
by original equipment manufacturers (OEMs) or users. Groups which differ
in approach have been working on the problem. **Data Base Task Group,**
a subcommittee which does research and development for the Committee

FIGURE 9.4
The data base manager, DDL, and DML

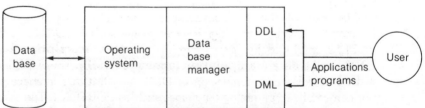

Source: Adapted from R. Clay Sprowls *Management Data Bases* (New York: John Wiley
& Sons, Inc., 1978), pp. 71–72.

on Data Systems Language (CODASYL)[1] composed of volunteer professionals, has concentrated on specifics of design. **GUIDE/SHARE,** a coalition of business and scientific users of IBM equipment, has adopted a more conceptual approach, focusing on determination of requirements based on users' desires. These two groups have both published major sets of reports with proposals for implementation.[2] DDL and DML described in the preceding section of this text belong to the data base management system under development by Data Base Task Group. GUIDE/SHARE proposes DBDL (Data Base Description Language) and DBCL (Data Base Command Language) with equivalent capabilities. The two groups also differ in terminology. Neither has developed a complete and definitive system. For example, Data Base Task Group has identified many areas where software is lacking, such as a device media control language to assist data administrators in assigning storage devices and the need for additional recovery techniques, but has left these areas to the realm of individual implementors.

It will take time for a common stand and a single DBMS implementation design to emerge. This is to be expected though the evolution of DBMS has proceeded at a slower pace than many other developments, such as that of COBOL. (A comparison of DBMS with COBOL is shown in Table 9.1) Since the work of all parties engaged in DBMS research cannot be covered in a single chapter, the sections which follow will concentrate on DBMS design features developed by Data Base Task Group, a group known in the field by its acronym, DBTG.

OPERATIONS OF A DBMS

The operation of a DBMS is shown in Figure 9.5. Each step is identified by a numbered arrow and takes place in the sequence shown.

1. User program 1 (UP 1) issues a request for the retrieval (or storage) of data using a DML (Data Manipulation Language).
2. The DBMS analyzes the request and extracts structural information regarding the part of the data base involved in the request from a stored **data-structure-diagram** specified by means of a DDL.
3. Based upon request and structure information, the DBMS will call on the operating system to perform one or more read or write operations.
4. The operating system establishes contact with the data base.
5. The operating system may transfer data requested between primary and secondary storage, using one or more data buffers. (A **buffer** is a temporary storage device.)

---

[1] CODASYL develops proposals for improving COBOL for ANSI, (American National Standards Institute), which is responsible for standard COBOL.

[2] GUIDE/SHARE Data Base Requirements Group, "Data Base Management Systems Requirements" (New York: SHARE, November 1970), and *CODASYL Data Base Task Group Report* (New York: Association for Computing Machinery, April 1971).

TABLE 9.1
Evolution of COBOL and DBMS

COBOL

Year	Compared to starting year	Event
1959	$t^* + 0$	Trying to understand problem
1960	$t + 1$	Published report
1961	$t + 2$	Several implementations
1963	$t + 4$	Publications—many implementations
1965	$t + 6$	Activity to initiate a standard begins
1967	$t + 8$	Draft standard
1968	$t + 9$	USA Standard COBOL X3.23
1979	$t + 20$	Revised Standard

DBMS

Year	Compared to starting year	Event
1965	$t + 0$	Trying to understand problem
1971	$t + 6$	Published DBTG report
1973	$t + 8$	Few implementations at this level
1974	$t + 9$	Activity to initiate a standard begins
?	?	Draft standard
?	?	Standards
?	?	

* $t =$ starting year.

6. The DBMS will transfer data between data buffers and a particular **user work area** (memory space for user).
7. The DBMS will also transfer various status information on the operation performed. This information is available to the user in some **system communication locations** in the user program.
8. Data will be available for further processing in the user work area.
9. The DBMS will control all data buffers, which are common to all programs interrogating the data base. It will also provide the answers and results requested.

FIGURE 9.5
Conceptual DBMS

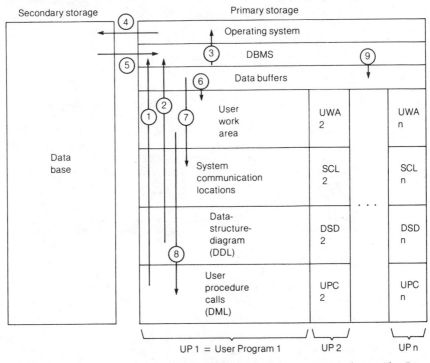

Source: This diagram and the text description is adapted from Sven Eriksen, "The Data Base,": *Honeywell Computer Journal,* (1971), p. 16; and Harry Katzan, Jr., *Computer Data Management and Data Base Technology* (N.Y.: Van Nostrand Reinhold Co., 1975), p. 210.

In essence, the Data Base Task Group has designed a structure to facilitate the association and retrieval of data. The hierarchy of data has been redefined and new levels added. Many terms such as *file management* (the mapping of logical files to physical storage space), a capability encompassed in the DBMS, have definitions that are widely accepted by others (see Table 9.2 for sample definitions), but other terms with multiple meanings in the field have specialized definitions. For example, the term *data management* means an administrative position in government, comprehensive data packages to software manufacturers, access methods to vendors, and DBMS to others.

ARCHITECTURE

One set of definitions in the DBTG report concerns architecture. Applications programmers generally need not view the entire data base, the **schema,** but only a logical subset of the base, a **subschema.** Many applications may invoke the same subschema, subschemas may overlap, or they may even

TABLE 9.2
Some definitions from the DBTG (CODASYL)

An *Area* is a named subdivision of the addressable storage space in the data base and may contain occurrences of records and sets or parts of sets of various types.

A *Data-item* is the smallest unit of named data. An occurrence of a data item is a representation of a value.

A *Data aggregate* is a named collection of data-items within a record.

A *Record* is a named collection of zero, one, or more data-items or data aggregates.

A *Set* is a named collection of record types. As such, it establishes the characteristics of an arbitrary number of occurences of the named set. Each set type specified in the schema must have one record type declared as its OWNER and one or more record types declared as its MEMBER records. Each occurrence of a set must contain an arbitrary number of occurrences of each of its member record types.

Source: "CODASYL Data Description Language," *NBS Handbook* (Washington, D.C.: Government Printing Office, January 1974). This source stresses the evolutionary nature of these specifications.

encompass the entire data base. Programmers that deal with a subschema have a **local view** of the data base, not a **global view.** Both local and global views consist of DDL entries that define parts of the data base required. The one-step separation of application from schema allows for logical and physical data independence. That is, changes can be made to the schema of the data base or to the physical structure and representation of the data without affecting applications, due to the DDL interface. This is of great importance because hardware changes and data modifications occur constantly and they are now insulated from the applications user. Remote terminal users may invoke the global schema or a local subschema by use of a **query language.** Two additional levels of DBMS architecture are defined: the **storage schema** and the **device level.** These latter levels concern the physical representation of data. Figure 9.6 is a graphic representation of the levels of DBMS architecture.

Data relationships are expressed by models in the DBTG's design of a DBMS. To explain model details fully would require a textbook on data structures. Briefly, there are three main data models: **hierarchical, relational,** and **network.**[3] Each model is evaluated by the user for its degree of data independence, for the danger of creating anomalies, for performance, and other criteria of relevance to use in determining which model is appropriate for each application.

A data model not only represents the schema but also subschemas. This is shown in Figure 9.7, where three applications (manufacturing, financial,

---
[3] For a survey and comparison of data models see *ACM Computing Surveys,* vol. 8, no. 1 (March 1976).

FIGURE 9.6
Levels of DBMS architecture

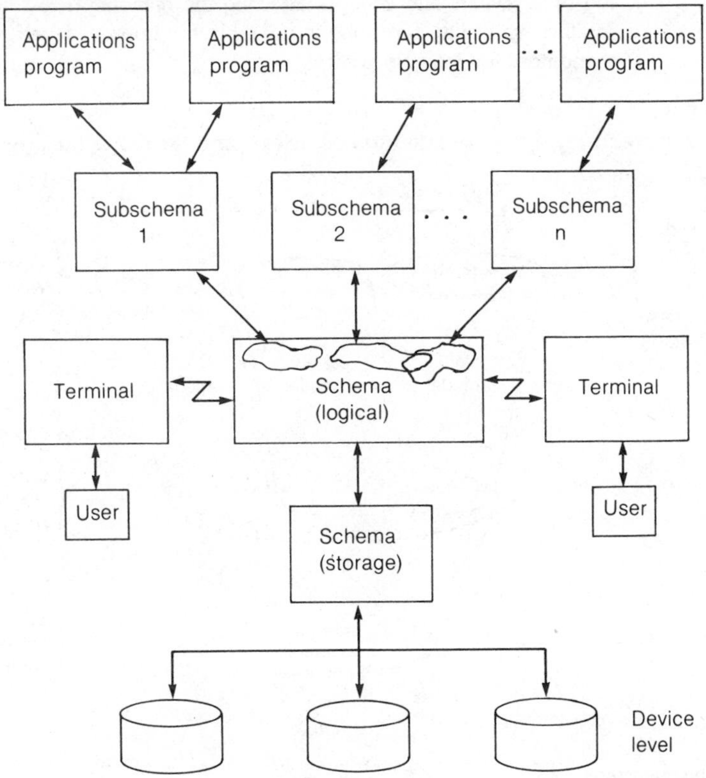

Source: S. M. Dean, *Fundamentals of Data Base Systems* (Rochelle Park, N.J.: Hayden Book Co., Inc., 1977), p. 51.

and personnel) illustrate model use. The users and language facilities at each level are also identified.

FEATURES AND FUNCTIONS OF DBMS

Two important features of the DBTG design for a DBMS have already been mentioned in this chapter: data independence and data models. Other features and a list of DBMS functions appear in Table 9.3. The data manager, which performs many of the support functions listed in the table, has been well described by Everest.

> The database manager is the single, controlling door through which all access to the database is accomplished. It is the run-time module providing data services for programs while they are in execution; it is the module which responds to all requests to access and manipulate data in the database; it is the security

guard which intercepts and checks all such requests for proper authorization as well as syntactic and semantic legality; and it is the auditor who keeps a log of all events and changes affecting the database. Providing a single door for the availability functions is desirable for improved performance, but it is mandatory for integrity control.[4]

FIGURE 9.7
DBMS architecture, showing data models, users, and language facilities

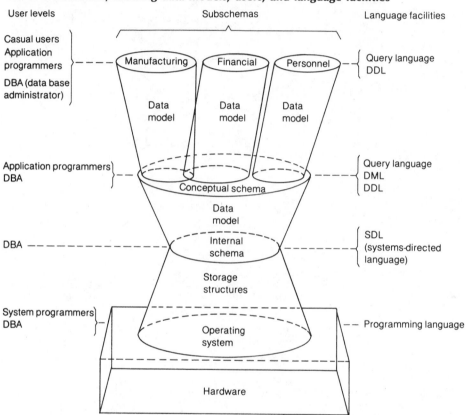

Source: Adapted from D. C. Tsichritzis and I. H. Lechovsky, *Data Base Management System* (New York: Academic Press, Inc., 1977), p. 97.

DATA BASE ADMINISTRATOR

Although a **data base administrator** has many duties (see Chapter 8), administering the DBMS is a major responsibility. For a large DBMS, a staff will be required, since no one individual can perform all the necessary activities. The duties of a DBA and staff in a DBMS environment are listed

---

[4] Gordon C. Everest, "Data Base Systems Tutorial," *Readings in Management Information Systems* (New York: McGraw-Hill Book Co., 1976), p. 170.

TABLE 9.3
Features and functions of DBMS

Data creation and structure
Data definition, creation, and revision
Data models
Data independence

Support
Access control
Security
Auditing
Integrity control
Performance monitoring
Usage monitoring
Data base administrator

Retrieval
Interrogation
User facilities

in Table 9.4. Most of the activities are self-explanatory but a few comments about integrity and backup will be helpful.

Integrity of data is a broad concept. Data must be accurate, complete, and continuous, which means that it must be protected from failure of the system. This integrity can be achieved by control over validation criteria and parameters, control over updating, and procedures for **backup** and recovery, should data be lost due to midstream termination of transactions. Some systems make periodic backup copies of the data base and restart from the backup point in the event of failure. A DBA must study the vulnerability of

TABLE 9.4
Duties of DBA and staff in a DBMS environment

Design and administration
Define schemas and subschemas
Select and maintain data model
Select and maintain DBMS software

Administration
Liaison with users
Training and assistance of users

Operation
Formulate and enforce procedures for security and privacy
Initiate and enforce procedures for recovery and integrity
Define, create, update, and retire data

Monitoring
Measure and monitor performance of DBMS resources
Log and monitor usage of DBMS resources
Schedule usage
Monitor security threats

FIGURE 9.8
Areas of DBA responsibility in a DBMS environment

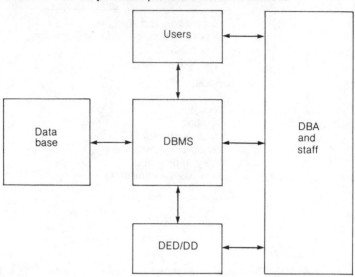

the data and make a cost-benefit analysis of possible recovery procedures and then initiate and enforce procedures to protect the data base.

Figure 9.8 is a representation of a DBA's responsibilities in a DBMS environment.

RETRIEVAL

DBMS retrieval may be in the batch mode or online responses to queries. The language in which queries are made will depend on the type of query and the class of user demanding information. The query itself may be one of several types. These are discussed below.

Types of queries

A **projection query** is a request for a whole set of data elements. For example: List the names of all sales representatives. A query might also be for a listing of values for a data element that have one attribute in common. This is called **mapping.** An example of this type of query would be: What are the names of all sales representatives in California? Or, what are the names of all sales representatives who sold more than 100 percent of their quotas?

Boolean operators like OR/AND/NOT can be added to the listing request. A **Boolean query** might be: List sales representatives in California who did not sell more than 100 percent of their quotas.

A user may require retrieval of information on a whole set of related data elements. This is called a **selective query.** An example would be: Give the record of sales representative John Dole.

Values of given **functions** can also be queried. For example: Print the sum of sales made. Software for deriving frequently used functions (MAXIMUM, MINIMUM, AVERAGE, RANGE, and SUM, for example) are available on call by programs.

Combination queries actually involve two outputs, one being input for the other. For example: Find the sales representatives who sold more than 100 percent of their quotas and print the names of their sales territories.

There are other types of queries that require some mathematical sophistication. For example, an understanding of predicate calculus, and knowledge of programming and the data base. These technical queries are used less frequently by management and will not be discussed.

Query languages

The characteristics and requirements of languages suitable for queries of a DBMS have been the subject of much research.[5] Managers with programming expertise may use host or self-contained languages for information retrieval but nonprogrammers, dependent on intermediaries to translate their requests into machine language, have urged development of computer-directed languages or natural language software. Research has shown that artificial query languages such as SEQUEL may actually be more effective than natural languages for retrieval purposes. For example, Schneidermann, one researcher in the field, has found that artificial languages structure queries so that users are far less likely to pose unanswerable questions than when using natural languages. His conclusions are worth quoting.

> These results should not be interpreted as a condemnation of natural language usage, but as an aid in determining which applications are suitable for natural language front ends and what training users should be given. User knowledge of the applications domain seems to be critical: without this prerequisite, natural language usage would be extremely difficult. Secondly, user knowledge of the structure of the data in the computer and what each item means appears to be vital. Finally, experience in asking questions against a specific database is probably helpful. Thus the ideal candidate for natural language usage may be the experienced frequent users of a manual information system, but these users are likely to appreciate the simplicity, brevity, and precision of a structured query language. The casual user with little knowledge of the application area, understanding of the data structure, and experience in posing queries may find natural language facilities more confusing. Realistic applications for natural language would be situations where people have familiarity with the application

---

[5] For a survey of query language research, see J. C. Thomas, "Psychological Issues in Database Management," *Proceedings Third International Conference of Very Large Data Bases* (New York: Institute of Electrical and Electronic Engineers, Inc., 1977), pp. 169–85.

area, data structure, and queries, but are infrequent users. Typical situations that fit this description include library card catalogs, airline schedules, or banking transactions. More research is necessary to support these hypotheses.[6]

In retrieving information, questions must be framed in the same form as data is stored in the data base. This is true regardless of the query language used. For example, the answer to the question, "Who was hired before 1980?" would require that values for the data element "year of hire" be stored in the data base. If the question were rephrased as "Who has served more than 10 years?" the system would be unable to answer. Thus the structure of the data base does affect the validity of queries.

Classes of users

No single query language is appropriate for all users of a large information system, for users vary in background, mathematical knowledge, and programming skills. Data processing professionals concerned with efficiency in processing generally employ host or self-contained languages. The type of information requested requires mathematical knowledge and familiarity with the data base. Skilled, frequent users are generally less concerned with machine efficiency than with minimizing time spent programming. These users frame Boolean or combination-type queries using computer-directed languages. Clerks and other users at the operational level with little or no knowledge of programming are dependent on the computer-directed mode for listings, built-in functions, selection, and projection-type queries. Casual users are the most difficult group to please. These users are generally intimidated by computers, preferring that human intermediaries retrieve information on their behalf. If they must query the system directly, they favor natural languages or natural-like languages. This class of user needs help framing requests in terms understood by the system, help that the prompting of the dialogue mode can provide. Of the four groups of users mentioned, this group is potentially the largest.

COSTS AND BENEFITS OF A DBMS

Personnel is one high cost component in a DBMS. Another is hardware, especially for storage, although the unit cost of storage is dropping significantly. Yet 500,000 characters of main memory for a DBMS are not unusual, and three times more extra disk memory is required for a DBMS than for an information system without a DBMS. Hardware for this much storage represents a considerable investment. And DBMS requires a larger CPU. Another expensive component is DBMS software which ranged between $30,000–160,000 per system in 1978. In addition, DBMS processing is costly.

---

[6] Ben Schneidermann, "Improving the Human Factors Aspect of Database Interactions," *ACM Transactions on Data Base Systems,* vol. 3, no. 4 (December 1978), p. 437. Copyright 1978 Association for Computing Machinery, Inc.; reprinted by permission.

A study at Ford Motor Co. showed that 70 percent of instructions executed involved DBMS overhead.[7]

All of the costs of a DBMS can be reliably measured. It is well established that EDP budgets increase significantly with implementation of data base technology. Figure 9.9 illustrates the upward shift in cost during the stages of EDP evolution. This figure is based on a hypothesis of Nolan regarding growth stages of information systems.[8] Note that EDP expenses rise sharply

FIGURE 9.9
Costs and stages of EDP evolution

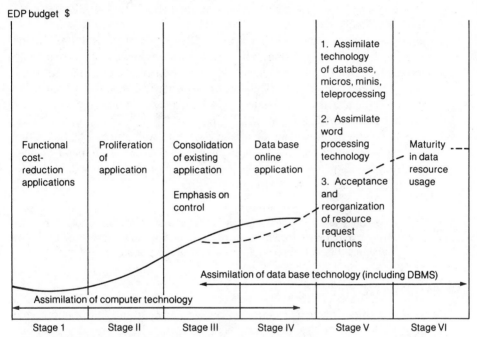

Source: Adapted from Richard L. Nolan, "Thoughts about the Fifth Stage," *Data Base,* vol. 7, no. 2 (Fall, 1975), pp. 6 and 9.

at the end of Stage II and during part of Stage III. The proliferation of applications at this stage means maintenance becomes cumbersome, and development starts getting out of control. New applications become less attractive without a change in technology. At a point in Stage III, organizations initiate a DBMS, adding to the system through Stages III and IV. Costs continue to rise significantly through Stage V, leveling off at the mature Stage VI.

---

[7] Richard G. Cannery, ed., "Planning for DBMS Conversions," *EDP Analyzer,* vol. 16, no. 5 (May 1978) p. 3.

[8] Richard L. Nolan, "Thoughts about the Fifth Stage," *Data Base,* vol. 7, no. 2 (Fall, 1975), pp. 4–10. This subject is discussed again in Chapter 21.

The question should now be asked: Do benefits of a DBMS warrant such expenditure?

A representative company with a medium-scale computer and a budget of approximately $750,000 annually was analyzed by McFadden and Suvey in 1978. The firm's initial DBMS cost was calculated as $525,000: the 5-year total cost of DBMS as $1,080,000. Cumulative benefits during this period were estimated at $3,289,250.[9] The benefits were calculated from increased sales, savings in production, improvement in performance, and the reduction of operating costs. A firm with less diverse activities would benefit less from a DBMS. Companies with few users, where shared information and data independence were not major concerns, might well find a DBMS system uneconomical.[10]

However, intangible benefits from a DBMS should also be taken into account. Improved discipline that results from company efforts to organize and support DBMS is hard to measure. Integration of data and online retrieval, two additional benefits of a DBMS, are also hard to quantify. We also lack the tools to give a dollar value to improved availability, accessibility, and timeliness of information.

It has certainly been demonstrated that a DBMS raises EDP to a high level of sophistication, a level that justifies the expense in many business applications. Data base technology may even prove to have far reaching effects on society. James Martin predicts that:

> In centuries hence, historians will look back to the coming of computer data banks and their associated facilities as a step which changed the nature of the evolution of society, perhaps eventually having a greater effect on the human condition than even the invention of the printing press.[11]

IMPLEMENTATION

Management must first define its decision system and information needs in operational terms so that these needs can be adequately addressed by a DBMS. Then installation of the DBMS can take place. Overcoming organizational resistance to the new system and promoting dialogue and cooperation between technicians and users are two areas of implementation that test managerial skill. As E. Sibley, chairman of CODASYL, has stated, "There are hardly any technical problems involved with installing a DBMS, only people problems and managerial problems."[12] The subject of human resistance to

---

[9] Fred R. McFadden and James R. Suvey, "Costs and Benefits of a Database System," *Harvard Business Review*, vol. 56, no. 1 (1978), p. 138.

[10] For a good discussion on not using a DBMS, see George Schlussel, "When Not to Use a Data Base," *Datamation*, vol. 21, no. 11 (November 1975), pp. 82, 91, 98.

[11] James Martin, *Computer Data-Base Organization* (Englewood Cliffs, N.J.: Prentice-Hall, Inc., 1977), p. 2.

[12] From a paper presented at the 1977 IFIP Congress and quoted in *EDP Analyzer*, vol. 16, no. 5 (May 1978), p. 3.

computer technology in general is a subject discussed in detail in Chapter 17.

Finding technical personnel to run the system poses additional difficulties, since the supply of experienced data base technicians has not kept pace with the demand. DBAs, analysts, and systems programmers are all scarce commodities. Training technicians in-house is both time-consuming and costly. It takes 4–8 months for a programmer to learn to use a DBMS, and 6–9 months to turn an analyst into a DBA.

When to implement

The decision to implement a DBMS should be based on a benefit/cost analysis. The need for a DBMS is generally indicated when a firm needs at least three of the following:[13]

1. An integrated data environment.
2. Rapid retrieval of data from large files.
3. A query/update language for use at terminals.
4. Sophisticated backup and recover procedures.
5. Elaborate privacy/security protection.
6. Handling of complex data structures.

Preparing for implementation

Once a decision is made to implement a DBMS, management should take steps to ensure success of the new system. These include:

1. Authorizing a central authority with total control over data definitions and all DBMS-related activities.
2. Identifying organizational and transitional problems on which management should focus to minimize company disruption and resistance to the new system.
3. Establishing auditing standards and auditing independence.
4. Instituting DBMS training for users and all levels of management.
5. Anticipating privacy and security issues and establishing policies and procedures for control.

GROWTH OF DBMS

The use of data base management systems is steadily on the rise. The first system was introduced at General Electric in 1961. By 1970, there were 100 users of DBMS; by 1975, 300, or roughly 10 percent of data processing organizations.[14] Some experts have predicted that by the early 80s, 75 percent of data processing organizations will be DBMS users.

---

[13] Adapted from John L. Berg, ed., "Data Base Directions," *Data Base,* vol. 8, no. 2 (Fall 1976), p. 15.

[14] Schlussel, "When Not to Use a Data Base," p. 83.

This use increase can be explained in part by the decreasing cost of minis and the growing availability of DBMS software for minis.[15] Both factors make a DBMS attractive to small businesses.[16] Not all minis, however, run large data base management systems efficiently due to their small word size and their small range of instructions. Some of the sophisticated features of data handling must therefore be sacrificed. But since small businesses do not always have large data files, the reduced capabilities (for example, restricted query capabilities and less data independence) do not adversely affect operations. Many of the stripped features were perhaps not applicable to a small business environment in the first place.

The availability of DBMS software for small organizations does not permit firms to skip the agonizing early stages of EDP evolution depicted in Nolan's growth hypothesis (Figure 9.9).[17] Experience has shown that firms trying to leapfrog directly into Nolan's third or fourth stage lack the proficiency to implement the requisite technology. The organizational and technical experience of coherent systems planning that is gained in Stages I and II is needed to absorb the "upheaval factor" of a DBMS and to control the new system.

However, advances in data base technology may make leapfrogging a possibility in the future. Computer equipment with operating systems integrated with DBMS are being planned; and special separate CPUs to control access to the data base are envisioned. Such equipment would let firms leap to Stages III or IV without experiencing previous growth phases. Also projected is a computer specially designed for a DBMS, a **data base machine,**[18] that would have optimum performance and data security designed in its architecture.

Distributed data bases and distributed DBMSs can be expected in the future.[19] (These subjects will be discussed in Chapter 18.) Deciding what data to distribute and what data to keep centralized will pose new problems for management as will control of distributed data bases. There is also hope that the near future will see the development of more models, additional generalized languages for DBMS such as EUFTG (End user facilities) and DBAWG (Management tools for DBA), standards for data technology, and DBMS oriented toward the casual user.

---

[15] J. Aaron Zornes, Jr., "Data Base Management Systems on Minicomputers," *Data Base,* vol. 9, no. 1 (Summer, 1977), pp. 9–13.

[16] Izak Benbasat and Robert C. Goldstein, "Data Base Systems for Small Business: Miracle or Mirage?" *Data Base,* vol. 9, no. 1 (Summer 1977), pp. 5–8.

[17] For a more recent view on the stage hypothesis, see R. L. Nolan, "Managing the Crises in Data Processing," *Harvard Business Review,* vol. 57, no. 2 (March–April 1979), pp. 115–126.

[18] For an excellent survey of this subject, see Eugene I. Lowenthal, "A Survey—the Application of Data Base Management Computers in Distributed Systems," *1977 International Conference on Very Large Data Bases* (New York: Institute of Electrical and Electronic Engineers, 1977), pp. 85–92.

[19] James B. Rothnie and Nathan Godman, "A Survey of Research in Distributed Data Management," *1977 International Conference on Very Large Data Bases* (New York: Institute of Electrical and Electronic Engineers, 1977), pp. 48–62.

SUMMARY AND CONCLUSIONS

Interface between a large and complex data base and the user can be provided by a DBMS. This interface necessitates hardware, software, and personnel resources. Hardware requirements include more storage and processing capability by the CPU and terminals than is needed for non-DBMS information systems. The software consists of a data base manager, an extension of the operating system, and both DDL and DML to provide data independence, user access to the base, and a vehicle for schema and subschema description.

A DBMS is used to request listings or responses to Boolean queries, projection queries, selective queries, built-in functions, or combination queries. Users with programming knowledge may employ high level languages like COBOL, FORTRAN, or PL/1, which host DDL and DML, or self-contained languages for retrieval. The nonprogrammer can retrieve information through a human intermediary (expensive in personnel cost), or may use a natural language (expensive in CPU time and not very effective) or a computer-directed language. Casual users favor natural languages. Clarification dialogues to help frame requests in terms understood by the computer are helpful when casual users query the system.

A data base administrator supervises the hardware, software, and personnel of a DBMS. A staff of assistants may be required if the system is large. The duties of a DBA include control of the DED/DD system and formulating definitions for schemas and subschemas. Monitoring security, privacy, integrity, operations, and user liaison are other areas of DBA responsibility. The job requires authority over all data definitions and all DBMS activities.

The cost of a DBMS includes the acquisition of hardware, specialized software, and technical personnel, the latter often proving the most expensive and scarce resource of all. Some of the benefits of a DBMS are largely intangible: data independence, fast retrieval, and better integration of data. Factors such as the amount of shared data and the diversity of functions are more important than the size of the data base when assessing the need for a DBMS.

The availability of DBMS software for inexpensive minicomputers has recently made DBMS feasible for small businesses. The main constraint is that small businesses often lack the organization and technical expertise with EDP to successfully implement a data base management system.

Though use of DBMS is on the rise, many firms are hesitant to make the large capital and organizational commitment required. They prefer to await the emergence of DBMS standards, the abatement of debate on data models, and the production of data base machines. At the present time, much research is being conducted on DBMS topics,[20] including research on query languages, graphic interfaces, data base definitions, data base restructur-

---

[20] For a report on ongoing research with 415 references, see C. Mohan, "An Overview of Recent Data Base Research," *Data Base,* vol. 10, no. 2 (Fall, 1978), pp. 1–24.

ing, data and applications migration, and distributed data bases. Results should be forthcoming in the next few years. The 1980s will undoubtedly see widespread and profitable use of DBMS in business and industry.

Figure 9.10 is a summary diagram of activities related to the data base, activities discussed in the preceding chapters of Part Two. This diagram shows both the sequence of activities in establishing a common data base and the supplementary software and personnel needed to administer the base. Information systems, the development of which are described in Part Three, are based on data technology.

FIGURE 9.10
Activities related to a data base

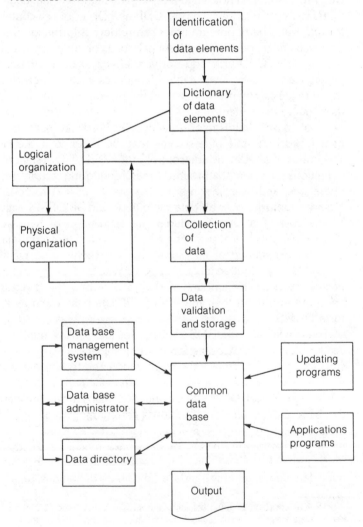

KEY WORDS

Backup
Boolean query
Buffer
Classes of uses
Combination query
Data Base Administrator (DBA)
Data base machine
Data Base Management System
  (DBMS)
Data Base Task Group (DBTG)
Data description language
  (DDL)
Data manager
Data manipulation language
  (DML)
Data-structure-diagram
Device level
Function
Global view
Guest language

GUIDE/SHARE
Hierarchical model
Host language
Integrity
Local view
Mapping
Network model
Nolan's growth curves
Projection query
Query language
Relational model
Schema
Selective query
Self-contained language
Storage schema
Subschema
System communication
  location (SCL)
User work area (UWA)

DISCUSSION QUESTIONS

1. What is the difference between the users' view of the data base and the programmers' view of the data base?
2. What is the difference between a schema and a subschema?
3. What is the difference between the logical and the storage schema in a data model? Identify the user and the language facility for each.
4. What is the role of the DBA in relation to a DBMS?
5. What are the main components of a DBMS?
6. Under what conditions in a business is a DBMS justifiable?
7. What are the managerial implications of a DBMS?
8. What is the role of a DBMS in a EDP system?
9. List the advantages and limitations of a DBMS seen from the viewpoint of a:
   a. User of output.
   b. DBA.
   c. Programmer.
   d. Data clerk.
10. What is the role of the DBTG and GUIDE/SHARE in the development and standardization of a DBMS? Have they helped or hindered toward standardization or have they just added to the confusion surrounding the DBMS?
11. What is the role of a data model in a DBMS? Why are there so many different models? Does it add to flexibility and choice for the user, or merely add to the uncertainty and confusion surrounding the DBMS?

12. List types of query languages you would use for each of the following situations:
    a. Clerk preparing and retrieving data.
    b. Manager requiring output.
    c. Client retrieving relevant information.
    d. Programmer accessing data base.
    e. Engineer using data base.

13. Is it desirable to have a natural language to access the data base? Why? What are the limitations?

14. How does the role of a DBA differ with and without a DBMS?

15. Explain the three main disadvantages or limitations of a DBMS.

EXERCISE

1. Draw a diagram showing the interrelationship of the following:
    a. Data manager.
    b. Data base.
    c. DDL.
    d. User.
    e. Query language.
    f. High level language.

SELECTED ANNOTATED BIBLIOGRAPHY

ACM Computing Surveys, vol 8, no. 1 (March 1976).

This is a special issue on data base management systems. It has an introductory survey of the evolution of DBMS followed by detailed discussions on three data models: relational, CODASYL, and hierarchical. A final article is a comparison of the relational and CODASYL data models.

The articles are by experts in the field and written for the nontechnical person. Highly recommended reading.

Everest, Gordon C. "Database Management Systems—A Tutorial. In *Readings in Management Information Systems,* edited by G. B. Davis and G. C. Everest. New York: McGraw-Hill Book Co., 1976.

An excellent tutorial written by a member of the CODASYL Systems Committee which authored the *Feature Analysis of Generalized Data Base Management Systems.* Discusses the concepts and functions of a DBMS.

Martin, James. *Computer Data-Base Organization.* 2d ed. Englewood Cliffs, N.J.: Prentice-Hall, Inc., 1977.

A well-organized textbook on both physical and logical data structures and DBMS. The tracing through problems using different colors makes it easy to follow. It places technical material in boxes as supplementary reading without breaking the continuity of the text.

Palmer, Ian. *Data Base Systems: A Practical Reference.* Wellesley, Mass: Q.E.D. Information Sciences Inc., 1975.

A detailed discussion of functions, facilities, software, and installation of DBMS. Also an excellent appendix on DBMS systems.

"Planning for DBMS Conversions." *EDP Analyzer,* vol. 16, no. 5 (May 1978), pp. 1–13.
Discusses case studies and "war-stories" on DBMS conversions. Outlines steps for implementing a DBMS.

Schlussel, George. "When Not to Use a Data Base," *Datamation*®, vol. 21, no. 11 (November 1975), pp. 82, 91, and 98.
A short article cautioning users against joining the bandwagon of DBMS.

Sprowls, R. Clay. *Management Data Bases.* Santa Barbara, Calif.: John Wiley & Sons, Inc., 1976.
A text structured around the implementation of a DBMS for a sales application. Also includes a discussion of DMS-100, ADABAS, SYSTEM 2000, DL/1, IDMS, and TOTAL.

PART THREE

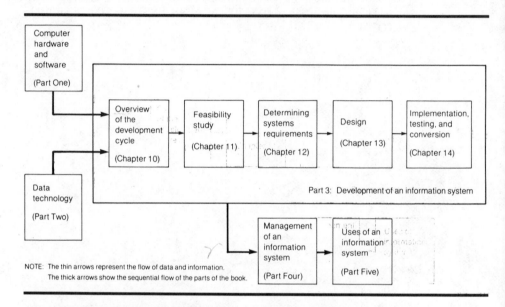

Computer
hardware
and
software

(Part One)

Overview
of the
development
cycle

(Chapter 10)

Feasibility
study

(Chapter 11)

Determining
systems
requirements

(Chapter 12)

Design

(Chapter 13)

Implementation,
testing, and
conversion

(Chapter 14)

Data
technology

(Part Two)

Part 3: Development of an information system

Management
of an
information
system

(Part Four)

Uses of an
information
system

(Part Five)

NOTE: The thin arrows represent the flow of data and information.
The thick arrows show the sequential flow of the parts of the book.

DEVELOPMENT OF AN
INFORMATION SYSTEM

Parts One and Two discussed hardware, software, and data: all being components of an information system. This section, Part Three, tells how to mobilize these components to provide the informational needs of a business organization.

System development takes careful planning. First, the output needed for decision making must be ascertained. Then a feasibility study needs to be conducted to determine whether or not a system can be designed to produce the desired output, given the firm's objectives and constraints. Systems specifications must next be defined in operational terms. Computer programs need to be written, forms for collecting data designed, and operational procedures established. Once the system is tested and the results are satisfactory, conversion must take place. This entire process is called the **development of an information system.** It is this development that is the subject of Part Three. A schematic view of the chapters in this section is shown in diagram form.

Chapter 10 introduces the reader to information system development, providing a general overview of all developmental activities. Subsequent chapters in Part Three discuss these activities in detail. The feasibility study is the subject of Chapter 11, Chapter 12 discusses determination of systems requirements, Chapter 13 design, and the final chapter, Chapter 14, deals with implementation, testing, and conversion.

10

DEVELOPMENT CYCLE OF AN INFORMATION SYSTEM

A computing time of a few seconds is all that is required for many reports produced by information systems. But to generate these same reports may take months or years of development. This is because the planning, design, and implementation of every computer output requires a set of activities that must be performed in a predetermined sequence.

The cycle of development of an information system is the subject of this chapter. Each main activity will be introduced and those activities for which the manager in a business has prime responsibility will be identified. This chapter presents an overview of developmental activities. Subsequent chapters will discuss the activities in detail.

THE DEVELOPMENT PROCESS

The main activities of development of an information system are shown in Figure 10.1. Although this figure does not show the recycling process (an integral part of developing an information system) the figure is useful as a frame of reference in the discussion that follows.

Feasibility study (Activity 15–20)

Once a decision to add a new system is made, the next stage in a systems development is a **feasibility study.** The study will determine whether the problem can be solved by traditional manual methods or whether a computerized information system is necessary. If the latter, different approaches to a solution are formulated and the organizational environment is checked for constraints. Many alternatives are eliminated at this point as unfeasible. For each approach that is feasible within the given constraints, the costs and benefits are identified and evaluated. Then the best alternative in the judgment of the manager is selected for implementation.

Overall systems planning (Activity 20–30)

After the feasibility study, the proposed new system should be evaluated in the context of the firm's overall operating system. Will the proposed system

FIGURE 10.1
Development of an information system

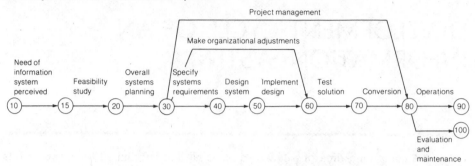

produce redundancy or overlap with ongoing systems? Do the desired objectives of the new proposed system satisfy corporate goals? Will the new system contribute to orderly growth? Meet long-range planning objectives? What adjustments or changes need to be made?

Specifying the systems requirements (Activity 30–40)

Following the decision to implement a solution, the problem needs to be defined more precisely than it was in the feasibility study. At this stage the objectives, policies, and constraints of the user must also be stated completely and in operational terms. These statements and the detailed job specification constitute the **systems requirement statement.**

Design (Activity 40–50) and implementation (Activity 50–60) of the system

The systems requirement statement is the basis of a blueprint developed by a systems analyst detailing the following: **data base, physical preparation, procedures,** and **program solutions.** The design and subsequent implementation of each of these four areas can sometimes be done in parallel. The complete system is an assembly of all four implemented parts of the blueprint.

DATA BASE

The contents of the **data base** must be determined after a careful analysis of the output needs and must be responsive to the changing environment and needs of the user. Too much data leads to inefficiency in storage and processing; too little will lead to ineffectiveness because the desired output will not be available. The data must be organized and stored so that it can be readily retrieved and used as a shared resource by many managers. This sharing across division and department lines complicates data base design specifications because not all users will have the same needs for reliability, validity, integrity, and security of data.

PHYSICAL PREPARATION

The **physical preparation** for a system is primarily the selection and installation of equipment (that is, computer equipment and peripherals). This usually involves technical choices made by specialists and consultants, but the final decision on equipment procurement must be made by the manager since this requires a large commitment of funds (one-time and recurring costs) and the allocation of space.

PROCEDURES

A **procedure** states how, why, and when a function is to be performed. Procedures for the information system need to be designed, implemented, and tested. The manager who is responsible for procedures when the system is fully operational should participate in this developmental activity.

PROGRAMS

Programs are computer instructions prepared by professional programmers. However, managers, with the aid of analysts, must specify what the programs should achieve and must define the decision rules necessary in reaching the solution. This requires on the part of management some knowledge of program capabilities and limitations.

Organizational adjustments (Activity 30–60)

The implementation of an information system requires **organizational adjustments.** These might encompass transferring, adding, retraining, or firing personnel. Such changes may result in a broadened (or narrowed) span of control for managers and alterations in the organization chart of the business. This activity, involving user personnel, need not wait until the technical design and implementation of the system is completed. It can and should be done in parallel with Activities 30–40, 40–50, and 50–60. This helps reduce the overall time needed to prepare the system for testing.

Testing the solution (Activity 60–70)

Once the solution is programmed, procedures prepared, physical preparation completed, and organizational changes implemented, the system is ready for **testing.** There are many approaches to testing. The new system may be tested while the old is still operational, or it may be tested by a pilot system on a small scale. Testing may also be done in progressively comprehensive stages. Another testing approach would be the use of statistical sampling; testing of sample data from which inferences can be made about the whole system. Whichever method is used, the test results are then compared with the specifications stated in the determination of the systems requirement stage. If unsatisfactory, the system is redeveloped. If satisfactory, the system is ready for operation.

Conversion (Activity 70–80)

Conversion is often the most traumatic phase of developing a new system. At this stage, personnel, procedures, manuals, forms, files, and equipment of the old system are changed to meet the requirements of the new system. The dislocations, readjustment, and forging of new relationships make conversion a difficult but crucial activity in the new systems development.

Project management (Activity 30–80)

By the time the conversion of a new system is complete, a large number of activities have been performed. For each main activity shown in Figure 10.1 many subactivities have taken place. For example, installing new equipment might require a false floor and rewiring of the electrical system. One actual case showed 242 subactivities related to equipment installation alone. Each subactivity needs to be scheduled, allocated resources, and completed within time constraints. The entire set of activities and subactivities from the feasibility study through conversion needs planning and coordination. This is called **project management.** In developing large information systems, project control techniques such as the Gantt chart, CPM, or PERT will be required. These techniques utilize computer programs to calculate the **critical path,** or paths of development, that is, the sequence of activities that cannot be delayed without prolonging the entire project.

Operation (Activity 80–90) and evaluation (Activity 80–100)

Once the system is operational, it should be evaluated. If evaluation indicates that the system is unsatisfactory, the system must be **redeveloped.** Once redeveloped, the system is reevaluated. The cycle of evaluation and redevelopment continues until the system is operating efficiently and effectively. Reevaluation also occurs periodically throughout the life of the system as part of regularly scheduled maintenance checks.

Recycling

Evaluation is not the only stage in the development process that may trigger **recycling.** A negative answer to the questions, "Is the proposed system feasible?" or "Are test results satisfactory?" will also lead to redevelopment of the system. Figure 10.1 does not identify the points where logical decisions leading to recycling are taken because this is a PERT chart and the universally accepted notation of PERT charts does not show recycling although it is implied. Recycling, also referred to as **looping,** can be shown, using GERT (Graphic Evaluation Review Technique), but since there are not as many computer programs for implementing a GERT chart as there are for CPM or PERT, GERT is used less frequently. To identify logical decisions leading to recycling in the development process of an information system, see flowchart Figure 10.2.

The perception of the need of a new system (Circle 1 in Figure 10.2) may come from the manager or the systems analyst. The need initiates a feasibility study (Box 2). The proposed system is then tested for feasibility (Box 3). If unsatisfactory (NO exit, Symbol 3), it is examined for potential of further study (Box 4). If the proposed system is totally unfeasible, the effort is terminated (Circle 5). For example, if the minimum resources required for a minimum system are more than the resources available, the study is terminated. If, however, another design of the system with revised objectives and constraints is feasible, then a second feasibility study would be conducted (Box 2) and the process would recycle (from Symbol 4, to 2 and 3) until the proposed study is accepted as feasible (YES exit, Symbol 3) or the project is terminated (Circle 5).

If the feasibility study is approved (Exit YES, Symbol 3), then the stages of determining the systems requirements (Box 6) through the testing of the solution (Box 10) are executed along with the parallel set of activities on organization changes (Box 9). These activities correspond to those shown in Figure 10.1 discussed earlier in this chapter. If the test proves unsatisfactory (Exit NO, Symbol 11), then the process will begin to recycle (Box 12). Recycling may start with a minor change in the implementation procedures (Box 8), or change in the design of the system (Box 7), or even a redetermination of the systems requirements (Box 6). The system is then tested (Box 10) and recycled until the test results prove satisfactory (Exit YES, Symbol 11). After conversion (Box 13) the new system is operational (Box 15). A large or complex system will be controlled under project management (Box 14) until the system is operational.

While the system is operational, it is controlled for quality of information (Box 16) and is evaluated (Box 17). If the evaluation is satisfactory (Exit YES, Symbol 18), operations continue. If unsatisfactory (Exit NO, Symbol 18), then maintenance (Box 19) or recycling (Box 12) is initiated. The development recycle may start at any of Boxes 6, 7, or 8, depending on the nature of the problem involved. The recycling may even start with a new feasibility study (Box 2) if the situation has changed radically and another feasibility study is required.

The **cycle of development** shown on the flowchart should be followed for all information systems, large or small, simple or complex. However, it is possible to combine several activities, add activities, or use other names for the activities. At this point in time, there is no common agreement among authors or industries on the names or definitions of activities. This is due

FIGURE 10.2
Flowchart for system development and redevelopment process

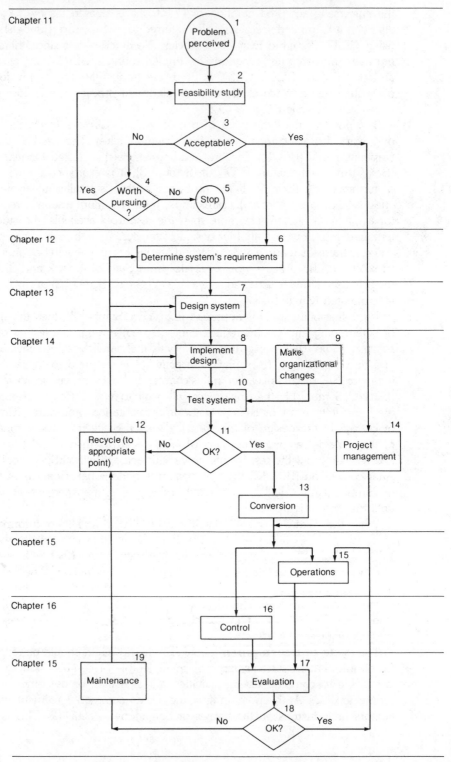

to the newness of computerized information systems themselves. Table 10.1 shows eight different schemas for the development cycle.

ROLE OF MANAGERS

An important resource in the development of an information system is the investment of time and effort by company personnel at all levels. The level of management involved will depend on the type of information system under development. Generally speaking, managers approve the development of systems one level below them in the organization structure, and participate in developing systems at their own functional level. Operational personnel should assist in the development of operating systems. This set of rules is depicted in Figure 10.3.

According to Figure 10.3, systems which affect only operational matters do not need the approval of top-level managers. For example, a business spending $20,000 per year at the factory for production could automate this function within the $20,000 without involving top management. The approval of a middle-level administrator such as the manager of production would suffice. However, if the system required additional resources—even on a one-shot basis, if the change affected institutional policies in the organization, if it violated institutional constraints, or if it might create interdepartmental rivalries, then approval of top management would be needed.

The necessity and importance of manager participation in developing information systems has been borne out by empirical evidence such as a survey by Garrity.[1] Garrity studied 27 different companies in 13 different industries using computerized information systems. He divided the companies into two groups: companies that were unmistakably successful in their use of computer systems and those that had had marginal success at best. In analyzing the characteristics of the successful lead companies, Garrity states:

> . . . executive management devotes time to the computer system program in proportion to its cost and potential and in relation to the executives' other responsibilities. This time is spent not on the technical problems, but on the management problems involved in integrating computer systems with the critical management process of the business. In particular, top management time is spent in reviewing the plans and programs for the computer systems effort and then in following up on the results achieved.
>
> Through formal progress reviews (taking place at least quarterly), lead company executives ensure that the computer effort focuses on high-leverage applications. They also see to it that current projects are proceeding on schedule. On projects that are not panning out, they look for the trouble spots and institute corrective action. In short, the lead company corporate executives are personally involved in making the computer pay off. . . .[2]

---

[1] Reprinted by permission of the *Harvard Business Review*. Excerpts from "Top Management and Computer Profits" by John J. Garrity (July–August 1963). Copyright © 1963 by the President and Fellows of Harvard College; all rights reserved.

[2] Ibid., p. 10.

TABLE 10.1
Schemas by eight authors for the development cycle*

Awad (1977: p. 344)

Feasibility study
Analysis
Design
Testing
Implementation

Blumenthal (1969: p. 91)

Feasibility study
Systems implementation
a. Phase 1: Completion of functional requirements
b. Phase 2: System specifications
c. Phase 3: Programming and testing
d. Phase 4: Conversion and cutover (to full operation)

Carter (1968: p. 105–114)

Feasibility study
Information analysis
System design
Program development
Procedure development
Conversion
Operation and maintenance
Post audit

Glans (1968: p. 4)

1. Study and design
   a. Problem recognition
   b. Determination of objectives
   c. Study present system
   d. Determine system requirements
   e. Design new system
   f. Propose solution
2. Implement and install
   a. Detail system design
   b. File design
   c. Develop test criteria and data

d. System test
e. Conversion
3. Operate, evaluate, and modify
   a. Operation
   b. Efficiency
   c. System modification and maintenance

Gore and Stubbe (1975: p. 16)

Study phase
Design phase
Development phase
Operation phase

Gross and Smith (1976: p. 46)

Preliminary systems analysis
Preliminary systems design
Systems engineering and design engineering
Systems development, testing, and implementation

Haden (1978: p. 123)

Recognition of need
Conception of possible solution
Feasibility evaluation
Systems-analysis
Programming
Control

Heany (1968: p. 46)

Develop or refine an information requirement
Develop gross systems concepts
Obtain approval
Detail the design
Test
Implement
Document
Evaluate

* Sources:

Elias M. Awad, *Introduction to Computers in Business* (Englewood Cliffs, N.J.: Prentice-Hall, Inc., 1977).

Sherman C. Blumenthal, *Management Information Systems: A Framework for Planning and Development* (Englewood Cliffs, N.J.: Prentice-Hall, Inc., 1969).

Norman H. Carter, *Introduction to Business Data Processing* (Belmont, Calif.: Dickenson Publishing Co., Inc., 1968).

Thomas B. Glans, Burton Grad, David Holstein, William E. Meyers, and Richard N. Schmidt, *Management Systems* (New York: Holt, Rinehart & Winston, Inc., 1968).

Marvin Gore and John Stubbe, *Elements of Systems Analysis for Business Data Processing* (Dubuque, Iowa: William C. Brown Co., Publishers, 1975).

TABLE 10.1 *(continued)*

Paul Gross and Robert D. Smith, *Systems Analysis and Design for Management* (New York: Dun-Donnelley Publishing Corp., 1976).

D. Haden, *Total Business Systems: Computers in Business* (St. Paul, Minn.: West Publishing Co., 1978).

Donald F. Heany, *Development of Information Systems: What Management Needs to Know* (New York: The Ronald Press Co., 1968).

FIGURE 10.3
Management's role in development of an information system

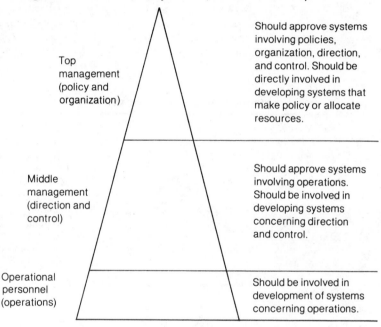

Top
management
(policy and
organization)

Should approve systems involving policies, organization, direction, and control. Should be directly involved in developing systems that make policy or allocate resources.

Middle
management
(direction and
control)

Should approve systems involving operations. Should be involved in developing systems concerning direction and control.

Operational
personnel
(operations)

Should be involved in development of systems concerning operations.

Even for new systems at the operational level, the attitude of top management toward computerized information systems is crucial. Garrity states:

> Obviously, the close involvement of operating management is essential if a company is to apply computer systems effectively to inventory management, equipment scheduling, demand forecasting, and the like. The lead companies have achieved it by a combination of factors, including productive missionary work by the technical staff. But top management's attitude seems to be the principal ingredient. Where top management has fostered a tradition of effective line-staff relations, where top management has created an atmosphere favorable to an innovating, inquiring approach, operating executives have been much

more willing to participate in the effort. Indeed, in some cases they have been the prime movers.

But over and above this indirect encouragement, top management in most lead companies has specifically spelled out to operating executives the corporate commitment to the computer effort, its objectives, and operating management's responsibility for achieving the anticipated return. One operating manager commented: "I did not volunteer to be a guinea pig for the computer. But the message came through loud and clear. I was expected to use the computer and show results.[3]

Table 10.2 shows the activities in the development cycle for which management has prime responsibility. However, managers should also understand and oversee the activities delegated to analysts (also listed in Table 10.2). In fact, a smooth and successful developmental process depends to a large extent on a close working relationship between management and technical personnel. This is difficult because the two groups have differences in back-

TABLE 10.2
Personnel responsible for development activities

Activities of development	*Person with prime responsibility*
Feasibility study	Manager*
System requirements	Manager*
Design system	Analyst
Implement system	Analyst
Test system	Analyst and manager*
Organizational changes	Manager*
Conversion	Analyst
Evaluation	Manager*
Maintenance	Analyst

* Manager of the relevant application area or manager directly involved.

ground, training, and perspective. The two often disagree in their perception of what can be done and what should be done. Problems of interpretation and communication arise. The cartoon in Figure 10.4 shows what can happen when objectives are not clearly understood by the technician. A common vocabulary and knowledge about the developmental process of information systems will usually minimize such understandings and reduce the noise in communications. One of the purposes of this text is to provide this common foundation.

Many managers in business complain that the promises of an information system are rarely achieved. Two reasons contribute to this credibility gap: systems analysts often promise more than they can produce, and managers,

---

[3] Ibid., p. 12.

FIGURE 10.4
Lack of communication in project development

As envisioned by the development team.

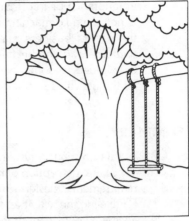

As specified in the product request.

As designed by the senior designer.

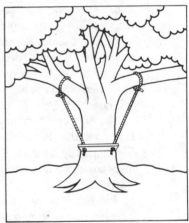

As perceived by the implementor.

As installed.

What the customer wanted.

in ignorance of information systems, often expect too much. The computer is not a magic machine that will produce instant results. Misconceptions on the part of business managers and the overenthusiasm of systems analysts reinforce one another with the result that managers feel let down. This can be avoided to some extent if management understands and participates in all the activities in the development of the information system.

SUMMARY

All information systems must be developed by a prescribed set of activities. These are: perception of need, the feasibility study, specification of the systems requirements, design, implementation, testing, conversion, and operations. Paralleling the activities, from the feasibility study through conversion, is management control and implementation of organizational changes. After conversion and during operations, the system must be controlled for quality of information and evaluated. If the evaluation is found unsatisfactory, the system recycles. This recycling may also begin during the testing activity.

During the development process, the manager must make decisions concerning the systems specifications, implementation, and evaluation. If the manager abdicates this responsibility, these decisions will be made by default by the analyst with the result that the system developed may not meet the manager's needs.

Manager and analyst each have prime responsibility for different activities. But in all phases of development manager and analyst should work together. This can only be done if they know each other's perspective and understand a common body of knowledge relating to the development of information systems.

The sequence and naming of activities of the development cycle will vary with the nature of the business and the style of managers and analysts. One sequencing expressed in poetry is as follows:

(Canto the first: Proposal)
"An information system," said the president, J.B.,
"Is what this company sorely needs, or so it seems to me:
An automated, integrated system that embraces
All the proper people, in all the proper places,
So that the proper people, by communications linked,
Can manage by exception, instead of by instinct."

(Canto the second: Feasibility study)
They called in the consultants then, to see what they could see,
And to tell them how to optimize their use of EDP.
The consultants studied hard and long (their fee for this was sizable)
And concluded that an information system was quite feasible.
"Such a system," they repeated, "will not only give you speed,
It will give you whole new kinds of information that you need."

(Canto the third: Installation)
So an information system was developed and installed
And all the proper people were properly enthralled.
They thought of all the many kinds of facts it could transmit.
And predicted higher profits would indeed result from it;
They agreed the information that it would communicate
Would never be too little, and would never be too late.

(Canto the last: Output)
Yet when the system went on line, there was no great hurrah,
For it soon became apparent that it had one fatal flaw:
Though the system functioned perfectly, it couldn't quite atone
For the information it revealed—which was better left unknown.[4]

KEY WORDS

Conversion	**Physical preparation**
Critical path	**Procedure**
Cycle of development	**Programs**
Data base	**Project control techniques**
Design	**Project management**
Evaluation	**Recycling**
Feasibility study	**Redevelopment**
Looping	**Systems requirement statement**
Organizational adjustments	**Testing**
Overall systems planning	

DISCUSSION QUESTIONS

1. Do all information systems go through the same stages of development? Why do many stages have multiple names? Is this confusion over names avoidable?

2. Why is the development of an information system a cycle? When (if ever) does the cycle end?

3. What phases of the development process must be recycled? Why does recycling take place?

4. How long does it take to develop an information system? What are the factors that determine the lapse time for development?

5. Does every information system require a development cycle? Explain the conditions under which a development cycle is essential.

6. What is the role of a manager in the development cycle of an information system? How does it conflict with or supplement (or both) the role of analysts?

7. What background, knowledge, and experience is necessary for a manager to participate effectively in the development of an information system?

---

[4] Marilyn Driscoll, "An Information System," *The Arthur Young Journal,* (Winter 1968), p. 318.

8. How do the stages in the development of an information system differ from stages in a redevelopment cycle?

9. List the stages of development of an information system in sequence. Under what circumstances can some of these stages be omitted?

10. Explain factors that lead to the development of an information system. Explain factors leading to redevelopment. Who initiates development and redevelopment? What units are responsible for implementation?

EXERCISES*

1. Draw a chart showing activities in the development of an information system for generating a monthly report which identifies sales per salesperson by product and sales area, and for comparing these figures with quotas for each sales representative. Specify any simplifying assumptions of the environment that you make.

2. Assume that the report prepared in the above exercise has been used for three years and needs to be modified in format. Draw a diagram showing the activities needed for such modification.

3. Draw a diagram for the development of an online real-time information system for a large warehouse with five sites annually handling 500 different products worth $5 million.

* Note: Keep your solutions to all the above exercises. Do the same exercises after studying Part Three and again after Part Four. You will probably find many differences in your answers. Analyze these differences.

SELECTED ANNOTATED BIBLIOGRAPHY

Davis, Gordon B. *Management Information Systems: Conceptual Foundations, Structure, and Development.* New York: McGraw-Hill Book Co., 1974, pp. 413–39.
A tightly written description of the development cycle with a good discussion of the human factors involved in development.

Kanter, J. *Management-Oriented Management Information Systems.* Englewood Cliffs, N.J.: Prentice-Hall, Inc., 1977, chap. 4, pp. 92–133.
This chapter discusses three main sets of activities in the development and implementation cycle: analysis, synthesis, and implementation. Detailed activities are also identified. Unfortunately, the pie diagrams used do not emphasize the sequential and cyclic relationship of the activities. There is, however, an excellent discussion of economic analysis as part of the feasibility study.

Kirk, F. G. *Total System Development for Information Systems.* New York: John Wiley & Sons, Inc., 1973.
Chapter 4, pp. 31–40, has an excellent diagram showing the interrelationship of the different phases of development. Each of these phases is subsequently discussed in a full chapter.

McDonough, A. M., and Garrett, L. J. *Management Systems: Working Concepts and Practices.* Homewood, Ill.: Richard D. Irwin, Inc., 1965, chapter 15, pp. 199–209.
This is an excellent review and summary of management systems. This reference

is old, but the process of development and the development cycle have not changed.

Orlicky, J.   *The Successful Computer System.* New York: McGraw-Hill Book Co., 1969, chapter 7, pp. 135–50.

This chapter contains a good review and summary of the information system development process. The phases discussed are: programming, supporting procedures, education, conversion planning and development of auxiliary procedures, file cleanup, program testing, debugging, and conversion.

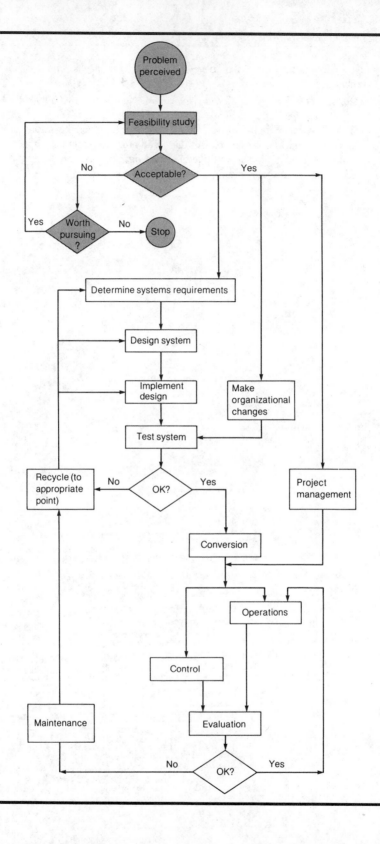

11

FEASIBILITY STUDY

Once the need for a new information system is perceived, a **feasibility study** determines whether or not desired objectives of a proposed information system can be achieved within existing constraints. The study identifies the cost of proposed changes (monetary and organizational) and estimates the benefits of the new system. On this information, the manager decides whether to implement the new system or discontinue the study.

A feasibility study is usually recommended when a proposed system involves major change such as the installation of a faster data processing system (with computerized processing). But feasibility studies are themselves costly. Many experts feel that they are a waste of valuable time, talent, and money. They argue that unless a firm is breaking new ground or desires to be on the leading edge of technology, it is wiser to follow the lead of firms that have already developed systems for achieving the desired objectives. Before a firm commits scarce resources to a feasibility study, it is generally advisable to undertake a preliminary study to decide whether to adopt the solution of another firm or to undertake development of a new system by reviewing objectives, ascertaining company resources and constraints, and surveying existing solutions. A preliminary recommendation to proceed with development of a customized information system would then lead to a detailed feasibility study.

Though a feasibility study postulates a new system, it does not guarantee success. The system may still fail in the testing phase of implementation. This risk, however, is minimized since the study identifies and anticipates problems to be solved.

There are four phases to a feasibility study:

1. Organizing for the feasibility study.
2. Search for a solution.
3. Feasibility analysis.
4. Choice of a solution.

PHASE ONE: ORGANIZING FOR A FEASIBILITY STUDY

The first phase in any feasibility study is preparing for the study itself. A flowchart representation of this organization is shown in Figure 11.1. This

FIGURE 11.1
Phase One: Organizing for feasibility study

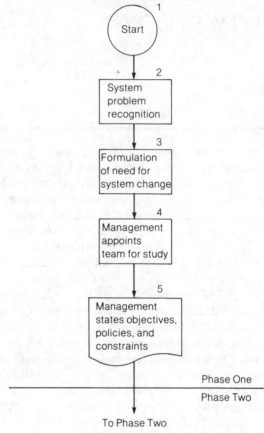

phase may be initiated by a manager when the need for a new information system is recognized (Box 2, Figure 11.1). Triggering the redesign may be:

1. Changes in organizational goals, plans, and information requirements.
2. Changes in organizational structure (e.g., appointment of new top management).
3. Changes in the environment (e.g., legislation requiring the company to supply new data to government agencies).
4. Changes in technology that may make new systems feasible.

Phase One may also be initiated by systems personnel who may be first to recognize potential benefits to the firm of technological developments in the computer industry. In addition, a firm with an operate-now-integrate-later approach to information systems development may rely on systems personnel to signal the need for expanding subsystems within the overall system.

Once the need for change has been recognized, the problem must be defined and formulated by management (Box 3, Figure 11.1). Then personnel must be appointed to make a feasibility study of problem solutions (Box 4, Figure 11.1). Members of the study team should have the following qualifications:

1. Knowledge of systems techniques. Whether this should be knowledge of operation research, statistics, computer science, information science, business functions (i.e., accounting, marketing, finance, and production) or a combination of these will depend on the nature of the problem. Experience with computer systems (hardware and software) is useful, especially if the systems change involves designing a large or complex information system. A specialist in computer systems is not always essential, though an understanding of the potentials and limitations of computer systems is helpful in making full use of technological developments.
2. The ability to work with people. Projected systems changes disrupt the status quo. People often feel their jobs threatened and manifest this insecurity by lack of cooperation, even open hostility, toward the feasibility study group. Working in this environment requires tact and discretion.
3. An understanding of the organization, its structure, philosophy, objectives, policies, and operations.
4. Skill in perceiving the overall picture, combined with a willingness to handle details.
5. A position in management. This provides the status and authority necessary to elicit cooperation when collecting information for the study from all organizational levels.
6. Experience in the type of project under consideration.

The above qualities are seldom found in one individual but all should be represented in the team. Often a firm will not have personnel experienced in the systems change under review. In such cases consultants will have to be hired and added to the team. Their presence has the advantage of bringing an outsider's scrutiny and a certain objectivity to the study.

Team size generally varies from two to eight. There is greater division of labor on large teams and more flexibility in staffing, making it easier to ensure that all the desired qualities are found in the membership. But as size increases so does the potential for personality conflicts, conflicts that can delay decision making and hinder the team's functioning. The selected committee chairman must be skillful in managing groups, and also be knowledgeable about the firm's goals and policies, for the team may need guidance in interpreting the organizational environment. Experience has shown that feasibility studies have more impact when the chairman is drawn from the upper levels of management for large and complex systems.

After the team has been appointed, management must state the objectives of the study and specify related policies and constraints (Box 5, Figure 11.1). This step is delayed until the feasibility study group has been assembled because a team-management dialogue is necessary during this organizational phase. The team's questions about variables and demands for clarification and/or elaboration help management define the study objectives in operational terms. Without this interaction, objectives tend to be stated in ambiguous, generalized terms such as "more accurate information" or "faster reporting." A team will demand specifics. What error rate is permissible? To how many decimal points should results be calculated? Does a response time of two weeks constitute faster reporting time or is one day, or one hour required? Sometimes management is reluctant to state goals, not knowing what can realistically be achieved. But the purpose of the study is to determine feasibility of goals. If the development of technology and the firm's resources make the goals unfeasible, management will be so informed and the goals can accordingly be scaled down, or resource constraints relaxed so the objectives can be achieved.

A good example of a seemingly unrealistic goal was stated by American Airlines in 1954. Realizing that the company was losing potential profits because the airline lacked timely information on the availability of seats on their flights, the following objective was formulated: The new system should provide company agents anywhere in the United States with immediate reservation confirmation and accurate information on schedules and seat occupancy. Such fast response time was technologically impossible at the time. Yet this objective was achieved in 1963 by the SABRE System[1] and today computerized reservation systems are taken for granted by the airline industry.

Discussions between team and management during the organizational phases of the feasibility study will also ensure that the resources available for the project and the limits of acceptable organization change are specified. Personnel policies regarding displacement or unemployment resulting from possible acceptance of a new system should also be stated in advance of the study. Without such a policy, valuable employees who feel their jobs threatened may leave the firm. Usually the best workers leave first, even before the new system is installed, thereby adding to the problems of conversion. Policies regarding reclassification of jobs, retraining, and transference of personnel, when stated well in advance of the actual feasibility study, can help alleviate unemployment fears and might contribute to keeping needed workers in the company's employ.

Authorization to cross departmental boundaries for collecting information should be granted the study team during the organizational phase. In cases of complex systems changes, this authority must come from top management.

PHASE TWO: SEARCH FOR SOLUTIONS

A flowchart for the steps in Phase Two is shown in Figure 11.2. The first step in the search for a solution is usually to study the existing system

[1] R. W. Parker, "The SABRE System," *Datamation*, vol. 11, no. 9 (September 1965), pp. 49–52.

FIGURE 11.2
Phase Two: Search for solutions

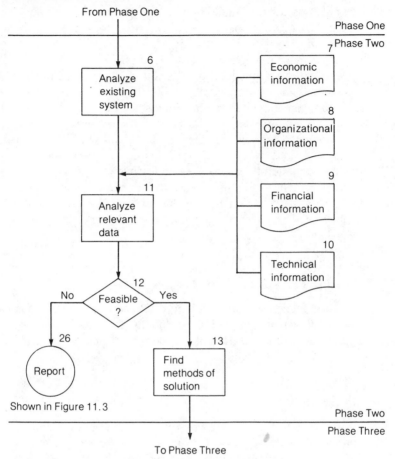

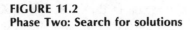

and to collect and analyze all relevant information on the environment so that the current performance can be evaluated, and required changes determined (Box 6, Figure 11.2).[2] However, some systems analysts feel that teams become biased when such a detailed study is made and argue that a fresh approach, disregarding existing systems, is needed. A look at the objectives and constraints of management will usually guide the team in how to initiate the study. When subsystems within the basic structure are to be changed, the first approach, a study of the existing system, is generally appropriate. For major overhauls, the fresh approach is usually advisable.

In either case the team must decide on the detail and depth of their study,

---

[2] For one view of this approach, see D. F. Heany, *Development of Information Systems* (New York: The Ronald Press Co., 1968), p. 165.

and how much information should be collected and analyzed (Boxes 7–11, Figure 11.2). If implementation follows the study, the committee's groundwork will prove useful, but should the study terminate, the time and effort invested is lost. For this reason, only a broad survey-type analysis should be made at this stage to determine whether or not to proceed further. For example, if management has allocated only $10,000 for the operation of a terminal system and the team discovers that the minimum equipment cost for such a system is in the range of $30,000, the team should report its findings, and management either terminate the study or restate its objectives and constraints. If, however, no glaring reasons for declaring the project unfeasible are apparent (YES exit for Symbol 12, Figure 11.2), the broad search for solutions should continue, (Box 13, Figure 11.2) with the collection of additional information if necessary. An unfeasible project terminates with a report to management to that effect (NO exit, Symbol 12, and Circle 26). In some cases, simple rules of decision making will produce solutions. In other cases, sophisticated models of operations research and management science will be required.

PHASE THREE: FEASIBILITY ANALYSIS

Phase Three, the formal testing of alternative solutions derived in Phase Two, is shown in Figure 11.3. Solutions are tested (Box 14, Figure 11.3) against four primary constraints: economic, financial, organizational, and technical (Box 15–19, Figure 11.3).

Economic feasibility

Theoretically, **economic feasibility** is conceptually simple: a cost-benefit analysis. The expected benefits must equal or exceed the expected costs. However, in designing information systems, the cost half of the equation is rarely computed with accuracy during the feasibility stage. User's requirements tend to be understated so that costs invariably increase as the project develops, and analysts often underestimate expenses.

Assigning a precise monetary value to the benefit side of the equation is equally difficult in practice since most benefits of information systems cannot be measured in dollars. For example, how can one measure the value of an analysis of consumer preferences, or timely information on sales or production? Fortunately it is not always necessary to measure the **cardinal utility** of benefits. **Ordinal utility** is sufficient, that is, the benefits must be of a higher order than the cost. If an information system is projected to cost $20,000, the manager need only decide whether expected benefits are worth the price, a decision that can be made on an intuitive basis.

Another way to estimate benefits is to ask management how much the company would be willing to pay to an outside firm for the information.

FIGURE 11.3
Phase Three: Feasibility analysis

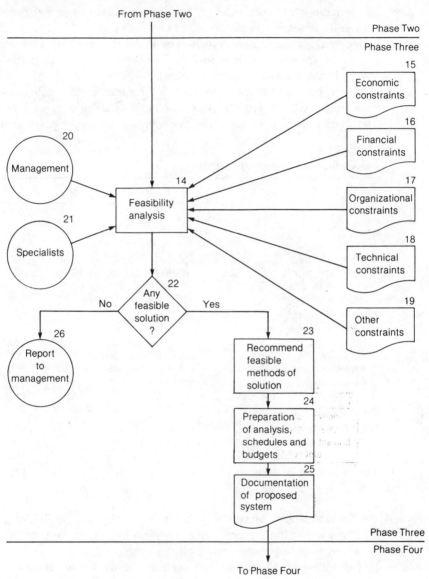

One technique for comparing costs with benefits is to state costs in terms of an **operational variable.** For example, the cost of the information system may be equated with a 0.2 percent increase in inventory turnover, or a 3 percent increase in sales. The value of information derived from the proposed system (management's judgment of intangible benefits plus the tangible benefits) would then be compared to the necessary increase in operations required to offset this calculated cost.

Estimations of costs and benefits are generally **range estimates,** with probability assessments for the values within the range. Managers will choose either pessimistic or optimistic values or an in-between value within the range, depending on their aversion to risk. The benefits-cost analysis that follows will be based on these expected values.

Where benefits can be quantified, the computed benefits can be placed on a table similar to Table 11.1, a hypothetical but fairly realistic case study.[3] The figures derived in the table can then be weighed against costs, as in

TABLE 11.1
Calculations of benefits (in $000)

	Year				
	1	2	3	4	5
Marketing benefits					
Sales forecast					
Present system	20,000	21,000	22,000	23,200	24,300
New system	20,000	21,500	23,700	26,000	28,600
Increase in sales	0	500	1,700	2,800	4,300
Increase in profits	0	50	170	280	430
Production benefits					
Inventory carrying costs					
Finished goods	0	25	25	25	25
In production	0	60	60	60	60
Replenishment avoided	0	125	0	0	0
Factory labor	0	0	20	30	50
Total production benefits . .	0	210	105	115	135
Other benefits					
From purchasing and					
other agents	0	60	70	70	70
Total benefits	0	320	345	465	635
Cumulative net benefits	0	320	665	1,130	1,765

the **benefits-cost analysis** in Table 11.2. The sample Tables 11.1 and 11.2 show that the project under consideration would be profitable within an approximate pay-back period of four years.

Not all benefits-costs analyses are this simple. Many refinements would be required in a more sophisticated capital budgeting decision. Expertise in business finance and accounting is generally needed when making a benefits-costs analysis for determining economic feasibility.

---

[3] This data and the following section on financial feasibility is adapted from Harold J. McCormack, "Measuring the Benefits of an MIS and a Case" (unpublished), 1979. The basic data came from Fred R. McFadden and James D. Suver, "Costs and Benefits of a Data Base System," *Harvard Business Review,* vol. 56, no. 1 (January–February 1978), pp. 131–39.

TABLE 11.2
Benefits-cost analysis (in $000)

	Year				
	1	2	3	4	5
Costs					
Hardware					
CPU	150				
Central memory	75				
Data storage	60				
Terminals	15	15			
Software and conversion					
DBMS	100				
Communications	15				
Training	20	5	5		
Conversion	25	25	25	25	
Other (mostly personnel)					
DBA-related	75	90	90	90	90
Maintenance	20	20	20	20	20
User costs	20	20	20	20	20
Total costs	575	175	160	155	130
Cumulative costs	575	750	910	1,065	1,195
Cumulative benefits					
(from Table 11.1)	0	320	665	1,130	1,765
Cumulative benefits less					
costs (net cash flow)	−575	−430	−245	65	570

An additional comment about benefits is in order here. Since the goal of any information system is to reduce a decision maker's uncertainty by predicting the future, the potential value of the information system under development should be compared with a calculation of the **expected value of perfect information (EVPI)** sometime during the early stages of the feasibility study. Of course, no system will be a crystal ball, but if expected benefits prove far from the ideal, the system is probably not worth developing.

Financial feasibility

Often a proposed system with a high benefits-cost ratio is economically feasible, but a lack of money prevents implementation. **Financial feasibility,** checking costs against available funds, is therefore an essential at this stage.

The study team often considers economic and financial constraints jointly, issuing a single decision on economic and financial feasibility. But, conceptually, two feasibility decisions have been made. Though computer analysts assist in determining costs, users determine economic feasibility. Financial feasibility requires technical advice from personnel knowledgeable about the availability of capital and methods of financing. Decisions on whether borrowed money would be available for the project, whether internal financing would suffice, or whether a combination of external and internal financing would be advisable are decisions that can only be made by financial personnel.

Capital budgeting decisions in large firms generally require complex calculations to determine the relative merit of projects competing for funds. For example, management might have to choose between allocating available resources to R&D, to plant renovation, or to the development of a new information system. In the feasibility study for an information system, the time value of money, the accounting rate of return on investment, the discounted return on investment, and the profitability index might be calculated and be decisive factors in recommending the system's implementation or rejection. These calculations are described briefly below.

TIME VALUE OF MONEY

The benefits-cost analysis is meaningful only when the estimated benefits are discounted to determine their present value, for the value of money changes over time due to inflation, changing rates of interest, and so forth. Costs are incurred when a project is initiated. Benefits come later. A comparison of benefits with the **present value (PV) of future amounts** is determined by the following formula:

$$PV = \frac{\text{amount in future}}{(1 + \text{discount rate})^n}$$

where n = number of years from present. For example, $100 two years in the future discounted at 22 percent would be $67.19 ($100 \div (1.0 + .22)^2 = 100 \div 1.4884 = 67.186$). (The 22 percent discount rate in this example is the rate estimated to reflect the changing value of money over a two-year period. This estimate would vary among businesspersons and would change in time as financial conditions and the cost of capital varies.)

NET PRESENT VALUE (NPV)

Calculations can be performed to discount the entire cash flow for a project to **net present value (NPV).** The formula for this calculation is:

$$NPV = \sum_{n=1}^{\text{years}} \frac{\pm (\text{cash flow})_n}{(1 + \text{rate})^n}$$

The data in Table 11.2 discounted at 22 percent to determine *NPV* yields a total positive benefit of $67,000 (see Table 11.3). That total benefit figure would then be weighed against benefits that might accrue from other projects that are competing for the limited financial resources of the firm. It would be during the financial feasibility study of a projected information system that this comparison would be made.

RETURN ON INVESTMENT (ROI)

Return on investment is the percentage return for a project based on the PV of benefits. Conceptually, ROI is the interest rate which makes the

TABLE 11.3
Calculation of NPV

	Year				
	1	2	3	4	5
Net cash flow (see Table 11.2).........	−575	145	185	310	505
NPV at 22 percent	−575	119	124	171	228

Total positive benefits = 119 + 124 + 171 + 228 − 575 = 67
(i.e., $67,000)

investment produce the expected returns. Mathematically, ROI is the discount rate which brings the NPV of the project to zero, calculated by iteration for various rates until one is found which satisfies:

$$\sum_{n=1}^{\text{Years}} \frac{\pm (\text{cash flow})_n}{(1+\text{rate})^n} = 0$$

The calculations for the above formula, using the data from Table 11.3, are shown below.

	1	2	3	4	5	NPV
Net cash flow	−575	145	185	310	505	
27 percent PV factors $(1+0.27)^n$	—	1.27	1.6129	2.0484	2.6014	
PV =	−575	114.17	114.70	151.34	194.13	$-1 \approx 0$

Since *NPV* at 27 percent = 0, therefore the ROI = 27 percent.

The above calculations (which assume that money is due or spent at the beginning of the year) gives *NPV* closest to zero. Other iterative calculations that do not give a zero NPV are:

NPV at 22 percent = +$67,000
NPV at 32 percent = −$58,000
NPV at 26 percent = +$12,000

The ROI for the information system (synonymous with **IRR, internal rate of return**), would be compared with the ROI of other projects under consideration and be a factor in deciding priorities for a firm's financial resources.

ACCOUNTING RATE OF RETURN (ARR)

Accountants use the average net income over the life of a project divided by the value of the investment as a supplement to ROI. Net income is directly affected by accounting conventions, such as depreciations that are excluded from the cash measures. Five years is the life of information systems generally used in the calculation since advances in computer technology make most systems obsolete after that length of time. This rule of thumb is applied to software as well as hardware, for systems are generally redeveloped within a five-year time period.

Using the data in Table 11.2, the **accounting rate of return (ARR)** on investment is 40 percent [(145 + 185 + 310 + 505)/5] ÷ 575 = 229/575 = 40 percent.

PROFITABILITY INDEX (PI)

Another index used when comparing the relative merits projects is the **profitability index (PI)** calculated by the formula:

$$PI = \frac{\text{Present value of benefit returns}}{\text{Present value of investment}}$$

For data in Table 11.1 and Table 11.3, the PI = 1.12 (119 + 124 + 171 + 228)/575 = 1.12).

CRITERIA SELECTION

Whether ROI, PV, and/or other criteria are used in economic and financial feasibility studies depends on the personnel conducting the study. The figures in Table 11.4, based on a 1975 study by Petry, show the percentage of surveyed companies using ROI, PV, NPV, and ARR. Most firms used more than one calculation when comparing projects competing for funds. The average number of criteria was 2.24, which explains why the total percentage in Table 11.4 exceeds 100 percent.

Organizational feasibility

Proposed solutions must also be tested against **organizational constraints.** For example, when a new information system requires combining two departments into one, the manager of the absorbed department may

TABLE 11.4
Preferences of investment criterion

	Percent
ROI—Return on investment (discounted)	61
PB—Payback period	58
NPV—Net present value (discounted)	33
ARR—Accounting rate of return (undiscounted)	
on initial investment	33
on average investment	27
Other approaches	12

Source: Glenn H. Petry, "Effective Use of Capital Budgeting Tools," *Business Horizons,* vol. 19, no. 5 (October 1975), p. 58.

strenuously object. If top management agrees that the merger is inadvisable, an organizational constraint exists. Sometimes the person who would be responsible for the new system lacks the qualities necessary to make the change viable. Clerical personnel may be unwilling to prepare data by the new method or unable to use terminals instead of cards for preparing input. A new system is feasible only when personnel with technical and administrative competency are available, and when employees are willing to make changes in procedures, to accept experimentation, to operate in an atmosphere of change, and to accept the risk of making errors, should the system design prove faulty.

Major systems change needs the support of top management. Support at operational and middle management levels is also important. Without such support, it requires courage to implement a new system. The availability of qualified systems personnel is a less decisive factor in deciding whether or not to adopt a new system, since that situation can often be corrected. Consultants can be hired to select, employ, and train needed personnel. It should be recognized, however, that the full support of management is necessary to attract and retain competent personnel. At the present time, the demand for analysts exceeds supply and this shortage is expected to continue in the near future. Instead of fighting nonsystems-oriented management, analysts will choose employment in a supportive working environment, assuming pay incentives are equal.

Sometimes corrective action can be taken to make a proposed system feasible in spite of the opposition of a key manager at the operational or middle management level. Top management might remove the incumbent, either by transfer or dismissal,[4] change the job (e.g., withdraw duties from one position and assign them to others), or, preferably, change the incumbent's views to support of the system through counseling and training. Ways in which management can mobilize employee support are described in detail later in this text. Indeed, the key to success in utilizing computer technology in decision making is often dependent on the ability of management to motivate and integrate people involved with the new system rather than on the solution of technical problems regarding machine integration. Because of the importance of human relationships in an information system, an entire chapter, Chapter 17, is devoted to this subject.

Table 11.5 is a decision table for determining organizational feasibility.

Technological feasibility

Sometimes no solution is feasible because of **technological constraints.** Examples include the present lack of mathematical and statistical techniques for determining optimal solutions in some unstructured decision-making situations, and the lack of equipment to perform certain types of operations, such as machine reading of handwriting.

---

[4] W. H. Newman, C. E. Summer, and E. K. Warren, *The Process of Management*, 2d ed. (Englewood Cliffs, N.J.: Prentice-Hall, Inc., 1967), pp. 272–73.

TABLE 11.5
Decision table for testing organizational feasibility

	Rule 1	Rule 2	Rule 3	Rule 4	Rule 5	Rule 6	Rule 7	Rule 8
Top manager support	N	N	N	N	Y	Y	Y	Y
Operational and middle management support	Y	Y	N	N	Y	Y	N	N
Experienced analysts available	Y	N	Y	N	Y	N	Y	N
Discontinue study		X	X	X				
Hire consultants (assume available)						X		X
Train analysts						X		X
Continue study with caution	X						X	X
Continue with enthusiasm					X			

Key: Y = Yes.
    N = No.
    X = Action to be taken.

Other feasibility considerations

Additional constraints, both internal and external, may also exist. One example of an **internal constraint** is **time.** A project may have little or no value unless completed by a given date. Competition or national unions may impose **external constraints,** as may federal and state regulatory agencies.

Feasibility decision

Feasibility deliberations in Phase Three are made by the study team though management and specialists may participate as advisers and counselors (Symbols 14, 20, and 21, Figure 11.3).

When a number of alternatives are possible, the study team must develop priorities for ranking solutions. For example, in selecting one of many departments to be automated, a unit that is the source of basic data for other departments in the organization might be given preference. Weight might be given to small and isolated departments since automation could provide experience in systems change without adversely affecting the rest of the organization in the event of miscalculation. The team may decide to start with small jobs having a high probability of success, situations where a high volume of repetitious work is done by clerks. Systems designers generally prefer jobs where the assignment is well defined and there is adequate time for planning and implementing the change. They prefer to avoid areas where employees are strongly opposed to change.

Once solutions have been weighted with priority values, the study team will choose and recommend to management the adoption of the highest ranking feasible solution with the best probability of success (Box 23, Figure 11.3). But alternate solutions in order of preference should also be presented with documentation for each possibility included (Boxes 24 and 25, Figure 11.3). The report should list:

1. Dollar resources required.
   a. Developmental costs
      Equipment
      Personnel
      Space
      Other
   b. Recurring costs
      Personnel
      Other
2. Anticipated consequences of proposed project
   a. Organizational changes
      Structural
      Personnel
      Procedures
   b. Informational changes
   c. Anticipated problems
3. Limitations of proposed project
4. Benefits of project
   a. Economic
   b. Organizational
   c. Overall systems
   d. Other
5. Time schedule
   a. Time schedule of project
   b. Priority reassignment of other jobs.

The above information should be supported by examples of output and performance figures from other case studies. In addition, a detailed statement of the objectives and the scope of the feasibility study should be prepared for management to accompany the recommendations.

A report to management is also necessary when the study team finds no feasible solution (Circle 26, Figure 11.3).

PHASE FOUR: CHOICE OF A SOLUTION

The fourth and last phase of the feasibility study, shown in Figure 11.4, is initiated when the study team presents its findings to management (Box 26, Figure 11.4). Before management adopts the proposed systems change the team's recommendations must be studied with care (Box 27, Figure 11.4). It is management's responsibility to ensure that all relevant variables are specified and that all estimates are checked. Consulting help may prove advisable at this stage. It should be recognized that overruns on expenses and delays in schedules are the norm in the history of information systems, especially in the area of computer installations, so provision for such miscalculations

FIGURE 11.4
Phase Four: Choice of solution

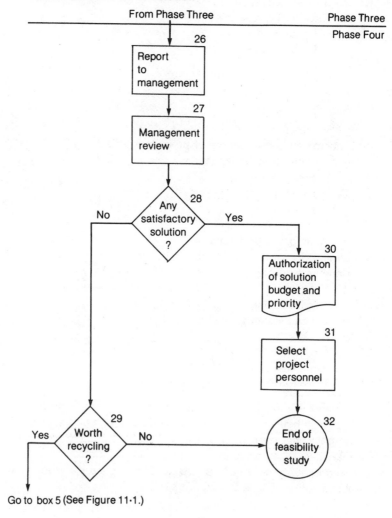

Go to box 5 (See Figure 11·1.)

should be made. In their defense, systems personnel claim that they cannot make predictions or estimates with accuracy since their job is developmental, untried, and full of uncertainties. There is some truth to this assertion. But in recent years the profession has gained experience. Many new techniques and rules for predicting costs have been developed. Some business firms exist solely by preparing and marketing computer systems for determining costs. Feasibility teams should be able to provide management with more reliable time/cost figures than in the past.

Management must also carefully study the feasibility report so that bias or omitted considerations are noted. For example, studies that dismiss organizational impact as unimportant should be viewed with skepticism. Many systems changes have organizational implications, especially on future job classifications and employment. These must be anticipated and plans for the future carefully prepared.

Although the feasibility team recommendations are generally accepted, the final decision on whether or not a new information system should be adopted rests with management. Management should have participated in the team's deliberations when costs and benefits were weighed, when values to intangible variables were imputed, when effects of conflicting factors were estimated, and trade-offs evaluated, but a reassessment of these value judgments after the study is complete is advisable. Committing the firm's resources to a new system is, in the final analysis, a policy decision that only management can make. In selecting projects to be implemented, the short- and long-range significance of each project must be considered and a balance between subsystem and total system implementation maintained. Management must guard against the tendency of combatting local brush fires while neglecting overall long-range planning needs. Some firms allocate systems personnel exclusively for long-range systems planning, but this requires top level commitment of resources and is too costly for small organizations.

When management decides the proposed solutions are unacceptable (Exit No, Symbol 28; Figure 11.4) recycling may be initiated (Exit Yes, Symbol 29 to Box 5, Figure 11.1). Constraints might be relaxed or objectives scaled down in order to find an acceptable feasible solution. A positive acceptance of a solution from the alternatives proposed by the feasibility study team (Yes exit, Symbol 28) must be followed by decisions necessary for implementation (output Symbol 30, Figure 11.4) such as authorization of a budget, the establishment of a time schedule, framing necessary policy and procedural changes, and possibly even reassigning existing priorities of systems effort. In some cases, statements concerning organizational policies on personnel are necessary.

In authorizing a new system, management must take actions necessary to ensure that the promised benefits of the system are fully realized. There are many cases on record where a department manager has supported the claim of savings made in the feasibility study, such as the replacement of clerks, but once the system has been implemented no savings appear. The clerks have merely been assigned unproductive work, what economists call disguised unemployment. This can be prevented if management sets a date when the funds representing the promised savings resulting from the new system will be withdrawn from the department concerned. If this be organizationally feasible, then the action has two important effects. One, it ensures that the savings from the new system are realized and, two, it motivates departments concerned to cooperate with systems personnel so that the proposed project can be completed effectively and on time.

Selecting project personnel

The final step in Phase Four is the appointment of a **project director,** one with knowledge and proven experience in managing systems changes, and assignment of a development team. The team will determine the requirements of the system, analyze and design the new system, and oversee implementation and conversion (Box 31, Figure 11.4). It will be disbanded and given new assignments when the system is turned over to users and operational personnel.

There are several approaches to the organization of this development team. A **functional organization, project organization,** or **matrix organization** are possibilities.

Traditional management philosophy is based on line and staff concepts with a vertical flow of authority and responsibility. The project team might be organized as a functional unit with assigned development responsibilities, keeping traditional line-staff relationships.

However, most information system projects require cooperation and resources from many line units. As M. Stewart states:

> The essence of project management is that it cuts across, and in a sense conflicts with the natural organization structure. . . . Because a project usually requires decisions and actions from a number of functional areas at once, the main inter-dependencies and the main flow of information in a project are not vertical but lateral. . . . Projects are characterized by exceptionally strong lateral working relationships, requiring closely related activity and decisions by many individuals in different functional departments.[5]

When functional organization is inappropriate, **project organization,** the creation of a separate organizational unit for the sole purpose of completing the project, may work. In this schema, professional, technical, and administrative staff are hired for the duration of the project. But there are serious problems in attracting competent personnel when projects are organized in this manner. Project jobs are temporary, with fluctuating work loads. Professionals are unwilling to join projects that offer no job security.

---

[5] M. Stewart, "Making Project Management Work," in D. I. Cleland and W. R. King, *Systems, Organizations, Analysis, Management: A Book of Readings* (New York: McGraw-Hill Book Co., 1969), pp. 295–96.

A **matrix organization** combines functional and project approaches to project management. In a matrix organization, the staff is "borrowed" from functional divisions. In the case of a development team, the team members might be drawn from the accounting division, marketing, operations research, the EDP department, and so forth. Which employees are borrowed is negotiated by the project manager with functional department heads, the choice usually being based on the availability of personnel and the qualifications demanded by the project. Sometimes department heads are reluctant to release competent personnel, but there are advantages to being represented on the development team that most department heads recognize. Certainly the department's interests will be promoted with a representative on the team.

However, the matrix organization means that project members have two bosses. They are responsible to the project manager for work assignments, yet their permanent supervisors retain jurisdiction over personnel matters such as salary and promotions. The two "bosses" may clash in values and objectives, with the project member caught in between. This potentially explosive situation can be defused if ground rules are negotiated between the project manager and functional heads regarding shared authority and responsibility over project members before the team is constituted.

The advantages of matrix organization may be summarized as follows. Matrix organization:

1. Provides a project manager with authority to cut across vertical organizational divisions.
2. Involves functional departments, and is responsive to their needs, because representatives of most departments will be on the project staff.
3. Has access to the resources in functional departments (on a negotiated basis).
4. Provides a "home" for the project personnel after the completion of the project.
5. Does not permanently disrupt organizational subgroupings or the continuity of fringe benefits.

When a development team must be chosen for complex projects, a User and Administrative Committee is often formed to aid the project leader in interpreting the firm's policies and in clarifying users' needs. This committee may also monitor the progress of the project at predetermined checkpoints.

Once a systems change is authorized and the project leader and team appointed, with responsibilities clearly defined, the feasibility study is terminated (Circle 32, Figure 11.4).

DURATION OF A FEASIBILITY STUDY

The feasibility study may take a few days if the system change is a simple one, or years if the proposed system change is complex. The duration of the study is also a function of systems personnel and managers, the state of documentation of the existing system, the amount of detailed analysis to be prepared, the number of departments involved in the study, the urgency of the project, and the systems orientation of personnel involved. The study should not be rushed at the expense of quality and thoroughness, for it serves not only as the basis for a decision on implementation, but as the basis for design and evaluation after the feasibility decision is made. Additional time spent on the study may well contribute to the relevancy and effectiveness of the project and furnish materials for starting system development after approval.

SUMMARY AND CONCLUSIONS

A feasibility study is primarily a fact-finding effort that provides the information necessary for the decision whether or not to implement a new information system. A secondary function is to provide the basic data necessary for the design, evaluation, and scheduling of the system, should it be adopted. Potential benefits and related problems will be identified during the course of the study.

There are four phases to a feasibility study: the organization of the study, a search for solutions, the feasibility analysis, and the decision on implementation. Steps in each of these phases and their interrelationships are shown in Figure 11.5.

Proposed solutions are checked for economic, financial, organizational, and technological feasibility, though not necessarily in that order. For example, when new equipment is under consideration, a technological decision must be made before economic and organizational feasibility can be examined. In some cases all feasibility checks are done in parallel.

The lack of necessary funds is the most frequent reason for rejecting a systems change. Economic nonfeasibility—costs exceeding benefits—comes next. Noneconomic reasons include time constraints, the lack of necessary organizational environment, or the technological inability to achieve objectives.

Two important documents must accompany the decision to implement a new system. One identifies what can be achieved and the resources required, a document prepared by systems personnel. The second is authorization for the project, management's commitment, stating resources available and outlining policies for procedural and organizational changes necessary for implementation.

Figure 11.5 identifies three important decision points. Two are taken by the feasibility team, Symbols 12 and 22, where recommendations to either continue or terminate the feasibility study are made. The third is management's, Symbol 28. This decision is crucial. If management errs and decides to discontinue the study when the project should have been implemented, the firm has lost benefits that could have accrued from a systems change. An implementation when the project should have been discontinued will result in a loss of the firm's resources and unnecessary organizational disruption.

FIGURE 11.5
Flowchart for feasibility study

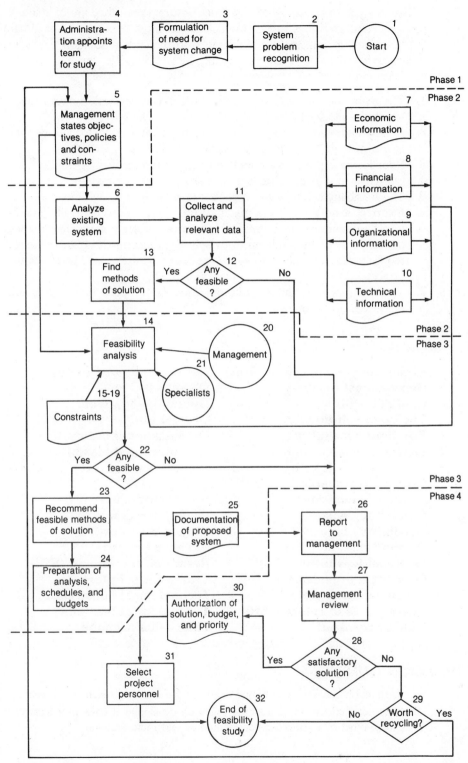

Feasibility studies are costly and time-consuming but they are of value. If properly conducted they reduce the risk of making a wrong decision. When the team fails to anticipate problems or recommends a solution that later proves unfeasible, the cause can usually be attributed to one or more or the following errors:

1. The team used a crash approach which did not provide sufficient time for all the phases of the study.
2. A nonintegrated approach was used, the team failing to consider the role of change in the long-range plans of the firm.
3. Poor leadership and poor staffing of the feasibility team existed.
4. Objectives and constraints were not adequately specified.
5. The feasibility study lacked organizational support.
6. Incorrect estimations were made by the team. These generally include errors in estimating organizational resistance to change, in underestimating the difficulty of the problem to be solved, in incorrectly stating resource requirements, or failure to recognize the organizational impact of the project.
7. The user management of application area did not participate and review objectives of the project.

KEY WORDS

Accounting rate of return (ARR)	Net present value (NPV)
Benefits-cost analysis	Objectives
Cardinal utility	Operational variable
Choice of solution	Ordinal utility
Economic feasibility	Organizational constraints
Expected value of perfect information (EVPI)	Organizational feasibility
	Present value of future amounts (PV)
External constraint	Profitability index (PI)
Feasibility analysis	Project director
Feasibility decision	Project organization
Feasibility study	Range estimates
Feasibility study team	Return on investment (ROI)
Financial feasibility	Search for solutions
Functional organization	Technological constraints
Internal constraint	Technological feasibility
Internal rate of return (IRR)	Time value of money
Matrix organization	

DISCUSSION QUESTIONS

1. Distinguish between tangible and intangible benefits. Give examples of each.
2. It is not sufficient to concentrate solely on development costs in a feasibility study. What other considerations should be taken into account?

3. What are the potential costs and benefits of an information system?
4. Describe and compare methods of determining financial feasibility.
5. List examples of intangible costs and intangible benefits. How would you calculate or estimate each?
6. Distinguish between:
    a. Objectives and constraints.
    b. Technical and organizational feasibility.
    c. Economic and financial feasibility.
    d. Economic and financial constraints.
    e. Feasible and optimum solution.
7. Describe how you would organize a development team to design and implement an inventory control system for six warehouses and a $30 million volatile inventory? Would the team composition change if the system were to be OLRT, as opposed to a batch system?
8. Is a feasibility study important in the development of an information system? Why? Is it essential for all information systems?
9. What types of feasibility should be examined?
10. Who should initiate a feasibility study? When should the study be initiated?
11. Give two examples each of economic, financial, organizational, and technical constraints.
12. Compare different approaches to capital budgeting for computer resources. Cite one example when each of the approaches might be used. Substantiate your choice.
13. What considerations lead to a "GO" decision following the feasibility study? Who makes that decision? Which approach is most suited for an EDP environment? Substantiate your position.
14. What project organization would you choose for an inventory project estimated at $800,000 over a span of three years and involving approximately 20 worker years? What types of persons would you want on the project team? Why?
15. What qualifications and qualities would you recommend for the project manager in Question 14.
16. Why are the future returns discounted in the economic criteria used to evaluate investment proposals for an MIS?
17. Explain why more than one financial criteria might be used to evaluate proposals for a MIS?

EXERCISE

1. Two MIS proposals are competing for a limited capital budget. They have the following net cash flows.

*Net cash flows
($000)*

	Year					
	1	2	3	4	5	6
Proposal 1	−440	100	180	180	200	220
Proposal 2	−180	60	80	20	160	200

The company has a target rate of return on investments of 24 percent before considering taxes. Using the financial criteria discussed in this chapter, evaluate these two proposals. Treat all cash flows as occurring at the *end* of each year and discount them at the end of year 1.

SELECTED ANNOTATED BIBLIOGRAPHY

Alexander, Tom. "Computers Can't Solve Everything." *Fortune,* vol. 80, no. 5 (October 1969), pp. 126–29, 168–71.
   This is an excellent reminder that computers have limitations which must be kept in proper perspective. The author discusses the gap between computer capabilities and their use, and problems arising in the development of computer applications. Though this was written many years ago the reasoning still applies.

Asimov, M. *Introduction to Design.* Chap. 4. Englewood Cliffs, N.J.: Prentice-Hall, Inc., 1962, pp. 18–23.
   Although written specifically for engineers, the concepts presented are applicable to the design of any system and can be easily grasped by the non-engineer. Chapter 4 includes an excellent treatise on the stages of the feasibility study and their interrelationships. The chapter is supplemented by a flowchart showing inputs and outputs of the feasibility study phase of development.

Couger, J. Daniel, and Knapp, Robert W., eds. *System Analysis Techniques.* New York: John Wiley & Sons, Inc., 1974.
   This book of readings has a section on cost effectiveness analysis in Part III including an excellent article by James Emery. "Cost/Benefit Analysis of Information Systems, (pp. 395–425). His discussion of the value and cost of quality information, the problem of selectivity of data, and techniques for analyzing benefits, both tangible and intangible, are especially informative. Another interesting article is by Boyd and Krasnow on the economic evaluation of management information systems (pp. 425–46).

Emery, J. C. "Costs and Benefits of an Information System." In *Information Processing,* edited by A. Rosenfeld, Amsterdam: North-Holland Publishing Co., 1974, pp. 967–71.
   This article discusses prices versus costs, efficiency versus effectiveness, and problems in estimating intangible benefits and determining costs.

Freilink, A. B., ed. *Economics of Informatics.* New York: North-Holland Publishing Co., 1975.
   This book is on proceedings at an international symposium held in Germany. Especially good are the papers by Dorothy Pope on cost estimation of EDP (pp. 304–13) and by Frank Land on "Criteria for the Evaluation and Design of Effective Systems" (pp. 239–50).

King, John Leslie, and Schrems, Edward L. "Cost-Benefit Analysis in Information Systems Development and Operation." *ACM Computing Surveys,* vol. 10, no. 1 (March 1978), pp. 19–34.
   A good discussion of the elements in estimating costs and benefits and how to avoid the major problems encountered. The article has a flowchart, a table, and some equations but nothing too technical. A good survey of 27 references.

Phister, Montgomery, Jr. *Data Processing Technology & Economics.* Santa Monica, Calif.: Santa Monica Publishing Co., 1974, pp. 167–238.

An excellent discussion of cost components: hardware costs, development costs, sales and marketing costs, maintenance costs, and life cycle costs. Has numerous cost figures in table and charts.

Rosenblatt, Meir J., and James V. Tucker. "Capital Expenditure Decision Making: Some Tools and Trends." *Interfaces,* vol. 9, pt. 1, no. 2 (February 1979), pp. 63–69.

A discussion of the use of discounting methods, the determination of discount and cut-off rates, the use of mathematical programming and capital rationing, and approaches to risk and uncertainty. The discussion is based on 15 surveys of the actual use of these approaches in business and industry.

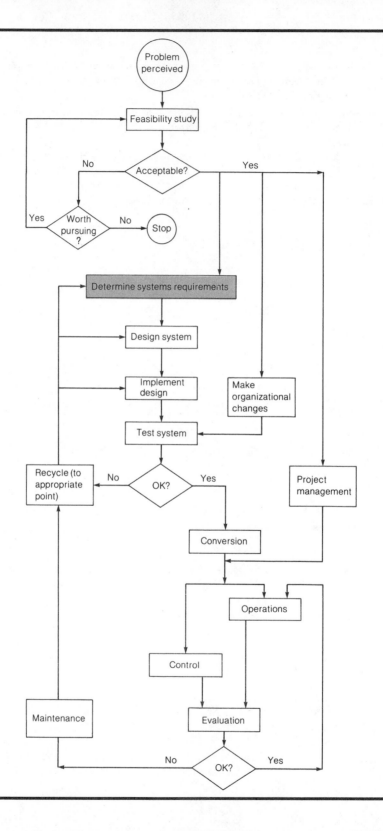

12

DETERMINING SYSTEMS
REQUIREMENTS

Determining users' needs and preparing system specifications follow the feasibility study. At this stage, the objectives stated in general terms in the feasibility study are restated in greater detail to provide the operational framework for the systems design.

According to a 1975 survey of 120 managers and systems professionals, "the identification of information needs of management is the most critical factor associated with successful management information systems." The study also noted that deficiencies in information systems can be partially avoided by properly defining the required content of the system. The steps in this crucial phase of development are shown in Figure 12.1.

In order to determine systems requirements, a series of design sessions are held so that top and supervisory management, as well as operating personnel, can express their informational needs as users (boxes 3, 4, 6). Systems analysts participate in these sessions but primarily as coordinators, catalysts, and documentors. A final design session (Box 7) resolves conflicts between users' groups.

There are two basic strategies that can be used in defining systems design: bottom-up analysis or top-down design. In a **bottom-up approach,**[1] the need for subsystems is identified, and modules are designed and tested as independent units and then integrated into a total system. The approach is evolutionary in nature, for operational modules of transaction files can first be designed, with later additions of modules for updating, control, and planning as the need develops.

The **top-down approach,** also called **structured design,**[2] starts by

---

[1] For a discussion of this approach see Sherman Blumenthal, *Management Information Systems* (Englewood Cliffs, N.J.: Prentice-Hall, Inc., 1969), pp. 20–24. Blumenthal also discusses the approaches of organization chart, data collection, data bank, integrate later, and integrate now.

[2] For a discussion by one of the earliest and strongest proponents of the structured approach, see Edward Yourdon and Larry L. Constantine, *Structured Design* (Englewood Cliffs, N.J.: Prentice-Hall, Inc., 1979), 473 p. See also Tom D. Marco, *Structured Analysis and System Specification* (N.Y.: Yourdon, Inc., 1978), 352 p.; and Chris Gane and Trish Sarson *Structured Systems Analysis: Tools and Techniques* (Englewood Cliffs, N.J.: Prentice-Hall, Inc., 1979), 231 p.

For a comparison of the structured approach with other approaches—Jackson Methodology, META Stepwise Refinement (MSR), and Higher Order Software (HOS)—see Lawrence J. Peters defining goals of the organization, the means to achieve these goals, the actions necessary to implement the means, and finally, the information needed for these actions. This approach is one of elaboration and clarification. The skeletal version of the new system is first designed before the system is subdivided into manageable components for development. The logic of the top-down structured design can also be utilized in programming, called **structured programming.**

At the design sessions, users must decide specifications for the new system, including:

1. Objectives, goals, and criteria of performance.
2. Outputs to be produced.
3. Inputs to be used.
4. Processes to be performed.
5. Resources to be available.
6. Procedures to be followed.
7. Organizational and other constraints to be met.

The key to determining users' requirements is data collection, for only by gathering facts and opinions about operating procedures and changes needed can designers draw up a list of such specifications.

This chapter opens with an analysis of three alternative approaches to data collection that can be employed to gather information needed in the design sessions. It is followed by a discussion of the tools and techniques used in each approach. The method of drawing up systems requirements is also explained and approval procedures outlined. Finally, a brief discussion on project management is presented.

DATA COLLECTION

The traditional approach

The main thesis of the **traditional approach** to data collection in determining users' needs is that no new information system can be designed without first considering the organizational and operational environment to be changed. An analysis of the current system identifies problem areas and areas of potential gain, and provides clues to system solutions. The detailed fact-gathering required aids not only in the analysis but in the subsequent design of the new system.

The list which follows shows the kinds of questions that must be asked when the existing system is studied.[3]

---

and Leonard L. Tipp, "Compare Software Design Methodologies," *Datamation*®, vol. 23, no. 11 (November 1977), pp. 89–94.

[3] Adapted from G. B. Davis, *Computer Data Processing* (New York: McGraw-Hill Book Co., 1974), p. 468.

FIGURE 12.1
Determining system specifications

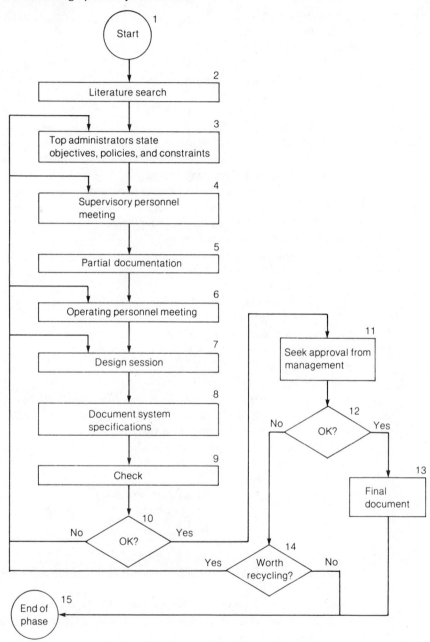

1. Related work
   What related work is being done?
      How is it being done?
2. Preparation and processing
   Who originates source data?
      Who prepares documents?
      How often is processing performed?
      How long does it take?
      Where is the processing performed?
      Who performs it?
      What equipment and supplies are used?
      How many copies are prepared? Who receives them?
      Is there unused processing capacity?
      What is the volume of documents (maximum, minimum, and average?)
      What has been the historical growth rate?
3. Form and timeliness of documents
   Are documents in a useful form?
      What are their limitations?
      Is exception reporting used?
      Can two or more documents be combined?
      Is greater accuracy needed?
      Can lesser accuracy be tolerated?
      Is faster reporting desired? Is it needed?
4. User of documents
   Who receives the document?
      Does the document initiate decision? What decision? By whom?
      Is there a part of the document that is ignored or rarely used?
      What additional information is needed?
      What processing is performed by the user of the document?
      What is the flow of the document?
5. Storage and retrieval
   Is the document retained? How? For how long?
      What are the procedures for retention and purging?
      How often is data purged and updated?
      How often is it retrieved?
      What are the procedures for retrieval?
      How large is file (in number of records and average size per record)?
6. Cost
   What is the cost of processing the document?
      What is the change in cost resulting from a change in frequency or accuracy of processing?
      How much of present cost of processing will be eliminated by computer processing?
      What is the cost of storage and retrieval?

The main disadvantage of this list is its length. Gathering information in so much detail is a very time-consuming task, especially for firms that have accumulated many forms and lack updated documentation on procedures. It took 10,000 hours, an equivalent of about five man-years, for a firm of only 300 employees to collect such information when considering a system change.[4]

One reason the traditional approach is favored is that many users want only to match current performance when a new system is designed, preferring to continue the pattern of decision making and processing existing instead of trying something new. They do not even attempt to find optimum solutions nor do they look ahead to predict future information needs.

Because so many users specify that new systems should simply match the old, many firms fail to take advantage of advanced technology. Too many information systems merely duplicate manual, card, and noncomputer data processing systems. The equipment used represents an outdated generation of technology, an inefficient and wasteful use of resources. But a fresh look at systems, discovering a new approach to achieving corporate goals while optimizing performance through the exploitation of technical advances, is difficult when the traditional approach to data collection is used.

The innovative approach

In this approach, the systems designers do not examine in-place systems, which may compromise their objectivity and channel their thinking. Instead, the systems favored by other firms with similar operations are studied and the latest computer technology searched. Novel ideas are considered, ideas which might be dismissed as impracticable by those who had first studied existing procedures. Users specify what information is desired even though this might seem idealistic and unobtainable. A drawback to this approach is that resulting systems often require changes in company policies and procedures, and organizational restructuring. The risk and disruption of such major overhaul makes firms hesitant to use the **innovative approach** when determining systems requirements.

The hybrid approach

The **hybrid approach** combines the two preceding methods of determining users' needs. First, a totally new system is explored (innovative approach), then the tentative specifications are checked to make sure the new system matches the performance of the old (traditional approach). A variation of the hybrid method is to supplement the traditional approach with recent innovative tools for data collection such as ADS (Accurately Defined System)

---

[4] Richard G. Canning, "Managing the Systems Effort," *EDP Analyzer,* vol. 6, no. 7 (July 1968), p. 4.

discussed later in this chapter. The main disadvantage of the hybrid method is that it compounds the weaknesses of the traditional approach: it is both time-consuming and costly.

The choice of method in data collection depends on the nature of the problem, the resources (money and personnel) available, the orientation of management, and the attitudes of systems personnel. The traditional approach is most commonly used. It has, therefore, been chosen as the basis for the flowchart in Figure 12.1.

TOOLS AND TECHNIQUES OF DATA COLLECTION

A literature search, interviews, meetings, the Study Organization Plan, and Accurately Defined System are ways of collecting data to assist users in defining their needs.

Literature search

A **literature search** may be used by management to review and update knowledge of information systems. Or it may be a study by systems personnel of the firm's annual reports, catalogs, and publicity material in order to learn about the organization, its size, operations, products, internal structure, and stated objectives. A search might also be made of monographs, periodicals, professional journals, house organs, and books to learn of systems changes in other firms.

An important aspect of the literature search is to help establish a common vocabulary of technical terms for developmental personnel. Lack of agreement on terminology is often a source of confusion, resulting in inaccuracies and wasted effort. The profession is too young and changing too rapidly for a settled body of definitions to exist. Yet development requires common definitions by users and technicians. A literature search should acquaint both groups with terms and be the basis for arriving at definitions to be clarified early in the project.

Interviews

Interviews are used extensively in the social sciences as a means of collecting data. Structured interviews of users, asking a predetermined set of questions, help ensure that essential data is collected, that nothing important is left out. Unstructured interviews are much more time-consuming, but often their impromptu and spontaneous nature provides insights that result in better system design.

Meetings

The systems design sessions themselves can prove a fruitful technique of data collection. Brainstorming, gathering a group of people with different backgrounds and training for discussions, is a method businesses and industry successfully use in problem solving. When determining users' needs, the meetings would involve managers, systems personnel, and specialists, including consultants when needed. Design sessions also provide an occasion for exchanging reservations, concerns, and objections, and for resolving differences in design philosophies. The strengths of management and systems personnel can be identified and supported, and compensation made for weaknesses. During the course of the discussions, management must ensure that the systems objectives and organizational policies are not compromised unnecessarily and that systems personnel acquire a good conceptual understanding of the problem. An important side effect of such meetings is that all parties usually become interested and involved in the project and gain a better appreciation of interrelationships which affect successful operation of.an information system.

Design sessions can be held at many points in the systems development. The flowchart in Figure 12.1 shows only one such meeting (Box 7) but additional sessions could be held following meetings with top management and supervisory personnel.

In all cases, design sessions should be conducted after careful planning and preparation. The participants should be selected with care, the meetings should have a suggestive and provocative agenda, and all relevant documents should be made available, with adequate lead time for study. For complex systems projects, the design sessions may last from two hours to two weeks. Experience has shown that the meetings are more productive when they are held away from constant interruptions.

Design sessions on systems changes tend to result in flowcharting and decision tables. A useful technique is to photograph these before they are erased, to provide documentation for the ideas that emerge from the discussions.

Study organization plan (SOP)

SOP is a systematic method of collecting information and designing a new system as developed by IBM. It was originated for breakthrough types of information systems and has been used with great success. SOP consists of three phases; understanding the present system; determining systems requirements; and designing the new system. Phases 1 and 2 correspond to this chapter, Phase 3 to the next chapter in this book. Phase 1 determines "what is done in the existing system, using what inputs, with what resources, and to achieve what results. Information is collected and organized into a meaningful pattern to permit an accurate understanding of the business as it presently operates and reacts to its environment." Phase 2 "reviews the input of these basic questions about the new system. What must it do? How well must it do it? What resources have management specified be used? To answer these questions and to arrive at a valid set of systems requirements,

Phase 2 blends known facts about the present system with projections concerning the future."[5]

The SOP method involves the completion of a number of forms: the Resource Usage Sheet showing the resources (personnel, equipment, and materials) consumed by each organizational unit; the Activity Sheet identifying the inputs, outputs, and file usage of each activity; the Operation Sheet listing the volumes and lapse times of each operation; the File Sheet specifying each file's characteristics; the Message Sheet identifying recorded or unrecorded communications entering or leaving an operation; the Input-Output Sheet showing the input-output specifications; the Required Operation Sheet recording details of operational elements within flowchart diagrams; and Resource Sheets providing quantity and cost data on each resource used.

The SOP method[6] is the traditional approach to data collection. Like other traditional approaches, it is time-consuming and costly, but it is also systematic and very thorough. The detailed data collected does help analyze bottleneck areas and identify areas where change can bring added efficiency and effectiveness. It also provides a sound basis for the design activity to follow.

Accurately defined system (ADS)

National Cash Register Company designed **accurately defined system (ADS)** for data collection. One version uses five forms for collecting information on outputs, inputs, data files, computations, and system logic. The forms are designed to make certain there is consistency among data fields; to identify relationships of input, computation, and output; to determine validation rules and ranges of values; and to specify the boundaries of the system.

Other instruments of data collection

Process charts, an additional technique for gathering information, need explanation. The sample process chart in Figure 12.2 is used to analyze an accounts receivable procedure. Each step is traced, the time taken is recorded, and the volume handled noted. An analysis of the chart will quickly identify bottlenecks as well as duplicated and redundant steps, suggesting areas of potential savings in time and effort.

Other instruments of data collection are **flowcharts, data flow diagrams** and **decision tables,** all of which have been employed in this text and

---

[5] *IBM Basic System Study Guide,* Form F20–8150 (White Plains, N.Y.: International Business Machines Corporation, 1963), p. 2.

[6] For a discussion of the SOP Method, Phase 1 and 2, see *IBM Study Organization Plan, The Method Phase I,* No. 7–20–8136–0, and *The Method Phase II,* No. F 20–8137–0, pp. 38 and 27, respectively. For an application using SOP, see Thomas B. Glans et al., *Management Systems* (New York: Holt, Rinehart & Winston, Inc., 1968), pp. 91, 123.

FIGURE 12.2
An example of a process chart

PROCESS CHART WORK SHEET

Please read instructions on other side before completing this form.

Job: Accounts Receivables   Page 1 of 1

Charted by: J. Williams   Date: 02-05-80   Procedure __ Method

Number	Details of Step	Delay / Operation / Transportation / Storage / Check/Control	Time Required	Number	Comment
1	Wait for daily receipts and log them	○ ● □ △ ▽	2-3-4 h		
2	Wait for batch	● ○ □ △ ▽	2-3-4 d		
3	Glance verification	○ ○ □ △	50-90-120 m		
4	Corrections made	○ ● □ △ ▽	2-4-7 h		
5	Sent for keypunching	○ ○ ■ △ ▽	1-2-4 h		
6	Key punching	○ ● □ △ ▽	2-3-4 h		
7	Sent to Computing Center	○ ○ ■ △ ▽	10-20-60 m		Recycled 2
8	Run edit program	○ ○ □ △	1-2-8 h		times at an
9	Return diagnostics to A/R	○ ○ ■ △ ▽	1-2-4 h		average
10	Errors await correction	● ○ □ △ ▽	1-4-16 h		
11	Correct errors	○ ● □ △ ▽	40-60-120 m		
12	When no errors, logged	○ ● □ △ ▽	5-10-12 m		
13	Records stored	○ ○ □ △ ▽	5-8-10 m		
14	Payment sent to bank	○ ● □ △ ▽	4-8-10 m		
15	Enroute to bank	○ ○ ■ △ ▽	4-4-8 hrs		
16		○ ○ □ △ ▽			
		○ ○ □ △ ▽			
		○ ○ □ △ ▽			
		○ ○ □ △ ▽			

Abbreviations used   d = days   h = hours   m = minutes

need no further comment. Forms and charts for design can also be purchased from equipment and form vendors.

DOCUMENTATION

SOP and ADS are essentially techniques of **documentation,** but other instruments of data collection, especially interviews and design sessions, should also be documented. This must be done soon after the event, while memories are fresh, and should be verified by the individuals involved. Analysts should integrate this documentation periodically as shown in Boxes 5, 8, and 13 of Figure 12.1.

The need for documentation cannot be over emphasized. It should be a complete recording not only of discussions, but of definitions used and assumptions made. This will prevent later misunderstandings.

IDENTIFYING USERS' OBJECTIVES, POLICIES, AND CONSTRAINTS

On the basis of collected data using the approaches and tools discussed in the preceding sections of this chapter, users' requirements must be identified at each organizational level shown in Figure 12.1: top management (Box 3), the supervisory level (Box 4), and the operational level (Box 6). This means defining **objectives** (what the user wishes to accomplish), **policies** (guidelines that determine the course of action for accomplishing the objectives), and **constraints.**

Stating objectives, policies, and constraints

Stating **objectives** is often difficult but it must be done. Information systems should be uniquely designed for each organization, and this can be accomplished only in context of the specific goals of each firm. The importance of defining objectives on the performance criterion is emphasized by R. N. McKean:

> There is a great danger of forgetting, or at least neglecting, the significance of criteria selection. If extreme care is not exercised in this part of the task, all the researcher's ingenuity and scientific tools may be wasted in deriving right answers to wrong questions—which are sometimes diametrically wrong answers to the real questions.[7]

Theoretically, a study of stated **policies** should help clarify objectives. In practice, however, policies are often not helpful. Policy manuals either do not exist or they are outdated. The missing information is usually crucial, for that is what caused them to be outdated in the first place. The process of determining short- and long-range objectives means examining how the system project fits into the organizational plan and verbalizing unwritten policies, preferences, priority rankings, biases, and prejudices. **Constraint** limitations imposed on the system by either internal or external factors, must also be specified.

Consider, for example, a business with the objective of reducing the length of its check-out lanes to specified limits. This is a classic problem in queuing theory that can be solved, provided the value of several rates and cost coeffi-

---

[7] R. N. McKean, "Sub-Optimization Criteria and Operations Research," in M. Alexis and C. Z. Wilson, *Organizational Decision Making* (Englewood Cliffs, N.J.: Prentice-Hall, Inc., 1967), p. 165.

cients is known. One cost coefficient required is the hourly cost of clerks servicing each station. This is a known value: the wage rate (plus fringe benefits) per clerk. The other cost coefficient needed is the value of the customer's time while waiting to be served, a difficult if not impossible value to state. One might use the average hourly wage of the average store client (if that is known), but what about psychic costs, the annoyance, and inconvenience to customers? How can the loss of income be determined, should a customer, irritated by the queue, begin shopping at a competitor's store? How could you assign a value to grumbling that might make other buyers leave? A crude estimation of the cost of waiting might be derived from the store records and interviews. But this is often not possible. The usual method is for the manager to assign a figure, the amount the business would pay to avoid customer waiting. It is this latter type of value judgment that must be formalized by management when stating objectives. If not, systems personnel will make the judgment by default.

PERFORMANCE SPECIFICATIONS

Objectives, policies, and constraints as they relate to users' requirements must next be specified in operational terms at desired performance levels. The following list shows the detail required.

Output: Content, format, quantity, availability, response time, frequency, distribution list, retention.

Processing: Decision rules, accuracy, ratio or absolute range, significance of results, current and future capacity.

Input: Source, media, procedures, validity checks.

Security: Input, organization, maintenance, decision rules, output, nature of access, list of those allowed access, control of access, identification, hardware, software, audit, general or specific, internal or external.

Backup system: Items needing backup, nature of backup procedures, and maintenance.

The preceding list is a general list of specifications. Each problem will vary in actual specification needs. The following sample, a partial list of systems requirements, shows the detail that was required in defining users' needs when the Universal Product Code (UPC) was developed by the Symbol Standardization Subcommittee of the Uniform Grocery Product Code Council, Inc.[8]

Mode	online real time
Size of code	12 decimal characters

---

[8] For details see D. Savir and G. J. Laurer, "The Characteristics and Decodability of the Universal Product Code Symbol," *IBM Systems Journal,* vol. 14, no. 1 (December 1975), pp. 16–34.

Area of symbol . . . .   ⊁ (not more than) 1.5 square inch
Speed of scanning . . . .   ⊁ 100 inch/sec
Scanning reject rate . . . .   ⊁ 0.01 percent
Undetected error rate . . . .   ⊁ 0.0001 percent
Normal conditions of abrasion, dirt, etc. allowed.

Output, processing, input, and security, the major headings in the performance specification list, have been mentioned earlier in this text and will be examined further in Chapters 15 and 16. Users must also consider **backup.** What happens if the new system breaks down, if input data is physically destroyed or lost during computer processing? Can the data be re-created at the source or must the system have the capability of regenerating such losses? Keeping backup data is one solution to this problem but adds to the cost of the system. During this phase, systems personnel can estimate backup costs and users can decide what backup is advisable, but the final decision whether or not backup is worth the cost is the responsibility of management.

APPROVAL PROCEDURES

Once users' requirements have been expressed and documented as **systems specifications,** the proposal should be checked for factual and statistical accuracy and the procedures analyzed to make sure they accomplish stated objectives. Then a series of approval decisions must be made on the proposal. The users and systems personnel who participated in the project must first decide whether the systems specifications are adequate (Symbol 10, Figure 12.1). If information is missing, the job recycles to the relevant point in the flowchart (Boxes 3, 4, 6, or 7). Management next evaluates the proposal (Box 11). If dissatisfied, recycling may be initiated (Boxes 3, 4, 6, 7). Management may also decide at this point to terminate the project (Exit No, Symbol 14). This may be the result of disapproval with the systems specifications or could be due to reevaluation of the project in light of changed environmental conditions such as the unavailability of expected resources, changes in assumptions made during the feasibility study, changes in priorities, or the appointment of new personnel in management.

Only if management decides to implement the project (Exit Yes, Symbol 12) will the document on systems specifications be finalized. This completes the stage of determining systems requirements. The final document, the bill of goods the users want from the new system, outlines the framework for the design of the new system which follows.

PROJECT MANAGEMENT

Determining system requirements is just one of the responsibilities of the development team. **Project management,** initiated after the feasibility study, continues through conversion. (Development of an information system is treated as a project since it begins and ends at target fixed points in time, and because special resources, techniques, and methodology are required.) Successful development is accomplished "not through providential guidance nor through any unique expertise, but rather through the application of time-tested methods which are wholly dependent on adequate resources, both personnel and financial, and on a well-developed plan."[9]

Project management is not used exclusively for systems development. Businesses apply project management techniques to complex projects of many

FIGURE 12.3
Network diagram of activities related to project management

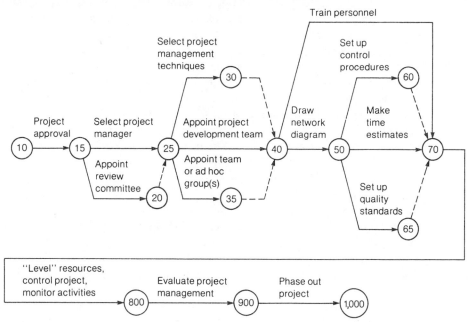

types. This discussion in this text, however, is limited to information systems development.

The essence of project management is planning: selecting management techniques, establishing standards and procedures for quality control, and drawing up a schedule with time estimates for each activity of development. The project director oversees the work of the development team, making sure standards and schedules are met. All of the activities of project management are shown in the network diagram, Figure 12.3.

---

[9] N. J. Retza, Jr., "Insuring Successful System Implementation," *Data Management,* vol. 10, no. 5 (May 1969), p. 24.

Selection of project management technique

There are many formal techniques of project management. The simplest is the Gannt chart where every activity is represented by a horizontal bar on a time scale. But if one activity is delayed, there is no way of telling which other activity or activities will be affected. A path or network diagram may be used instead. These show interrelationships, clearly establishing which activities must be completed before others can begin. The critical path can also be calculated (that is, the set of activities where delay retards the entire project); this information is needed to determine how long the project will take. If the time for each activity is known with certainty, **CPM (Critical Path Method),** a computerized technique for scheduling, can be used. When times can only be estimated, **PERT (Program Evaluation Review Technique)** can be applied. This latter technique allows for three types of time estimates: optimistic time, pessimistic time, and most likely time. PERT is more commonly used than CPM in project management for information systems because the time needed for development activities is generally uncertain.

Another computerized scheduling technique, **GERT (Graphic Evaluation Review Technique)**[10] is frequently favored over PERT because it allows **looping.** A loop occurs when three activities (A, B, and C) must be completed before another (D) is initiated, but A must be done before B, B before C, and C before A, as depicted in Figure 12.4. Such loops frequently occur in information systems development. GERT also allows alternative paths (either E or F in Figure 12.4), whereas PERT conventions require that all activities be performed in a set sequence. That is, PERT allows "AND" relationships, whereas using GERT, one can specify the probability of alternative paths in an OR relationship such as E or F in Figure 12.4. The time of project completion is then calculated with probability (p) associations. For example, the completion time might be 20 weeks with $p = .6$, and 26 weeks with $p = .8$. This additional information is valuable for scheduling and control in project management.

GERT has disadvantages, however. It requires more data than PERT (data on probabilities which are difficult and expensive to collect), and few computer programs exist for calculating GERT. Computer programs for PERT are readily available[11] and many include refinements such as optimization (of cost and time) as well as management and equipment leveling. PERT is, therefore, more commonly used than. GERT for information system development. It is perfectly adequate as long as the user makes allowance for its limitations. For example, when calculating time estimates, the PERT user should include time estimates for possible looping.

---

[10] For an excellent introductory discussion, see E. r. Clayton and L. J. Moore, "GERT vs. PERT," *Journal of Systems Management,* vol. 2, no. 2 (February 1972), pp. 11–19. For a detailed discussion, see the book by L. J. Moore and E. R. Clayton, *GERT Modeling and Simulation* (New York: Petrocelli/Charter, 1976), 227 p.

[11] For a survey of 43 software packages and a critical discussion of such software, see Perry Peterson, "Project Control Systems" *Datamation®,* vol. 25, no. 7 (June 1979), pp. 147–148 ff.

FIGURE 12.4
Illustration of GERT

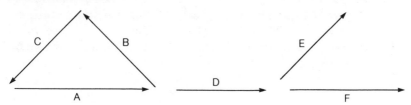

SUMMARY

The stage in the development process after the feasibility study is the specification of users' requirements. It is in this stage that users at different levels ask what, why, how, and when is information needed. Figure 12.1 shows the activities in determining the systems specifications. Users must identify objectives and constraints during the course of these activities, and specify inputs, outputs, resources, processes, security, and backup to be used. Needed data on which to base specification decisions may be gathered by the traditional, innovative, or hybrid approach, using literature searches, interviews, meetings, SOP, ADS, and other instruments of data collection.

The goal in this phase of a new systems development is to define users' needs completely and accurately. Since these needs are forever changing and expanding, the process can continue indefinitely at great cost. The other extreme, defining users' needs hastily, is equally unwise for the system developed may prove ineffective. A judicious middle ground should be found.

Once the feasibility study is terminated, development activities must be planned and scheduled. The Gannt chart can be successfully used for small projects. More complex projects with many interrelated activities require a planning technique that shows sequencing and precedence, and calculates the critical path of project completion. PERT and GERT are two techniques commonly used with computer programs for scheduling and control.

KEY WORDS

Accurately Defined System (ADS)
Backup
Bottom-up approach
Constraints
Critical Path Method (CPM)
Data flow diagram
Decision table
Documentation
Flowchart

Graphic Evaluation Review Technique (GERT)
Hybrid approach
Innovative approach
Interviews
Literature search
Looping
Meetings
Objectives
Performance specifications

Policies	Structured programming
Process chart	Study Organization Plan (SOP)
Program Evaluation Review	System specifications
Technique (PERT)	Top-down approach
Project management	Traditional approach
Structured design	

DISCUSSION QUESTIONS

1. What information is relevant when specifying users' needs? How is this information gathered and synthesized?

2. What is systems analysis? What are essential features? Why is systems analysis important when developing a computerized information system?

3. What are some of the tools and techniques of systems analysis to be used for EDP?

4. How are informational requirements influenced by:
   a. Function (that is, planning, control, and so forth)?
   b. Level of management?
   c. Size of organization?
   d. Types of decisions?
   e. Style of management?

5. Why do analysts study existing systems prior to studying alternate solutions? What other approaches can be used?

6. Distinguish between:
   a. Literature search and study of existing system.
   b. Innovative and hybrid approach.
   c. System requirements and users' requirements.
   d. Objectives and requirements of system.

7. Who should state the objectives and constraints of the future system? In what detail should specifications be made?

8. How is the user and system specification at this stage different from specifications drawn up during the feasibility study?

9. Empirical studies have shown that the user specification stage is the most difficult developmental stage. Why?

10. What is the difference between ADS and SOP? Which would you prefer? Would your choice depend on the project? If so, why?

11. Why is a process chart a useful technique for data collection? Cite two examples when the chart could be used.

12. What are differences between Gannt, CPM, PERT, and GERT? Which would one use for an EDP project that is:
    a. Large and complex with most time estimates known with certainty?
    b. Small, simple?
    c. Large and complex with only probability time estimates known?
    d. Complex with much looping and alternative branchings?

EXERCISES

1. Specify in detail a reporting system for Exercise 1, Chapter 10 for use by a manager:

   a. For reference of salesperson's performance.

   b. For posting information on each salesperson (by name or number. Assume that there is a unique ID number of ten digits).

   c. For other purposes, such as ranking salespersons and calculating bonuses.

2. Read Russell L. Ackoff, "Management Misinformation Systems," *Management Science,* vol. 14, no. 4 (December 1967), pp. B147–B156, and Alfred Rappaport, "Management Misinformation Systems—Another Perspective," *Management Science,* vol. 15, no. 4 (December 1969), pp. B133–B136. (Both articles are available in books of readings, including U. T. Dock, et al., *MIS, A Managerial Perspective* (Chicago: Science Research Associates, 1977), pp. 119–30.

   Why does Ackoff argue that managers do not know what they need? What information do managers need, and why? Who understands these needs? Do Ackoff's statements made in 1967 hold true in the 1980s? Does Rappaport effectively answer arguments?

3. State the specifications needed for an office terminal to perform calculations for production and finance. These specs should be detailed enough to be used as a basis for bids.

SELECTED ANNOTATED BIBLIOGRAPHY

Burch, John G., Jr., et al. *Information Systems: Theory and Practice,* 2d ed. New York: John Wiley & Sons, Inc., 1979.
This textbook has an extensive coverage of the development cycle including the phase of specifying users' needs. A case study includes calculators, flowcharts, memos, and documentations generated. A good nontheoretical presentation.

Canning, Richard G., ed. "Progress in Project Mangement." *EDP Analyzer,* vol. 15, no. 12 (December 1977), pp. 1–14.
Project management systems packages are discussed. The experiences of the city of Tacoma with SPECTRUM–1 and the Airborne Freight Corporation with SDM/70 are discussed.

———, ed. "The Analysis of User Needs." *EDP Analyzer,* vol. 17, no. 1 (January 1979), pp. 1–13.
Two techniques are discussed: IA (Information Analysis) used extensively in Europe and SA (portion of Structured Analysis and Design Techniques). These techniques are not yet automated but may soon be.

———, ed. "Getting the Requirements Right." *EDP Analyzer,* vol. 15, no. 7 (July 1972). pp. 1–14.
This article discusses the experiences of business organizations in stating the requirements of their application systems.

Cleland, David I., and King, William R. *Systems Analysis and Project Management,* 2d ed. New York: McGraw-Hill Book Co., 1975.
This book is not specifically on information system project management but is

nonetheless relevant to such projects. The first edition of the book got the McKinsey Foundation Award. The second edition is updated and has excellent coverage on the project environment and how to plan and organize for it.

Couger, J. Daniel, and Knapp, Robert W. *System Analysis Techniques.* New York: John Wiley & Sons, Inc., 1974, 509 p.

This is an excellent set of readings on techniques of analysis, including optimizing techniques for system design and implementation. Specifically included are chapters on ADS, SOP, HOSKYNS, decision tables, gridcharting, and SYSTEMATICS.

Munro, Malcom C., and Davis, Gordon B. "Determining Management Information Needs: A Comparison of Methods." *Management Information System Quarterly,* vol. 1, no. 2 (June 1977), p. 43–54.

This is a comparison of the effectiveness of decision analysis (top-down) and data analysis (bottom-up). The results of information obtained by these methods, evaluated by college executives for values and other attributes, are discussed.

Rosove, P. E. *Developing a Computer-Based Information System,* chap. 3. New York: John Wiley & Sons, Inc., 1967, pp. 67–93.

The book is written by personnel of the Systems Development Corporation with extensive experience in the development of large-scale computerized information systems for defense. Several development strategies are introduced, but Rosove emphasizes deductive strategy and planned evolution of information.

Sauls, Eugene. "The Use of GERT." *Journal of Systems Management,* vol. 23, no. 8 (August 1972), pp. 18–22.

An excellent tutorial for management. Somewhat technical but easy to follow because of the excellent diagrams.

Taggart, W. M., and Tharp, M. "A Survey of Information Analysis Techniques." *ACM Computing Surveys,* vol. 9, no. 4 (1977), pp. 273–90.

This article surveys 29 references on the subject and includes an annotated bibliography of an additional 40 references. It also suggests directions for profitable research in the future.

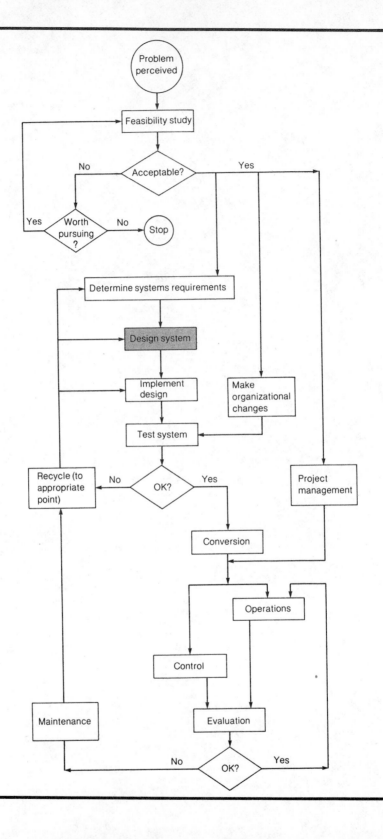

13

DESIGN OF A SYSTEM

The design phase of a new systems development is the detailed specification of the systems requirements. This phase is analogous to preparing blueprints for the construction of a new house. Once users' needs have been determined (general house layout, square footage, style), particulars must be decided (roof slant, room dimensions, location of electrical outlets). When designing a new system, a development team draws up users' requirements in specific operational terms, designating input, output, the flow of information, standards for personnel, forms to be used, and equipment performance required. Computer programming specifications and system test specifications must also be determined and the role of the new system defined in the overall system plan for the organization.

Figure 13.1 is a network diagram showing the activities in this phase of

FIGURE 13.1
Network diagram for design stage in system development process

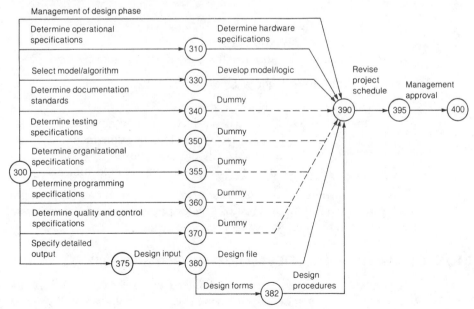

development. Since the activities are performed in parallel from 300 to 390, dummy activities (requiring no resources or time) are inserted in some paths so a numbering system to uniquely identify each activity is possible.

Users should participate in the development team in this phase to ensure that the final version of the systems design reflects users' needs. Since implementation of the completed design is the responsibility of the technicians, the activities described in this chapter end active user involvement until testing and conversion.

DESIGN MANAGEMENT (300–390, Figure 13.1)

As standards and specifications are detailed during the design phase, they must be checked to see that they comply with overall system objectives. Also, projects need to be kept on schedule. It is the responsibility of the project director to oversee and coordinate the many activities that take place during this stage of development.

OPERATIONAL AND HARDWARE SPECIFICATIONS (300–310–390)

In the preceding phase, determining systems requirements, overall operational and hardware specifications were decided. In the design phase, technical decisions regarding standards and hardware characteristics are made. In many instances the firm already has adequate computer facilities so no new computer hardware is needed. But specifications on input and output equipment would still have to be made. For example, if scanning equipment for reading input data has been recommended, operational specifications prepared in the design phase might be:

Speed $>$ (more than) 1600 documents/hour
Error rate $= 1/10,000$ markings
Maintenance $\not>$ (no more than) 24 hours at any one time

Hardware specifications might include:

Cost $\not>$ (no more than) \$4,000/year
Capability $=$ Read markings on document and convert to
        cards at least 400 markings per document.
        Document size should be about 8½" x 11".
        Medium darkness of markings should suffice.

The development team generates a document with such detailed specifications for the use of technicians responsible for physical preparation, programming, and testing of the new system.

MODEL SELECTION AND DEVELOPMENT (300–330–390)

The **model** necessary for computation must be selected (300–330) and developed (330–390). It defines mathematically the manipulation of variables leading to a solution. In simple applications—such as payroll, accounts payable, or generating reports—flowcharts and decision tables can be used as long as relationships are stated in detail and all decision rules necessary for computation appear. For planning purposes, complex linear programming models may be required. Computer applications such as inventory control, queuing, and scheduling needed for management control use complex models. The use of models will be discussed in Chapter 20.

DOCUMENTATION STANDARDS (300–340)

In developing a new information system, standards for documentation should be established in the design phase.

Documentation in this context is a written description of choices and decisions during the development process. There is both **developmental** and **project control documentation.** The former is a description of the system itself (objectives, characteristics, decision rules); the latter concerns project development organization (personnel, time, materials, money). Developmental documentation is needed for operation and use of the new system. Control documentation is for auditing and evaluating the project.

If properly prepared, the documentation package has many advantages.

1. It is a record and evidence of all the commitments and expectations.
2. It helps initiate and train newcomers to the system.
3. It provides information needed to change the system, should the environment or management's needs alter.
4. It prevents dislocation and cost which occurs when knowledge of the system is centered in a few individuals who subsequently resign, relocate, or are assigned to other duties.
5. It facilitates routine evaluation, auditing, and control.

Programmers and systems analysts have a reputation for disliking documentation and for procrastinating over its completion, for it is tedious and time-consuming work. They often argue that they are too busy, or that documentation should wait until the system stabilizes. Since systems are constantly redesigned, stabilization occurs over a long period of time and documentation tends to be indefinitely postponed. Some companies will contract a system job for a 20 percent reduction in cost if no documentation is required. This is a penny-wise pound-foolish proposition. Documentation is too important to be compromised.

The fact that documentation is not a popular activity means that the development team must carefully spell out documentation standards and insist upon compliance. When standards for previously developed systems exist, they should be checked by the team to make sure they are applicable to the system under development. It may be necessary to supplement these standards to meet the unique needs of the new system.

Documentation should be divided into four manuals: a **Systems Man-**

ual—general information on the system and its objectives; a **Programmer's Manual**—description of programs; an **Operator's Manual**—directions for running programs; and a **User's Manual**—procedures for use of the system, including data flow diagrams, decision tables, and program descriptions written in terms that users understand. This division allows simultaneous access to documentation information by groups with differing needs. No single user can withdraw all documentation from circulation. The development team must prescribe what material is to be contained in each manual and establish the format for recording information. Abstract, detailed, and summary documentation should appear in each manual. The team must also specify the timing for completion of the documentation, for it loses its value if not available when needed. The dates of documentation completion should be included in project planning charts.

Testing standards for the documentation must also be outlined by the development team. Persons who prepare documentation are often so immersed in the system that assumptions are taken for granted. It is helpful to have personnel unfamiliar with the system try to operate it on a test basis by following documentation guidelines. Incompleteness, inadequacies, and ambiguities will soon be revealed.

Finally, the team should establish control standards for the documentation. Personnel (librarians) responsible for the manuals should be assigned and given authority to control access, and a physical location for the manuals must be chosen. Persons authorized to use and/or modify the documentation must be identified and procedures for documentation revision and validity testing should be set.

Documentation standards should be sent to all personnel involved in the development of the new system. This would include personnel in project management, programming, operations, testing, physical preparation, and also personnel responsible for organizational changes.

TESTING SPECIFICATIONS (300–350)

As part of the design of an information system, testing standards and requirements must be determined. This includes the choice of an approach to testing. One approach is a **pilot study.** The new system is designed and tested on a small scale and only after it is found to be successful does full-scale system implementation take place. This reduces and localizes the losses and disruption that may result from design errors.

When a pilot study is not feasible, testing may be a **parallel** or **dry run.** This involves testing the new system while the old is still in operation. This approach lets management observe the new system and check performance standards before discontinuing the old. Management may insist on this approach if skeptical about the new system, or if the consequences of system failure are so great that a trial run is essential. There is, however, a price that must be paid for test assurance. Two systems running simultaneously often cause confusion. Time and personnel costs are involved. Both pilot studies and dry runs produce considerable organizational strain.

Sometimes management chooses no testing after weighing testing costs against consequences should the system fail to perform. In automated information systems, however, this course is not recommended, because one unidentified variable, one unstated decision rule, one transcription error, or one incorrectly stated programming instruction can cause the entire system to malfunction.

One design policy that makes a system suitable for testing and conversion is modularity. This subject will be further discussed in Chapter 14.

New systems need a **factor of safety,** a factor determined by the development team and used in testing. For example, if an information system were designed for 10,000 employees, a safety factor of 2 would require the system to be tested for 20,000. Designing a system to function under unexpected conditions assures management that it can operate when conditions are normal. The magnitude of the safety factor should be decided by the team after weighing incremental costs against benefits.

In this design phase, what to test and how to test are determined. For example, for an online terminal system, the stated requirements for a particular output might be a response time of no more than five seconds. When the new system is implemented, performance will be checked against this specification or, using a factor of safety of 2, a response time of no more than 2½ seconds. Establishing such testing rules and standards is the responsibility of management working in conjunction with the development team.

Test design would also include the assignment of personnel to perform the tests, identification of control points and controls to be used in testing, the establishment of procedures for recording results, and finally, the setting up of a liaison between user and systems personnel for the purpose of evaluating test results.

ORGANIZATIONAL SPECIFICATIONS (300–355)

New systems require changes in a firm's organizational structure. Some jobs will be eliminated. Others will be created. Existing personnel may have to be retrained and/or new employees hired. Not all staff needs will be known at this stage in the development process. For example, the number and skills of operational personnel required for the new system will depend on the equipment selected. But as soon as these requirements are known, the persons responsible for personnel planning should be informed.

Since a general knowledge of the information system is needed if it is to be operated effectively and efficiently, the development team should specify what types of educational programs are necessary and who should participate. Employees requiring intensified retraining should be identified. In some cases, specifications for staffing may call for a retrenchment of personnel. Since a long gestation period is usually needed when making organizational changes, the development team should document personnel requirements as early as possible to ensure that employees are trained and available when it is time for conversion to the new system.

PROGRAMMING SPECIFICATIONS (300–360)

Programming specifications should include information on the capability and features of the programs to be written. The programming language(s) to be used should also be stated. Sometimes language choice is constrained by limitations of equipment. Too often, programmers simply use the language they know best, a language which may not be the most efficient or effective for the demands of the new system. This happens because programmers, under pressure of production work, have little time to keep abreast of their fast-moving field. Time should be spent in language evaluation before the team makes the final language selection. For example, many languages, especially machine languages, are machine-dependent though these languages have certain advantages such as fast processing time. Machine-independent languages provide flexibility, facilitating future changes in computer systems. Programmers for such languages are also easier to find. The development team must evaluate such trade-offs in their choice.

Establishing programming standards, such as structured programming, is another responsibility of the development team. Uniform standards have been widely adopted and undoubtedly the firm has incorporated them for other systems in use. Or they can be found in textbooks or manuals.[1] Standards should facilitate interchangeability between programmers.

QUALITY AND CONTROL SPECIFICATIONS (300–370)

Quality and control are related because the function of control is to ensure specific levels of quality. This is achieved by setting up quality standards and making sure that they are met.

Control is exercised with each system component, such as input, output, and processing. Control is discussed in different sections of this chapter when design of these components is considered. There is, however, one important aspect of control that affects all components of the system, the **audit trail.**

An audit trail is the path of data flow in a transaction. In manual processing, points are established along this trail for recording information about the transaction, permitting, for example, a given monetary transaction to be traced from original entry to its termination in the general ledger. The records are then later examined by auditors. In a manual accounting system, arithmetical accuracy and correct posting of figures from one set of documents to another would also be checked as part of quality control.

---

[1] See Dick H. Brandon, Arnold D. Palley, and A. Michael O'Reilly, *Data Processing Management: Methods and Standards* (New York: Macmillan Information, 1975), 520 p.

Audit trails also exist in computerized systems, but control is different since the computer has eliminated the detailed recording that is done in manual processing. Auditors concentrate on verifying input documents and seeing that subsequent procedures are carried out as planned. They are more concerned with checking the system than in checking the individual items being processed by the system. When designing a new information system, costs versus benefits of audit trails must be evaluated and the degree of trailing must be decided. Management may have little choice, however, for government and regulatory agencies specify auditing requirements for many applications.[2]

Control and quality specifications generate a document that is sent to testing personnel who make sure that the quality standards set are met by the new system. The document is also sent to the programming group so that these capabilities can be programmed.

INPUT AND OUTPUT SPECIFICATIONS (300–375–380–382–390)

In a functional sense, input comes before output. But from a design viewpoint the order is reversed. It is necessary to know output requirements first because these determine the input that is required. File design (needed in processing) generally comes last since input determines the records which constitute the file, though in some cases a preliminary file will be designed before input.

Output (300–375)

In specifying detailed output, users on the development team should be sure that the new system provides all the information that is needed for both current and future use. The incremental cost of producing added information is relatively small at the design stage compared to the cost of redesigning the system at a later date. An analogy would be including a public address system in the blueprints for a building under construction as opposed to the high renovation cost of adding such a system to an existing structure.

But care must be taken not to over-specify output needs. Users should not demand output that is simply nice to have. Unnecessary information can be a burden and have a negative benefit. It can crowd out needed information, making essential information difficult to find and use. There is also a cost involved in producing useless information. The development team must weigh the benefits of output against costs before determining exactly what output the new system should produce.

The details of content of the output may have already been determined as part of the users' requirements. If not, then details must be specified now. For example, parameters and input variables for each computation required for the output should be stated along with their spatial relationships, if these

---

[2] The subject of auditing is discussed later, in Chapter 16.

are desired. Requirements such as totals, subtotals, and figures in absolute values or percentages must also be specified.

One characteristic of good output is that it can be understood and accurately interpreted by any user, even one who has not participated in the development of the system and is ignorant of the environment. The output can be checked by asking: Is the output readable? Does it have an adequate, unique, and meaningful title? Are the different types of reports easily accessible? Are pages numbered? Are all abbreviations and codes adequately identified? Are assumptions clear? Is the period for which the data is relevant apparent? Is the output dated? Is the run number given when more than one run is made per day? Is the output complete? Is it accurate? Is it easy to store and retrieve?

These questions may seem trivial but attention paid to seemingly small and inconsequential matters often determines the effectiveness of an information system. For example, a university using an information system to produce a class schedule discovered that many students were attending class at the wrong time or going to the wrong room at the start of the semester. The format of the schedule made it hard to read. The eye had to move across ten columns of course information (course number, section number, credit hours, instructor, and so forth) before reaching the columns for time and location. The close spacing of horizontal lines resulted in frequent misalignment of information, the students' eyes wandering to the line above or below before reading the final columns. In this case, faulty output design meant ineffective use of the information produced by the system. The problem was corrected by reformatting the output, keeping relevant information, such as room number and class times in the left-hand columns and lengthy and less consequential information, such as course title, in the right-hand columns. A further solution was to leave spacing at the end of each department's course information, and to use output paper with colored horizontal stripes.

The design of output will vary with the user's style of management. The mode of processing (real time versus batch) and the nature of output (printed versus terminal, or print versus graphic) will also influence design. Nevertheless, there are some basic design principles that apply to all output. They are as follows:

1. Legends, headings, and output formats should be standardized whenever possible.
2. Acronyms, abbreviations, and terms used in the output should be defined. Examples and explanations may serve this purpose. Or a glossary can be appended.
3. Algorithms and assumptions on which calculations are based should be available to users of the output. This assures correct interpretation of output.
4. Output should be hierarchical in presentation so that the user can access data easily at each level required without having to search through all the data.

5. The amount of data, its accuracy, and precision should be governed by how the output is to be used. For example, too much output can overload the user and prove as ineffective as too little.
6. Exceptional data should be displayed in a manner which facilitates comparison of actual values with expected values, the comparison being in meaningful units. For example, percentage increase or decrease in dollar sales might be more useful than absolute dollar values.
7. The contents of the output should be listed in a menu, especially when output appears on a terminal.
8. Users have psychological and intellectual constraints in the amount of data that can be absorbed at any one time.[3] These constraints should be recognized and taken into consideration when designing the quantity and format of output data displayed per frame.[4]
9. Users needs should govern the level of aggregation of output.
10. The age of data affects the usefulness of output. Outdated information, data no longer needed for decision making, should be excluded.

Output specifications, once determined, are sent to the personnel involved in programming, physical preparation, and testing. The specifications are also prerequisites for the next set of activities to be performed, the design of input.

Input (375–380)

As with output, there is input data that is not essential but nice to have. It is tempting to collect such data because the incremental cost of added input is often very small. However, useless input has the same negative benefit as useless output. Data for future use should be collected but users must be able to show benefits for such input.

Care must be taken to collect data at the lowest level of aggregation needed for present and future use. For example, data on total sales per month per sales representative could not be used to generate a report on company sales for each state unless the input also included information on the location of each sale. What if management five years hence requires historical information on sales per product? The system will be unable to produce such a report unless the input of sales data includes information on products sold.

---

[3] See George A. Miller, "The Magical Number Seven, Plus or Minus Two: Some Limits on Our Capacity for Processing Information," *The Psychological Review,* vol. 63, no. 2 (March 1956), pp. 81–97.

[4] For designs of display output, see James Martin, *Design of Man-Computer Dialogues* (Englewood Cliffs, N.J.: Prentice-Hall Inc., 1973). For a discussion of human factors in output design, see Henry M. Parsons, "The Scope of Human Factors in Computer-Based Data Processing Systems," *Human Factors,* vol. 12, no. 2 (April 1970), pp. 165–75, and Lance A. Miller and John C. Thomas, Jr., "Behavioral Issues in the Use of Interactive Systems," *International Journal of Man-Machine Studies,* vol. 9, no. 5 (September 1977), pp. 509–36.

Files (380–390)

The development team must determine the nature of **files** required for the new information system, the content of each file (what data elements are to be used) and the storage media for each file.

The concept of files was discussed in Chapter 6. Every application will use at least one file. When multiple applications and files exist, files need to be integrated with other files in the data base. For **horizontal integration,** that is, integration between files, one or more linking data elements is needed. For **vertical integration,** integration between the different levels of management, a common set of data elements is required. For **longitudinal integration,** data compatibility over the years is needed. These integrations must be approved and coordinated by the data base administrator. The topic of integration will be discussed in greater detail in Chapter 21.

Within one functional file or subsystem (that is, sales, manufacturing, advertising, or personnel), there may be many related or derived files, as shown in Figure 13.2. The **master file** is designed to contain all basic operational information and should also contain current information on transactions by being regularly updated from the **transaction file.** Updating adds to the master file. It would soon become bulky and inefficient unless stripped of data no longer needed for processing. Stripped historical data, including that used in occasional operational processing and data kept merely for the record, should be stored in an **archive file.** In government-regulated industries, such as utilities, length of time records must be stored is specified by law.

A master file containing data for the current year may still prove cumbersome. Files of 10,000 to 50,000 records, each containing up to 500 characters, are not uncommon for employee, vendor, or customer files. Since only part

FIGURE 13.2
Types of files

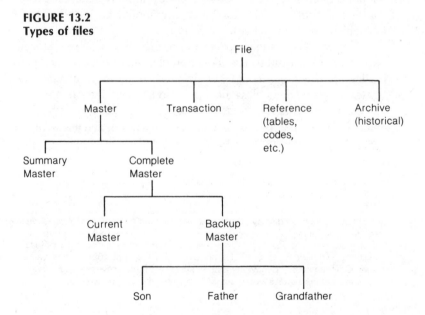

of these records affect transactions, a **summary master file** can be extracted for regular updating and frequent use, while the complete master is updated less often and processed only when required.

Backup is needed for the master file when the loss of data on that file would disrupt or interfere with operations. If the master file is processed daily, retention of the superseded file would constitute one level of backup (first generation). Yesterday's file would be a second backup (second generation), and the file from the day before yesterday would serve as the third generation of backup. These respective files are commonly called **son, father,** and **grandfather files.** They should be stored in secure and disperse locations. If the location of the master makes it vulnerable, the amount of backup and the degree of security required are factors to be decided by management and the development team. Allowance should be made for accidental master file loss due to operational errors, loss due to natural disasters such as fire or flood, and possible sabotage or theft. But creation of backup will be tempered by processing costs necessary to create backup and the cost of storage.

Figure 13.2 also shows a **reference file.** Generally tables and codes are kept in a reference file because they are commonly shared by several programs, or because they are too lengthy to be incorporated into a program. Which tables and codes to include in the reference file is also a design specification.

Forms (380–382)

Output and input often require preprinted forms. There are principles of design that apply to all forms. They must be unambiguously titled and worded; the color of the forms should be chosen for emphasis and ease of reading (light brown and light green print have been found empirically to be easy on the eye); the forms should be shaded for horizontal reading of lines of data without the drifting of sight; the print must be spaced to facilitate reading; related data should be grouped together; the form size should fit into standard binders and file cabinets; no information should be lost when the form is punched or bound; and finally, the paper used should satisfy requirements at minimum cost.

Other **form design** principles that apply specifically to output were covered in the discussion on output in this chapter. In checking design of input forms, the following questions should be asked:[5]

1. Are the instructions for completing the form adequate and easily understood?
2. Are input codes (if used) unique and unambiguous?
3. Is there sufficient space for completing information without crowding?
4. Are the questions worded unambiguously?
5. Are the questions in proper sequence to avoid confusion?

---

[5] For details, see C. B. Randall and S. W. Burgly, *Systems & Procedures for Business Data Processing* (2d ed.; Cincinnati, Ohio: South-Western Publishing Co., 1968), pp. 235–36.

6. Are lines to be filled in by typewriter spaced to conform to typewriter spacing?
7. Is the vertical alignment on forms to be typewritten such that clerks can use the typewriter tabular-stop device?
8. Does the form provide larger spaces for handwritten data than for type-written data?
9. If the form is to take information from, or pass information to, another form, do the items appear in the same order on both forms?
10. Does the form have all recurring items printed so that only variable values need to be filled in?
11. Is all known and fixed information preprinted?
12. Have all relevant facts been collected?
13. Is the form designed so that no information is lost when the form is filed or bound?
14. Is the form printed on the size and weight of paper that meets the requirements of the form without being more expensive than necessary?
15. Can the form be easily referenced by document number, date of origin, or some other identification?

The importance of careful form design cannot be overemphasized. A firm with an application asking for name, address, birthdate, father's name, and date of high school graduation found that many persons entered their father's date of graduation whereas the information desired was the applicant's own high school graduation date. In this case, poor sequencing of questions or poor clarification of the question resulted in misinformation. Such problems should be anticipated. Careful form design should minimize such misunder-standings. Pretesting a form by sample users is one method of detecting such design errors.

The entry of numbers on forms is a frequent source of errors. For example, handwritten ones and sevens often look alike. The use of boxes on forms for numerical data seems to encourage the average user to write numbers legibly. Data processing personnel commonly use the European convention of placing a dash on the stem of a seven ($\not{7}$) to distinguish it from a one. They also place a dash on the Z ($\not{Z}$) so it won't be mistaken for a 2, and a slash through the zero ($\emptyset$) to distinguish it from the letter O. (Unfortunately, this latter convention is the opposite of the practice in the military).

Date entries such as 3/1/52 can also cause problems of interpretation since the American convention of month/day/year is reversed for Europeans.[6] Here again the use of boxes is advisable. By using the box form design

MONTH	DAY	YEAR

---

[6] The convention proposed for interchange of data regarding dates is Year/Month/Date. For details, see *Communications of the ACM,* vol. 13, no. 1 (January 1970), p. 55.

the danger of reversing the date order is eliminated though there still remains the possibility that Mo, meaning Monday, may be filled in as day of birth. But well-written instructions for filling out the form, coupled with sample correct and incorrect responses, should eliminate such errors.

The box technique has other advantages. It can keep units separate, such as cents from dollars, and can also ensure that all digits of a number are entered, such as the nine digits of a social security number. An empty box assigned to a social security number can be detected more easily by a glance than a missing number in a string of nine numbers written on a line.

Boxes are also used for coding. Some forms have a space reserved on the right-hand column with boxes used by a coder to code information written on the left-hand side of the form. The form is then used as a document for direct key punching.

Another variation is a series of boxes which users check to indicate a condition. One such example is:

MARITAL
STATUS ☐ 1 ☐ 2 ☐ 3 ☐ 4
SINGLE MARRIED DIVORCED OTHER SPECIFY_____

Input boxes are also used on machine-readable forms, though these boxes must be marked by a special pencil. This technique, called **mark-sensing,** reduces processing time and inaccuracies in processing since data need not be manually converted into machine language.

Forms are costly. They must be designed, printed, processed, stored, and controlled. Yet forms have a tendency to proliferate. In designing a new system, the development team should carefully scrutinize not only the design of forms but their need, guarding against the collection of unnecessary information or duplicating information previously gathered.

Procedures (382–390)

In using an information system, especially when using equipment preparing input or disseminating output, a specific set of steps and instructions called **procedures,** must be followed. These procedures are:

> . . . a predetermined sequence of actions which should be taken to carry out some task or job, specifying what shall be done, how it shall be done, who shall do it and when . . . System procedures provide a link among the men, machine, and computer programs within the system, a link which can be used to orient and educate the users before the system is installed and operated, and which will guide them when it is put into use.[7]

The above definition emphasizes the descriptive and prescriptive nature of procedures. But procedures also have a heuristic character, since they

---

[7] L. A. Friedman, "Design and Production of Systems Procedures," in *Developing a Computer-Based Information System,* ed. P. E. Rosove (New York: John Wiley & Sons, Inc., 1967), pp. 201, 203.

are exploratory methods for solving a problem and are improved by evaluation and experience.

The importance of procedures can perhaps best be illustrated by a case study. Figure 13.3 shows the procedures used by a large firm for handling accounts receivable. Careful analysis by the reader should reveal a major procedural weakness costing the firm loss of interest income. According to the flowchart, no check is sent to the bank until all check data is validated

FIGURE 13.3
Procedure for processing accounts receivable

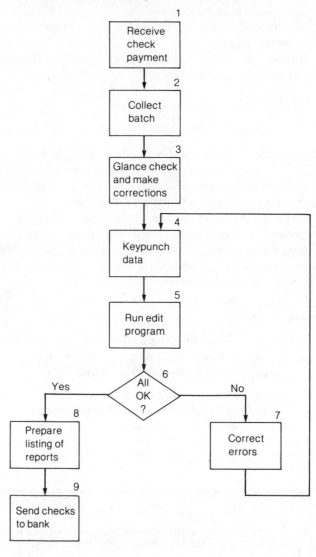

(Box 5). In this firm, only 6 percent of the entries needed recycling, yet they held up the deposit of all accounts receivable an average of four days. By changing the decision rule in Symbol 6 to "OK?" instead of "All OK?", valid checks could be sent to the bank immediately to earn interest and only bad entries recycled. This change gave three days of previously lost interest on the valid checks to the firm, and increased cash flow.

Batch collection (Box 2) may also result in a loss of interest income if processing is delayed until a large number of checks are received. If batch size is small, response time will improve but the overhead cost of processing may be more than the interest accrued by faster processing. The procedures should therefore specify optimal batch size. This can be calculated, given the cost of processing, the average rate of arrivals, and the average amount per check. In some cases, the batch size will be one, in which case an online real-time system is needed, as found in many warehouses and large urban banks.

As shown by the above example, procedures affect cost and response time. They also affect accuracy and the effectiveness of the system so they must be designed with care. Since many procedures are custom-designed, the participation of management is needed on the development team to interpret the organizational environment and to decide which procedures best serve the interests of the firm.

Some principles of procedure design are:

1. Human considerations should not be overlooked when designing procedures. Tasks should not be monotonous and the opportunity for job enlargement should exist.
2. Skills required for each procedure should be indicated. If special authorization is required, such as security clearance, this should also be stated.
3. The boundaries and domain of each employee's job and responsibility should be well defined. Rules must be established yet should allow for flexibility of action. Priorities should be stated. The degree of specificity of procedures will vary with the nature of the environment and projected external disturbances such as illness, strikes, or natural disaster.
4. Procedures should be standardized whenever possible.
5. Similar procedures having only slight modifications to fit particular circumstances should be performed by different individuals. For example, when data for a system being tested must be coded simultaneously with coding for the existing system yet each system uses different codes, two individuals, a coder for each system, should be assigned. If only one employee is available, processing of the similar procedures should be staggered in time. Switching back and forth between procedures that are alike causes confusion resulting in inaccuracies.
6. Procedures should allow for feedback and evaluation. Statistics should be maintained on the frequency of errors by type of error so that informa-

tion is available for procedure evaluation. For example, statistics on high error rates in coding might later be used to trace a coder who is poorly trained or incapable of meeting operational standards.

A member of the development team, an analyst, or a technical writer assigned the task should document all procedures in a clear, complete, and unambiguous manner in a **Procedures Manual.** This manual should be tested before being used and periodically evaluated to ensure continued validity.

FORMAL DESIGN TECHNIQUES

Some techniques of systems design are integrated with computer program development. That is, a computer will generate the necessary sets of programs for the implementation of an information system, given the systems specifications as input. PSA (Program Statement Analyzer) and HOSKYNS (named after the designer) are examples of such an automated design technique. So is a decision table processor that produces COBOL code from a decision table specification. PSA does not go so far as to produce program code but does produce program specifications.

Other techniques such as HIPO (Hierarchy Plus Input-Process-Output) integrate design with stages of system analysis and system specification. Still other design techniques include programs for optimizing design. SODA (System Optimization and Design Algorithm) claims to generate an optimal design and hardware specifications from a statement of processing requirements. ISDOS (Information System Design and Optimization System) automates systems development, operations, and maintenance.

Although all these design techniques are technical, generally implemented by systems analysts, management should be aware of their capabilities and limitations in order to ensure that the design technique adopted will produce desired results.

REVISE PROJECT SCHEDULE (390–395)

An additional activity in the design phase is revising the project schedule. Once detailed design specifications have been determined, more accurate time estimates for completing activities can be made. Also, some activities may have been added which were not anticipated when the schedule was first drafted.

MANAGEMENT APPROVAL (395–400)

The revised schedule, the system definition and the specification documents, are presented to management for approval at the conclusion of the design phase. Although management may have been represented on the design team, a review of the total design package by user management is needed at this stage, and a formal decision on implementation must be made. Lack of approval of the system definition means either termination of the project or recycling of those activities designated unsatisfactory by management. Approval is followed by implementation, the subject of the next chapter of this text.

SUMMARY AND CONCLUSIONS

This chapter is conceptually a continuation of the previous chapter. Both chapters concern system specifications. There are, however, two main differences: detail and responsibility. In Chapter 12, overall specifications, determined primarily by users on the development team, were examined. In this chapter, detailed specifications, made primarily by systems analysts on the team, are described. But in both these phases of development of the new system, analysts and management should work closely together to ensure that the real objectives of the system change are fully achieved. Both are needed to interpret the internal and external environment in which the new system will operate. Factors in these environments influencing system design are summarized in Figure 13.4.

FIGURE 13.4
Internal and external environment affecting system specifications

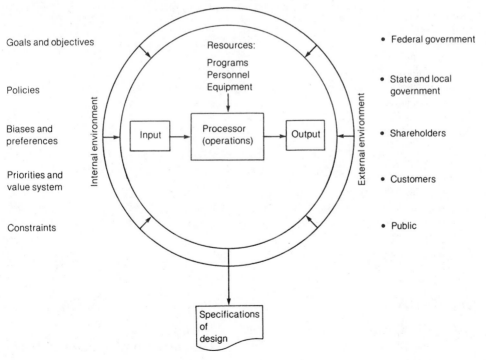

The discussion of design activities in this chapter has followed the generic network diagram in Figure 13.1. In actual practice, system design may deviate somewhat from this schedule of activities. For example, programming and testing design specifications may be combined for small systems, and no need may exist for making organizational changes or for determining hardware specifications.

The product at the end of the design phase is the set of specification documents listed in Table 13.1. These are sent to various groups, also identified in the table, where they serve as the basis for implementation.

TABLE 13.1
Users of documents generated in the design phase

Documents	Pro-gram-ming group	Physi-cal prepa-ration group	Test-ing group	Organi-zational change group	Other develop-ment per-sonnel	Data base adminis-trator
Overall systems plan ...	*	*	*	*	*	*
Systems specifications ..	*	*	*	*	*	*
Operational specifications	*	*	*			*
Hardware specifications	*	*	*			*
Documentation specifications	*	*	*	*	*	*
Testing specifications	*	*	*	*	*	*
Organization specifications				*		
Programming specifications	*		*			*
Quality and control specifications	*	*	*			*
Model definition	*		*		*	*
Output specifications ...	*	*	*			
Input and file specifications	*	*	*			*
Forms and procedures specifications	*	*	*			*
Revised schedule	*	*	*	*	*	*

KEY WORDS

Archive file
Audit trail

Backup
Developmental documentation

Dry run
Factor of safety
Files
Form design
Hardware specifications
Horizontal integration
Longitudinal integration
Mark-sensing
Master file
Model
Operational specifications
Operator's manual
Parallel run

Pilot study
Procedures manual
Programmers' manual
Programming specifications
Project control documentation
Reference file
Son, father, and grandfather
  files
Summary master file
Systems manual
Transaction file
User's manual
Vertical integration

DISCUSSION QUESTIONS

1. Suppose you were responsible for developing a new accounts receivable application for a medium-size organization of medium complexity having a variety of accounts. Describe the development team you would like to have appointed.

2. What are the responsibilities of management systems analysts and programmers in the design process?

3. Describe some of the tools of systems design.

4. What are the main components of a good computerized report for management?

5. Explain how flowcharts are used in designing an information system? Why are decision tables not always used?

6. What are the advantages of assigning to a steering committee responsibility for the design of a large and complex system?

7. What is the role of an accountant and auditor in the design phase? Why cannot accounting and auditing considerations be left until implementation and operations?

8. What are procedures? What role do they play in an information system? When should procedures be designed? Who should be responsible?

9. What is the significance of forms in an information system? Describe different types of forms. Who should design forms?

10. What are the objectives of a systems flowchart?

11. Suppose an application were designed to incorporate a Sales Order File for batch processing. What changes will be necessary for real-time processing?

12. What types of files (master, transaction, and so forth) would be required for the following types of processing:
    a. Payroll?
    b. Accounts receivable?
    c. Student admission?
    d. Student grades?
    For each of the four cases, what storage media would you use?

13. List the components of a document package? Why should they be in distinct modules for user, programmer, operator, and so forth?

14. Describe the importance of documentation.

15. When should documentation begin and end within the development cycle?

16. Who should be responsible for documentation?

17. Why is documentation so unpopular? Can it be subcontracted?

18. What are the components of a procedures manual?

19. What are the differences between system feasibility documentation, program documentation, and system documentation?

EXERCISES

1. Design detailed outputs for the file in Exercise 1, Chapter 10 for managerial use.

2. Draw a systems flowchart for Exercise 1, Chapter 10.

3. Draw a programming flowchart for the system in Exercise 1, Chapter 10.

4. Is the file in Exercise 1, Chapter 10 a master file or a transaction file? Is any other file required for this application?

5. Design a form for collecting the data for Exercise 1, Chapter 6.

6. Consider an environment using tapes for accounts payable processing. Tape A is the master with information on all the vendors and amounts owed; Tape B is a transaction file with the day's transactions of amounts paid to vendors during the day. At night, in batch, the master tape is updated by the transaction tape giving the remaining amounts due to vendors. What tapes result in output? What happened to tapes A and B? What is used for the next day's processing? What happens if the new master tape is lost or destroyed in error?

7. What is the difference between a systems flowchart and a programming flowchart? Draw an example of each. Assume any one application for both flowcharts.

SELECTED ANNOTATED BIBLIOGRAPHY

Daniels, Alan, and Yeates, Donald. *Systems Analysis.* Palo Alto, Calif.: Science Research Associates, 1971, pp. 37–117.
This text has three chapters on design: the design of input, output, and files. It includes numerous check lists and tables.

Herchauer, James C. "What's Wrong with System Design Methods? It's Our Assumptions." *Journal of Systems Management,* vol. 29, no. 4 (April 1974), pp. 25–29.
The author criticizes the common assumptions: dominance of information technology; humans are inferior to machines; noncomputer technology is not optimal; and humans lack understanding of using computer technology. The author recommends a sociotechnical system of information and communication within the complexity of an existing organizational structure. The author's design methodology is highly output- and user-oriented.

Kinzer, J. G. "A Model for System Design." *Journal for System Management,* vol. 23, no. 9 (October 1972), pp. 24–30.

Kinzer presents a model (not mathematical, but conceptual) for the evolutionary design of an information system. The author emphasizes the detailed nature and iterativeness of the design process.

Meyers, Gibbs. "Forms Management." *Journal of Systems Management,* vol. 27, nos. 9–11 (September–November 1976).

This is a series in three parts on forms management. Part One discusses the use of forms for greater organizational efficiency and smoothness of operations; Part Two is on the design of business forms; and Part Three is on cost-saving techniques for designing ten different types of forms, including form construction and production.

Mixon, S. R. *Handbook of Data Processing Administration, Operations and Procedures.* New York: AMACOM, Division of American Management Association, 1976, pp. 127–258.

This text includes eight chapters on system design: input forms design, output/report design, DED, systems control, data base design, program functions, modular programming, and program specifications design.

Rubin, Martin L. *Introduction to the System Life Cycle,* vol. 1. New York: Brandon/Systems Press, 1970, pp. 61–100.

This is a multivolume handbook with a chapter in Volume 1 on system design, including sections on detailed analysis, design decisions, design objectives, and system specifications. The next two volumes are on documentation forms and standards.

Teichroew, Daniel, and Gackowski, Z. "Structured System Design," *Ideas for Management.* Cleveland, Ohio: Association for Systems Management, 1977, pp. 45–58.

Teichroew has long been associated with a project at the University of Michigan for automating the design and implementation of an information system. In this article a computer-aided technique for structured documentation and analyses of an information system is described; numerous charts are used. Highly recommended for one view of the future of automated design. Tiechrow's work can also be found in *Systems Analysis Techniques* edited by J. D. Couger and R. W. Knapp published in 1974 by Wiley and Sons. This book also includes chapters on HOSKYNS, ISDOS, TAG, SOP, ADS, and SYSTEMATICS.

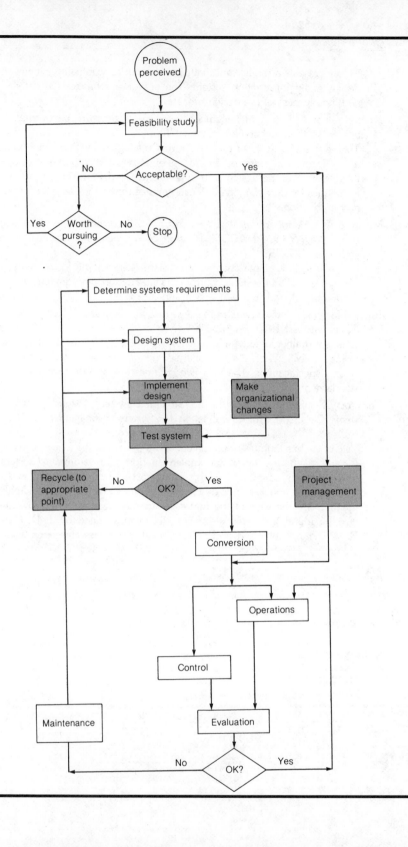

14

IMPLEMENTATION, TESTING, AND CONVERSION

Following design of the new system, implementation takes place although it is not always possible to pinpoint exactly where design ends and implementation begins. Programming the solution, for example, is usually a major activity of implementation but some development teams provide so much detail in the design phase that programmers need only translate each design specification into a computer instruction. Other teams, however, merely specify logic in general terms when designing the system, leaving implementation of this logic to programmers.

Hardware installation and testing are other activities of implementation. Organizational changes are also initiated in this phase of development and files prepared. Then the system is tested and the development process evaluated. Finally, conversion takes place. Figure 14.1 is a network design showing implementation activities in relation to testing, conversion, and evaluation.

FIGURE 14.1
Partial network diagram of programming, testing, and conversion

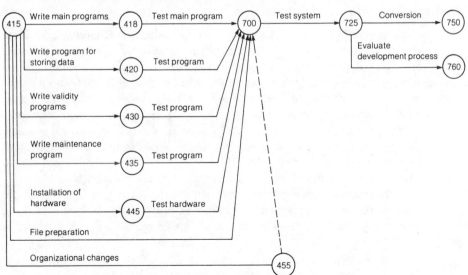

This chapter is the last in Part Three describing the development process of an information system. Some aspects of design and implementation are mentioned only briefly in this part, to be examined in detail in Part Four about management of an information system. Problems of operations, evaluation, maintenance, and redevelopment, for example, are discussed in Chapter 15; quality control and security are the subjects of Chapter 16; behavioral and organizational questions, the crux of successful implementation, are in Chapter 17; and distributed data processing is the subject of Chapter 18.

IMPLEMENTATION

Programming activities

All computerized information systems require programming effort. The main program(s) must be written so that the system produces the information expected. At the same time, programs for storing data, checking data, and maintenance must also be prepared. Once the needs of management have been spelled out, programming is left to programmers. A detailed discussion of this technical activity is beyond the scope of this text. However, it should be noted that not all programs needed for the new system have to be written by the firm's programmers. Software programs, designed to perform a specific or general-purpose function, can be purchased. Many are available for functional information systems, such as marketing, advertising, and financial accounting, and for solving operations research problems. The value of such packages must be weighed against their cost and the expense of adapting them to local equipment configurations.

Hardware selection and installation

Responsibility for the selection and implementation of hardware for large and medium-size computerized systems is generally delegated to hardware and systems personnel. However, operational managers are increasingly assuming the responsibility for selection of minis, micros, and input-output equipment. The principles of analysis described in the feasibility study should be used in evaluating costs versus benefits when making equipment decisions.

Site preparation, installation, and testing of the new equipment are also part of this phase of implementation. These activities may be complex and technical for larger systems. An IBM manual[1] lists 222 activities in a critical path diagram for installation of a computer system, for example.

In the field, sequencing of hardware activities varies. Figure 14.2 is a sample network diagram, representing the common practice. In any given situation, sequencing will be a function of equipment complexity, the time available

---

[1] IBM, *Management Planning Guide of Data Processing Standards*, No. C20–1670–1 (White Plains, N.Y.: International Business Machines Corporation, n.d.), p. 13.

FIGURE 14.2
Equipment-related activities

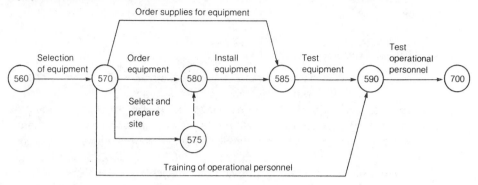

for project completion, and the level of knowledge and experience of existing personnel.

File preparation

File specification was discussed in Chapter 13 and file design in Chapter 6. The implementation of a file according to file specifications is done in one of two ways: **file creation** or **file restructuring.** Files are created from new, or predominately new, raw data. Collection of this data may require special forms and procedures. Large volumes of data may be collected on special mark-sense sheets or on documents that are optically scanned. If coded or collected from documents, the data must be converted to machine-readable form. Whatever the approach to data collection and conversion, the data must be stored on storage media chosen for the new file. File creation is done by a special program, sometimes called a **start-up program.** Either before or after storage the file must also be validated and checked for completeness.

In file restructuring, an old file is converted into a new one. Restructuring may be triggered by the addition of data elements and consequent expansion of a file, the need for additional width of one or more data elements, the rearrangement of data elements to facilitate processing, the need to change format to conform to a new standard form, or the need to revise an old file to make it complete and accurate.

To restructure a file, selected parts of the old file have to be retrieved and added to newly created raw data or new derived data calculated from other files. A start-up program can also be written for this purpose. It should contain special checks like subtotals, totals, and cross-totals to ensure that no data is lost in the restructuring process. Also, special procedures must be adopted so data generated during the time the old file is being converted to the new one is not lost. This problem is critical when transactional data is being continuously generated in real-time systems. Again, as with newly created files, restructured files must be checked for data validity and completeness.

Organizational considerations

Many new information systems require organizational changes. Positions may be eliminated, others created, and the job descriptions of employees altered to incorporate new responsibilities. Restructuring jobs may affect departmental span of control so that the firm's organization chart may change.

After planning for such changes and management approval of the plans, training programs must be established to teach employees how to operate the new system. This involves preparation of teaching materials and selection of personnel to perform the training. An alternative to in-house training is to send employees to commercial training institutes or schools run by manufacturers.

Figure 14.3 is one example of sequencing **training** activities. Note that each type of training is based on the specifications drawn up in the design phase. Activity sequencing, however, will vary from project to project. A small organization, for example, may train a single individual for updating, equipment operation, and input/output procedures, so consecutive training sessions

FIGURE 14.3
Activities related to training and operation

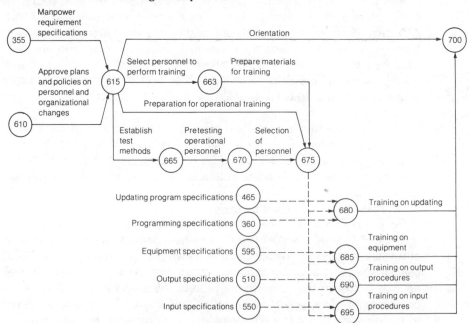

rather than parallel sessions would be required. The project manager will determine sequencing based on the nature of the project and the resources (time and personnel) available for training.

If the firm lacks systems analysts, they may have to be hired from outside the firm, but often it is more difficult to train a person in the intricacies of the company's power structure, its practices, terminology, and procedures than it is to train as an analyst a person already within the organization. Furthermore, loyalty to the firm of an outsider is hard to assess, whereas the loyalty of an individual already in the firm's employ is known. For these reasons, many managers prefer to train analysts from existing personnel, selecting individuals that show interest and aptitude for this work.

But what makes a good analyst? M. Wofsey lists 24 characteristics,[2] though obviously not all will be found in one individual. The main desirable characteristics are: an inquisitive mind, a flair for detail, ability to work with people at all levels, an open mind, logical ability, thoroughness, resourcefulness, imagination, and ability to communicate (verbally and in written documentation). Technically, systems analysts should be knowledgeable about computer subdisciplines such as hardware, software, data structures, and data management. Also, the analysts must have good business backgrounds so that they can communicate readily with management and the applications staff. However, since these fields are growing, becoming increasingly complex and specialized, no systems analyst can be expected to have expertise in all these areas. If the EDP department is weak in one of these subdisciplines, consultants may have to be hired when selecting equipment, developing specialized software, making feasibility decisions, or even when orienting and training operating personnel.

Orientation, the introduction of users to the new system, should also take place during implementation. Organizing orientation would be similar to the organization for training. Traditionally, orientation has been directed exclusively toward managers and supervisors. However, to ensure system effectiveness, workers and clerks in affected areas should also participate, though the material covered should be modified according to the level of personnel being oriented. Orientation should establish favorable attitudes toward the new system, once employees know how the system operates and how each operation contributes to final results.

The content of the orientation sessions should include:

1. Objectives of system
        Short term
        Long term
        Relationship to:
            Organizational goals
            Overall systems goals

---

[2] Marvin W. Wofsey, *Management of Automatic Data Processing* (Washington, D.C.: Thompson Book Co., 1968), p. 54.

2. Limitations of system
3. Systems environment
   Applications
   Equipment
4. Process of development
   Nature
   Stages
5. Resources required
   Time
   Critical path
   Monetary
   Personnel
6. Role of
   User
   Systems personnel

TESTING THE SOLUTION

The testing process involves comparison of desired performance (as stated in the users requirement specifications) with actual performance, identifying deviations and eliminating them outside the allowed tolerances.

First, the actual system test must be planned. This means preparing the test data and selecting knowledgeable persons who represent the users to perform the test.

Reliability testing standards state the allowable occurrence of error in processing. For example, one error in a thousand may be the reliability specification of a warehouse inventory system. If the system, when tested, exceeds this error allowance, the system will have to be redeveloped or testing conditions reestablished. This is an example of the iterative recycling nature of the development process: design, test, redesign, retest, and recycle until the test is satisfactory; or, state systems specifications, design, test, restate specifications, redesign, and retest. (Some steps in the development process have been excluded to emphasize the relationship between design and testing.) **Performance testing standards** include specifications of response time, throughput, and staff and equipment efficiency. **Load specifications** state the factor of safety needed for peak periods, emergencies, and future expansion.

Next, test data must be collected. The team must decide how **test data** will be generated, what data to use, and the amount of data required. In many cases historical data is available for testing. For example, in converting from a manual to a computer system, the new system can be tested against the results of the old, using data collected in the past. However, in projects performing functions never done before, test data must be created. This should be done by the manager who can anticipate the conceptual problems and exceptions that may arise and need testing, in cooperation with the systems designer, whose experience makes it possible to anticipate operational problems.

What data to use and how much to use is a problem of sampling. A well-designed sample produces results as significant as results from the data collected from the population as a whole, and processing of the sample is cheaper and faster as well. Unfortunately, few people working with systems have training or applied experience in empirical experimental techniques. It may be necessary for the development team to add consultants knowledgeable in experimental design when test data is being prepared. Also, the consultants could help with the entire scope of testing, which should extend from the collection of input to the usage of output.

Levels of testing

Testing a new system is done at four levels: component testing, function testing, subsystem testing, and system testing.

Component testing is checking the parts of the system, such as a piece of equipment, the performance of an individual operator, or the effectiveness of a form, procedure, or program (for example, when desk-checking a computer program, the methodical manual check of each output, watching for omissions and possible misinterpretations, is one type of system component test).

Sometimes a component cannot be isolated. For example, one person's work may be so integrated with that of other employees that testing the individual's output would not be meaningful. In this case, the component to be tested would be the aggregate work of a group of employees.

The testing phase should begin with component testing because it is easier to identify errors and problems at this level than it is to isolate problems when testing interrelated components. Also, the earlier a problem is detected, the less effort is required to correct it.

Function testing is at a higher level of aggregation, measuring the performance of related components in a functional subsystem. This level of testing should be done after components of the function have been tested individually and found satisfactory.

Subsystem testing evaluates how related functions operate. For example, in testing an input subsystem, input procedures, input preparation, validity checking, and procedures for correcting errors would be assessed. Testing at this level checks the interrelationships of functions tested individually earlier.

System testing, checking overall results (that is, the performance of all subsystems in aggregate), is the final test phase. This can be done by **pilot tests, parallel runs,** or **simulation.**

The four testing levels are illustrated in Figure 14.4. The terms will perhaps be more meaningful when a practical example is given. A financial system can be subdivided into financial subsystems of accounting, manufacturing, engineering, marketing, and inventory subsystems. Each of these subsystems has many functions. The accounting subsystem includes accounts payable, accounts receivable, general ledger, costing, assets, liabilities, income, expenses, and tax functions. Each function is further subdivided into components. The payroll function includes wages, social security, W2 form, editing, balancing, journal, register, check writing, and payroll statement components. Testing begins at the component level of this hierarchy, continues at higher levels of aggregation, and ends up with the total systems check.

Testing is a very labor-intensive activity and takes a great share of the total effort required for the development of a computerized information system. This is reflected in Figure 14.5, which shows that testing takes about 45 percent of the total development effort.

The testing process ends when test results at the system level are satisfactory.

FIGURE 14.4
Levels of testing

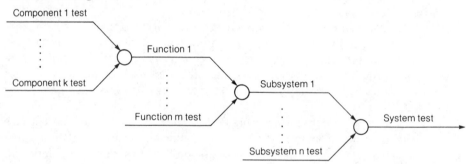

Unsatisfactory testing requires recycling, as in Figure 14.6, where possible cycles are depicted.[3] In complex systems, the value of *n* may be 3 or 4. If *n* is larger, responsibility may lie with users who failed to adequately specify needs, with systems personnel who did a poor design job, or with the development process itself which was not carefully planned and controlled. The value of *n* is seldom 1, even with capable personnel. Management should recognize that recycling is part of the development process and be prepared for it. Formal recycling controls should be established, such as procedures for recording the need for change and documenting modifications accomplished. Information about these changes must then be channeled to affected groups.

At the conclusion of favorable testing, the test results should be presented to management for approval. This is management's final check to see that the system satisfies goals and objectives for the system. By formalizing user acceptance, the development team minimizes the possibility that users will complain at a later date that the system fails to satisfy requirements.

---

[3] For a detailed discussion, see Z. D. T. Bross, *Design for Decisions* (New York: The Macmillan Company, 1953), pp. 171–82.

FIGURE 14.5
Share of effort in the development of an information system

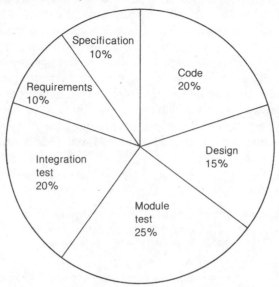

Source: M. V. Zelkowitz, "Perspectives on Software Engineering," *ACM Computing Surveys* (New York: Association for Computing Machinery), vol. 10, No. 2 (June 1978), p. 198.

Testing responsibility

Responsibility for testing lies with both users and systems personnel. Users can best formulate the conditions for **outside testing,** for example, examining systems' response to varying conditions of input, including instability and overload. **Inside tests,** examining the structure of the system for complete-

FIGURE 14.6
Recycling of testing process

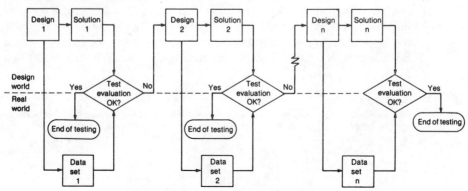

ness, consistency, reliability, and linkages, fall to systems personnel, particularly programmers.

Sometimes the individual performing a job does the testing. For example, programmers generally **debug** programs [4] they have written, though programs can also be tested by systems designers who know the system and can antici- pate some of the problems. To ensure objectivity, it is advisable to leave testing to analysts assigned to other responsibilities in the firm who have not participated in the development of the new system. A side benefit is that the expertise the tester acquires during testing serves as job enlargement for the analyst, while giving to the firm backup personnel knowledgeable in the system. In cases of programs involving funds or an accounting procedure, an internal auditor should be involved in the test function.

CONVERSION

The development process concludes with the cut-over or **conversion** from the old system to the new. Old documentation and outdated forms and files must be withdrawn and equipment no longer required removed. Any delay in removing unnecessary equipment can result in additional rental costs.

There are many approaches to conversion. Three of the most common are shown in Figure 14.7. The **sequential approach** means the complete switchover from old to new system is made on a given date. Sometimes old and new systems are run in **parallel** for a period of time. Large and complex information systems are generally phased in one **module** or **subsystem** at a time, "bottom-up," even though the design may be "top-down." This reduces the work load on personnel responsible for conversion and at the same time helps isolate problems of the new system while minimiz- ing the consequences of potential system failure.

Phasing in the new system must be carefully planned. Orientation and training sessions should have been completed. Manuals should have been distributed to affected personnel, and employees of departments involved in the changeover should be briefed on the scheduled cut-over date.

There is a tendency among users to delay phasing out old systems. Continu- ation of a parallel run beyond the planned schedule, for example, gives users an added sense of security. This costly practice should be discouraged. Once the new system has achieved desired performance levels, the old system should be discontinued. Confidence in the new system will develop only when it stands on its own.

---

[4] This term originates from the early days of computers when vacuum tubes were used. One such computer gave false results. The programmers spent many days trying to trace the error but with no success. Then, by accident, an operator found a bug on a contact that was causing the machine to malfunction. The bug was removed and the program, once debugged, worked perfectly.

FIGURE 14.7
Approaches to conversion

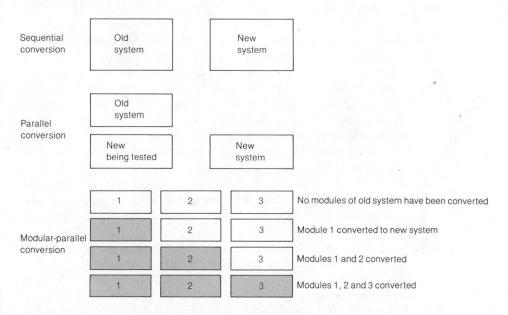

EVALUATING THE SYSTEMS DEVELOPMENT PROCESS

Before the development team is dispersed, **evaluation** of the systems development process should take place. Mistakes should be identified and analyzed as to why they were made and how they could have been avoided. The purpose of such an analysis is not to exchange accusations and recriminations, but to learn from the past so that similar mistakes won't be repeated when future information systems are developed. The efficiency and effectiveness of the new system should be scrutinized and the benefits versus costs assessed. A critical review of the need for recycling during the development process, of liaison and communication problems that arose, and of schedule slippage should lead to improved procedures and approaches for other projects.

SUMMARY

Design and implementation of an information system are closely allied. The exact point where design ends and implementation begins is difficult to pinpoint. Generally, however, implementation is left to technicians following design guidelines made during the design phase. Programs are written, files prepared (either created or restructured), equipment purchased and installed, and orientation and training sessions take place. Testing, a comparison of expected operational performance with desired performance as stated in the systems specification stage, follows. This testing stage provides an opportunity for further training of employees that will eventually be responsible for operation of the new system.

The actual tests are done on several levels: component tests, functional tests, subsystem tests, and tests of the entire system. All functions must be tested, including those of hardware, input data, input instruments, formats, codes, feedback, programs, training, and procedures for both normal and exceptional conditions. Performance must be evaluated not only for content quality but for timing and sequence as well, using the safety factors specified in the system specification stage. During testing, management must ensure that the new system performs as desired and needed.

Training is an important part of implementation. It has a long period of gestation and must be started early. Conversion should take place as soon as the new system achieves desired performance levels. All interested personnel should be carefully and regularly informed of the status of conversion and project completion. Silence and absence of information can start rumors resulting in low morale.

Testing and conversion cause a period of organizational strain and disruption. Unforeseen difficulties arise, and recycling is generally required. Recycling is usually done under great pressure of time, requiring higher work loads than usual. Normal service is unavoidably affected. The stress of conversion can be minimized if such problems are understood and anticipated and if the phase-out of the old system takes place swiftly on schedule. Organizational breakdowns are most likely to occur during long parallel runs.

A final duty of the development team is to present an evaluation of the development process to management. This report should include mistakes and insights of both users and system personnel to aid future teams in formulating new information systems for the firm.

KEY WORDS

Component testing	Parallel runs
Conversion	Performance testing standards
Debug	Pilot tests
Evaluation	Programming
File creation	Reliability testing standards
File restructuring	Sequential conversion
Function testing	Simulation
Inside tests	Start-up program
Load specifications	Subsystem testing
Module	System testing
Modular-parallel conversion	Test data
Orientation	Testing
Outside tests	Training
Parallel conversion	

DISCUSSION QUESTIONS

1. Distinguish between:
   a. Creating and restructuring a file.
   b. Training analysts and orientation of management.
2. Describe four programming activities.
3. Describe different approaches to conversion.
4. Describe five sources of file changes which would require updating of the files.
5. What redesigning of an information system is necessary for an expected change of equipment?
6. For whom should orientation sessions be planned?
7. Why should management be trained in system use?
8. Why should system orientation permeate all through the organization?
9. What type of training should be provided to managers and supervisors?
10. What are the activities of implementation of an EDP project?
11. How can the systems implementation be humanized?
12. Why is testing necessary? Should testing be done after each component of the system is implemented or should the testing be done for each subsystem or the total system? What are the advantages and limitations of each approach?
13. Distinguish between:.
    a. Pilot and parallel testing.
    b. Component and subsystem testing.
    c. Subsystem and system test.
    d. Historical data and test data.
14. How should the training differ in content, depth, detail, and terminology for managers, supervisors, operators, and data clerks?
15. Suppose that the completion of programs for a project were scheduled for December 1, but on October 1, two programs in COBOL were each three man-months behind. What action would you recommend? What if the December 1 deadline could not be changed?

EXERCISES

1. Write a program to produce the report requested in Exercise 1, Chapter 10. Specify procedures needed in operations.
2. Read Dan Appleton, "A Manufacturing System Cookbook, Part 3," *Datamation*, vol. 29, no. 9 (August 1979), pp. 130 ff. Do you agree with the author's list of characteristics for successful and unsuccessful implementations? How would you rank these characteristics? Substantiate your ordering.
3. Fill in the network diagram provided below, naming the activities in the proper sequence.
   a. Write main program.
   b. Dummy.
   c. Dummy.
   d. Conversion.
   e. Write other program.
   f. Install equipment.

g. Dummy.
h. Dummy.
i. Test main program.
j. Select equipment.
k. Orientation of management.
l. Test other program.
m. Test equipment.
n. Dummy.
o. Dummy.
p. Test system.
q. Test all programs.
r. Test operational personnel.
s. Specify manufacturer requirement.
t. Dummy.

Diagram for Exercise 3

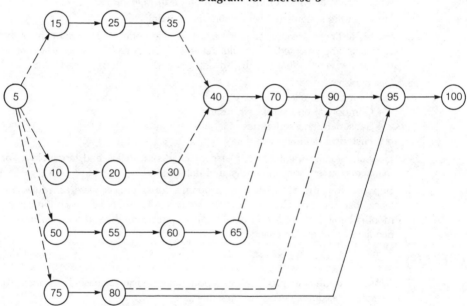

SELECTED ANNOTATED BIBLIOGRAPHY

Benjamin, Robert T. *Control of the Information System Development Cycle.* New York: John Wiley & Sons, Inc., 1971, pp. 41–90.
    This is a good discussion of the development cycle, including the phases of feasibility study, systems specification, design, implementation, and alterations. The author's use of numerous charts and tables is helpful.

Daniels, Alan, and Yeates, Donald. *Systems Analysis.* Palo Alto, Calif.: Science Research Associates, 1971.
    Chapter 7 is an excellent chapter on implementation of an information system.

Topics discussed are: selection of tasks, training, file conversion, cut-over, and the management of implementation. The chapter on testing is also recommended reading.

Lehman, John H. "How Software Projects Are Really Managed." *Datamation,* vol. 25, no. 1 (January 1979), pp. 119–29.

This is a mine of statistics collected from a stratified sample of 37 computer users. The article includes numerous statistical tables covering the management not just of software but of the entire development cycle of an information system. It discusses methods of estimating costs and schedules, documents required, project team composition, personnel turnover, testing tools, aids and methodology used, and approaches to project planning and control.

Mixon, S. R. *Handbook of Data Processing Administration, Operations, and Procedures.* New York: AMACOM, 1976.

This text has an excellent chapter on system testing (pp. 259–70). It discusses the organization of testing, system test plan, test data development, and acceptance testing. There are many checklists provided. The book also has good sections that relate to implementation: project implementation (pp. 45–125) and documentation standards (pp. 271–354).

Rubin, Martin L. *Introduction to the System Life Cycle,* vol. 1, New York: Brandon/ Systems Press, 1970, pp. 101–04.

This is a handbook on the development process with three chapters relating to implementation discussing the subjects of programming, documentation, and system installation. Well written with numerous illustrations.

Scharen, Laura L. "Improving System Testing Techniques." *Datamation,* vol. 23, no. 9 (September 1977), pp. 115–17 ff.

The author strongly argues that systems testing should follow a standard set of procedures. Extensive checklists for preparation, test operations, unit-test evaluation, system test evaluation, and acceptability test are provided.

PART FOUR

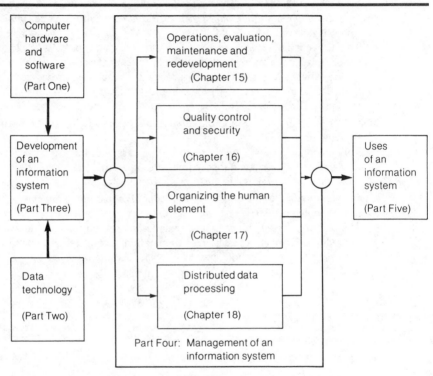

Computer hardware and software

(Part One)

Development of an information system

(Part Three)

Data technology

(Part Two)

Operations, evaluation, maintenance and redevelopment
(Chapter 15)

Quality control and security

(Chapter 16)

Organizing the human element

(Chapter 17)

Distributed data processing

(Chapter 18)

Part Four: Management of an information system

Uses of an information system

(Part Five)

NOTE: The thin arrows represent the flow of data and information.
The thick arrows show the sequential flow of the parts of the book.

MANAGEMENT OF AN INFORMATION SYSTEM

Part Four is closely related to Part Three. In fact, it is difficult to separate the two since many aspects of management of an information system (such as evaluation, redevelopment, control, and organization) need to be planned when the system is being designed. Yet integration of all the material in Chapters 15 through 18 into a discussion on development would have been cumbersome indeed. The operational considerations which are raised in Part Four must be well understood by the development team and this knowledge used in determining design specifications. However, the organizational problems raised in Part Four also affect daily operation of the system, which explains why the material is introduced following sections on development. An overview of the chapters in this part is shown in diagram form.

Chapter 15 examines operations, evaluation, maintenance, and redevelopment. Normal operations include periodic evaluations for efficiency and effectiveness, but evaluation may also be triggered by user complaints or changes in EDP management. Should system performance prove unsatisfactory, either maintenance (minor modifications) or redevelopment (major redesign), following the steps of development described in Part Three, will also be required. Chapter 15 also discusses evaluation criteria and modification methodology.

Control measures are designed to prevent inadvertent errors in processing and breaches in system security. Procedures, corporate policies, software, and specialized hardware all can contribute to control. In Chapter 16, points are identified where information systems are most vulnerable to security violations and most susceptible to error, and control recommendations are outlined.

The human element of a computerized information system must also be managed. Schemas for organizing EDP departments are described in Chapter 17. How the mobilization of EDP personnel has changed as computer technology has evolved is also explained. In addition, this chapter discusses the problem of human resistance to computers and recommends ways to overcome this resistance.

Chapter 18, on distributed data processing (DDP), is an extension of Chapter 17, describing in detail an alternative organizational structure for processing. A separate chapter has been devoted to this topic because of the newness and importance of DDP and the effect DDP will have on equipment, software, and personnel in the management of information systems.

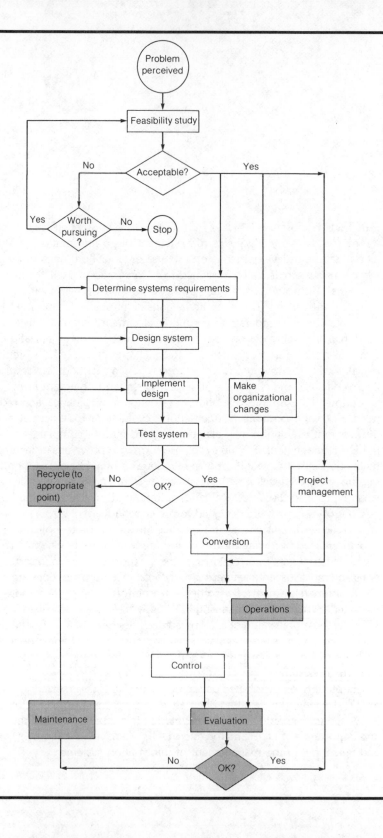

15

OPERATIONS, EVALUATION, MAINTENANCE, AND REDEVELOPMENT

Once a system is developed and converted, operations begin. In many business organizations, operations are performed by an EDP department. Operations should be evaluated periodically, where evaluation is the comparison of actual performance with objectives. When a predetermined level of error tolerance is exceeded, system modification is necessary. The corrections themselves are technical matters. What concerns management is evaluation leading to a decision to modify the system, and control of modification procedures.

Modifications may be minor, called **maintenance,** or major, requiring **redevelopment** of the system following the cycle of development discussed in Chapters 11–14. In this chapter, the interrelationship of operations with evaluation, maintenance, and redevelopment is discussed. Evaluation criteria are listed and the methodology of maintenance and redevelopment is described.

OPERATIONS

Operations in small systems (for example, operations using a mini-computer) are administered by line management. In large systems and systems with a common data base, however, a specialized department handles operations. Organizations differ in how this department is named. It may be called a Computer Center or Data Processing Department. In this text, the term EDP (Electronic Data Processing) department will be used.

A prime responsibility of EDP departments is **efficiency** of operations, efficiency being the ratio of output to input. Efficiency of operations is dependent on good documentation of procedures such as:

1. Run sheets for computer operators.
2. Instructions for error corrections during operations.
3. User procedure manuals.
4. Library procedures.
5. Project control procedures.

Optimization of operations means either maximizing output within a given departmental budget, or minimizing input for the production of a required output. How hardware (CPU and peripherals), software (systems and application programs), the data base, and EDP personnel are deployed will determine results. The department may change equipment or reorganize existing equipment in a new configuration to improve efficiency, organization logic may be revised, software rewritten, the data base restructured, and/or data on storage devices reorganized. All of these technical decisions will affect both efficiency and critical factors of performance such as timeliness, accuracy, and quality of information,[1] factors by which users measure the **effectiveness** of the information system. Whenever **evaluation** of the system shows that either efficiency or effectiveness have dropped below acceptable levels, corrective action must be taken.

EVALUATION OF OPERATIONS

Evaluation of operations may be initiated periodically or may occur when changes in EDP management take place. (Mobility is high in EDP management due to competition among businesses for qualified, experienced EDP personnel.) Users may also request a review of operations when dissatisfied with service.

Factors considered in the evaluation of operations include:

1. Timeliness of operations and reports generated.
2. Validity and completeness of reports.
3. Achievement of predetermined acceptable levels of operations.
4. Frequency of errors or discrepancies.
5. Response time required to meet users' requests.
6. Effectiveness of measures to control data and protect both security and privacy of information.
7. Software performance.
8. System reliability.
9. Achievement of long-range goals.
10. Frequency of unscheduled down-time and its percentage of total scheduled time.
11. Availability and usefulness of documentation.
12. Degree of incorporation of latest technology.
13. Quality and turnover of EDP personnel.
14. Availability and effectiveness of training programs.
15. User perception of EDP quality and service.
16. Openness of communication lines between users and EDP personnel.

Many of the above factors can only be measured subjectively. But much data can be collected on operations to assist management in the evaluation process. For example, **hardware monitors** can collect data on the utilization of the CPU and peripherals as well as data that can be analyzed to identify

---

[1] For formal measures of these factors, see David P. Norton, and Kenneth G. Rau, *A Guide to EDP Performance Management* (Wellesley, Mass.: Q.E.D. Information Sciences Inc., 1978), p. 310.

bottlenecks, down-time, and saturation conditions of channels, storage devices, and other peripherals. **Software monitors,** such as account or auditing programs, can provide management with information on how the systems resources have been used, by whom, and for what application. **Monitor programs** embedded in software may keep track of applications programs in demand, languages favored, as well as software features and routines used. Such data is useful for analysis but has a price tag, for the cost of processing this data must be considered. Monitors can also interfere with optimal operating efficiency.

Monitors aid in the evaluation of EDP operations in the aggregate but have limited value in reviewing the efficiency and effectiveness of individual applications. Generally users are less concerned with overall operation of a system than with application specifics. Methods of evaluating each application (or subsystem) are described in the next section of this text.

EVALUATION OF APPLICATIONS

The evaluation of input, process, and output for applications is conceptually similar to the evaluation of general operations. What differs is that user management is responsible for the evaluation process. Users, not EDP personnel, determine the efficiency and effectiveness of the application. An unsatisfactory assessment of performance will lead to maintenance or redevelopment.

Efficiency

In the development of an application, analysts try to maximize output for a fixed input, or minimize input for a fixed output. They are often able to identify areas in which output can be substantially increased at very little marginal cost. Once the system is operational, however, users can often spot inefficient design features. Data preparation, for example, is still a very labor-intensive activity, constituting a high recurring cost. Users are frequently able to recommend changes in procedures, redesign of forms or program modifications that will help reduce this cost (recommendations that should have been made, but were not, during design). The run time of applications programs is also a cost that users are highly motivated to reduce. Rewriting programs, perhaps using a clever algorithm, restructuring data, and better utilization of hardware to reduce processing time are technical improvements that users, analysts and programmers often initiate to improve efficiency.

Effectiveness

The objectives stated in the feasibility study and in the detailed specification of systems requirements are compared to actual performance to determine the effectiveness of an application. One problem with this measure of effectiveness is that the objectives themselves may be outdated, invalid because of internal or external environmental changes, or because the decision maker has reordered priorities. In such cases, user objectives must be restated in detailed operational terms. To do so, users must follow the procedures for determining objectives that were originally followed during the developmental cycle of the application.

Monitors can assist in the collection of quantitative data used to evaluate effectiveness, but qualitative evaluation requires a survey of user attitudes. Questionnaires are one method of gathering user opinion. Sometimes users are asked to rank their responses on a scale of 1 (very satisfied) to 5 (very dissatisfied). The answers of all users can then be weighted. Interviews are another technique for gathering user opinion on application effectiveness. Observation and study of documentation, such as logs recording complaints or error frequency, can also be used.

In addition to measuring performance against stated objectives, users should be asked to evaluate the application in general terms. The answers to the following questions would be a good indication of the effectiveness of the system.[2]

1. Have original system objectives been undesirably compromised in an attempt to satisfy other objectives the system was designed to encompass?
2. Is all system output used?
3. Are meaningful data reduction and exception reporting techniques employed to produce digestible, usable decision-oriented information?
4. Do adequate procedures exist governing preparation and control of input data?
5. Does the system employ sufficient data edits and audits?
6. Are precision standards and the accuracy of the system's results understood by users?
7. Are processing turn-around times satisfactory?
8. Are processing delays frequent in occurrence?
9. What is the general level of confidence placed in system output by the users?
10. Are obsolete or unused data retained in system files unnecessarily processed?
11. Is processing logic straightforward, easily understood and properly documented? Or, are routines unnecessarily complicated?
12. Do adequate processing operation procedures exist?

The process of evaluation and monitoring is summarized in Figure 15.1. Changes in operations to improve effectiveness and efficiency are sometimes called **fine-tuning.** A 25 percent improvement in efficiency is not uncommon; 100 percent improvement is not unknown. With constant technological development in hardware and software, the importance of regular evaluation cannot

---

[2] Adapted from J. G. Kirzer, "A Model for System Design," *Journal of Systems Management,* vol. 23, no. 10 (October 1972), p. 30.

FIGURE 15.1
Efficiency and effectiveness of computer application

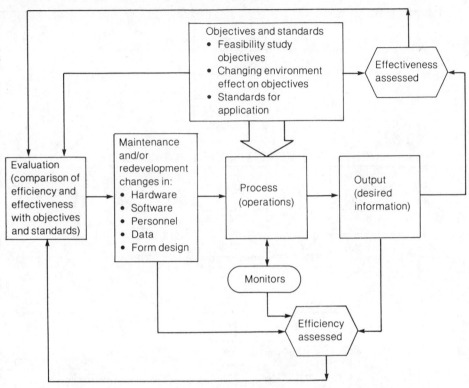

be overstressed. Internal and/or external evaluation teams may be used, depending on the size and complexity of the operation. J. Kanter claims that outside evaluators are used by three out of five large companies, and two out of five small and medium-sized companies.[3] Regular evaluation should identify problems before **crash maintenance** is required. Balancing cycles of evaluation and maintenance is part of **maintenance management,** the subject of the last section of this chapter.

MAINTENANCE AND REDEVELOPMENT

Maintenance and redevelopment are illustrated in Figure 15.2. The process begins when an application (system or subsystem) is ready for implementation (Box 1) at the conclusion of the development cycle. After operations begin (Box 2), the system is evaluated (Box 3). If satisfactory, procedures are estab-

---

[3] Jerome Kanter, *Management-Oriented Management Information Systems* 2d ed. (Englewood Cliffs, N.J.: Prentice-Hall, Inc., 1977), p. 166. Kanter does not cite the year of his findings or his source. But the numbers seem plausible.

FIGURE 15.2
Process of maintenance and redevelopment

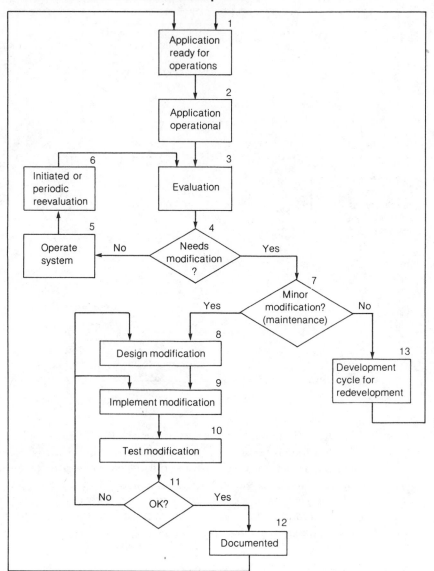

lished for periodic reevaluation, or reevaluation initiated by users or analysts (Box 6). If modification is needed (Exit Yes, Symbol 4) then a decision must be made whether the modification required is major or minor (Symbol 7). Minor design changes are made (Box 8), and these changes, once implemented (Box 9), are tested (Box 10). Satisfactory results lead to documentation (Box 12), and operations (Boxes 1 and 2). Major modifications, however, require redesign of the system following the stages outlined in Chapters 11–14 (Box 13).

The questions unanswered by the flowchart are: Why does the need for modification arise, and when should modifications be undertaken? What criteria determine whether maintenance or redevelopment are required? What are the problems of maintenance management? These questions will now be addressed.

System modification

Many reasons for modification were suggested during the earlier discussion on evaluation. Because of the importance of this subject, the reasons are summarized below.

MODIFICATIONS IMPOSED BY EXTERNAL ENVIRONMENT

New laws or changed government regulations are two reasons systems must commonly be modified. Competitors may also so alter market conditions that system redesign must be initiated. Flexible programs can be written that make modification part of routine maintenance when regular changes in the external environment are anticipated, such as revision of tax rates, but sometimes unexpected modification is required.

MODIFICATIONS INITIATED BY USER MANAGEMENT

System modification is sometimes triggered by a change in the management and user environment. A different style of decision making may lead to the need for a different threshold of information (level of information detail). Or management may simply learn to use information systems more effectively. An increase in awareness of a system's potentialities often causes management to place increased demands on the system. Policies of an organization may change, requiring new algorithms for calculations such as new depreciation methods. Or frequent errors and inconsistencies resulting from poor system specification, bad design, or hasty and incomplete testing may become apparent to users when the system is put into operation. A user may also have a wish list of features to be added to the system when finances permit.

MODIFICATIONS INITIATED BY EDP PERSONNEL

A system generally requires modification when new equipment is acquired. For example, more storage would mean a larger data base and increased processing would be feasible. Technological advance in the computer industry is swift-paced. Organizations adopting new technology or merely expanding their systems with more sophisticated computers will find that their information systems need modification.

Analysts also may detect errors in a system resulting from poor design and implementation or invalid assumptions once the system is operational. EDP personnel, like management, may also have a wish list not included in the original development because the design was frozen or because development resources were lacking at the time. The list might include reorganization of data, new output form design, or even new programming solutions. Generally these ideas were conceived and documented during development. Once the system is made operational, the suggestions are renewed and reevaluated, and often the changes proposed are added during regular maintenance or redevelopment cycles.

MAINTENANCE AND REDEVELOPMENT MANAGEMENT

Every firm needs a policy to differentiate between maintenance and redevelopment, to answer the question posed in Symbol 7 of Figure 15.2. In general, minor modification is defined as a change that affects few users, one that does not require much effort or many resources (not more than one month of a senior programmer's time or two days of the time of a senior analyst). Maintenance jobs can also be defined as routine or expected tasks, or preventive action to minimize errors. Some firms add adjustment to new equipment to the category of maintenance, including the training of user personnel in the new technology. On the other hand, redevelopment requires a major allocation of resources and personnel. Many firms have a committee to help draw the line between minor and major modifications, an important distinction because procedurally the two may differ since minor modification may skip some of the stages of development.

Once the maintenance tasks are defined, responsibility must be assigned and resources allocated. (An estimated 30–70 percent of all systems effort goes to maintenance). Usually authority to review and evaluate operations, and responsibility for approving minor modifications, are given to a senior EDP analyst or an internal auditor. A committee composed of the DBA, an auditor, and users' representatives generally assigns priorities to maintenance requests and reconciles conflicts between user departments, settling jurisdictional problems of maintenance when they arise. The committee also sets guidelines for identifying emergency maintenance and establishes rules for maintenance control. This latter activity, **maintenance control,** is exceedingly important for statistics show that security violations often occur during maintenance procedures. There is also a tendency to cut corners in maintenance work to get to more exciting projects. Control of maintenance procedures should ensure that one job is fully completed before the next is begun.

Even routine maintenance should not skip the steps outlined in the development cycle of an information system. Too often there is a tendency to hastily patch programs, to omit the need specification and testing stages due to time pressures. This can lead to monumental blunders such as the error which resulted when a university programmer patched a grade report, and in the process changed the statement numbers of the program. Figure 15.3 is a flowchart showing both the original statement numbers (to the left of each box) and modified numbers (to the right). The "Go To" statement, however, remained unaltered. The program was run without testing. As a result, 14,000 grade reports were mailed by the university to the first student on the list, L. C. Able, instead of grade reports being sent to each of the university's 14,000 students. In this case, the original fault lay with the maintenance programmer who skipped an important step in the development process, testing. But maintenance procedures were also inadequate, for a supervisor should have caught the error. And it is incredible that no one running the program, printing results, bursting and decollating the reports, and stuffing envelopes caught the mistake. Similar errors can well occur in business environments. Mistakes of this nature can be expensive, disruptive, and ruin a firm's credibility.

All modifications, both major and minor, must be economically justified. The cost of development is a sunk cost, so the justification is based on a

FIGURE 15.3
Partial flow chart of a program carelessly maintained

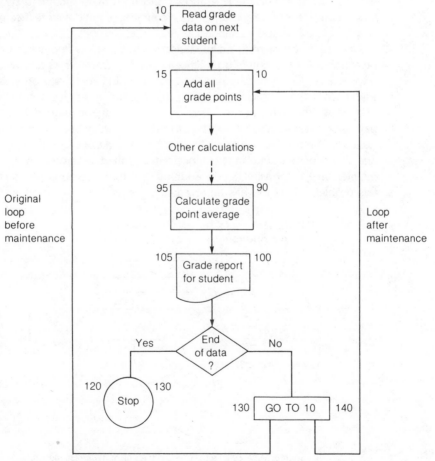

Note: the numbers on the left are those before maintenance, those on the right after maintenance.

marginal analysis: that is, the additional marginal cost compared to the marginal benefits of modifications. The techniques of economic analysis described in the feasibility study apply.

When a system has been repeatedly modified, often by different programmers, it becomes cumbersome and inefficient to operate. You might compare the system to an old car which becomes increasingly unreliable and costly to maintain with age. Some systems are junked as are old cars but others can be redeveloped. A redevelopment decision should be economically justified, but in practice the decision is often judgmental. The resulting redevelopment, however, can sometimes be supported since integrating new technology should make the new system cost-effective.

There is a strong correlation between high standards in the original development process and low maintenance. Planning ahead for equipment and software compatability, for example, will obviously reduce maintenance. Errors and inconsistencies should be identified and corrected during testing of the system, before it is made operational and the errors become a problem of maintenance. Rigid standards of documentation should also reduce time and effort required to make changes.

One major problem in maintenance management is finding and retaining personnel with the skill and patience needed to trace errors and weaknesses of programs. Correcting, testing, and documenting changes is often less interesting work than attacking a new project from an analyst's point of view. The need for maintenance often results from inadequate documentation, patchwork design, and unrealistic procedures. Senior programmers and analysts who should be engaged in maintenance because of their experience and skill generally shun maintenance duties. Job enlargement, giving analysts maintenance responsibilities in addition to other duties, is one solution to this problem. Rotation has other advantages as well, for a pool of analysts

FIGURE 15.4
Effort distribution

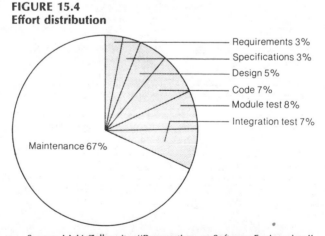

Source: M. V. Zelkowitz, "Perspectives on Software Engineering," *ACM Computing Surveys* (New York: Associations for Computing Machinery), vol. 10, no. 2 (June 1978), p. 202.

for maintenance provides system backup in addition to a variety of approaches and fresh solutions to maintenance problems.

Maintenance is very costly and takes a large share of effort when compared to the effort spent in the initial development of an information system, as shown in Figure 15.4. Note that the shaded part of the figure is the effort required for the initial development, corresponding to Figure 14.5.

SUMMARY

After an information system has been implemented and is operational, periodic changes will be required to keep it running efficiently and effectively. The altered state of variables both within the organization and in the external environment may mean operations no longer meet the objectives of the system. Minor changes made to a system are called maintenance. Major modifications are called redevelopment.

The need for maintenance or redevelopment is identified during evaluation of system performance. Evaluation is the comparison of actual with expected performance. When the need for major modifications is indicated, a decision for redevelopment should be made by a committee that includes user representatives and EDP personnel responsible for maintenance.

Maintenance and redevelopment are extensions of the development process described in Chapters 11–14 (see Figure 15.5). The development cycle is

FIGURE 15.5
Development cycle

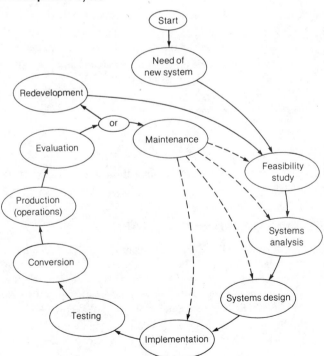

never ending, triggered whenever evaluations indicate that performance is unsatisfactory. Evaluation may be either regularly scheduled or be initiated by dissatisfied users and EDP personnel.

KEY WORDS

Crash maintenance	**Maintenance**
Effectiveness	**Maintenance control**
Efficiency	**Maintenance management**
Evaluation	**Monitor programs**
Fine-tuning	**Redevelopment**
Hardware monitors	**Software monitors**

DISCUSSION QUESTIONS

1. What is system maintenance?
2. What is system redevelopment?
3. How are system maintenance and system redevelopment related?
4. How long can the life of an information system be extended by modification and redevelopment? How can it be determined whether such maintenance is cost-effective?
5. Describe how an information system is evaluated. When should evaluation take place? Who should be responsible?
6. What is a monitor? What are the functions of monitors?
7. How can components of an information system, such as hardware, software, and procedures, be evaluated separately? Is such evaluation desirable?
8. What is the role and the importance of maintenance programmers? Why is maintenance often an unpopular assignment?
9. What is the difference between efficiency and effectiveness of an information system? How can they be evaluated?

EXERCISE

1. What resources would you require to generate the report requested in Exercise 1, Chapter 10?

SELECTED ANNOTATED BIBLIOGRAPHY

Canning, Richard, ed. "That Maintenance Iceberg." *EDP Analyzer,* vol. 10, no. 12 (October 1972), pp. 1–14.
    This article has a very apt title. The author discusses why more than 50 percent of all programming costs are due to maintenance. Problems of maintenance are described. Two case studies are presented.

Herzog, John P. "Systems Evaluation Technique for Users." *Journal of Systems Management,* vol. 26, no. 5 (May 1975), pp. 30–35.

This article is specifically addressed to the line manager and describes a scoring system by which a system can be evaluated in terms of problems solved, objectives satisfied, and reliability of input, output, and processing.

King, William R., and Rodriques, Jaime I. "Evaluating Management Information System." *MIS Quarterly,* vol. 2, no. 3 (September 1978), pp. 43–52.
This article describes an evaluation model that measures attitudes, value perceptions, information usage, and decision performance. The model is applied to a strategic planning information system.

Lucas, Henry C. "Performance Evaluation and Monitoring." *ACM Computing Surveys,* vol. 3, no. 3 (September 1971), pp. 79–91.
A good survey of the topic of evaluation, including hardware and software evaluation. Also discusses performance monitoring. Has 59 bibliographical citations.

Luit, Peter. "Why You Shouldn't Neglect Systems Maintenance." *Canadian Data Systems,* vol. 8, no. 2 (February 1976), pp. 37–38.
An excellent brief discussion on the importance of maintenance. Conditions that impair the effectiveness and efficiency of a system are listed and ways in which companies can organize for maintenance are suggested.

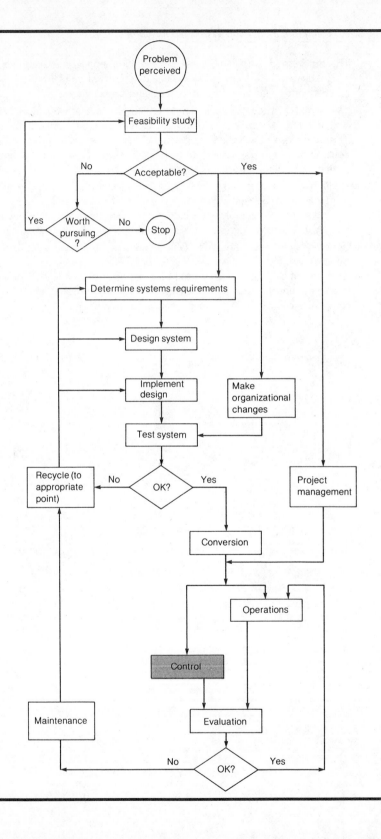

16

QUALITY CONTROL AND SECURITY

Information systems should be controlled for accuracy, timeliness, and completeness of data. Procedures must be adopted and checkpoints established to guard against unintentional human errors such as the use of an outdated code, the wrong input tape, or incorrect output distribution. Some errors are built into the system by poor design; many result from careless programming.

Preventing such errors is one aspect of control. Security, protecting information from unauthorized access and illicit use, is another.

The need for control and security of business data predates the use of computers. For example, marketing strategies and product development have always been closely guarded business secrets. However, the volume of confidential data processed by information systems today means the rewards for theft or industrial espionage are of a higher magnitude than in the past. Consider, for example, the large sums of money being transferred daily by EFT (electronic fund transfer). Furthermore, modern data communications technology makes remote theft a possibility. Computerized systems can be breached from a location thousands of miles from a data base. In addition, an estimated 2 million persons in 1977 had knowledge of computing systems, a knowledge that could be used for nefarious purposes.

Another reason control is so important is that never before in history has it been possible to make so many mistakes in so short a time. Undetected errors compound at an alarming rate due to the rapidity of computer calculations and the repetitious nature of computer operations. No wonder the issues of control and security occupy so much management attention.

The determination of technical control measures is generally the responsibility of EDP personnel. However, management should specify control standards, identify the data that needs protection, and specify the degree of control and security needed after weighing costs versus benefits and considerations of risk.

PROTECTION OF DATA

Data must be protected from accidents and natural disasters as well as from intentional theft. A breakdown in an air-conditioning system may result in loss of computing capabilities. Fire, flooding, hurricanes, even a heavy snowfall causing a roof to collapse can cause destruction of data and valuable equipment. Poor machine maintenance may be at fault. Human errors such as inadequate input preparation, poorly drawn user specifications, programming oversights, or careless machine operation may also cause failure of the system to provide needed information.

Establishing control measures for the above is far less taxing than protecting information systems from intentional damage or theft. Disgruntled employees have sabatoged computer operations in the past; so have members of the public. Computers have been shot, short-circuited with metal objects, and doused with gasoline and set afire. Damages for acts of vandalism alone run into the millions.

Industrial espionage and fraud are other security threats that are hard to control. When all computer equipment and data were centralized, physical access to the system could be controlled, but with widespread use of teleprocessing networks, data is in far greater jeopardy. Communication lines can be infiltrated through **wiretapping** (electromagnetic pickup of messages off communication lines); **masquerading** (pretending to be a legitimate user to access the system); **piggy-backing** (interception and switching of messages), and **reading between the lines** (engaging the system illicitly when a user is connected to the computer but is "thinking," and the computer is idle). Infiltration may involve manipulation of data, the alteration of computer programs, pillage of data, or unauthorized use of the computer itself. In 1979, for example, a 15-year-old boy was charged with felony, grand theft, and vandalism for using 200 hours of unauthorized time, worth about $10,000, at the University of California at Berkeley, accessed from a second-hand terminal costing $60. In another case of remote entry fraud, 277 freight cars of Penn Central, worth over $1 million, were diverted to a spur track and sold.

The Stanford Research Institute did a study of 148 cases of computer fraud made public that occurred between 1964–73. (Many cases of fraud are kept "hush-hush," firms being reluctant to announce their losses to the public.) In 65 of these cases, the average loss was $1.39 million (excluding one case of $2 billion). The study disproved the supposition that computer theft is a crime requiring a high level of education: 56 percent of the infiltrators had only completed high school. In cases of internal theft, the culprits ranged from clerk to vice president. Fifty-two percent of the cases studied represented corporation fraud, 16 percent were crimes against banks and savings and loan associations, 28 percent were perpetrated against state and local government, and 4 percent against the federal government. Detection in many cases was accidental, not due to established EDP control measures or auditing by accountants. A summary of the findings of the study appears in Table 16.1.

The Stanford Research Institute statistics are an indication of the alarming dimensions of computer crime. And professionals predict that computerized

TABLE 16.1
Job position of perpetrator, scheme of fraud, method of manipulation

Job position	Transactions added	Transactions altered	Transactions deleted	File changes	Program changes	Improper operation	Miscellaneous (unknown)
Data entry/ terminal operator	9	4	0	1	0	0	1
Clerk/teller	9	6	0	1	0	0	0
Programmer	0	0	0	0	14	0	1
Officer/manager	8	4	3	1	3	1	1
Computer operator	1	4	0	1	0	3	0
Other staff	1	0	1	1	0	0	2
Outsider (nonemployee)	3	1	0	0	0	0	1
Unknown	0	1	0	3	0	0	0
Totals	31	20	4	7	17	4	4

Schemes of fraud used							Totals*
Payments to employee and other individuals	40	2	6	2	2	4	56
Accounting/inventory control/disbursements	44	3	3	7	1	11	69
Billings/deposits	17	2	1	5	0	2	27
Miscellaneous	0	0	2	0	0	2	4

* These totals are not mutually exclusive. Some cases are entered under more than one category.

Source: Adapted from: Brandt Allen, "The Biggest Computer Frauds: Lessons for CPAs," *The Journal of Accountancy*, vol. 143, no. 5 (May 1977), pp. 56 and 59. Copyright © 1977 by the American Institute of Certified Public Accountants, Inc.

systems will be assaulted with increasing frequency in the future. The saying, "Temptation makes a thief," appears to be applicable to computer theft. The increasing use of telecommunications, the large amount of data being processed and huge sums of money involved in electronic transfer make computer theft highly lucrative. Unfortunately, cheap minicomputers and tele-processing capabilities favor the embezzler rather than the controller.

COUNTERMEASURES TO THREATS

Security of an information system should be tight, the detection of fraud not dependent on luck. Validation of data, coding, and access directories, measures to counter threats to computer systems, have been discussed in earlier chapters of this text. Access control and auditing are additional counter-measures that will be examined in greater detail at this point.

Access control

For centralized CPUs in batch mode, access control is easily achieved. The computer center can be physically closed to unauthorized personnel—a closed shop, denying unauthorized personnel the capability of submitting jobs to the computer. Badge systems, locked doors, a guard at the entry: all procedures common to restricted areas in security-sensitive factories or research divisions can be adopted. In addition, the computer can reference an access directory, described in Chapter 8, when use of the data base is requested.

With telecommunications, access control has three dimensions: (1) **authentication:** verifying the identity of the user requesting service; (2) **identification:** verifying the user's right to access a requested file or portion of the data base; and (3) **authorization:** verifying the type of access permit-ted, that is, read, write, update, or no access. A security matrix stored in the computer can control dimensions 2 and 3. (See Table 8.4 for a sample.) The user's identity may be authenticated by a machine-readable badge, a voice print, fingerprints, or handprints, though such equipment is expensive at the present time. More common is the use of **passwords.** The secrecy of passwords can be guarded by frequently changing the password, by using a system to generate passwords for each user or by techniques for generating passwords for each session, called **session passwords.** The user can also be identified by a project or account number, and be constrained by time locks (system operational only during specified times), hardware locks (physi-cal locks on machines), and the amount of computer time allocated per job. In addition, the security matrix may control the access to the data base of each individual terminal. For example, the terminal in the data base administra-tor's office may be the only one permitted to access all files and programs, and the only terminal that has access to the security matrix itself.

Auditing

There are two approaches to auditing: auditing around and through the computer. Auditing is used to detect accidental errors as well as fraud.

AUDITING AROUND THE COMPUTER

In this approach, output is checked for a given input. It is assumed that if input is correct and reflected in output, then the processing itself is also correct. The audit does not check computer processing directly, hence the term **auditing around the computer.** This type of audit does not require computer expertise. Instead, traditional auditing methods and techniques are used: that is, tracing who did what, when, in what sequence.

The problem with this approach is that processing errors may exist even though no errors are apparent in input and output. Furthermore, computer calculations provide few intermediate results for auditors to check by traditional trailing methods.

AUDITING THROUGH THE COMPUTER

To check both input *and* process, **audits through the computer** can be made. This auditing approach may use test data, auditor-prepared programs, auditor-software packages, or audit programming languages.

a. Use of test data. In this technique, a selected set of data is checked for reasonableness, validity, and consistency. Auditors search for extreme conditions, out-of-sequence data, out-of-balance batches, and so forth, the type of errors frequently found when testing applications programs. The accuracy of the computer program itself in performing calculations is examined, and operation procedures used by the firm are scrutinized and checked for consistency with corporate policies.

b. Auditor-prepared programs. In this approach, specially written programs prepared by the auditors are used to check specific conditions and to identify situations that need further study and analysis.[1] The programs also spot check for unauthorized manipulations by programmers and operators, and provide listings of before and after changes which facilitate auditing.

c. Auditor-software packages. Standard auditing programs can be purchased. These are not as specialized as programs written by auditors for a specific information system but they are less expensive and relatively easy to use.

d. Audit programming languages. Special programming languages can be used to generate output needed by auditors. System 2170, for example, developed by the accounting firm Peat, Marwick and Mitchell, is a language that can be learned in about one week, and has 21 audit commands.

All through the computer auditing approaches create problems when used

---

[1] For a further discussion and examples, see W. T. Porter, *EDP Controls and Auditing* (Belmont, Calif.: Wadsworth Publishing Co., Inc., chap. 8, 1974), pp. 112–33.

on real-time systems, for sample data can get mixed with the live stream of data unless extreme care is taken and expensive precautions are adopted. One solution to this problem is to create a representative set of data that would represent the company and use it for auditing independent of the live data system. This approach is referred to as the **mini-company approach,** since the test data base is a miniature representation of the company.

Auditing approaches should be decided during the early stages of development of an information system. For example, the generation of reports to trace calculations on intermediate results and generation of listings of exceptional and suspicious situations can be programmed with little effort during the design phase. Grafting these auditing and control features after the system is operational is both expensive and disruptive. At the time design specifications are under consideration, auditors must indicate output needs; specify decision rules of computations (e.g., rounding rules); establish editing, backup and recovery procedures; and set document and testing standards. Auditors should also participate in testing the system and have a voice in the decision of system acceptance. Once the system is operational, auditors play a role in control and evaluation throughout the life cycle of the system.

An auditor of a computerized information system should be not only a competent accountant and auditor, but also knowledgeable about computer systems, especially the implementation of data bases, documentation, data security, and recovery. In addition, programming skills are needed since computer programs are used in the audits themselves, COBOL being the language most commonly employed. For example, programs control calculations, comparisons, and verifications; perform intermediary operations such as sampling and extractions, and also perform the functions of monitors, collecting data on operations.

There are many texts on the subject of computers and auditing.[2] What needs to be stressed here is that computers are used by auditors in auditing computerized systems. But current computer audit techniques are not as advanced as the technology being audited and the computer profession shows no sign of waiting until auditors catch up.

HOW MUCH CONTROL AND SECURITY?

In deciding how much control is needed to protect a computerized information system from inadvertent errors and security violations, the monetary cost to implement control measures must be considered as well as the psychic cost of delays and inconvenience from controls. Companies can go too far, causing production to fall off because computers are so difficult to access

---

[2] See John G. Burch, Jr., and Joseph L. Sardinas, Jr., *Computer Control and Audit: A Total Systems Approach* (New York: John Wiley & Sons, Inc., 1978), 492 p.; William C. Mair et al., *Computer Control and Audit* (n.p., Institute of Internal Auditors, 1978), 489 p.; and W. Thomas Porter, *EDP Controls and Auditing* (Belmont, Calif.: Wadsworth Publishing, Inc., 1974), 240 p.

by bona fide users and because procedures to monitor errors impede performance. A well-conceived system of control can be visualized as rings of protection (see Figure 16.1), designed uniquely for each system, with complex controls when the cost of data loss by accident or criminal intent is high.

Every information system should include in its design control points for monitoring the system. Figure 16.2 shows where controls are needed, where information systems are most vulnerable to security violations and most susceptible to error. The remaining sections of this chapter will be a commentary on each of these control points. Potential threats to data quality and security

FIGURE 16.1
Rings of control and security defenses

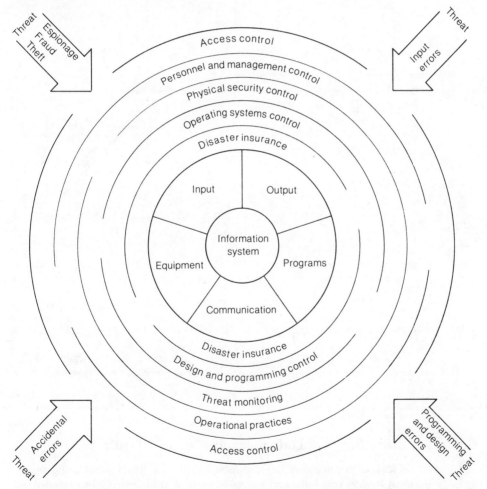

Source: Adapted by permission of the *Harvard Business Review*. Exhibit from "Plugging the Leaks in Computer Security" by Joseph J. Wasserman, (September–October 1969), p. 124. Copyright © 1969 by the President and Fellows of Harvard College.

FIGURE 16.2
Stages of processing and quality control points

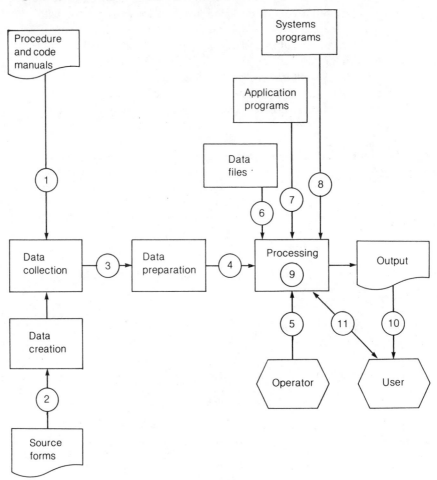

at each point will be discussed, countermeasures to these threats will be suggested, and the personnel responsible for control will be identified.

CONTROL POINTS

Control of procedure and code manuals (Circle 1, Figure 16.2)

Table 16.2 summarizes the common sources of errors when using procedure and code manuals and suggests control solutions. Control is shared between user management and EDP personnel supervising manual preparation, updating, and distribution. Many businesses designate a single office

TABLE 16.2
Control of manuals

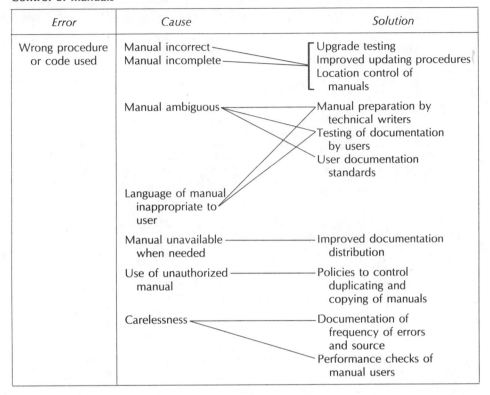

Error	Cause	Solution
Wrong procedure or code used	Manual incorrect Manual incomplete	Upgrade testing Improved updating procedures Location control of manuals

	Manual ambiguous	Manual preparation by
		  technical writers
		Testing of documentation
		  by users
		User documentation
		  standards

	Language of manual
	  inappropriate to
	  user	

	Manual unavailable
	  when needed
		Improved documentation
		  distribution

	Use of unauthorized
	  manual
		Policies to control
		  duplicating and
		  copying of manuals

	Carelessness	Documentation of
		  frequency of errors
		  and source
		Performance checks of
		  manual users

under the data base administrator as the keeper of codes. This office coordinates assignment of codes according to the needs of users to eliminate redundant coding schemes, and is responsible for establishing all codes needed by the system. Publication, maintenance, and distribution of a uniform code manual is usually discharged by this office.

Form control (Circle 2)

A common method of collecting data for an information processing system is through the medium of forms. Though error-free data collection may be impossible, errors can be minimized by having well-designed forms with easy-to-follow directions. Analysts who design forms and program input validity checks are primarily responsible for controlling errors at this checkpoint. **Turnaround documents** are being increasingly used by businesses to reduce errors. For example, banks provide customers with deposit slips already printed with their name, address, and account number. Only spaces for date and amount need to be filled. By reducing the amount of information the customer must provide, the opportunity for error is minimized. Other examples of turnaround documents are the tear-off sections of utility and credit card bills that must accompany bill payment, and preprinted complaint forms that come with mail order merchandise.

Table 16.3 summarizes frequent causes of errors in filling out forms and possible control solutions.

TABLE 16.3
Form control

Error	Cause	Solution
Forms filled incorrectly	Directions ambiguous	Forms prepared by analysts experienced in form design
	Format poor	Upgrade testing, including testing by user groups
	Substitute or unauthorized person filling out forms	Distribution and collection controls
		Requiring identification of user
	Poor motivation	Instructions should emphasize positive benefits of correct data and negative effect of wrong information
	Carelessness	Use of turnaround documents
		Validity checks of data during processing (a solution at Checkpoint 9)

Data collection (Circle 3)

One of the most important points in data control is data collection. Data collection is not only the source of many careless errors, but is also the focus of much criminal activity.

For example, a Blue Shield-Blue Cross claims examiner mailed forms to relatives who filled them in with real names and policy numbers to defraud the system of $128,000. In another recorded case of fraud, 11 employees of the County Department of Social Services in Los Angeles issued checks to themselves using terminated welfare accounts. Other cases of manipulation of input data include: an IRS clerk who awarded a relative unclaimed tax credits; the theft of $100,000 from a bank account using the MICR number found on a discarded deposit slip; and a conspiracy between an accounting clerk and grocer resulting in a theft of more than $120,000 over the years by issuing false invoices for undelivered food. Inadvertent errors can be equally harmful to an organization. The code of equipment costing $20,000 was erroneously used to code the price of 50 manuals of that equipment. This mistake resulted in an inflated inventory value of one million dollars.

Table 16.4 summarizes common errors in data collection and suggests possible control solutions.

TABLE 16.4
Data collection control

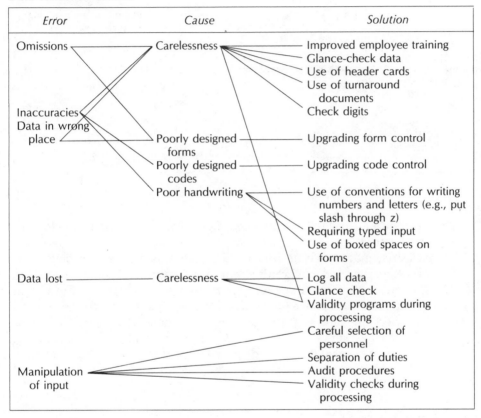

Error	Cause	Solution
Omissions	Carelessness	Improved employee training
		Glance-check data
		Use of header cards
		Use of turnaround documents
Inaccuracies		Check digits
Data in wrong place	Poorly designed forms	Upgrading form control
	Poorly designed codes	Upgrading code control
	Poor handwriting	Use of conventions for writing numbers and letters (e.g., put slash through z)
		Requiring typed input
		Use of boxed spaces on forms
Data lost	Carelessness	Log all data
		Glance check
		Validity programs during processing
		Careful selection of personnel
		Separation of duties
Manipulation of input		Audit procedures
		Validity checks during processing

Data preparation (Circle 4)

Errors in data preparation occur when data is incorrectly converted into machine-readable form. Control is exercised by the department responsible for the data preparation. Recommended control measures are summarized in Table 16.5.

Ways to detect error and procedures to correct mistakes are not all that is needed. The source of the errors should be traced and procedures amended so that the same errors do not reoccur. By reorganizing the location of data preparation, for example, one firm reduced input errors from 15 percent to

TABLE 16.5
Summary of data preparation errors and solutions

Error	Cause	Solution
Incorrect data	Poorly written ——————————— keypunch instructions	Upgrade procedures manual, include visual aids
	Hardware error ———————————	Proper maintenance
	Carelessness	Verification of keypunching by a second operator
		Use of check digits
Card handling errors (cards misplaced, put out of order, damaged, or duplicated inadvertently)	Carelessness	Glance check
		Validity programs
		Upgrade employee selection and training
	Poor procedure	Upgrade procedure testing
		Log data

2 percent. Originally clerks had coded information on forms from user transactional records, the forms later being used to keypunch input at the EDP center. By moving keypunchers for EDP to user departments, coding forms were eliminated and input cards keypunched directly from source documents. The cards were then given in batches to the processing center for validation by computer, the computer generating error listings. The cards, once returned for correction by the keypunchers, were then submitted as input. This procedural change, with responsibility for data preparation no longer shared (each department blaming the other for errors), helped reduce input errors significantly.

Operations (Circle 5)

Though employees can be trained in emergency procedures should flood, earthquake, fire, or an explosion interrrupt operations, a safeguard for an information system against such disasters is backup data files stored in a secure vault at another location. Also, complete backup processing facilities at another computer center tested for restart and recovery may be provided. Backup is good insurance against sabotage. Incidents of willful damage to computer equipment and data files have augmented in recent years, particularly in industries engaged in politically sensitive research such as nuclear energy or chemical warfare.

In handling sensitive information, the following basic operating precautions are also recommended. There should always be two operators present. This is a good security measure, and a good safety practice as well. Work schedules should be changed frequently so that no single operator handles the same programs over a long period of time. No employees should be assigned processing tasks when a conflict of interest might arise (for example, bank employees should not handle programming that will affect their accounts). Finally, proof of authorization and sign-in/sign-out controls for handling sensitive files should be initiated and neither programmers nor analysts should be assigned routine operating tasks.

Though many controls are needed to prevent malicious intrusion during operations, information systems being exceedingly vulnerable during this activity, most breakdowns and errors can be traced to lax procedures and careless operators. And these incidents can be costly indeed. For example, the running of an accounts payable program using an out-dated price list cost one firm $100,000. Another expensive mistake: A bank shredder fed a printout of sensitive data on depositors with the line of print parallel to the blades instead of at right angles. As a result, strips of readable confidential data were thrown in the trash where they were spotted, retrieved, and peddled at a local bar by a drifter. The cost to the bank: reward money for return of the strips and an incalculable loss of customer confidence.

More stringent control procedures could also have prevented the following incident. A Chicago hotel mixed address tapes, sending letters to vendors instead of to past guests explaining recent hotel renovations and urging the guests to return. Instead of good will, the hotel received irate calls from vendors whose spouses were citing the letters as evidence of their infidelity.

Failure to test control procedures produced the following fiasco. When a fire broke out in a computer center, employees discovered that narrow doors barred passage of fire extinguishing equipment.

But who was to blame when a corrosive leak in an air-conditioning system destroyed a computer several floors below? It simply isn't practical to devise control methods for all possible threats to an information system. Controls are costly, and too many controls can impede operation. The controls summarized in Table 16.6 are those most frequently adopted for operations.

Data files (Circle 6)

If data files are centrally stored, a librarian generally is assigned responsibility for control. Otherwise the owner of the data is responsible. Table 16.7 summarizes the types of control needed to protect data files.

There are numerous cases of errors and fraud relating to data files cited in computer literature. Stolen programs have been held for ransom. Disgruntled employees have maliciously scratched or destroyed tapes. At the Arizona State Finance Center, a backup card file was used for making Christmas decorations. An employee moving files to storage in another organization wedged the vault open but forgot to remove the wedge after the move was

TABLE 16.6
Control of operations

Error	Cause	Solution
Incorrect operation	Poor instructions ——————— Carelessness ————	Upgrade personnel selection, training, and procedure testing / Checking of data file labels
Machine breakdown	Poor maintenance ———— Careless operators ————	Upgrade maintenance / Upgrade testing / Upgrade personnel selection / Upgrade training
	Act of nature (flood, storm)	Backup equipment / Shutdown devices
	Fire	Emergency training / Heat and smoke alarm / Fire extinguishers / Panic switches
Fraudulent operation	Sabotage	Intrusion detectors / Police patrol
	Desire for personal gain	At least two people on duty / Steel or steel mesh on windows and doors / Control physical access / Control access to files / Remove conflict of interest / Vary work schedules / Strict supervision / Upgrade personnel selection / Bond personnel
Data not processed on time	Documents lost or or misrouted ————	Establish documentation procedures (logging, checking record totals, etc.)

complete. Though the vault was fireproof, a fire swept through the open door and destroyed hundreds of tapes.

In most cases, destruction of data files can be attributed to lax security. Since files are particularly vulnerable to industrial espionage, the need for data safeguards at this control point is vital.

Programming controls (Circles 7,8)

Many mistakes in computerized systems can be attributed to faulty programming. One bank, for example, lost $300,000 by paying customers interest on 31-day months. A hyphen omitted from a programming card caused a rocket being tested to head for Rio. It had to be destroyed mid-flight, at a loss of $18,500,000. Unintentional errors may result from an incorrect algo-

TABLE 16.7
Summary of data file controls

Error	Cause	Solution
Warped cards, dirty tape or disks	Poor physical storage	Controlled humidity storage "Clean room" conditions Special cabinets Periodic cleaning
	Lack of clearly defined responsibility for data files	Centralized storage under a librarian
	Inadequate procedures	Upgrade storage procedures
Destruction of files	Natural disaster	Special vaults Backup data
	Theft, fraud, or sabotage	Controlled access to files: Data librarian Lock words Control labels

rithm, erroneous programming logic, or a cause as minor as one out-of-sequence programming statement. Training care, strict adherence to standard programming procedures and proper documentation should minimize such problems.

The controls summarized in Table 16.8 should trace inadvertent errors and also help prevent fraud. Control measures should be initiated and enforced by EDP personnel responsible for systems analysis and programming. Unfortunately, programming fraud is exceedingly difficult to detect and the crimes themselves are often quite ingenious. The first federal prosecution of computer crime in 1966 was against a bank programmer who programmed the system to omit his name from a list generated daily of overdrawn accounts. He withdrew large sums of money before being caught. Control measures, however, did not bring about his downfall. The overdrafts were detected when the computer broke down and the bank had to revert to manual processing.

Another programmer assessed a ten-cent service charge to each customer and put the amounts in a dummy account under the name of Zwicke. By chance, a PR man decided to award a bonus to the first and last name on the firm's alphabetical list of customers. The bogus Zwicke was accordingly discovered.

Nibble theft, stealing small amounts of money over a period of time, is more difficult to detect than bite-size fraud, the embezzlement of large sums. The latter can be uncovered by auditing and checking for unreasonable values or control totals. But no matter how well designed the controls, someone

TABLE 16.8
Programming controls

Error	Cause	Solution
Incorrect solution	Out of sequence programming	Upgrade training of programmers
		Establish standard programming procedures
	Wrong algorithm	Upgrade testing: Desk check
	Programming instructions wrong	Manual check Compare historical results Cross-check totals
	Peculiarities of programming language give wrong results	Program in two different languages
	Poor documentation	Establish and enforce documentation standards
Unauthorized changes	Lax security	Check programs against original version periodically
		Team program auditing

will think up a new technique for cheating the system. Constant vigilance is required, especially when technology changes and new hardware and software are used.

Processing (Circle 9)

At the time of processing, data which passed control points 2, 3, and 4 can be reevaluated by computer programs. Validation programs, described in Chapter 7, can check for completeness, accuracy, format, range, reasonableness, consistency, sequence, and number of transactions. Input errors can also be detected during processing when self-checking codes are used.

Processing control, the responsibility of EDP personnel, is closely related to operations control. Measures that specifically guard against careless processing are listed in Table 16.9.

Output (Circle 10)

Output is the product of all input and processing. If proper control is exercised in each of the steps discussed earlier, the output should be free of error. But most firms add output controls in an information systems design

TABLE 16.9
Processing controls

Error	Cause	Solution
Records lost	Carelessness	Validity checks
		Upgrade training of personnel
		Log jobs
Use of incorrect file	Carelessness	Use standard labels for all files
		Programs to automatically generate updated data
Lack of necessary supplies	Carelessness	Upgrade planning and inventory control

to cross check for errors that may have slipped past earlier controls. Responsibility for these controls is divided between EDP personnel producing output and management using the output. These controls are summarized in Table 16.10.

Many output mistakes can be caught by cursory sight checks. For example, a payroll run of checks issued without decimal points could be easily spotted by an alert operator, for the amounts would be unreasonable. In addition, many of the validation programs used for input can be run to control output.

Teleprocessing (Circle 11)

Access controls discussed earlier in this chapter are one method of protecting data during teleprocessing. The use of cryptography, transformation of

TABLE 16.10
Output control

Error	Cause	Solution
Inaccurate output	Processing errors	Audits
		Validation programs
		Interfile comparison
		Defer large-volume printing until proof data checked
		Sample check of output with corresponding input
	Operation error	Sight check
Incomplete output	Operation or processing error	Check page counts
		Check control totals for each process or report

data, protocols, packet switching, parity checks, and self-checking codes, described in Chapters 5 and 7, are additional control techniques.

CONTROL RESPONSIBILITY OF MANAGEMENT

The responsibility for control and security of information is ultimately management's. A firm's survival is at stake when decisions are based on inaccurate data or when losses must be absorbed due to sabotage or theft. Goodwill and a firm's reputation for quality service are also threatened when controls prove inadequate. Though EDP personnel participate in technical control decisions, it is up to management to identify needed points of control, to establish and document control procedures, and to assign personnel to enforce these procedures. In designing an overall security plan, information needing protection must be identified, resources for this protection must be allocated, and corrective actions must be outlined for procedure revision should the security prove inadequate. Regulations should be flexible, selective, effective, and enforceable.

Control of an information system is facilitated by dividing the system into five basic functions: programming and system development; handling input media; operation of data processing equipment; documentation and file library; and distribution of output. The duties of employees should not cross these functional lines. When no single individual performs all the steps in a transaction, the opportunity for fraud is diminished. If controls at one level are bypassed, errors can be detected at the next control point. This separation of duties may not be practical in small institutions, but the principle should be followed whenever possible.

All controls should be periodically reviewed and problems that have arisen analyzed. What types of errors occurred? At what cost? Why? Could the errors have been prevented? How? Depending on the answers to these questions, controls should be tightened (or relaxed).

SUMMARY AND CONCLUSIONS

This chapter examines controls for documentation, forms, data collection, data preparation, operations, data files, programming, processing, and output. A management dilemma is deciding how much control is necessary. Too much control is costly: it can impede work and affect morale. Too little control permits inaccuracies and security infractions, reducing the usefulness of the system.

The importance of carefully designed controls cannot be overstressed. Most readers will have personally experienced the frustration of trying to correct a billing error resulting from inadequate control procedures. Indeed, a major source of public distrust of computers can be traced to such experiences, the feeling of consumers that they are being victimized by computerized systems. In a survey reported by Sterling,[3] four or more contacts were required by one third of the individuals negotiating clarification or solution of computer errors. Billing mistakes were by far the most common category of error (81 percent), the types of errors falling into the following categories:

Payment not credited	7.9%
Incorrect amount of payment credited (overcharged)	12.8
Incorrect amount of payment credited (undercharged)	4.3
Billed for already settled account	7.3
Charged for nonexistent expenditure	29.9
Not given credit on returned item	5.5
Charged interest without cause	14.0
Billing error caused by misdirected bill	7.3
Other	10.9
All billing errors	100.0%

Distribution of error by type of transaction was as follows:

Credit service and special credit card	16.7%
Oil company (heating, gasoline)	9.9
Utility company (gas, phone, electric)	16.7
Department store	22.2
Mail order business	16.0
Insurance	1.9
Bank or savings institution (not including checking)	4.3
Checking account	4.9
Government (municipal)	0.6
Government (federal)	2.5
Other	4.3
All errors	100.0%

Since a firm's reputation depends on the quality of its customer service, inadequate controls over computerized information can lead to decrease of clients, a decline of profits, and a loss of goodwill.

Control measures should be planned, implemented, tested, and evaluated during the development of an information system. It is both expensive and disruptive to add controls at a later date. However, whenever computer fraud is reported, security experts must devise counter procedures to prevent future incidents of the same nature. Unfortunately, firms are reluctant to publicize security breaches lest their credibility suffer. This means that analysts designing security measures are not always aware of the tricks and techniques used by perpetrators of fraud to breach information systems. And the widespread use of home computers makes information systems today even more vulnerable to security infractions than in the past, for every terminal has the potential for infiltrating information networks.

---

[3] T. D. Sterling, "Consumer Difficulties with Computerized Transactions: An Empirical Investigation," *ACM Communications,* vol., 22, no. 5 (May 1979), pp. 285–87.

Common countermeasures to security threats are summarized in Table 16.11.

TABLE 16.11
Countermeasures for threats to security

Access Control	*Physical controls*
Authorization/authentication, (e.g., passwords, cards)	Vaults
	Fire extinguishing equipment
	Physical restrictions to:
Hardware locks	Peripherals
Logging access	Libraries
Time locks	CPU
Librarian control of:	
Data	*Organizational controls*
Programs	Separation of duties
Documentation	Rotation of duties
	Bond personnel
	Identify disgruntled personnel
	Train personnel
	Remove conflicts of interest
Processing controls	Disaster insurance
Transformation of data	Background check
Ciphering/deciphering	Appoint security officer
Validity checking	
Control totals	*Monitoring controls*
Form control	Auditing
Procedure control	Internal
Backup	External
Equipment	Standards
Personnel	Testing

KEY WORDS

Access control	**Mini-company approach**
Auditing around the computer	**Passwords**
Auditing through the computer	**Piggy-backing**
Authentication	**Processing control**
Authorization	**Reading between the lines**
Control	**Security**
Control points	**Session passwords**
Identification	**Turnaround documents**
Masquerading	**Wiretapping**

DISCUSSION QUESTIONS

1. Identify methods of access control to:
   a. The data base.
   b. Programs.
   c. The CPU.

How effective is each control?

2. What is an audit trail? How is it different in a computerized business firm compared to a noncomputerized firm?

3. How does auditing through a computer compare to auditing by a computer and auditing around a computer?

4. Distinguish between:
   a. External and internal control.
   b. Organizational and administrative control.
   c. Process and operational control.
   d. Physical and access control.

5. Comment on the statement: A computer system adds to the probability of errors, fraud, and destruction of data and information.

6. Describe types of crimes perpetrated against computerized systems.

7. Describe five situations in which personal identification might be required before access to a computer is granted. In each case, which of the following methods would you recommend:
   a. I.D. card?
   b. Password?
   c. Signature identification?
   d. Hand form identification?
   e. Voice identification?
   f. Handprint identification?

8. Comment on the statement: Computers never make mistakes. People do.

9. What are some of the common causes of errors in computer systems? Classify them in terms of:
   a. Source.
   b. Motivation.
   c. Importance.
   d. Difficulty to trace.
   e. Difficulty to correct.

10. Why is privacy of data important to business clients and customers? What other segments in business are affected and why? How can each problem be successfully approached?

11. How can the conflict between need for data privacy and need for data access be resolved? What trade-offs can be made?

12. What is a password? Are passwords cost-effective? When should passwords be used?

13. Give two examples of unexpected results that might be produced because of:
    a. Malfunction.
    b. Mistakes.
    c. Fraud.
    d. Theft.
    e. Sabotage.
    How might security be improved to prevent incorrect results caused by *a*? By *b, c, d,* and *e*?

14. What are some common abuses of computerized information systems? How can these abuses be prevented?

15. What is the difference between the design and implementation of control? Where does each start and end? How do they overlap?

16. Has your privacy been invaded by business computers? How can invasion of privacy be prevented?

17. Can a computer system ever be completely secure? What are the trade-offs in costs? What are the social and nonmonetary costs?

18. Can error-free data be guaranteed? Can error-free results be guaranteed? Explain your answers.

19. Identify control points where measures should be taken to ensure security of data. Explain what measures you would require and why?

20. How can careless errors be reduced?

21. What should be management's role in planning system security?

EXERCISES

1. Assume that a firm has a privacy policy which states that salary data should be known only to the immediate supervisor of employees and higher level managers. Design controls to implement that policy.

2. Read about computer fraud of Equity Funding in *Fortune,* vol. 88. no. 2 (August 1973), pp. 81 ff.

    a. How was the fraud discovered?

    b. What levels of management were involved?

    c. Why was the crime not uncovered by auditors?

    d. Why did it take so long to discover?

    e. How could the crime have been avoided?

    f. How can a system be designed and operated to prevent such a crime from recurring?

SELECTED ANNOTATED BIBLIOGRAPHY

Allen, Brandt. "The Biggest Computer Frauds: Lessons for the CPAs." *The Journal of Accountancy,* vol. 143, no. 5 (May 1977), pp. 52–62.
This is an analysis of cases of computer abuse described in a study by Stanford Research Institute. The author explains how such examples of fraud can be prevented and how the accounting profession can aid in preventing criminal activity.

ACM Computing Surveys, vol. 11, no. 4 (December 1979), pp. 281–413.
This is a special issue on cryptology and data encryption addressed to the nontechnical reader. The articles recommended include one on the history and state of the art on application of encryption to secure data bases, communications, and networks, and one examining cryptographical weaknesses.

Comer, Michael J. *Corporate Fraud.* London: McGraw-Hill Book Company Limited, 1977, 393 p.
A comprehensive book on the classification, concealment, detection, and defense against corporate fraud. Thirty cases of computer crime (pp. 153–88) are described and many cases analyzed.

Diraff, T. E. "The Protection of Computer Facilities and Equipment: Physical Security." *Data Base,* vol. 10, no. 1 (Summer, 1978), pp. 15–24.

A good discussion of considerations of location, access control, personnel control, and systems recovery as it relates to physical security of an information system.

Hoffman, Lance J., ed. *Security and Privacy in Computer Systems.* Los Angeles, Calif.: Melville Publishing Co., 1973, 422 p.
This is a technical book but written in nontechnical language. It includes a cram course in threats and countermeasures, and sections on privacy transformations, models for secure systems, and security in existing systems.

La Bjork, L. A., Jr. "Generalized Audit Trail Requirements and Concepts for Data Base Applications." *IBM Systems Journal,* vol. 14, no. 3 (1975), pp. 229–45.
This article hypothesizes what information must be retained in the audit and presents a scheme for organizing the contents of the audit trail so as to provide the required functions at minimum overhead. Types of audits, audit assumptions, time domain addressing, time sequences required to support versions of data, and audit trails and their implementation are discussed.

Lowe, Ronald L. "Auditing the Corporate Information System." *The CPA Journal,* vol. 47, no. 11 (November 1977), pp. 35–40.
This article discusses the weak spots of an information system from the point of view of control and security. Presents check lists and flowcharts suggesting how the system should be audited and controlled.

Mair, William C., Wood, Donald R., and Davis, Keagle W. *Computer Control and Audit.* Wellesley, Mass.: Institute of Internal Auditors, 1978, 489 p.
The authors are partners in the accounting firm of Touche, Ross & Co. They discuss concepts of auditing, auditing tools and techniques, and the role of the auditor in the development and operation of a computerized information system.

Martin, James. *Security, Accuracy and Privacy.* Englewood Cliffs, N.J.: Prentice-Hall, Inc., 1973, 626 p.
This is an advanced text of topics related to computer control and security. It has a good appendix including a checklist on computer auditing and programs for cryptography.

Perry, William E. "Designing for Auditability." *Datamation®,* vol. 23, no. 8 (August 1977), pp. 46–50.
Perry argues that internal audit functions of the system must be considered throughout the development cycle, starting with project definition and extending to conversion. The author also identifies conditions necessary before internal auditing of a computerized system is effective.

Pritchard, J. A. T. *Risk Management in Action.* Manchester, England: National Computing Center Ltd., 1978, 160 p.
An excellent discussion of the trade-offs in security management of a computing center. Discusses the identification and measurement of threats, countermeasures, auditing, contingency planning, and a risk control program.

Van Tassel, Dennis. *Computer Security Management.* Englewood Cliffs, N.J.: Prentice-Hall, Inc., 1972, 220 p.
A very detailed discussion of techniques and strategies for control and security of a computer system. The book has checklists and bibliographical references after each chapter.

17

ORGANIZING THE HUMAN ELEMENT IN INFORMATION SYSTEMS

Though computerized societies are often pictured as machine-dominated, with humans insignificant in the production of information and in decision making, in fact computers exist to serve people, to aid humans in reaching decisions. Furthermore, a computer requires a large number of professionals and support personnel for the execution of a given task (see Figure 17.1). Input, be it data, operating instructions, or applications programs, is initiated by humans. It takes skilled analysts to assess the needs of users and to convert these needs into bits, the only medium understood by machine. Collection and updating of data is an iterative human activity. Skilled programmers are needed for the preparation and evaluation of operating instructions, and many technicians are required for operating and servicing the computer itself. Output must be interpreted and evaluated by management, and then both distributed and stored. Without analysts, applications and systems programmers, systems engineers, operators, and librarians to provide ancillary services, a computer simply cannot produce the information that users request.

This chapter opens with a discussion of the organization and mobilization of EDP personnel, both departmental organization and vertical and horizontal relationships of EDP departments with other divisions of a firm. The nature of human resistance to computers is then analyzed and steps to minimize this resistance proposed. The chapter concludes with a brief introduction to human engineering.

LOCATION OF EDP

Firms vary in their placement of EDP on their organization charts. Figure 17.2 shows five alternative plans of organization. When data processing was in its infancy and applications were limited, Case 1, EDP as a subdepartmental unit, was common. However, as more resources were devoted to computers and applications became diversified, EDP rose in the organizational hierarchy of most firms, with personnel reporting directly to department heads (Case 2) or division chiefs (Case 3). Since payroll and accounting applications predominated in the 1950s, EDP often fell under the jurisdiction of a firm's comptroller. Then, as applications extended to all functional areas, decentralized parallel computing facilities in several divisions developed.

FIGURE 17.1
Interaction between humans and machines

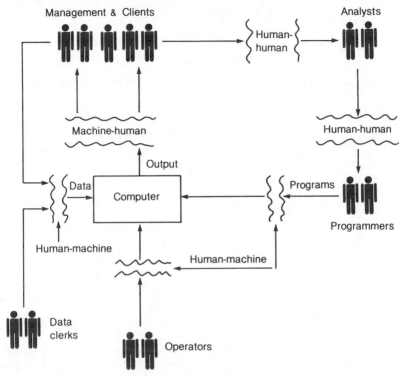

As the need for expensive data processing resources grew, sharing of data and equipment across divisional lines was initiated to cut costs in many firms. This gave impetus to the centralization of data processing, the establishment of EDP departments reporting directly to top management (Case 4). Still another organizational schema is the use of service bureaus to supplement a company's internal computing facilities or to handle all of its data processing (Case 5).

Many variables, such as equipment needs, personnel considerations, and data base use influence management's choice of EDP location. Economies of scale, and Grosch's law, that computer effectiveness is proportional to the square of cost, were factors that promoted **centralization** in the past,[1] but technological developments of microelectronics and the dramatic drop in the cost of computers have given impetus to **decentralization** in recent years.

On the other hand, decentralized personnel is more vulnerable to high

---

[1] For a discussion of these studies and of Grosch's Law, see William F. Sharpe, *The Economics of Computers* (New York: Columbia University Press, 1969), pp. 314–22.

FIGURE 17.2
Alternative locations of EDP within a firm's organization structure

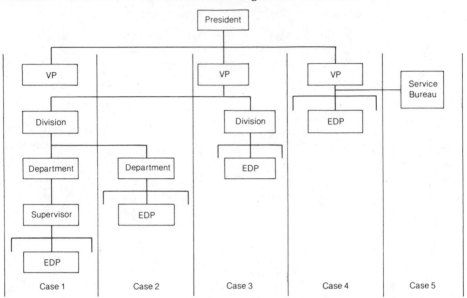

turnover,[2] and studies show that personnel costs are lower for a single large installation than for small dispersed processing facilities.[3] In addition, many firms claim that they are better able to attract and retain competent personnel when equipment is easily accessed at a central location. But this latter argument has lost some of its validity with the common use of terminals, telecommunications, and remote job entry. Furthermore, firms supporting decentralization counter that distributed centers are more sensitive to users and are better able to implement and maintain applications.[4] Though common data bases must be centralized, modern technology permits segmented, replicated, and/or distributed bases under local control.

All of the arguments for and against centralization are discussed in greater depth in the next chapter, Chapter 18, on distributed data processing. The point to be made here is that there is simply no conclusive advantage to either centralization or decentralization of all EDP departments. What often tips the scale is personalities and/or the existing organizational structure of a firm. A strong manager may insist on retaining control of all resources

---

[2] For a discussion of computer personnel turnover and approaches to improve staff retention, see Richard G. Canning, "Managing Staff Retention and Turnover," *EDP Analyzer*, vol. 15, no. 5 (August 1977), pp. 1–13.

[3] Martin Solomon, "Economics of Scale and Computer Personnel," *Datamation®*, vol. 16, no. 3 (March 1970), pp. 107–10.

[4] See Peter Berman, "A Vote against Centralized Staff," *Datamation®*, vol. 16, no. 5 (May 1976), pp. 289–90.

necessary for profit making, including EDP. Reorganization may be resisted even when decentralization is indicated because of new equipment or expanded operations.

A combination of centralized and decentralized EDP functions is quite common (see Table 17.1). Planning is generally centralized even under distributed data processing to ensure equipment compatibility and to minimize duplication of effort. Alternative 4, compromising between user' demand for decentralized operations, development activities and personnel, and the value of centralized control of the data base and planning has become increasingly popular in recent years.

TABLE 17.1
Some alternative centralization-decentralization combinations

Alternative	Development personnel	Equipment and operation	Development activities	Data base	Planning
1	C	C	C	C	C
2	D	C	C	C	C
3	D	D	C	C	C
4	D	D	D	C	C

C = Centralized.
D = Decentralized.

EDP RELATIONSHIP WITH USER DEPARTMENTS

To facilitate coordination between functional departments that are heavy users of computer and EDP personnel, many companies place these groups under the jurisdiction of a single vice president in their organizational charts (see Figure 17.3). The vice president's title varies from firm to firm, though VP for Information Services is frequently used. This plan of organization helps coordinate teleprocessing by EDP personnel with telecommunications under the Director of Communications, for example. It minimizes bureaucratic red tape for record managers who handle large volumes of computer output and rely on EDP equipment for retrieval and storage. A link with EDP ensures access to analysts and programmers for planners, reference service personnel, and word processor users. In deciding placement of EDP within a firm's organizational structure, the horizontal relationship of EDP with user departments is as important as EDP's vertical integration in the organization's hierarchy.

EDP DEPARTMENTAL ORGANIZATION

The development of increasingly sophisticated computer equipment and the expansion of computer applications in business has led to changes in the need for EDP personnel and altered job descriptions over time. In early

FIGURE 17.3
Organization chart for a VP for information services

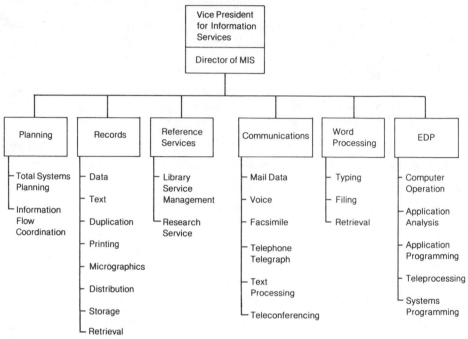

EDP shops, a single employee often functioned as analyst, programmer, and operator. As the demand for computing services grew, operations became a full-time job and a programmer-analyst was added to the staff. By the early 1960s, computers were performing tasks that required systems programmers, applications programmers, and systems analysts. By the late 1960s, specialization was needed in all EDP positions. The generalist could no longer keep abreast with technological advances. Qualifications for all EDP positions were upgraded. Operators, for example, needed experience with online realtime, multiprocessing and multiprogramming environments, and some knowledge of data management and programming as well. Programmers specialized in either scientific or business applications with business programmers in large organizations further specialized in functions such as accounting and production. Likewise, EDP staff expanded to include systems programmers, maintenance programmers, data base programmers, and functional analysts. Though computers have eliminated many manual jobs for workers, a multiplicity of new positions to provide ancillary computer services have been created. Coordinating the activities of these numerous positions and providing job backup has become a major managerial problem.

Figure 17.4 shows diagrammatically how EDP personnel configurations have changed since computers were introduced in the 1950s. The temporal evolution corresponds to the growth of EDP departments in size. That is, firms with limited EDP may consolidate operation, programming, and analysis in one position even today: the job array at the base of the figure corresponds to that found in large EDP departments. Note that some jobs listed for the 1970–1980s are not offshoots of earlier positions but are completely new. These include the data base administrator, specialists for applications such as numerical and process control, problem analysts who might be compared to earlier time-and-motion-study experts tracing back to Taylor, and policy analysts who evaluate EDP input and output for policy implications.

FIGURE 17.4
EDP personnel configurations

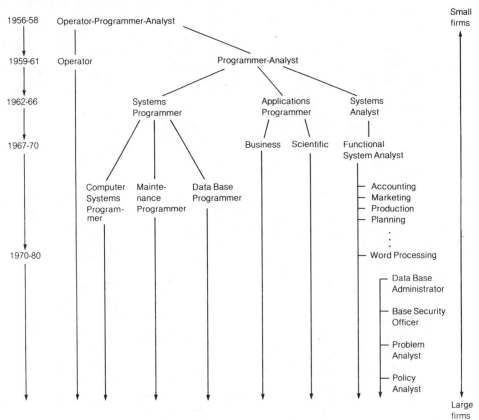

The organizational structure of EDP departments, which has changed over the years as a result of altered staff configurations, has also been affected by a redefinition of the role and responsibilities of EDP personnel and users. For example, when computers were first introduced, users participated in the development of new information systems but EDP departments had the major responsibility for the development effort. In the 1980s, however, widespread use of decentralized and distributed processing will shift some systems development to users. The EDP role will become largely advisory. Hardware selection, acquisitions, installation, operations, and maintenance will also be transferred to users. One reason this transference of responsibility is possible is that less technical knowledge is needed for the operation of today's minis, micros, and packaged systems than was required for early models of computers.

A switch in roles has also occurred with reference to data base control. Originally local data was kept by users. With the centralization of EDP and the advent of common data bases, data processing departments assumed jurisdiction over data. However, today's minis enable local sites to manage local data, and distributed data processing technology permits users to control replicated and/or segmented parts of the common data base as well. So users have again assumed data base responsibility.

All of these shifts, summarized in Figure 17.5, have required constant readjustment in the structure of EDP departments. For example, system development was the responsibility of EDP departments until the mid-1970s, when it

FIGURE 17.5
Changing responsibilities of user and EDP departments

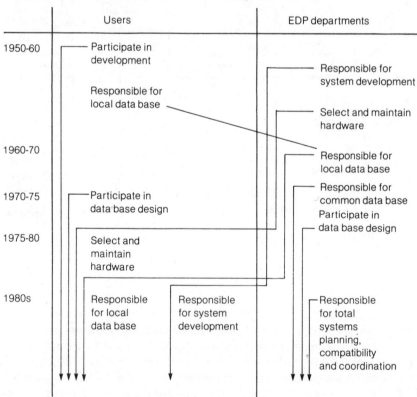

shifted to users. Responsibility for the data base, however, rested with users in 1950–60, moved to EDP departments 1960–75, then back to users after 1975. In the 1980s, EDP at the corporate level will include systems planning, and coordination and maintenance of the common data base which will necessitate compatibility of hardware and systems development at all levels. Users will be responsible for hardware, software, and development of their information systems. They will also inherit problems of human engineering, meshing human with machine, that heretofore have fallen to EDP management.

NATURE OF HUMAN RESISTANCE

In the preceding section of this chapter, changes in the location, structure, and duties of EDP departments were discussed. These changes, reflecting the expanded role of computers in business, have disrupted the traditional power structure in many firms. Some employees have lost jobs; others have been transferred to learn new skills in different working environments. Every change—even changes for the better (that is, higher pay, better working conditions, job enlargement)—evokes **human resistance.** Empirical evidence shows opposition to computerized information systems is the rule, not the exception. This should come as no surprise to managers, for the phenomenon of resistance to change has been well documented in businesses. For example, the 1958 Hawthorne Study at Western Electric noted that factory conditions alone did not explain worker attitudes. Actions perceived as a threat to job security triggered a strong emotional response. Another example is the negative reaction by managers when techniques to apply mathematical and statistical methods to decision making were first introduced by management scientists.

The resistance to computers is found at all levels of an organization. Though an assembly line worker may have different reasons for fearing computers than management does, the reaction is no less intense. Both groups are disturbed by disruption of the status quo. Procedures change, jobs gain or lose status, and totally new relationships must be forged as departments are restructured in accordance with the expanded role of machines. Resistance can often be traced to job insecurity, fear of displacement, or loss of income. But personal ego and feelings of self-esteem are also involved. It is a blow for workers to learn that their former duties have been reassigned to machines in the interests of efficiency, to find computerized systems installed without forewarning.

Managers themselves realize that fundamental changes are required in their personal styles of management, their thought patterns and their job behaviour when computerized information systems are installed. Many feel increasingly hemmed in, believing that their choices are restricted, since information systems seem to centralize all important decisions. Local managers resent having daily goals defined, the action to achieve these goals specified, and performance evaluated by a system in which personal relationships play no role. Furthermore, the information produced by the system may reveal staff incompetence, or provide data that managers would prefer to suppress.[5] For example, a report by one company comparing monthly sales showed a correlation between low performance and deer season. Managers lax in controlling unexcused absences of hunters were easily identified.

A final explanation for managerial resistance is that computers alter the decision making process. Decisions are no longer based on intuition but on data provided by the system. This type of decision making requires a different type of conceptual thinking. Many managers find their former style of decision making under attack and are not able to adjust to new technology in time.[6]

Some individuals express their opposition to computers by quitting their jobs. These are usually personnel the firm can least afford to lose for only those with good qualifications have job mobility. Those that remain may express resistance by griping, sloppiness, failure to meet deadlines, and possibly even sabotage of data. Sometimes resistance is mobilized by unions. Most often it is simply a reluctance, a hesitation, a lack of confidence in the new system that slows achievement of projected benefits. How to overcome this resistance is the subject of the next section.

OVERCOMING RESISTANCE

A sensible approach is to anticipate and identify pockets of resistance. For example, studies show that the intensity of resistance is proportional to the age of an employee, the number of years an individual has performed the task to be consigned to machine, the degree of planning, education given to employees affected by the change, and the rate of the introduction of change. Policies should be adopted in the early stages of planning a new system to defuse this hostility. The policies selected will depend on the nature of the resistance. For example, if it's economic, a combination of policies to relocate, reclassify, and retrain personnel as well as liberal policies on compensation or early retirement should help. If resistance is a function of the rate of change, pacing implementation of the new information system to allow time for readjustment should be a solution.

Often seemingly irrational resistance to computers is based on a lack of understanding of machine capabilities. Orientation sessions and in-house training are two techniques that help change employee attitudes. Change in attitude also occurs when employees participate in systems development, helping identify problems and the need for additional information. When possible solutions are proposed by the development team, employees begin to see computers are valuable business aids, and the mystique, the fear of the unknown, fades.

---

[5] Chris Argyris, "Resistance to Rational Management Systems," *Innovation,* no. 10 (1970), pp. 28–35. Also reprinted in Gordon B. Davis and Gordon C. Davis, *Readings in Management Information Systems* (New York: McGraw-Hill Book Co., 1976), pp. 245–51.

[6] Some authors predict automation of management. See John E. Steeley, Jr., "When Management Is Automated," *Datamation®,* vol. 24, no. 4 (April 1978), pp. 172, 174, 176.

In many cases resistance is based on employee resentment of computer specialists. Technicians often appear insensitive to users, talking in computer jargon, using acronyms that have no meaning to laymen, showing contempt when proposed solutions are not readily accepted. Instead of using tools of persuasion, they dictate change, ignoring psychological factors altogether. Indeed, many computer technicians lack the most elementary aspects of common sense and tact in dealing with people.

The personality of programmers has been described by Dick Brandon, a well-known author and EDP consultant as follows: "The average programmer is excessively independent—sometimes to a point of mild paranoia. He is often eccentric, slightly neurotic, and he borders upon a limited schizophrenia."[7]

Perhaps Brandon's description is too severe, but an antagonism between users and computer specialists is indeed very common.[8] The problem is further aggravated by the fact that programmers and analysts have high mobility, their turnover rate deterring the development of company loyalty and deep interpersonal relationships.[9]

In some instances, resistance may prove beneficial. If management and the development team examine the objections of employees and improve the proposed system by listening to constructive criticism, resistance can serve a useful purpose. Perhaps technicians have not paid enough attention to human needs in designing the work environment, perhaps the stress has been on technology, ignoring human-machine interface on which success of the new system depends. A careful assessment of employee objections may help avert a costly flop. Those who assume that all resistance is the grumbling of malcontents do their firm a disservice.

Once management has decided that the proposed information system is indeed in the best interests of the firm, steps must be taken to change the attitude and behavior of employees resisting the system's implementation. Change may be **participative change,** from within the individual, or be initiated by management, called a **directive change.**

A participative change starts with new knowledge (formal education, self-instruction, or observation), knowledge that kindles new attitudes which in turn affect behavior—first individual, then group behavior. Such change can be nurtured by the environment. For example, it may be corporate policy to reward employees financially if they join educational programs. A directive change is imposed by management. Policies are formulated that require altera-

---

[7] Quoted in Jac Fitz-enz, "Who Is the DP Professional?" *Datamation®*, vol. 24, no. 9 (September 1978), p. 125.

[8] Ibid., pp. 124–28. In a profile of computer personnel, Fitz-enz examines the DP professional in terms of Herzog's five motivators: achievement, recognition, work, responsibility, and advancement. See also D. Couger, J. Daniel, and R. A. Zwacki, "What Motivates DP Professionals?" *Datamation®*, vol. 24, no. 9 (September 1978), pp. 116–23.

[9] R. A. McLaughlin, "That Old Bugaboo, Turnover," *Datamation®*, vol. 25, no. 11 (October 1978), pp. 97 and 99.

tion of group behavior (e.g., all employees are *required* to attend orientation sessions), which in turn should alter the attitude of individuals and their knowledge.

Which of these two approaches works best in an EDP environment? Generally a participative change is most desirable. Self-motivated employees tend to infect others with their enthusiasm, and their willingness to try new ideas often serves as a catalyst to a change in attitude of co-workers. But when

FIGURE 17.6
Participative and directive changes

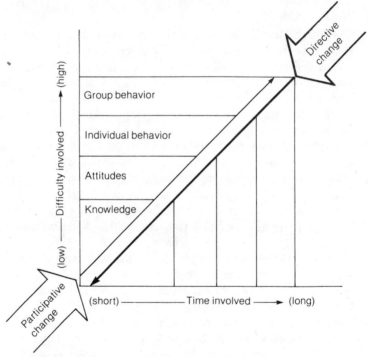

Source: Adapted from Paul Hersey and K. H. Blanchard, *Management of Organizational Behaviour: Utilizing Human Resources* (Englewood Cliffs, N.J.: Prentice-Hall, Inc., 1977), pp. 281–82.

no employees voluntarily engage in activities that lead to an alteration of behavior, management must implement strategies to encourage an attitude change. Figure 17.6 shows that the impetus for change comes from opposite points in participative and directive change, but that the end results are the same.[10]

---

[10] This conceptual framework originates with Mayo and is well discussed in Paul Hersey and Kenneth H. Blanchard, *Management—A Behavioural Approach* (Englewood Cliffs, N.J. Prentice-Hall, Inc., 1977), pp. 2–3, 280–84.

HUMAN FACTORS

What makes human resistance to computers different from the resistance of human to machine during the industrial revolution and later automation is that EDP adds two more dimensions to the human machine relationship: specialized computer hardware and software. As illustrated in Figure 17.7, EDP requires machine-software interface (A), human-software interface (B), human-machine interface (C), and human-machine-software interface (D).[11]

FIGURE 17.7
Relationship between human, machine, and software

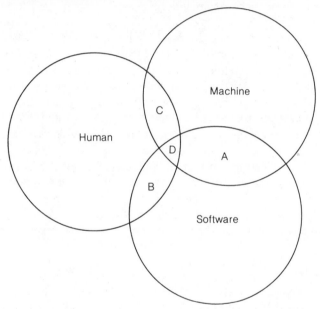

A = Machine-software interface. C = Human-machine interface.
B = Human-software interface. D = Human-machine-software interface.

Human factors, sometimes called **man-machine studies (ergonomics in Europe)** is a field currently researching human-computer relationships.[12] Some of the problems and recommended solutions are quite mundane. Are work stations comfortable and pleasing? The arrangement of furniture and

[11] For a similar diagram and an excellent discussion, see Gloria Grace in her preface to a special issue on human considerations in information processing, *Human Factors,* vol. 12, no. 2 (March–April, 1970), pp. 161–64.

[12] See Thomas Martin, "The User Interface in Interactive Systems," in Carlos A. Cuadra, *Annual Review of Information Science and Technology,* vol. 8 (Washington, D.C.: American Society for Information Sciences, 1973), pp. 203; and K. D. Eason, L. Damodaran, and T. M. Stewart, "Interface Problems in Man-Computer Interaction," in E. Mumford and H. Sackman, eds., *Human Choice and Computers* (Amsterdam, Netherlands: North-Holland Publishing Co., 1975), pp. 91–105.

work space around a terminal can affect user morale: an inconvenient layout may contribute to employee errors. The size of the keys, the angle of the screen, the flickers on the screen, the size of the characters on the screen, and color of displays are all important to the user.

Many human engineering problems arise from the diverse and wide range of knowledge and computer experience of information system users. Managers use computers primarily for output, but the same machine must serve clerks (who use terminals primarily as input devices), professionals (analysts, programmers), and product designers using CAD (computer-aided design). Technicians designing computerized systems see information problems that need resolution, and manipulate hardware, software, and technology toward this end. They often fail to recognize the communication barriers of nonprofessionals with computers, the need for interactive and conversational modes, and the need for techniques, training methods, and documentation aids to assist users in taking full advantage of the potential of computers for problem solving. As David McCarn states, computer experts who tend to be highly rational and mechanistic in their thinking often deny the existence of individuals who see broad patterns and total pictures rather than well bounded problems that can be solved by computer. As a result systems design is not always appropriate for all classes of users.[13]

The literature on human engineering is quite extensive (over 1,000 references as early as 1971), a clear indication of the importance of this subject. Management should keep abreast of current research in this field, for no computerized information system can achieve its full potential as a tool in management decision making when aspects of human engineering are ignored.

SUMMARY

Figure 17.2 shows alternative organizational plans for EDP departments within a firm's hierarchy. Their location has been influenced over time by the expanding nature of EDP responsibilities and the introduction of new technology, such as DDP (distributed data processing) equipment, which permits decentralization of data processing. Even within EDP departments, organization has not remained static. As the demand for information has increased, a multiplicity of new jobs to provide ancillary computer services have been created. Job descriptions have also been continually altered in response to technological developments. At the present time, for example, DDP and the widespread use of minis have shifted many former responsibilities of technicians to users.

The growth of EDP has not proceeded smoothly in all cases, however. Employee resistance to change, fear of job displacement, and unwillingness to learn new procedures and skills have hindered the development of informa-

---

[13] David B. McCarn, "Getting Ready. . . . ." *Datamation®*, vol. 16, no. 8 (August 1970), p. 26.

tion systems. How to eliminate human resistance and design computers with human-machine interface is the subject of much research at the present time.

KEY WORDS

Centralization   Human factors
Decentralization   Human resistance
Directive change   Man-machine studies
EDP departmental organization   Participative change
Ergonomics   Personnel configurations

DISCUSSION QUESTIONS

1. Why are some people against automation?

2. Why is there resistance to computerized information systems by:
   a. Managers?
   b. Data clerks?
   c. Clients/customers?
   How does each group react? What can be done to reduce the resistance from each group?

3. Describe the skills required for computer processing and comment on:
   a. The relative importance of these skills.
   b. The changing demand for these skills.
   c. The supply of persons with these skills.

4. What is the difference between human factors in computer processing and human engineering of information systems?

5. What are the problems of human-machine interface in computer processing? Give examples in business, and propose solutions.

6. What steps should be taken to improve the probability that an information system will be accepted by users?

7. How can resistance to computerized information systems be overcome?

8. How and why is the involvement of users in development useful in reducing resistance to computerization?

9. Does computerization support the centralization or decentralization of management in a business firm?

10. How are the personnel problems in EDP departments unique?

11. Where in the organization structure of a business firm should EDP be located? Justify your answer.

12. How would you organize EDP in terms of organization structure, span of control, and supervision?

13. What are the major functions to be performed at an EDP installation? What personnel is required to perform these functions?

14. What are the advantages of having a single analyst-programmer rather than an analyst and a programmer?

15. What personal and professional qualities are required by each of the following employees:
    a. Computer programmer?
    b. Systems analyst?
    c. Data clerk?
    d. Computer operator?
    What schooling is necessary for each job? What on-the-job training is required?

16. Why is there a high turnover among computer personnel? How could this turnover be minimized?

17. Why is displacement important when a computerized information system is initiated? What are the variables that affect the importance of displacement?

EXERCISES

1. What personnel would be required for generating the report in Exercise 1, Chapter 10 and implementing the policy in Exercise 1, Chapter 16? Would a firm have to hire personnel specially for these tasks?

2. Suppose you are consulting for a firm about to initiate an EDP center with 50 persons, including 20 programmers to operate a batch as well as an OLRT computer system for marketing. What EDP organization structure would you propose? What employees will be needed?

3. Read R. Boguslaw, *The New Utopians* (Englewood Cliffs, N.J.: Prentice-Hall, Inc., 1965). The author calls computer people the new utopians, the social engineers of our times. What dangers does Boguslaw identify? Do you agree with Boguslaw's hypothesis?

4. Identify the principal jobs in business data processing and compare them in terms of:
   a. Education required.
   b. Experience required.
   c. Relationship to user management.
   d. Position in the organizational structure.
   e. Salary range.

SELECTED ANNOTATED BIBLIOGRAPHY

Argyris, Chris. "Resistance to Rational Management Systems." *Innovation,* no. 10 (1970), pp. 28–35.
This is a psychologist's perspective of resistance to computerized information systems. Specifically, Argyris discusses the impact of computers on management power structure, style, and behavior.

Glaser, George. "The Centralization vs. Decentralization Issue: Arguments, Alternatives and Guidelines." *Data Base,* vol. 2, no. 3 (Fall/Winter 1970), pp. 28–35.
A very well-written, excellent survey of the issues of centralization and decentralization.

Patrick, Robert L. "Decentralizing Hardware, and Dispersing Responsibility." *Datamation®,* vol. 22, no. 5 (May 1976), pp. 79–84.
This is a detailed discussion of the relationship of computer power as a function

of hardware, supply cost, and complexity, not just cost as postulated by Grosch's Law. Patrick also discusses the limits to centralization, and the movement toward decentralization and distributed processing without entirely giving up the centralized facility.

Reynolds, Carl H. "Issues in Centralization." *Datamation®,* vol. 23, no. 3 (March 1977), pp. 91–93, ff.
This is a description of centralization at Hughes Aircraft Co. The author specifically discusses the following variables: hardware, personnel required, applications, data base/data communications systems, maintenance, and motivation of the organization.

Tomeski, Edward A., and Harold Lazarus. *People-Oriented Computer Systems.* New York: Van Nostrand Reinhold Co., 1975, 299 p.
The authors argue that computers have failed to serve people and organizations. The book is a plea to vendors and users to adopt policies and practices that will make computerized information systems sensitive and responsive to human and social needs.

18

DISTRIBUTED DATA PROCESSING

Distributed data processing (DDP) is one way of organizing equipment and personnel to implement a management information system. Generally, a decision to utilize this processing structure is made during the development stages of a new information system, but sometimes an ongoing system is converted to DDP. In either case, operations shift from a centralized EDP center to dispersed locations. This chapter describes in detail how daily operations and management are affected by this change. The material could have been included in Chapter 17, but has been allocated a separate chapter due to the newness of this processing organization and the importance of this approach for the 80s.

DDP combines features of both centralized and decentralized processing. Managers view this innovation with some apprehension, however, for widespread use of DDP will change organizational structure and patterns of corporate decision making. This chapter provides background information on the evolution, architecture, and features of DDP and identifies implementation considerations.

EVOLUTION OF DDP

When EDP was first introduced, firms commonly established small data processing centers in divisions needing information. These centers were physically dispersed and had no centralized authority coordinating their activities. Data processed in this manner was often slow to reach middle and top management, and frequently failed to provide the information needed for decision making. In addition, this type of organization structure did not take advantage of Grosch's law, a law applicable to early computers which states that the increase in the computational power of a computer is the square of the increase in costs, that is, doubling computer cost quadruples computational power. Processing by small dispersed computers was, therefore, unnecessarily expensive. Furthermore, due to the scarcity of qualified computer specialists, the centers were often poorly run.

The need for centralized computing facilities was soon recognized. Firms hoped that costs would drop, that information processing would be responsive to management needs, that the delivery speed of information would increase, that redundancy in processing and files would be eliminated, and that security and control of information would be tightened. However, not all of these expectations were realized when centralization took place. Lack of communication between users and analysts continued to exist. Users felt isolated from the computing facilities, complaining that analysts were unresponsive to their needs and resenting the hours required to justify and document requests for service. The bureaucracy created often proved inept at mediating conflicting interests. Analysts chaffed at criticism, believing that the length of time required for system development was simply not understood by users.

This dissatisfaction led to reconsideration of dispersed processing. Technological developments in the meantime made DDP economically feasible. Minicomputers with capabilities exceeding many former large computers were now on the market at low cost. Chip technology had increased CPU and memory capacity while reducing computer size. Strides in telecommunications meant that no processing center would be isolated. In addition, experience with data processing had given users confidence that they could manage and operate their own processing systems. By the late 1970s, DDP was a commercial reality.

WHAT IS DDP?

Distributed data processing is the linking of two or more processing centers **(nodes)** within a single organization, each center having facilities for program execution and data storage. However, this definition—which excludes computer networks like ARPA (Advanced Research Projects Agency) and EFT (Electronic Fund Transfer) because they serve many clients in business, industry and government—is still evolving.

The linkage provided by DDP permits centralized control over policies and processing while the system retains the flexibility of decentralization. The facilities at sites are tailored to local needs and controlled by local management, avoiding the rigidity of centralized hardware and personnel, while integration of the sites minimizes duplication of effort.

Distributed systems vary in architecture, software, protocols, controls, and data transmission capabilities according to the needs of the organization served. A number of equipment configurations will now be discussed.

EQUIPMENT CONFIGURATIONS

The difference between DDP and earlier dispersed processing is the linkage between processing centers. Formerly, stand-alone computers processed information: DDP involves a network of processors. Figure 18.1 shows sample DDP configurations. In the **star network,** failure of the central computer impairs the entire system. The **ring** structure overcomes this problem, for rerouting is possible should one processing center or its link fail. The ring allows interaction and **offloading** (the transference of processing from one site to another) without dependence on a central host. Both star and ring configurations are essentially **horizontal systems,** that is, each processor is an equal. The hardware may be unique at each center, which means that equipment may be purchased from any number of vendors, an advantage when the market responds to technological developments and new models are made available. But this flexibility has a negative aspect: it increases problems of linkage and compatability between nodes. There are combinations

FIGURE 18.1
DDP configurations

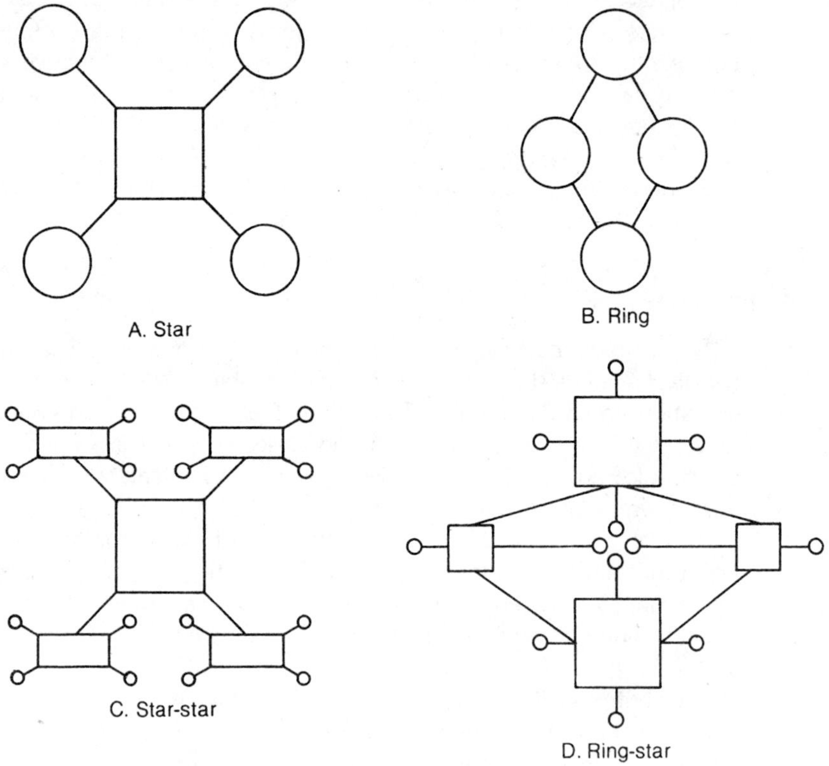

A. Star

B. Ring

C. Star-star

D. Ring-star

of rings and stars, like star-star and ring-star as shown in Figure 18.1 C and D, respectively, but the basic weaknesses remain.

Hierarchial distribution is the configuration that many firms prefer since it requires the least reorganization, corresponding to the hierarchial structure that is already in existence within the corporation. This system, illustrated in Figure 18.2, has a central host computer and common data base with minis and micros at dispersed sites. Generally, all equipment and software are supplied by the same vendor, minimizing problems of compatibility between nodes. Because many computers have either a fail-safe capability (ability to continue operations in spite of breakdown due to the existence of backup) or a **fail-soft capability** (the ability to continue with a degraded level of operations) a breakdown in the hierarchy does not incapacitate the entire system; all computers have independent processing capabilities to some extent. Of course, the exact configuration of any hierarchial system of DDP would vary according to the needs of the organization being served.

FIGURE 18.2
Hierarchical distributed data processing

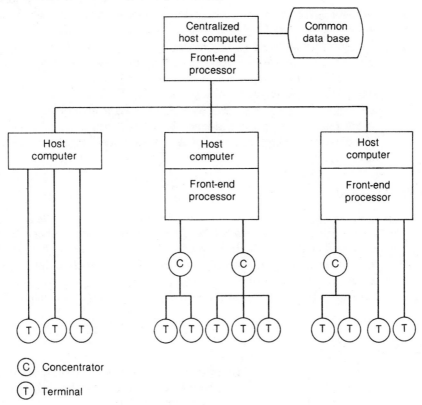

Ⓒ Concentrator

Ⓣ Terminal

SYSTEMS ARCHITECTURE

DDP, regardless of configuration, requires a system for data control, for resource sharing, and for coordination of dispersed processing. Procedures, software, hardware, and personnel are all needed to support DDP. How these resources are combined is part of the **systems architecture.** Systems architecture is not merely a design. It includes protocols for running DDP as well. Many computer vendors market architecture systems. In 1977, 16 different systems were in use in the United States alone.[1] Others were available abroad.

However, choice of systems architecture is more limited than these figures imply. Vendors design software for specific equipment to encourage purchase of that hardware. Furthermore, lack of industry standards and rapid changes in technology add to problems of equipment interface with the network systems. Users often find that only one network architecture can be adapted to their equipment configurations.

The most widely used architecture is **SNA (Systems Network Architecture).** IBM first introduced SNA in 1974 for hierarchial distributed processing.[2] In 1978, the IBM 8100 was placed on the market, a computer specifically designed for DDP using SNA. Because of IBM's dominance in the computer industry, its investment in SNA and the 8100 has legitimized DDP as a concept and made it a commercial reality. An important feature of the 8100 is that it is a stand-alone computer designed for online processing and need not be linked to a host computer. Furthermore, installation does not require technical expertise. As an IBM press release notes, ". . . portions of the new system can be installed by users—with a set of easy to follow directions—in much the same way as a basic household stereo system might be set up."[3]

DDP DATA BASES

There are many ways to organize DDP data bases.[4] All data can be centralized, or processing centers can keep **segments** of the data base. Sometimes dispersed centers keep data needed for local processing that **replicates** data stored in the central repository. A **hybrid approach** to data organization is also possible in which dispersed processors keep both segmented and replicated data. These approaches to data base organization will be explained next.

Centralized data base

When dispersed processors draw all data from a centralized data base, transmission costs are high. This system is appropriate when infrequent access

---

[1] For a detailed comparison, see Anthony Durniak, "Special Report: New Networks Tie Down Distributed Data Processing Concepts," *Electronics,* vol. 51, no. 25 (December 7, 1978), pp. 101–22. For another editorial comparison, *see* Ralph G. Berglund, "Comparing Network Architectures," *Datamation®,* vol. 24, no. 2 (February 1978), pp. 79–85. Both discuss American network architectures, but Durniak also discusses architectures commonly used in Europe and Japan.

[2] For detailed study of SNA, read R. J. Cypsen, *Communications Architecture for Distributed Systems* (Reading, Mass.: Addison Wesley Publishing Co., Inc., 1978), 711 p.

[3] Quoted by Larry Woods, "IBM's 8100: First Impressions," *Datamation®,* vol. 25, no. 3 (March 1979), p. 142.

[4] For a further discussion of this subject, see a set of articles on distributed data bases in Burt H. Leibowitz and John H. Carson, *Distributed Processing* (Long Beach, Calif.: IEEE Computer Society, 1978), pp. 381–444.

to the centralized data is needed and when updating needs to be strictly controlled.

Segmented distributed data base

Under this system, parts of the data base are stored at dispersed sites. The segments might be data from a function or data pertaining to a geographic area. The data is segmented according to local processing needs so that each site is basically independent though other sites may draw on the distributed data base as a shared resource.

Replicated distributed data base

When more than one dispersed processor needs the same data, a common approach to data base organization is to store the data base at a central repository with duplicate segments needed for local processing stored at decentralized computers. This is called a **replicated distributed data base.** The local bases used for processing, including online real-time operations, are then periodically used to update the centralized data, which in turn updates all distributed data bases.

Large regional banks frequently adopt this system. Central processing takes place after banking hours and distributed data bases are then created for branch offices. These latter bases are essentially working files used for local transactions such as deposits and withdrawals. At the end of each working day, the central data base is again updated and the cycle begins once again with the creation of (updated) distributed data bases for the branch offices.

In general, the centralized data base has all control and summary data bases, whereas transactional data and local data is in the distributed data bases. Branch offices might still have to access the centralized data during the course of the day. This would occur when a customer of the bank wished to cash a check at a branch that did not have a record of his or her account, for example. In this case, the transaction would have to be routed through the central data base.

One advantage of replicated data bases is that they provide backup, so the system is less vulnerable should failure at the central location occur. An additional advantage is that systems are more responsive to local needs when data is managed locally. (An advantage that applies to segmented data bases as well.) In particular, maintenance and updating of large and complex data bases are more effective when sections of the bases are under local control. Certain types of processing are also more efficient. For example, retrieval by indexes requires careful cross-indexing. Personnel on location with a need for the retrieved data will be more highly motivated and more knowledgeable about the task than programmers at a centralized data base.

A major problem with replicated distributed data bases is minimizing redundancy. For efficient processing, no more data than absolutely necessary should be stored at remote sites, but the exact need of distributed centers for data is not easily determined. Another problem arises when more than one dispersed processor attempts to access the same data at the same time from the central data base. Such concurrent communication problems also occur with segmented distributed data bases when two processors attempt to access the same data at the same time. Much research is currently being conducted in this area.

Hybrid approach

Some firms combine a segmented and replicated approach to organization of their data bases—the hybrid approach. For example, a national business may segment the base geographically, and then provide branches within each region with replicated data from geographical headquarters. Warehouse inventories are often controlled in this manner.

In a DBMS environment, both distributed DBMSs and a central DBMS are possible. Though the distributed systems would satisfy local needs, the central DBMS would have the overall schema of the entire logical data base, and be concerned with problems of security, integrity, and recovery for all data, including data at distributed centers.[5]

DDP ORGANIZATIONAL STRUCTURE

There is no standard DDP structure because a range of choices exists with three organizational variables: degree of centralized control, hardware configurations, and data base distribution. A number of combinations of these three variables is possible, as seen in Figure 18.3. In this figure, the three axes represent control, hardware, and the data base. The shaded area represents a clear-cut case for DDP: multiple computers or a single computer with remote access; hierarchical or decentralized cooperating nodes; and distributed data, either segmented or replicated. Except for the squares at the lower level (marked with X), firms with a number of combinations of control, hardware, and data base might utilize DDP. For example, a firm with national sales which manufactures products at a single factory may use DDP but retain centralized administrative control and a centralized data base.

Though Figure 18.3 is helpful conceptually, in practice firms cannot be categorized so simply. Many firms have mixed processing modes, combining features of centralized, decentralized,[6] and distributed processing. For example, Hewlett Packard manufactured 4,000 products in 38 plants in 1978, and had 172 sales offices around the world. The company's 1400 computers

---

[5] For a further detailed discussion see James Martin, *Security, Accuracy and Privacy in Computer Systems* (Englewood Cliffs, N.J.: Prentice-Hall, Inc., 1973), and Jan Palmer, *Data Base System: A Practical Reference* (Wellesley, Mass.: QED Information Sciences Inc., 1977), chap. 2, pp. 2.26–2.41.

[6] Decentralized processing refers to physically separated, stand-alone processing entities.

FIGURE 18.3
Three dimensions of DDP

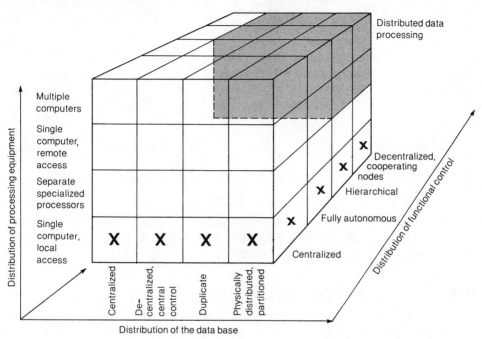

Source: Adapted from Anthony Durniak, "Special Report: New Networks Tie Down Distributed Data Processing Concepts," *Electronics,* vol. 51, no. 25 (December, 1978), p. 110. Copyright © McGraw-Hill, Inc., 1978.

served 4500 employees, mixing all processing modes. For example, materials services, legal reporting, and employee benefits were centralized; customer service, inventorying, payroll, and personnel decentralized; with production information, orders, and accounts receivable handled by the distributed mode.[7]

WHEN TO IMPLEMENT DDP

There is no formula or precise decision rule for determining when to implement DDP. However, one technique to help identify situations that should be considered for the distributed mode is **grid analysis.** A sample grid analysis is shown in Table 18.1. Here a hypothetical firm with sites A, B, C, and D (X axis) has informational needs that Processes (applications or programs) 1–3 and Files 1–3 (Y axis) satisfy. A check is made of the informational requirements of each site. Note that the grid shows that Process 2 and File 1 are needed by only a single site. These are possible candidates

[7] See Cort Van Renssalear, "Centralize? Decentralize? Distribute?" *Datamation*®, vol. 25, no. 9 (April 1979), p. 90.

TABLE 18.1
Illustration of grid analysis

Informational Sites / Needs	A	B	C	D
Process 1	X	X	X	X
2	X			
3			X	X
Files 1	X			
2	X	X	X	X
3			X	X

for the distributed mode. Since all sites require Process 1 and File 2, centralization is advisable. The principle of grid analysis can be used to help determine whether a need for DDP is indicated.[8]

IMPLEMENTATION CONSIDERATIONS

Before a company commits itself to distributed data processing, it should investigate costs and determine how EDP organizational structure will be affected. The exact operations to be performed at the distributed site must be decided and personnel be prepared for the shift in power that accompanies DDP. A discussion of all these implementation considerations will follow.

Costs

One component of cost is CPU hardware. Grosch's law is no longer applicable. Today's minis and small computers are dropping in price while increasing in computing power due to recent technological advances. For example, a computer equaling the PDP-1 that sold for $150,000 in 1965 could be purchased in 1979 for $700. And a computer such as the Amigo 300, a small business model with a megabyte memory having the purchase price of $32,000 in 1979, has a computing capacity that exceeds that of any even conceived in 1965. These reduced costs in computing power mean DDP is feasible for many businesses that formerly could not afford dispersed processors.

Terminal hardware is also dropping in cost, but as users demand more sophisticated units, such as intelligent terminals with local processing capabilities, actual terminal expenditures may rise. Figure 18.4 shows a cost curve for various types of terminals.

At the present time, transmission costs are not dropping as dramatically

---

[8] For details, see P. J. Down and F. E. Taylor, *Why Distributed Computing?* (Oxford, England: The National Computing Center Ltd., 1976), p. 41.

FIGURE 18.4
Cost of terminals for varying degrees of distribution

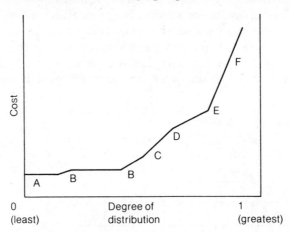

A = Unintelligent terminal
B = Introduction of some limited intelligence
C = Provision of more software to use local processing capability
D = Conversion of the intelligent terminal to a full blown mini-
    computer system with peripherals
E = More software to process more applications locally
F = Tending towards complete independence from the central site

Source: P. J. Down and T. E. Taylor, *Why Distributed Computing?* (Oxford, England: The National Computing Center, Ltd. 1976), p. 78.

as the cost of hardware, so it is tempting to install additional processors in the distributed mode rather than transmit data to a centralized computer. This is due, in part, to the monopolistic character of the transmission industry. Changes in federal regulations may alter this situation so that firms implementing DDP may need to make an economic reassessment of their equipment configurations in the future.

EDP reorganization

Distributed data processing requires that EDP personnel be shifted to dispersed centers for operations and even for systems development. Acquisition decisions may also be made on site. The transition to decentralization should be gradual to allow employees time to adjust to the change, and time to acquire experience making decisions at the local level.

EDP personnel will still be needed at the corporate center for administering overall control of data processing, and for coordinating and counseling the dispersed sites. These responsibilities mean that the EDP group at the center should be of high caliber with a global view of the system. Reorganization under DDP may produce a structure similar to the chart in Figure 18.5.

Control over budgets and auditing procedures will still be centralized under DDP. The center will also be responsible for developing and enforcing performance standards for equipment, software, and personnel at the distributed sites. DDP does help safeguard a company's data files since not all of the data is stored in one place, and access control is easier to administer at

FIGURE 18.5
Organization chart with DDP

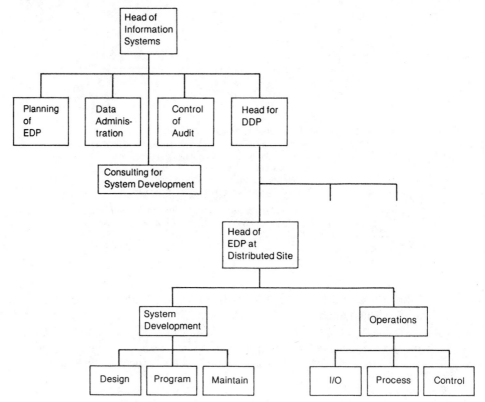

small processing sites. DDP, however, is vulnerable to wire-tapping, so new types of security precautions must be taken.

Before implementing DDP, a reorganization plan must be developed by management for distributing functions and a workable timetable established for the transition period. The prime objective of the reorganization should be to match DDP capabilities and architecture with users' needs. It may be necessary to call in consultants to assist in the decentralization process. A team of outside consultants plus analysts drawn from within the organization to supervise decentralization has many advantages. The consultants provide objectivity, experience, and adequate staff when it is needed; the analysts provide knowledge of company policies, procedures, and personalities most affected by the reorganization.

A data base administrator will have added responsibilities during the period of transition. For example, conflicts over data jurisdiction will have to be resolved. The DBA will also have to decide whether the data base should be segmented and how, what data should be replicated, and what schedule of data distribution should be followed. Care must be taken to see that uniform procedures for control, protection, and recovery of data exist at all dispersed sites. The units responsible for updating and maintaining data files must be designated. Procedures for establishing common data definitions must be determined.

Operations and staffing

The reorganization plan will assign operational responsibilities to each distributed processor. Equipment acquisition and system development may also be allocated to dispersed centers. Staffing is a major problem because persons at each local site must know how to run a computer center and be knowledgeable about distributive processing as well. This includes knowledge of systems architecture, communication equipment, protocols, and security unique to DDP. Staff may need special training and/or additional professionals may have to be hired. Officials at the corporate center must also be able and willing to take on additional responsibilities since decentralization redefines the role of management. Operations must be coordinated and a total system approach for the organization formulated and managed.

Power restructuring

Redevelopment of data processing functions will cause upheaval and disruption to the power structure of a firm. The EDP staff at the corporate center will be dismantled, managers will loose "empires," and new sets of interpersonal relationships will have to be forged. Even when job security is not threatened (employees merely transferred to new duties at the dispersed sites), physical dislocation can be traumatic. Conversion to DDP is a problem requiring management savvy in industrial relations.

FUTURE OF DDP

The future of DDP is clouded due to uncertainty in two major areas: standards and federal regulations.

Lack of agreement over network standards has prevented coordination of DDP research and development. The Europeans utilize X.25 standards;

the Americans, SNA and SDLC (Synchronous Data Link Control).[9] DDP will not be widely implemented until universal standards are adopted and DDP equipment and software of competing manufacturers can be integrated into a single DDP system.

Another area, uncertainty over federal regulations, is also slowing development of DDP. Will AT&T be allowed to extend its communication monopoly to include DDP? Will IBM be permitted to enter communications through Satellite Business Systems? Competiton between these corporate giants should lower communication costs, a benefit to DDP users.

Once DDP is cost-effective and hardware, systems architecture, and communications are integrated into reliable, robust systems, DDP will become more viable. Advances are being made in distributed data base technology and software so that data can be accessed with ease no matter where it is stored in the distributed network. Solutions to problems of deadlock and optimal routing of queries are presently being researched. Future systems must be less vulnerable to failure and more easily restructured in response to growth or changed informational needs. DDP applications will undoubtedly broaden from current use for data entry and validation to full office automation and shop floor control.

Widespread DDP (particularly widespread use of intelligent terminals) should give computing power to large segments of the population heretofore lacking efficient and speedy access to information processing. Perhaps DDP's greatest impact will be democratization of the computer. Once computer mysticism fades and DDP use is as common as telephoning, then computers will be used extensively in the office and in the home, a subject discussed further in later chapters (Chapters 24 and 25).

SUMMARY

DDP takes computing power from one large centralized computer and disperses this power to sites where processing demand is generated. The equipment used is a mix of terminals, minis, and small business computers integrated by appropriate systems architecture. Some computers are being specially designed for DDP applications, such as the IBM 8100. The computers themselves can be linked in a variety of configurations, such as star, ring, or hybrid configurations, though the hierarchical structure with fail-soft capability is more common.

DDP is an attempt to distribute processing capability and intelligence. The move away from centralization has been prompted by user dissatisfaction with central processing, a willingness and ability of EDP personnel to manage local computer centers, and technological advances such as chip technology and advances in telecommunications which have made DDP feasible.

Deciding when to distribute depends on how much processed data is

---

[9] See F. P. Corr and D. H. Neal, "SNA and Emerging International Standards," *IBM Systems Journal,* vol. 18, no. 2 (1979), pp. 244–62.

needed by the corporate center and how much is utilized at branches. One rule of thumb states that distributed processing is indicated when 20 percent of the processed information is needed by the center and 80 percent at local sites. Other factors indicating the need for DDP are decentralization of responsibility, distributed functions, and limited information flow to headquarters.

A major advantage of DDP is that systems can begin simply and grow modularly. DDP can also be adapted to various organization structures and modified when necessary to adapt to changing patterns in the flow of information. These and other advantages are listed in Table 18.2. Limitations appear in Table 18.3. Most of the technological limitations will be overcome in time, for the computer industry is already researching systems architecture, equipment, software, and data base management systems in response to user's

TABLE 18.2
Advantages of distributed data processing

1. Offers decentralized processing and satisfies desire for local autonomy and local application development. Facilitates user accessibility to computer centers.
2. Local control over needed segments of the data base is retained at the distributed centers.
3. Quality of input and processing is improved because of greater sensitivity to local conditions.
4. Users feel analysts at dispersed sites are more responsive to their needs.
5. Enables modular growth with little disruption at central site.
6. Enables use of different equipment at sites, provided interface problems are resolved.
7. Provides stand-alone operations with fail-soft capability for hierarchical structures and alternative routes for ring structures.
8. Provides middle management at distributed level unique, relevant, and timely information, and consequently a measure of independence from top management.
10. Enables use of heterogeneous equipment and resource sharing, including dynamic load balancing (by moving around and distributing load) to maximize throughout.

TABLE 18.3
Limitations of DDP

1. Can be more expensive than centralized processing in spite of low-cost minis, largely because of the cost of transmission, software necessary for DDP, and the overlapping of equipment (especially disks in cases of replicated data bases).
2. The interface of expensive equipment from different vendors at dispersed nodes is a problem, for equipment may differ in instruction sets and operating systems.
3. Most existing software packages are designed for stand-alone computers and need to be adapted for DDP.
4. Communication systems of DDP are vulnerable to security violations.
5. National and international standards for network communication do not exist, causing problems of interfacing and implementing DDP.
6. With autonomous distributed sites, corporate standards of development, integration, and data base are more difficult to enforce.

needs. Resistance to change will slow the spread of DDP, but once a firm restructures its data processing and new relationships are forged, DDP will prove its value to users and technical personnel.

KEY WORDS

Centralized data base	Offloading
Distributed data processing (DDP)	Replicated distributed data base
Fail-soft capability	Ring network
Grid analysis	Segmented distributed data base
Hierarchical distributed data processing	Systems Network Architecture (SNA)
Horizontal system	Star network
Hybrid approach	Systems architecture
Nodes	

DISCUSSION QUESTIONS

1. Describe the essential elements of a distributed processing system.
2. What are the characteristics of DDP?
3. When would you select a star computer configuration as opposed to a ring or hierarchical configuration? Why? Give examples of each in business and industry.
4. What configuration of computer equipment in a DDP environment would you select for the following situations:
   a. A bank with many branches?
   b. A wholesaler with many warehouses?
5. What problems arising out of personnel conflicts and power struggle should be expected in the transition from centralized EDP to DDP? What can be done to minimize the harmful effects?
6. What are the problems of control, security, and privacy to be expected in a DDP environment? How can one overcome such problems?
7. What is the role and importance of telecommunications and teleprocessing in a DDP environment?
8. Comment on the following statement: DDP democratizes computing by making it more accessible.
9. What is distributed in DDP?
10. Can DDP be implemented in modules?
11. What effect will DDP have on organization structure, management style, and the decision-making process in business?
12. What is involved in the conversion from centralized EDP to DDP? What additional equipment, software, or personnel will be required under the new structure?

EXERCISE

1. Would you want the systems in Exercises 1, Chapter 10 and 1, Chapter 16 to be processed at a central facility or a distributed facility, assuming both options were feasible? Explain your choice.

SELECTED ANNOTATED BIBLIOGRAPHY

Becker, Hal B. "Let's Put Information and Networks into Perspective." *Datamation®*, vol. 24, no. 3 (March 1978), pp. 81–86.

Becker identifies the pitfalls and unresolved problems of distributed data processing. The author is optimistic that all the problems will be resolved.

Champaine, G. A. "Six Approaches to Distributed Data Bases." *Datamation®*, vol. 23, no. 5 (May 1977), pp. 69–72.

This is a good discussion of centralized versus distributed data processing (and distributed data bases) with a description and evaluation of six actual approaches used: ARPANET (a national nonbusiness-oriented system), SITA, Celanese, Bank of America, Aeroquip, and Loews Companies, Inc.

Down, P. J., and Taylor F. F. *Why Distributed Computing?* Manchester, England: National Computing Center Ltd., 1976, 168 p.

This book is the result of a project to investigate the alternatives and implications of DDP for the corporate planner in the business environment in England. The concepts discussed and even some of the cost data are applicable to this country. It is an excellent overview of the subject of DDP, including operational and design considerations.

Durniak, Anthony. "Special Report: New Networks Tie Down Distributed Processing Concepts." Electronics, vol. 51, no. 3 (December, 1978), pp. 107–20.

An excellent article on network architecture, including both American and foreign approaches. Somewhat technical but not difficult reading.

Katzan, Jr., Harry. *An Introduction to Distributed Data Processing.* New York: Petrocelli Books, 1978, 242 p.

This book is in three parts: Management Overview of the Distributed Concept; Data Communications Concept; and Distributed Systems Concepts. In other words, the communications link is emphasized. A well-written, easy-to-read, nonmathematical text that is generously illustrated.

Kaufmaun, Felix. "Distributed Processing: A Discussion for Executives Travelling over Difficult EDP Terrain." *Data Base,* vol. 10, no. 1 (Summer 1978), pp. 9–13.

A pleasure to read. Many terms are defined and concepts are well stated.

Liebowitz, Burt H., and John H. Carson. *Distributed Processing Tutorial,* 2d ed. Long Beach, Calif.: IEEE Computer Society, 1978.

This book is not a tutorial nor is the text limited to a discussion of DDP. It is a set of over 50 articles on topics such as communications, networks, intelligent terminals, multiprocessors, and distributed data bases. As with most sets of readings, it is a mix of excellent and mediocre articles. But overall, it is a good collection, including both survey-type and technical articles.

Lorin, H. "Distributed Processing: An Assessment." *IBM Systems Journal,* vol. 18, no. 4 (1979), pp. 582–603.

This article discusses the potential benefits and pitfalls of DDP: centralized management, historical relationship of DDP with online systems, the reliability and growth of fail-soft systems, and adjusting DDP to the organization structure of the firm. Lorin concludes, "We do not know, in general, whether complexity will increase or decrease distributed processing systems, nor how operational costs will evolve. We are just discovering an art."

McLaughlin, Michael J., and Katz, Michael S. "Distributed Processing—The Second Generation." *Infosystems,* vol. 26, no. 2 (February 1979), pp. 38 ff.

The author analyzes the first generation of DDP and concludes that it was difficult to implement, operate, and maintain. The author then discusses the second generation and the continuing need for distributed data base management software, applications programs, operating systems, and user acceptance.

Patrick, Robert L. "A Checklist for System Design." *Datamation®,* vol. 26, no. 2 (January 1980), pp. 147–53.

This article is an excerpted version of the author's *Design Handbook for Distributed Systems,* discussing 15 ideas on systems design (out of 186 ideas in the book) describing how each idea has been successfully implemented in practice. The article is especially good on the human factors of designing and implementing a distributed system.

Scherr, A. L. "Distributed Data Processing." *IBM Systems Journal,* vol. 17, no. 4 (1978), pp. 324–43.

This article discusses different configuration choices of distributed data processing and evaluates them in terms of price-performance ratio, organizational needs, communications, and software. This is a scholarly but nontechnical article.

Thierauf, Robert J. *Distributed Data Processing.* Englewood Cliffs, N.J.: Prentice-Hall, Inc., 1978, 305 p. The fact that a textbook is published on this new and controversial topic is an indication of the importance of this subject and its approaching maturity. This book includes some material from the author's previous work, *Systems Analysis and Design of Real-time Management Information System.* Both books are packed with lists, tables, and diagrams and are very tightly written.

PART FIVE

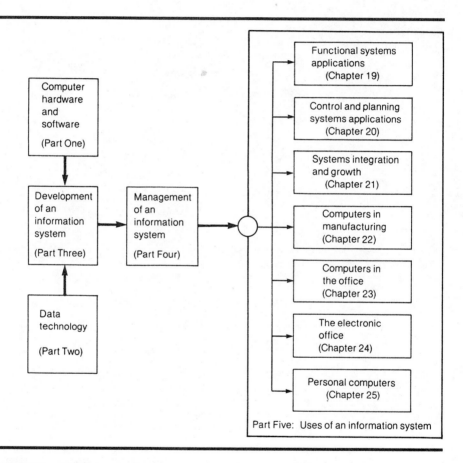

Part Five: Uses of an information system

USES OF AN
INFORMATION SYSTEM

The overview of Part Five appears in diagram form. Most information systems are at the operational level of a business. In Chapter 19, four case studies are presented to show functional computer applications: airlines reservations, a travel agency, a hotel, and a car dealership.

Computerized decision making by middle and top management for planning and control, the subject of Chapter 20, often requires decision support systems with data management, analytical, and interactive capabilities. Other special features that need to be considered in planning and control information systems are the scope of data, time horizon, degree of quantification, degree of detail, mode of operation, and display media. A brief discussion on artificial intelligence attempting to answer the question, "Will machines replace management?" will conclude the chapter.

Though functional applications discussed in Chapter 19 and control and planning applications discussed in Chapter 20 can be developed and maintained independently, integration of subsystems to encompass all levels of management is more effective. Chapter 21 introduces horizontal, vertical, longitudinal, and total system integration, discussing their implementation and analyzing the advantages of each type of integration. The chapter concludes with a section on growth, describing how a firm's capacity to absorb computer technology can influence speed and direction of growth.

Chapter 22 analyzes specialized and somewhat advanced computer applications in manufacturing. One section is devoted to smart products. Another to the automation of manufacturing processes, including numerical control, use of robots, and process control. The chapter also reviews the use of computers in product design.

Chapter 23 describes advanced office applications of the computer, including electronic mail, teleconferencing, the war room, electronic fund transfer, and word processing.

The last two chapters, 24 and 25, look to the future, describing electronic offices and the use of personal computers. An attempt is made to alert readers to economic and social implications once home computers are linked to data bases and have access to the computing power of external computers.

19

FUNCTIONAL SYSTEMS APPLICATIONS

The use of a computer in a function such as accounting, marketing, finance, manufacturing, or production is known as a **functional computer application.** Payroll, invoicing, asset depreciation, inventory forecasting, scheduling, labor distribution, and job costing are examples of such applications. Some applications are strictly at the operational level, but many assist management by making decisions formerly made by executives, such as production scheduling, or provide information needed for decision making, such as sales information, job costing, or forecasting used in planning. In this chapter, functional computer applications will be discussed for airline reservations, travel agencies, a sample hotel, and a car dealership.[1]

Airline reservations has been selected since most readers are familiar with this application and because there are many spin-off applications such as reservations for hotels and credit authorizations, EFT, loan payment processing, message switching in telecommunications, police car dispatching, and teller postings in a bank. One system chosen for study is SABRE of American Airlines since this was the first large-scale commercial real-time system developed. But all airlines today have systems similar to SABRE. For equipment configurations necessary for reservations, the United Airlines system will be examined. Also, the use by small travel agencies of inexpensive minis requiring little training will be explored.

Hotels in many ways resemble airlines for similar reservation systems are required, and both use computers for subsystems such as accounting, general ledger, and payroll. However, hotels have many unique computer applications, such as monitoring energy consumption. A case study will be presented to demonstrate computer use in a medium-size business in a hotel chain.

Finally, the chapter will discuss computer use by an automobile dealer. This example has been selected because of the diversity of input and output required by small businesses.

---

[1] For books with details on functional systems, see M. J. Alexander, *Information Systems, Theory and Applications* (Chicago: Science Research Associates, 1974), chaps. 10–14; A. L. Eliason and K. D. Iitts, *Business Computer Systems and Applications* (Chicago: Science Research Associates, 1979), chaps. 4–18; and R. J. Mockler, *Information Systems for Management* (Columbus, Ohio: Charles E. Merrill Publishing Co., 1974), chaps. 4–9.

AIRLINE RESERVATIONS

The SABRE system

The need for a computerized information system for reservations was recognized by American Airlines in 1954 because the company was finding it increasingly difficult to maintain accurate and timely manual records of passengers. The conventional system of assigning agents quotas for seats was also unsatisfactory. When local agents sold out their seat allotments, passengers were often lost to the airlines due to delays in locating a vacancy held by an agent in another part of the country. Lost revenues resulted.

It took ten years of development and more than $30 million to make the desired computerized **central reservation system** operational. Originally the reservations project was called SABER, an acronym for Semi-Automatic Business Environment Research. This choice of words was significant. The term "research" was used since reservation confirmation in 2–3 seconds as requested by management was technologically unfeasible at the time the project was initiated. "Business environment" stressed the fact that designers were not concerned solely with the internal operation of the system but considered the user environment of great importance. The word "semiautomatic" was recognition of the human role in information systems, for no computer is *fully* automatic.

The SABRE system works as follows. A client inquires about a flight. The agent keys the coded flight number and proposed date of travel on a terminal. An average of 2.3 seconds is required before the agent receives information regarding seat availability and answers to client questions such as total plane capacity, number of seats in first class, meals served, and plane connections. Once the client reaches a decision on flight and date, this information is keyed along with the client's name, phone number, number of seats requested, and passengers' names. Special service needs such as a salt-free diet, a wheel chair or assistance in boarding, car rental, and escorts for children changing planes can be added to the client's record. After a code to identify the agent is entered, a key is pressed which signals the terminal to print out the input message for visual recheck by the agent. If no mistakes are identified, the reservation is confirmed and the reservation transaction completed.

In addition to making reservations and keeping passenger records, SABRE has control functions. For example, the system will not accept incorrect data, such as a code for a nonexistent flight or a family booking where the number of names does not match the number of seats requested. Incomplete input is also refused. Should a flight be canceled, each agency having made bookings is informed and told which clients to notify. The system automatically releases seats when a cancellation is made. If a passenger desires a connecting flight, the system will make the reservation, even on another airline. This latter service is provided for more than one third of all passengers.

Reservation information is also used internally by the airlines. For example, the information provides caterers with estimates of the number of meals to be prepared, arrival and departure desks receive passenger lists, and flight control is given weight and loading information which also guides management in assigning crew and maintenance personnel. Furthermore, the system keeps accounts of funds receivable for each day, month, flight, and route. Such statistical data is exceedingly useful to management for planning. SABRE processes all flight information received from dispatch centers, adjusting scheduled flights and stops as well.

Reservation systems similar to SABRE are now standard in the entire airlines industry. The original SABRE has been completely redesigned, incorporating new technology and additional information services, but before it was replaced, other airlines had improved upon SABRE, developing more sophisticated systems,[2] leapfrogging over AA to become leaders in automation. Both Eastern and United, for example, used CRT terminals, which provide faster and quieter output than typewriters, before AA made the switch.

Reservations hardware

The hardware configuration of the United Airlines reservation system is shown in Figure 19.1. Note that the large computer in the IBM line, the 370/195, is integral to the system. Two IBM 195s serve the centralized data base at Denver, each computer capable of handling all the load of more than 5,000 terminals scattered throughout the United States. In practice, one of these 195s is used as backup, and in addition, processes information on maintenance, assists in the development and testing of new systems, and is a utility selling computer time. The IBM 195 processing reservations is fed by two front-end processors (IBM 360 Mod 44) from major cities in the United States, each city having an additional backup line. For example, if the line from New York were interrupted, reservations could be sent via Philadelphia (or vice versa), though at a somewhat lower level of service. Subsystems in other cities also tie in, such as maintenance in San Francisco, flight operations in Chicago, and a finance and accounting system from headquarters outside Chicago.

Performance

United Airlines's hardware supports a fleet of 370 aircraft, operating over 20,000 flight miles, and involving 49,000 employees. The computer system processes information on all phases of operation, including the generation of management and control reports on passengers, cargo, crews and personnel, scheduling, and equipment utilization. In 1980, system characteristics included:

---

[2] See William E. Jenkins, "Airline Reservation Systems," *Datamation®*, vol. 15, no. 3 (March 1969), pp. 29–32.

The capacity to process 36,000 reservations per hour.

A real-time response of less than two seconds 50 percent of the time; four seconds 90 percent of the time.

Average dialogue: two and a half to three minutes.

Average input message: 15 characters.

Average response: 130 characters.

Sequential transaction files are retained as backup and the entire real-time data base copied once a week as additional backup.

The purpose of these performance statistics and Table 19.1, summarizing functional subsystems of airline information systems, is to demonstrate the

FIGURE 19.1
Hardware configuration for United Airlines

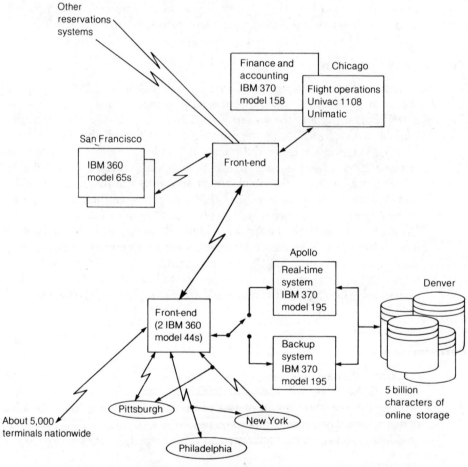

Source: Adapted from Douglas H. Haden, *Total Business Systems* (St. Paul, Minn.: West Publishing Co., 1978), p. 345.

TABLE 19.1
Functions performed by an airline information system

Provides information to potential customers on flight times, fares, and availability, as well as information on routes, schedules, hotels and car rentals, meals in flight, movies, and so forth.

Makes cargo reservations.

Maintains passenger inventory and availability lists.

Maintains passenger waiting lists, confirmation, cancellations, and no-show lists.

Keeps track of special requirements for wheelchairs, pets, and so forth.

Checks in passengers.

Generates tickets, including self-service issuance of tickets using credit cards.

Prepares boarding manifests.

Provides a meal count prior to departure.

Makes cargo load calculations prior to departure.

Makes passenger load and trim calculations prior to departure.

Calculates an optimal passenger route (for minimum time or minimum fare).

Provides information for:
Crew scheduling.
Maintenance scheduling.

Integrates automated ticketing, boarding control, and baggage delivery at all airports.

Keeps profile of passengers, including information on seat preferences (aisle, window, nearness to exits, smoking or nonsmoking), choice of drink, special dietary requests, wheelchair needs, and so forth.

Navigates the route for the pilot to optimize fuel consumption, given the number of passengers, cargo weight, wind velocity, wind direction, and air and cloud currents.

Integrates the microprocessors in an aircraft.

Integrates maintenance and monitoring of crucial parts of the airplane under stress or strain.

Schedules pilots (3,500 in AA) and flight attendants (4,800 in AA), giving consideration to their preferences and seniority within the constraints of time flown and projected earnings.

Provides automatic rerouting when bad weather exists or in the event of flight cancellations.

speed and capabilities of an OLRT system. Pressures of competition are continually upgrading services offered. For example, calculation of fares and ticket printout by computer is presently being implemented: Eastern has automated 85 percent of ticketing. The variety of fares and discounts available impedes total implementation at this time. United, Eastern, and Pacific Southwest are presently testing self-servicing ticketing machines at airports. The magnetic strip on the back of accepted credit cards provides information that is used to verify credit, create a billing record, and issue a ticket in the card holder's name.

What slows new applications is the problem of integration, the subject of Chapter 21. Because of the size of the airline industry, development and integration of new subsystems takes years of planning and the allocation of substantial resources. Automation of this large complex industry (in 1979, 615 million air fares were provided) taxes even computers.

RESERVATIONS BY TRAVEL AGENTS

Airline reservations today are made primarily by travel agencies. No longer do most passengers buy their tickets directly from the airlines. These agents utilize minicomputers or terminals with access to airline data bases. Both American Airlines and United are selling access to their own reservation systems to travel agencies, but these have only limited flight information about other airlines. Approximately 42 percent of all agents (over 6,000) are so equipped.

The SABRE system designed by AA for travel agencies is essentially the same system accessed by AA agents described earlier. It requires about a week of training for personnel to learn procedures for calculating the numerous options for fares and for mastering the large number of codes utilized. This system is utilized by Schmal Travel, a travel agency in the town of 50,000.

A sample of the coding as it appears on the passenger hard copy given by Schmal to clients and as it appears on the input terminal (with slight modifications in format) is shown below:

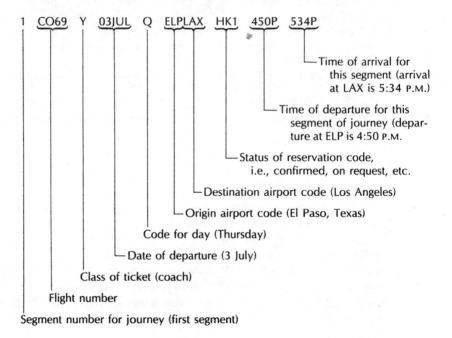

1   CO69   Y   03JUL   Q   ELPLAX   HK1   450P   534P

─Time of arrival for this segment (arrival at LAX is 5:34 P.M.)

─Time of departure for this segment of journey (departure at ELP is 4:50 P.M.

─Status of reservation code, i.e., confirmed, on request, etc.

─Destination airport code (Los Angeles)

─Origin airport code (El Paso, Texas)

Code for day (Thursday)

─Date of departure (3 July)

Class of ticket (coach)

Flight number

Segment number for journey (first segment)

The system also prints a schedule for passengers (see sample, Table 19.2), though many clients find this output hard to read, preferring a simple typed schedule with only essential noncoded information including travel date, flight numbers, and arrival and departure times.

TABLE 19.2
Sample output for airline reservation

```
*A
  1.1HUSSAIN/K M DR ──────────────────── Name of passenger
  1 CO  69Y 03JUL Q ELPLAX HK1    450P  534P ⎫
  2 CI   7Y 03JUL Q LAXHND HK1   1020P  700A │ Information on
  3 PA   2C 10JUL Q NRTLAX HK1    730P 1205P ⎬ 4 segments of
  4 CO  74Y 10JUL Q LAXELP HK1    200P  533P ⎭ the journey
 T-TAW10DEC/ ────────────────────────── Date of reservation
 P-ELP915-882-3836-A ───────────────── Phone number of agent
 ELP505-646-1206-0 ─────────────────── Phone number of passenger
 M-07                                         ⎫
 CALL DR FOR RECFN                            ⎬ Other codes required
 R-P                                          │ for tracing the record
 C3U*MS 1719/29OCT RCS6KX H                   ⎭ and reconfirmation
```

Note the highly formulated and coded form. The codes are sometimes obvious, such as 03JUL = 3d July. Codes such as HND = Haneda Airport in Tokyo, and NRT = Narita Airport, also in Tokyo, are less obvious. All data is coded in a prescribed sequence and format, requiring a trained person to operate the system.

The cost of American's reservation system (two CRT terminals and one printer) to Schmal Travel is $690/month with line charges paid by the airline. The salary of one clerk performing the same services would be approximately $700/month plus fringe benefits, so on strictly economic grounds the system is cost-effective. Intangible benefits include faster and more accurate information, less monotonous work for clerks, and greater customer satisfaction. An increased load by the agency could improve the cost-benefit ratio because one printer can service two additional terminals. The principal disadvantage to travelers is that the system is biased toward AA reservations, providing little information on competing flights.

Another system, called MARS (Multi-Access-Airline Reservation System), whose development cost a reported $17 million, is being marketed by IT&T. This system gives travel agents direct access to each airline's data base and flight reservation system, and can be used to book an entire trip, even flights abroad, including reservations in airline-owned hotels.

MARS equipment configurations vary. One 1980 option: three CRTs and two printers for $850/month in addition to a service charge of 35¢ per valid ticket up to 500, and 15¢ per ticket thereafter. Or the same equipment could be purchased for $23,000, with a monthly service charge of $526.[3]

───────────
[3] Karin Rubin, "IT&T Offering CO-OPS MARS-PLUS to Sell Their Member Agents," *The Travel Agent,* vol. 168, no. 4 (October 15, 1979), p. 1.

HOTEL COMPUTER APPLICATIONS

It was stated in the chapter introduction that an airline reservation system has spin-off applications for hotel reservations. Hotels also use computers for applications such as accounting, inventory, and payroll. These applications will now be discussed in the context of an actual case study. The hotel chosen for the study, Hotel West (a fictitious name), is a private business, though part of a chain, in a town of 50,000. It has 200 rooms, 175 employees, and a variety of facilities, including an indoor pool, conference rooms, banquet halls, shops, bars, and a restaurant servicing primarily upper-middle class families and traveling businessmen.

Hotel reservations

The input required for hotel reservations is name, address, phone, date and time of arrival, length of stay, number in party, room preference (size, price, location; e.g., poolside, quiet wing), and special services requested (crib, wheelchair). Because desk clerks and receptionists are generally unskilled and nonpermanent staff, reservation equipment is designed to be simple to operate. In Hotel West, a terminal with a standard typewriter keyboard is used for entering name, address, and phone number of the client, and a special-purpose terminal with 76 keys and 16 lights is used to input other

FIGURE 19.2
Two terminals for hotel reservations

Courtesy International Business Machines Corporation

reservation data. The two terminals are shown in the photo in Figure 19.2. The keyboard for the special-purpose terminal is shown in Figure 19.3. Though this latter terminal appears confusing at first glance, it is actually easier and faster to operate than airline reservation systems. For example, when an October booking is requested, the clerk need not remember a month code such as 10, but merely presses the key marked Oct. in a group of 12 keys for months set in a row. Additional keys represent other crucial data such as code keys for hotel identification, date, number and type of rooms required, or action requested (cancel, reserve), and all related keys are grouped together. The lights identify the status of the equipment (ready, in use), availability of different types of rooms (single, double), and room availability in nearby hotels. Equipment so specialized is expensive and can only be justified if

FIGURE 19.3
Keyboard of special terminal for hotel reservations

the number of reservations and hotel size are sufficiently large to permit it to be cost-effective.

Reservations for a room at Hotel West can be made by another hotel in the chain or reservations can be made by the client calling a reservation center. When Hotel West initiates a room request on behalf of a customer for a room at another hotel in the chain, a computer tie-in with central reservations checks availability. Confirmation of the reservation and a copy of notification to the hotel in question are messages that the operator in Hotel West receives as printout, and which the client can use as a reservation confirmation. Table 19.3 shows how such a request is coded.

If the requested hotel has no bookings available, central reservations will

TABLE 19.3
Sample hotel reservation dialogue

Mr. John Doe, staying at Hotel West, asks the desk clerk to make reservations at another hotel in the chain, Hotel Polka, code 352 for June 5th for one person for two nights for a single room with guaranteed payment. Doe's address is 4943 Karen Drive, Las Cruces, NM 88001. Telephone 505-523-1427.

INPUT
TYPED BY
CLERK:

Doe, John	(name of guest, last name first)
4943 Karen Dr.	(street address)
Las Cruces, NM 88001	(City, State, Zip code)
5055231427	(Area code plus phone number)
SK	(operator's initials for Kathy Stacy)

Clerk also keys in data on the special terminal, 352 for the hotel code, June 5 for the date of arrival, the 1 key for the number of rooms required, 1BD 1PR key for 1 bed for one person, and the 2 key for the two nights desired, the action key AVAIL to inquire about availability of the room, and finally, the ENTER key to enter the data for processing.

COMPUTER
MESSAGE
CONFIRMING
RESERVATION
AT HOTEL
WEST:

CONF 1RM 1BD 1PR 2NT MON JUN 05
GUARANTEED PAYMENT DUE IF NOT CANCELLED BE-
FORE 6PM

MESSAGE
TO HOTEL
POLKA:

SOLD 1RM 1BD 1PR 2NT MON JUN 05
GUARANTEED PAYMENT
4943 Karen Dr.
Las Cruces, NM 88001
SK

supply data on room options at the nearest hotel in the chain. Table 19.4 is a sample output message conveying information on alternative hotel booking possibilities.

The tie-in to central reservations costs Hotel West $8,000 per year with $1 charged for each reservation made by the system. Line charges vary from one chain to another, some underwriting the expense as part of their service to member hotels. One can measure the gain from a centralized reservation system for many of the figures are available for a cost-benefit analysis: cost of reservation service, number of rooms reserved through the system, income from reservations, income otherwise lost from unoccupied rooms. However,

TABLE 19.4
Sample of information on alternative hotel accommodations

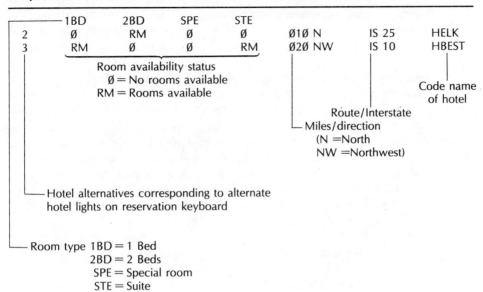

intangible benefits, such as convenience to customers, should also be recognized.

The central reservations network can also be programmed to provide other information services as well. In 1979, when gas shortages discouraged travelers, one hotel chain relayed information on filling-station hours, and dollar and volume limits per vehicle of stations within a five-mile radius of each hotel in the 1,500 member chain. Travelers or hotels could phone to obtain the information. The purpose was to prevent cancellations or empty rooms by providing information on gas availability to clientele.[4]

Other business applications

Hotel West also has a minicomputer for other business applications that is independent of the reservation system. This minicomputer has five CRTs: a main office terminal, three at points of sale (restaurant and bars), and one at the housekeeper's station. These terminals are used for room assignments, registration and billing (front desk activities), and for processing payroll, accounts receivable, general ledger, cash posting, printing of statements, and management reporting, as well as energy and inventory control (backroom accounting). Larger hotels often have two computer systems for these functions, separating front desk and backroom accounting, and also providing

---

[4] *Computer World*, vol. 13, no. 27 (July 2, 1979), p. 1.

backup in the backroom computer should the frontroom system fail at the check-in counter.

Hotel West's minicomputer is located in an alcove of the front office. Maintenance and training are provided by the small out-of-state firm that installed the equipment and developed the software, Communications Diversified, Inc. This firm, with only 45 professionals, can compete with large conglomerates like IT&T because it specializes, providing software packages that apply to only a few industries. The hotel management software, for example, required little modification to fit Hotel West's needs, whereas the purchase of a general business application package would have required Hotel West to hire a programmer or systems analysts to adapt the package to local conditions. This specialization of software entrepreneurs, coupled with the drop in the price of minis, is what has made computer applications cost-effective for small businesses. In the following sections, several of Hotel West's specialized business applications will be described.

ROOM STATUS

In order for a desk clerk to assign rooms to clients, the status of hotel rooms (occupied or empty) must be known. At Hotel West, room status is one report provided by the minicomputer. To obtain room status information, the clerk first requests the display of a menu of reports or programs on the CRT of the front desk terminal by pressing a key code to this effect. From this list, the code for room status report is determined. This code is keyed and the RETURN key pressed to indicate end of choice of report. The terminal will then display the number of rooms available on any given date (up to 20 years in the future) and rooms currently ready for occupancy by room number and type (single, double). Occupancy status is updated in real-time mode from the housekeeper's terminal as maids complete cleaning. This information not only serves the front desk for registrations, but pinpoints the location and progress of each maid, and identifies rooms ready for inspection.

REGISTRATION AND CHECK-OUT

Registration is done on the CRT by the front desk clerk. The input required, listed in Table 19.5, is keyed line by line from top to bottom, the terminal validating each entry by character and range validity checks. When a required field is not provided, the system locks (does not proceed) until all required information is entered. In processing registrations, the computer updates the room inventory, informs the housekeeper (on a terminal) of the room assignment, and generates a guest folio of all registration information keyed by room number. Included is data such as time and date of check-in, which the computer automatically records. A guest account is also created (room rent and tax) to be updated in real time for charges such as telephone calls or restaurant bills.

At check-out, the computer will print an itemized customer bill upon a simple keyed command by the desk clerk. When payment is received, the clerk enters the method of payment (cash, check, credit card) and amount into the system for auditing purposes. The computer automatically updates the room inventory and signals the housekeeper that the vacated room is ready for cleaning.

Check-out using the computer system is fast and accurate, saving the client time since the system instantly generates the bill. But registration by computer takes longer than traditional manual registrations primarily because more information is requested, information that the desk clerk manually keys into the system.

TABLE 19.5
Terminal input for hotel registration

Number of days stay

Guest's name (Last, First)

Guest address _____

                   Street,   City   State,   Zip

Number in party

Rate

Representing

Method of payment code

(1. Cash, 2. Prepayment, 3. Credit Card, 4. City Acct.)

Credit Card _____

                 Number   Date expires (MM/YY)

CONTROL APPLICATIONS

Stock inventory, especially food and beverages, is one important control function performed by computer at Hotel West. Another is auditing: shift audits (done three times a day) and the night audit (an audit summary of all three shifts). The audits list all transactions, amounts, mode of payment, transaction clerk, and shift supervisor. These computer audits eliminate the need for daily bookkeeping by an accountant. In addition, the audits serve as financial reports to management. Table 19.6 lists still other types of reports generated by computer at Hotel West.

In addition, the computer regulates energy consumption at Hotel West. Upon registration of a client, room heat (or air conditioning) is automatically turned on: at check-out, the system turns heat off. Air circulation in unoccupied rooms is also maintained by automatically switching on heat or cooling periodically. At Hotel West the computer is programmed to control demand during peak periods to reduce energy surcharges by switching off heat for short

TABLE 19.6
Hotel's reference and control reports

For front desk
  Directory of guest folios for any date
  Directory of guests' names for any date
  Inventory of rooms available for any date
  Folio details for any guest
  Advance deposits received
  No shows
  Stayovers
  Arrivals
  Advance deposit transferred
  Entire content of current room folios or city accounts
  Check-out listings

Guest accounting
  Folio copies for each check-out
  Shift audits
  Credit card account totals
  Shift audits for each POS terminal
  Account code summaries for each POS terminal
  Room summary balance due and method of payment

Inventory control report

Energy consumption report

time spans when energy demand reaches a predetermined level. The computer also regulates power-consuming devices such as pumps, lights, and signs. This automation and control reduces energy consumption at Hotel West, saving an estimated 15–30 percent on the hotel's energy bill.

WAKE-UP SERVICE

Wake-up is automated, the computer telephoning clients at the time requested.

COST VERSUS BENEFITS

Are the functional applications and information generated by the computer at Hotel West cost-effective? Though costs can be determined, many benefits are hard to quantify (see Table 19.7). One simply cannot subject the benefits to a rigorous monetary analysis. One can merely say that management, knowing costs, deems the computer systems worthwhile.

AN AUTOMOTIVE DEALER

Not all businesses can afford a mini nor require real-time capabilities. Many turn to a computer utility for processing business information. The car dealer in the following study is a case in point. Though this businessman has net assets over $2 million and employs 65 persons, he utilizes a computer located

TABLE 19.7
Hotel's cost-benefit analysis

Costs

$1,000/room for hardware and software (one-time costs)
$700/month for maintenance
$8,000/year for tie-in to national reservation system,
   including communications

Benefits

Energy expenditure reduction of 15–30 percent
Increased employee productivity
Real-time accounting including restaurants and telephone
Personalized, fast service to client
Accurate information regarding room availability
Control and reference reports

1700 miles from his car lot for accounting reports, entering all data online from the terminal (shown in Figure 19.4) and receiving output, including periodic management reports, on that same terminal overnight. This terminal has all of the features of a typewriter terminal plus many lights and special keys. In addition, it utilizes two cassettes simultaneously for input or output, and storage.

The input mode is conversational, the system asking for relevant data. Incorrect data, such as alpha characters in a numeric field, will cause the system to lock up until corrections are made. If data is suspicious but not necessarily incorrect (e.g., sales price less than cost), a light and beep alert the operator though the coded data will be accepted.

Let us trace an input transaction. Invoice No. 26772, for a part costing $4.46 is manually assigned a control number (CTL 170) by the accounts payable clerk, and the department to which it is charged is coded (1250). The invoice data is then keyed onto the terminal in the format shown in Table 19.8. The system's responses are explained above the code line: the operator's below.

All input is transmitted online to the computer utility (and a copy for the dealer is stored on cassette) where it is processed overnight. The output is transmitted to the dealer before 8:00 A.M. the next morning, where it is recorded on tape. Daily output is generally coded, used for reference, checking, or operational control by employees familiar with the codes. The output may also be processed by computer, according to a prescribed format programmed on a second cassette. This auto dealer has seven programs on tape for performing editing, summary, and utility functions.

The computer service also periodically generates and mails reports, such as a listing of deviations between forecasted and month-to-date sales, inventory control reports, and accounting reports such as a balance sheet and profit and loss statement. One such report is shown in Table 19.9. This is a financial statement, completed and printed by computer monthly and annually. The

FIGURE 19.4
Terminal for auto dealer accounting application

balance sheet and profit and loss statement are necessary for businesses in all industrial sectors if they are public corporations, for they are required to file this information with the Securities and Exchange Commission. In this case, the auto dealer is not a public corporation but the information is useful for internal control, auditing, and tax purposes.

Another sample report, Analysis of Accounts Payable, is shown in Table 19.10. This report shows transactions from Lohman Auto Parts, including invoice 26772 used in Table 19.8. In addition to listing date, source number, and invoice number of each transaction with vendors, the report shows total payments, the closing balance, and year-to-date purchases.

Note that this report is not coded. Since it is mailed, not sent by telecommunications, length is not an overriding cost consideration. Readability is more important than condensation. But for daily input and output, coding is essen-

TABLE 19.8
Sample input dialogue

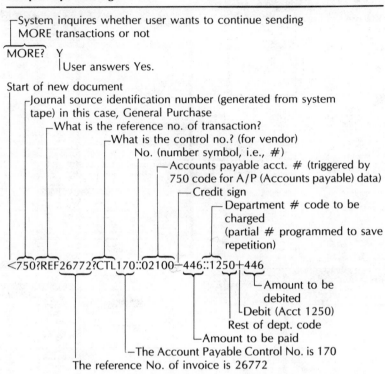

tial. Though data per transaction is small, total volume to be processed is large. Coding reduces input time, the need for storage space, the duration of computer processing, and the expense of data transmission. In addition, coding classifications facilitate processing and reporting, and minimize the danger of ambiguity.

The way these reports reach the dealer (coded output transmitted by telecommunications, and noncoded reports sent by mail) is depicted in Figure 19.5.

Cost-benefit analysis for accounting applications

The costs and benefits of computer accounting services in this case study are summarized in Table 19.11. Though costs are $7,970 higher than tangible benefits, this dealer estimates intangible benefits at $52,000, making the system cost-effective. The manager claims that the major benefit of information provided by the computer is timely reporting, a benefit which can only be given a subjective value. Other benefits, however, are tangible. For example, 90 percent of claims against car warranties are paid within 14 days when pro-

TABLE 19.9
Blank financial statement report for auto dealer to be completed by computer

TABLE 19.10
Sample accounting report for auto dealer

				ANALYSIS OF ACCOUNTS PAYABLE		ACCOUNT # 02100		10/31/79
				REPORT # 15				PAGE 12
CTL #	VENDOR NAME	TELEPHONE NUMBER	DATE SRC	REF #	OPENING BALANCE	CURRENT PURCHASES PAYMENTS	CLOSING BALANCE	YEAR-TO-DATE PURCHASES
169	L C RADIATOR SHOP	524-4152	09-28		261.00-			
			10-04 750	38547		17.50-		
			10-04 750	39872		20.00-		
			10-04 750	39860		24.75-		
			10-19 600	1867			261.00	
			10-29 750	38939		31.16-		
			10-31 750	35991		12.50-		
			10-31 750	33756		40.00-		
	* TOTAL *						145.91-	2,358.97-
170	LOHMAN AUTO PARTS	523-7559	09-28		88.88-			
			10-09 600	1721			88.88	
			10-17 750	26715		6.28-		
			10-22 750	26772		4.46-		
			10-22 750	26393		4.47-		
			10-22 750	26739		4.52-		
			10-23 750	26850		2.19-		
			10-24 750	26882		40.50-		
			10-24 750	26786		44.40-		
			10-24 750	26829		46.65-		
			10-25 750	26919			14.49	
	* TOTAL *						138.98-	2,968.73-
171	LORDS LOCKSMITHING	524-3651	09-28		43.00-			
			10-09 600	1722			43.00	
			10-15 750	4241		7.50-		
			10-16 750	4079		14.04-		
			10-31 750	4096		32.00-		
	* TOTAL *						53.54-	871.15-
173	MAC TOOLS OF LAS CRUCES	524-4535	09-28		.00			
			10-22 750	517435		33.80-		
	* TOTAL *						33.80-	73.11-
174	MANNIES	524-3646	09-28		.00			
			10-24 750	12110		2.34-		
	* TOTAL *						2.34-	22.40-
176	MESILLA VALLEY LINC MERC	524-2481	09-28		235.47-			
			10-11 750	2306		4.73-		
			10-11 750	27320		11.66-		
			10-11 750	27337		23.48-		
			10-11 750	27310		71.40-		
			10-19 600	1873			235.47	
			10-23 750	27333		1.91-		

cessed by computer. The remaining 10 percent must be documented by mail with an average of 35 days elapsing before payment is received. The early payment of claims increases cash flow and working capital, producing a saving for this dealer of $4,200 annually.

Intangible benefits include increased inventory control. Information on inventory is of value to all businesses, but a car dealer's inventory represents many thousand dollars per car type. Very close monitoring of inventories, peak sales months, and customer preferences is essential in this high turnover and high cash flow business.

Other computer applications

In addition to utilization of a computer service for accounting reports, the car dealer has a minicomputer for making computations regarding auto financing. This mini serves the financial manager (sometimes called contract officer) of the firm in determining monthly payments for a client once auto and accessories are selected. Monthly payments depend on a number of variables: rate of interest, trade-in value, credit-life or disability insurance costs, starting date of payments, cash down payment, number of payments, and so forth. Tax and license fees must also be reckoned. The computer speeds answers to such questions as, "What will be my monthly payment if I put

FIGURE 19.5
Flow of data and information to the auto dealer

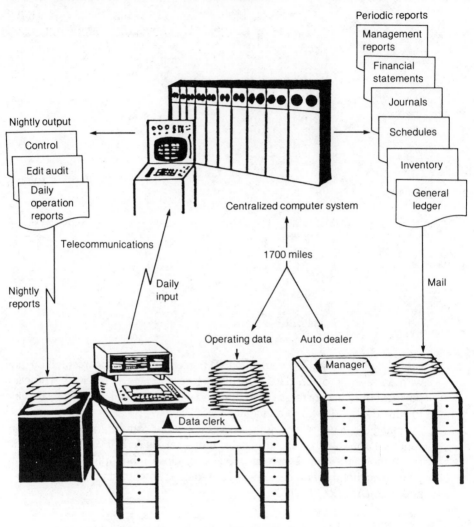

$1,500 down instead of $500? If I pay over 20 months instead of 24?" By hand, the answers to such questions take an average of 16–18 minutes to calculate, and errors occur on an average of once every 15 computations. The minicomputer takes about 3 minutes to arrive at and print answers with an average of one input entry error per 1,000 entries. The use of the minicomputer thus saves considerable time for both client and financial manager and proves more accurate as well.

The minicomputer also assists in contract preparation. Once the amounts to be specified in a contract are decided between client and agent, a lapse

TABLE 19.11
Cost-benefit analysis for accounting applications (annual)

Cost	
Payroll, including fringe benefits of part-time data clerk	$ 7,680
Rental of equipment	16,200
Transmission cost	420
Other (supplies, etc.)	110
Total costs	$24,410
Benefits	
Savings over manual costs of doing essential accounting and inventory reports	$12,240
Benefits from faster accounts receivable	4,200
	$16,440
Intangible benefits estimated by management of the additional reports and sales resulting from faster ordering	$52,000
Total benefits	$68,440

time of 1–2 hours is required for contract preparation if the figures are typed into a contract by a secretary. This includes a wait period while the secretary completes priority assignments and 8–12 minutes of actual typing. The mini-computer can prepare the same contract document much faster. The financial manager selects the contract form desired by a one-digit code and keys in the variables in a given sequence. The content format is stored in computer memory. The entire document is printed with the variables inserted, ready for the customer's signature in approximately 3 minutes.

With each contract, numerous forms and letters are generated by the agency (see Table 19.12). Again the minicomputer is utilized, inserting names and address of customer, odometer reading, stock number of auto sold, and so forth, in appropriate spaces in standard letter and document formats. For example, a letter of thanks to the customer is prepared, the content of which varies, depending on whether a new car or second-hand model was purchased.

TABLE 19.12
Forms and letters prepared for auto dealer

Title application
Power of attorney
Odometer statement
Agreement on insurance
Credit-life and disability
Tax affidavit
Bank draft for mortgage and loan payoff
Thank-you letter to customer

Once an operator keys the type of purchase, the computer collates prewritten paragraphs with customer name and address and prints a personalized letter and addressed envelope. (This is a word processing rather than data processing application, a topic to be discussed later in Chapter 23.)

This same mini is also used in inventory control and the preparation of reports on sales per salesperson. Data on sales is stored on a floppy disk (a random storage device as opposed to sequential storage on a cassette), agents being represented by the last four digits of their social security numbers. From this stored information, weekly control reports are generated (see Table 19.13). These reports serve as the basis for managerial decisions on quotas, bonuses, vacation schedules, salesperson-of-the-month awards, and so forth.

TABLE 19.13
Content of one report generated from contract manager's mini-computer

For each salesperson
Number of cars sold
  Old
  New
Number of trucks sold
  Old
  New
Number of deals financed
Number of credit life policies sold
Number of extended summer plans
Ranking

A cost-benefit analysis of the mini appears in Table 19.14. In view of the fact that the life of the mini is an estimated five to ten years, the mini is clearly cost-effective.

The authors were surprised that payroll is not handled by computer at this dealership. It was explained that payroll was one of the first systems automated at this agency, but by NCR noncomputer data processing equipment. Neither the computer utility nor the mini have taken over the payroll application, a problem of integration to be discussed in Chapter 21.

SUMMARY AND CONCLUSIONS

In this chapter examples of functional applications of computers in business, primarily at the operational level, have been presented, the applications being for airline reservations, a travel agency, a hotel, and a car dealer. Table 19.15 summarizes characteristics of the applications discussed. In each example, terminals with online capabilities were used. This is by no means the universal

TABLE 19.14
Cost-benefit analysis of minicomputer applications

Costs

Equipment	=	$38,000; initial investment
Clerk plus fringe benefits	=	$13,000/year
Supplies	=	$500/year

Tangible benefits

Savings of $26,000/year in clerical help

Intangible benefits

Speed of computer in answering "What if" questions makes great impressions on customer
Reduces errors
Saves the time of contract officers

mode of operation though it is becoming increasingly common and proving cost-effective for a wide spectrum of businesses.

The examples cited varied in development effort, dialogue, and the required training of personnel. But all applications had the following advantages:

1. Customer service improved and expanded.
2. The level of efficiency was raised, as sales and office staff saved both time and effort recording information necessary for operations and control.
3. Load potential increased.
4. Information accuracy improved, enhancing the firm's image and reducing losses due to errors.
5. The query and interactive capabilities provided the right information at the right time to the right person.

There are, of course, many other applications of computers to business (see Table 19.16). Some of these will be discussed in detail in later chapters (computers in manufacturing is the subject of Chapter 22, and office applications appear in Chapter 23). Contrasting the use of information systems for control and planning with operational use is the subject of the next chapter.

TABLE 19.15
Summary of characteristics of functional applications discussed in Chapter 19

Characteristic	Airline reservations		Hotel (non-reservation) applications	Auto dealer	
	Airline	Travel agent		Accounting	Contract management
Mode	OLRT	OLRT	OLRT	Online input and batch output	Online and batch
Use of teleprocessing	Yes	Yes	No	Yes	No
Nature of input	Coded	Coded	Menu	Coded but prompted	Formatted but not much coded
Nature of output	Coded	Coded	Listings, tables, and reports	Listings, tables, and reports	Letters, contracts, and reports
Levels of application	Operational	Operational	Operational and control management	Operational and control management	Operational and control management
Location of computer system	Owned Centralized	Accessed	On site and rented	Utility	Owned on site
Size of computer "on site"	Large	None	Mini	None	Mini
Data base	Own data base accessed	Central base accessed	Local data base	Data sent by teleprocessing	Local data base
Capital costs	High	None	Small	Almost none	Small

TABLE 19.16
Sample of computer operational applications in business

Accounting and finance
    Accounts payable
    Accounts receivable
    Asset accounting
    Auditing
    Billing
    Budget analysis
    Budgeting
    Capital budgeting
    Cash disbursements
    Cash receipts
    Check writing and
      reconciliation
    Cost accounting
    Equipment inventory
    Funding
    General ledger
    Invoicing
    Payroll
    Purchasing
    Warranty administration

Administration
    Facilities control
    Information retrieval
    Operations research
      models
    Personnel records
    Record keeping
    Recruiting
    Regulatory reporting
    Skills inventory
    Training management
    Wage and salary
      administration
    Word processing

Agribusiness
    Farm and crop rotation
    Financial and accounting
    Optimal feed blending
    Optimal fertilizing program

Banking
    Automatic cash dispensing
    Bill-paying service
    Checking account
    Credit card subsystem
    Electronic funds transfer
    Investment analysis
    Loan management
    MICR routine
    Mortgage control
    Proof and reconciliation
    Savings accounts

Construction
    Design analysis
    Project control (CPM, PERT,
      GERT)
    Scheduling of labor and
      materials
    Stress and strain calculations

Financial
    Cost accounting
    Financial reporting
    Ledger accounting
    Payroll
    Tax accounting

Hotel and restaurant
    Accounting
    Auditing
    Billing
    Checkout subsystem
    Energy control
    Inventory control
    Personnel management
    Registration
    Reservation
    Room service

Insurance
    Actuarial computation
    Claims
    Customer policy records
    Dividend management
    Estate planning
    Revenue management
    Risk analysis
    Underwriting

TABLE 19.16 *(continued)*

Manufacturing
  Bill of materials processing
  Equipment inventory
  Inventory control
  Job costing
  Labor accounting
  Materials control
  Numerical control
  Plant and tooling
  Process control
  Production scheduling
  Purchasing
  Quality control
  Robots
  Routing and standards
  Shop floor control
  Simulation models
  Smart products
  Stores control
  Tool control
  Vendor file

Marketing
  Advertising and promotion
  Client file
  Credit control
  Dealer analysis
  Forecasting—short- and
    long-range
  Market research
  New product scheduling
  Order entry
  Physical distribution
  Sales analysis
  Sales control
  Warehouse control

Purchasing and order entry
  Billing
  Inspection
  Invoice matching and payments
  Materials procurement
  Ordering
  Pricing
  Receiving

Real estate
  Financial computation
  Investment portfolio analysis
  Listing services
  Mortgage loan accounting
  Property management
  Tax analysis

Research and development
  Computer-aided design
  Engineering control
  Engineering scheduling
  Experimentation control
  Product testing
  Project control
  Scientific computing
  Simulation

Reservations
  Airlines
  Car rentals
  Camping
  Hotel
  Theaters

Retailing
  Accounting
  Auditing
  Billing
  Credit checking
  Inventory control
  Marketing analysis
  Point-of-sale subsystem
  Sales forecasting

Word processing

Utilities
  Accounts receivable
  Customer billing
  Facilities
  Maintenance accounting
  Maintenance scheduling
  Rating

KEY WORDS

Accounting applications
Airline reservation application
Auto dealer application

Backroom accounting
Central reservation system
Contract manager applications

Cost-benefit analysis	Hotel applications
Functional computer	SABRE system
application	Travel agency applications

DISCUSSION QUESTIONS

1. Give three examples of computer applications in different functional areas in business. In each case, identify:
   a. Output.
   b. Input.
   c. Equipment required.
   d. Mode of processing used (batch, OLRT, etc.).
   e. Functions performed.
   f. Benefits achieved.

2. Give examples of information systems that are used for:
   a. Calculations.
   b. Storage and retrieval.
   c. Report generation.
   d. Combination of above.

3. Describe briefly the operational information generated by all information systems for:
   a. Production.
   b. Marketing.
   c. Research development.
   d. Personnel.
   e. Accounting.
   f. Finance.

4. What are some of the problems of operational management in business that can best be resolved by a computerized system?

5. What are common business functions? Can data files be organized to correspond to these functions?

6. What effect will the POS terminal have on marketing?

7. Discuss functional applications of computers in the following industries:
   a. Airline.
   b. Banking.
   c. Construction.
   d. Insurance.
   e. Real estate.
   f. Retail.
   g. Agriculture.
   h. Government.

8. Identify functional applications relating to personnel records in a business firm.

9. List three computer applications. Identify their common characteristics.

10. List five functions in a business that are currently done manually and should be done by computer. In each case, specify the reasons you think the functions should be computerized.

11. Is it possible for a manual system, such as the airline reservation system in the United States, to be cost-effective? (Manual reservations exist in many countries, including the Soviet Union.) Specify the reasons for your answer.

12. Suppose that you were in charge of an MIS in a large car rental firm without any computer system. Suppose further, your firm has just been bought by a conglomerate owning an airline with a sophisticated airline reservation system. How could you adapt the airline reservation system to car rental operations? What functions could it perform?

13. Suppose that you were given a large interest in Hotel West described in this chapter. What other ways could the computer be used, if any? Explain.

14. Why is it difficult to measure all the benefits of a functional system? Are there different approaches you would follow in different environments? Explain.

15. List five new computer applications in business in the last two years.

EXERCISE

1. How would you classify Exercise 1, Chapter 10? Is it functional? Is the application at the operational level?

SELECTED ANNOTATED BIBLIOGRAPHY

Eliason, Alan L., and Kitts, Kent D. *Business Computer Systems and Applications.* 2d ed. Chicago: Science Research Associates, 1979, 348 p.
This text examines operational applications in business. In each case, the application is described, output and input displayed, data elements in the file listed, systems flowcharts presented, and the implications to management discussed. These are not case studies but actual realistic data is used. This book is a very detailed walk-through of the design stage of the development process.

Gessford, John Evans. *Modern Information Systems Designed for Decision Support.* Reading, Mass.: Addison-Wesley Publishing Co., 1980, 511 p.
This text has six chapters on computer applications in business, including systems for administration, payment, financial control, operations data, planning, and strategic information. The applications are described with varying detail, but many are explained by flowcharts and lists of file contents.

Haden, Douglas H. *Total Business Systems: Computers in Business.* St. Paul, Minn.: West Publishing Co., 1978, 463 p.
This textbook has chapters on computer applications, retail systems, one-statement booking, motels, hotels, Standard Oil of Ohio, Norwich Pharmaceutical, Cuyahoga County Welfare Department, Blue Shield, Provident Insurance, and United Airlines. These applications cover businesses of all sizes using different modes of processing (online, OLRT, and batch). The cases are well researched and described.

Thierauf, Robert J. *Systems Analysis and Design of Real-Time Management Information Systems.* Englewood Cliffs, N.J.: Prentice-Hall, Inc., 1975, 607 p.
The first half of the book deals with theory and concepts; the second half describes ten different subsystems. Most of these subsystems are at the operational level and all are real-time systems. The text is very tightly written with numerous lists, tables, and diagrams. It is not an introductory book but highly recommended for the serious student.

20

PLANNING AND CONTROL SYSTEMS APPLICATIONS

This chapter contrasts computer assistance in decision making for control and planning with computer applications at the operational level as described in Chapter 19. First, the chapter classifies control decisions, describing the types of problems computers can solve. Then data needs at different levels of management are analyzed. Finally, special design features required by decision support systems for middle and top management are examined, features not required for functional applications. An information system used by American Airlines for planning and control is presented as a case study. The chapter concludes with a brief discussion on artificial intelligence in answer to the question, "Will computers replace management in making planning and control decisions in the future?"

MANAGEMENT DECISIONS CLASSIFIED

A decision is a choice among alternatives. Some business decisions are judgmental, based on intuition. But many others can be stated in terms of decision rules, the problems being well structured and conceptually simple. Software to make programmed decisions is possible for this latter type of problem, the assistance of computers being particularly valuable when structured problems must be solved routinely and repeatedly. A nonprogrammed decision is generally required for nonstructured, complex problems with variables that cannot easily be quantified.

To answer the question "What control and planning decisions can be and should be made by information systems?" one must first classify decisions and then check the applicability of computerized solutions to each classification. Anthony divides business decision making for control and planning into operational control, management control, and strategic planning:

1. Operational control is the process of assuring that specific tasks are carried out effectively and efficiently.
2. Management control is the process by which managers assure that resources are obtained and used effectively and efficiently in the accomplishment of the organization's objectives.
3. Strategic planning is the process of deciding on objectives of the organiza-

tion, on changes in these objectives, on the resources used to attain these objectives, and on the policies that are to govern the acquisition, use, and disposition of these resources.[1]

When analyzing decisions at each of these levels, one finds that problems arise requiring both programmed and nonprogrammed solutions. For example, prediction models can be programmed for management control. However, hiring, layoff, and the assignment of personnel are nonprogrammed management control decisions, for at the present time no decision theory exists that permits the statement of personnel decision rules. This may change. In 1969 Herbert Simon predicted that by 1985 "we shall have acquired an extensive and empirically tested theory of human cognitive processes and their interaction with human emotions, attitudes and values."[2] And Norbert Wiener predicts that whatever man can do, the computer of the future will also do, though he does not specify a point in time when information systems will automate all decision making.[3]

Not all experts accept these views, however. Many believe that there are areas of business decision making that can never be automated. Psychologists such as Reitman call such problems "ill-defined";[4] the term "ill-formed" is used by computer scientist Uhr;[5] in the context of architectural design Ritter refers to the "wicked problem."[6] "Many management commentators prefer the classification "ill-structured."

Though time may prove Simon and Wiener correct, at present individuals, not computers, make decisions that require the ability to recognize and infer patterns for nonquantifiable data variables, especially human variables. Table 20.1 represents the structure of decision making today, with both programmed and nonprogrammed decisions made at all levels. The actual percentage of programmed versus nonprogrammed decision making varies from one industry to another, but approximately 80 percent of all decisions are programmable, given the current state of the art, especially in areas such as accounting, finance, and manufacturing.

---

[1] Robert N. Anthony, *Planning and Control Systems: A Framework for Analysis* (Cambridge, Mass.: Harvard University, Division of Research, Graduate School of Business Administration, 1965), pp. 16–18. For another set of definitions in the context of higher education, see R. L. Ackoff, "Toward Strategic Planning of Education," in *Efficiency in Resource Utilization in Education* (Paris: Organization of Economic Cooperation and Development, 1969), pp. 339–57.

[2] J. M. Bergey and R. C. Slover, "Administration in the 1980s," *S.A.M. Advanced Management Journal,* vol. 34, no. 2 (April 1969), p. 31.

[3] Ibid., p. 26.

[4] W. R. Reitman, *Cognition and Thought* (New York: John Wiley & Sons, Inc., 1965), pp. 148–64.

[5] L. Uhr, *Pattern Recognition, Learning and Thought* (Englewood Cliffs, N.J.: Prentice-Hall, 1973), pp. 268–84.

[6] For an excellent discussion of Ritter's characteristics of the wicked problem, see Lawrence F. Peters and Leonard L. Tipp, "Is Software Design Wicked?" *Datamation®,* vol. 22, no. 8 (May 1978), p. 127. See also Derek Partridge, "A Philosophy of 'Wicked' Problem Implementation," *Proceedings of the AISB/GI Conference on Artificial Intelligence* (Hamburg, 1978), p. 245.

Peter Keene and Michael Morton, who equate structure with programmed decisions and nonstructure with nonprogrammed decisions, would add an intermediate layer to Table 20.1: semistructured problems. "These are decisions where managerial judgment . . . will not be adequate, perhaps because of the size of the problem or the computational complexity and precision needed to solve it. On the other hand, the model or data alone are also inadequate because the solution involves judgment and subjective analysis. Under these conditions the manager *plus* the system can provide a more effective solution than either alone."[7]

Keene and Morton also point out that there are no rigid divisions between cells as shown in Table 20.1, for factors such as time available for decision making may require a nonprogrammed solution when the writing of a programmed solution would also be possible. In addition, the use of operations research techniques and the development of new technology continually blurs arbitrary divisions: yesterday's ill-structured problem may be solved by computer today.

TABLE 20.1
Classification of decisions

Function / Type of decision	Operational control	Management control	Strategic planning
Programmed	1	3	5
Nonprogrammed	2	4	6

Note: Though all problems in Cells 1, 3, and 5 are theoretically programmable, the shaded area approximates current computerized problem-solving effort.

Table 20.2, listing sample control and planning business problems that fall into structured, semistructured, and nonstructured categories, should be studied with Keene and Morton's criticism of arbitrary divisions in mind. The chart is included to provide examples of applications with programmed solutions, and to show types of problems for which software is of no assistance to managers in decision making at the present time.

DECISION-MAKING STAGES

How can problems solvable by computer be identified? How can management determine whether programmed solutions are feasible? Problem solving, according to John Dewey, requires answers to three questions. What is the

---

[7] Peter G. W. Keene and Michael S. Scott Morton, *Decision Support Systems: An Organizational Perspective* (Reading, Mass.: Addison-Wesley Publishing Co., Inc., 1978), p. 86.

TABLE 20.2
Sample decisions classified by level of decision making

Type of decision	Operational control	Management control	Strategic planning
Structured	Inventory control Accounts payable Accounts receivable Queuing Sequencing Plant scheduling Transportation models Assignment models	PERT/GERT for project control Linear and mathematical programming for resource allocation Prediction models Inventory control Break-even, marginal or instrumental analyses	Resource allocation using mathematical programming
Semistructured	Cash management Bond trading	Short-term forecasting Budgeting Marketing models Long-term forecasting	Capital acquisition Portfolio analyses New product planning Mergers and acquisitions
Unstructured	Designing products	Hiring and firing Predicting consumer preference	R & D planning

problem? What are the alternatives? Which alternative is best? This corresponds to Herbert Simon's division of the decision-making process into three stages: intelligence, design, and choice (see Figure 20.1). Only after gathering intelligence and analyzing options will the structure of the problem be revealed and the applicability of information system decision models become apparent. Each of these stages is described in greater detail below.

FIGURE 20.1
Stages of decision making

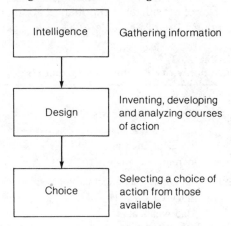

Intelligence — Gathering information

Design — Inventing, developing and analyzing courses of action

Choice — Selecting a choice of action from those available

Intelligence[8]

Intelligence in this context is defined as in the military: the gathering of information. Data must be collected on objectives, organizational constraints, resources available, and on the external environment (for example, competition and legal framework). Study of this data, recognizing patterns and trends, leads to the next phase, design.

Design

When examining alternative courses of action, mathematical and statistical models for decision making should be considered. See Table 20.3 for a list of models commonly used in solving business problems. The models fall into three categories: those that utilize the data base but can be manually processed; those that utilize the computational capability of computers but utilize external data; and those that process by computer data kept in the data base.[9]

---

[8] For an excellent discussion of this phase of decision making, see Gordon B. Davis, *Management Information Systems* (New York: McGraw-Hill Book Co., 1974), pp. 322–30.

[9] There are numerous other ways of classifying models. See Jay W. Forester, *Industrial Dynamics* (Cambridge, Mass.: MIT Press) 1961. For a discussion on the role of models in decision making see J. D. C. Little, "Models and Managers: The Concept of a Decision Calculus," *Management Science*, vol. 16, no. 8 (April 1970), pp. 3466–85.

The first group includes simple prediction models, trend analysis, and break-even analysis where simple plotting of data stored in the data base is sufficient.

Models requiring the computing capability of computers but utilizing external data form a far larger group. PERT and GERT for project management fall into this category. Even though only simple mathematical operators are needed (add, subtract, multiply, divide, compare), numerous computations are required, and computations for each set of data are run repeatedly during the life of the project to produce a variety of reports (sorted by earliest target date, by highest slack, by management responsibility, and so forth). In addition, speed is a factor of considerable importance. For models with similar characteristics, a computer is indispensable.[10]

TABLE 20.3
Taxonomy of decision-making models

1. Using data base:
     Simple prediction models
     Break-even analysis
     Marginal analysis
     Incremental analysis

2. Using computing capability of computer:

PERT/GERT	Sequencing
Mathematical programming	Plant scheduling
	Plant location
Queuing	Exponential smoothing
Inventory	Transportation models
Simulation	Assignment models
Sensitivity analysis	

3. Using computer and data base:
     Budget simulation
     Inventory
     Markovian chain
     Multiple regression for prediction

Mathematical programming for resource allocation is another model in the second group. Computers are valuable in solving this type of problem, for not only must a large number of calculations be performed, but the calculations themselves are cumbersome, requiring coefficients correct to stated decimal places. The mathematics involving matrix manipulation is also complicated. Here again the data utilized is primarily external.

---

[10] Computer programs for OR (operations research) models are often provided by the vendor of large computers or sold by software houses. In the case of CPM/PERT, there are some 87 programs available. See Perry Peterson, "Project Control Systems," *Datamation,* vol. 25, no. 6 (June 1979), pp. 147–53.

Repetitive calculations are also needed for simulation models and sensitivity analysis, problems that again are best solved by computer.

The final group of models includes those that utilize both the data base and processing capabilities of computers. An example is inventory models where data on demand, lead time, and supplies are provided by the data base and numerous complex calculations are made.

After analyzing the problem, it may become apparent that information systems cannot provide a solution. Instead, data is manipulated, risks evaluated, and alternative solutions postulated based on management's past experience, knowledge, perception, creativity, and intuition. Several solutions should be developed, including solutions with probability associations indicating the chance of success for each decision.

Choice

The final decision will be generated by computer when information systems are applicable. In semistructured situations, a model may be of assistance by classifying and displaying relevant information that will aid management in making a nonprogrammed decision. For example, a sensitivity analysis may indicate the consequences of changes in selected variables and parameters. Nonstructured problems will require judgmental decisions.

Note that in all types of decisions, choice is essentially a human activity. Even programmed decisions are based on rules and criteria originally established by the decision maker.

DECISION SUPPORT SYSTEM

When information systems are used to assist management in problem solving, the term **decision support system (DSS)** is used to describe the human-machine interplay in reaching decisions. In spite of the predictions of early commentators (Leavitt and Whistler in 1958;[11] Simon in 1965[12]), computers have not replaced management, not even middle management, though it is argued that growth at this middle level has not kept pace with management growth at other levels of corporate organization.[13] Instead, computers complement management, aiding, not eliminating, the decision maker. Today managers rely on computers ranging from small minis to sophisticated OLRT systems with a DBMS accessible by conversational high languages.

---

[11] H. J. Leavitt and T. L. Whistler, "Management in the 1980s," *Harvard Business Review,* vol. 36, no. 6 (November–December 1958), pp. 41–48.

[12] Herbert Simon, *The Shape of Automation for Man and Management* (New York: Harper & Row Publishers, Inc., 1965).

[13] J. G. Hunt and P. F. Newell, "Management in the 1980s Revisited," *Personnel Journal,* vol. 50, no. 1 (January 1971), pp. 35–43.

DIFFERING INFORMATIONAL NEEDS FOR OPERATIONS, CONTROL, AND PLANNING DECISIONS

How do planning and control decisions vary from one organizational level of decision making to another? Entire textbooks have been written on this subject.[14] But briefly, planning by top management determines *what* must be done, direction by middle management specifies *how* it is to be done, and operations *do* it. The feedback of *what* is done in operations is then evaluated and controlled. These activities and the levels of management responsible are graphically illustrated in Figure 20.2, with arrows indicating

FIGURE 20.2
Functions of planning and control by different levels of management

At left: Anthony's framework of business decision making.
At right: Corresponding levels of management.

the continual recycling of information throughout the corporate structure. This is a theoretical framework. In practice, the responsibilities of management vary from one industry to another and depend on management style.

Each level of decision making for planning and control requires different data. For example, Table 20.4 shows informational needs according to functions at the levels of operational control, managerial control, and strategic planning. Before information systems can be designed, the nature of information required at each level of decision making must be explicitly stated in operational and quantitative terms. Variables include: type of questions asked, time horizon of data, the information environment, degree of quantification, degree of detail, mode of operation, and display media.

---

[14] For a good definition and discussion of corporate planning and control in the information system context, see Z. S. Zanvetas, "Towards Intelligent Management Information Systems," *Industrial Management Review,* vol. 9, no. 3 (September 1968) p. 22.

TABLE 20.4
Information needed for strategic planning, management control, and operational control

Type of information	Operational control	Management control	Strategic planning
Accounting	Accounts payable Accounts receivable Costing	Budgeting reports with discrepancies and exceptions	Budget projections
Finance	Cash on hand	Investment alternatives	Long-term financial needs
Manufacturing	Engineering specs Work-in-progress Work to be started	Equipment loading and utilization Optimization of resources Performance measurement	Product enlargement Resource allocation
Marketing	Sales orders (A/R) Sales distribution	Projection of sales	Projection of markets and products
Purchasing	Inventory on hand Physical distribution Orders (A/P)	Inventory control Vendor evaluation	Planning new sources for purchasing
Personnel	Personnel records	Union negotiation	Manpower projection
R&D	R&D work-in-progress and its schedule	R&D progress reports for monitoring	Evaluation of long-range pure and applied research

Type of question asked

A computerized information system must answer different types of questions according to the levels of management being served. Operational management wants descriptive responses to questions that ask What is? Planners want answers to What if? (for example, What will happen if parameter X is increased by 2 percent?).

The distinction is important to system development because different resources are required for solutions to different types of questions. A descriptive report can best be written in COBOL, RPG, or languages such as BASIC, PL/1, APL, or FORTRAN. "What if?" questions usually require simulation models using languages like GPSS and SIMSCRIPT. Query and conversational languages, such as those described in Chapter 3, are also appropriate for planning and control. In addition, familiarity with special techniques such as the Critical Success Factors (CSF) and Business System Planning (BSP) developed by IBM is required of analysts developing systems for planning and control. Unfortunately, analysts and programmers specialize. Those who are knowledgeable and skillful in designing descriptive information systems generally have little experience with languages and techniques appropriate for planning models.

Time horizon of needed data

Operational management is concerned with current information. Today or this week. The timeliness of data can be crucial. Strategic planning looks ahead 1–10 years, depending on the volatility of the business. Management control falls in between. Current data must be compared with horizontal and longitudinal data to identify undesirable discrepancies in order for corrective action to be triggered. The time horizon is generally 1–5 years, though some middle managers evaluate monthly or yearly data only.

Informational environment

The source of information for decision making varies at the three levels of management. Generally, internal information relating to performance is generated from the data base for operational control, though some external information such as the price of raw materials and lead time for delivery may be required. This external data, however, is usually gathered by telephone or telex, not derived from the data base.

As one moves upward in management hierarchy, the need for internal information decreases and more external information must be evaluated in reaching decisions. Strategic planning requires data from demographic and industry studies, as well as information on sources and suppliers of materials, data regarding government regulations (federal and state), data on competitors' policies, and data on customer preferences. Formerly such external data was not included in the data base. It was too voluminous. The cost of converting it into machine-readable form was excessive, and retrieval systems were inadequate. Recent advances in computer technology have altered this situation. There has been a drop in hardware costs, and data, such as industry reports or macro data on the economy, is now available on tape or readable by OCR readers.

Retrieval of relevant information, however, remains a problem. It can be done to some extent by a manager on a terminal using conversational and dialogue languages such as those discussed in Chapter 3. Computer input on microfilm also aids in the retrieval of management information in much the same manner as online inquiry systems. In addition, special computer programs can be written to retrieve information. But then there is the problem of analyzing and interpreting the information for its policy and planning implications. This is part of intelligence in decision making referred to earlier and also part of nonprogrammed decision making.

Degree of quantification

Whereas operational and managerial control require numeric data, strategic planning places a heavy reliance on subjective data, such as qualitative evaluations of products and services.

Degree of detail

Operational management needs detailed information such as sales per sales representative, quantity of each product sold, or cost figures for each unit in production. At the level of management control, figures on branch or division performance are required. For strategic planning, information must be further aggregated, providing decision makers with figures for the organization as a whole. Once the lowest level of aggregation is identified and common definitions of data elements accepted by management throughout the organization, software can process data at any level of aggregation specified. Often operational information must be accurate to two decimal places. But future projections cannot be calculated with the same degree of accuracy. Tolerance ranges for information accuracy are another difference in the degree of detail required by the three levels of management.

Another aspect of detail is **exception reporting.** This is information on deviations, both good and bad, from expected or targeted values. Such deviations may alert managerial control to problems in need of solution, or may result in rewards such as bonuses when sales exceed quotas. Sometimes exceptional reporting triggers a decision by top management to revise policies and procedures.

An information system that provides exception reporting saves middle management from having to monitor *all* phases of operation. The use of information systems for making decisions based on exceptional data is known as **management by exception.**

Mode of operations

By definition, real-time systems are those that generate information so fast that the results of computations are useful in guiding a physical process. OLRT has its primary use at the operational level for businesses with continuous processes where changes in the environment will have important consequences.

Strategic planners in the past generally relied on overnight batch processing. Today's planners, however, are more dependent on instantaneous results, utilizing the inquiry capability of OLRT. This capability can be provided by a war room or a communications center, though the reduced cost of terminals and minis means many managers today are installing OLRT in their corporate offices.

Display media

All levels of management use printouts for long reports, and will, in all likelihood, have access to a CRT and/or a typewriter terminal for short reports. Operational and control management utilize interactive display terminals sometimes with plotting and graphing capabilities. In addition, microfilm or microfiche units to display historical or archival data are frequently employed. Strategic planners have a greater need for graphic displays. Since their requirements need not be online information, the graphics can be generated.

MANAGEMENT STYLE AND THRESHOLD

There are still other factors which contribute to the type of information needed by management: style and the threshold of information desired by an individual manager. Driver and Rowe[15] classify managers into four groups: the **flexible manager** who relies heavily on intuition and personal affability; the **decisive manager** who makes quick decisions after examining alternatives and summary data, satisfied with a "good enough" decision; the **hierarchical manager** who makes up his mind after evaluating lots of data, seeking the "best solution"; and the **integrative manager** who uses logic to sift through data and alternatives. These differences in style pose a dilemma for designers of information systems because tailoring a system to one style of management may mean redevelopment when managers change.

The **threshold of information** desired also varies from one manager to another. In Figure 20.3 the shaded area A represents a manager who

---

[15] Michael Driver and Alan Rowe, "Decision Making Styles: A New Approach to Management Decision Making," in *Behavioral Problems in Organization,* ed. Cary Copper (Englewood Cliffs, N.J.: Prentice-Hall, Inc., 1979), chap. 6.

relies on exceptional information, staff reports, and summary presentations prepared specifically for top management. In contrast, B is a manager at the top level who also utilizes selected detailed information on control and operations in reaching decisions. Of course, many other variations exist, the shape of the shaded area depending on an individual manager's personality, style, span of control, and professional background, as well as on factors such as the complexity of the organization and the confidence of the manager in the abilities of subordinates. A good information system is one that can be easily modified when changes in management style or threshold occur.

FIGURE 20.3
Different information thresholds

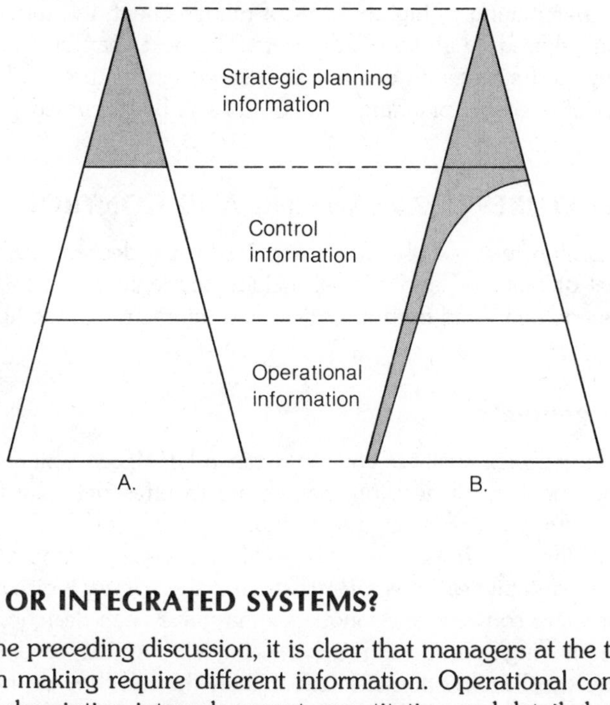

INDEPENDENT OR INTEGRATED SYSTEMS?

From the preceding discussion, it is clear that managers at the three levels of decision making require different information. Operational control needs are largely descriptive, internal, current, quantitative, and detailed, demanding a high degree of accuracy. Strategic planning information is primarily prescriptive, external, qualitative, aggregated, directed toward the future, with a wide range of accuracy permissible. Management control lies in between. These different needs suggest that three separate information systems might be advisable. Indeed, managers have often insisted on tailored information systems for they have not wanted to share information nor been willing to conform to the rules, definitions, and procedures of common information systems. Computer analysts have encouraged this posture in the past because of limited processing and memory capability of computers and their inability to manage large data bases.

But computer technology has now changed. DBMSs have been developed to handle large data bases and memory capacity has expanded. At the same time, hardware prices have dropped, making use of the new technology economically feasible. Meanwhile, problems with parallel independent systems have been recognized by both managers and analysts. The inability to relate data at different levels is a serious drawback. So is the high cost of parallel systems in terms of duplicated equipment, personnel, and effort in creating, verifying, and maintaining data bases. Most important, the information generated by parallel systems is often inconsistent, impeding, not abetting, decision making.

An integrated system, on the other hand, collects and validates raw data only once before processing. The resulting information is refined and reformatted, percolating to higher levels of management, the same basic information being shared by all bona fide users. The next chapter, Chapter 21, discusses integrated systems in detail. But first, design features to be included for the special needs of planning and control will be discussed.

DESIGN FEATURES FOR PLANNING AND CONTROL

Design features specifically required for a decision support system at the level of planning and control include access to the data base through data management, and both analytical and interactive capabilities.

Data management

In complex business environments, a DBMS capability is required if planning and control decision makers are to effectively use the data base. But planners also need languages that are analytical and have conversational capabilities such as those discussed in Chapter 3, and also languages with query capabilities for a DBMS such as the software discussed in Chapter 9. There are software and languages that have been designed for business decision making approaching such capabilities. TROLL[16] and TSP,[17] for example, have excellent econometric capabilities though they do not have very good capabilities for accessing and using large data bases.

Analytical and modeling capability

Available data that cannot be analyzed has little value. Analysis may be done by statistical packages (including packages utilizing standard operations

---

[16] National Bureau of Economic Research, *TROLL Reference Manual* (Cambridge, Mass.: NBER, 1974).

[17] R. E. Hall, *TSP Manual,* Harvard Technical Report, No. 12 (Cambridge, Mass.: Harvard Institute of Economic Research, 1975).

research techniques),[18] or specially written software. Programming should correspond to the human thought process and aid decision makers by suggesting solutions. The system should also encourage factoral thinking. That is, large problems should be factored (subdivided) into smaller subsets of decisions. Also, the computer should assist managers in interpretation, what Newell and Simon describe as "bringing the problem-solving methods into effective correspondence with each problem-solving situation."[19]

Many systems are being developed to help planning and control managers analyze problems. For example, STRATANAL is useful in planning corporate strategies[20] and GIDS (Generalized Intelligent Decision System) has the "ability to comprehend English-like queries and subsequently formulate models, interface appropriate data with these models and execute the models to produce some facts or expectations about the problem under consideration."[21] AIDS (An Interactive Decision System), written in common BASIC, rationalizes the judgmental process on a broad range of topics,[22] and GMIS (General Management Information System) uses an interactive relational data base management system and a high level language SEQUEL (discussed in Chapter 3) to give it enhanced analytical and statistical capabilities.[23]

Interactive capability

A decision support system that utilizes human-computer interaction, a dialogue with the computer, is particularly helpful for problems with the following characteristics, problems commonly found in planning and control.

1. The problems are not known in advance.
2. Solutions are open-ended (that is, there is no single correct answer).
3. Problems can be factored and tackled incrementally.
4. Limited human patience is a major consideration.

---

[18] Statistical routines are available either from vendors, software houses, or universities. For an excellent survey, see W. R. Schucany, B. S. Shannon, Jr., and P. D. Minton, "A Survey of Statistical Packages," *Computing Surveys,* vol. 4, no. 2 (June 1972), pp. 65–79.

Other packages include: *IBM Mathematical Programming System Extended/370 (MPSX/ 37), Basic Reference Manual,* For: SH19–1127 (White Plains, N.Y.: IBM, 1975); and K. W. Smillie, ed., *STATPACK,* Publication No. 17, 2d ed. (Edmonton, Canada: Department of Computer Science, University of Alberta, 1969).

[19] Allen Newell and H. A. Simon, *Human Problem Solving* (Englewood Cliffs, N.J.: Prentice-Hall, Inc., 1972), p. 91.

[20] F. T. Paine and W. Naumes, *Strategy and Policy Formulation* (Philadelphia: W. B. Saunders Co., 1974).

[21] Robert H. Bonczek, Clyde W. Holsapple, and Andrew B. Whinston, "Computer-Based Support of Organizational Decision Making," *Decision Sciences,* vol. 10, no. 2 (April 1979), pp. 268–91.

[22] Peter R. Newsted and Bayard E. Wynne, "Augmenting Man's Judgment with Interactive Computer Systems," *International Journal of Man-Machine Studies,* vol. 8, no. 1 (January 1976) pp. 29–59.

[23] John J. Donovan, "Data Base Systems Approach to Management Decision Support," *ACM Transactions on Data Base Systems,* vol. 1, no. 4 (December 1976), pp. 344–69.

5. The data is rapidly changing.
6. The policymaker's perception is also changing over time.
7. The problem is complex and needs raw data analysis, transformations, projections, and so forth.
8. The environment is dynamic.
9. Decisions must be made rapidly.

Though problems at the operational level often meet the above criteria, a decision support system is primarily used for decisions that are more abstract—complex problems as found in management control. A DSS is also used for problems in strategic planning that need to be graphically portrayed for easy assimilation and comprehension.

Designing interface equipment that provides interactive capabilities requires a knowledge of human engineering. One strategy, for example, is to lock out the user at selected points in the human-machine dialogue. This forces the user to concentrate on the problem for a given time period before proceeding with the solution. Presumably the delay ensures better decisions.[24] Some critics, however, believe delays, intentional or otherwise, add a factor of distress which negatively affects the quality of decisions.[25] Unfortunately, studies of human behavior have a long gestation period. By the time issues are resolved, computer technology has changed and the answer is often irrelevant.

CASE STUDY: AIRLINE USE OF INFORMATION SYSTEMS FOR PLANNING AND CONTROL

Chapter 19 described a functional application of an airline information system: reservations. This section will briefly describe AAIMS used by American Airlines for planning and control. This system, which was called AEMS (Airline Econometric Modelling System) when it was first introduced, was operational as early as 1970. By 1972 the system adopted a new name, AAIMS (An Analytical Information Management System),[26] while its jurisdiction extended to include operations research modeling, and reports on traffic analysis, freight administration, flight departures, maintenance engineering, and economic regulation needed for management control and strategic planning. Studies and forecasts performed by the system appear in Table 20.5. The system also performed many statistical routines, some of these being listed in Table 20.6.

AAIMS is user-operated and user-controlled, requiring no knowledge of programming. The system prompts managers in an interactive conversational

[24] See B. W. Bochum et al., "Interactive Problem Solving—An Experimental Study of 'Lockout' Effects," *Proceedings of Spring Joint Computer Conference,* ACM, 1971, pp. 205–21.

[25] Jamie R. Carbonell et al., "On the Psychological Importance of Time-Sharing Systems," *Human Factors,* vol. 10, no. 2 (March–April 1968), pp. 135–42.

[26] This discussion relies heavily upon Janet M. Taplin, "AAIMS: American Airlines Answers the What Ifs?" *Infosystems,* vol. 20, no. 2 (February 1973), pp. 40–41 ff., and Richard L. Klaas, "A DDS for Airline Management," *Data Base,* vol. 8, no. 3 (Winter 1977), pp. 3–8.

mode using industry terminology, not computer jargon. It is a computational system with a repertory of 60 verbs, including DISPLAY, PLOT, MINUS, and TIMES—the computations being tested for validity and consistency. The AAIMS system is also a retrieval system, using coded commands. For example, P5; AA; SYS; 5136; 6401 will generate an operating expense quarterly report (code P5) for American Airline (AA) systems (SYS) personnel expenses (code 5136) related to the DC–9–30 (code 6401).

What does this system cost? In 1973, after a capital investment of $62,500 (including online storage), roughly $18,000 was spent for data collection and $540 for associated directories in an 18-month period. The benefits for this same period were estimated at $361,000 in cost savings and increased passenger revenues. The research time was one sixth of the time required without AAIMS.

TABLE 20.5
Studies and forecasts in AAIMS

Aircraft utilization	Productivity measurement
Financial ratios	Revenue/yield
Load factors	Seating configuration
Market shares	Traffic and capacity growth
Operating statistics	Unit costs

TABLE 20.6
Statistical routines used in AAIMS

Graphic analysis	*Time series analysis*
Time-series plots	Exponential smoothing
Scatter diagrams	Moving averages
Statistical analysis	Period-to-period ratios
Correlation	Year-end totals
Descriptive statistics	Year-over-year ratios
Regression	

This description of AAIMS is already outdated, for like all computerized information systems it is continually evolving and improving. Will such planning systems ever replace middle or top management? What are the limits of a computerized information system? This chapter concludes with a discussion on artificial intelligence, the capacity of machines to perform functions normally associated with human intelligence.

ARTIFICIAL INTELLIGENCE

A major problem in a discussion of whether computers will ever match human intelligence is defining the term *intelligence*. Computers are intelligent if intelligence is reasoning, adaptability, or the ability to solve structured problems, to work mathematical equations, or prove theorems in geometry. The computer's intelligence even outstrips mankind's (according to this definition) insofar as a computer possesses the ability to process numerical data at super-human speed without error or fatigue and the ability to store and retrieve far larger amounts of data than can be handled by the human mind.

Sometimes a capacity to learn is defined as a key characteristic of intelligence. Can computers learn? Arthur Samuel answered this question affirmatively with his checkers program in the 1950s. This program included rules of thumb to identify and incorporate successful game strategies so that the computer improved its game in time. At first, Samuel, a mediocre player, beat the machine, but the computer "learned" and soon was able to defeat checker champions.

When defining intelligence as the ability to think and be creative, again the question of semantics arises. Does a problem such as, "What is the minimum number of colors needed for countries on a world map so that no two adjacent areas have the same color?" require thinking? If so, machines can think for the answer, 4, was generated by computer in 1977. Computers have constructed original proofs in Euclidean geometry and can design electric motors, activities many professionals define as creative.

Alan Turing's solution to this controversy has been to establish a test for thinking. He suggests an individual match wits with a computer and with another person communicating through a terminal. If computer performance cannot be distinguished from human performance, the machine thinks. There have been many applications of Turing's test premise. In 1978, for example, David Levy played chess against a computer version, Chess 4.7, at an international chess match. He was unable to determine whether he was competing against a human or machine, a proof according to Turing, that a computer can think.

One criticism of Turing's test lies in the nature of communication used. But perhaps the premise of the test is also at fault. Why should a machine have to be equal to humans before it can be called creative and intelligent? After all, a plane cannot fly as well as a bird, but nevertheless flies. Without doubt, computers today contribute greatly to management decision making and problem solving. Machine intelligence, called **artificial intelligence,** still has a limited problem-solving range. But perhaps computers will be used to make design improvements in hardware and software, so that future computers may eventually equal or even surpass human problem-solving capabilities. We may produce what Jack Good calls the **ultra-intelligent machine (UIM),** which might in turn make design improvements, creating a second generation of UIMs, and so on, and so on.

Joseph Weizenbaum, an eminent computer scientist, argues in his book *Computer Power and Human Reason* for a halt in research on aritifical intelligence.[27] He believes our society cannot handle the social, psychological,

---

[27] For another strong criticism of artificial intelligence, see Hubert L. Dreyfus, *What Computers Can't Do* (New York: Harper & Row, Publishers, Inc. 1972), p. 259, and a reply by Senon W. Pjlyshyn, "Minds, Machines, and Phenomenology: Some Reflections on Dreyfus' 'What Computers Can't Do,' " *Cognition,* vol. 3, no. 1 (1975), pp. 57–77.

TABLE 20.7
Differences in information content required by three levels of management

Nature of information	Operational control	Management control	Strategic planning
Question asked	What is? (descriptive)	What was, is, and will be? (descriptive and prescriptive simulation)	What will be? What if? (prescriptive) simulation)
Time horizon	Current (What is happening today and this week?)	Past and current	Future (What will happen in 1–5 years?)
Information environment	Mostly internal current information: Resources Utilization	Some internal and some external: Past and current performance Predictive future information	Highly dependent on external information
Degree of quantification	Quantitative	Quantitative	Not quantitative

ethical, and human implications of aritifcial intelligence, foreseeing culture shock many magnitudes greater than that described by Alvin Toffler in *Future Shock.* But can we stop development in artificial intelligence? And should we? Management at present benefits greatly from decision support systems, and most professionals support further research to extend the problem-solving range of machines. Weizenbaum, however, reminds us that trust, courage, and sympathy cannot be programmed. Do we want all human emotion excluded from decision making?

Exactly how artificial intelligence will alter society and businesses remains unknown. What is known is that computers assist and supplement human intelligence in problem solving, and that computers will play an expanded role in business decision making in the future, even at the higher levels of management.

SUMMARY

Not all problems can be solved by computer. Programmed solutions are feasible for structured problems, computer assistance in decision making being most effective when speed is essential and a large number of routine, repetitive computations must be performed.

Information systems for control and planning must provide a different type of data than information systems at the operational level. Variables include types of questions asked, time horizon of data, informational environment, degree of quantification, and degree of detail (see Table 20.7). In addition, information systems must respond to differences in the mode of operation in reaching decisions at the three levels of management, and to preferences regarding display media. Management style and threshold are also factors to be considered in a systems design. Special features required for planning and control decision support systems are data management, an analytical and modeling capacity, and interactive capability.

At present, computers complement, support, and extend a decision maker's range but management is in no immediate jeopardy of being replaced by machine. Too many "wicked problems" exist, defying programmed solutions. However, research in artificial intelligence, data management, linguistics, and psychology will undoubtedly expand the role of machines in decision making in the future.

KEY WORDS

**Analytical and modeling
  capability**
Artificial intelligence
Choice
Data management
Decision-making models

Decision-making stages
Decision support system (DSS)
Decisive manager
Degree of detail
Degree of quantification
Design

Display media	Nonprogrammed decisions
Exception reporting	Operational control
Flexible manager	Programmed decisions
Hierarchical manager	Semistructured problems
Informational environment	Strategic planning
Integrative manager	Structured problems
Intelligence	Threshold of information
Interactive capability	Time horizon of data
Management by exception	Type of questions asked
Management control	Ultra-intelligent machine (UIM)
Mode of operations	

DISCUSSION QUESTIONS

1. Describe five examples of computerized systems used by middle management. In each case, identify:
   - a. Information provided.
   - b. Models used (if any).
   - c. Nature of information (quantitative or qualitative).
   - d. How the information can be used.
   - e. Benefits (of the information).

2. What is exception reporting? Cite an example. Specify the trigger rules for initiating such a report.

3. Can a computer be a catalyst in management decision making? If so, how?

4. What can middle and top management do to ensure and maximize the beneficial use of computers?

5. Can techniques of operations research and management science be used in an information system? Cite examples. In each case, identify the model used and the function performed.

6. Can decisions be programmed? What decisions cannot be programmed? Give examples of programmed and nonprogrammed decisions in a business firm where the primary activity is:
   - a. Marketing.
   - b. Production.
   - c. Service.
   - d. Financial.
   - e. Consulting.

7. Can a computer think? What kind of an impact will computers have on middle and top management? Will they help or hinder the decision-making process?

8. What is a model? What is simulation? What is a simulation model? How can such a model be used in business? Cite four examples of simulation models identifying the functions performed by computer.

9. Can computers make managerial decisions? How can the unintentional decisions be avoided?

10. What is the difference between algorithmic and heuristic decision making? In

what business situations are each type of decision made? Which type of decisions do computers make?

11. Give six examples of models used by computers in business problem solving? Is the main reason for using the model to:
    a. Compute quickly and accurately.
    b. Process large masses of data.
    c. Correlate the data in the common data base.
    d. Compute complex mathematical relationships.
    e. Combination of the above.

12. Describe the different informational needs of middle and top management in terms of:
    a. Source.
    b. Aggregation.
    c. Period covered.
    d. Accuracy.
    e. Other considerations (specify).

13. Suppose Hotel West were part of a large chain under your management. What information would you require from each hotel in the chain for purposes of planning and control?

14. What types of decisions can computers make that humans cannot? Explain.

15. What are the comparative advantages of computers over humans in making business decisions and vice versa? How will these relative advantages change once computers become faster and cheaper with greater information storage and retrieval capabilities?

16. Will advances in artificial intelligence result in replacement of middle and top management? Describe the nature of advances that would promote such a situation.

17. How will traditional structure of management hierarchy change because of computers? What adverse effects will reorganization have and how can these be minimized or eliminated?

EXERCISES

1. Suppose the manager in Exercise 1, Chapter 10 wanted to:
   a. Compare the sales of each salesperson with that of the average last month.
   b. Compare sales by each salesperson by age group to establish a predictive relationship.

   What additional input, if any, would be required? Are applications *(a)* and *(b)* at the operational, planning, or control level? Would these applications be cost-effective? State assumptions you need to make.

2. Read Joseph Weizman, *Computer Power and Human Reason* (San Francisco, Calif.: W. H. Freeman and Co., 1976), or one of Weizman's articles on artificial intelligence, such as "On the Impact of the Computer in Society," *Science,* vol. 1176, no. 4035 (May 12, 1972), pp. 609–14. List arguments against future research on artificial intelligence.

SELECTED ANNOTATED BIBLIOGRAPHY

Alter, Steven L. *Decision Support Systems: Current Practice and Continuing Challenges,* Reading, Mass.: Addison-Wesley Publishing Co., 1980, 316 pp.
This Ph.D thesis is a supplement to *Decision Support Systems: An Organizational Perspective* by Peter G. Keene and Michael S. Morton. It includes many cases of DSS implementation, such as AAIMS of American Airlines. A good discussion of difficulties in system usage, implementation patterns, strategies, and implementation risk factors is presented.

Carlson, Eric D. "An Approach for Designing Decision Support Systems." *Data Base,* vol. 10, no. 3 (Winter 1979), pp. 3–15.
This article, written by a staff member of IBM Research Laboratory, is not technical. It is an excellent discussion of DDS in business, including many flowcharts and examples of terminal-oriented query systems for middle and top management.

Evans, Christopher. *The Mighty Micro.* London: Victor Gollancz, Ltd., 1979.
This book looks at short-term computer technology (up to 1990) and also makes long-term predictions for 1991–2000. Included are three chapters on intelligent machines. These chapters discuss the pro and con of artificial intelligence. The author represents the minority of computer scientists in his opposition to artificial intelligence. His views are worth reading.

Keene, Peter G., and Morton, Michael S. *Decision Support Systems: An Organizational Perspective.* Reading, Mass.: Addison-Wesley Publishing Co., Inc., 1978.
An excellent book in a series on decision support. It traces the underlying theory, discusses models for DSS and then their implementation (including design, evaluation, and strategies for DSS development).

Naylor, Thomas H. *Corporate Planning Models.* Menlo Park, Calif.:) Addison-Wesley Publishing Co., Inc., 1979, 390 p.
A good book on models for planning and control, integrating a discussion of decision-making models with a look at the informational needs of management and information systems.

Weizenbaum, Joseph. *Human Power and Human Reason.* San Francisco, Calif.: W. H. Freeman and Co., 1976, 300 p.
This is a powerful assault on artificial intelligence from a prominent researcher. It is a provocative book to read even if one disagrees with the author's views.

21

SYSTEMS INTEGRATION AND GROWTH

Computer applications at the operational level were discussed in Chapter 19; control and planning applications in Chapter 20. Many of these applications can be developed and maintained independently though integration of subsystems is far more efficient and effective. In this chapter, different types of integration will be examined (horizontal, vertical, longitudinal, and total systems), and the advantages of each described.

Integration leads to growth of information systems. How users and analysts evaluate growth perspectives will also be discussed in this chapter along with the effect of technology on growth.

TYPES OF INTEGRATION

Integration of an information system is the unification of subsystems through linkage. There are four types of integration: **horizontal, vertical, longitudinal,** and **total systems integration.**

Horizontal integration

A firm with three levels of decision making (operations, control, and planning) has horizontal integration when functional information subsystems such as production, marketing, accounting and finance are integrated at one level, as illustrated in Figure 21.1, sharing a common data base. There does not have to be direct linkage between all files to achieve integration as long as **chaining** exists. That is, key data elements can be used to link Files 1 and 3 indirectly as long as Files 1–2 and 2–3 have direct links.

Integration has two advantages: data stored in several files can be correlated and used to generate new information otherwise not available; and collection, preparation, storage, and processing of duplicate data are eliminated. An example of horizontal integration is the use of sales information in a marketing file to send invoices for payment collection, an accounting function. Another example would be the use of the sales file to determine production quantities and schedules.

In the past, it was necessary for a manager to spend a great deal of time combining information contained in operational reports prepared in different

FIGURE 21.1
Horizontal integration at different levels of management

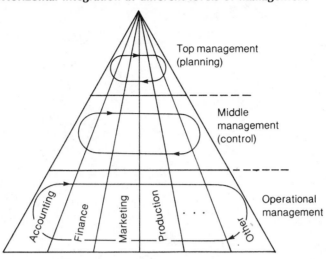

functional areas. Often these reports were produced in a manner which made it necessary to re-sort the information so that meaningful correlation could be produced from different functional areas. Now all this can be done automatically in an integrated system.

Vertical integration

In vertical integration, an information system for a single function (e.g., production) serves all levels of management but is not integrated with other functional systems (see Figure 21.2). For this type of data flow, common definitions or definition equivalencies are essential. For example, if the code for married were 1 in the operational personnel file and M in the planning personnel file, this must be known at the time of data access. Such information is stored in tables for automatic reference by the computer, a process known as **table look-up.**

One advantage of vertical integration is efficiency, for data need be collected only once for use at all levels of management. Consistency, accuracy, and timeliness of information are added benefits, for the information conveyed to control and planning is working operational data aggregated by software for management's needs. Information and feedback also flow in two directions, a feature lacking in horizontal integration.

Longitudinal integration

Another dimension of integration is time. Managers are interested not only in operations today, but in historical trends (such as trends in demand,

FIGURE 21.2
Vertical integration

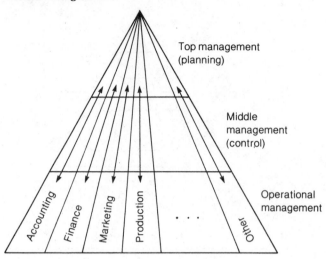

supply, and performance). Such data is needed for evaluating performance (comparing past with present records) and is useful when making predictions for future values of sales, market share, production, and so forth. Longitudinal integration need not be for the entire system, as illustrated in Figure 21.3, but may be for only selected functions of the system. The time period for longitudinal integration is shown in Figure 21.3 as five years, but this will vary from one firm to another depending on the nature of the product and industry.

Unfortunately, past data is not always available when needed. It may not have been collected, may be lost, or simply may be aggregated in units not comparable with present data. Integration over time requires both completeness and continuity of data, called **data integrity. Equivalence tables**

FIGURE 21.3
Longitudinal integration

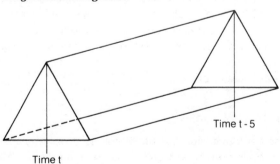

can be used if the incompatability is a trivial coding difference and software can generate compatibility when new classifications of data are composites of two or more former classifications. But disaggregation, such as the division of account x into x_1 and x_2 means that the new x_1 has no historical counterpart. Such disaggregation of codes should therefore take place only when absolutely necessary, with managers aware of the fact that this disaggregation will disrupt continuity of data.

Total systems

Most firms want horizontal *and* vertical integration so that data is shared by all functions and information flows between all levels of management. When longitudinal integration is also incorporated, the system is referred to as a **total system,** or an **integrated management information system.** Sometimes the acronym **MIS** is also used, though this latter name has many other interpretations and connotations.

EXAMPLES OF INTEGRATED AND NONINTEGRATED SYSTEMS

In Chapters 19 and 20, computer applications were described for an airline, travel agency, hotel, and automobile dealership. Each of these applications will now be reexamined for horizontal, vertical, and longitudinal integration.

Airline integration

The airline reservation application discussed in Chapter 19 was integrated horizontally with related functions such as aircraft loading, meal catering, crew scheduling, aircraft maintenance, and so forth. Baggage control, however, was omitted. Why? Primarily because of the large capital investment needed to develop scanners for data collection on luggage which varies in size, shape, material, and position. At the present time airports lack the special facilities required for computerized baggage control.

Another application that can be integrated horizontally with airline reservations is hotel reservations. Pan Am, for example, has structured its data base and added necessary software to make the reservation system for Pan Am's chain of InterContinental Hotels compatible with their airline reservation system. The data base of Best Western Hotels is also being integrated with United Airlines so that similar reservation services can be offered. It takes planning and capital investment for such integration, but the advantages are recognized by both airlines and passengers. Undoubtedly other hotel chains, car rentals, and tour companies will be integrated with airline reservations in the future.

Chapter 20 described the DSS for American Airlines called AAIMS. This system has been extended to all U.S. carriers, providing horizontal integration of airlines, so that the Civil Aeronautics Board can receive compatible reports from all carriers under its jurisdiction. AAIMS consists of an extensive standard data base, with files for traffic capacity, head count, and financial data, the latter including income, expense, and balance sheet data with the data itself broken down into six dimensions: airline, marketing, function, account, aircraft, and time. See Figure 21.4 for the hierarchical structure of this data base. One path in the data hierarchy, expense, is traced through all six dimensions.

This system enables the calculation of expenses for every airline for each marketing entity for every function and account, for each aircraft type, and for different time periods such as daily, or quarterly. Reports specified by

FIGURE 21.4
Data base structure for AAIMS

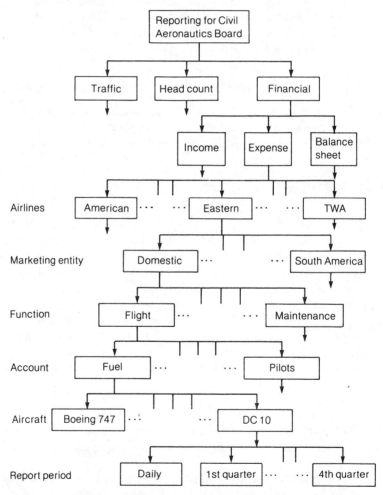

Source: Adapted from Richard L. Klaas, "A DSS for Airline Management," *Data Base,* vol. 8, no. 3 (Winter 1977), p. 3.

the CAB are used by the entire airline industry, including the airlines themselves, the Air Transport Association, and even engine and airframe manufacturers. Quarterly reports vary from 50–75 pages per airline, depending on company size, aircraft type, and route structure.

AAIMS is also longitudinally integrated, containing over 20,000 monthly and quarterly time series data values, each set covering four to ten years. The AAIMS system has the capability of manipulating the time series data for forecasting and prediction, partly because of the language used, APL (A Programming Language), an interactive language with a powerful vector manipulation capability. But this time series orientation, while it is a strength, is also a weakness for it limits modeling capabilities such as simulation. Still, the AAIMS reporting system has conceptually many applications in industries other than the airline, such as banking, manufacturing, and transportation.

Travel agent application

Use of computers at Schmal Travel is a strictly functional application at the operational level with no other computerized subsystems at higher levels of management (and hence no integration). The agency has no horizontal integration, such as accounting with reservations, even though such software is available, the stated explanation being cost. An unstated reason is that Schmal Travel is a family business, and an automated accounting application would have replaced the accountant, who, in this case, is the son-in-law of the owner. The reservations system does have longitudinal integration because the accessed data base is so integrated.

Hotel West application

Hotel West has two information systems: reservations, and a horizontally integrated system for operations, including registration, accounts, payroll, and so forth. Why this separation when reservations should logically be integrated with registration? The answer is that software for the two systems came from different sources (the reservation system developed by the chain, and the applications programs developed by a software company, Communications Diversified, Inc.), neither system designed for integration with the other. As a result the two systems are incompatible. The desk clerk at Hotel West manually enters reservation data into the registration system for there is no linkage between the two systems. In hotels where reservations and registration are linked, guests merely verify registration data that has been processed by computer from the original reservation request, sign the registration form, and pick up the key without having to provide duplicate information at check-in.

Energy regulation could be an independent application handled by a microprocessor, but at Hotel West, energy is integrated horizontally with other operational functions. The computer system also generates management reports for control (e.g., on utilization and distribution) but its vertical integration does not extend to planning, for no planning models are needed for this type or this size of business. Expansion and planning decisions are based on the judgment of the manager, not on a computer model of business data.

Longitudinal integration exists at Hotel West but integration includes future reservation data (up to 20 years in advance), not past data needed for forecasting, as most firms require.

Auto dealer

The auto dealer described in Chapter 19 has three independent information systems: a NCR data processing system for payroll, a minicomputer for sales contracts, and a terminal connected to a computer utility for accounting and inventory applications. The processing modes of these three systems differ and the hardware is incompatible. Why? Because the systems evolved independently and the software purchased has no integration capability. The manager recognizes the need for horizontal integration, but says separate systems have been beneficial, giving the company operating experience with modules and subsystems, preparing them for a larger integrated system which they hope to acquire in the future. The manager is currently studying alternative integrated systems, talking with other dealers to learn their experiences and recommendations, and waiting for hardware and software costs to drop. Asked if vertical integration and a decision support system for planning is contemplated, the manager answered no. The control reports presently generated are adequate, and future sales can be predicted by studying economic indicators, the money market, and interest rates without the need for a planning model. The value of DSS was recognized, however, the manager being particularly impressed with DSS retrieval capabilities and the advantage of being able to ask "What if?" questions, such as, "How will demand for pickups change, given shifts in population? Industry?" But the acquisition of DSS is a distant goal.

PLANNING FOR AN INTEGRATED SYSTEM

Total systems are not always required. For example, the auto dealer cited above has no need for vertical integration. This is true of many small firms.

The sample case studies also reflect another truism. Many firms fail to integrate systems even when the need is apparent. The primary reason for this is lack of compatible hardware, particularly when subsystems are implemented by minicomputers. In addition, subsystems with their own data base require software and linking data elements, perhaps even a DBMS, to implement and maintain an integrated data base. Such integration requires planning, as described in Part Three of this text, and coordination of personnel. The more people involved, the more complex the planning becomes, for a linear increase in personnel means a geometric increase in cross currents and interaction. There is one path for two persons, three paths for two, six paths for four, ten for five, and so forth. Note that the fifth person increases personnel by 25 percent, whereas the paths increases 66.6 percent. This phenomenon, called the **geometric organization syndrome,** adds to the time and resources that must be allocated to integration. Furthermore, in the past, firms have been unable to find systems personnel with knowledge of structured programming and skill in analysis and design combined with a business background to implement integration. This is changing. There are now over 60 schools and colleges of business in the United States with formal MIS undergraduate programs giving students a good foundation in business principles while providing training in programming and systems analysis.

Another impediment to total integration is that few businesses have the monetary and human resources to implement large integrated systems all at once. Instead, modular systems are added and integrated gradually within an overall plan for an integrated system. Large, complex, mature firms with subsystems already in operation find vested interests, and entrenched personalities impede system integration. The difficulties of implementation, however, should not forestall integration efforts. With planning, time, and patience, a total system can be achieved.

CASE STUDY OF SUBSYSTEM INTEGRATION: MATERIALS REQUIREMENTS PLANNING SYSTEM

When total integration is not financially feasible, limited integration is often possible. Integration of subsystems related to the flow of materials needed for production can be implemented by the **Materials Requirements Planning System (MRP),** for example. In this system, products that need to be produced, quantities, and times of production are specified in a Master Production File. This information, combined with data from a Production Requirements File and Materials Availability File is used to calculate materials needed for each product, and to ensure that materials are ordered and available at the time of production, no later and no earlier. This reduces the investment in inventory and maintains the flow of materials without which production would be slowed or even stopped.

The integrated MRP System is shown in Figure 21.5. Subsystems include inventory accounting, production scheduling, shop floor control, procurement, customer order entry, and bill of materials. Several models used by middle management are part of the system, including an economic order quantity model for production, least unit cost model, least total cost model, and a part-period balancing model.

MRP integrates not only horizontally but vertically between operational and control management levels. The system orders materials (expediting some orders, canceling others), allowing for discounts. It does both production shop scheduling and vendor scheduling, and enables management to react promptly

FIGURE 21.5
The MRP system showing linkage between subsystems and files

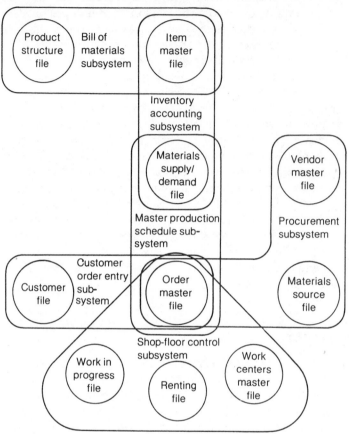

to changes in the master schedule or market availability of materials. These prompt reactions are facilitated not only by performance reporting and accounting reporting but by status reports on demand and supply schedules of materials.

MRP is costly. For one manufacturer with $50 million annual sales, annual cost of processing MRP in 1979 was approximately $360,000, plus an initial investment of $2 million with $60,000 allocated for systems support and $80,000 for support clerks.[1] MRP also requires discipline and careful handling of bills and supply orders. In fact, "The extreme operating discipline placed on inventory managers and material planners by MRP may cause cultural shock to the point of passive or active resistance by these groups—the very

---

[1] William S. Donelson, "MRP—Who Needs it," *Datamation®*, vol. 25, no. 5 (May 1, 1979), p. 194.

same people MRP is supposed to help."[2] Most firms implementing MRP, however, find the system is extremely helpful to management, well worth the cost.

ADVANCED INFORMATION SYSTEMS

Seldom are **advanced information systems** exactly alike. Equipment configurations will vary, for example. So will decision support models, languages, hardware, and organization of the data base. One firm may limit applications to planning, inventory control, and scheduling: another to production and accounting. However, basic components of advanced information systems will be common, as listed in Table 21.1. All advanced information systems must be adaptive, designed to incorporate change without disrupting information flow and generation of reports.

An example of an advanced information system is the use of the simulation model for planning shown in Figure 21.6. This model can determine consequences when different subsets of internal and planning variables are manipulated in a given environment. First the manager analyzes and evaluates the firm's performance (Box 3) in the context of its societal environment (Box 2), which is determined by external variables such as manpower and labor unions. (Box 1). The evaluation may lead to a reassessment of goals and objectives (Box 4), which in turn affects company priorities and policies (Box 5). A trial set of planning variables selected by management (Box 6) is then entered as input, the planning model simulating results (Box 7) based on data in the common data base (Box 9), which is composed of both environmental data (Box 1) and corporate data (Box 8). The results of the calculations are then displayed as analytical reports (Symbol 10).

After reviewing the consequences of the trial decision, the manager may wish to change the values of the planning variables and recalculate consequences. The cycle of Boxes 6–10 continues until the decision maker is satisfied with results. Decisions are then translated into budgets and resource allocations (Box 11) and the plan put into operation (Box 12). The analytical reports from the planning model are evaluated (Box 3), with the planning cycle repeated periodically.

INTEGRATION ACROSS NATIONAL BORDERS

System integration (both limited and total system integration) in firms with foreign operations may result in **transborder data flow.** This flow has been the subject of much political controversy, leading to national restrictions on data flow. As expressed by Louis Jorvet, Magistrate of Justice in France, "Information is power, and economic information is economic power.

---

[2] Ibid., p. 187.

TABLE 21.1
Components of an advanced information system

Common data flows
Common [or compatible] source documents, common input media, and a common data base are utilized so that unnecessary processing activities involving storage files, input data, and output information are eliminated.

Immediate data entry
Data created from transactions and operations is entered directly into the computer system from the point of origin, which may be a local or remote terminal.

Real-time processing
Data is processed in real time.

Common data base
Current and historical data, forecasts, plans, standards, decision rules, mathematical models, and other analytical techniques are stored in a direct access data base for use by all subsystems.

Integrated information subsystems
The major categories of business information systems are integrated into a single information system which provides an efficient and effective flow of information to management.

Decision support orientation
The computer system utilizes decision rules and models, and other tools and techniques to evaluate the contents of data bases, the data being processed, and the information produced. As a result, the computer may specify decisions to be taken, identifying unusual conditions that require management intervention and integrating the decision maker's insights and judgments into an interactive decision-making process.

Conversational computing
Data communications terminals, data base management software, and other computer system capabilities encourage conversational computing. Computer users can simply and instantly direct the computer to solve problems, answer questions, process data, update files, and produce output in any format desired.

Source: James A. O'Brien, *Computers in Business Management: An Introduction,* rev. ed. (Homewood, Ill.: Richard D. Irwin, 1979) p. 335. © 1979 by Richard D. Irwin, Inc.

Information has an economic value and the ability to store and process certain types of data may well give one country political and technological advantage over other countries. This, in turn, may lead to a loss of national sovereignty through supernational data flows."[3]

Some Third World countries are concerned that cultural and institutional bias accompanies data flow, fearing that imported information may not be in their national interest. Other countries fear loss of employment when multinationals integrate systems. It is estimated that Canada will have lost 23,000

---

[3] Quoted by John Eger in "Transborder Flow," *Datamation®,* vol. 24, no. 2 (November 15, 1978), p. 50.

FIGURE 21.6
Simulation model for planning in an advanced information system

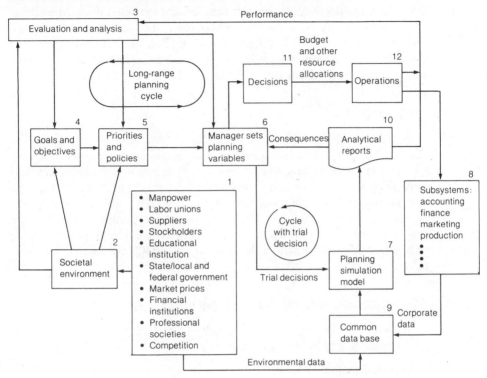

jobs worth $1.5 billion by 1984 due to system integration of U.S. firms with Canadian outlets.[4]

To control transborder flow of data, many countries have passed restrictive legislation. In France, for example, a fine of $400,000 and five years of prison is the penalty for transborder data flow of what is defined as "sensitive." In England, the post office has the right to read all transmitted messages, a right that implies that firms must share their cryptographic codes. In Italy, a proposal has been made that transmission cost be proportional to the volume of messages, which could increase transmission costs tenfold. Some countries require that all transborder data flow be handled by public carriers. This results in loss of control by the user and often means degraded service. A data act in Sweden in 1973 empowers a Data Inspection Board to approve all transmissions of personal data crossing its borders. There are over 20 countries with data privacy acts, many using the acts as a way to monitor data for their own economic and political objectives.

---

[4] Rein Turn, "Transborder Data Flow," *Computer World,* vol. 14, no. 9 (March 3, 1980), p. 62.

The response of U.S. firms has been to stress the need for balance between privacy and freedom of economic opportunity, and the right of unhampered flow of information.[5] At the present time, efforts are being made to establish international conventions on transborder data flow at the United Nations and through the OECD (Organization of Economic Cooperation and Development).[6] Just how such conventions will impede or promote growth and integration of information systems of U.S. firms remains to be seen.

GROWTH PATHS

As subsystems are added and integrated, information systems grow. The direction of growth is a management decision influenced by users' requests for additional applications, analysts' recommendations for expansion, available technology, and the size and complexity of the existing system. The growth path favored by users may prove inadvisable from a technological standpoint, however, or factors such as lack of operational expertise within the firm may preclude new applications favored by analysts. The considerations to be weighed by management in choosing a growth path are described in detail below.

CRITERIA DETERMINING PRIORITIES OF GROWTH

In recommending priorities for growth, users rank potential applications on the basis of the following criteria:

Projected tangible payoff.

Projected intangible payoff.

Time and cost of implementation.

Opportunity costs.

Human factors.

Development risks.

Potential impact on competitiveness.

What other companies have done.

Placement of application in project sequencing.

Requirements of local, state, or federal legislation.

When analysts list priorities for growth, they choose applications on the basis of:

Ease of implementation.

Contribution to learning.

---

[5] Peter Safirstein, "How to Best Control the Flow of Electronic Information across Sovereign Borders," *AFIPS Conference Proceedings 1979* (New York: AFIPS Press, 1979), pp. 279–82.

[6] Ibid., p. 281.

Minimal operational problems.

High visibility and a large number of users.

Contribution to an integrated system.

Experience and capabilities of EDP personnel.

Support of top management.

Minimal resistance of personnel.

Not included in these two lists is a factor that is often decisive in choosing which applications should be implemented: personal and financial power. The saying, "Whoever has the gold gets first priority," is relevant, for generally the priorities of financial officers, who control funding and often have organizational responsibility for computer operations, are adopted. The fact that financial applications are usually the first implemented may be justified since many such applications are structured, repetitive, serve multiple users, have a high benefit-cost ratio, and involve a large volume of transactions. However, many other applications have the same characteristics. When implementation decisions are made in committee, power, including vocal power, wins.

Often the growth of information systems is impeded by lack of available resources or technological limitations. Projects high on a list of priorities may have to be delayed, whereas minor applications low in priority may prove feasible. Furthermore, Nolan's growth curve, described below, is a significant factor in determining a firm's ability to assimilate computer technology.

NOLAN'S GROWTH CURVES

According to Richard Nolan, information systems (reflected in EDP costs), follow a S curve through four stages of learning and growth: initiation of EDP, expansion, control formalization, and integration. This curve is the same shape curve used by Arnold Toynbee to explain the histories of societies, and by others to explain success patterns of peoples and organizations, product development, market development, and the absorption of technology. That is, slow early acquisition of knowledge and skill is followed by a period of rapid learning and growth, then a slowdown in learning rate and a final plateau. For EDP, however, Nolan adds a second S to the curve and two more growth stages to include the assimilation of data base technology (see Figure 21.7).

Tables 21.2 to 21.4 describe characteristics of management and organization during Nolan's six growth stages.[7] These include equipment variations, and differences in types of applications and modes of processing. These are listed to show readers that implementation decisions on new applications have a relationship to the phase of growth an organization has reached. Some applications desired by users and analysts may be inappropriate due

---

[7] For details see Richard L. Nolan, "Managing the Crises in Data Processing," *Harvard Business Review,* vol. 57, no. 2 (March–April 1979), pp. 115–26.

FIGURE 21.7
Growth curves postulated by Nolan

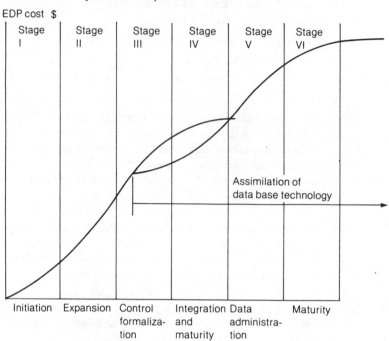

Source: Richard L. Nolan, "Thoughts about the Fifth Stage," *Data Base,* vol. 7, no. 2 (Fall 1975), p. 9.

to the firm's lack of maturity and experience, or lack of appropriate technical personnel.

It is often asked whether a firm can leapfrog over stages of growth. This is possible in small firms when software is purchased for a minicomputer. Such firms are often pressured by competition to adopt real-time systems as was Hotel West, described in Chapter 19, which started with a centralized online real-time system and integrated accounting applications without experiencing earlier stages of EDP development. The auto dealer, however, was more cautious, following Nolan's growth curve (using a minicomputer in decentralized functional applications), in spite of the purchase of software.

Larger firms may also skip growth stages if management and analysts have learned their lessons elsewhere. But leapfrogging is inadvisable in most cases. Generally, large complex businesses opt to follow an orderly growth curve, as did American Airlines with SABRE and AAIMS.

Nolan's growth curves are theoretical. In actual practice the slopes of the S's vary from one organization to another, depending on the firm's ability to absorb computer technology. The term **absorptive capacity** originally applied to economic development: the recognition that underdeveloped coun-

TABLE 21.2
Applications in the six growth stages

I	II	III	IV	V	VI
Initiation of decentralized jobs	Proliferation of applications	Consolidation of application Some networks	Selected data base application Individual networks	Integrated data resource management Integrated switched networks Satellite transmission Integrated voice data, facsimile, text editing	
Initiation of: Payroll Accounts payable Accounts receivable	Initiation of: Budgeting Cash Management Inventory Materials control Marketing Order processing Purchasing Stores control	Initiation of: Cost analysis Scheduling Financial and capital investment planning Personnel	Initiation of: DSS OLRT CAD Process control Numerical control	Initiation of: Electronic office DSS for strategic planning Advanced robots and CAM Word processing Personal computing	Refinement of: Text management CAI Heuristic modeling
Selected reduction of cost and labor-intensive jobs	Initiation of: Data base and telecommunication Minis and micros			Integration of data base, telecommunication with minis and micros	

TABLE 21.3
Processing mode in the six stages of growth (percentage)

Modes of processing	Stages					
	I	*II*	*III*	*IV*	*V*	*VI*
Batch	100	80	70	50	20	10
RJE		20				
Data communications processing				40	60	60
Data base processing			15			
Inquiries processing			10			
Time sharing			5			
Personal computing				5	5	5
Mini and micro computing				5	15	25
Total	100	100	100	100	100	100

Source: Reprinted by permission of the *Harvard Business Review.* Exhibit from "Managing the Crises in Data Processing" by Richard L. Nolan (March–April 1979). Copyright © 1979 by the President and Fellows of Harvard College; all rights reserved.

tries need an infrastructure, knowledge, and discipline to absorb massive aid. EDP also requires learning and experience before a firm can operate and manage a sophisticated integrated system. The lessons learned in extending applications progressively, adding new equipment and software with each phase of growth, enables firms to absorb and effectively utilize EDP technology. This absorptive capacity will affect the slope of each firm's growth curve.

Furthermore, no single growth curve can describe a firm's level of development in all applications at any given point of time. Instead, a series of parallel growth curves may be required. For example, a firm may be in Nolan's second stage in implementing word processing, the third stage in telecommunications, and fourth in its applications portfolio. Each organization's mix will be unique. Nevertheless, growth should be orderly, with a long-range systems plan for EDP expansion.

SUMMARY AND CONCLUSIONS

Integration of subsystems requires the linking of files and compatability of data. This integration can be horizontal, vertical, or longitudinal. When these three types of integration are combined, the system is a total system or an integrated MIS. The three dimensions of a total system are shown in Figure 21.8.

Integration can be initiated "top-down" as discussed in Chapter 12. The

TABLE 21.4
Organizational mode for the six stages of growth

Function	I	II	III	IV	V	VI
DP organization	Decentralized	Centralized computer	Centralized computer	DDP, utilities	Data resource management	
DP control	Lax, to encourage utilization	Lax, but controlled to facilitate growth	Formalized to contain supply of services	Formalized control to match demand with supply of resources Steering committee	Formalized control to contain demand	Formalized control to balance supply with demand
					Data administration	
User attitude and responsibility	Hands off	Superficially enthusiastic	User directly involved and accountable for quality and value added		User and EDP jointly accountable for quality and effectiveness of system	

top-down structured approach has the advantage of ensuring that the organizational goals and objectives filter throughout the design of the system.

Integration reduces the redundancy of data; eliminates duplication in preparation, validation, storage, updating, and filing; and permits calculations and report generation from multiple files for the production of information not previously available.

An example of limited integration described in this chapter is MRP, Materials Requirements Planning Systems. This system integrates procurement, customer order entry, bill of materials, production scheduling, shop floor control, and inventory accounting to minimize the cost of materials inventory and to ensure that materials required for production are available when needed. The components of advanced information systems are also described.

System integration of firms with foreign subsidiaries results in transborder

FIGURE 21.8
Three dimensions of total integration

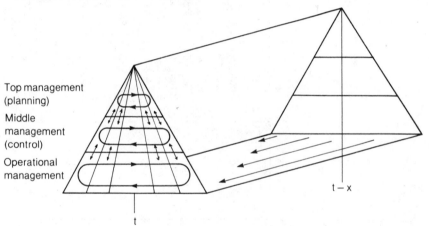

Top management (planning)

Middle management (control)

Operational management

data flow. Many countries consider this flow a threat to their sovereignty and have reacted by passing restrictive legislation on data transmissions.

Growth of EDP systems is stimulated by integration. The growth path favored by users may not be that recommended by analysts, for the two groups evaluate potential applications on the basis of different sets of criteria.

The ability of a firm to assimilate computer technology will also influence speed and direction of growth. The growth curves postulated by Nolan, representing six stages of development, apply to most firms. However, an additional S may have to be added to Nolan's curve to represent assimilation of recent computer technology (see Figure 21.9). The same slow acquisition of knowledge and experience may be required before a period of rapid implementation, growth, and integration of word processing, microtechnology, personal computers, glass fibers, lasers, conversational, graphic and intelligent terminals,

FIGURE 21.9
Current and possible future growth curves

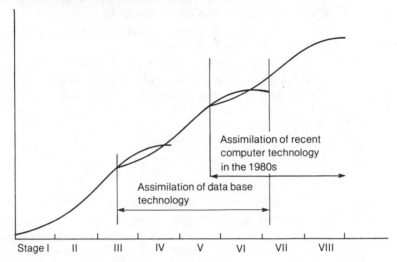

more powerful CPUs using Josephson junctions, large memory systems, and telecommunications.

KEY WORDS

Absorptive capacity
Advanced information systems
Airline integration
Analysts' priorities of growth
Chaining
Data integrity
Equivalence tables
Geometric organization
  syndrome
Growth paths
Horizontal integration

Integrated management
  information system
Longitudinal integration
Materials Requirements
  Planning System (MRP)
Nolan's growth curves
Table lookup
Total systems
Transborder data flow
Users' priorities of growth
Vertical integration

DISCUSSION QUESTIONS

1. What is an integrated system?
2. "A total MIS is a myth." Comment. Justify your position.
3. What is the difference between an MIS and an information system used by management in business?
4. What are the essential prerequisites of an MIS?
5. Why is a total MIS difficult to achieve in a large and complex organization?

6. Can an MIS be achieved modularly? Or must it be implemented all at once?

7. How are the basic functions in a business firm related to one another? How can they be integrated in an information system?

8. What are the stages in the growth and use of computer systems? Is it necessary to follow all the stages in sequence?

9. Why must a firm go through stages of growth for an information system?

10. What is the shape of the growth path for EDP operations? Is the same growth path followed for all types of applications or does each application have a unique path?

11. Distinguish between:
    a. Horizontal and vertical integration.
    b. Vertical and longitudinal integration.
    c. System and subsystem.
    d. Total information system and MIS.

12. What determines the boundaries of a system and subsystem?

13. What are the advantages and disadvantages to systems integration?

14. Can systems integration be achieved during operations after experience is gained with the system or should it be planned in the stage of system design?

15. Is it desirable and practical to plan and strive for a total system? Why?

16. Is the SABRE system a total system? If not, why not?

17. Why are many business systems not integrated even under desirable conditions? What is needed to achieve an integrated system?

18. Do you believe that there will be a third S curve above the two curves suggested by Nolan? Where will it start and end? For what industries? What will trigger and sustain a third curve?

EXERCISES

1. Can the applications in Exercise 1, Chapter 20 be independent of Exercise 1, Chapter 10 or should the applications be integrated? How can this integration be accomplished?

2. Suppose that your firm is planning a computerized information system for marketing and production records. Should this system be integrated with the finance file or should the system and the file be separate? Is integration beneficial to the manager? Explain.

3. Read John Dearden, "MIS is a Mirage." *Harvard Business Review,* vol. 50, no. 1 (January–February 1972), pp. 90–99 and one response by James C. Emery and C. R. Sprague, "MIS: Mirage or Misconception," *Harvard Business Review,* vol. 50, no. 3 (May–June 1972), pp. 22–23. Both are printed in V. T. Dook et al., *MIS—A Management Perspective.* Chicago: Science Research Associates, 1977, pp. 131–47. Do you agree with Dearden's arguments or the response by Emery and Sprague? Explain.

SELECTED ANNOTATED BIBLIOGRAPHY

Alexander, M. J. *Information Systems Analysis: Theory and Applications.* Chicago: Science Research Associates, 1974, p. 424.

Chapter 15 is on integrated information systems, including a case study on the POS-integrated application at Sears, Roebuck and Co.

Haden, Douglas H. *Total Business Systems: Computers in Business.* St. Paul, Minn: West Publishing Co., 1978. 463 p.

This text describes many applications of integrated and total systems.

Nolan, Richard L. "Managing the Crises in Data Processing." *Harvard Business Review,* vol. 57, no. 2 (March–April 1979), pp. 115–126.

This is one of many articles that Nolan has written on his growth hypothesis since its original publication in *ACM Communications,* July 1973. This article discusses the six stages in terms of applications portfolios, EDP planning and control, data base software, and investment benchmarks. Many good diagrams and tables are included.

Strassmann, Paul A. "Stages of Growth." *Datamation®,* vol. 22, no. 10 (October 1976), pp. 46–50.

An excellent discussion of growth theories (including Nolan's and Withington's), their limitations and refinements, as well as growth trends.

22

COMPUTERS IN MANUFACTURING

Computers are used to generate reports for operations, control, and planning in all functional areas of a business, including manufacturing. In addition, computers can be added as components to manufactured products, giving the products intelligence. Computers can also be used to automate manufacturing processes, for example, numerical control, the use of robots, and process control to monitor a continuous operation. They are also used in product design. The development of intelligent terminals with color graphic capabilities has made the latter use increasingly common. CAD, computer-aided design, can be implemented without other computer applications in manufacturing, but when integrated, CAD provides input for the other applications in manufacturing.

All of these diverse uses of computers in manufacturing, either as integral parts of a manufactured product or as a tool in the actual manufacturing process itself, will be discussed in this chapter. The nature and need for each computer application will be identified, the advantages and limitations will be presented, costs and hardware/software needs will be evaluated, and future use of each application will be considered. The importance of these subtopics differs with each application so that the emphasis and sequence of subtopics in each section will vary.

REPORT GENERATION

In manufacturing, as in all functional areas of a business, information must be gathered on operations for purposes of evaluation and control. Managers also require data for planning future production. Computerized information systems for job costing, production scheduling, shop floor control, equipment inventory, and so forth are common in manufacturing concerns. Table 19.16 (in Chapter 19) lists other operational computer applications that can be applied to manufacturing; Chapter 20 describes the use of computers to assist managers in planning and control.

SMART PRODUCTS

Computers can also be used as a component in a manufactured product. A **smart product** has a microprocessor embedded in its design which gives the product arithmetical capabilities, the ability to make choices (logic), and memory. Such products entered the market as a result of chip technology which has made microprocessors very inexpensive. Microprocessors of the type used in many smart products range in price from $2 to $5, depending on their capabilities and the lot size of production. Furthermore, microprocessors are tiny and reliable. Because they still need protection from oil, dust, and vibrations, manufacturers are constantly seeking to improve their design so that in the near future they will be robust, and be able to withstand rough environments. Examples of smart products include the following:

Smart taxi meters

A microprocessor can keep track of charges for up to five persons sharing a cab, each passenger with bags traveling to a different destination (luggage handling per piece is added to each bill).

Smart postal scale

A microprocessor has the capability of calculating the exact postage of weighed packages once the destination (either zip code or country code) is keyed in. The scale's postal rate charts are stored in the microprocessor's memory. The use of a smart scale saves labor costs, replacing employees that were formerly needed to calculate postal rates. Union Bank of Los Angeles calculated a savings of $8,000 in 1976 due to reduced labor costs (at a time when a smart scale cost $305.) An estimated 8 percent of all outgoing commercial mail is stamped with excess postage, so the accuracy of a smart scale is also a money-saver.[1]

Smart phone

A smart phone can store both emergency numbers (fire, police) and frequently used numbers, and will dial them when users press a specific key. The phone microprocessor will also keep dialed numbers in memory until a call is connected. Upon receipt of a busy signal, the line will be monitored until free and the call then automatically redialed. In addition, the phone can serve as an answering service, recording incoming messages for later reply, and can also be used as a home intercom system.

Smart microwave oven

Many ovens have time-bake capabilities but the timers cannot be set with great accuracy for the setting options are generally 15-minute blocks. Smart ovens can be set to the second, and can furthermore be programmed to

---

[1] *Business Week,* no. 2439 (July 5, 1976), p. 29.

perform a sequence of activities. For example, the user may preset a microwave oven to first defrost four pounds of rump roast for 2 minutes, followed by a 25-minute time delay for temperature equalization, and a cooking period of 56 minutes at temperature level five, and finally, an indefinite keep-warm at "hold" until the meat is served and the oven turned off. It took Amana four years to develop its smart microwave oven, but being the first among oven manufacturers to apply microprocessors to cooking, it was breaking new ground. Additional Amana smart products should take less development time. Each industry must acquire knowledge and experience in electronic-oriented production if it plans to produce smart products.

Smart clock

A smart clock can also be programmed to perform a sequence of activities. For example, the clock might be set to buzz gently at 6:38 A.M.; to turn on both the radio and coffee pot at 6:40 A.M.; to automatically retune the radio dial to music with a fast rhythm at 6:51 A.M.; and to ring the alarm loudly at 6:55 A.M.

Smart pilot

Microprocessors can be a cockpit aid to pilots by taking readings on temperature, wind velocity, direction and engine performance, then calculating optimum altitude for minimum fuel consumption, given the number of passengers. Flight testing has shown a fuel saving of 2–5 percent when such calculations are made.

Smart TV

TV game programs can be stored on cassettes and displayed on TV screens by microchip processors. Favorite TV programs can be recorded and stored for later replay. A smart TV connected to a phone is able to access information on theater bookings, weather, sales, and even information in the *Encyclopaedia Britannica*. Some of these services are offered by VIEWDATA in Great Britain. AT&T is currently testing EIS, Electronic Information Service, for such purposes in this country. With keyboard and interface, the smart TV can become a rudimentary home computer.

Future of smart products

Smart products will have even greater potential when chip technology merges with voice recognition technology. Imagine the convenience of departing for work after having left verbal instructions with a home computer to vacuum the house at 4:30 P.M. in preparation for dinner guests. The computer would turn on the vacuum at the prescribed hour and direct its path according to the house floor plan stored in its memory. Unexpected objects would be detected by a TV camera and appropriate deviations made. After cleaning all rooms, the vacuum would return to the closet and the computer would record a message to the effect that the task has been completed.

It is not the lack of technology that limits applications of smart products. Rather high program development costs limit the number of smart products on the market. Sales must either be voluminous so that the fixed initial cost is shared by many users, or multiple uses of programs in other products must be found. Sometimes additional applications of the microprocessor in a product will add to its appeal at little extra cost. For example, the smart clock might be used for thermostat control, or locking house doors at night. Smart products will sell only if the price is right and price is directly related to quantity produced and sold. Manufacturers must therefore be shrewd in assessing customer preferences and needs. There is great scope for creative designers and salespeople in the smart-product marketplace.

ROBOTS

Another use of computers in manufacturing is the addition of microprocessors to machines in order to automate control of machine processes. When the microprocessor controls performance of a specific manual task, the machine is called a **robot.** Robots are of particular value under conditions that are intolerable or dangerous to the human body. For example, following the 1979 nuclear accident at Three Mile Island robots were used to take samples to determine whether the degree of radioactivity was high and possibly dangerous to humans. Robots have also been used extensively in space exploration.

But many practical applications of robots involve no element of risk. A coffee cart programmed to negotiate corridors and stop at specific locations (the stops based on a historical record of demand) is one such application. Robots do not report late for work, get sick, or tire. Service goes on uninterrupted. Neither coffee breaks nor shift changes lower robot productivity. Robots do not demand pay hikes or rally against management. In the past, cost constrained their widespread use, but rising wage scales and the dramatic reduction in price of microchip technology have made robots economically viable today. A closer look at their capabilities, limitations, and potential is therefore in order.

How do robots work?

A photograph of an early industrial robot appears in Figure 22.1. The main components of a robot are schematically represented in Figure 22.2. Data is collected on the environment through a sensor, a device such as a photo cell with an amplifier having on-off light sensitivity. The sensor locates objects

FIGURE 22.1
Shakey, the robot developed at Stanford Research Institute

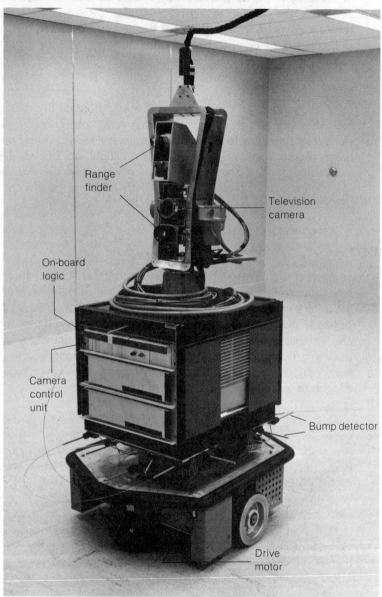

Courtesy Systems Research International

FIGURE 22.2
Components of a robot

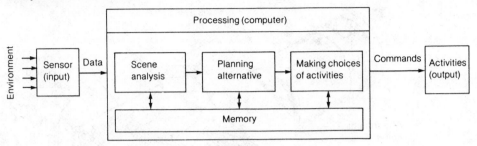

and a range finder determines their distance. Three-dimensional data is collected so that spatial images of the objects and their motion can be determined.

The data from the sensor is then processed by computer. First, scene analysis is performed. Light and shade patterns and densities are studied by the computer and spatial relationships of objects determined. TV cameras are sometimes used as sensors but their current effectiveness is limited, since technology for processing data from pictures is not highly developed. Next, alternatives for performing necessary actions are evaluated, given the environmental context by a procedure called **context-dependent processing.** That is, information stored in the memory of the computer regarding operational steps must be coordinated with environmental data collected by the sensors, so that the optimal strategy for the operation can be determined. Techniques incorporating artificial intelligence are used to analyze the data and choose the best operation alternative. The actual choice is then translated into commands to direct an actuator which performs the desired activity.

This activity may require robot arm movement. Figure 22.3 shows a sample robot arm. Maneuverability of such an arm will depend on arm sensors and size.[2] A warehouse, for example, might need arms for handling fragile items and arms with different capabilities for large, heavy crates.

Use

Robots are most effective in dangerous or hostile environments and for tasks that are structured and highly repetitive. For example, in an assembly environment, they can be used to stack parts. They may be activated by toggle switches, push buttons, joysticks, handlebar controls, or instructions from a keyboard. Though some voice recognition software has been developed, robots which can receive verbal instructions have very limited capabilities at the present time. Instructions accepted are of the following nature: go

[2] For an excellent discussion on sensors, see Charles A. Rosen and David Nitzan, "Use of Sensors in Programmable Automation," *Computer,* vol. 10, no. 12 (December 1977), pp. 12–23.

FIGURE 22.3
View of the arm of a robot

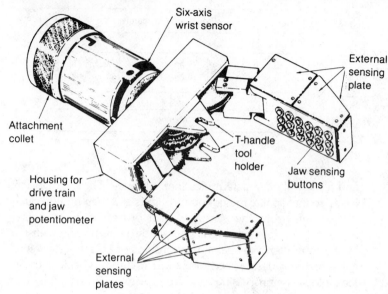

Courtesy Systems Research International

higher, stop, repeat last step, go two inches backward, and so forth. At present, robots have limited dexterity of movement and are not cost-effective for all activities. Trained employees are still needed to identify defective, soiled, worn, deformed, or cracked parts found in an assembly line. Robots also are unable to assist in assembly lines where turn-around parts are handled and they do not always recognize parts assembled in the wrong position. (Advances in pattern recognition should help alleviate this problem.) In addition, robots are still unable to coordinate activities with other machines in an autonomous multirobot environment.

Future of robots

Robots are being increasingly used in business operations. In 1979, for example, GM had 150 robots and planned for 330 other models. Ford, with 236 robots in 1979, planned a 50 percent increase in robot use for 1980. An obstacle to even greater expansion of robot use is labor union resistance rather than economic feasibility, because many workers, even highly skilled ones such as welders, can now be economically replaced by robots. (A $45,000 UNIMATE welding robot can replace two human welders and pay for itself in about one year).[3] Technological unemployment raises many social

---

[3] *Business Week,* no. 2578 (March 26, 1979), p. 75.

issues as well. Can man control robot machines? Will the widespread replacement of workers by labor-saving devices like robots mean that mankind will lose its sense of human value and purpose? It is time for our society to carefully evaluate the social implications of a robot world.

An advantage of increased use of robots and microprocessors is that they will help make U.S. industry more competitive on the world market, both in the price and quality of goods. This should expand sales. Though robots

FIGURE 22.4
Where robots could help

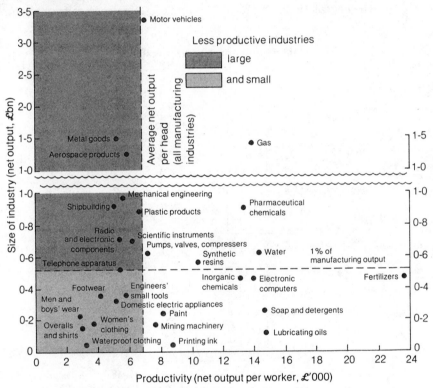

Source: *The Economist,* vol. 273, no. 7106 (November 10, 1979), p. 111.

may replace some workers, the net result should be an increase in jobs. The actual contribution of robots to productivity, however, will depend on the size and nature of the industry, as shown in Figure 22.4.

At present, robots are only economically produced in large batches. In the 1980s, smaller batches (e.g., 50) are forecast. This will enable the production of robots for specialized needs. The leasing of robots, as is now done in Japan, will also make robots available to small businesses.

NUMERICAL CONTROL (NC)

Computers have an increasingly important role in the manufacturing process itself. Formerly, operators played a far larger role on the factory floor than they do today. In the 1940s, for example, all drilling machines were manually controlled. Metal was placed in the machine by an operator who set the tool for the exact operation to be performed and turned on the power. Later the metal was removed, or perhaps turned, so new operations at different angles could take place and tools were adjusted for wear and tear.

In the 1950s, the operator's role was eliminated by hard-wired circuitry. In the 1960s, computers began controlling tools for machining as shown schematically in Figure 22.5. A computer generates instructions for operations

FIGURE 22.5
Offline numerical control machines

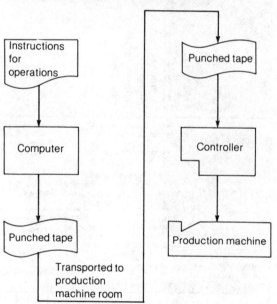

on paper tape or other input modes such as magnetic tape cartridges, cassettes, or more recently, floppy disks. The instructions may be coded sets of holes in cards or tape representing numeric data which tell the machine what operations to perform. From this the name **numerical control** was derived. In many cases, instruction preparation takes place on offline equipment, far away from the factory floor. The instructions are subsequently fed into a **controller** attached to a given machine which is a smart product or a full-fledged computer. The controller interprets the instructions on the tape and generates appropriate impulses that govern the positioning and operation of the tools. It even selects the necessary tools. For example, in boring a large hole, a series of small holes must be drilled. The numerical control machine will select the optimal number and tool sizes needed to perform the task as well as the optimal sequence, and then position the tool by three coordinates and dictate the speed of the drilling. The computer can also be programmed to make allowances for wear of the tool as experienced human operators do.

The precision of numerical control machines makes them invaluable. For example, in making a turbine blade which tapers in thickness to a fine edge, the blade can be tooled within a fraction of a millimeter of design specifications. If the same machine were needed for another similar operation, a new tape could be fed into the controller to direct the new operation.

Automation of factory machines has reached a high level of sophistication. It is currently possible to draw on a graphic terminal the shape of a two-dimensional machine cut desired. A printer will list the coordinates of the drawing, which are then converted on a keyboard device into punched paper tape, which is then fed into a controller which activates the cut on a numerical control machine and monitors it for accuracy. In the online version the image drawn on a terminal can be converted directly to instructions for the NC machine.

More complex operations in three dimensions can be programmed in special languages such as APT (Automatically Programmed Tool). Many factory operations have been programmed by software vendors and are available as software packages that can be adapted to a variety of production tasks. Large firms often have a library of programs for different operations, different combinations of which may be used to automate complex sets of operations.

Configurations for numerical control machines

One configuration of numerical control machines, represented schematically in Figure 22.6, is for **direct numerical control (DNC)** by a single large computer over different tools and production equipment. This centralized system was favored in the late 60s and early 70s when computers were expensive, but conflicts in priorities and delays often occurred, since a single computer was often overburdened and subject to breakdown.

Micro technology of the late 1970s made distributed and decentralized computers economically feasible. A computer used for NC costing $350,000 in 1965 dropped to $35,000 in 1970. By 1975 the cost was $3,500. This dramatic drop in price, if it continues, means that one computer per production machine or tool will soon be a reality. Distributed computers dedicated to a special task are optimized in design, which further reduce costs. The use of distributed computers also permits relatively autonomous modular growth of numerical control assembly lines. New equipment can be added with no disruption to the line, a departure from the "throw-away" philosophy that prevailed in earlier days when entire systems were uprooted when new numerical control machines were installed.

FIGURE 22.6
Direct numerical control machines

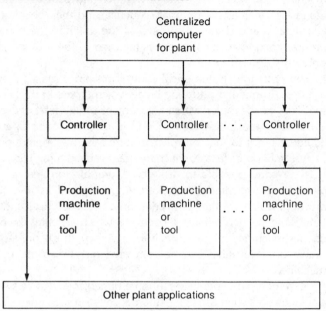

A schema for a **dedicated numerical control** system is shown in Figure 22.7. In this schema, a centralized computer schedules operations and monitors a number of numerical control computers attached to dedicated different production machines, thereby maximizing throughput and minimizing waiting time between jobs. The main purpose of the central computer is to coordinate and optimize the work of all numerical control machines, thereby improving overall plant efficiency. The **scheduling computer** receives its numerical control instructions from a NC programming computer on which NC programs are written online. Once debugged, these programs are forwarded by the scheduler to the appropriate NC machine for production.

The computers in numerical control machines, in addition to directing machine operations, can also run diagnostic tests to ensure that the operational steps are performed in the proper sequence and on schedule. For example, they can monitor temperatures and torques to see that they fall within allowable limits. Such testing need not interrupt the work of the machine but can be fitted into time slices when the machine is otherwise idle.

Future of numerical control

The low cost of minicomputers and microprocessors will definitely increase the use of numerical control. What is presently needed is the development

FIGURE 22.7
Network of dedicated numerical control machines

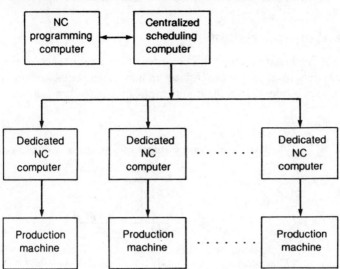

of new numerical control architecture with software and diagnostic packages for new applications. The greater use of distributed computers in tools and machines, each with stored NC programs, will eliminate the need for most human operators on the factory floor. Machine operations will be directed by commands keyed in from the console of a central computer. In this automated environment, manual operations would be limited to restocking raw materials and removing finished products.

PROCESS CONTROL (PC)

Another application of computers to production is **process control.** Unlike numerical control which deals with the manufacture of a discrete product or process (such as cutting a sheet of metal or milling a part), process control monitors a continuous activity, and checks key variables to detect variations from prescribed allowable tolerances; for example, monitoring the production of chemicals, the manufacture of paper, or the generation of electricity. When deviations of prescribed norms occur, corrective action is quickly taken and/or human operators are alerted to prevent production from falling below standard, the ramifications of which could be very adverse, varying in magnitude according to the nature of the process being monitored.

The concept of process control is not new. What *is* new is the low price of computers, making computerized process control economically feasible for many plants that formerly could not afford it. The first process control computer cost $300,000 in 1958. In 1976 the price was $3,000, a decrease in cost by a factor of 100.[4] This is another example of how microtechnology has reshaped jobs performed by factory workers.

Nature of process control

The basic structure and components of a process control system are shown in Figure 22.8. In this figure, manipulated variables and disturbances are input, while intermediate and control variables are output.

FIGURE 22.8
Basic inputs and outputs of a process control system

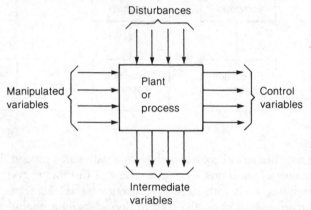

Source: Adapted from Cecil L. Smith, "Digit Control of Industrial Processes," *Computing Surveys,* vol. 2, no. 3 (September 1970), pp. 211–41.

Manipulated variables are predominately the flow of raw materials, but temperature and process would also be examples of variables that fall in this category. Disturbances may be environmental, such as air temperature and humidity, or relate to the quality of raw materials. Since adjustments must be made to ensure uniformity of the product when variables occur in the environment or materials, these input variables are labeled **disturbances.**

It is the computer's role in process control to evaluate performance of the system, to ensure that the process keeps within prescribed limits of factors such as production rate, product quality, and dimensions of product. These output variables, which must be constantly monitored, are called **set points.** Since set points for the limits must be controlled, the term ***control variables*** is used. The computer also checks intermediate variables, the output at given points during production, again comparing the results with predetermined

---

[4] *Business Week,* no. 2439 (July 5, 1976), pp. 42.

standards. The purpose of process control is to adjust manipulated variables to keep the system operating within the set points of control variables.[5]

To control a process, three components are necessary: **sensors,** a **processor,** and an **actuator.** Figure 22.9 shows how these components are interrelated. Sensors gather information on intermediate and control variables. The computer compares this information with set points stored in its memory to determine whether corrective action is necessary. If so, the actuator is instructed to make necessary adjustments to the manipulated variables. These adjustments have also been predetermined, based on given conditions, and instructions for corrections are also stored in computer memory. The corrections are then monitored by the sensors and the process reevaluated by the computer in a new control cycle.

FIGURE 22.9
Components of process control

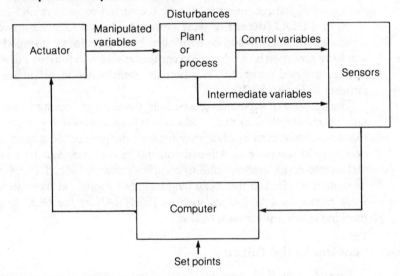

How often factory processes should be monitored is an important management decision. Frequent process control ensures high quality of output, but also entails high computing costs. There is also the possibility that conflicting demands for computing service may arise if several factories and/or several processes are being monitored by a single computer at frequent intervals. Timing for sampling must be balanced against the cost of sampling and how critical the control loop is to the manufacturing process. One rule of thumb that is widely applied is: sample every second for flow loops, every 5 seconds for pressure loops, and every 20 seconds for temperature loops.

---

[5] The terms *manipulated variables* and *control variables* are often confused. Though manipulated variables are under the control of a factory manager, control variables are preset by higher management, and are not within the floor manager's jurisdiction.

But each industry is unique and production methods vary, so optimal sampling frequency will obviously vary from one situation to another.

Equipment required for process control

Process control requires an online real-time computer, one that has the capability to activate sampling at timed intervals and take immediate corrective action. Because continuous processes have a long start-time, breakdown can be exceedingly disruptive and expensive. Computer backup and recovery capabilities are therefore very important. The process control system must include a digital computer with an analog-digital converter so data on flow and changes in pressure and temperature, for example, can be analyzed.

Though many processes can be controlled by one computer, microtechnology has reduced computer costs so much that it is now economically feasible in many cases to dedicate a computer to a single control process. If the dedicated digital computer is directly connected to sensors and actuators, it is called a **DDC (direct digital computer).** In a fully automated system, a number of DDCs would be controlled by **supervisory computers** which would be governed by a scheduling computer, which in turn would be regulated by a centralized computer. A schematic representation of such a hierarchy appears in Figure 22.10.

The purpose of supervisory, scheduling, and central computers is to coordinate process control so that production will be optimized in accordance with management objectives while making periodic production adjustments when necessary in response to external constraints and changes. To take all these factors into consideration requires complex software indeed. Programs should be written in efficient assembly language, but more and more programmers favor higher level languages such as FORTRAN at the DDC level, trading machine efficiency for ease of use.

Process control in the future

Process control is becoming increasingly attractive as a strategy for production and manufacturing, primarily because of the reduced cost of computer processing as a result of microtechnology. With greater development of software packages written in high level languages, usable on a variety of equipment and applicable to a wide range of problems, process control will certainly spread in use. Program packages under current development will perform diagnostic and maintenance monitoring in the future, help optimize processing, and provide management with needed data and comparative information for control purposes.

COMPUTER-AIDED DESIGN

Another production application for computers is **computer-aided design (CAD).** A design on a visual device such a graphic terminal can be

FIGURE 22.10
Hierarchy of computers for process control

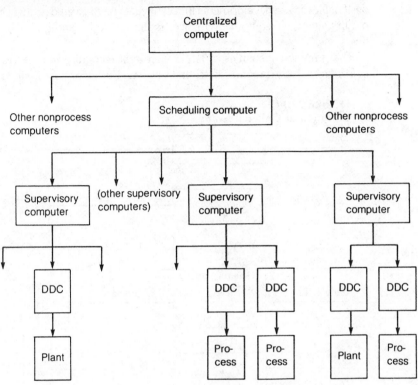

scaled, moved around on the screen and rotated in desired perspectives. The computer can perform calculations on the critical variables of a design and can also determine the effect of design alterations and modifications. Specifications can be stored in computer memory and then integrated with numerical control for actual manufacture of the designed product. Of course, there are many degrees of CAD sophistication. In this section, the discussion of CAD will open with a look at CAD hardware and software, followed by examples of industrial use, and an analysis of cost. Finally, CAD problems and future prospects will be examined.

Evolution of CAD hardware

A view of the evolution of CAD hardware is shown in Figure 22.11. Early keyed manual inputs were replaced by **digitizers** that used a hand-held pen-like device to trace diagrams and convert them into signals. These signals were processed by preprocessors (and later by computers) and converted into alphameric data.

Later versions of CAD introduced high level programming language statements and the use of a CRT with either offline or online plotting for product design. Hardware developments in recent years have given designers improved plotting and CRT equipment, minicomputer networks, and time-sharing facilities.

The graphic capabilities of CRTs were first recognized in the early 1960s in a doctoral dissertation, "Sketchpad," by Ivan Sutherland. Since then research

FIGURE 22.11
Evolution of CAD hardware

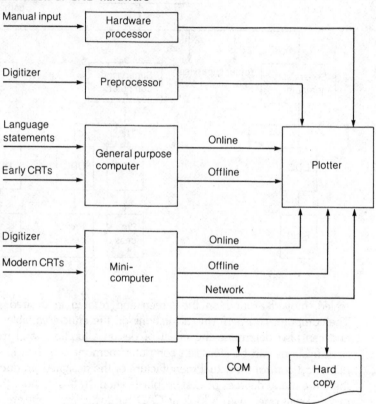

has refined CRT graphics. Circles and geometric shapes can be drawn or preprogrammed on CRTs and called to the screen by keying a command, then figures can be moved, scaled, or rotated by designers. A light pen sketch of these figures can be geometrically corrected (e.g., a circle can be drawn accurately for a given radius, or a hand-drawn line straightened). In addition, some modes of hardware offer designers 128 color choices. Texture can be added by a method called **collage.** A mix of texture and color, called **image mixing,** can give a screen design the illusion of a three-dimensional figure.

The most recent development in CAD is that image manipulation, collaging, and mixing can now be done by a minicomputer, either as a stand-alone mini or in a mini network. Specifications can then be sent to a printer, plotter, photo machine, or stored on microfilm for reference and further processing.

CAD software

The intelligence of CAD systems resides in software. Though approximately 1,600 CAD programs developed under NASA funding are in the public domain, many manufacturers prepare their own programs. In addition, graphic packages are available from software houses. A *Datapro* survey showed that 63 percent of the software purchased in 1976 required no modification; 19 percent required modification by the vendor; and only 23 percent by the user, so these packages have proved portable from machine to machine and to different products.[6]

CAD software aids in new product design by providing timely and complete information about proposed designs (that is, materials, weight, costs, performance criteria, and so forth). Such information is needed quickly, at the time new ideas are conceived, not hours or days later when the designer has turned to other projects. This quick access of information and feedback increases productivity by keeping designer involvement and interest at a peak, focusing designer attention on a single project. As a result, design lapse time is considerably shortened and any necessary changes or corrective action to design errors can be made quickly.

Increased designer productivity resulting from CAD was shown in a comparative study made of two firms that had contracted to design a complex traveling wave tube. The firm with CAD assembled 15 tubes and 10 qualifying prototypes in six months at a cost of $30,000 for software. The other firm, which used the conventional trial and error design process, built over 100 tubes at a cost of $300,000 and at the end of a year did not have a single prototype that met set specifications.[7] Of course, in this case both designers and design environments differed, so perhaps factors other than CAD influenced results, but there is considerable empirical evidence that CAD increases productivity by a factor of 6 to 15.

Firms using CAD systems can store their designs by software in a data base for archival purposes. These stored designs can be used as working drafts for future modifications, or for reference by other authorized designers working on similar design problems. Software may also be developed to integrate design specifications with production, coordinating and automating the steps leading from design to manufacture of the new product.

---

[6] Max J. Shindler, "Computer-Aided Design by Trial and Error—Just Find the Software," *Electronic Design,* vol. 12, no. 6 (June 7, 1977), p. 45.

[7] Shindler, "Computer-Aided Design by Trial and Error," p. 44.

Applications of CAD

Despite the high cost of CAD equipment and software, many firms believe that the reduction of time spent in designing products makes CAD cost-effective. As might be expected, the computer industry is in the forefront of CAD use. LSI (large-scale integration), for example, was primarily designed by CAD.[8] In other industrial applications, CAD has been used to:

Design and proportion bottle shapes, perform modeling and volume calculations for bottle molds, generate tooling of fixtures, jigs, and pumps, and prepare engineering drawings for a bottle molding and manufacturing facility.

Generate technical illustrations, both 2D and 3D, for instrument housings, assemblies, schematic and wiring diagrams, layouts, and so forth, for use in technical manuals of an electronics company.

Perform the mechanical design and layout of gear boxes, axles, springs, drive shaft, and so forth, for the undercarriage of truck models.

Design specifications for production machines of a company specializing in the manufacture of electrical wire fittings and plumbing fittings for the construction industry, since these machines cannot be purchased commercially.

Generate high quality, accurate engineering drawings to be used to perform manufacturing and assembly operations in an automotive firm. The drawings include designs of sheet-metal parts, electrical schematics, wiring diagrams, control panels, and so forth.

Produce layout drawings for architectural design, including plumbing, electrical, and heating for office buildings and factories.

In all the above applications, CAD is used to advantage both in the original product design and in later changes made in response to new contract specifications or altered marketplace preferences. All firms claim that the reduced drafting turn-around time provided by CAD gives them a critical competitive edge.

Note that the above applications in manufacturing are independent of numerical control. However, numerical control and CAD can be integrated. Figure 22.12 depicts such an integrated production process. Engineering drawing control receives data on product definition which is used by CAD to produce engineering drawings. This is shown in the top half of the figure. The lower half is concerned with manufacturing. Data of product design, provided by CAD, is sent to the numerical control program where data on routing (the sequence of operations), machine and work center data (the data on the machine to be used in each work center for producing each product), and tooling data (what tools are needed for each production stage)

---

[8] For details, see William Rosenbluth, "Design Automation: Architecture and Applications," *Computer*, vol. 9, no. 2 (February 1976), pp. 12–17.

FIGURE 22.12
Relationship of CAD and numerical control

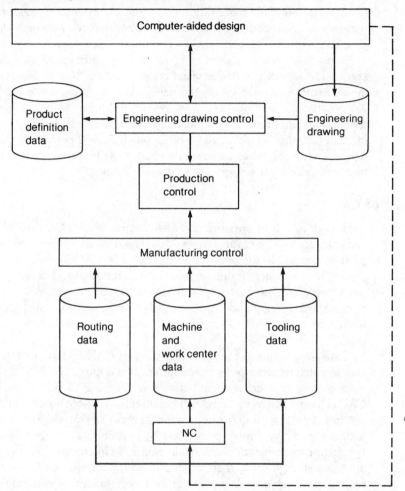

are specified. This data is needed for manufacturing control and production control. The direct link between CAD and numerical control is not essential to manufacturing (hence the broken line connection), but it is the ultimate objective of an integrated system.

The integration of numerical control with other operations in manufacturing is called **computer-aided manufacturing (CAM).**[9] Integration with CAD

---

[9] For an excellent case study of CAM, see Jerome F. Rickett, "On-Line Support for Manufacturing," *Datamation®*, vol. 21, no. 6 (June 1975), pp. 46–48. Discussed are six subsystems for sales order entry, shipping orders, materials control, shop floor control, and financial subsystems. For a case study of CAM at Levi-Strauss, see James R. Bensen, "The Intelligent Warehouse," *Datamation®*, vol. 22, no. 9 (September 1976), pp. 107–18.

is referred to as **CAD/CAM.** The extended meaning for this terminology is not yet accepted by everyone in the field of computer science but in a rapidly changing field names must constantly be adjusted to cover new developments or expanded operations. Unfortunately, name changes seldom keep pace with dynamic technology like computer technology.

Firms differ in the amount of computing resources they allocate to CAM and CAD. Generally, CAM is given priority, but at General Motors, a leader in CAD since the early 1960s, the reverse is true. A 1978 internal GM study "found that the use of computers in manufacturing now lags behind both design and data processing." The study concluded that "the use of computers in manufacturing would increase by as much as 400 percent in the five-year period ending in 1982 compared to just a 40 percent increase for design functions and 9 percent growth in data processing."[10]

Cost of CAD

How does a firm measure cost-effectiveness of CAD? Prices of hardware and software can be calculated, but how can a dollar value be given to better product design? In the application examples of CAD listed in the preceding section, the firms cited found improved product design and design turn-around more than offset hardware and software costs. CAD results in savings because of improved drafting and drawing capabilities as well. A cost study by Daniel Mullen shows a CAD saving/cost ratio of 2:1 (for a project of $154,000/year).

Costs vary with the sophistication of each CAD system. In 1975, though an integrated minicomputer-based system cost approximately $125,000, there were 500 such systems operational; one measure of how industry valued CAD. These systems included combinations of graphic input stations, digitizers, function keys to generate specific symbols or figures, joysticks to move a cursor in a two-dimensional plane or keyboard, an output station drum, light beam, microfilm or electrostatic plotter, an interactive CRT, large secondary mass storage (disk, tape, or drum), and a communications interface for remote processing.[11] The price of such equipment is currently dropping. Though this trend may not continue indefinitely, additional features will surely be added to CAD in the future that will increase the usefulness of CAD to industry and still keep it cost-effective.

Future of CAD

A recent survey sponsored by the Society of Manufacturing Engineers predicts that by 1985 there will be over 5,000 CAD installations, an increase by a factor of five over 1977.

---

[10] Robert W. Decker, "Computer-Aided Design and Manufacturing at GM," *Datamation®*, vol. 24, no. 5 (May 1978), p. 160.

[11] See Tric Teicholz, "Interactive Graphic Comes of Age," *Datamation®*, vol. 21, no. 12 (December 1975), p. 52.

CAD will continue to improve its cost-effectiveness and future technological developments will further reduce turn-around time from design to production. But a burden has been placed on designers who now find that industrial design requires knowledge about computers. A designer must learn about software capabilities and limitations, and must be able to communicate with a computer, to structure problems that the data base and the software can solve. The field of design now includes human-machine interface. As with all new technology, it will take time before the full benefits of CAD can be exploited.

PREDICTIONS FOR FUTURE USE OF COMPUTERS IN MANUFACTURING

The president of General Motors was quoted in 1978 as saying, "I think it is fairly safe to say that within ten years computers will control about 90 percent of all machines in GM's manufacturing and assembly plants. This doesn't mean computers will be replacing men nearly as much as it means that they will be helping our employees to do a better job."[12]

Certainly there is every indication that the use of computers in production will grow dramatically in the future. A Delphi study[13] conducted jointly by the University of Michigan and the Society of Manufacturing Engineers makes the following predictions:

By 1982

5 percent of assembly systems will use robots.

At least 50 percent of manufacturing managers will use computers for inventory control materials management.

Computer-aided design techniques for automatic designing of parts will be available.

By 1984

The technical problem of automated sensing and replacement of broken or damaged tools will be solved.

By 1985

Lasers will also be used extensively for in-process control.

Software systems will be available which will predict accurately the manufacturing cost based on part definition only.

Parts storage and retrieval will be integrated automatically in assembly production systems.

By 1986

NC and computer-controlled machines will produce 50 percent of all metalcutting machine tools.

---

[12] Robert W. Decker, "Computer-Aided Design and Manufacturing at GM," *Datamation®*, vol. 24, no. 5 (May 1978), p. 160.

[13] This technique requires respondents to express their opinions on a numerical scale. They are then informed of the statistical results of answers in relation to their responses. This process is iterated until there is a stability of opinion.

By 1987

15 percent of assembly systems will use robot technology.

20 percent of all companies will use computer-aided design.

66 percent of all manufacturing companies will find computerized management information systems suitable for their use.

About 38 percent of all manufacturing systems will be equipped with diagnostic sensors and associated software for implementing indicated changes or actions.

Software information for locating every individual part in a manufacturing facility will be in wide use.

The expanding use of computerized controls will permit prime contractors to transmit cookpiece configurations via leased wire to subcontract shops, and thereby reduce or eliminate the use of blueprints by 10 percent.

By 1988

50 percent of all direct labor for small component assembly will be replaced by programmable automation.

80 percent of all in-process and finished products will be controlled by computer.

30 percent of all manufacturing plans will be automatically generated by computers.

50 percent of all work force on the floor will be skilled persons operating automated plants.[14]

SUMMARY AND CONCLUSIONS

There are many applications of computers in manufacturing. Some are data processing applications as discussed in Chapter 19: the generation of management and operational reports on production subsystems such as ordering, materials handling, and product control. Numerous other applications which increase production efficiency include the use of microprocessors for activities such as the regulation of current amperage and speed to machine motors, or making energy-saving adjustments according to the load on the motor. In this chapter, specialized production applications were discussed; the use of computers in smart products, robots, process control, numerical control, and computer-aided design.

Smart products have embedded microprocessors that give them intelligence for decisions or choices based on calculations the computers perform. Robots are smart products used in industry. Initially they were introduced to replace employees in dangerous, unpleasant, monotonous or inhospitable environments. But they now are used in all types of production activities, for robot prices have dropped while labor costs are on the rise. Even skilled jobs, like welding and assembly line work, can now be done by robots.

In numerical control, computers direct machines for operations such as boring, planing, or milling. Each machine may have an individual microprocessor under the control of a supervisory scheduling computer. Computers also

---

[14] See *Delphi Forecast of Manufacturing Technology* (Dearborn, Mich.: SME Technical Division, 1977), 94 p.

process analog data provided by sensors in continuous processes as found in factories such as steel and paper mills. Microprocessors check sample data against standard performance criteria and initiate corrective action if necessary. As in numerical control, process control computers can be linked in a network so as to optimize overall plant production and throughput.

Computers are also used in product design. Critical variables in design can be simulated, and design alternatives studied from varying perspectives. CAD can also provide drawings and specifications for production which can be integrated with numerical control for the automation of all steps from design to manufacture of a product.

The use of computers will disrupt the labor force. Many workers will have to be retrained. Others will be displaced and face unemployment. However, computers, especially micros in production, will increase U.S. productivity, which is essential because our competitive industrial edge in the modern world is being seriously challenged. Currently, the incompatibility of micros limits our ability to exploit micros to full advantage. The large number of micro manufacturers, 4,000 in the United States alone, is one reason for this incompatibility.

Though the United States is an acknowledged leader in computerized automation, both quantitatively and qualitatively we presently lag behind many nations in the industrial use of robots. ASEA, a robot designed in Sweden and produced in Japan, is more sophisticated than any robot produced in the United States. Volvo in Sweden and Peugot in France use highly complex robots in their factories, perhaps the most sophisticated robots in the world.

One reason Japan is being increasingly successful in computer technology and applications is that the Japanese government has supported private business in computer use and manufacturing. At the end of the 70s, a three-year annual subsidy of $360 million was given Japanese business for the coordination of computer development. The Japanese government has also launched a $50 million project to foster the use of robots in industry and has spent $55 million (as of 1979) toward an experimental fully automated factory scheduled for completion in 1983. In the United States, advances in computer technology rely almost exclusively on private enterprise.

A great surge in smart products will occur when voice output units are economically feasible for mass production at low cost. These units added to microprocessors will result in a proliferation of new products. Imagine a stove which gives oral recipe directions or a thermometer that recommends clothing on the basis of weather conditions. How about a freezer that announces food needing restocking? The production of such items will not only create new jobs but will add enjoyment and comfort to our lives.

KEY WORDS

Actuator
CAD/CAM
Collage

Computer-aided design (CAD)
Computer-aided manufacturing (CAM)

Context-dependent processing	**Manipulated variables**
Controller	**Numerical control (NC)**
Control variables	**Process control (PC)**
Dedicated NC computer	**Processor**
Digitizer	**Robots**
Direct digital computer (DDC)	**Scheduling computer**
Direct numerical control (DNC)	**Sensor**
Disturbances	**Set points**
Image mixing	**Smart product**
Intelligence	**Supervisory computers**

DISCUSSION QUESTIONS

1. What is a smart product? What is a smart terminal?
2. Discuss functional applications of computers in manufacturing in:
   a. Design of product.
   b. Manufacture of product.
   c. Testing of product.
   d. Control of manufacturing process.
   e. Performance of product.
3. What are the implications of CAD on the manufacturing process?
4. How can robots be used in:
   a. A house?
   b. An office?
   c. Manufacturing of a part?
   d. An assembly plant?
   e. A continuous industrial process?
5. There are more industrial robots in Japan than in the United States, yet some of those are manufactured from U.S. patents. Why is this the case? What limits robot use in the United States?
6. What are the economic and social implications of industrial robots?
7. What is the difference between numerical control and process control? Give examples (other than from text) of each.
8. How can numerical and process control be used in fully automating production? What industries and tasks are most appropriate for each type of control? Give examples from industry.
9. What is the potential of CAD in industry in the United States? How will CAD use vary between industries? Why this variance?
10. What is needed to integrate NC, PC, and CAD? What would be the effect of this integration?
11. Do you believe that the predictions of the Delphi study on use of computers in industry are optimistic or realistic? Do you dispute the predictions or the dates?
12. What is the effect of CAM on:
    a. Productivity?
    b. Competitiveness?

       c. Unemployment?

       d. Society?

13. Comment on the statement: A computer is nothing but a fast arithmetic machine. It is an obedient intellectual machine that can do only what it is told to do.

14. Describe briefly smart products not mentioned in the book now available on the market.

EXERCISE

1. Draw a diagram showing the use of robots:
       a. In an assembly plant.
       b. In an office.
       c. In production.
       d. In connection with numerical control.
       e. In connection with process control.

SELECTED ANNOTATED BIBLIOGRAPHY

Arbib, Michael A. *Computers and the Cybernetic Society.* New York: Academic Press, Inc., 1977, pp. 283–97.

    The author has a background in artificial intelligence and so the discussion focuses on whether robots can think and how artificial intelligence can be used to make robots perform human activities.

Barash, M. M. "The Future of Numerical Controls." *Mechanical Engineering,* vol. 101, no. 9 (September 1979), pp. 26–31.

    This is a survey of hardware and software for numerical control with predictions for technology of the future. According to Barash, inspection, parts handling, and even some management functions will be incorporated into computer-controlled automated manufacturing systems by the year 2000.

Bertram, Raphael. *The Thinking Computer.* San Francisco: W. H. Freeman and Co., 1976. 322 p.

    This book, one of a series of books in psychology, describes the use of computers in problem solving and intellectual activity. There is an excellent chapter on robots, including a case study on the earliest robot, Shakey.

"Computer-Aided Design and Manufacturing." *Manufacturing Engineering,* vol. 83, no. 4 (October 1979), pp. 73–82.

    This is a bimonthly report on CAD/CAM. This issue discusses minis in process planning and inventory control and also the evolution of a computer-based manufacturing system.

Smith, Cecil L. "Digital Control of Industrial Processes." *Computing Surveys,* vol. 2, no. 3 (September 1970), pp. 211–41.

    This is an old reference when it comes to computer hardware and software, but it is still valid when it comes to basic concepts of process control. This is a well-written article by an authority on the subject. It has a rich bibliography of 23 references, each with a very short annotation.

Willette, Edward J. "The Computer's Role in Numerical Control." *Manufacturing Engineering,* vol. 19, no. 3 (September 1977), pp. 36–37.

    Each page of this article is rich in content. This is certainly one of the best short articles on numerical control.

23

COMPUTERS IN THE OFFICE

Computer office applications are the subject of this chapter. Electronic mail, teleconferencing, the war room, electronic fund transfer, and word processing will be examined. The applications can be implemented independently or integrated in an electronic office. In this chapter, each application will be treated independently; the integrated approach in an electronic office is the subject of Chapter 24.

ELECTRONIC MAIL

Using computer technology, especially teleprocessing, to transfer messages is called **electronic mail. Instant mail** is another term used, emphasizing the speed with which messages are conveyed. Though speed is lacking in conventional mail delivery, the U.S. Postal Service provides home delivery of mail at low cost. Electronic mail can be delivered only to other computer terminals at a cost exceeding postal rates at the present time, but electronic mail may overcome cost limitations in the near future. This section will discuss electronic approaches to message transfer, the efforts being made to increase public convenience, and the prospects of electronic mail in the future.

Use of electronic mail

At the end of the 1970s, the U.S. Postal Service was spending $13 billion annually on mail delivery. Only 20.2 percent of this mail originated with individuals. The rest represented communications from one office to another (that is, government to business, government to government, or business to business), or from government or business to private households. Seventy percent of all first-class mail was generated by computers, much of this mail being destined for other computers. Computer output mailed conventionally must first be burst into sheets (*to burst* means to break the perforations in a roll of computer output to produce pages), then stuffed into envelopes, transported to a mail room for stamping, delivered to the post office, taken to port of destination, re-sorted, and distributed. These steps could be eliminated if the output were transmitted electronically to a terminal of the recipient.

According to James Martin, 45.5 percent of all mail is potentially deliverable by satellite, bypassing traditional mail sorting and delivery methods.[1]

Much of the mail in the 1980s will be deliverable to end users by systems such as SBS and XTEN described in Chapter 5. Order acknowledgments from one business to another, for example, fall into this category. In addition, an estimated 22.8 percent of mail might be delivered by satellite to a post office for local distribution. For example, monthly bills to individual households might be sent in this fashion. It is estimated that available technology could electronically deliver the equivalent of 50 billion pieces of mail per year in the 1980s. If only 1 percent of this volume were actually transmitted, it would pay for a large satellite system. No wonder so many firms are researching improved transmission technology at low cost, for electronic mail has the potential of reducing costs substantially.

Business persons in all fields have a vested interest in the development of inexpensive electronic mail, for many firms conduct a large share of their business by mail. One division of a $500 million company reports that it generates an average of 800 printouts daily, many of which are duplicated for distribution, requiring 1.3 tons of paper monthly and a mail room staffed by five full-time clerks. This commitment of resources to mail is not uncommon.

The telephone is another communication device on which many firms rely. Busy signals, no answer, or equipment failures cause an estimated loss of 200,000 man-years of caller-time per year in the United States, or a $3 billion waste (based on $15,000 per man-year).[2] Electronic mail equals telephone communications in speed yet permits the storage of the message should the intended party be unavailable.

There are many **modes** of electronic message transfer that can be categorized as electronic mail. A message sent from one computer terminal to another is only one of these modes. Mailgram, a joint venture of Western Union and the U.S. Postal Service for overnight delivery of business messages, is another. So is TELEX by Western Union, and FAX; the latter electronically transmits text or graphic materials to a service such as Datapost, which then sorts and packages the messages by zip codes in 25 cities and gives them to the post office for next-day delivery. FAX currently has problems of machine compatibility and is slow in transmission, taking between 1½ to 6 minutes to transmit a document copy comparable in quality to a Xerox copier. The process is also costly. A document page in facsimile form requires 200,000 bits. That is 1,000 times the number of bits required for a typical telegram, and 60 times that of a typical office memo.

Electronic mail requires that the addressee have access to a computer for receipt of messages. Currently, electronic mail is used predominantly for telegrams, memos, and short office messages. Citibank of New York City[3]

---

[1] James Martin, *Wired Society* (Englewood Cliffs, N.J.: Prentice-Hall, Inc., 1978), p. 105.

[2] *Ibid.*

[3] For details, see Fredrick W. Miller, "Electronic Mail Comes of Age," *Infosystems*, vol. 24, no. 11 (November 1977), p. 64.

has an operational service, and several national networks for electronic mail exist, such as the **ARPA (Advanced Research Projects Agency),** though ARPA was originally designed to facilitate the sharing of hardware, software, and data resources. In 1969 when it was initially put into operation, the network consisted of only four terminals for the U.S. Department of Defense. By the late 1970s, thousands of users had access to the expanded network as a substitute for telephone calls, letters, memos, and even conferences, the latter being multiperson dialogues transmitted to and from several network stations.

When host computers on the ARPA net are not of the same manufacture or model, a network interface is required. **Interface message processors (IMP)** then handle and route messages in packages to connected host computers, the speed of transmission varying between one and two seconds. Connected terminals which have terminal IMPs are called **TIP.**

The exact capabilities of electronic mail systems vary, depending on their hardware and software configurations, but the following scenario is technologically feasible at the present time and may become commonplace in the future.

Scenario of future use of electronic mail

The secretary's office has a CRT-typewriter terminal with a programmable 10-key pad sitting on a desk cleared of paper stacks. When the secretary keys a message into the computer, it is validated by a spelling-checking routine, centered, and spaced with both right and left margin justification by software. Input messages are addressed to an individual, or keyed by subject to be sent to all persons on a distribution list for that key. A hard copy of the message is automatically printed for the files, and the message itself conveyed to the CRT of the addressee(s) on which an identification number of the intended recipient flashes to announce the arrival of a message. The message itself appears on the screen once a code or password is keyed into the computer identifying the recipient, the code or password which matches that specified by the sender. After reading the message, the receiver can have it stored or deleted. When more than one message has arrived, a request for a list of senders to be displayed on the CRT can be keyed. The recipient can then decide in which order the messages should appear on the screen, or simply command last-in-first-out (LIFO) or the reverse, first-in-first-out (FIFO).

A traveling sales representative or manager may carry a portable terminal for communications with the home office, or use equipment at branch offices to query the home electronic mail box. Messages received may be rerouted from the home terminal to the traveler, who can then relay instructions electronically to a secretary regarding what responses to make. A draft message can be modified or corrected, then transmitted to the terminal of the addressee directly, with a hard copy of the message produced for home office files or stored in computer memory. If the intended recipient of the message does not have access to a terminal, the message can be directed to a computer service in the vicinity of the addressee, which prints a hard copy in batch processing and mails the message to the addressee for next-day delivery.

Sometimes a manager wishes to reference previous correspondence when drafting a message response. The computer can retrieve past correspondence or memos by subject, key word, name of addressee, date, or a combination of identifiers when programmed to do so. Other information from the data base can be referenced, extracted, and chained to standard letter formats to constitute a message.

Advantages and disadvantages of electronic mail

Electronic mail increases secretarial performance by a factor of between two and three.[4] Retrieval and file management capabilities are particular strengths. In addition, the system is quieter than conventional typewriters and reduces the need for office storage since cabinets with filed correspondence are replaced by computer memory. Firms with computerized information systems already possess most of the hardware needed. It is only when terminals or minicomputers are used exclusively for electronic mail that hardware becomes a significant cost consideration.

In spite of obvious advantages, managers tend to be ambivalent in their attitude towards electronic mail. They like the speed, retrieval, and cross-indexing capabilities; like being shielded from constant interruptions by jangling phones; and like receiving and responding to messages when convenient. But management style must change. Margin notes can't be jotted when messages appear on a screen, mail can't be taken home for late night work sessions, nor can management pass copies of messages to associates in conferences unless hard copies are printed, in which case one raison d'être of electronic mail is defeated. Furthermore, electronic mail eliminates the need for voice or personal contact in many business situations. Gregarious businessmen miss the human interplay lost when visual messages replace a phone call or office visit with an associate.

Future of electronic mail

The extent to which telecommunications will be allowed to compete in mail and message transfer with the U.S. Postal Service will determine the future of electronic mail. Cost will become competitive with traditional delivery once competition is allowed, for large-volume message handling will reduce transmission costs and be incentive for innovative technological developments. Once firms are allowed freedom to use electronic resources for communications, systems will be designed for transmission not only of data and text, but voice, video, and facsimile as well. Communication centers will be struc-

---

[4] Richard G. Canning, ed., "The Automated Office: Part I," *EDP Analyzer,* vol. 16, no. 9 (September 1978), p. 4.

tured with integrated equipment, procedures, and data processing resources. Business will find it necessary to revise their whole approach to office communications, for electronic mail will become merely one feature of an electronic office (discussed in Chapter 24).

The future of electronic mail will also depend on how television is combined with computer technology. A VIEWDATA system already exists in England in which TV screens serve as terminals for display of requested information. Were this system expanded and widespread, messages sent by electronic mail might be received by TV owners, but in the United States such a system would further erode the prerogatives of the Postal Service. Television receipt of electronic mail would also require considerable refinement of existing TV equipment, for at the present time TV does not have the resolution to reproduce fine print, or even a letter in small fonts.

TELECONFERENCING

Whereas electronic mail is primarily for two-party communication, **teleconferencing** serves multiperson communication, linking conference rooms within a large company, or conference rooms between firms. Terminals provide access to the firm's data base and serve as electronic flip charts, displaying specially prepared materials stored in the base for participants at distant locations (information that might be presented on a flip chart at a conventional conference). Subgroups with access to terminals can communicate during the teleconference, and even "whisper" bilaterally. Travel time and travel expense can be eliminated. A study by Ferrera and Niles, comparing the cost of visual teleconferencing with travel in the New York-Chicago-Washington triangle, found a 1.2 advantage in teleconferences for a group of two; and advantage of 32 for a group of six.[5] Computers can also provide a recording of proceedings in teleconferences and give participants flexibility in scheduling meetings.

However, many executives prefer live meetings, relying on interpersonal relationships for conducting business. Teleconferences also require the development of new communication skills.

WAR ROOM (MULTIMEDIA CENTER)

War rooms originally served the military, being large halls with maps and multiple display screens where battles were planned and, more recently, strategies simulated, as in the SAGE system. NASA used the war room concept when establishing a communication and information center for space flight at Houston. Large businesses today have **multimedia centers,** an equivalent to military war rooms, where OLRT systems retrieve and process information

---

[5] Joseph Ferrera and Jack M. Niles, "Five-Year Planning for Data Communications," *Datamation®*, vol. 22, no. 10 (October 1976), p. 53.

needed for decision making and models simulate answers to "What if?" questions. Information is displayed on CRT screens, many of which have graphic and color capabilities. Top management, for example, might use the center to display statistics for the firm's predicted share of the market for five years, and then simulate "What if?" questions to weigh alternative marketing strategies. Or the center might be used to simulate results were a PERT chart for a major project altered. Sometimes such centers add teleconferencing capabilities, closed circuit TV, videotapes and other types of equipment to aid management decision making. The war room concept was used by the consortium Alyeska during construction of the Alaskan pipeline. It also serves small companies such as Gould Corporation of Rolling Meadows, Illinois.

ELECTRONIC FUND TRANSFER

In 1965, Thomas J. Watson, the then chairman of IBM made the following prediction:[6]

> In our lifetime we may see electronic transactions virtually eliminate the need for cash. Giant computers in banks, with massive memories, will contain individual customer accounts. To draw down or add to his balance, the customer in a store, office, or filling station will do two things: insert an identification into the terminal located there; punch out the transaction figures on the terminal's keyboard. Instantaneously, the amount he punches out will move out of his account and enter another.
>
> Consider this same process repeated thousands, hundreds of thousands, millions of times each day; billions upon billions of dollars changing hands without the use of one pen, one piece of paper, one check, or one green dollar bill. Finally, consider the extension of such a network of terminals and memories—an extension across city and state lines spanning our whole country.

This prediction is today much closer to reality. Technology for such electronic transactions exists, but resistance by individuals, banks, corporate firms, and regulatory agencies has slowed implementation. Known as **electronic fund transfer (EFT)**—an unfortunate name since the term implies physical transfer of funds—transactions are completed by computer and telecommunications. Information on checks (payee, amount, account number, check writer, depositor, institution) converted into electronic impulses is sent from one bank to another, a process known as **check transaction.** The check itself, that is, the paper on which the information is written, is not physically moved from one location to another. This is no trivial difference, for in 1978, 30 billion checks were written in the United States and a 7 percent annual growth in check writing has been forecast. EFT can eliminate the need for checks altogether if transactions are done on terminals such as **point-of-sale systems (POS)** in restaurants or department stores. Martin forecasts that eventu-

---

[6] Reprinted by permission of IBM.

ally there will be 50 billion such electronic POS transactions per year in the United States.[7]

Terminals can be used not only for fund transfers but to check bank balances to see whether customers do, in fact, have adequate funds to pay for purchases, or to check customer credit, reducing the risk of bounced checks. Systems can also check for reported stolen credit cards and monitor for possible stolen cards by analyzing frequency of use. While providing EFT service, terminals in retail stores can also collect information of interest to market planners and help monitor inventories. Other terminals can be used for automatic payments of bills, payment of insurance premiums, and cash dispensing.

EFT uses

Potential EFT users fall into three categories. These are organizations transferring funds through a bank, banks themselves making interbank transactions, and individuals in need of banking services. (In this context, banking includes all depository institutions, including savings and loan associations and credit unions.) How these three groups might use EFT, were it widespread, is described below.

ORGANIZATIONAL USE OF EFT

Organizations which regularly write large numbers of checks (for payroll or accounts payable, for example) can use EFT profitably, eliminating check writing for these applications entirely. Accounts payable information can be keyed on tape, listing names of payees, accounts, and banks to which deposits should be sent. This information can be sent electronically to the nearest **automated clearing house (ACH),** a computerized version of the traditional check clearinghouse. The ACH then transfers funds into banks where vendors hold accounts, sending the information on through the ACH network for nonlocal banking institutions if necessary. The transactions to the depository institutions are completed by the close of the banking day.

EFT BETWEEN BANKS

In terms of monetary value transferred, banks use EFT more than any other group. Early experiments with EFT included Fed Wire, CHIPS (Clearing House Inter-Payments System), and Bank Wire, a system developed by the Monetary and Payments System Committee of the American Banking Association. Bank Wire II replaced Bank Wire in 1978, after a $10 million, three-year study. The revised system is 30 times faster, sending 18,000 messages per day between 185 member banks with a daily value of transferred funds exceeding $20 billion.[8] The system sends administrative messages and miscel-

---

[7] Ibid., p. 100.

[8] Edith Meyers, "EFT: Momentum Gathers," *Datamation*®, vol. 24, no. 10 (October 1978), p. 53–55.

laneous reimbursement messages in addition to fund transfers. It has a 100 percent redundancy, with its backup system capable of switching into operation within seconds.

SWIFT (Society for Worldwide Interbank Financial Telecommunications) has provided international EFT service between banks since 1973. As of 1978 nineteen countries had participating banks with network expansion projected for the future, particularly for banks in Southeast Asia and the Pacific. The system is a ring network connecting major cities with backup circuits to provide alternative EFT routings should the primary circuits fail. Figure 23.1 illustrates this concept. The dark lines in this figure represent primary circuits, the broken lines backup. Should New York–Brussels be inoperative, electronic funds destined to Brussels could be transferred from New York through Montreal and Amsterdam.[9]

FIGURE 23.1
Segment of SWIFT ring network

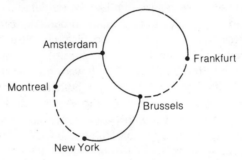

EFT USE BY INDIVIDUALS

Individual EFT transactions can also take place on terminals. These terminals, frequently located in retail stores (POS terminals) instantly debit a customer's account and simultaneously credit the keyed amount to a merchant's account. Terminals can also perform many of the functions of a bank teller. Called **automatic teller machines (ATM),** these terminals can accept deposits or payments on loans and bills, can authorize transfer of funds from one account to another, and can even dispense cash. They can also retrieve financial data from the data base for reference. When placed in a shopping mall, 24-hour service for routine banking operations is available to the public. (Tax counseling, loans, and investment services still require a visit to a bank.) In the past, ATMs have had problems keeping supplied with money for cash dispensing. One solution to this problem has been to place ATMs near supermarkets that wish to keep cash supplies minimal for security reasons. Regular deposits by the markets at the ATMs keep the terminals solvent.

---

[9] Angeline Pantages, "Is the World Building Data Barriers?" *Datamation*®, vol. 23, no. 12 (December 1977), pp. 90 ff.

Resistance to EFT

Terminals for the electronic transfer of funds have raised legal and regulatory issues. Court battles are being fought over laws regarding interest payments and branch banking, for example. The uncertainty of the law has caused many banks to be cautious, if not to resist, the use of EFT. Resistance also stems from the high cost of EFT, loss of float, problems regarding privacy and security of data, and fear of monopolistic control. Each of these considerations will now be discussed.

LEGAL ISSUES

Whether terminals performing banking functions are, in fact, branch banks subject to branch banking regulations was contested in 1974. A decision by the Comptroller of Currency, who regulates banking activity, stated that terminals did not constitute a branch, but a court challenge later partially overruled the comptroller, based on an interpretation of the McFadden Act passed in 1927. All parties recognize that laws as outdated as the McFadden Act need revision to fairly regulate computers in banking. But recommendations by a 1971 Presidential Commission on Financial Structure and Regulation and a 1974 National Commission on Electronic Fund Transfer calling for increased competition in the banking industry were not translated into law. The battle has now shifted to state courts, for both federal and state-chartered banks must follow state laws of branching. A patchwork of regulations currently exists. In general, states with heavy population densities support statewide branching, whereas rural states limit branching. Federal legislation will be required before interstate EFT or nationwide EFT networks can be established.

Another legal issue has been raised by the use of EFT by thrift institutions such as savings and loan associations which offer third-party payment facilities to customers through EFT terminals. This puts thrifts in competition with commercial banks but with a decided advantage since thrifts give interest on checking accounts. This restructuring of the traditional relationship between banks and thrifts is being contested by banks which demand laws to regulate EFT use by competitors.

The fact that EFT strains the resources of small institutions due to the high cost of terminal equipment also has legal implications. Small businesses find themselves unable to offer EFT services which large institutions can afford. Many states have passed mandatory sharing laws for EFT terminal equipment, but the Department of Justice has recently declared these laws in violation of antitrust legislation. Here, again, legislators must grapple with the implications of EFT in a free enterprise system.

Given the inadequacy of present laws and uncertainty over future legislation, it is not surprising that resistance to the spread of EFT exists.

COST

The capital cost of EFT is very high. Citibank, for example, has spent $150 million on its EFT network. A 1978 IBM study estimating 1985 EFT equipment needs forecasts 32,000 ATMs and 50 ACHs to handle 15 percent of all check-type payments through direct deposits, and 400,000 POS terminals to replace another 6 percent of the check volume. The total cost: $2.7 billion.[10]

FLOAT LOSS

There is generally a four to seven day interval between the time a check is written and the time a check is cashed. The value of checks or drafts in transit and not yet collected is known as **float.** In effect, float constitutes an interest-free loan to check writers during this period. Many corporate firms invest float amounts in short-term loans, in many cases using sophisticated mathematical models to optimize the employment of float funds. Both advantages, interest-free loans and short-term investments are lost with EFT, for the speed of electronic processing reduces float to one day. Of course, if all payments were made by EFT the loss of float funds would be regained by accounts receivable. There is even the possibility that EFT would be profitable should accounts receivable exceed accounts payable. But firms have no control over how clients pay their bills. A company using EFT for bill payment but receiving income by traditional checks stands to lose money. No wonder cash managers oppose EFT.

On the other hand, fast processing of transfers and exact information on the status of funds enable firms to reduce demand deposits and mobilize idle money. Funds can be transferred on a daily basis. This movement will have an important effect on our economy because of the magnitude of funds involved ($20 trillion in checks per year translates into $54.8 billion for a one-day float). A detailed discussion of macro effects of EFT is beyond the scope of this book,[11] but briefly, increased demand for demand deposits and the conversion of liquid holdings into "near-money assets" such as Treasury bills and commercial paper would cause a rise in profits and a corresponding rise in the GNP. The normal increase in income velocity of money (the ratio of GNP to demand deposits and currency) is 3 to 3.5 percent a year. Should EFT cause a spurt in this velocity by encouraging the flight of demand deposits, the Federal Reserve would initiate policy to curb the exodus and help bankers hold on to their demand balances. It might recommend payment of competitive interest rates on demand deposits for example, but this would require a change in the legal framework of current banking practices and would profoundly affect all financial intermediaries.

PRIVACY AND SECURITY CONSIDERATIONS

The ease with which financial records can be accessed by EFT raises concerns about individual privacy and the security of financial data. EFT systems

[10] Frederick W. Miller, "Checkless Society Gets Closer," *Infosystems,* vol. 26, no. 3 (March 1979), p. 52; and Kathryn H. Humes, "The Checkless/Cashless Society? Don't Bank on It," *Futurist,* vol. 12, no. 5 (October 1978), p. 303.

[11] See Rose Stanford, "More Bang for the Buck: The Magic of Electronic Banking," *Fortune,* vol. 95, no. 5 (May 1977), pp. 202–09.

have all the security problems generic to data processing systems as discussed in Chapter 16 and two additional weak spots: input identification and telecommunications.

Most terminal systems for EFT are accessed by a plastic card identifying the user's account, but the danger of theft or loss of a card makes this control inadequate. Keys can be stolen for locked terminals and a determined thief will breach a password code. Voice, hand form, or fingerprint recognition are the best security. However, such systems are not economically feasible at the present time.

The use of codes and both encryption and decryption equipment help protect data in transmission. Fewer incidents of attempted theft are reported with EFT than with conventional methods of fund transfer, but the potential loss per incident is much greater. The vulnerability of telecommunications and the limit of liability to the customer prescribed by law makes many financial institutions cautious about embracing EFT.[12]

In an effort to protect privacy of financial data, Congress passed the 1978 Right to Financial Privacy Act, incorporating recommendations of the Privacy Protection Study Commission for safeguarding records of individuals and small partnership customers of financial institutions from unauthorized governmental access. Another law, the Electronic Fund Transfer Act, requires financial institutions to periodically document to customers all transfers. Maximum liabilities and steps for the correction of error are also prescribed. There is still concern that individuals are not adequately protected by legislation in the electronic age, that EFT is an additional threat to individual privacy. This is another reason resistance to EFT exists.

CONCERN OVER MONOPOLIES

Small banks and thrifts are afraid EFT will lead to concentration of deposits in fewer and fewer banks. There is some evidence to support this concern. For example, Chase Manhattan estimated in 1977 that over $50 million of the $250 million received by EFT would have gone to smaller banks were it not for the bank's EFT service.[13] Alarmists see Citibank spreading westward and Bank of America eastward, swallowing smaller financial institutions in their paths. Though antitrust laws, and legislation regarding branch banking, should prevent bank monopolies, resistance to EFT is partially based on this fear.

For many employees, receipt of a paycheck is the best part of the workweek. A check in hand or cash in pocket gives a sense of well-being and accomplishment that is lost in electronic fund transfer. For such individuals, cash and checks will remain the primary media for monetary transactions, though such persons will probably use cash dispensing terminals and other services of

---

[12] For a detailed discussion of this subject, see Linda Flato, "EFT and Crime," *Computer Decisions,* vol. 7, no. 10 (October 1975), pp. 30–33.

[13] Sanford, "More Bang for the Buck," p. 204.

EFT, such as credit verification. A greater effort to humanize EFT, for example, designing pleasing terminal environments and providing personnel to assist users, should help reduce consumer resistance to EFT.[14]

Pros and cons of EFT

Table 23.1 summarizes the advantages of EFT and the reasons EFT is resisted. The fast processing of EFT is cheaper than handling cash, credit cards, and checks. Credit card processing exceeds 50 cents per transaction, with every indication that this cost will rise. The equivalent transaction by

TABLE 23.1
EFT pro and con summary

Party	Advantages	Reasons for resistance of EFT
Corporate firms	Better cash management	Loss of float
Supermarkets and retailers	Quick check and credit card approval, which contribute to higher sales and market share	Capital cost of EFT
Financial institutions	Low cost of processing electronic transactions	Fear of monopolies
	Automated teller machine services	Insecurity of data
Consumer	Provides convenience of: Automatic cash dispensing Direct deposits Direct payments of bills Home terminal transfer	Loss of float Potential loss of privacy Lack of "in-hand" cash

EFT costs only seven cents and this cost should drop with improved technology.[15]

A benefit not listed in Table 23.1 is that street muggings and hold-ups should occur less frequently when most transactions are by EFT rather than the actual physical exchange of money. Individuals will simply not carry cash to be stolen.

---

[14] For a consumer advocate's viewpoint, see Cary Maple and Blair C. Shick, "Consumers: Forgotten Factors in the EFT Formulae," *Bank Administration,* vol. 5, no. 2 (February 1977), pp. 20–25.

[15] Martin, *Wired Society,* p. 93.

WORD PROCESSING (WP)

Word processing is another major application of computers for office management. The data processed is not numbers but text. In 1976, 15 million secretaries, typists, and clerks were employed in the United States. With office costs rising yearly, businesses have begun to recognize the value of WP, a computerized system of hardware and software for transforming ideas into printed text. Computers can compose and format correspondence, and can edit, revise, update, duplicate, and file data for memoranda, contracts, reports, manuals, and reference materials. Word processors can also automate conversion of documents into machine-readable form, provide copy storage, and facilitate the flow of information in an office through reference and retrieval capabilities. In short, WP aids document creation and record keeping. Linkage with equipment for electronic mail speeds office communications considerably.

Nature of word processing

An overview of word processing is shown in Figure 23.2. Input may be in the form of printed material such as documents or mail converted into machine readable text by means of **OCR (optical character recognition)** or facsimile equipment, it may be gathered by voice recognition equipment, or may be entered by keystroking on a hard copy terminal or CRT system, a process similar to typing. Word processors may also draw upon data (text) stored in computer memory for input. For example, a computer memory can store an encyclopedia of statistics, quotations, standard responses to common queries, and text previously processed. Information from trade journals may also be extracted and placed in storage for references, or articles may be entered in their entirety after being indexed for retrieval. There are currently 100,000 magazines on the market. Computer retrieval of information in these magazines helps businesspersons keep abreast of the latest developments in their fields for future document generation.

The text chosen for output is formatted under software control. This includes centering, left and right justification, and horizontal and vertical spacing on a page. In conventional text preparation, 38 percent of all copy goes into the wastebasket because of typewriting errors. The nervousness a typist feels, particularly near the end of a page when an error will require retyping the entire page, is eliminated in word processing since corrections can be made one letter, one word, one line, or one paragraph at a time, the word processor making all the necessary format adjustments for corrections automatically. Insertions and deletions can also be performed easily by one command. A dictionary stored in memory can be referenced quickly to check on spelling and syllable divisions.

Text stored in memory, once edited, can be reproduced without mistakes, a tremendous saving over conventional typing where each retyped copy is subject to error. However, text in memory may have to be updated or revised.

FIGURE 23.2
Overview of word processing

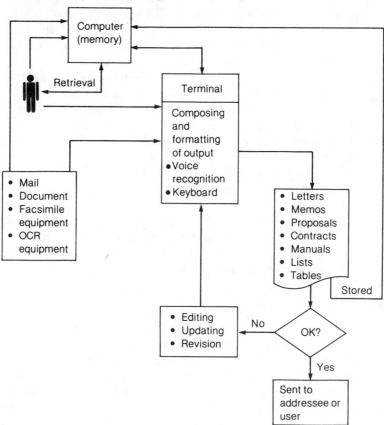

A final check must therefore take place after the output text is composed to be sure all editing has, in fact, been done. The document can then be printed at 400–900 words per minute. When the text has been prepared on a CRT, a code releases the text from the screen into memory and starts the printing. A second page of text can be composed while the first is being printed, or can be stored in auxiliary memory for later printing in batch mode if desired.

When the output is correspondence, the computer can be programmed to personalize letters, with names, addresses, and salutations added to the text. This capability was available in the mid-1960s with the magnetic tape Selectric Typewriter. What makes WP different is that sentences or entire paragraphs can be extracted from the data base and collated with other information provided through dictation or reading by an OCR device in preparing the text. A change in wording, such as substituting the words "recreation vehicle" for "trailer" whenever it appears in the text can be done by a simple command under program control. Names and address lists can be drawn from computer memory, and letters for a selected list printed, such as letters to vice-presidents in a particular industry in zip code 88001, for example. The system may also be directed to print letters and envelopes with a font chosen from a large variety of styles and sizes. In addition, the system can keep track of time spent on each job to facilitate charging customer accounts for service. This feature is particularly valuable for law and consulting firms.

If the word processor has telecommunications equipment and addressees have terminals, electronic mail with instant delivery can be transmitted instead of preparing copies of text. Text storage can be in the computer memory on microfilm, microfiche,[16] floppy disk, or a computer peripheral instead of hard copy.

General Mills is an example of a company using WP for correspondence. Some 10,000 letters composed from a set of 550 paragraphs stored in memory are mailed each month in response to letters regarding Betty Crocker products. The letters appear customized. So do documents such as contracts and manuals prepared by word processors. The wide variety of office applications for word processors, and their speed, accuracy, and convenience are reasons business people are turning to this office use of computers.

When word processing?

Word processors will never replace secretaries entirely. Personal correspondence and documents directed to a particular situation or recipient require conventional methods of preparation. WP is of value primarily for documents with a large receivership, for messages that are repetitive, and for documents that must be regenerated periodically with only minor revisions and updating of text. For such documents, word processing reduces lead time up to 50 percent, and proofreading by 10–95 percent.[17] In addition, reproductions are highly accurate and have cosmetic formatting and lettering.

The need for word processing should be established by a cost-benefit analysis before firms invest in the equipment. Fortunately, WP can be acquired in modules so that receptive departments can initiate word processing and demonstrate its value to other departments in the firm.

Computer resource requirements of word processing

Current hardware for WP falls into one of four categories:

1. Stand-alone hardcopy WP

    This system with limited editing and processing capabilities can produce repetitive letters and merge prerecorded text on cassettes to produce

---

[16] For a discussion of such technology, see Michael P. Zampino, "Microimage Technology and Practice," *Datamation®*, vol. 23, no. 10 (October 1977), pp. 96–108.

[17] B. W. Tartaglia, "The Economics of Word Processing," *Journal of Systems Management*, vol. 24, no. 11 (November 1973), p. 10.

hard copy. This system is "blind," permitting no visualization of the text before the output is produced.

2. Stand-alone display WP

    Composition and editing are done on a CRT screen with a minicomputer editing and processing the text. The system is intelligent, with many of the capabilities described earlier in this section.

3. Terminals

    Terminals attached to a large computer system with word processing software provides users with shared-logic WP. Users who share a centralized system pay less for hardware and software, but problems of equipment conformity, CPU availability, and priorities inherent in all sharing systems arise.

4. Time-shared services

    WP services may be provided to customer firms by computer utilities. Time-shared services are appropriate when word processing volume is small, when sophisticated equipment for pictorial or graphic processing is required, or when access to large data banks is needed, such as access to libraries of manufacturing, engineering, or architectural specifications. Large firms might combine internal time-sharing systems with contracted external time-sharing.

Regardless of CPU, WP requires extensive memory hardware. Text requires more space than numerical data since the size of field and record length are variable, not fixed as in many data processing applications. This means that text cannot be stored sequentially in predetermined fields, but must be kept in random storage linked by pointers. The software required for this type of access is not new nor limited to WP. What is new is the software to retrieve and then edit textual data. The newspaper industry has made large investments in software for composition and text editing, so firms can acquire WP packages for as little as $75 per month lease or $400 purchase. Sophisticated packages, however, cost up to 40 times as much.

What is still lacking is software to integrate WP with data processing telecommunications and applications such as electronic mail and teleconferencing. Also needed are packages for quick retrieval of correspondence and memorandum from a context index (or by subject, names, or dates).

Future of word processing

At present, word processing technology exists and the equipment itself is easy to operate. Secretaries already trained in the use of magnetic tape Selectric Typewriters show little resistance converting to WP, and productivity of WP is high (see Figure 23.3.)

However, there are problems that limit widespread use of word processors. The capital cost is high; equipment ranges from $5,000–200,000. Units cannot be justified economically unless systems do more than simply replace typists.

FIGURE 23.3
Productivity of alternative means of typing

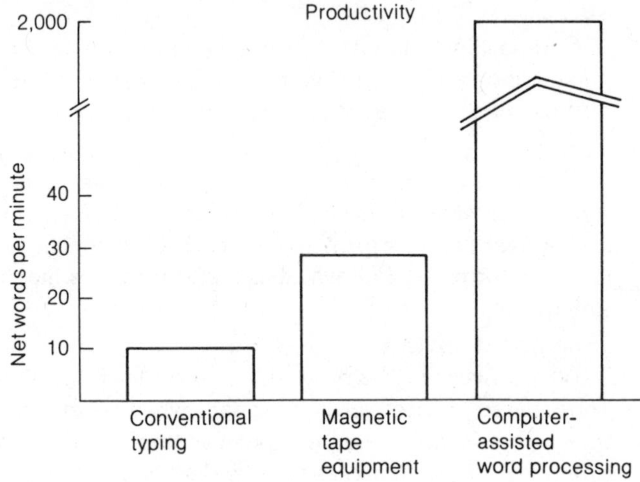

Source: B. W. Tartaglia, "Economics of Word Processing," *Journal of Systems Management,* vol. 24, no. 11 (November 1973), p. 10.

Applications such as filing and retrieval, electronic mail, account and record keeping, appointment scheduling, selective dissemination of information, trade magazine browsing, and so forth, must be added. As more and more applications are developed and as secretaries become competent in their use, the market demand for WP will increase. With greater demand, economies of scale will send prices tumbling down.

WP also raises organizational questions. What units should be responsible for WP? Should WP and EDP be integrated? Secretaries may resist being assigned to a clerical pool for sharing WP equipment and managers may prefer private secretaries to the impersonality of WP. With WP, verbal exchanges in the office are replaced by instructions on a CRT typewriter terminal, and users must rely on the magnetic image of data on a screen instead of paper copies of text that can be handled. Users must also learn to index and code data for storage and procedures for retrieval. Though changes in long-established habits and work patterns will take time, increased office reliance on word processors is definitely the trend of the future.

SUMMARY

Electronic mail, teleconferencing, war rooms, electronic fund transfer, and word processing are five computer applications that are restructuring office work in business.

Electronic mail is still in its infancy. Since a large percentage of mail delivered is generated by computers and destined to business and government with computer access, office-to-office message transfer will be the first wide-spread implementation of electronic mail. Service networks, which receive messages electronically destined for individuals in their area, mailing these messages for overnight delivery, may be next. But the extent to which federal regulatory agencies permit the electronic industry to compete in communications will determine the future of electronic mail.

The impact of computers in the office is felt in other ways as well. Teleconferencing and war rooms are changing managerial methods of gathering information for decision making. Electronic fund transfer revises accounting procedures for accounts payable and receivable, minimizing the handling of checks and cash. The alteration of traditional relationships between savings and loan institutions and banks, the potential rise of banking monopolies, and the accelerated income velocity of money under EFT are some of the side effects of EFT that have legal ramifications. Corporate managers must also contend with losses of float funds due to the speed of electronic monetary transactions, and the possibility that security and privacy of financial data may be breached due to the vulnerability of telecommunications networks. The adoption of EFT requires new office procedures, revised job descriptions, retraining of personnel, and a change in the physical environment of business offices.

Word processing has an equally disruptive effect on traditional patterns of office management. WP can be used not only for text preparation of correspondence, contracts, manuals, memos, and so forth, but can be used for retrieval of data needed for decision making, whether it be internal data from the data base such as transactional accounting or corporate financial data, or external data from a linked data base such as stock market and economic reports, or data from *The Wall Street Journal* and other daily newspapers.[18]

An office with integrated computer applications is called an **electronic office.** This is the subject of the next chapter.

KEY WORDS

ARPA	**Float**
Automated clearing house (ACH)	**Individual use of EFT**
	Instant mail
Automatic teller machines (ATM)	**Interface message processors (IMP)**
Check transaction	**Mode**
EFT between banks	**Multimedia center**
Electronic fund transfer (EFT)	**Optical character recognition (OCR)**
Electronic mail	

---

[18] For more on this subject, see Kenneth Edwards, "The Electronic Newspaper," *Futurist*, vol. 12, no. 4 (April 1978), pp. 79–84.

Organizational use of EFT
Point-of-sale systems (POS)
Resistance to EFT
SWIFT

Teleconferencing
TIP
War room
Word Processing (WP)

DISCUSSION QUESTIONS

1. Why doesn't the U.S. Postal Service set up an electronic mail system for public use?

2. Will electronic mail and EFT require a greater degree of centralization than is now allowed by antitrust laws?

3. Should government-sanctioned monopolies (e.g., the telephone company) be used to provide standardized EFT/electronic mail services?

4. Will advances in electronic office technology eventually make the use of paper obsolete for office purposes (e.g., money, letters, and office documents)?

5. What new communication skills are required by teleconferencing?

6. To what degree is the "human element" necessary in teleconferencing systems? How can a cybernetic environment be humanized?

7. What are the weak points of a computerized credit and moneyless society? How can these weak points be controlled?

8. What are the effects of EFT as seen from the following viewpoints:
   a. Micro?
   b. Macro?
   c. Economic?
   d. Social?

9. Can EFT systems be made as secure as present-day fund transfer systems (e.g., checks and drafts)?

10. Should the government implement a nationwide EFT network?

11. What is the difference between data processing and word processing?

12. Comment on the statement: Word processing will do for society what data processing did earlier.

13. State the ways in which computers will affect your chosen major field of interest. Explain.

EXERCISES

1. Read K. L. Kraemer and K. W. Colton, "Policy, Values and EFT Research: Anatomy of a Research Agenda," *ACM Communications,* vol. 22, no. 12 (December 1979). List topics on EFT research relevant to businesses.

2. Collect articles from newspapers or magazines describing computer applications or implications of computer use. Analyze the effect of these news items on business and society.

3. Keep a log for a week of all your activities that involve a computer. Analyze the impact of computers on your personal life.

SELECTED ANNOTATED BIBLIOGRAPHY

Benton, John B. "Electronic Fund Transfer: Pitfalls and Payoffs." *Harvard Business Review,* vol. 55, no. 4 (July–August 1977), pp. 16–17 ff.
Benton discusses uncertainty about costs, consumer questions that must be resolved, and the legal and regulatory issues that must be handled before any of the payoffs of EFT result.

Canning, Richard D., ed. "The Automated Office: Part I. *EDP Analyzer,* vol. 16, no. 9 (September 1978), pp. 1–13.
The author includes topics such as electronic mail and word processing in his discussion of an automated office. Many examples of automation in business are cited.

Communications of the ACM, vol. 22, no. 12 (December 1979), pp. 636–39.
This special issue on electronic fund transfer is the publication of a selected set of papers presented at a national conference on EFT held in June 1977. Included is a paper by Donn Parker examining threats to EFT posed by accidents, white-collar crime, organized crime, and extortion. Robert Long views issues faced by consumers and assesses the roles of policymakers, providers, and third-party institutions. Allen Lipis discusses the comparative costs of cash, credit card, checks, and EFT and concludes that "EFT systems are likely to be implemented without a valid assessment of whether they are profitable or justifiable."

Cross, Frank, and Lennox, Donald D. "Teletransportation—An Answer To 21st Century Problems." *Management Review,* vol. 64, no. 1 (January 1975), pp. 54–56.
A short, well-written article on the use of telecommunications and computers to replace some of the traveling now done by businessmen.

Getz, C. W. "MIS and the War Room." *Datamation®,* vol. 23, no. 12 (December 1977), pp. 66–70.
This article has a detailed discussion of the use of a control room for operations and management. The author argues that EDP resources can be used by management for appreciating, knowing, and analyzing data through a management control system using the war room as a nerve and communication center.

Humes, Kathryn H. "The Checkless/Cashless Society? Don't Bank on It." *Futurist,* vol. 15, no. 5 (October 1978), pp. 301–06.
This article combines a look into the future of a cashless society with an excellent survey of the development of EFT, the laws and regulations EFT has sprouted, and the micro and macro effects on the economy of EFT.

Johansen, Robert; Vallee, Jacques; and Spangler, Kathleen. "Electronic Meetings: Utopian Dreams and Complex Realities." *Futurist,* vol. 12, no. 5 (October 1978), pp. 313–19.
This article is based on the authors' book, *Electronic Meetings: Technical Alternatives and Social Choices,* 1978.
The article compares the use of audio, video, and computer teleconferencing with face-to-face meetings supported by examples of teleconferencing use in industry and results of studies on the social effects of the media. It argues that teleconferencing "borrows its terminology from computer science even though its purpose, culture and evaluation strategies are all more closely tied to communications."

Kling, Rob. "Value Conflicts and Social Choice in Electronic Fund Transfer System

Developments." *Communications of the ACM,* vol. 21, no. 8 (August 1978), pp. 642–56.

Kling discusses the incentives for EFT developments and the social problems that arise in the context of conflicts between five different value positions that are often implicit in analyses of proposed EFT arrangements. These conflicts reflect the relative importance of certain problems for specific groups. The five value systems are: private enterprise model, the statist model, the libertarian model, the neopopulist model, and the systems model. Kling also discusses the significant social, legal and technical questions that must be resolved if full-scale systems of EFT are not to cause more problems for the general public than they solve.

Martin, James. *Future Developments in Telecommunications.* Englewood Cliffs, N.J.: Prentice-Hall, Inc., 1977, pp. 297–302.

These pages are devoted to "alternative modes of travel" and include a discussion of telephone conference calls, picturephones, facsimile, still video, electronic flip charts, communications via a data base, teleconference rooms, radio paging, and two-way mobile radios.

Miller, Frederick W. "Electronic Mail Comes of Age." *Infosystems,* vol. 24, no. 11 (November 1977), pp. 56 ff.

A good survey of the history, economics, limitations, and future of electronic mail.

Rose, Stanford. "More Bang for the Buck: The Magic of Electronic Banking," *Fortune,* vol. 95, no. 5 (May 1977), pp. 202–09. A good article on the macro effects of EFT.

Tartaglia, Benjamin W. "The Economics of Word Processing." *Journal of Systems Management,* vol. 24, no. 11 (November 1973), pp. 8–14.

An excellent discussion with numerical data on the cost of WP. Also an excellent survey of WP and a guide to its implementation.

24

THE ELECTRONIC OFFICE

The **electronic office** has many names. It is sometimes called an automated office, an office system, or the office of the future. These names signify a change in the nature of office work. A modern office is no longer a place but a system—an electronic system. This system claims higher office productivity, more detailed and easily accessed data and information, and faster communications both within and between organizations at low cost.

The fact that approximately 15 million persons were engaged in office work as secretaries in 1977,[1] with 7–21 percent of all operating expenses[2] attributed to office costs, explains why business managers are seeking systems to improve office efficiency. In 1974, Americans spent $22 billion for secretarial services.[3] Though office productivity is increasing (4 percent a year[4]), office work load is increasing much faster, particularly with regard to processing information for government reports. The Federal Register listing government regulations for business has tripled in length in ten years, up to 20,466 pages in 1978. In 1979, 58,000 pages of new regulations required an estimated 92,000 man-years of processing.[5] The Cyclops Corporation with sales of approximately $800 million/year estimates that it requires 50,000 hours of employee time annually just to satisfy government requirements.[6]

The electronic office solves the business community's dilemma of increased office work load and rising labor costs by integrating telecommunications with computers for fast, inexpensive processing (especially word processing), storage, and retrieval of information. Fortunately, the price of important components in an electronic office is dropping. Communication equipment is

---

[1] Quoted from a U.S. Department of Labor Bulletin by Jo Ann Hennington, "Is There Need for Shorthand in the Business Curriculum of Tomorrow?" *21 Century Reporter* (Spring 1979), p. 1.

[2] J. Christopher Burns, "The Office in the 1980s," *Information Systems in the 1980s* (n.p.: Arthur D. Little, Inc., n.d.), p. 24.

[3] Richard Lowerstein, "Office System Studies," *Guide 47* (Chicago: GUIDE Interest Group, 1978), p. 94.

[4] Richard G. Canning, ed., "The Automated Office: Part I," *EDP Analyzer*, vol. 16, no. 9 (September 1978), p. 8.

[5] Edith Myers, "Shiny Plastic Cards," *Datamation®*, vol. 25, no. 11 (October 1979), p. 53.

[6] "Regulatory Paperwork: A Company Assesses Its Costs in Time and Money," *Management Review*, vol. 68, no. 7 (July 1979), p. 46.

down 11 percent annually, computer hardware logic down 25 percent, and computer memory down 40 percent.

This chapter will describe the tasks performed by an electronic office, and the equipment components needed to perform these tasks. In addition, the problems a manager faces when implementing an electronic office will be examined.

OFFICE TASKS

Before the value of office automation can be assessed, activities performed in an office need to be studied and electronic equipment identified that is used to perform these activities. In Table 24.1, office work is analyzed for a firm of 1700 employees that produces both consumer and industrial

TABLE 24.1
Office activities performed by different levels of employees: Percent of time (average)

Activity	Level 1	Level 2	Level 3	All
Dictation to secretary	4.9%	1.7%	0.4%	1.9%
Dictation to machine	1.0	0.9	0.0	0.6
Writing	9.8	17.2	17.8	15.6
Proofreading	1.8	2.5	2.4	2.3
Mail handling	6.1	5.0	2.7	4.4
Telephone	13.8	12.3	11.3	12.3
Scheduled meetings	13.1	6.7	3.8	7.0
Unscheduled meetings	8.5	5.7	3.4	5.4
Planning or scheduling	4.7	5.5	2.9	4.3
Traveling outside headquarters	13.1	6.6	2.2	6.4
Copying	0.1	0.6	1.4	0.9
Reading	8.7	7.4	6.3	7.3
Calculating	2.3	5.8	9.6	6.6
Conferring with secretary	2.9	2.1	1.0	1.8
Filing	1.1	2.0	2.5	2.0
Retrieving filed information	1.8	3.7	4.3	3.6
Using equipment	0.1	1.3	9.9	4.4
Other	3.1	6.7	11.4	7.7
Total number in sample	76	123	130	329

Level 1 = Upper management.
    2 = Other managers and manager equivalent personnel.
    3 = Nonmanagerial personnel.
Source: Adapted from: G. H. Engel et al., "An Office Communication System," *IBM Systems Journal,* vol. 18, no. 3 (1979), pp. 403. © 1979 by International Business Machines Corporation.

TABLE 24.2
Secretarial and clerical activities: Percent of time spent (average)

	Secretary	*Clerk*
Writing	3.5%	7.3%
Taking shorthand	5.5	
Typing	37.0	7.8
Proofreading	3.9	
Mail handling	8.1	
Bulk envelope stuffing	1.4	
Pick up or delivery	2.2	0.8
Copying or duplication	6.2	3.9
Filling out forms		8.3
Telephone	10.5	9.2
Scheduling and dispatching		1.2
Meetings or conferring		
with principals	4.3	1.9
Checking documents		10.4
Looking for information		10.2
Keeping calendars	2.6	
Reading	1.7	2.9
Calculating		10.3
Filing	4.6	5.9
Pulling files	2.8	
Collating/sorting	2.6	5.2
Using equipment	1.3	6.3
Other	2.0	8.4

Source: Adapted from: G. H. Engel et al., "An Office Communication System," *IBM Systems Journal*, vol. 18, no. 3 (1979), pp. 404–06. © 1979 by International Business Machines Corporation.

products.[7] The percentage of time spent in each office activity is listed for three levels of employees. Secretarial and clerical activities are further detailed in Table 24.2.

ELECTRONIC OFFICE COMPONENTS

Activities in these lists that are most affected by electronic technology are **data creation, data capture, processing, output creation, output distribution,** and **scheduling.** For example, the creation of input in machine-readable form by offline data processing equipment or an online terminal with a dialogue or interactive mode can replace conventional office procedures for recording and storing data. Data capture refers to machine-reading of hard copy data from correspondence, documents, forms, reports, or memos. Electronic processing replaces filing clerks and storage cabinets, and speeds

[7] For other analysis, see H. Minzbug, "The Manager's Job: Folklore and Facts," *Harvard Business Review*, vol. 53, no. 4 (July–August 1975), pp. 49–61.

computations and retrieval of data. It minimizes clerical tasks and time spent in report generation when terminals have word processing capabilities.

In an electronic office, output may appear on a terminal screen or be printed according to programmed instructions, often replacing the need for typing pools. Software can prepare charts and tables, check spelling by validation programs, and regulate spacing, headings, footnotes, and so forth in reports. Electronic mail, as described in the preceding chapter, will alter traditional office communication patterns. Even scheduling of meetings and conferences can be done electronically. For example, if updated calendars of employees and their fields of specialization and areas of responsibility are in the data base, the participants who should attend meetings on a given subject can be identified by a program and the meetings scheduled so no one has a conflict. The computer can also coordinate travel arrangements with meetings (recommend departure time from office, flights, and so forth), prepare an agenda, retrieve relevant documents, and even send reminder notices to participants automatically.

The electronic components that can perform office functions are listed in Table 24.3. It is from this list that equipment and software will be selected for office **workstations,** a workstation being a configuration of electronic

TABLE 24.3
Components of an electronic office

Data creation and capture	Processing (continued)
Computer console	Interactive languages
Keyboard terminal	Interactive graphics
CRT terminal	Bibliographical search capability
POS terminal	Word processing
Light pen	CAI (Computer-assisted instruction)
Voice recognition unit	Decision support systems
Graphic unit	
Data tablet	Output
Telephone	Printer
Pattern recognition unit	Plotter
Micrographic reading equipment	CRT display units
(for microfilm and microfiche)	COM
OCR	Audio
Card reader	
Tape reader	Copying and distribution
	Electronic mail
Processing	Intelligent copiers
Routine software	Smart facsimile devices
Scheduling capability	Automatic typesetting
Indexing systems	Teleconferencing
Retrieval systems	Integrated communication of data,
Personal calendar system	word, voice, graphics, and images
Information packaged services	Networks access
(for example, on industry status,	internal
stock market, newspapers, journals)	external
English-like query languages	

equipment designed for employees according to their work assignments. For example, an administrative secretary may require electronic storage, filing, and retrieval capabilities;[8] a correspondence secretary, a keyboard terminal for handling electronic mail and an output device for printing quality hard copies. A manager, however, might need voice I/O capability, a push button terminal, and a light pen. In some offices, workstations may be shared by several users. In others, jobs may have to be processed at an EDP center in batch mode. Since each organization will have differing needs, it will be up to management to install appropriate workstations for maximum effectiveness at minimum cost.

In comparing tasks in Tables 24.2 and equipment and capabilities in Table 24.3, one can identify that not all office activities have electronic equivalents. For example, there is no electronic means to speed or reduce time spent reading and assimilating reports. Teleconferencing can minimize business travel but meetings will never be totally replaced for planning, and evaluation. Most of the components of an electronic office listed in Table 24.3 have been described in general terms in other parts of this text. In the next few sections, the special application of electronic equipment and software to office tasks will be examined. Because compatibility of equipment and software purchased from a number of vendors is a major problem for office managers, many companies are turning to consulting firms for the feasibility, selection and installation of automated office equipment and procedures.

Software

An important requirement of software for office applications is ease of use. Knowledge of computers and experience in programming should not be necessary. This means complex sets of commands must be avoided, English-like languages should be employed, and the system should be tolerant of errors, able to prompt when input is omitted, and both edit and validate data. Furthermore, a large choice of programs should be available for performing routine office tasks. For example, software might include existing programs such as SCRIPT for formatting letters; PROOFER to check spelling; LABELPRT to print labels; CIPHER to invoke DES for encryption; CALENDAR to announce events taking place in the building; GETNEWS for retrieval, using keywords; PREP2 for help in preparing files; HELP to query online manuals; MAIL to provide standard headings for correspondence; and REMEMBER to store messages for future reminders. TTF might also be available for composing multicolumn pages, and YMFP for formatting technical text. YMFP, for example, uses the Bell Lab language EQN to print formulas such as

---

[8] For an excellent discussion of this subject, see D. K. Ischay, "Word Processing: File and Retrieval," *Information and Records Management,* vol. 11, no. 8 (August 1977), pp. 25–29.

$$y = \sum_{x=1}^{5} \frac{1}{x^4}$$

for which the following command would be needed:

eq y = *sum of* x = 1 to 5 of 1 over x sup 4

In addition to the above software,[9] the electronic office of the future will need **query languages,** languages with a dialogue capability as discussed in Chapter 3. These will help clerical staff determine what information is needed and assist in online retrieval.

Security should be part of office software as well. Passwords, for example, might be programmed to ensure only bona fide users have access to the system. Pattern recognition stations will undoubtedly be used in the future, granting access to the data base by speech, fingerprints, or hand forms, but currently such equipment is too expensive for common use and not sufficiently developed to be foolproof.

Processing, storage, and retrieval

The amount of paperwork necessary for processing, storage, and retrieval of office information is staggering (see Figure 24.1). In addition to the clutter of correspondence, memos, reports, and computer printouts, indexes of state and federal regulations must be on hand, and most managers keep trade journals and reference material on their shelves. Microfilm and microfiche can greatly reduce volume and storage cost, but information on film is not always easy to access and read, and space is required for specialized reading equipment. Direct computer storage can reduce storage space for office documents and information. For example, the computer can process and store electronic mail for reference and later retrieval, passing along pages or copies of documents to specified individuals through telecommunications for screen reading, eliminating hard copies altogether. Reports can be stored in memory, their existence indicated by a menu of reports that can be flashed on request onto a CRT screen. Terminals may be connected to services such as VIEW-DATA for transmission of stock market prices, industry surveys, market surveys, or even newspapers and magazines.[10] By the late 1980s it is predicted that some electronic journals will be available which eliminate the delay of publication and distribution, transmitting articles to subscribers as soon as they are written.

Information stored by computer must be indexed for retrieval, and potential users need to understand retrieval procedures. Some indexing may be automatically generated by software such as the indexing of correspondence by name

---

[9] For details, see A. M. Gruhn and A. C. Hohl, "A Research Perspective on Computer-Assisted Office Work," *IBM Systems Journal,* vol. 18, no. 3 (1979), pp. 432–56.

[10] Kenneth Edwards, "The Electronic Newspapers," *Futurist,* vol. XII, no. 4 (April 1979), pp. 79–84.

FIGURE 24.1
Daily paper on desk of an average clerical employee in the United States.

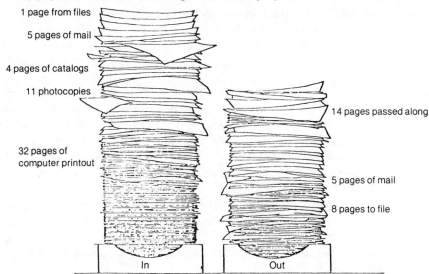

1 page from files

5 pages of mail

4 pages of catalogs

11 photocopies

32 pages of computer printout

14 pages passed along

5 pages of mail

8 pages to file

In   Out

Source: J. C. Burns, "The Office in the 1980s," *Information Systems in the 1980s* (n.p.: Arthur D. Little, 1978), p. 22.

of addressee, date, and reference number. In many cases, however, a clerk may have to assign key words from content. In addition, the storage media, length of storage, and security/privacy levels for access have to be identified. **Coding** speeds this process but codes need first be designed by analysts, then learned by users. It should be apparent, therefore, that though the computer eliminates much paper shuffling, it creates new operational and management problems. But the demand for retrieval programs will undoubtedly spur software firms in the development of such programs as independent packages or as part of a generalized office management package.

The components used by managers for office applications can be multipurpose, serving other managerial needs as well, such as project control, forecasting, and planning. For example, a manager's office workstation may include decision support models on graphic terminals such as PERT and GERT. The terminal used for scheduling may also serve computer-assisted instruction.

Copying and distribution components

Copying information for distribution is an important office function. Stencil and spirit duplications were common in the past; more recently, copy machines have become widely used. In an electronic office, the need for hard copies will not be totally eliminated. Contracts, for example, will still be required for customer signature and not all clients will have workstations for receipt of electronic copy. But electronic office technology includes a fast online intelligent copier that responds to electronic signals from a CPU or from a terminal. A nonimpact printer can also be used which burns text on a photoconductive drum, converting the text to paper by a toner. Magnetic cards control spacing, justified margins, and pagination. Electronic mail, of course, will revolutionize correspondence and interoffice communications, as will teleconferencing.

Technological improvements in copier equipment and message delivery systems can be expected in the future because large businesses such as Xerox, 3M, and Kodak in graphics and copiers; IBM in computers; and AT&T in communications are all competing to increase or at least protect their markets. For example, IBM has developed the 6670 Information Distributor, basically a copier/printer machine, but one capable of performing a number of office functions. At its simplest level, the 6670 is an ordinary copier capable of producing 36 pages per minute. But it can also receive input from mag cards or from a remote but communicating computer or word processor which can be combined with other material to create original documents, output being in a variety of fonts and formats. The capabilities of the system are shown in Figure 24.2.

Other corporate giants will undoubtedly develop competing subsystems, providing the consumer with a wide choice of equipment components. One can expect that the electronic office of the future will encompass a wide variety of copy and distribution equipment, as envisioned in Figure 24.3.[11] However, offices will not necessarily have the same equipment configurations. Small businesses may choose typesetting copy equipment as peripherals to their computers, whereas large firms may connect copiers in intrafirm and/ or interfirm electronic networks. Intrafirm networks can be financially justified in large companies for an estimated 90 percent of the paper that crosses office desks is internally generated.[12]

A DAY OF WORK IN AN ELECTRONIC OFFICE

Knowing the components of an electronic office already in production and prototype models, it is possible to describe a possible scenario in an electronic office of the future. Upon arrival at work, the manager (Adams) requests a CRT display of the day's calendar. A request for a list of correspondence is keyed on the terminal at Adams' workstation, letters chosen in order of importance from a display menu, their contents read on the screen. A dictaphone is used for replies to be sent by hard copy. Other responses are typed online and delivered by telecommunications to the addressee. One

---

[11] For another diagram, see J. Christopher Burns, "The Evolution of Office Information Systems," *Datamation®*, vol. 23, no. 4 (April 1977), p. 61.

[12] Robert White, "A Prototype for the Automated Office," *Datamation®*, vol. 23, no. 4 (April 1977), pp. 83–90.

FIGURE 24.2
Configuration of an IBM 6670 word processing system

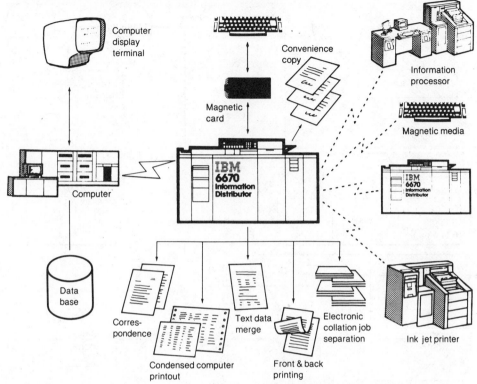

Courtesy International Business Machines Corporation

response requires a meeting with Williams. Adams types a message on the terminal to the office secretary asking that a meeting be arranged later in the day.

Adams then keys a request for a list of jobs to be done. Included in the list is a message from the office of project control stating, "Project B85 Activity 10–15 completion due yesterday. Off schedule." Adams displays the PERT chart on the screen, locates activity 10–15 on the critical path, and retrieves the name of the employee responsible (James) from a menu for the PERT program. A message is typed to James, delivered directly to his workstation, requesting an explanation for the delay.

Manager Adams is alerted to the receipt of an urgent communication by a two-star flash on the screen. Secretarial messages such as "Meeting with Williams OK for 15:30 today," or "Dictated correspondence ready for signature," receive a one-star flash. A buzzer and screen announcement interrupt work at 9:55, reminding Adams of a teleconference scheduled for 10:00.

FIGURE 24.3
Equipment configuration in an electronic office

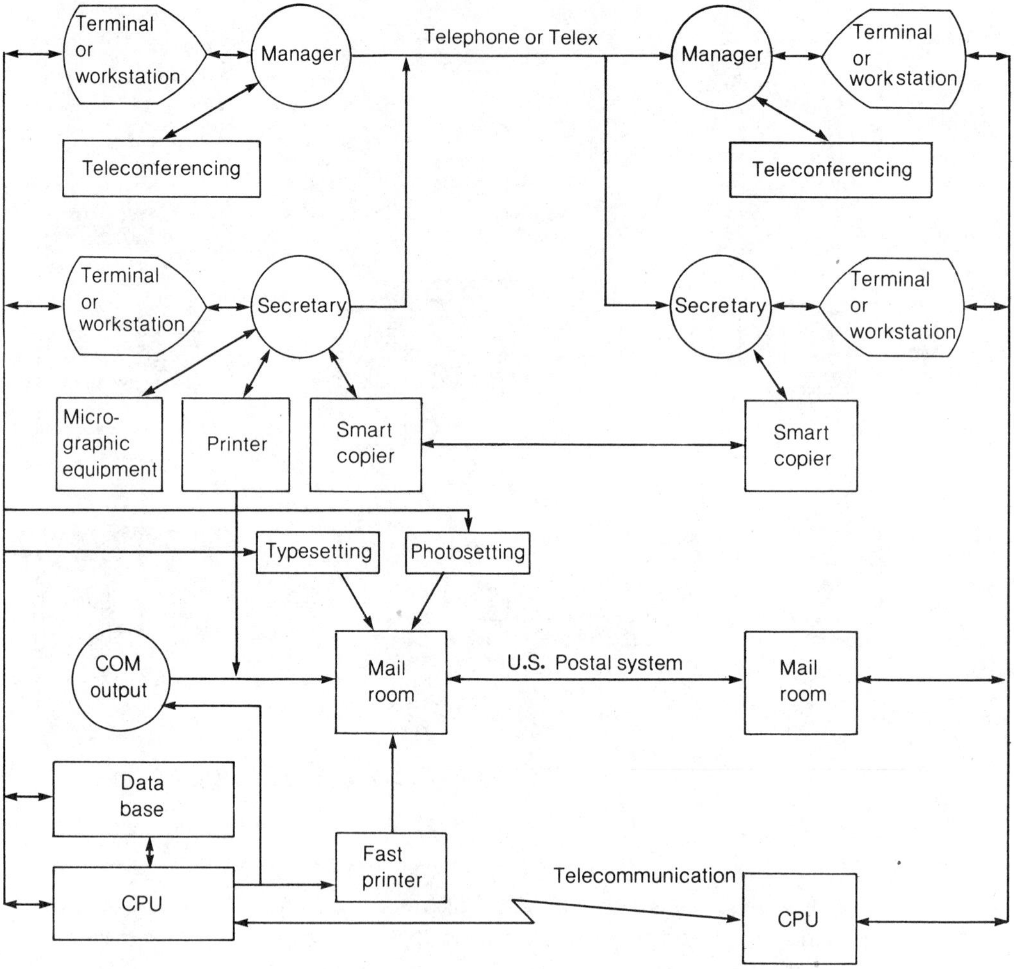

Note: Not shown are detailed telecommunication interfaces.

Reports and documents needed for the meeting have been automatically retrieved and transmitted to the teleconference room, hard copies preprinted when so specified.

After lunch, correspondence prepared by the secretary is called to the screen, changes made where necessary. The workstation is linked to an information network, so by a touch of a button Adams is able to obtain accounting and financial information, current news reports, directories, and other pertinent information. A CAI course on electronics is sandwiched between scheduled meetings. A list of outstanding tasks keeps Adams informed of jobs that require attention, but priorities are decided by Adams, not by the computer.

One activity, listening to conference proceedings on tape, is prepared for the homeward car journey. The tape is fed into a speech compressor that accelerates the proceedings to reduce listening time.

In conventional offices, 35 percent of an executive's time is spent on the telephone, responding to correspondence, and traveling. An increase in productivity in any one of these areas would be a significant saving. In Adams' electronic office, no jangling telephones or drop-in visitors interrupt the pace of work. Adams is alerted to important communications but can delay receipt until convenient. Little time is lost waiting for files to be located or reports typed. (The use of word processing increases typing productivity itself by an estimated factor of 10). And telecommunications, including teleconferencing, eliminates the need for much business travel.

The electronic office, however, is less personal than conventional offices, for social contacts are minimized. Adams has few opportunities for chats with co-workers, few excuses for walks down the hall. This all-work environment requires self-discipline and both a willingness to interact with machines and knowledge of their capabilities. Successful implementation of electronic technology in offices will require a major adjustment in the skills, work habits, and attitudes of office personnel.

CASE STUDY RESULTS

Electronic offices do exist, although implementation has been limited to date.[13] At IBM, experience with electronic offices in two divisions over a four-year period has led to the following observations:[14]

1. An electronic office improves the quality of office services.
2. Operations are efficient, a savings of 5.25 percent in the time of the principal (manager or professional user); a 15–35 percent savings in secretarial time.
3. Five to ten hours of personal instruction to new employees reduces frustration with electronic components and provides the background needed for new personnel to follow regularly scheduled training courses.
4. Managers tend to initiate their own reference sequences. This apparently reduces the impersonality of the system, giving individuals a sense of having a system of their own responsive to unique needs.
5. Users are able to cope with the new tools of an electronic office and able to incorporate these tools into established work patterns.
6. Enthusiasm grows as computerized aids augment in numbers and sophistication.

---

[13] For a case study of Bank of America, see Howard Anderson, "Consider the Bank of America," *Datamation®*, vol. 24, no. 9 (September 1978), pp. 153–55.

[14] G. H. Engel et al., "An Office Communications System," and A. M. Gruhn et al., "A Research Perspective on Computer-Assisted Office Work," *IBM Systems Journal*, vol. 18, no. 3 (1979), pp. 402–31 and 432–56, respectively. © 1979 by International Business Machines Corporation.

Another study done by Booz, Allen, and Hamilton shows that enhanced decision making is the prime benefit of office automation, as ranked by those executives polled who had implemented electronic office technology. The executives also listed higher managerial and clerical productivity, an improved competitive position, and the ability to pinpoint managerial accountability as additional benefits of importance.[15]

IMPLEMENTATION CONSIDERATIONS

The implementation of electronic technology requires capital investment in hardware, the allocation of resources for software development, environmental planning, organizational changes, and managerial skill in smoothing the transition to electronic processing, all topics discussed in other chapters of this text. Table 24.4 summarizes activities specially related to the implemen-

TABLE 24.4
Implementing an electronic office

Developmental considerations	*Environmental considerations (cont.)*
Indexing	Aesthetics
Directory maintenance	Noise reduction
Filing and retrieval subsystems	Security
Text and file transmission protocols	
Security and privacy of data	*Organizational considerations*
protocols	Changes in job content
Equipment use procedures	Changes in supervisory relationships
Integration of EDP, WP, and	Displacement of personnel
telecommunications	Unemployment
Short-term plans within long-range	Training
system plan	Human factors
Capital investment	Fear of work invisibility
	Resistance to change
Environmental considerations	Fear of machines
Space	Social isolation
Reorganization	

tation of an electronic office. One unique problem is the need to integrate word processing with the corporate data base. This permits bona fide employees throughout the organization access to this subsystem, not limiting word processing to office applications. Another special problem is the strong resistance encountered when altering the traditional secretary-manager bond. Many firms have experienced this resistance when trying to organize typing pools. When McGraw-Hill first attempted to introduce an electronic office, resistance was so intense that the company was forced to withdraw implementation plans.

---

[15] See Harvey L. Pappel, "The Automated Office Moves On," *Datamation*®, vol. 25, no. 13 (November 1979), p. 75.

FUTURE OF THE ELECTRONIC OFFICE

World sales of electronic office components are on the rise (see Figure 24.4). New equipment for office applications is also under development. For example, **intelligent workstations** are projected with private switchboards which will store messages and forward calls. So are multifunction units that are either stand-alone intelligent machines that can "talk" to one another or machines integrated with larger office systems.

Laws, especially in the field of telecommunications, and the development of international equipment standards will largely shape the electronic office of the future. For example, an international standard to regulate fax and facsimile machines was drafted in the late 1970s. At that time, Japan had 250,000 fax machines (word processing is less useful to Japan than fax machines due to the large character set in the Japanese language), the United

FIGURE 24.4
Growth in sales of electronic office components

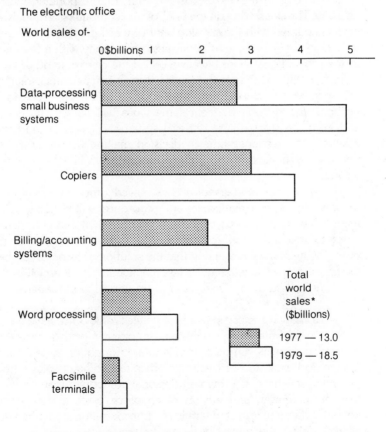

* Total for all electronic office products.
Source: *The Economist*, vol. 273, no. 7113 (December 29, 1979–January 4, 1980). p. 56. Data from EIU estimates.

States, 150,000, and Europe, 65,000, based on different standards. The draft standard regulating compression of data and rates of transmission should spur equipment development in the fax industry and promote tie-ins between industries across national frontiers.

Another international standard allows the scanning of more than one line at a time with a two-dimensional code and transmitting only differences between the two consecutive lines. This improves speed and gives better resolution of data. Further improvements would also enable these machines to be intelligent, able to "talk" to one another and to a central computer with a common data base. The central or shared computer, designed not just for data processing but also for word processing, large data bases, and information retrieval will then make the electronic office not only more efficient but more effective and with easier and faster access.

SUMMARY

Office costs in the 1970s rose without a corresponding increase in productivity. The steady drop in the price of minicomputers, terminals, and storage devices coupled with the development of word processing and micrographic technology have provided the business community with a feasible alternative to the conventional labor-intensive office: the electronic office.

In the 1980s, terminals and minis will replace typewriters, intelligent copiers will be linked by telecommunications, OCRs and microfilm readers will scan documents and correspondence, messages will be sent by electronic mail, and magnetic storage and retrieval systems will reduce the need for filing cabinets. The response time in decision making will decrease as stacks of paper are eliminated and use of teleconferencing will minimize travel by management.

Though computer technology will speed office information processing, the transition to new equipment and procedures will be costly. Capital investment will be high, and psychic costs must be taken into consideration. Resistance to machines and fear of change will affect employee morale and productivity. Managers will find that the solution of technical problems during the transition period will require less managerial skill than will solving human problems caused by the disruption of traditional work patterns and relationships.

In this chapter the components of an electronic office have been described. These components, when integrated with office information systems and data processing systems can be part of a total information system for a firm.

A logical extension of electronic office technology is placing workstations in employees' homes. Providing personal computers may be less expensive than brick, mortar, and utilities of an office. Such a change would affect not only office structure, but family life, transportation, and urban development as well. This is the subject of the next chapter.

KEY WORDS

Automated office	**Office system**
Coding	**Output creation**
Data capture	**Output distribution**
Data creation	**Processing, storage, and**
Electronic office	**retrieval**
Electronic office components	**Query languages**
Implementation considerations	**Scheduling**
Intelligent workstations	**Workstations**
Office software	

DISCUSSION QUESTIONS

1. List several dangers of the future computerized office.
2. List functions of the office that computers cannot perform well.
3. Comment on the following statement: An electronic office is more effective and more efficient than a conventional office.
4. In what areas can bottlenecks in office procedures be eliminated by computers?
5. What are some of the unique problems of an electronic office? What special human engineering problems arise?
6. List the advantages of a desk terminal or minicomputer in an office as compared with the traditional office system. Examine these advantages from the viewpoint of a:
   a. Secretary.
   b. Clerk.
   c. Manager.
7. How can a computer assist in the following areas:
   a. Correspondence?
   b. Information storage, filing, and retrieval?
   c. Text production, such as preparation of manuals?
   d. Conferences?
8. Why is it difficult for computers to retrieve information about correspondence?
9. Why is there resistance to an electronic office? What groups of people resist and why? How is this resistance manifested?
10. Some persons claim that computers, especially home computers used for office work, will create new office jobs. Others claim that computers will cause unemployment among office workers. Which claim do you think is true? Explain your choice.
11. Do you agree with the following statement: The computer will remove tediousness and monotony from offices and make office work more creative, stimulating, pleasant, and easy? Justify your answer.
12. If workstations were being designed for you as manager and for your secretary, what features (hardware and software) would you want included?
13. If a conferencing network were established between offices in your building

and 20 branch headquarters throughout the country, what features would you like the network to have?

SELECTED ANNOTATED BIBLIOGRAPHY

Burns, J. Christopher. "The Evolution of Office Information system." *Datamation®*, vol. 23, no. 4 (April 1977), pp. 60–64.
An excellent discussion of the technology, costs, and operations of an electronic office.

Canning, Richard G., ed. "The Automated Office: Part I." *EDP Analyzer*, vol. 16, no. 9 (September 1978), pp. 1–13.
A good discussion of the components of an electronic office, and two case studies.

———. "The Automated Office: Part II." *EDP Analyzer*, vol. 16, no. 10 (October 1978), pp. 1–13.
A discussion of the implementation of an electronic office.

Driscoll, James W. "People and the Automated Office." *Datamation®*, vol. 25, no. 12 (November 1979), pp. 106–12.
This is an excellent article. Driscoll traces the reasons for early unsuccessful attempts to introduce electronic offices. He argues against the individual workstation, and the Prussian bureaucratic approach to the office organizational design.

Engel, G. H.; Groppuso, J.; Lowenstein, R. A.; and Frank, W. G. "An Office Communication System." *IBM Systems Journal*, vol. 18, no. 3 (1979), pp. 402–31.
This is an excellent survey on the future of electronic offices. The article discusses studies of time spent by office personnel on different types of activities and then analyzes how these activities can be automated. Also discussed is the implementation of an electronic office in the Account Customer Marketing Department at IBM in 1972, including numerous displays of output.

Gruth, A. M., and Hohl, A. C. "A Research Perspective on Computer-Assisted Office Work." *IBM Systems Journal*, vol. 18, no. 3, (1979), pp. 432–56.
This article is actually a case study of the electronic office implemented in the IBM Watson Research Center in Yorktown. It describes the tasks that have been computerized, the hardware and software facilities that were used, training required, and the reactions of people who used the electronic office.

Holmes, Fenwicke W. "IRM: Organizing the Office of the Future." *Journal of Systems Management*, vol. 30, no. 1 (January 1979), pp. 24–31.
This article describes the future electronic office and discusses the merging of the data, voice, text, and image technology. It also discusses the organizational changes necessary for such an office.

Morgenbrod, Horst, and Heinz, Schwartzel. "How New Office Technology Promotes Changing Work Methods." *Management Review*, vol. 68, no. 7 (July 1979), pp. 42–45.
A survey of the issues involved in an electronic office, drawing from the study done by a task force in a West German firm.

Stewart, Jon. "Computer Shock: The Inhuman Office of the Future." *Saturday Review*, vol. 6, no. 13 (June 20, 1979), pp. 14–17.
This article takes a broad look at the social and economic implications of comput-

ers in society, offices, and factories. It is rich in U.S. statistics and statistics from abroad.

White, Robert B. "A Prototype for the Automated Office." *Datamation*®, vol. 23, no. 4 (April 1977), pp. 83–88.
An excellent discussion of how an electronic office could operate and the problems that might arise.

25

PERSONAL COMPUTERS

The sale of personal computers for home use is a development of the late 1970s. Though the price is beyond many family budgets at the present time (approximately $500 in 1980), costs per unit are dropping dramatically due to technological innovations and production economies. In addition, growing sales have spurred competition among manufacturers, and so lowered prices. Also, the continuing decrease in prices in the chip industry has contributed to less expensive computers. Personal computers may soon be a fixture in every home.

A personal computer is a micro or small mini, desk-top in size. In this text, the terms **personal computer** and **home computer** are used interchangeably to identify units designed primarily for family use, though they can also be used in business, either as a stand-alone computer or connected through an interface to a large computer. Though the stand-alone home computer is limited in computational capability and storage, many small businesses do find them adequate for their needs. Personal computers become an even greater home and business asset when connected by telecommunications with other computers and/or large external data bases. A separate classification is made for **hobby computers.** This chapter will describe current and potential applications for home computers and the communications infrastructure needed for implementation of many applications. In addition, many of the changes the personal computer will bring to our social structure will be evaluated.

COMPUTERS FOR HOBBYISTS

In 1976, the Venture Development Corporation surveyed over 1500 computer hobbyists. Of those surveyed, nearly ¾ used computers on their jobs, and ⅔ were either programmers, engineers, or technicians. Most knew machine or assembly language in addition to BASIC or FORTRAN. Computer reliability of 3.8 on a scale of 0–5 was acceptable to these hobbyists since they were computer system builders, able to diagnose and correct hardware problems. Twenty percent of those surveyed spent 20 percent of their income on their **hobby computers.**[1] Though the computer industry caters to this market, a hobby computer has little relevance to business management and will, therefore, not be discussed further.

THE HOME COMPUTER

The user of a home computer, unlike the hobbyist, has little knowledge of programming. System reliability must be high and cost low. Furthermore, a variety of easy-to-use applications programs for personal use must be available. Preferably the software should be conversational,[2] able to determine user's needs, and permit simulation and experimentation. Editing and retrieval should be designed for "casual users." The entire system should be easy to install, operate, update, and maintain. The potential market for home computers is an estimated 75 million U.S. households (250 million households in the Western world). According to a study done at the University of Southern California, 40 million personal computers will have been sold by 1990, primarily to professional people and small businesses.[3]

Uses of stand-alone home computers

Applications for home computers are continually expanding. See Table 25.1 for a partial list of functional software currently available for home

TABLE 25.1
Applications of a home computer

• Address records	• Correspondence
• Calendar, diary, appointments, and reminders	• Dictionary and thesaurus
	• Games and home entertainment
• CAI (computer-assisted instruction)	• Homework
• Check-book balancing	• Invitations and menu listings
• Christmas card list	• Inventory record and control
• Computations	• Tax record keeping

use. The potential for expanded applications is limitless. France, for example, that has nationalized PT&T (post, telephone, and telegraphic service), has calculated that the cost of printing and distributing phone books coupled with the salary of 4,500 operators to provide directory assistance is greater than the cost of providing each phone household with a liquid crystal or

[1] Alan R. Kaplan, "Home Computers Versus Hobby Computers," *Datamation*®, vol. 23, no. 7 (July 1977), p. 74.

[2] For special languages for personal computers like LOGO and SMALLTALK, see Alan C. Ray, "Microelectronics and the Personal Computer," *Scientific American*, vol. 257, no. 3 (September 1977), pp. 232 and 234.

[3] This estimate is for first-time buyers of computers. See *The Economist*, vol. 274, no. 7115 (January 2, 1980), pp. 93–94.

plasma display home computer for retrieving directory information. Toward this end, over $3 million has been invested in production of a facsimile machine (projected for 1981) that will receive and send full page texts. The system, once implemented, will give each phone subscriber not only the ability to retrieve phone numbers, but electronic mail capability as well.

Most owners of home computers purchase packages from software houses or personal computer vendors, but some write programs themselves. On occasion, quality programs of this latter type are bought by vendors, then resold under the vendor's trademark to the general public. What is still not commonly available is software to integrate general-purpose home computers with specialized home minis and micros, an integration that would minimize redundancy.

The home computer can serve business in a variety of ways. For example, one popular application of home computers is **games.**[4] Currently, about 1 million U.S. households have TV games. By 1982, an estimated 5 million households will have TV games; by 1987, 42 million; by 1992, 80 million.[5] Though many TV game units are microprocessor-controlled video games that cannot be classified as home computers since they lack read/write memory and cannot be reprogrammed for other purposes, personal computers as defined earlier can accept software modules for game playing in addition to performing other functions.

Most games are strictly for entertainment, but business games can be quite educational. In fact, these are often included in the curricula of business schools. Inventory and marketing games, for example, can simulate variables such as lead time, elasticities of demand and supply, transportation differentials, costing by products and regions, and so forth, providing players with valuable decision-making experience.

Another business use of home computers is **computer-assisted instruction.** Educational programs are for adults as well as children. In many fields based on technology, the half-life is approximately five years; that is, half of the information is obsolete after five years. Professionals in such fields must constantly upgrade and update their knowledge. The home computer can provide self-paced instruction, replacing traditional classroom learning. This demands great self-discipline, for the routine of classes and exams is lacking and teacher-student contact is eliminated, but a major advantage is that instruction can take place in the home at the learner's convenience.

Home computers can also store information for professional reference. A dictionary of generic and trade name medicines might be stored for quick retrieval by doctors. Bibliographies, foreign language dictionaries, lists of fellow professionals (names, addresses, publications), or supply houses and price

---

[4] For listings and discussions of such games, see David W. Zuckermann and Robert E. Horn, *The Guide to Simulation/Games for Education and Training* (Lexington, Mass.: Information Resources, Inc., 1973), 501 p.

[5] Joseph P. Martino, "Telecommunication in the Year 2000," *Futurist,* vol. 13, no. 2 (April 1979), p. 97.

lists of chemicals might be the information stored by others. Zeitlin computes that the storage required for a college education of 64 books (the size of Samuelson's *Economics*) would require only three cubic centimeters, using magnetic bubble technology.[6]

The home computer also serves business indirectly when managers who have used such computers gain confidence in machine capabilities and recognize parallels between functional applications at home and potential business applications. For example, it may be realized that computer programs for tax accounting, address management, and invoice accounting are applicable to small businesses. It may be recognized that a program controlling water and fertilizer schedules for the garden would be of value in nurseries, or for inventory control. If letters can be typed, stored, and retrieved on a home computer, why not the same facility for lecture notes, research, or office correspondence?

Most home computers are inappropriate for heavy-duty business use. Supplementary hardware, especially for storage and output, is required.[7] For example, a typewriter terminal would suffice for typing letters and printing short output at 20–30 c/s (characters per second), but for longer reports and invoices, a dot matrix printer with a capability of 150–200 c/s is desirable.

But many small businesses find home computers satisfactory. Business software can be bought off the shelf from $500–1500. For example, **turnkey packages** are available that combine word processing and data processing capabilities along with a compiler such as BASIC or an interpreter such as PASCAL (this language is named after a famous French mathemetician.) Training, documentation, development, and maintenance can all be purchased from the software vendor. A home computer system with 65 K bytes of random access memory, 400 K bytes of online storage, a keyboard, a CRT, and applications programs for accounting and inventory could be bought for about $5,000 in 1980.

A major disadvantage of home computers for business use is their limited software repertory and limited processing capability. Furthermore, software packages commercially available often prove inappropriate for the specialized needs of a business. Making adaptions (or writing programs) for minis and micros is difficult. It is far harder to write programs for a computer with a limited instruction set and small memory than to write for larger machines. Programs and adaptations therefore require skilled programmers, a scarce resource. Furthermore, to use a small computer for business applications, the manager should be knowledgeable about capabilities and limitations, and participate in the development cycle of the application as discussed in Part 3.

---

[6] Lawrence R. Zeitlin, "The Ultimate Personal Computer," *Datamation®*, vol. 23, no. 5 (May 1, 1977), pp. 131–37.

[7] For some burned fingers in applying home computers to small business, see Terry Kepner, "The Failure of a Micro in Business," *Microcomputing*, no. 33, (September 1979), pp. 68–69.

HOME COMPUTERS CONNECTED TO OTHER COMPUTERS

Thus far in this chapter only stand-alone computers have been considered. But once telecommunications connect personal computers with a network of other computers and data bases, a wide range of applications will be available. Most important from a business standpoint: extension of EFT, home shopping, and electronic home offices.

Extension of EFT

Were EFT extended to the home, the personal computer would act essentially as a POS terminal. Payments of bills for utilities, loans, charge accounts, even tax payments could be transacted from a personal computer. The payers would first have to be identified by a password or unique account number, either keyed or read by machine from a card, but once identification was acknowledged by the machine "shaking hands," the transaction would instantly take place, a record being kept of all transactions at the bank which would make the actual fund transfers.

Home shopping

Another potential use of home computers is for shopping. If information on a store's inventory could be accessed by a home computer, a customer could obtain information on goods, prices, quality, size options, and special features, information such as one would commonly find printed in a store catalog. If pictures of goods were in the store's data base and the home user's terminal had graphic capabilities, products could be displayed, rotated, and scaled. After comparing offerings at several stores, an order could be placed through the home computer by a menu-directed or parameter-driven system, home delivery specified, and payment authorized through EFT. Such home shopping is not yet a reality, but this is not because technology is lacking. It is primarily because not enough computers are in homes to make such systems cost-effective.

Home shopping, once it becomes widely implemented, will change our current advertising and marketing practices. For example, stores themselves may reorganize, eliminating salespersons and goods on display, becoming warehouses instead. In addition to reduced overhead costs, shoplifting would no longer be a problem. How will this alter the shape of cities? Streets, highways, parking, and city centers would all be affected.

In the future, entrepreneurs may market access to data bases that match "wanted" requests with available goods and services. Do you wish to rent a cottage on the French Riviera during the month of July? Do you have cocker spaniel puppies for sale? Are you searching for a babysitter for New Year's Eve? This is a form of shopping that is also a potential on home computers.

Electronic home offices

Assuming the existence of a telecommunications infrastructure, the electronic office described in Chapter 24 could consist of terminals located in employees' homes. This would minimize the need for downtown office space, a savings to the firm, and reduce work-related expenses for employees (transportation to work, parking, dress clothes, restaurant meals, and so forth). Work schedules would also be more flexible. For example, persons who function best at night might choose 9:00 P.M. to 4:00 A.M. to be on duty. The schedules of workers need not overlap since all communications would be sent and stored by the terminal for retrieval at each employee's convenience. Urgent messages could be brought to the attention of even off-duty employees by being flashed on the screen, a flash reinforced by an audio buzzer. A weekly work contract, specifying hours on duty, might be keyed in Monday morning to assist a scheduling program in coordinating teleconferences.

Planning and evaluation sessions, however, will still require meetings and face-to-face conferences might prove the only way to clear up ambiguities and misunderstandings. The annual Christmas office party is another get-together that electronics can't replace—at least, not yet.

IMPLICATIONS OF ELECTRONIC HOME OFFICES

The electronic home office is not feasible for all firms. Service industries, for example, rely on personal contact. Office controllers of large and expensive manufacturing equipment will have to remain on site. But the electronic home office will be widely implemented in many industries in the future. It already exists in computer software firms: programmers develop programs on a home terminal, submitting them by remote job entry. Technical writers and accountants may be the next groups to utilize terminals at home.

The electronic home office will inevitably expand the nation's available work force. Flexible scheduling will enable parents to work who have child-rearing responsibilities that keep them home. Many handicapped persons will be added to the labor pool. The employment of more part-time workers may prove cost-effective if the capital investment of a home workstation plus the wage is less than the value of the worker's contribution. This enlarged work force will result in more competition for jobs. It is possible that unions, to protect members from unemployment, may resist.

The nature of supervision will also change with home electronic offices. Less personal contact between boss and employee may reduce motivation and lower productivity. It will be easy to lodge a complaint, but also easy to ignore it. Employees may be more readily fired when management does not know individuals or family circumstances first-hand. But this is merely speculation. The actual effect of home electronic offices on employer-employee relationships will take a long time to assess.

The automobile industry, highway builders, and office construction firms will all be adversely affected by widespread implementation of electronic home offices. Telecommunications industries, however, will benefit. There will also be a positive benefit to the nation in terms of energy conservation. Just think how much gasoline will be saved when employees no longer drive to work. With the elimination of rush hour traffic, pollution will also diminish.

HOME COMPUTERS CONNECTED TO DATA BASE SERVICES

Terminal access to information of public interest such as the weather report, latest stock market quotations, or movies being shown at local theaters is another potential use of home computers. Such information, collected and stored by entrepreneurs, can be accessed for a small fee by home computers connected to such **data base services.** A partial list of potential applications appears in Table 25.2.[8] Widespread implementation will require telecommunications networks, but already such services are operational on a limited basis, such as The Source and Micronet. Micronet, for example, can be accessed through a telephone modem. The cost? Nine dollars installation fee and $5 per connect hour (in 1980). The service provides 8 programming languages, 5 text editors, 17 utility routines, 18 games, and 2 financial applications as well as word processing and statistical packages.

An extension of information services would be to enable individuals to make reservations directly from a home computer. The technology would be the same as that used by the travel agent who accesses an airline's data base from a computer, identifies the availability of seats, and makes an online reservation for a customer. Why not the same facility for customers at home terminals? Payment could be by EFT or credit card, the ticket itself picked up at the airport. Similar reservation services might also be offered by the entertainment industry.

Were the data base queried by a home computer part of a computing system, a matching response could be made. For example, a medical diagnosis might be requested. The symptoms, keyed on the home terminal, would be compared with symptoms and diagnosis stored in the data base. In the same manner an individual's reading profile might be matched with a list of recent library acquisitions, or golf partners identified with a given handicap. The accuracy of any match is subject to programming decision rules, the data stored in the data base, and the correctness and completeness of data input in the query. With so many variables, the quality of information provided will differ from one data service to another. The home computer owner will have to be as careful "shopping" for information as shopping for quality merchandise.

A major advantage of computer information services over directories, indexes, or other traditional references is **selective processing.** For example, were the San Francisco telephone book in a computer's data base, all persons

---

[8] For a detailed list, see James Martin, *Wired Society* (Englewood Cliffs, N.J.: Prentice-Hall, Inc., 1978), pp. 154–57.

TABLE 25.2
Applications of a home computer using a telecommunications network

Static informational services

Addresses	Investment information
Airline information	Library search information
CAI	Matching (dates, tennis
Car rental	partners, etc.)
City information	Medical diagnosis
Dictionary, thesaurus,	Real estate information
encyclopedia	Restaurant information
Electronic newspaper	Shopping information
Employment information	Sporting conditions
Entertainment information	Stock market information
Games	Telephone numbers
Housing, education, and	Travel information
welfare information	Vocational counseling
Income tax preparation	Weather information
Insurance information	Yellow pages

Interactive services

Access to local officials	Medical counseling
Advertising and ordering	Psychiatric counseling
merchandise	Public opinion polls
Bidding at an auction	Quiz shows
Computer-assisted instruction	Reservations (airline, hotel,
Consumer guidance	theater, etc.)
Debates on political issues	Shopping
Entertainment guide	Television ratings
Gambling	Travel counseling
Job counseling	Voting

living on Sunset Drive could be listed, or a list generated of all restaurants that serve seafood. In addition, the computer can assist individuals in their search for information by ensuring through menu selection that all necessary input is entered in the system in the correct sequence.

Sample data base services of the future

Home computers may be used to access news, journals, even library books in the future. Stock market quotations may also appear on the home CRT screen. These potential applications of home computers will now be explored, as samples of the types of information services that will be brought into the home once personal computers are connected to large external data bases.

ELECTRONIC NEWS AND BOOKS

Newspapers in the future may no longer appear in print. Instead, news will be accessed (for a fee) electronically from the data base of a news agency. A format of traditional newspapers might be used to present daily events on the home CRT screen so viewers can glance quickly at headlines and choose articles of interest. The viewer might then select articles to be read from a menu of headlines. The home screen might also be used for receipt of foreign newspapers transmitted by satellite. Past newspapers could be accessed, or all current and past information retrieved on a particular topic. The real-time nature of electronic news means that reports on events could be transmitted to homes as soon as the news was keyed into the computer at the news center.

Electronic magazines and journals, like electronic news, are also forecast. Books might also be stored in a computer's data base for access from a home computer. Imagine being able to ask a computer to prepare a bibliography on a given topic, then being able to request a given book from the list, selecting pages for viewing from an index, and having only those pages displayed. Entire libraries may be stored in computer memory in the future, books accessed simultaneously by hundreds of readers, perhaps printed in hard copy for some readers by printers connected to their personal computers.

Before such systems can be implemented, however, many problems must be resolved. For example, how can a writer's work be protected from unauthorized use? How will royalties be assessed and collected? Will telecommunications costs be subsidized by funds now allocated to public libraries? Will public terminals exist for persons who do not own personal computers?

STOCK MARKET SERVICES

OLRT stock market quotations are currently available to brokers. There is no technological reason why such services cannot be connected to home computers. For a fee, service agencies specializing in stock market data might also provide programs to calculate ratios relevant to investment such as the PE (price-earnings) ratio. Though such programs would not guarantee a "killing" on the stock market (the advice being a product of decision rules in programming that might be in error), access to past historical records of stock market behavior, plus access to business economic indicators and other related data would give weight to any advice proffered.

Stock market data might also be utilized in a game mode on home computers. With an imaginary $100,000, the home computer could be used to simulate buying and selling based on real market conditions accessed from a stock market data base. Similar games can also be used to simulate production and marketing decisions. Many such games, however, require a larger memory than personal computers have available, and such game programs can be costly to purchase or rent.

EQUIPMENT CONSIDERATIONS

The above applications of personal computers depend on an infrastructure of telecommunications and terminal equipment at a cost individuals can afford. In addition, information services must be profitable to entrepreneurs who must have programmers to write software and technicians to collect and maintain large data bases for the public.

The final section of this chapter will describe applications of home computers when telephone, TV, and Cable TV systems serve as the link between home computers and information sources.

Telephone

To connect home equipment with remote data bases or other computers, telephone lines may be used. A hard-wired line is feasible between offices in a building or between adjoining buildings of a corporation, but when distances are great, a public carrier must be used.

One information service currently in existence using a telephone lines for telecommunications is **PRESTEL,** the trade name for England's **VIEWDATA** system. The initial investment in PRESTEL was $35 million; an additional $36 million will have been spent through 1981 enlarging and refining the system. In 1979 over 180,000 pages of information on shopping, entertainment, exhibitions, gardening, travel, and news were available to customers for a fee based on number of pages accessed and telephone line charges. The data service is projected to expand to millions of pages in the 1980s.

The information itself is provided by newspapers, advertisers, and computer consultants (163 in 1979) who regularly update the data. It is indexed by code and appears in menu form on a TV screen on call. The user keys in the code for information desired on a remote control device which has buttons for numerical input, a device which resembles a TV remote control unit and calculator combined. See Figure 25.1 for a schematic representation of PRESTEL. Samples of output appear in Figure 25.2.

Future plans for PRESTEL include a printer and audio recorder attached to the home unit which can record messages. The service will also be able to be used for teleshopping, for the system will have a two-way capability that permits users to place orders for later delivery. A disadvantage of VIEW DATA equipment is that it has only limited compatability with other telecommunication equipment.

In the United States, a similar service, called **EIS (Electronic Information Services),** was being tested by AT&T in 1979 in mid-state New York. The system covered 10,000 square miles and 80,000 New York telephone subscribers. EIS, however, does not use TV, as in England, but uses special CRT terminals hard-wired to a standard telephone. Plans call for EIS to include teleshopping, electronic mail, stock market quotations, library information retrieval,[9] theater reviews, and remote computing. A similar telephone-based system was tested in 1980 in Canada at an estimated cost of $9.7 million for 1,000 terminals and 10,000 pages of information including airline schedules and classified ads.

[9] For the electronic library in the United States, see Robert Perry, "The World's First Electronic Library," *Personal Computers,* vol. 1, no. 1 (October 1979), pp. 18–19.

FIGURE 25.1
Representation of the PRESTEL system

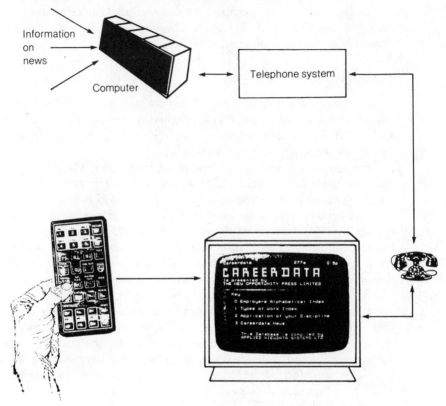

TV

Television can also be used to transmit information to individuals in their own homes. **TELETEXT,** an information service in England using this method of telecommunications, codes information for transmission on 40 of the 625 lines available on a TV screen to supplement conventional TV programming. TELETEXT is implemented by both BBC and IBA (Independent Broadcasting Authority), their systems called **CEEFAX** and **ORACLE,** respectively. Neither CEEFAX nor ORACLE interfere with regular TV programming except when urgent messages are superimposed at the bottom of the screen. The coded information is only displayed when the viewer presses keys on a remote control unit (or buttons directly on the TV set) which activate a decoder. The viewer can select the type of information displayed and has the option of using either part or the entire TV screen.

Samples of CEEFAX output are shown in Figure 25.3. The viewer can choose to display instant news (100 pages) or background news (200 pages). This option suggests that news in the future will be customized. Other facilities

FIGURE 25.2
Sample output from the PRESTEL system

include preprogrammed warnings flashed on the screen at predetermined times such as "5 minutes to school." Answers to crossword puzzles may also be requested. The main emphasis, however, is news, sports, weather, entertainment, shopping, farm, and financial information, features of a limited electronic newspaper. Unlike VIEWDATA, TELETEXT is not encyclopedic in nature, nor does it include articles such as those found in a magazine.

Cable TV

Currently in the United States no system like TELETEXT is under development. But the fact that the largest producer of TELETEXT decoders is a

FIGURE 25.3
Sample output of CEEFAX system

```
140        CEEFAX 140   Tue 18 Sep   10:34/54
```

```
■■■■SPORT■■■■
```

```
■ FOOTBALL
2 Tuesday's match    ..........        mm
  UEFA Cup team news ..............157
  Nattrass injured again ..........158
  Villa pay £250,000 for Bremner ...151
  Hay gets Chelsea youth team post .142
■ TENNIS
  Stewart and Riessen win doubles ..147
■ SQUASH
  British team confident of success 159
■ RACING
  Yarmouth .........................153
  Lingfield ........................154
■ CYCLING - SKOL 6
  Banbury and Hermann go one better 145


    Sport on BBC 2 Index 230
```

```
100        CEEFAX 100   Tue 18 Sep   10:32/08

    BBC  CEEFAX
```

```
2
NEWS HEADLINES ....101    TV and RADIO
NEWS IN DETAIL 102-119      .....171-174
NEWS FLASH ........150
NEWS INDEX ........190    WEATHER and
                         TRAVEL INDEX
FINANCE HEADLINES .120      ...........180
FINANCIAL NEWS 121-130
                         FULL INDEX
SPORT HEADLINES ...140    A-F.......193
SPORT NEWS ....141-159    G-O.......194
                         P-Z.......195
FOOD GUIDE .......161
FARMING PAGES ...168-9    CHESS   149

CEEFAX subtitling for the deaf ....189
```

United Kingdom factory owned by Texas Instruments means that the technology is known to United States industry. Cable TV is a logical network for implementation of this technology.[10] The Sloan Commission has estimated that by 1980 cable will be in between 40–60 percent of U.S. households. This figure is projected to rise to 90 percent in urban areas by the 1990s. By the year 2000, U.S. homes having Cable will number 100 million. Optical

---

[10] For a further discussion, see M. V. Jones, "How Cable Television May Change Our Lives," *The Futurist,* vol. 7, no. 5 (1973), pp. 196–99.

fibers, instead of the wire and coaxial cables in current use, will permit two way communication in the future. The Cable network will then be able to provide a channel for electronic mail to households.

SUMMARY AND CONCLUSIONS

The continuing drop in the cost of minicomputers and storage will soon make personal computers economically feasible for most American households. (Table 25.1 summarized uses of stand-alone home computers.) When connected by telecommunications with other computers or large external data bases, the range of applications expands dramatically. The home computer can then serve as an extension of an electronic office and can be part of a larger information system. Indeed, when integrated with computer networks and large data bases, even a small home computer can be a useful component in a firm's total information system.

This expansion will have far-reaching effects on our society. The electronic home office, for example, will affect the size of the labor force, urban development, transportation, the relationship of employer to employee, and personal work patterns. Teleshopping, EFT, electronic mail, and the many analytical and informational services (listed in Table 25.2) will all be brought into the home.

In England, the fact that the post office, telephone system, and TV are nationalized has fostered innovative applications for home computers. In the United States, the government regulates the telecommunications industry through the FCC, but has not subsidized research or implementation. Uncertainty about FCC rulings, the failure of legislation to keep pace with rapid technological advances, and the slowness of U.S. judicial process in resolving disputes are all factors that have hampered the development of the network of telecommunications needed for realizing the potential of home computers. Cost is also a factor, but a communications network will cost less than the $70 billion spent in a recent ten-year period for national highways.

Once a telecommunications infrastructure is a reality, the home computer will reshape our lives. With cheap and miniaturized storage devices, information equivalent to a college education may soon be available to every household in a space as small as a dental filling. This knowledge will be supplemented by paperless, cardless libraries that can be accessed selectively, quickly, and easily. Problems and obstacles are not technological but political (regulatory) and social (resistance to change and fear of machines). Will society benefit when government, business, and private individuals have access to so much information? Or will the knowledge that computers provide us be misused? Only time will tell the answers to these vital questions.

KEY WORDS

Cable TV
CEEFAX

Computer-assisted instruction
Data base services

EFT   ORACLE
EIS   **Personal computer**
Electronic home office   PRESTEL
Electronic news   **Selective processing**
Games   **Stand-alone computer**
Hobby computer   TELETEXT
Home computer   **Turnkey packages**
Home shopping   VIEWDATA

DISCUSSION QUESTIONS

1. Distinguish between a home computer and a:
   a. Personal computer.
   b. Hobby computer.
   c. Minicomputer.
   d. Small business computer.

2. What trend do you foresee for personal computer use in the United States in the near future?

3. What specifications in the following areas would you choose for a home computer used for education, pleasure, and business purposes?
   a. Make.
   b. Storage
   c. Speed.
   d. Peripherals.
   e. Software.
   f. Other desired capabilities.

4. The home computer will have a sociological, psychological, and economic impact on individuals and on society. Comment on this statement.

5. Discuss problems of hardware, software, and maintenance when home computers are used in a small business.

6. What are the potential effects of home computers on business? How can adverse effects be minimized?

7. Why is it desirable to increase the speed of acceptance of home computers?

8. Explain the national infrastructure required if home computer use is to extend beyond mere entertainment and home computing. How can such an infrastructure be financed?

9. How can home computers be used in business training? How is this use dependent on the type and size of the business or industry? Is such training cost-effective?

10. How will EFT affect and be affected by the home computer? What are obstacles to EFT extension to homes? How can these obstacles be removed?

11. What will be the economic implications of the home computer on:
    a. GNP?
    b. Workweek?
    c. Unemployment?
    d. Displacement?

12. Describe the interrelationship between public data bases and home computers. How can this interrelationship be of benefit to business and society?

13. What is slowing the integration of home computers? To what extent is that desirable? How can integration obstacles be overcome?

14. How will widespread use of home computers change society? State any assumptions that you may make.

15. Now that you have completed this text, state your agreement or disagreement with the many fictional views of computers described in Chapter 1. How do your present opinions differ from your evaluation of computers when you first began reading the text?

16. Do you believe that all students of business should have a basic understanding of computers? How about all citizens of the United States? Explain your answers.

SELECTED ANNOTATED BIBLIOGRAPHY

Barden, William. "Personal Computers; Are They Right For You?" *Radio Electronics,* vol. 49, no. 6 (June 1978), pp. 38–43.
An excellent survey of 30 home computers manufactured by 23 vendors. The author compares both hardware and software features, and factors that should be considered in acquiring a home computer.

Canning, Richard G., and McNurlin, Barbara. "Micros Invade the Business World." *Datamation*®, vol. 24, no. 8 (August 1978), pp. 93–95.
Canning, the editor of *EDP Analyzer,* summarizes two articles that appeared in his magazine, "Personal Computers for Business Computer Sources for Small Sites" and "Distributed Systems and the End User," in relation to home computers. Hardware, software, and support that must be considered in using a mini or personal computer for business purposes are also examined by the authors.

Koy, Alan C. "Microelectronics and the Personal Computer." *Scientific American,* vol. 237, no. 3 (September 1977), pp. 230–44.
A good discussion of the use of personal computers, especially the use by children. Includes a discussion on graphics.

Martin, James. *Wired Society.* Englewood Cliffs, N.J.; Prentice-Hall, Inc., 1978, chap. 14, pp. 151–70.
This chapter, "Home," is an excellent discussion of the effect of telecommunications on home use of personal computers. Political and social problems are also discussed.

Martino, Joseph P. "Telecommunications in the Year 2000." *Futurist,* vol. 13, no. 2 (April 1979), pp. 95–103.
This article looks into the future of all telecommunication applications, including the personal computer. Martino discusses the comparative advantage in many application areas of telephones, cable TV, and satellites.

APPENDIX

GLOSSARY IN PROSE

This glossary will introduce information systems terminology in a   1
meaningful context. The definitions are informal, designed to give   2
the reader an intuitive appreciation and understanding of computers   3
and information systems. An index at the end of this glossary will   4
enable quick reference to the line on which each term is used or   5
defined. A conventional glossary in alphabetical sequence follows.   6

EQUIPMENT   7

One of the earliest examples of mass processing of data was the   8
use of a **punched card** by Herman Hollerith in 1880 to process   9
census data. The card was redesigned in 1889 and since then has   10
been produced in very large quantities by IBM. It is referred to as   11
an **IBM card** or a **Hollerith card.** The card has 80 **columns.**   12
Holes are punched in each column according to a code to represent   13
a character of data. The cards are then fed into special equipment,   14
passing one at a time between **photo cells** carrying electric current.   15
Wherever the punched holes appear the current passes through the   16
card. The characters represented by the holes are then read by ma-   17
chine in the form of electrical impulses and interpreted as the charac-   18
ters the holes represent, be they data or instructions on how to process   19
data. Machines predating the computer such as calculators, sorters,   20
and collators followed the instructions for simple processing such   21
as adding, subtracting or classifying the data. This is known as **data**   22
processing.   23

In the early years of data processing, handling cards required much   24
special equipment. A **keypunch,** used like a typewriter, punched   25
holes in a **data card** to represent data or processing instructions;   26
a **verifier** identified errors in keypunching; a **reproducer** generated   27

duplicate cards and had the added capability of moving columns 28
of data to another position on a card; a **sorter** classified cards accord- 29
ing to coded data classifications; and a **collator** merged data cards, 30
combining two similarly sequenced sets of cards into one set. These 31
devices are sometimes still used in processing but today their use 32
is primarily for preparing data for a computer. They are referred 33
to as **input** and **peripheral equipment.** The latter also include 34
devices that handle processing results, called **output equipment.** 35
These include a **printer** that prints results in single or multiple copies; 36
a **decollator** that separates the carbon sheets from the multiple 37
sheets of output paper, called a multiple **ply** paper; and a **burster** 38
that breaks the perforations in the sheets, creating pages from the 39
long continuous sheets of paper. 40

The equipment mentioned above was originally used for account- 41
ing purposes. Those machines using electric impulses became known 42
as **electric accounting machines (EAM)** or **unit record equip-** 43
ment because each input card used by the machines usually repre- 44
sented one record of data. Since EAM equipment was used for auto- 45
mating office processing, use of the equipment was called **automatic** 46
data processing (ADP). 47

Much of this equipment is no longer used to perform the functions 48
of data processing, having been replaced by a **computer,** an elec- 49
tronic machine that is capable of complex operations with data at 50
fantastic speeds. The early computers in the 1950s performed arith- 51
metic operations that were measured in **milliseconds** (thousandths 52
of a second). As computers developed, the time for operations was 53
reduced to **microseconds** (millionth of a second). It is currently 54
measured in **nanoseconds** (billionths of a second), and will soon 55
be measured in **picoseconds** (a thousandth of a nanosecond). Many 56
computers still use cards for input and output, so supplementary 57
unit record machines are used as well. These supplementary machines 58
are also referred to as **offline devices** (the printer excepted) because 59
they are not connected directly to the **central processing unit** 60
(CPU) of the computer. The CPU has three parts, the **arithmetic** 61
and logical unit that performs arithmetic calculations (such as 62
add and subtract) and makes choices (Yes and No); the **internal** 63
memory unit that stores information temporarily; and the **control** 64
unit that selects the order of operations and coordinates the other 65
units. 66

The computer is **electronic** because the processing is done by   67
the movement of electronic pulses rather than electrical or mechanical   68
means as in ADP or EAM. Computer processing is therefore referred   69
to as **electronic data processing (EDP).**   70

One type of electronic computer is a **minicomputer.** It performs   71
simple applications economically, requires no environmental equip-   72
ment like an air conditioner in order to operate and is small enough   73
to be placed on a desk. When within the budget range of families,   74
a minicomputer may be purchased as a **home computer** or a   75
personal computer to keep track of household inventories, bank   76
accounts, monthly menus, or for other uses.   77

A **microprocessor** is not a **general-purpose computer** like   78
the minicomputer. It is hardwired by electrical connections to perform   79
a special task such as controlling a car carburetor or controlling a   80
factory operation. Such machines are extremely small, the size of a   81
fingertip, and require very little energy to operate. They consist of   82
one or more **chips** of a **semiconductor** such as **silicon** with   83
circuitry etched into it that enables it to perform computations like   84
a computer. These chips, when assembled and related together, form   85
an **integrated circuit (IC).** Large-scale integration of circuits may   86
consist of 10–20,000 **transistors** on one or several chips, each   87
transistor performing the function of the earlier **electronic tube,**   88
which was a small electronic device capable of processing data coded   89
in **binary values** (values of 0 or 1).   90

Microprocessors can also be built into configurations of chips that   91
have input/output capability as well as memory capacity. They then   92
constitute a **microcomputer.** Microcomputers, unlike microproces-   93
sors, can be tailored for several different applications by program-   94
ming, but these tasks can only be performed one at a time, contrasting   95
to minicomputers which can simultaneously perform multiple tasks.   96
Microcomputers are also slower and have less memory than minicom-   97
puters.   98

When devices are in direct communication with the CPU they   99
are referred to as **online equipment.** Examples are **printers** that   100
produce output and **terminals** that both receive input and produce   101
output directly from the CPU. Terminals may be **typewriter termi-**   102
nals or **cathode ray tubes (CRT).** A **CRT terminal** looks much   103
like a television set sitting on top of a typewriter. The terminal may   104
be physically part of the computer (in which case it is called a **con-** 105

sole) or it can be located apart, connected to the computer by direct 106
cable or by telephone (in which case the terminal is said to have 107
remote access.). With telephone transmission, terminal data must 108
be converted into telephone signals which are then reconverted into 109
data acceptable to the computer. This is done by a **data-phone** 110
with a **data transmission set.** The data phone in this case performs 111
the function of an **interface** between the terminal and the telephone 112
lines. 113

Other examples of computer-related equipment, also called 114
peripheral devices, are a **plotter** that plots input graphically; a 115
card reader that reads punched cards; a **magnetic ink character** 116
recognition reader **(MICR),** used in bank accounting, that reads 117
coded symbols such as those that appear on bank checks; and an 118
optical scanner or **optical reader** that recognizes marks and 119
special characters on documents such as invoices. The characters 120
read can be of different styles and sizes, referred to as **fonts.** Some 121
of this equipment is not directly connected to a computer. Such 122
equipment is called **offline equipment.** 123

The equipment discussed in this section may be grouped in many 124
combinations or **configurations.** All computer-related equipment 125
is referred to as **hardware.** 126

SOFTWARE 127

In contrast to hardware, physical objects that can be touched, 128
there is software, written as **programs,** that are stored on an input 129
medium such as cards. A program instructs the computer on the 130
algorithm to be used, that is, the specific computing procedure 131
to be followed in order to achieve the desired results and the sequence 132
in which the operations are to be performed. Computational opera- 133
tions such as adding, subtracting, finding logs and square roots, and 134
rearrangements of data are done quickly and accurately by computer 135
without further manual intervention. 136

Programmers are individuals who write programs instructing 137
the computer what to do. The computer only recognizes electronic 138
pulses which can be generated by a language using numbers for its 139
instructions. Such a language is called **machine language.** Machine 140
language is a **low level language,** in contrast to **natural lan-** 141
guages such as English, which are **high level languages.** There 142

is a spectrum of programming languages in between. The closer   143
the programming language is to a natural language, the higher it   144
is in the computer language hierarchy and the easier it is for program-   145
mers to write. Low level languages are more difficult to write but   146
are more efficiently run by the computer. A very low level language   147
is called **micro-code.** This term should not be confused with codes   148
and programs for microprocessors, which are referred to as **micro**   149
software.   150

High level programming languages have to be interpreted and   151
translated into machine language to be understood by a computer.   152
This is done by special machine language programs that convert a   153
program written in a high level language into machine language.   154
These sets of conversion programs are called **compilers, assem-**   155
blers, translators, and **interpreters.** Other computer programs   156
govern the scheduling of programming **jobs** and automate the rela-   157
tionship of the computer to its peripheral devices. These programs   158
are called **monitors** or **supervisors.** Still other computer programs   159
perform "household" duties (frequently performed operations of a   160
computer such as label checking and **listing** an information file).   161
These are called **utility programs.**   162

The compilers, assemblers, translators, interpreters, monitors, su-   163
pervisors, and utility programs are collectively referred to as **systems** 164
programs and are frequently provided together with computer   165
equipment by the manufacturers. These programs are distinct from   166
application programs that are typically provided by the user. Both   167
systems and application programs constitute what is known as **soft-**   168
ware. Sometimes software is used to redefine a computer's hardware.   169
These programs and the affected hardware are known as **firmware.**   170

Systems programs are called **operating systems.** The operating   171
system along with the hardware configuration is unique for each   172
computer model. This is why programs run on one computer system   173
cannot always be run on another. If two computer systems can run   174
the same set of computer programs they are considered **compatible**   175
with one another. One system can then serve as a **backup** for the   176
other in the event of a breakdown. Another type of backup is dupli-   177
cated data files and programs in case the originals are accidentally   178
or maliciously altered, destroyed, or stolen.   179

Most computer programs are written by the user or programmers   180
and are written in one of the higher-level programming languages.   181

Whereas each computer model has its specific machine language, 182
standard programming languages can be used for writing programs 183
for many types of computers. There are tens of high level program- 184
ming languages. **COBOL** and **RPG** are most commonly used for 185
information systems and business data processing. Many languages 186
are used in scientific programming though **FORTRAN** is most com- 187
mon in the United States and **ALGOL** is very popular in Europe. 188
Some languages serve dual purposes, being used for both scientific 189
and business data processing. Examples are **PL/1** and **BASIC.** 190
Languages like **APL** and **BASIC** are also **conversational** or 191
interactive languages, enabling fast responses on a terminal. Of 192
interest to business management are **simulation languages** like 193
GPSS and **SIMSCRIPT,** that are designed specially for business 194
problems in planning and control. Some languages are appropriate 195
for nonnumerical processing such as text processing. **SNOBOL** and 196
LISP are examples. 197

DATA
198

As mentioned, programs are sets of instructions for processing 199
data. This data must be organized and managed so that it can be 200
efficiently and effectively processed. This is known as **data manage-** 201
ment or **file management.** Organized data is a **data base,** also 202
called a **data bank,** consisting of a set of **integrated files.** A 203
file is a set of records; a **record** is a set of **data elements** where 204
a data element is a fact or an observation with a value that the 205
user needs to record. Each data element is represented in a **data** 206
field, which is a set of **data columns** on a data card. There are 207
80 such data columns per card, each representing a **character** of 208
data. A set of characters can be **alphabetic** (A to Z), **numeric** 209
(0–9), **alphanumeric** (or **alphameric**) such as the license plate 210
AEJ472, special symbols such as $ * +, or a combination of all 211
these types. For the character to be understood by the computer it 212
must be machine-readable. That is, the character must be represented 213
by a set of **bits** which are **binary digits** of 0 or 1. A set of electric 214
currents can be made to represent these digits by being off (0) or 215
on (1). By changing these states we can represent bits, which are 216
combined to represent unique characters. For example, the number 217
9 can be represented in binary digits as 1001 (on-off-off-on). Similarly, 218

letters and symbols can be represented by a unique permutation of   219
0 and 1 bits. In this way, bits can be made to represent the entire   220
hierarchy of data from data elements, records, and files to the   221
entire data base itself.   222

A data element is usually the lowest level of data a manager   223
uses. Each of these data elements is defined in a **data element**   224
dictionary (DED) prepared specially in each business according   225
to its data element needs. In large information systems, these data   226
elements have to be classified, indexed, and organized so as to facili-   227
tate their access and use. This function is performed by a **data direc-** 228
tory. The data directory and the DED are then used by a set of   229
computer programs to structure, access, and manage the data base.   230
This is known as a **data base management system (DBMS).**   231
There are many such systems sold by computer manufacturers and   232
software companies. These include **TDMS, MARK IV, TOTAL,**   233
ADABAS, IMS, and **SYSTEM 2000.**   234

There are basically two types of DBMS. One uses a high level   235
English-like programming language that enables a manager to **query**   236
the data base, retrieve data, and structure output to facilitate decision 237
making. The second type handles applications programs. Both are   238
independent of data storage techniques. Administering the DBMS   239
and acting as a liaison between users and the data base is a person   240
called the **data base administrator.**   241

Data and programs to be processed are stored on a **storage** or   242
memory device. There are many types of such devices. One is   243
called **core.** It is part of the CPU equipment and is referred to as   244
internal storage (internal to CPU) or as **primary storage.** It is   245
supplemented by additional storage on an **external memory de-**   246
vice. An example is a **magnetic tape** similar to that used in tape   247
recorders. Tape is especially suitable for recording data that must   248
be processed and retrieved **sequentially,** such as a payroll. Some   249
processing and retrieval is done in **random** order, allowing any word   250
in the memory to be accessed. The memory device appropriate for   251
such **random processing** is a **disk** which is similar to a phono-   252
graph record. On small computers, a smaller and less rigid disk,   253
called a **floppy disk** or **floppy,** is used. The tape **(magnetic** or 254
paper tape) and the disk are referred to as **auxiliary, secondary,** 255
or **external storage.**   256

Data is stored on tapes or disks as **bits** when representing one   257

character, or stored as **bytes,** sets of bits. The size of a byte is 258
eight bits. Data is also stored as a **word** which varies with computer 259
manufacturers but is between 8–64 bits. Large data bases are mea- 260
sured in **tons** of data where a ton is 40 billion bits of data. Many 261
businesses have tens of tons of data. The capability of storing large 262
amounts of data not only enables the use of large data bases but 263
also enables the use of large and complex programs, some being 264
many million bits in size. 265

Some data is kept in a **common data base.** This data is collected 266
and validated only once, then stored to be shared by all bona fide 267
users in the organization for many purposes. Such a system is 268
integrated. There are many types of integration. **Vertical integra-** 269
tion is sharing of data by all levels of management even though 270
this may be confined to one function only, such as marketing or 271
production. Other systems are integrated at one level of management 272
but integrated for all functions at that level. Such integration is called 273
horizontal integration. There is also integration over time, called 274
longitudinal integration, which is used, for example, in making 275
sales projections based on the past five years of data. When an infor- 276
mation system has all three types of integration it is then called a 277
total system of a **management information system (MIS).** 278

INFORMATION SYSTEMS 279

Thus far, computer technology, hardware, software, and data bases 280
have been discussed. If these components are organized as a whole 281
to produce desired information, an **information system** is created. 282
An **MIS** system produces information needed by managers for plan- 283
ning as well as for control and operational functions. However, infor- 284
mation systems are not a panacea to all of a manager's informational 285
needs. They do, however, provide information that can contribute 286
to better and more efficient management. 287

The careful reader will note that the term MIS has been defined 288
in two ways in this glossary. There are still other definitions. Many 289
terms used in this book have more than one definition, especially 290
terms such as *implementation* and *development.* This is because com- 291
puter science is a relatively new field. It will take many years to 292
develop universal standardization of terms. The **American National** 293

Standards Institute (ANSI) is one organization presently working on this problem. 294 295

Information systems are developed in **stages,** each consisting of a set of jobs called **activities.** The first group of activities (first stage) of the developmental process is a **feasibility study,** which examines alternative approaches to producing information for practicality within constraints of the organization. A **constraint** is a factor that places a limit on what is possible. 296 297 298 299 300 301

Once an alternative is chosen by management, the next stage in the developmental process is for the manager to define information needs specifically in order for the system to be designed to meet these needs. The **design** starts with the specification of the user's need of **output,** that is, determining what information the system should generate. From the output needs, the **input,** the resources put into the system, can be deduced. This includes a determination of equipment, data, and procedures needed to produce the output. The **procedures** are sets of instructions and rules governing the human-machine (user-computer) relationship. 302 303 304 305 306 307 308 309 310 311

The designed system is then **implemented.** This includes writing programs to manipulate data in order to generate the desired output. The system is then **tested,** comparing actual performance with desired performance. Further **debugging,** locating and correcting errors, may be necessary. Once the system performs as expected, it is **documented,** a process of stating all relevant facts about the system. This documentation includes **decision tables** which specify the logic of the **decision rules** and **flowcharts** which show the logic and the flow of data. The documentation and programs are then deposited in a **program library** and are handled and controlled by a **librarian.** 312 313 314 315 316 317 318 319 320 321 322

The system when satisfactorily tested and documented is then **converted,** the old system being **phased out** and the new system made **operational.** 323 324 325

MANAGEMENT OF AN INFORMATION SYSTEM 326

Computer operations have many **modes** of operation. One is **batch processing,** which involves collecting jobs into a **batch** before they are processed. Another is **time sharing,** where users take turns being serviced. However, due to the very fast processing speeds 327 328 329 330

of modern computers, users are serviced almost instantly, giving each 331
individual the illusion of having the machine to oneself, **dedicated** 332
to one's use. Time-sharing systems are used largely by programmers 333
and users for scientific computations. Some businesses require a **real-** 334
time system, which searches its data base and gives results in time 335
to affect the operating environment. 336

Developing, operating, and maintaining an information system 337
requires professional personnel, the most important being the 338
systems analyst, also referred to as **systems designer** and 339
systems engineer. Within a development team, expertise in syn- 340
thesizing systems is necessary as well as a knowledge of **operations** 341
research or **management science,** the use of mathematical and 342
statistical techniques for finding the **optimal** (best) solution in appli- 343
cations programming and experience in data management. The team 344
of systems analysts must also have some knowledge of **mathemati-** 345
cal and **numerical analysis** as well as knowledge of computer 346
hardware and operating systems, though it may call on **hardware** 347
and systems programming specialists for help when needed. 348

A systems analyst may do computer programming but often this 349
responsibility is assigned to a **programmer,** a professional at writing 350
programs. If the logic and flow of the program has been specified 351
in detail, the actual writing of the program can be done by a lower- 352
level programmer called a **program coder.** Another type of **coder** 353
is a clerk who represents lengthy data by shorthand **codes,** such 354
as representing colors by numbers (for example, 1 for red, 2 for 355
orange, 3 for yellow, etc.). 356

Keypunched data is prepared by a **keypuncher.** The cards are 357
then sometimes processed on EAM equipment by a **tab operator.** 358
Other professional and technical personnel involved in systems work 359
are **systems programmers,** who write systems programs and the 360
control clerk, who checks and controls the quality of input and 361
output. The checking of output should be done after each **run,** pro- 362
cessing of data by computer in the expectation of getting desired 363
output. If the output meets prescribed standards, it is distributed to 364
authorized personnel. 365

The **run time** of modern computers is a small fraction of time 366
compared to the **response time,** the time elapsed from the moment 367
the input starts being read to the moment the output is produced. 368
Response time includes the wait before the CPU is available and 369

the time required for reading and printing. When input-output opera-   370
tions are very slow compared to the time spent on computations,   371
the full capability of the computer is not utilized. Such computer   372
systems are **input-output bound.** Machines that are limited in com-   373
puting capabilities are **compute bound.**   374

In addition to the response time, preparation of input takes time,   375
as does control of output and its distribution. These are, relatively   376
speaking, more time-consuming and error-prone operations than   377
computer runs, since they are very **people-intensive,** jobs done   378
manually by people.   379

One other time concept concerns **lapse time.** This is the time   380
required from the start of a job to the finish, which is not the same   381
as the time actually spent on the job. For example, a manager may   382
spend ten minutes making a decision but it may take three weeks   383
of preparation before the necessary data is assembled on which the   384
decision is based. The lapse time in this case is three weeks, ten   385
minutes. Lapse time in preparing a computer program is often much   386
longer than the actual time spent writing the program, for included   387
are the hours spent in debugging. Extended lapse time for preparation   388
is one reason why the development of information systems takes   389
so long and why they must be planned with adequate **lead time**   390
for development.   391

During operations, the system is **controlled** for quality of informa-   392
tion. This includes checking of input data for validity, completeness,   393
accuracy, and errors. Controls are also designed to protect against   394
intentional tampering of data such as fraud and theft, but **security**   395
against tampering is not always completely successful. Part of the   396
problem is that design procedures and training for control do not   397
keep up with advances in technology, especially hardware develop-   398
ments.   399

During operations the system is regularly evaluated. This   400
evaluation is based on both efficiency and effectiveness. **Efficiency**   401
refers to the relationship between input and output while **effective-**   402
ness refers to the successful achievement of critical factors   403
of performance set by the user. Examples of critical factors are **accu-**   404
racy, a specified percentage of freedom from error; **timeliness,**   405
the availability of information when needed; and **completeness,**   406
the availability of all relevant data.   407

COMPUTER APPLICATIONS 408

Computers process data and perform calculations to generate in- 409
formation. Often during the operation of a system the data changes. 410
The recording of this change is a **transaction.** A file containing 411
transactions is called a **transaction file** or **detail file.** It is used 412
to change the data on the **master file.** This is done in a sequential 413
order. The reflection of the new transactions on the master file is 414
called **updating** and periodic updating of a master file is referred 415
to as **file processing.** The deletion of irrelevant data is **purging** 416
of data. Such processing takes place at the **operational level** of 417
a business; for example, payroll accounts receivable or payable, or 418
deposits and withdrawals from a bank. Other computer applications 419
are needed at the **control** and **planning levels** involving middle 420
and top managers. At these levels, statistical and mathematical com- 421
puter models of decision making and special programming languages 422
such as **GPSS** and **SIMSCRIPT** are needed. 423

In addition to producing information and performing calculations, 424
computers have other applications in business and industry. They 425
are used to control operations. **Numerical control** is **discrete** 426
where distinct operations are controlled, such as the movement of 427
a lathe or drill. Another type of control is **process control** for 428
continuous operations as found in a refinery or a steel rolling mill. 429
For such control, **minis** (minicomputers) and **micros** (microcompu- 430
ters) are used. These may be independent computers that have **stand-** 431
alone capabilities. Other computer systems are designed for lim- 432
ited operations such as game computers or use in **smart products.** 433
Some stores have **terminals,** each capable of recording a sale and 434
calculating the remaining cash to be paid and are connected to a 435
central computer. These terminals, called **point-of-sale terminals** 436
(POS terminals), are sometimes **interactive,** asking and answer- 437
ing questions in a **conversational mode.** 438

There are many other applications of terminals served by a central 439
computer. One example is **computer-assisted instruction (CAI),** 440
where terminals are used for teaching and drilling. Another is **com-** 441
puter-aided design (CAD), where products are designed on termi- 442
nals. Such terminals are CRTs having **graphic** capabilities on which 443
the user can draw and combine lines, symbols, and curves. Objects 444
thus drawn can be **scaled,** that is enlarged or contracted, or rotated, 445

and objects can be moved to any part of the screen. Once the desired   446
shape or design is drawn, a mathematical description of the design   447
is stored on paper tape which can then be used on numerical control   448
equipment to automatically direct the production of the actual prod-   449
uct designed on the CRT screen.   450

Some terminals have memory and are programmable. These are   451
called **intelligent terminals.** These may be miniature stand-alone   452
computers that are used, for example, in accounting applications,   453
data entry, data checking, and even for **cash dispensing.** The latter   454
will dispense cash on request after verifying that one's bank balance   455
will cover the amount. Others dispense cash on a credit card and   456
can communicate in several languages, selecting the preferred lan-   457
guage of the user by reading a code symbol on the credit card.   458
Intelligent terminals can also be used for **credit checking** when   459
accepting checks as in a grocery store. Some are connected to a   460
bank and will instantly debit your account for the amount of the   461
check. Funds are then transferred electronically from the buyer's to   462
the seller's account, a process called **electronic fund transfer**   463
(EFT). Similarly, funds may be transferred between banks electroni-   464
cally. With more common use of EFT and intelligent terminals, the   465
United States may become a **cashless** and **checkless society.**   466
This will require a greater use of **teleprocessing,** the processing   467
of data at a remote point. For this, the use of **telecommunications**   468
via telephone lines or even satellites for the transference of data   469
between remote points is necessary. Connections between a central   470
computer with intelligent terminals and other computers enable com-   471
puting power to be distributed to decentralized points and locations.   472
This is called **distributed data processing.**   473

Sometimes computers are interconnected and share peak loads   474
much like the grid connecting electric power stations. Another similar-   475
ity with electric power stations is when a **computer utility** sells   476
computing power to customers much as a power utility sells electricity.   477
Both systems have high equipment cost and require many customers   478
to reduce unit cost. Some businesses, however, are hesitant to use   479
a computer utility because they fear the loss of control over the   480
security of their data. Security in this context is protection against 481
unauthorized access.   482

Security in an information system is sometimes breached by acci-   483
dent or error on the part of a programmer or operator, though often   484

the breach is by sabotage or theft. There are two types of computer 485
theft. One is **bite theft,** a one-time theft where a large dollar amount 486
is stolen by unauthorized access to computerized accounts with the 487
thief disappearing or attempting to escape. The other is **nibble theft** 488
where the thief takes small amounts over a period of time, hoping 489
never to be discovered. A classic example is the salami technique 490
in which a programmer **truncated** small amounts in paychecks and 491
transferred the amount to his personal account. 492

Informations systems thus far discussed have been data processing 493
systems. Some systems, however, process words or text. These are 494
called **word processing systems.** A common use of this computer 495
application is typing correspondence and the preparation of manuals. 496
Text is stored in the computer, displayed on a CRT and then corrected 497
by **text editing capability.** The text, once corrected, does not 498
have to be retyped, thereby reducing labor and errors that may occur 499
in the retyping. Unfortunately, the system is not capable of processing 500
handwriting, pictures, or verbal text. However, input equipment is 501
being developed for **voice recognition, picture processing,** 502
handwriting recognition, and even **signature recognition.** In 503
all these areas there is an infinite set of possibilities to be recognized 504
and the problem is one of identifying the uniqueness of pattern, a 505
subject known as **pattern recognition.** Such recognition does not 506
use formulas or algorithms for its solution but uses rules of thumb 507
for the exploration of potential solutions. This is referred to as 508
heuristic problem solving. This approach is also used when writ- 509
ing computer programs for composing music, solving integration 510
problems in mathematics, and for playing games of chess and check- 511
ers. Some computer programs **learn** from experience, improving 512
their performance, as in the Samuel checker-playing program. Some 513
of this activity has been called **intelligent.** Much research is being 514
done to make computers approach the natural intelligence of human 515
beings. This field of research is called **artificial intelligence.** Suc- 516
cess in this area will have important implications for our society. 517

IMPLICATIONS 518

Computers, with or without artificial intelligence, affect our ways 519
of problem solving and decision making. Managers need to learn 520
how to effectively use this extension of their informational base and 521

computational capabilities. In the future, computers may replace some   522
managers at the operational and middle levels of management. There   523
will also be displacement of high level management though this will   524
occur less frequently because managers at this level are concerned   525
with problems that cannot be easily solved using computers. Compu-   526
ters will also replace factory workers and clerks at the operational   527
level, resulting in **unemployment.** In some cases, persons may lose   528
a job because of computers, but gain a job in computing itself, becom-   529
ing a keypunch operator, for example. This **displacement** often   530
requires retraining. The fear of losing jobs as well as ignorance of   531
computing often leads to **resistance,** a behavior that is common   532
in the computer revolution.   533

The location of decision making will change in the future. Cheaper   534
computers and minicomputers will enable processing and decision   535
making to be distributed to the plant or division site rather than at   536
the headquarters, although data in a data bank would still be pro-   537
cessed at the headquarters. The **common data bank** reduces the   538
cost per unit of processing and also increases the effectiveness of   539
processing by correlating data from the different files.   540

It was this concept that was the basis of the proposal in 1969   541
to create a national data bank. It would then have been theoretically   542
possible to relate personal data on each citizen (family history, school- 543
ing, and so forth) with checking accounts, records at credit bureaus,   544
and with records in the federal government, including the IRS and   545
FBI. This raised the possibility that the data could be also misused   546
for surveillance, thereby violating the individual's **privacy.** The term 547
privacy should be distinguished from *security.* Security is concerned   548
with protection against unauthorized access; privacy guards against   549
unauthorized use. While security is a technological problem, privacy   550
involves ethical and moral values. It is the concern for such privacy   551
that led Congress to reject the idea of the national data bank and   552
instead enact the 1974 Privacy Act. This act gives individuals the   553
right to know what personal data is collected and how it is to be   554
used. Furthermore, it provides controls for the validity and complete-   555
ness of data. The act applies only to federal agencies, but it has   556
been used as a framework for state laws on data privacy, and for   557
federal laws covering the private sector, including education, health   558
care, and business.   559

There are other legal problems unique to computers that are cur-   560
rently being defined in court: the liability for computer errors and   561
computer fraud; patenting of software; the use of computer media   562
as evidence; and perhaps most important, interpreting antitrust laws   563
in relation to computer manufacturers. Old laws need to be redefined   564
and new ones enacted as the industry evolves.   565

Along with the legal implications, there are social implications   566
of the still emerging computer industry. The combination of EFT   567
credit terminals with personal and home computers will affect the   568
way we do our shopping, and influence urban development and   569
the growth of shopping centers. The use of **numerical control,**   570
robots, electronic mail, electronic office, teleconferencing,   571
and **process control** will affect our nation's productivity. These   572
and other computer applications currently being developed will have   573
a significant impact on how we do business and even on how we   574
live in the future.   575

INDEX TO GLOSSARY IN PROSE

562

GLOSSARY

This glossary includes operational definitions of terms that are needed by users of computerized information systems. Since precise technical definitions too often obscure meaning, the definitions in this list have been simply written in an effort to promote understanding. For readers wishing a complete technical glossary of computer terms, the *American Standard Vocabulary of Information Processing* published by the American National Standards Institute is recommended.

This glossary draws heavily from James O'Brien's *Computers in Business Management* published by Richard D. Irwin, Inc., in 1979. Permission to utilize definitions from this text is gratefully acknowledged.

abacus: beads on wires in a wooden frame. Calculations are performed by moving the beads along the wires, using them as counters and memory aids.

acceptance test: a test for evaluating the capabilities and performance of a system in terms of specifications predefined by the user in the system specification stage.

access time: the time interval between the instant that the CPU requests a transfer of data to or from a storage device and the instant such an operation is completed.

accumulator: a register in which the results of arithmetic or logic operations are formed.

ADAPT: a language used for programming numerical control machines. A subset of APT.

address: a name, number, or code that identifies a particular location in storage or any other data source or destination.

ALGOL: ALGOrithmic Language. An international procedure-oriented language that is widely used in Europe. Like FORTRAN, it was designed primarily for scientific-mathematical applications.

algorithm: a set of well-defined rules or processes for the solution of a problem in a finite number of steps.

alphameric: see alphanumeric.

alphanumeric: pertaining to a character set that contains letters of the alphabet, numeric digits, and special characters such as punctuation marks. Also called **alphameric.**

analog computer: a computer that operates on data by measuring changes in continuous physical variables, such as voltage, resistance, and rotation. Contrast with **digital computer.**

APL: A Programming **L**anguage. A mathematically-oriented language originated by Kenneth E. Iverson of IBM. Real-time and interactive versions of APL are being utilized in many time-sharing systems.

APT: Automatic **P**rogramming **T**ools. A language for programming numerical control machines.

architecture: the physical and logical arrangement of a computer.

arithmetic-logic unit: the unit of a computing system that contains the circuits that perform arithmetic and logical operations.

arithmetic operation: binary operations of addition, subtraction, multiplication, and division. Also operations with negative and absolute values.

array: an arrangement of elements in one or more dimensions.

artificial intelligence: the capability of a machine (usually a computer) to perform operations associated with human intelligence, such as computations, reasoning, and learning. The term is often used synonymously with **machine intelligence.**

ASCII: American **S**tandard **C**ode for **I**nformation **I**nterchange. A standard code used for information interchange among data processing systems, communication systems, and associated equipment. The coded character set consists of seven-bit coded characters (eight-bits including a parity check bit.)

assemble: to translate a symbolic language program into machine language program by substituting absolute operation codes for symbolic operation codes and absolute or relocatable addresses for symbolic addresses.

assembler: a computer program that assembles.

assembler language: a programming language that utilizes symbols to represent operation codes and storage locations. Also called a **symbolic language.**

audio-response unit: an output device of a computer system whose output consists of the spoken word.

audit trail: the presence of data processing media and procedures which allow a transaction to be traced through all stages of data processing, beginning with its appearance on a source document and ending with its transformation into information on a final output document.

automatic data processing: data processing performed by electronic or electrical machines with a minimum of human assistance or intervention. The term is applied to both electromechanical punched card data processing and electronic data processing.

automation: the automatic transfer and positioning of work by machines or the automatic operation and control of a work process by machines, that is, without significant human intervention or operation.

auxiliary operation: an offline operation performed by equipment not under control of the central processing unit.

auxiliary storage: storage that supplements the primary storage of the computer. Same as **secondary storage.**

background processing: the automatic execution of lower priority computer programs when higher priority programs are not using the resources of the computer system. Contrast with foreground processing.

backup: standby equipment or procedures for use in the event of failure, damage, or overloading of normally used equipment and facilities.

BASIC: **B**eginners **A**ll-Purpose **S**ymbolic **I**nstruction **C**ode. A programming language developed at Dartmouth College which is widely utilized by time-sharing systems.

batch processing: a category of data processing in which data is accumulated into batches and processed periodically. Contrast with **real-time processing.**

binary: pertaining to a characteristic or property involving a selection, choice, or condition in which there are two possibilities, or pertaining to the number system which utilizes a base of two.

bit: a contraction of binary digit, which can have the value of either 0 or 1.

block: a grouping of contiguous data records or other data elements which are handled as a unit.

blocking: combining several data records or other data elements into blocks in order to increase the efficiency of input, output, or storage operations.

broadband: a communication channel with a capacity for high speed transmission of data.

buffer: temporary storage used to compensate for a difference in rate of flow of data or time of occurrence of events, when transmitting data from one device to another.

bug: a mistake or malfunction.

business data processing: use of automatic data processing in accounting or management.

business information system: information system within a business organization that supports one of the traditional functions of business; such as marketing, finance, production, and so forth. Business information systems can be either operational or management information systems.

byte: a sequence of adjacent binary digits operated upon as a unit and usually shorter than a computer word. In many computer systems, a byte is a grouping of eight bits which can represent one alphabetic or special character or be "packed" with two decimal digits.

CAD/CAM: an integrated system of computer-aided design and computer-aided manufacturing.

calculator: a data processing device suitable for performing arithmetical operations which requires frequent intervention by a human operator.

call: to transfer control to a subroutine.

card code: combinations of holes on a punched card to represent characters or combination of small magnetic fields on magnetic cards.

card column: the vertical set of punching positions on an IBM card.

card field: assigned card columns for data.

card punch: a device that will record information on cards by punching holes to represent characters.

card reader: a device that can sense and translate the information coded on a card for use in processing.

cathode ray tube: an electronic vacuum tube (television screen) which displays the output of a computer system.

central processing unit: the unit of a computer system that includes the circuits which control the interpretation and execution of instructions. In many computer systems, the central processing unit includes the arithmetic-logic unit, the control unit, and the primary storage unit. Also called the **CPU,** the **central processor,** or the **main frame.**

chain: a list of data records which are linked by means of pointers. Though the data records may be physically dispersed, each record contains an identifier by which the next record can be located.

channel: a path along which signals can be sent. More specifically, a small special-purpose processor which controls the movement of data between the CPU and input/output devices.

character: a letter of the alphabet, a number, or special symbol.

character reader: equipment which reads printed characters from a document.

check bit: a binary check digit such as a parity bit.

check digit: a digit in a data field which is utilized to check for errors or loss of characters in the data field as a result of data transfer operations.

clock: (1) a device that generates periodic signals utilized to control the timing of a synchronous computer; (2) a register whose content changes at regular intervals in such a way as to measure time.

COBOL: **CO**mmon **B**usiness **O**riented **L**anguage. A business data processing language.

CODASYL: **C**onference **O**f **DA**ta **SY**stems **L**anguages. The group of representatives of users and computer manufacturers who developed and maintain the COBOL language.

code: a string of characters to (1) identify data classifications; (2) use in transmission; (3) provide secrecy (see **cryptography**); (4) program instructions for a computer.

coding: developing the programming language instructions which direct a computer to perform a data processing assignment.

collate: to combine items from two or more ordered sets into one set having a specified order not necessarily the same as any of the original sets.

compile: to translate a high level programming language into a machine program.

compiler: a program that compiles.

computer: (1) a data processing device that can perform substantial computation, including numerous arithmetic or logic operations, without intervention by a human operator during the processing; (2) an electronic device that has the ability to accept data, internally store and execute a program of instructions, perform mathematical, logical, and manipulative operations on data, and report the results.

computer-aided design: utilization of a computer for the design or modification of a product.

computer-aided manufacturing: the use of computer technology in operation and control of a manufacturing process.

computer application: the use of a computer to solve a specific problem or to accomplish a particular job for a computer user. For example, common business computer applications include sales order processing, inventory control, and payroll.

computer graphics: the use of computer capability to create, transform, and display symbolic and pictorial representations.

computer industry: the industry composed of firms which supply computer hardware, software, and EDP services.

computer program: a series of instructions or statements in a form acceptable to a computer, prepared in order to achieve a certain result.

computer specialist: a person whose occupation is related to the providing of computer services in computer-using organizations or in the computer industry. For example, a systems analyst, programmer, computer operator, and so forth.

computer system: computer hardware and software as a system of input, processing, output, storage, and control components. Thus, a computer system consists of input and output devices, primary and secondary storage devices, the central processing unit, and the control units within the CPU and other peripheral devices. Computer software can also be considered as a system of programs concerned with input/output, storage, processing, and control.

computer user: anyone who uses the output of a computer system.

console: that part of a computer used for communication between the operator and the computer.

control: (1) the systems component that evaluates feedback to determine whether the system is moving toward the achievement of its goal and then makes any necessary adjustments to the input and processing components of the system to ensure that proper output is produced; (2) sometimes synonymous with **feedback-control;** (3) a management function that involves observing and measuring organizational performance and environmental activities and modifying the plans and activities of the organization when necessary.

control card: a punched card that contains input data required for a specific application of a general routine. For example, job control cards are a series of cards, coded in job control language (JCL), which direct an operating system to load and begin execution of a particular program.

control program: a program that assists in controlling the operations and managing the resources of a computer system. It is usually part of an operating system.

control unit: a subunit of the central processing unit which controls and directs the operations of the entire computer system. The control unit retrieves computer instructions in proper sequence, interprets each instruction, and thus directs the other parts of the computer system in the implementation of a computer program.

conversational computing: a type of real-time processing involving frequent man-machine interaction. A dialogue occurs between a computer and a user in which the computer directs questions and comments to the user in response to the questions, comments, and other input supplied by the user.

cryptography: the coding of data into an unrecognizable form (encryption) for purposes of security in transmission. After transmission, the message is translated back to its original state by decryption.

cursor: a visual pointer that can be moved on the display screen of a CRT. The hyphen symbol often serves as a cursor.

cybernetic system: a system that uses feedback and control components to achieve a self-monitoring and self-regulating capability.

cylinder: an imaginary vertical cylinder consisting of the vertical alignment of data tracks on each surface of magnetic disks which are accessed simultaneously by the read/write heads of a disk storage device.

data: a representation of facts, concepts, or instructions in a formalized manner suitable for communication, interpretation, or processing by humans or machines.

data bank: (1) a comprehensive collection of libraries of data utilized by an organization; (2) a centralized common data base which supports several major information systems of an organization.

data base: a superfile which consolidates and integrates data records formerly stored in several separate data files; that is, a personnel data base might consolidate data formerly contained in several files such as the payroll file, employee skills file, personnel action file, and so forth.

data base management system: a generalized set of computer programs which control the creation, maintenance, and utilization of the data bases and data files of an organization.

data base system: an electronic data processing system that utilizes a common data base for data processing and storage.

data communication: pertaining to the transmitting of data over electronic communication links between a computer system and a number of terminals at some physical distance away from the computer.

data communication system: an electronic data processing system that combines the capabilities of the computer with high-speed electrical and electronic communications.

data element: a fact or observation collected and recorded as data.

data hierarchy: the organization of characters, data elements, records, and files (data sets and subsets) to form a data base.

data management: control program functions which provide access to data sets, enforce data storage conventions, and regulate the use of input/output devices.

data medium: the material in or on which a specific physical variable may represent data.

data name: an unambiguous and unique word or phrase to identify a data element.

data-phone: an AT&T designation of a group of devices which utilize telephone channels for transmission.

data processing: the execution of a systematic sequence of operations performed upon data. Synonymous with **information processing.**

data processing system: a system which accepts data as input and processes it into information as output.

debug: to detect, locate, and remove errors from a program or malfunctions from a computer.

decision support system: a management information system which utilizes decision rules, decision models, a comprehensive data base, and a decision maker's own insights in an interactive computer-based process leading to a specific decision by a specific decision maker.

decision table: a table of all contingencies that are to be considered in the description of a problem, together with the actions to be taken.

decollate: to remove carbons when multiple copies of computer output are printed and to separate the sheets, called plys.

dedicated computer: typically, a general-purpose computer that has been dedicated or committed to a particular data processing task or application.

descriptor: a word or phrase used to identify, categorize, or index information or data.

device: mechanical, electrical, or electronic equipment used to perform a specific function.

diagnostics: messages transmitted by a computer during language translation or program execution which pertain to the diagnosis or identification of errors in a program or malfunctions in equipment.

digit: a single character, 0–9, A–Z, or a special symbol such as $, %, or +.

digital computer: a computer that operates on digital data by performing arithmetic and logical operations on the data. Contrast with **analog computer.**

direct access: pertaining to the process of obtaining data from, or placing data into, storage where the time required for such access is independent of the location of the data. Synonymous with **random access.** Contrast with **serial access.**

direct access storage device: a storage device that can directly access data to be stored or retrieved. For example, a magnetic disk unit.

direct address: an address that specifies the storage location of an operand.

disk pack: a removable unit containing several magnetic disks which can be mounted on a magnetic disk storage unit.

display: a visual presentation of data.

display tube: a cathode ray tube on which information appears.

distributed processing: also called **distributed data processing (DDP).** A decentralization of electronic data processing made possible by a network of computers dispersed through an organization.

document: a medium on which data has been recorded for human use, such as a report or invoice.

documentation: a collection of documents or information which describes a computer program, information system, or required data processing operations.

double precision: pertaining to the use of two computer words to represent a number.

down time: the time interval during which a device is malfunctioning or inoperative.

dump: to copy the contents of all or part of a storage device, usually from an internal device onto an external storage device.

duplex: in communications, pertaining to a simultaneous two-way independent transmission in both directions.

duplicate: to copy so that the result remains in the same physical form as the source. For example, to make a new punched card with the same pattern of holes as an original punched card.

dynamic relocation: the movement of part or all of an active computer program and data from one part or type of storage to another without interrupting the proper execution of the program.

echo check: a method of checking the accuracy of transmission of data in which the received data are returned to the sending device for comparison with the original data.

edit: to modify the form or format of data; for example, to insert or delete characters such as page numbers or decimal points.

electromechanical data processing: the use of electromechanical devices such as typewriters and calculators to process data into information.

electronic data processing: the use of electronic computers to process data automatically.

emulation: to imitate one system with another so that the imitating system accepts the same data, executes the same programs, and achieves the same results as the imitated system. Contrast with **simulation.**

executive routine: a routine that controls the execution of other routines. Synonymous with **supervisory routine.**

extended binary coded decimal interchange code: an eight bit code that is widely used by current computers.

external storage: any storage device separate from or outside the physical confines of a computer.

facilities management: the use of an external service organization to operate and manage the electronic data processing facilities of an organization.

feedback: (1) information concerning the components and operations of a system; (2) the use of part of the output of a system as input to the system.

feedback-control: a systems characteristic that combines the functions of feedback and control. Information concerning the components and operations of a system (feedback) is evaluated to determine whether the system is moving toward the achievement of its goal, with any necessary adjustments being made to the system to ensure that proper output is produced (control).

field: a subdivision of a data record that consists of a grouping of characters which describe a particular category of data. For example, a name field or a sales amount field.

file: a collection of related data records treated as a unit. Sometimes called a **data set.**

file label: a unique name or code that identifies a file.

file maintenance: the activity of keeping a file up to date by adding, changing, or deleting data.

file processing: utilizing a file for data processing activities such as file maintenance, information retrieval, or report generation.

firmware: the use of microprogrammed read-only memory modules in place of hard-wired logic circuitry. See also **microprogramming.**

fixed-length record: a data record that always contains the same number of characters or fields. Contrast with **variable-length record.**

fixed-point: pertaining to a positional representation in which each number is represented by a single set of digits, the position of the radix point being fixed with respect to one end of the set according to some convention. Contrast with floating-point.

fixed word-length: pertaining to a computer word or operand that always has the same number of bits or characters. Contrast with **variable word-length.**

floppy disk: a record of data on a flexible plate.

flowchart: a graphical representation in which symbols are used to represent operations, data, flow, logic, equipment, and so forth. A program flowchart illustrates the structure and sequence of operations of a program, while a system flowchart illustrates the components and flows of data processing or information systems.

font: type for printing (letters and symbols), sets of which may vary in style and size.

format: the arrangement of data.

FORTRAN: FORmula **TRAN**slation. A high level procedure-oriented programming language widely utilized to develop computer programs that perform mathematical computations for scientific, engineering, and selected business applications.

general-purpose computer: a computer that is designed to handle a wide variety of problems. Contrast with **special-purpose computer.**

GIGO: a contraction of "Garbage in, Garbage out," a computer cliché which emphasizes that data processing systems will produce erroneous and invalid output when provided with erroneous and invalid input data or instructions.

graphic: pertaining to symbolic input or output from a computer system, such as lines, curves, geometric shapes, etc.

hard copy: a data medium or data record that has a degree of permanence and that can be read by man or machine. Similar to document.

hardware: physical equipment, as opposed to the computer program or method of use, such as mechanical, magnetic, electrical, or electronic devices. Contrast with **software.**

hash total: the sum of the numbers in a data field which is not normally added, such as account numbers or other identification numbers. It is utilized as a control total, especially during input/output operations of batch processing systems.

header card: a card that contains information related to the data in cards that follow.

header label: a machine-readable record at the beginning of a file containing data for file identification and control.

heuristic: pertaining to exploratory methods of problem solving in which solutions are discovered by evaluation of the progress made toward the final result. It is an exploratory trial-and-error approach guided by rules of thumb. Contrast with **algorithm(ic).**

high level language: a programming language which is close to a natural language.

HIPO chart: a chart drawing its name from hierarchy + input/processing/output. Also known as an IPO chart. A design and documentation tool of structured programming utilized to record input/processing/output details of the hierarchial program modules.

Hollerith: pertaining to a particular type of code or punched card utilizing 12 rows per column and usually 80 columns per card. Named after Herman Hollerith, who originated punched card data processing.

host computer: the controlling computer in a multicomputer system.

human factors: physiological, psychological, and training factors to be considered in the design of computers and computer equipment and the development of operating procedures to ensure efficient and effective human interface with machines.

hybrid computer: a computer for data processing which utilizes both analog and digital representation of data.

index: an ordered reference list of the contents of a file or document together with keys or reference notations for identification or location of those contents.

index sequential: a method of data organization in which records are organized in sequential order and also referenced by an index. When utilized with direct access file devices, it is known as index sequential access method (ISAM).

information: (1) data that has been transformed into a meaningful and useful form for specific human beings; (2) the meaning that a human assigns to data by means of the known conventions used in their representation.

information processing: same as **data processing.**

information retrieval: the methods and procedures for recovering specific information from stored data.

information system: a system which utilizes manual, electromechanical, and electronic data processing systems, as well as user personnel and operating procedures, to collect and process data and disseminate information in an organization.

information theory: the branch of learning concerned with the likelihood of accurate transmission or communication of messages subject to transmission failure, distortion, and noise.

input: pertaining to a device, process, or channel involved in the insertion of data into a data processing system. Opposite of **output.**

input/output control system: programs which control the flow of data into and out of the computer system.

inquiry: a request for information from a computer system.

installation: (1) the process of installing new computer hardware or software; (2) a data processing facility such as a computer installation.

instruction: a grouping of characters that specifies the computer operation to be performed and the values or locations of its operands.

instruction cycle: the phase in the execution of a computer instruction during which the instruction is called from storage and the required circuitry to perform the instruction is readied.

integrated circuit: a set of related electronic circuitry packaged in a single unit. Integrated circuits are classified by size, SSI being small-scale integrated circuitry, MSI being medium-scale, and LSI large-scale.

intelligent terminal: a terminal that can be programmed.

interactive language: a programming language designed to allow a programmer to communicate with the computer during the execution of the program.

interactive processing: see **conversational computing.**

interactive program: a computer program that permits data to be entered or the flow of the program to be changed during its execution.

interactive programming: developing a computer program in real time with the assistance of a computer.

interface: a shared boundary, such as the boundary between a computer and its peripheral devices.

internal storage: storage within the computer proper.

interpreter: a computer program that translates and executes each source language statement before translating and executing the next one.

interrupt: a condition that causes an interruption in a data processing operation during which another data processing task is performed. At the conclusion of this new data processing assignment, control may be transferred back to the point where the original data processing operation was interrupted or to other tasks with a higher priority.

iterative: pertaining to the repeated execution of a series of steps.

job: a specified group of tasks prescribed as a unit of work for a computer.

job control cards: see **control card.**

job control language: a language for communicating with the operating system of a computer to identify a job and describe its requirements.

justify: (1) to adjust the printing positions of characters toward the left or right-hand margins of a data field or page; (2) to shift the contents of a storage position so that the most or the least significant digit is at some specified position.

K: an abbreviation for the prefix kilo, that is, 1,000 in decimal notation. When referring to storage capacity it is equivalent to two to the tenth power, or 1,024 in decimal notation.

key: one or more characters within an item of data that are used to identify it or control its use.

keypunch: (1) a keyboard-actuated device that punches holes in a card to represent data. Also called a **card-punch.** (2) The act of using a keypunch to record data in a punched card.

KWIC: Key Word In Context. An index to assist in retrieval of data.

KWOC: Key Word Out of Context. An index to assist in data retrieval.

label: one or more characters used to identify a statement or an item of data in a computer program or the contents of the data file.

language: a set of representations, conventions, and rules used to convey information.

leading zero: a redundant zero placed to the left of a number of fill space assigned to the number.

leased line network: a network reserved for the exclusive use of a single customer.

left justified: placement of characters in a data field from left to right. Used to facilitate reading of alpha characters. **Right justified** is used for numbers.

level: degree of subordination within a hierarchy, whether the hierarchy be the organizational structure of a business or a set of data.

library: a collection of files or programs.

library routine: a proven routine that is maintained in a program library.

light pen: a hand-held photo-sensing device used to communicate with a CRT by touching the screen.

line printer: a device that prints all characters of a line as a unit. Contrast with **character printer.**

linear programming: in operations research, a procedure for locating the maximum or minimum of a linear function of variables that are subject to linear constraints.

linkage: in programming, the coding that connects two separately coded routines.

list: (1) an ordered set of items; (2) a method of data organization which uses indexes and pointers to allow for nonsequential retrieval.

list processing: a method of processing data in the form of lists.

location: any place in which data may be stored.

log: a record of the operations of a data processing system.

logical data elements: data elements that are independent of the physical data media on which they are recorded.

machine instruction: an instruction that a computer can recognize and execute.

machine language: a programming language where instructions are expressed in the binary code of the computer.

magnetic card: a card with a magnetic surface on which data can be stored.

magnetic core: tiny rings composed of iron oxide and other materials that are strung on wires which provide electrical current that magnetizes the cores. Data is represented by the direction of the magnetic field of groups of cores. Widely utilized as the primary storage media in second and third generation computer systems.

magnetic disk: a flat circular plate with a magnetic surface on which data can be stored by selective magnetization of portions of the curved surface.

magnetic ink: an ink that contains particles of iron oxide which can be magnetized and detected by magnetic sensors.

magnetic ink character recognition: the machine recognition of characters printed with magnetic ink. Contrast with **optical character recognition.**

magnetic tape: a tape with a magnetic surface on which data can be stored by selective magnetization of portions of the surface.

main frame: the main part of the computer, generally referring to the CPU.

maintenance: keeping a system operational. This includes anticipating, detecting, and eliminating errors, as well as ensuring that system performance is relevant.

management information system: an information system that provides the information required to support management decision making.

manual data processing: (1) data processing requiring continual human operation and intervention and which utilizes simple data processing tools such as paper forms, pencils, filing cabinets, and so forth; (2) all data processing that is not automatic, even if it utilizes machines such as typewriters, adding machines, calculators, and so forth.

mark-sensing: the electrical sensing of manually recorded conductive marks on a nonconductive surface.

mass storage: (1) devices having a large storage capacity, such as magnetic disks or drums; (2) secondary storage devices with extra-large storage capacities (in the hundreds of millions of bytes), such as magnetic strip and card units.

master file: a data file containing relatively permanent information which is utilized as an authoritative reference and is usually updated periodically. Contrasts with **transaction file.**

match: a process used to correlate two or more records having an identical key, a process used in updating a master file from a detailed transaction file.

matrix: a two-dimensional rectangular array of quantities.

memory: same as **storage.**

menu: a displayed list of items from which a terminal operator makes a selection.

merge: to combine items from two or more similarly ordered sets into one set that is arranged in the same order.

message: an arbitrary amount of information whose beginning and end are defined or implied.

metal-oxide-semiconductor: technology for manufacturing semiconductors to produce integrated circuit logic components.

microcircuit: a small integrated circuit.

microcomputer: a small computer ranging in size from a computer on a chip to a small typewriter-size unit.

microprocessor: a microcomputer central processing unit on a chip and without input/output or primary storage capabilities in most types.

microprogram: a small set of elementary control instructions called microinstructions or microcodes.

microprogramming: the use of special software (microprograms) to perform the functions of special hardware (electronic control circuitry). Microprograms stored in a read-only storage module of the control unit interpret the machine language instructions of a computer program and decode them into elementary microinstructions which are then executed.

minicomputer: a small (for example, desk-top size) electronic, digital, stored-program, general-purpose computer.

mnemonic: the use of symbols which are chosen to assist the human memory, which are typically abbreviations or contractions such as MPY for multiply.

modem: **MO**dulator-**DEM**odulator. A device which converts the digital signals from input/output devices into appropriate frequencies at a transmission terminal and converts them back into digital signals at a receiving terminal.

module: a unit of hardware or software that is discrete and identifiable and designed for use with other units.

monitor: software or hardware that observes, supervises, controls, or verifies the operations of a system.

multiplex: to interleave or simultaneously transmit two or more messages on a single channel.

multiprocessing: pertaining to the simultaneous execution of two or more instructions by a computer or computer network.

multiprogramming: pertaining to the current execution of two or more programs by a computer by interleaving their execution.

nanosecond: one-billionth of a second.

noise: (1) random variations of one or more characteristics of any entity such as voltage, current, or data; (2) a random signal of known statistical properties of amplitude, distribution, and special density; (3) any disturbance tending to interfere with the normal operation of a device or system.

numeral: a discrete representation of a number.

numeric: pertaining to numerals or to representation by means of numerals. Synonymous with numerical.

numerical control: automatic control of a process performed by a device that makes use of all or part of numerical data generally introduced as the operation is in process.

object program: a compiled or assembled program composed of executable machine instructions. Contrast with **source program.**

offline: pertaining to equipment or devices not under control of the central processing unit.

operand: that which is operated upon. That part of a computer instruction which is identified by the address part of the instruction.

operating system: software that controls the execution of computer programs and that may provide scheduling, debugging, input/output control, accounting, compilation, storage assignment, data management, and related services.

operation: a defined action, namely, the act of obtaining a result from one or more operands in accordance with rules that specify the result for any permissible combination of operands.

operation code: a code that represents specific operations. Synonymous with **instruction code.**

operational information system: an information system that collects, processes, and stores data generated by the operational systems of an organization and produces data and information for input into a management information system or for the control of an operational system.

operational system: a basic subsystem of the business firm as a system which constitutes its input, processing, and output components. Also called a **physical system.**

operations research: the use of the scientific method to provide criteria for decisions concerning the actions of people, machines, and other resources in a system.

optical character recognition: the machine identification of printed characters through the use of light-sensitive devices.

optical scanner: a device that optically scans printed or written data and generates their digital representation.

original equipment manufacturer: a firm which manufactures and sells devices for use as components in the products of other computer hardware manufacturers.

output: pertaining to a device, process, or channel involved with the transfer of data or information out of a data processing system.

pack: to compress data in a storage medium by taking advantage of known characteristics of the data in such a way that the original data can be recovered.

page: a segment of a program or data, usually of fixed length, that has a fixed virtual address but can in fact reside in any region of the internal storage of the computer.

paging: a process which automatically and continually transfers pages of programs and data between primary storage and direct access storage devices. It provides computers with advanced multiprogramming and virtual memory capabilities.

parallel: pertaining to the concurrent or simultaneous occurrence of two or more related activities in multiple devices or channels.

parallel processing: concurrent execution of two or more programs.

parity bit: a check bit appended to an array of binary digits to make the sum of all the binary digits, including the check bit, always odd or always even.

parity check: a check that tests whether the number of ones or zeros in an array of binary digits is odd or even.

pass: one cycle of processing a body of data.

password: a unique string of characters that must be supplied by the user of a computer system before gaining access to it.

patch: to modify a routine in a rough or expedient way.

pattern recognition: the identification of shapes, forms, or configurations by automatic means.

peripheral equipment: in data processing, any unit of equipment distinct from the central processing unit that may provide the system with outside communication.

personal computing: the use of computers by individuals for educational, recreational, home management, and other personal applications.

PERT: Program Evaluation and Review Technique. A network analysis technique utilized to find the most efficient scheduling of time and resources when developing a complex project or product.

physical record: the physical data medium which contains one or more logical data elements. For example, a punched card is a single physical record which may contain several logical records.

picosecond: one-trillionth of a second.

PL/1: Programming Language 1. A procedure-oriented high level general-purpose programming language designed to combine features of COBOL, FORTRAN, ALGOL, and so forth.

plot: to map or diagram by connecting coordinate values.

plotter: an output device for making a hard copy of two-dimensional representations of data.

point-of-sale terminal: a computer terminal used in retail stores that serves the function of a cash register as well as collecting sales data and performing other data processing functions.

pointer: a data item associated with an index, a record, or other set of data which contains the address of a related record.

polling: periodically interrogating terminals to see whether or not computing service is needed in a time-sharing system.

position: in a string, each location that may be occupied by a character or binary digit and may be identified by a serial number.

precision: the degree of discrimination with which a quantity is stated.

preprocessor: a computer program that will prepare for another processing activity.

primary storage: internal storage within a computer.

printer: a device used to produce hard copy.

privacy: the protection of data from unauthorized use.

privileged instruction: a computer instruction whose use is restricted to the operating system of the computer and is not available for use in ordinary programs.

problem-oriented language: a programming language designed for the convenient expression of a given class of problems.

procedure: the course of action taken for the solution of a problem.

procedure-oriented language: a programming language designed for the convenient expression of procedures used in the solution of a wide class of problems.

process: a systematic sequence of operations to produce a specified result.

process control: the use of a computer to control an ongoing physical process such as industrial production processes.

processor: a hardware device or software system capable of performing operations upon data.

program: (1) a series of actions proposed in order to achieve a certain result; (2) an ordered set of computer instructions which cause a computer to perform a particular process; (3) the act of developing a program.

program library: a collection of available computer programs and routines.

programmed check: a check procedure designed by the programmer and implemented specifically as part of the program.

programmer: a person mainly involved in designing, writing, and testing computer programs.

programming: the design, writing, and testing of a program.

programming language: a language used to prepare computer programs.

protocol: a specific set of rules defining the exchange of special signals and characters when a connection is made between two data communications terminals, and before and after each transmission of a data communications message.

pseudocode: an informal design language of structured programming which expresses the processing logic of a program module in ordinary English language phrases.

punch position: a defined location on a card or tape where a hole may be punched.

punched card: a card punched with a pattern of holes or cuts used to represent data.

random access: same as **direct access.**

random access memory: one of the basic types of semiconductor memory used for temporary storage of data or programs during processing. Each memory position can be directly sensed (read) or changed (write) in the same length of time, irrespective of its location on the storage medium.

random data organization: a method of data organization in which logical data elements are distributed randomly on or within the physical data medium. For example, logical data records distributed randomly on the surfaces of a magnetic disk file.

raw data: data that has not been processed.

read: to acquire or interpret data from a storage device, a data medium, or any other source.

read-only memory: a basic type of semiconductor memory used for permanent storage. Can only be read, not written (changed). Variations are programmable read-only memory (PROM) and erasable programmable read-only memory (EPROM).

reader: a device which converts information from one form into another form.

real time: pertaining to the performance of data processing during the actual time a process transpires in order that results of the data processing can be used in guiding the process.

real-time processing: data processing in which data is processed immediately rather than periodically. Contrast with **batch processing.**

record: a collection of related items or fields of data treated as a unit.

refresh: the periodic renewing of electrical charges to restore data in semiconductor memory or on a CRT screen.

register: a device capable of storing a specified amount of data, such as one word.

remote access: pertaining to communication with the data processing facility by one or more stations that are distant from that facility.

report generation: producing complete reports from a set of rules which describe the input file and the format and content of output.

reproduce: to prepare a duplicate of stored data or information.

response time: the time that elapses from the end of a request until the beginning of desired action or receipt of information.

robot: an automated device that performs activities that would otherwise require human intervention.

rounding: the process of deleting the least significant digits of a numeric value and adjusting the part that remains according to some rule.

routine: an ordered set of instructions that may have some general or frequent use.

RPG: **R**eport **P**rogram **G**enerator. A problem-oriented language which utilizes a generator to construct programs that produce reports and perform other data processing tasks.

scan: to examine sequentially, part by part.

scroll: the movement of a CRT display upward with new lines continually being added at the bottom of the screen.

secondary storage: storage that supplements the primary storage of a computer. Synonymous with **auxiliary storage.**

security: control and protection of data.

segment: (1) to divide a computer program into parts such that the program can be executed without the entire program being in internal storage at any one time; (2) part of a computer program.

sensor: a device that measures external phenomena and converts it into machine-readable data for a computer.

sequence: an arrangement of items according to a specified set of rules.

sequential access: a sequential method of storing and retrieving data from a file. Contrast with **random access.**

sequential data organization: organizing logical data elements according to a prescribed sequence.

serial: pertaining to the sequential or consecutive occurrence of two or more related activities in a single device or channel.

serial access: pertaining to the process of obtaining data from or placing data into storage, where the access time is dependent upon the location of the data most recently obtained or placed in storage. Contrast with **direct access.**

service program: a program that provides general support for the operation of a computer system, such as input/output, diagnostic, and other utility routines.

set: (1) a collection; (2) to place a storage device into a specified state, usually other than that denoting zero or space character.

setup: to arrange and make ready the data or devices needed to solve a particular problem.

setup time: the time required to setup the devices, materials, and procedures required for a particular data processing application.

signal: a time-dependent value attached to a physical phenomenon which conveys data.

significant digit: a digit that is needed for a certain purpose, particularly one that must be kept to preserve a specific accuracy or precision.

simplex: pertaining to a communications link that is capable of transmitting data in only one direction. Contrast with **duplex.**

simulation: the representation of certain features of the behavior of a physical or abstract system by the behavior of another system. Contrast with **emulation.**

smart products: industrial and consumer products with intelligence provided by built-in microcomputers or microprocessors which significantly improve the performance and capabilities of such products.

software: a set of computer programs, procedures, and possibly associated documentation concerned with the operation of a data processing system. Contrast with **hardware.**

solid state: pertaining to devices whose operation depends on the control of electric or magnetic phenomena in solids, such as transistors, diodes, and so forth.

sort: to segregate items into groups according to some definite rules.

source program: a computer program written in a language that is an input to a translation process. Contrast with **object program.**

special character: a graphic character that is neither a letter, a digit, nor a space character.

special-purpose computer: a computer that is designed to handle a restricted class of problems. Contrast with **general-purpose computer.**

statement: in computer programming, a meaningful expression or generalized instruction in a source program, particularly in high level programming languages.

storage: pertaining to a device into which data can be entered, in which they can be held, and from which they can be retrieved at a later time.

storage allocation: the assignment of blocks of data to specified blocks of storage.

storage protection: an arrangement for preventing access to storage for either reading or writing, or both.

store: to enter or retain data in a storage device. Sometimes synonymous with **storage device.**

stored program computer: a computer controlled by internally stored instructions that can synthesize, store, and in some cases, alter instructions as though they were data and that can subsequently execute these instructions.

string: a linear sequence of entities such as characters or physical elements.

structure chart: a design and documentation technique used in structured programming to show the purpose and relationships of the various modules in a program.

structured programming: a programming methodology which involves the use of a top-down program design and uses a limited number of control structures in a program to create highly structured modules of program code.

structured walk-throughs: a structured programming methodology which requires a peer review of other programmers of the program design and coding to minimize and reveal errors in the early stages of programming.

subroutine: a routine that can be part of another routine.

subsystem: a system that is a component of a larger system.

supervisor: a control program which assists the computer in operations, controlling such functions as scheduling, queuing, and storage allocations.

synchronous computer: a computer in which each event, or the performance of any basic operation, is constrained to start on, and usually to keep in step with, signals from a clock.

system: (1) a group of interrelated or interacting elements; (2) a group of interrelated components that seeks the attainment of a common goal by accepting inputs and producing outputs in an organized process; (3) an assembly of methods, procedures, or techniques united by regulated interaction to form an organized whole; (4) an organized collection of people, machines, and methods required to accomplish a set of specific functions.

system library: the catalogued information in computer-usable form at a computer installation.

systems analysis: (1) analyzing in detail the components and requirements of a system; (2) analyzing in detail the information needs of an organization, the characteristics and components of presently utilized information systems, and the requirements of proposed information systems.

systems development: (1) conceiving, designing, and implementing a system; (2) developing information systems by a process of investigation, analysis, design, programming, implementation, and maintenance.

table: a collection of data in which each item is uniquely identified by a label, by its position relative to other items, or by some other means.

table lookup: a procedure for obtaining the value of a data element from a table.

tabulate: to form data into a table or to print totals.

teleconferencing: the use of teleprocessing and audio-video equipment to enable communication between conference participants not gathered in one location.

teleprocessing: data processing in which telecommunications is used for input, output, or both.

Teletype: the trademark name of the Teletype Corporation of a device which sends and receives data transmitted over long distances.

terminal: a point in a system or communication network at which data can either enter or leave. Also, an input/output device at such a point in a system.

throughput: the total amount of useful work performed by a data processing system during a given period of time.

time sharing: providing computing services to many users simultaneously, while providing rapid responses to each user.

top-down design: a methodology of structured design in which the design is organized into functional modules, with the main module being designed first, and then lower level modules.

track: the portion of a moving storage medium, such as a drum, tape, or disk, that is accessible to a given reading head position.

transaction file: a data file containing relatively transient data to be processed in combination with a master file. Synonymous with **detail file.**

transducer: a device for converting energy from one form to another.

translator: a device or computer program that transforms statements from one language to another, such as a compiler or assembler.

transmit: to send data from one location and to receive data at another location.

truncate: (1) to terminate a computational process in accordance with certain rules; (2) to remove characters from the beginning or ending of a data element, especially digits at the beginning or ending of a numeric quantity. Contrast with **rounding.**

turnaround time: the elapsed time between submission of a job to a computing center and the return of the results.

turnkey systems: computer systems where all of the hardware, software, and systems development needed by a user are provided.

unit record: pertaining to a single physical record that contains a single logical record.

update: to incorporate into a master file the changes required to reflect the most current status of the records in the file.

utility program: a standard set of routines which assists in the operation of a computer system by performing some frequently required process such as sorting, merging, and so forth.

variable: a quantity that can assume any of a given set of values.

variable-length record: pertaining to data records which contain a variable number of characters or fields.

variable word-length: pertaining to a machine word or operand that may consist of a variable number of bits or characters. Contrast with **fixed word-length.**

verify: to determine whether a transcription of data or other operation has been accomplished accurately.

virtual machine: pertaining to the simulation of one type of computer system by another computer system.

virtual memory: the use of secondary storage devices as an extension of the primary storage of the computer, thus giving the virtual appearance of a larger virtually unlimited main memory than actually exists.

visual scanner: an optical scanning device that can identify print or written data.

voice-grade line: a transmission channel capable of transmitting speech.

WATS: Wide Area Telephone Service. A telecommunications service for transmitting long-distance phone calls at a flat rate.

word: (1) a character string or bit string considered as an entity; (2) an ordered set of characters handled as a unit by the computer.

word processing: pertaining to the use of automated and centralized typing, dictation, copying, and filing systems that are utilized in modern offices.

write: to record data on a data medium.

zero suppression: the elimination of nonsignificant zeros in a numeral.

SELECTED LIST OF ABBREVIATIONS AND ACRONYMS

AA	American Airlines
AAIMS	An Analytical Information Management System
ACH	Automatic Clearing House
ACM	Association of Computing Machinery
ACS	Advanced Communication System
ADABAS	Adaptable DAta BAse System
ADP	Automatic Data Processing
ADS	Accurately Defined System
AEMS	Airline Econometric Modelling System
AI	Artificial Intelligence
ALGOL	ALGOrithmic Language
ALU	Arithmetic and Logic Unit
ANSI	American National Standards Institute
A/P	Accounts Payable
APL	A Programming Language
APT	Automatically Programmed Tool
A/R	Accounts Receivable
ARPA	Advanced Research Projects Agency
ARR	Accounting Rate of Return
ATM	Automatic Teller Machines
AT&T	American Telephone and Telegraph
BASIC	Beginner's All-Purpose Symbolic Instruction Code
BBC	British Broadcasting Corporation
BSP	Business System Planning
C	Centigrade
CAD	Computer-Aided Design
CAD/CAM	Computer-Aided Design/Computer-Aided Manufacturing
CAI	Computer-Assisted Instruction
CAM	Computer-Aided Manufacturing
CCD	Charged Coupled Devices
CHIPS	Clearning House Inter-Payments System
COBOL	COmmon Business-Oriented Language
CODASYL	Committee On DAta SYstems Language
COLINGO	Compile On LINe and GO
COM	Computer Output on Microfilm
CPM	Critical Path Method
CPU	Central Processing Unit
CRT	Cathode Ray Tube

CS	Computer Science
CSF	Critical Success Factor
DASD	Direct Access Storage Device
DBA	Data Base Administrator
DBCL	Data Base Command Language
DBMS	Data Base Management System
DBTG	Data Base Task Group
DD	Data Directory
DDC	Direct Digital Computer
DDL	Data Description Language
DDP	Distributed Data Processing
DED	Data Element Dictionary
DED/DD	Data Element Dictionary/Data Directory System
DES	Data Encryption Standard
DML	Data Manipulation Language
DNC	Direct Numerical Control
DP	Data Processing
DSL/ALPHA	Digital Simulation Language/ALPHA
DSS	Decision Support System
EAM	Electrical Accounting Machines
EDP	Electronic Data Processing
EFT	Electronic Fund Transfer
EIS	Electronic Information Services
ENIAC	Electronic Numerical Integrator And Calculator
EVPI	Expected Value of Perfect Information
FAX	Facsimile
FCC	Federal Communications Commission
FDS	Full Development System
FICA	Federal Insurance Contributions Act
FIFO	First-In-First-Out
FORTRAN	FORmulae TRANslator
GERT	Graphic Evaluation Review Technique
GIDS	Generalized Intelligent Decision System
GIGO	Garbage In Garbage Out
GIS	Generalized Information System
GM	General Motors
GMIS	General Management Information System
GNP	Gross National Product
HIPO	Hierarchy Plus Input-Process Output
IBA	Independent Broadcasting Authority
IBM	International Business Machines Corporation
IC	Integrated Circuitry
ID	IDentification Number
IMP	Interface Message Processor
IMS	Information Management System
I/O	Input/Output
IQF	Interactive Query Facility
IRG	Inter Record Gap
IRR	Internal Rate of Return
IRS	Internal Revenue Service

ISBN	International Standard Book Number
ISDOS	Information System Design and Optimization System
IT&T	International Telephone and Telegraph
JCL	Job Control Language
K	Kilo
KWIC	Key Word In Context Index
KWOC	Key Word Out Of Context Index
LIFO	Last-In-First-Out
LISP	LISt Processing
LSI	Large-Scale Integration
LSNLIS	Linear Sciences Natural Language Information System
MARS	Multi-Access Airline Reservation System
MIC	Magnetic Ink Characters
MICR	Magnetic Ink Character Recognition
MIS	Management Information System
MOS	Metal-Oxide-Semiconductor
MRP	Materials Requirements Planning System
NASA	National Aeronautical and Space Administration
NC	Numerical Control
NCR	National Cash Register
NPL	Natural Processing Language
NPV	Net Present Value
OCR	Optical Character Recognition
OEM	Original Equipment Manufacturer
OLRT	OnLine Real Time
OR	Operations Research
OS	Operating System
PB	PayBack Period
PC	Process Control
PERT	Program Evaluation Review Technique
PI	Profitability Index
PIN	Personal Identification Number
PL/1	Programming Language 1
POS	Point Of Sale
PR	Public Relations
PSA	Program Statement Analyzer
PV	Present Value
RAM	Random Access Memory
R&D	Research and Development
REQUEST	Restricted English QUESTion-Answering
RJE	Remote Job Entry
ROI	Return On Investment
RPG	Report Program Generator
SBN	Standard Book Number
SBS	Satellite Business System
SCL	System Communication Location
SCS	Small Computer System
SDLC	Synchronous Data Link Control

SEQUEL	**S**tructured **E**nglish **QUE**ry **L**anguage
SIMULA	**SIMULA**tion **L**anguage
SMF	**S**ystems **M**anagement **F**acilities
SNA	**S**ystems **N**etwork **A**rchitecture
SNOBOL	**S**tri**N**g-**O**riented Sym**BO**lic **L**anguage
SODA	**S**ystem **O**ptimization and **D**esign **A**lgorithm
SOP	**S**tudy **O**rganization **P**lan
SQUARE	**S**pecifying **QU**eries **A**s **R**elational **E**xpressions
SSI	**S**mall-**S**cale **I**ntegration
SWIFT	**S**ociety for **W**orldwide **I**nterbank **F**inancial **T**elecommunications
TDMS	**T**ime-shared **D**ata **M**anagement **S**ystem
TELEX	**TEL**etypewriter **EX**change (Western Union)
TIP	**T**erminal **I**nterface **M**essage **P**rocessor
TWX	**T**eletype**W**riter **EX**change Service
UIM	**U**ltra-**I**ntelligent **M**achine
UL1	**U**ser **L**anguage **1**
UP	**U**ser **P**rogram
UPC	**U**niversal **P**roduct **C**ode
VP	**V**ice-**P**resident
WATS	**W**ide **A**rea **T**elephone **S**ervice
WP	**W**ord **P**rocessing

INDEX

591

This book has been set Videocomp in 10 and 9 point Souvenir Light, leaded 2 points. Part numbers are 24 point Roma and part titles are 24 point Roma Semi-Bold. Chapter numbers are 52 point Roma and chapter titles are 20 point Roma. The size of the text area is 27 picas by 47 picas.